Canadian Politics

in the 21st century

Canadian Politics
in the 21st century

edited by

Michael Whittington
Carleton University

Glen Williams
Carleton University

THOMSON
꘎
NELSON

Australia   Canada   Mexico   Singapore   Spain   United Kingdom   United States

THOMSON
NELSON

Canadian Politics in the 21st Century,
Sixth Edition
By Michael Whittington and Glen Williams, editors

Editorial Director and Publisher:
Evelyn Veitch

Executive Editor:
Chris Carson

Senior Marketing Manager:
Murray Moman

Senior Developmental Editor:
Rebecca Rea

Senior Production Editor:
Bob Kohlmeier

Copy Editor:
Lisa Berland

Proofreader:
Margaret Crammond

Indexer:
Dennis A. Mills

Production Coordinator:
Helen Locsin

Creative Director:
Angela Cluer

Interior-Design Modifications:
Brenda Barratt

Cover Design:
Liz Harasymczuk

Cover Image:
Leon Zernitsky/The Stock
Illustration Source

Compositor:
Carol Magee

Printer:
Transcontinental

National Library of Canada Cataloguing in Publication

Canadian politics in the 21st century / edited by Michael Whittington & Glen Williams. — 6th ed.

Includes bibliographical references and index.
ISBN 0-17-641551-3

1. Canada—Politics and government. I. Whittington, Michael S., 1942– II. Williams, Glen, 1947– III. Title: Canadian politics in the twenty-first century.

FC635.C37 2004   971.064'8
C2003-904268-5

CONTENTS

CONTRIBUTORS

Yasmeen Abu-Laban, Associate Professor of Political Science, University of Alberta, Edmonton, Alberta

Michael M. Atkinson, Professor of Political Studies and Vice-President (Academic), University of Saskatchewan, Saskatoon, Saskatchewan

David V.J. Bell, Professor in Environmental Studies, Professor of Political Science, Professor of Social and Political Thought and Director of the York University Centre for Applied Sustainability, York University, Toronto, Ontario

Neil Bradford, Associate Professor of Political Science, Huron University College, University of Western Ontario, London, Ontario

Sandra Burt, Associate Professor of Political Science, University of Waterloo, Waterloo, Ontario

Alexandra Dobrowolsky, Associate Professor, Political Science, Saint Mary's University, Halifax, Nova Scotia

David Docherty, Associate Professor of Political Science, Wilfrid Laurier University, Waterloo, Ontario

Robert Everett, Ph.D., teacher of political science and Assistant Secretary of the University, York University, Toronto, Ontario

Frederick J. Fletcher, University Professor of Communication Studies and Political Science and Director, Joint Graduate Programme in Communication and Culture, York University, Toronto, Ontario

Radha Jhappan, Associate Professor of Political Science, Carleton University, Ottawa, Ontario

Laura Macdonald, Associate Professor of Political Science, Carleton University, Ottawa, Ontario

Kenneth McRoberts, Professor of Political Science and Principal of Glendon College, York University, Toronto, Ontario

Jon H. Pammett, Professor of Political Science and Associate Dean of the Faculty of Public Affairs and Management, Carleton University, Ottawa, Ontario

Miriam Smith, Professor of Political Science, Carleton University, Ottawa, Ontario

Daiva Stasiulis, Professor of Sociology, Carleton University, Ottawa, Ontario

Garth Stevenson, Professor of Political Science and Chair of the department, Brock University, St. Catharines, Ontario

Reg Whitaker, Distinguished Research Professor Emeritus, York University, Toronto, Ontario, and Professor of Political Science, University of Victoria, Victoria, British Columbia

Michael S. Whittington, Distinguished Research Professor of Political Science, Carleton University, Ottawa, Ontario

Glen Williams, Professor of Political Science, Carleton University, Ottawa, Ontario

INTRODUCTION: CANADA BEGINS THE TWENTY-FIRST CENTURY

Mike Whittington and
Glen Williams

At the turn of the previous century, Canada was a far different place from what it has become today at the beginning of a new millennium. Our population was just over 5 million people, 80 percent of whom lived on farms and in small rural communities. Today we number 31.5 million, with 85 percent living in urban centres. In 1900, Canada's House of Commons was composed of 213 MPs, all of whom were either Liberals or Tories, and our federal system featured only seven provinces. By contrast, in 2003 there are 301 MPs, 10 provinces, and three self-governing territories. Our two-party system is long gone: today no fewer than five political parties have significant representation in Parliament. The role of state at the turn of the last century was passive or laissez-faire, with total expenditures of all levels of government amounting to a mere 5 percent of the GNP. Today, government expenditures in Canada make up about two-fifths of our economy.

At the beginning of the twenty-first century, few aspects of our day-to-day lives are not touched in some way by government, whether through the provision of services to individual Canadians or through regulation of citizen behaviour. Reflecting this expanded role of the state, total employment in the publicly funded sector has mushroomed from about 2 percent of the labour force in 1900 to almost 20 percent of the total jobs in Canada today.

Canada's international role has also undergone a transformation in the past 100 years. In 1900, Canada was an outpost of the British Empire, and our trading relations were built on the intensive export of resources and bounded by a domestic industrial policy of protective tariffs and import substitution. In 2003, Canada pursues a foreign policy completely independent of Britain, actively participating in multilateral institutions such as the United Nations, the Group of Seven (G7), the Asia Pacific

Economic Cooperation (APEC) forum, the Commonwealth, La Francophonie, and North Atlantic Treaty Organization (NATO). In terms of trade, Canada has become a "free trader" through participation regionally in the North American Free Trade Agreement (NAFTA) and globally in the World Trade Organization (WTO).

On the domestic political scene, Canada today would be almost unrecognizable to anyone living in 1900. At the turn of the last century, not only did Canada lack a Charter of Rights and Freedoms but our political culture tolerated many practices that would be unacceptable today. For example, women, aboriginal people, and persons of Asian extraction were denied the right to vote by law, and few people at the time believed there was anything wrong with this. Homosexuality was a crime. Labour unions were thought to be subversive, and the right to strike was illegal in most jurisdictions. Interest groups and social movements as we know them today did not exist 100 years ago, the only "interests" significantly influencing policy decisions being the corporate contributors to party election chests and, perhaps, leaders of the major churches.

Although there have been enormous changes in the past 100 years of our history, many things have remained remarkably similar. The chapters in this sixth edition of *Canadian Politics* provide a snapshot of social and economic forces, political institutions and processes, and the issues and agendas of Canadian political life at the beginning of the twenty-first century. The authors have attempted not only to explain the nature of politics today in terms of its historical evolution but also to speculate about the trends that will prevail in our new century.

As in previous editions, contributors were asked to present a clear and uncluttered overview of their respective fields of specialization. Our objective is to explain in plain language the complex issues, institutional arrangements, and central processes that are part of the current Canadian political landscape. Our target audience is not our professional colleagues but students and other informed Canadians who are not specialists in economics or political science.

As in the past, the comments of our students and colleagues have been extremely useful in helping us to determine the nature and extent of the revisions required for this new edition. Thanks must go to the following reviewers who took the time to make this a better book: Paul Barker, Brescia College, University of Western Ontario; Lois Harder, University of Alberta; Lydia Miljan, University of Windsor; David Murphy, University of British Columbia; Nelson Wiseman, University of Toronto; and Peter Woolstencroft, University of Waterloo. Thanks as well to Rebecca Rea, at Nelson, and Lisa Berland for all their help in the production of this volume.

GOVERNMENT INSTITUTIONS AND PROCESSES

GOVERNMENT INSTITUTIONS AND PROCESSES

The five chapters of Part I survey the principal structures of Canadian government—the building blocks of our democracy. Although the study of state structures often requires learning details about the constitutional roles of individual political actors, the topics covered in this part of the text involve much more than mere memory work. Government institutions are essential to the orderly resolution of large and small political conflicts in Canadian society. Simply put, our democratic institutions of governance enhance social harmony by giving legitimacy to authoritative decisions that create political winners and losers. Students will also discover from a careful reading of Part I that the specific organizational architecture of Canada's government institutions actually helps shape the nature of laws that are enacted. In addition, Canada's political institutions reflect the basic values of our political culture (see Chapter 13 in Part III).

The core principles of parliamentary democracy remain much as they were in 1900. However, as Michael Atkinson and David Docherty describe in Chapter 1, the role of backbenchers, standing committees, and the opposition have recently changed to accommodate four opposition parties, a heavy legislative agenda, and demands by MPs for more input to policy decisions. While the authors have chosen, quite appropriately, to focus on the legislative process in the House of Commons, the reader is reminded that in the coming years the Senate may undergo the most radical transformation. The demands for reform or abolition of the upper chamber are growing, from Canadians in general and from opposition parties and individual MPs.

While the role of the prime minister and Cabinet has changed over the past 100 years, there remain several striking similarities in those institutions between 1900 and 2003. Besides the fact that the PM, then as now, is a Québécois, a lawyer, and a Liberal, Michael Whittington, in Chapter 2, makes the point that the executive branch is still the dominant actor in Canada's governmental process. As well, prime ministerial "style" and the personality of the prime minister are still important predictors of how Cabinet and the central bureaucratic agencies operate.

In Chapter 3, Reg Whitaker stresses that the power of the modern bureaucracy stems not so much from its size but from its monopoly over the expertise that our political leaders require if they are to make wise and effective policy decisions. This chapter traces the evolution of bureaucratic power from a time when politics and administration were separate processes, through the heyday of the "mandarins" when senior bureaucrats and politicians shared power, to the modern context in which technocrats now influence the policy process. This chapter also highlights the effects of more than a decade of downsizing on the quality and quantity of the senior bureaucracy's contribution to the policy process.

Garth Stevenson, in Chapter 4, explains how our federal system has become far more decentralized—with far more power in the hands of the provinces—than was intended at Confederation. At the same time, he points out that the system is actually quite integrated through executive federalism, fiscal federalism, and a complex network of intergovernmental relations. Moreover, as the subsequent Chapter 5 by Whittington on aboriginal self-government tells us, intergovernmental relations have become even more complex with the creation of the territory of Nunavut and with the potential evolution of aboriginal governments as a "third order" of government in the federation.

At the turn of the last century, aboriginal people were not allowed to vote, and "Indians" and Inuit in Canada were "managed" by "agents" assigned by the Department of the Interior in Ottawa. In fact, the topic of aboriginal self-government has become an item on the national political agenda only since the 1980s. At present, there are only a handful of aboriginal governments in place, and none of them has been in existence long enough to enable any firm conclusions about their effectiveness. The only certain conclusion of Michael Whittington's chapter is that the issues of aboriginal rights and self-government will continue to find a place on the agenda of political debate well into the next century.

CHAPTER 1

PARLIAMENT AND POLITICAL SUCCESS IN CANADA

Michael M. Atkinson and
David C. Docherty

INTRODUCTION: SUCCESSFUL GOVERNMENT

Parliament is the centre of government in Canada. Governments derive their ultimate authority from the electorate—the sovereign people at the ballot box—but their immediate fate is determined in the House of Commons and the Senate. It is in the legislative arena that policy is defended, successes celebrated, and failures dramatized. It is here that governments are tested, and here, in Parliament, where the pathologies of public policy are identified and diagnosed.

To help ensure that the will of the people, as expressed by their electoral choice, will in fact be done, Canada has created an executive-centred form of parliamentary government. We have placed a great deal of authority in the hands of the prime minister and Cabinet, especially during times of majority governments. The Cabinet, supported by a loyal set of followers in the House of Commons, is given an almost unlimited opportunity to pursue its agenda. Successful governments retain the support of Parliament and produce legislation that addresses national policy problems, attends to local interests, and meets the test of moral leadership.

But many governments are not successful. Some of the roadblocks to success are constitutional (such as the Senate) and others are informal (such as the media). Some are part of parliamentary procedures themselves (such as Question Period) and others (such as the government caucus) remain largely hidden from public view. Governments cannot escape these obstacles, but they also cannot escape the fact that the system was created to work. Unlike the U.S. presidential system—often described as a political system intentionally designed to discourage active, effective government—the Westminster system is designed to permit governments to govern. Governments in Canada have the tools necessary to provide successful leadership that is responsive to the needs of Canadians. Why then do many Canadians think of Parliament as a major culprit in creating a so-called democratic deficit? Is it because the rules and structures that allow for effective government somehow frustrate democracy? Can any government be genuinely successful if the men and women elected to represent Canadians are perceived as unable to do so?

ELECTORAL SUCCESS

The answer to the question of what makes a successful government depends very much on who is asked the question. Most political parties will measure their success by their capacity to get re-elected. A finance minister might argue success means meeting expectations or keeping promises. When a balanced budget is the declared goal or, even better, the core of an electoral contract, then anything short of that outcome is a failure. And while a fisheries minister may not be so foolhardy as to promise a rejuvenated northern cod fishery, there is little doubt that the return of the cod would be hailed as a victory. But asked to construct an agenda for the governing party, one on which success or failure could be pronounced, the voting public would be divided and confused on all but the most general and unhelpful of objectives. Some Canadians want reduced taxes, others want deficit reduction. Some want more public services, others want privatization. Differences of opinion on the scope, scale, and objectives of public policy provide governments with considerable latitude.

Success, like victory in battle, can be declared without necessarily being achieved. Declaring victory and asking for vindication is a common strategy of governments at election time. And once re-election is achieved, those in power argue with conviction, and some logic, that a new mandate constitutes a public endorsement of their achievements while in office. However, there are two problems with this argument. First, most governments in Canada are not elected by a majority of the electorate. Only twice since the Second World War has a national party captured more than half of the vote: the 1958 Diefenbaker and 1984 Mulroney Progressive Conservative victories. Typically, parties win office, and assemble majority governments, when more Canadians vote against them rather than for them.[1] Jean Chrétien managed three consecutive majorities but never captured over 42 percent of the popular vote. Second, voters seem more willing to punish governments they dislike than reward those of which they approve. Even when governments are re-elected a number of incumbents will inevitably lose their seats.[2] Jean Chrétien's third majority is unique in that the Liberals managed to improve their seat total from their second victory. However, their largest win was their first. Despite a badly divided opposition, Chrétien never improved on his first victory. In electoral terms, therefore, mere survival can equal success.

POLICY SUCCESS

Looking for success in policy terms is even more problematic. If there is a perfect balance of public goods, services, and taxes, no one has yet agreed on it. Perhaps if a government could redistribute wealth in a society with little adverse impact on those whose incomes would decrease while meeting all of society's needs (from health care to a reduction in greenhouse gases to combating homelessness) without running out of revenue (deficits and debts), then a consensus might emerge around the meaning of success. Normally, however, success at one of these endeavours results in failure, or at least less success, in the others. Governments constantly balance competing demands and interests: they have no blueprint for long-term economic prosperity. And even if they manage to please the median voter on one issue, they will alienate the same voter on another. Success in policy terms is never a complete victory, but rather the achievement of partial, and temporary, arrangements that are eventually found wanting.

Nor does simply "keeping election promises" neatly satisfy the definition of successful governments. While it may cost incumbent governments credibility with voters, governments must often go back on proposed policy plans or alter their campaign platforms to adjust to changing realities. The problems of terrorism that arose in the fall of 2001 had policy implications that could not have been foreseen during the 2000 election. From revisiting national security to dealing with a crippled airline industry, governments must react to unanticipated events. These unexpected developments require governments to re-assess campaign pledges, following through on what they can and altering what they cannot. Success does not necessarily mean keeping promises at any cost.[3]

PARLIAMENTARY SUCCESS

In the face of these difficulties, let us take a long-term view and suggest that a successful government in Canada is simply one that brings honour to democratic practice as embodied in the parliamentary system itself. If Canadians are left with more confidence in the parliamentary system at the end of a government's tenure, rather than less, then that government was successful. Admittedly, this kind of thinking suggests that a continuation of our parliamentary system is worthwhile and that no superior system awaits this one's demise. But that does not mean there cannot and should not be structural change, especially change that would make Parliament a more democratic institution. A government that is successful in Parliament adheres to its core constitutional responsibility—to be accountable for the exercise of the tools that the Westminster form of parliamentary government provides. The Westminster system allows MPs to bring local interests into the national forum, it supplies the Cabinet with the authority to steer national policy, and it gives the prime minister and his or her colleagues the forum from which to provide inspirational and morally sound national leadership. It also requires the government to justify and explain both general policy directions and specific policy decisions. Simply put, the Cabinet and the prime minister must be willing to be held publicly accountable for their actions and the actions of individuals working on their behalf, both members of their political staffs and public servants who implement and help develop public policy.

When Cabinet refuses to be held accountable, or when elected members are denied the ability to properly participate in the legislative process, the result is a democratic deficit. This does not mean that party discipline is always the enemy of democracy. Freeing up members to vote without fear of sanctions from their leaders might lead to brief improvements in the public's perception of legislators, but there is little evidence to suggest it will lead to increased parliamentary success as we have defined it. Members of Parliament must be given an opportunity to represent the opinions of constituents, but political parties, especially the governing party (or parties) must be given the opportunity to define and act on what they perceive to be the interests of all Canadians. If local and national interests coincide, all the better; but where they do not, the parliamentary system allows all competing interests to be heard. So we return to the original understanding that parliamentary government in Canada provides those in power with the capacity to articulate policies that express the national interest, and in so doing, give the sovereign people a strong sense of loyalty to a system that serves their collective needs. Of course, Parliaments can achieve this and still provide a greater role for members to participate. If done properly, Members of Parliament themselves can go some way to addressing the democratic deficit without changing the nature of parliamentary government.

THE TOOLS: GOVERNING IN PARLIAMENT

The Canadian Parliament now has three components: the lower house (the House of Commons), the upper house (the Senate), and the Crown (represented in Canada by the governor general). In Canada, the executive council (the Cabinet), exercises the Crown's prerogatives. This concentration of centralized authority is the most important tool available to any government. The Canadian Parliament is an executive-centred legislative body, in which those outside of Cabinet, private members, have little direct authority.[4] In the Canadian Parliament, with 301 MPs, this means executive authority is concentrated in a group of about 30 Cabinet ministers, approximately 10 percent of the House.[5]

Inside Parliament, Cabinet authority is manifested most prominently in control over the parliamentary agenda. In the nineteenth century, when ordinary members of Parliament assumed much of the initiative for legislation by offering proposals in the form of private bills and private members' bills,[6] even then it was the government-sponsored public bill that was used to change the general laws of the country.[7] Now almost all of the bills that Parliament finally adopts are government bills introduced by ministers of the Crown. Moreover, only ministers are permitted to introduce bills that authorize the raising or spending of money. Parliamentary procedure has gradually tightened to give the government sufficient time to enact its legislative program and to curtail lengthy debates, while the Speaker is counted on to dispose of dilatory motions.

The government has responsibilities other than the sponsoring of a legislative program. Every year, on or before March 1, the government lays before the Commons a request for funds to conduct business. This request, appearing in the form of "estimates," is followed by a supply bill, which is needed to give the estimates legislative authority. Supplementary estimates are tabled and further supply bills are introduced as required during the remainder of the fiscal year. The minister of Finance presents a budget, usually in February or March of each year, that announces the government's overall financial plan and intended tax changes. Major policy announcements often accompany the budget.

The Government House Leader is responsible for orchestrating all of this activity, ensuring that deadlines are met, that important government bills are not postponed indefinitely, and that the opposition is satisfied with the time that has been made available to discuss these measures. The week-by-week and month-by-month planning of the parliamentary session is in the hands of the parliamentary party leadership. The prime minister is responsible for summoning and proroguing Parliament and requesting that the governor general dissolve it. From the narrowest of details to the broadest of constitutional responsibilities, the government is in charge.

PRIME MINISTERIAL POWER

How does the government acquire and retain these responsibilities? The formal (and rather uninformative) answer is that the Cabinet enjoys the *confidence* of the House of Commons and is therefore able to offer advice to, and act on behalf of, the Crown. But behind this expression of confidence lie the machinery of the electoral process and the politics of party organization and cohesion. The parliamentary support that the Cabinet possesses has been garnered in the electorate, not in the House of Commons. The electorate has given one party more seats than the others and that party's leader almost always becomes prime minister and chooses a Cabinet. As individuals, members of Parliament have no special role in any of this. They have been elected, of course, but their electoral success cannot easily be interpreted as a personal endorsement.

Instead, it is the prime minister, the leader of the governing party, in whom the government's, and the party's, fate ultimately resides. He or she has the freedom to choose who will stand as a candidate for the party and who will serve in Cabinet and for how long. Members of the ministry all serve at the pleasure of the prime minister. This is an effective carrot for all members of the governing party, not just those initially asked to take a seat at the Cabinet table, and it is an effective stick to be used on ministers who are tempted to stray from the path laid out by the leader.[8] Prime ministers must be careful to keep the prospect of advancement real: once members have little hope for promotion, they have less need to remain loyal. But given the power of the executive, it is not surprising that the majority of MPs see Cabinet selection as a desirable career goal. Getting there can be a slow process, one that is largely in the prime minister's hands. Members who seek advancement within the House of Commons are careful, therefore, not to place too much distance between themselves and their leader.

Small wonder that once MPs arrive in Ottawa, the Westminster model assigns them a rather prosaic task. If they sit on the government side of the House, their job is to express confidence in their leadership by voting for government-sponsored measures; if they are opposition members, they are expected to oppose those measures, at least if directed to do so by the opposition party leadership. The team spirit that this exercise engenders is reinforced by the "confidence convention," the erroneous notion that the defeat of any government-sponsored bill requires the government's resignation.[9] No such requirement exists, except perhaps in the minds of MPs. Still, many MPs appear to be convinced that given the circumstances of their own election—namely, the indispensable role played by the prime minister and the rest of the party's leadership—an overt expression of independence is tantamount to a renunciation of that leadership. The result of this logic is that rigid party discipline, punctuated (on the opposition side at least) by leadership crises, is the standard behavioural dynamic in the House of Commons.[10]

Nonetheless, even this dynamic can break down. During his final eighteen months in office, Jean Chrétien has found himself facing a potential back-bench rebellion. As part of the retiring prime minister's legacy, the second Throne Speech of the 37th Parliament pledged to "introduce legislative changes to the financing of political parties." Members were surprised to learn that this would mean an end to substantial corporate and labour union support for the political parties. The notion that a departing prime minister was establishing rules that his successor would have to live under struck even some of his own caucus as hypocritical. The peculiar turned to bizarre when the prime minister declared this a matter of confidence and threatened to go to the people if the bill was defeated. The threat of an election (and the prospect of having Chrétien as leader for a fourth term) was enough to bring potential rebels into line. Governments that stick together are mighty forces; those that turn on themselves have short lifespans.

A government created and sustained by strong leadership is able to act decisively and can accomplish a great deal without delaying and equivocating until problems have reached crisis proportions. It has been argued that medicare and the social programs to which Canadians often point with pride have emerged not because of broadly based social democratic parties but "through the electoral dialectic of a powerful, centralized Cabinet and a mass electorate."[11] The Westminster model, it appears, is better suited to the development of integrative, national programs than to the cultivation of narrow, special interests. By the same token, the concentration of responsibility implicit in this model would seem to assist in the assignment of blame. Ministers can be held responsible for their actions (or inactions), and Cabinet, because it remains a cohesive political body, can presumably be censured collectively for poor performance. It is not surprising that this type of system, with its focus on the effectiveness of centralized decision making, is often referred to as *Cabinet government.*

THE SENATE

For most of Canada's history, the Senate, the upper chamber of Parliament, has been a tool in the hands of the government. Usually, but by no means always, the Senate has been controlled by the party controlling the House of Commons. Even when it is not, the Senate is an enormously convenient institution for the party leadership. Perhaps most important in this regard, the Senate is a "de-recruiting" ground for the governing party—one of the most popular post-elected spots for MPs is in the other chamber.

Using the Senate as a career inducement is not the only way prime ministers use the upper chamber to fulfill their legislative program. The Senate can also be used as a tool for successful governing in terms of regional representation. The qualifications that existed for the appointment of Canadian senators in 1867 are still present today.[12] These criteria provide some telling indications of whose interests these individuals are charged with representing. First, senators must be at least 30 years old. Second, they must hold at least $4000 worth of property. While this amount seems trivial today, in 1867 this represented a substantial value. The Senate was, at least in part, meant to represent propertied, or moneyed, interests.

But like the U.S. Senate, the Canadian red chamber was also supposed to represent regional interests. It was to be our institution of *intrastate* federalism, where regional interests were championed, not by premiers, but by senators working inside the central government. To this end, the Senate was initially divided along regional lines, 24 seats each for Quebec and Ontario, with Nova Scotia and New Brunswick to share an additional 24 seats. The intrastate principles of the Senate remain today, with Ontario and Quebec each still maintaining two dozen Senate seats. The four Western provinces also have 24 seats, as do the three Maritime provinces of Nova Scotia, New Brunswick, and Prince Edward Island. Six Senate seats were added when Newfoundland joined Confederation in 1949, and there are three senators for the Yukon, the Northwest Territories, and Nunavut.

The Senate can claim, at best, mixed success as a regionally representative body. During the Chrétien years there was little to suggest that senators effectively protected Western interests. Nor are Prince Edward Island's interests better protected with four appointed senators speaking on behalf of their concerns. Like most issues in Parliament, votes and debate break down along partisan, not regional, lines. The Senate represents a major, unrealized opportunity to address the democratic deficit in the country's central policy-making institutions. An elected Senate would

give regional interests democratic legitimacy in Ottawa. Effectivene
however, is another matter.

The Senate has acted as something of a representative safety val\
When the vagaries of the electoral system provide a government with
majority of seats but little or no representation from entire regions of the
country, the Senate fills this void. Using appointed senators as Cabinet
ministers, even in relatively minor positions, allowed Pierre Trudeau to
have Western voices heard during Cabinet deliberations.[13] When Joe Clark
won his short-lived minority government in 1979, he turned to the Senate
for Quebec representation in Cabinet. The national majorities that Canada
has witnessed from 1984 to the present have decreased the need for this
form of representational fillip.

THE ROADBLOCKS: LIMITS TO A GOVERNMENT'S POWER

We have emphasized to this point the array of tools the government has at
its disposal to be successful. It might appear that the government has a relatively easy job because the deck is stacked almost entirely in its favour.
Most Cabinet ministers and prime ministers would probably disagree.
Governing is not easy. True, the Westminster model of parliamentary government does confer opportunities on the government, but it also ensures
a constitutional balance. And while the checks and balances in the parliamentary system are not always located in separate institutions, as they are
in the U.S. congressional model, these checks and balances can be
imposing nonetheless, especially for governments that have lost their
capacity to articulate a sense of public purpose.

RESPONSIBLE GOVERNMENT

Foremost among these institutional checks is the principle of responsible
government. Responsible government is a constitutional formula
requiring the Cabinet to account for its actions, and the actions of government departments, to the House of Commons. In turn, the House of
Commons is responsible for ensuring that Cabinet answers for its use of
executive authority.

Primarily the result of the Durham Report, the Act of Union in 1840
had created a single parliamentary body for what had been Upper and
Lower Canada (Ontario and Quebec).[14] But the Report had also recommended responsible government in which the members of the executive

council (the precursor to the modern Cabinet) had to be members of, and have the confidence of, the legislative council. By 1848 this practice had been adopted in most of the North American colonies.

The critical requirement that members of Cabinet have the confidence of the House of Commons helped usher in political parties as electoral vehicles that would ensure unity of purpose among Cabinet's supporters. The development of political parties was "critical in the democratic struggle to secure responsible government" in the years leading to the adoption of responsible government in 1848 and eventually Confederation in 1867. Since then, parties have become the fundamental mechanism through which voters choose their government.[15]

MINISTERIAL ACCOUNTABILITY

The inclusion of the executive inside Parliament also means that the executive can be held to account, publicly within the legislature, for their actions. Among other things, this means that opposition members regularly scrutinize the actions of the executive. A responsible government has been defined as one that "has a continuing obligation to the legislature, and ultimately to the electorate, to either give a satisfactory account of itself or be defeated."[16] This formula nicely captures collective ministerial responsibility, but members of the government are also the heads of the various departments and ministries. Individual Cabinet ministers are theoretically responsible not just for their own individual actions, but also for the actions of those men and women in departments under their jurisdiction. They must be prepared to answer questions about the actions (or inactions) of their departments, correct problems, and explain matters in the House of Commons.

In practice, however, ministers are loath to resign following indiscretions or errors committed by their advisers. Ministers retain effective responsibility for actions undertaken in accordance with their instructions, but determining which actions are encompassed in this understanding can be a difficult task. The Federal Court of Appeal sought to make that task easier in 1988 by finding two ministers—Joe Clark and Flora MacDonald—personally responsible for the failure of their public servants to obey a court order. That decision sent a message to officials and politicians, but it did not produce resignations. So, ministerial responsibility has its limits. But even if ministers continue to treat individual ministerial responsibility as little more than a willingness to answer questions, parliamentary convention requires that new ministers be responsible for old problems. Among the more famous examples is the tainted blood scandal of 1996–97. As national health minister in 1997, Alan Rock was held politically responsible for an issue that pre-dated not only his government but also the government of Brian Mulroney.

THE INSTITUTIONALIZED OPPOSITION

In Canada it is difficult to discuss methods of accountability (let alone other forms of parliamentary practice) without emphasizing the primary role played by political parties.[17] Beyond parliamentary mechanisms of responsible government, with their emphasis on specific decisions, lies the task of ensuring electoral accountability. In this realm political parties are critical agents. In addition to their daily criticisms, parliamentary parties are supposed to provide a clear alternative to the government in power. Despite the fragmentation of political representation and recent threats to party discipline, political parties remain the dominant force for accountability both inside and outside of Parliament.

Inside Parliament, the government explains and justifies its action (or inaction) not to a sympathetic audience anxious to offer assistance, but to an organized, institutionalized opposition bent on demonstrating the inappropriateness and inefficiencies of government policy. Though it may never actually have the votes necessary to defeat the government, the opposition is nonetheless charged with ensuring that the responsibility of the government to the House of Commons is more than a formality. As one authority in this field has put it, "It is this public testing of governance, with the government and the opposition as institutionalized adversaries, that is the hallmark of contemporary Responsible Government."[18]

The strength of the opposition parties,[19] like the strength of government parties, is a function of the tools available to them including the quality and experience of their members. Most important, the opposition must be cohesive to be effective. When numerous parties are able to establish regional strongholds, the result is a highly fragmented opposition facing a cohesive government. Since 1993, this pattern of opposition fragmentation has plagued the House of Commons.

When it comes to experience, the Cabinet usually holds a great advantage over opposition parties. Recent Parliaments have been no exception. When Jean Chrétien became prime minister in 1993, he brought to Ottawa many new and talented members of Parliament. Yet when choosing Cabinet ministers, Chrétien bypassed most of these new MPs and appointed a host of veteran legislators. By contrast, the two main opposition parties, the Bloc Québécois and the Reform Party, had few members with any legislative experience, let alone in the House of

Commons. The result was a longer than usual "honeymoon" period for the government. The Reform Party's attempt to avoid what it considered unseemly partisan displays, in favour of constituent-oriented politics, only compounded the problem. The Cabinet was able to move ahead with its legislative agenda while the opposition parties were still finding their way around Parliament Hill and becoming acquainted with the formal and informal rules of life in Ottawa.

In a fragmented environment, an additional requirement is simply survival as a party. Since 1963, the House of Commons has defined survival in terms of the "12 member rule."[20] Today, parties with the minimum 12 members are eligible to participate in all legislative committees, can pose questions in Question Period on a regular basis, have representation on the all-important Board of Internal Economy, and are entitled to additional funds for caucus research and their leader's staff. Less obvious, but just as important, the House leaders of recognized parties meet and negotiate the House time schedule with the government House leader.

The ability of opposition parties to set forth a truly national alternative to the governing Liberals has also been compromised by the increasing regional nature of Canadian politics as amplified by the electoral system and party strategies. In the past decade, the Official Opposition parties have been either unable to break out of their Western roots (Reform and Alliance) or have seen their success tied to a single region (Bloc Québécois). Opposition fragmentation has made the job of governing easier. Cabinet is less accountable when those holding them to account are either internally divided or have too narrow a focus. Canadians now have the satisfaction of voting for parties that better reflect their regional interests, but at the expense of having a national alternative. Under these circumstances it has been easy for the governing Liberal Party to appear as the only national voice. The fact that the Liberals depend on one province, Ontario, for anywhere from 55 to 65 percent of their seats hardly makes them less regional. Multiple parties provide the illusion of more democratic choice, but not the reality of a more democratic government.[21]

OPPOSITION OPPORTUNITIES

There are three major opportunities for the opposition to construct roadblocks for the government of the day. One of these is during the *second reading* stage of government-sponsored legislation. First reading is nothing more than parliamentary approval to allow the bill to be printed and placed on the order paper. Second reading is the stage at which Parliament debates "the principle" of the bill; no amendments are permitted and strict rules of relevance are enforced. It is here that the minister defends the legislation and the opposition mounts a challenge. Governments prefer to believe that once the second reading stage is completed, Parliament is obliged to concentrate on the details of the bill, the main battle over principles having been fought. This interpretation of second reading is entirely in keeping with the idea that legislation is a government–opposition affair.

A second opportunity for opposition takes place during the *special debates* that are scattered throughout the parliamentary year. The Speech from the Throne and the budget debate are opportunities for the opposition to criticize the government's vaguely worded legislative program and its more precisely formulated tax and spending proposals. In addition, 25 "opposition days" are set aside in each parliamentary session during which motions proposed by the opposition parties form the basis for debates.

Unfortunately, none of these debates, whether on legislation or major speeches, can be considered a splendid success from anyone's perspective. One commentator puts the matter bluntly: "The action is slow, the dialogue is ponderous and interminable, the scene is sparsely populated and the wit has all the subtlety but none of the force of a Mack truck."[22] The essential problem is that the quality of parliamentary debate is simply not high enough to attract media attention. MPs simply do not bring enough independence of mind and oratorical skill to the task, with the result that a great deal of debate is simply for the record.

Oral *Question Period*, the third opportunity to construct roadblocks, has much more potential. For opposition parties, it is the most important part of any day in which the House is in session. Question Period provides an opportunity to talk to all Canadians, not just members across the aisle. The 45-minute period, and the media "scrum" that follows, is the most covered daily event in Ottawa.[23] As a result, a successful, well-researched question can garner national media attention. Such coverage can have the effect of raising the profile not just of the issue but of the MP who raised it.

For all that, Question Period has its critics. Derided as lousy theatre and gratuitous grandstanding, the effectiveness of Question Period as an accountability mechanism has long been suspect.[24] For years, the problem has been the small number of questions actually posed and the uncommon appearance of a straight answer. Question Period has become a platform for opposition taunts and government bravado. And much of the action is staged. Government and opposition House leaders and whips are in regular contact, letting each other know who will be present and who will be absent on any given day. Cabinet ministers are usually fully prepared for questions, with complete briefing notes to put a government "spin" on opposition charges. When the opposition is divided, Question Period can sometimes work to the government's advantage. A question from one party on the need for tax cuts, for example, can be played off against a question from a different party on the need for more spending in different program areas.

Yet opposition parties see Question Period as their premier opportunity to embarrass the government about its inability to successfully manage the nation's finances or its pressing policy issues. And they are probably right. Despite the resources at the disposal of Cabinet ministers, vigilant and inventive opposition MPs have frequently managed to derail a government's agenda by posing unexpected and embarrassing questions. Questions regarding government policy or a legislative agenda item rarely stymie the Cabinet. Instead it is questions of ministerial or departmental competence, questions that have minimal ideological or policy content, that are most avidly covered by the media and therefore most likely to have an effect.

If opposition parties cannot force a government to adopt their policies, they can often force a government to halt its agenda to deal with a wayward minister. Given that majority governments rarely fall, causing the resignation of a cabinet minister is about as good as it gets for opposition members. By that criterion, 2002 was a banner year and Question Period the prime theatre for this power struggle. In May, then Minister of National Defence Art Eggleton was found to have given untendered contracts to a former intimate acquaintance. For opposition parties this was the political equivalent of finding a winning lottery ticket. For the government, all policy initiatives were stalled while they dealt with the political fallout. Some of the damage was minimized by virtue of geography. Mr. Eggleton, from Liberal-thick Toronto, was relatively expendable. Once removed, the government could return to its legislative program.

Months later, when Solicitor General Lawrence MacAulay had to leave Cabinet under another cloud (he had apparently been lobbying for federal funds for a college headed by his brother), the dynamics of Canadian regionalism were once more at play. Mr. MacAulay hailed from Prince Edward Island, and his departure from Cabinet determined that a fellow Islander would certainly be promoted to ensure the province would continue to be represented. This meant that the prime minister's choices for a Cabinet replacement were slim. Mr. MacAulay's bad fortune (and questionable judgment) made the odds for promotion for his peers one in three. By contrast, Mr. Eggleton's bad fortune and questionable judgment made the odds for promotion for his regional peers about one in 12.

Political requirements influenced the outcomes of these cases, but the main lesson was how opposition parties, united in their quest, can effectively embarrass a government and block its agenda. Question Period gives them the platform and the media are happy to carry the message to the public. Prime ministers and Cabinet ministers must always be on guard for these moments. It is not the questions alone that stall a government but the follow-up media attention and the perception that the government is not competent at managing its own affairs. While members of Parliament often feed off the media, using the daily headlines to determine the questions they will pose in the House, the media are just as likely to follow the lead of members. When all opposition parties focus on one minister, it is almost a certainty that this minister's troubles will be the lead item in the nation's major media outlets.

The highly public nature of Question Period does distract public attention from some of the more constructive roadblocks, or hurdles, that the parliamentary system places in front of the government. More than any single institution, Question Period has created the impression that the only political test of importance is survival in combat conditions on the floor of the House of Commons. Members of the media, often untutored in the ways of the House or in the substance of policy, gravitate to these stylized confrontations because they offer the sound bites demanded by radio and television. Unfortunately, this over-attention to Question Period has diminished the significance of other debates and left the impression that adversarial politics is all that there is to the Commons.

NEGOTIATING SUCCESS: GOVERNING WITH PARLIAMENT

Successful governments must not only avoid the indiscretions and political miscalculations that lead to Question Period embarrassments, they must also construct and nurture a political agenda that is congenial to supporters. And when governments are in a minority situation and must rely on at least one of the opposition parties to survive a vote of confidence, their supporters must include at least some of those sitting across the floor of the House. Maintaining this ongoing support requires a government to negotiate a policy course that does not offend backbenchers or encourage formation of an opposition coalition united behind a clear policy alternative. Negotiating success is not something that governments, even majority governments, can take for granted.

GOVERNMENT CAUCUS

The government caucus consists of all supporters of the government, including MPs in the governing party, Cabinet members, and government supporters in the Senate. For back-bench MPs, the weekly caucus meeting is the primary vehicle for holding ministers to account. Always held in camera, these meetings give government supporters a unique opportunity to tell the Cabinet "what the people back home are thinking." In general, the role of the government caucus is "one of communications and consultation." Cabinet lets private members know their legislative and policy agenda, and caucus tries to warn Cabinet of danger, rein in politically damaging proposals or, occasionally, prod Cabinet to push their policy ideas a bit further. Usually, disagreements are tactical and subject to negotiation.

If a policy plan does not pass muster in caucus, it will never make it to the floor of the House of Commons. On occasion the government has dropped budgetary or legislative proposals in the face of an incipient backbench revolt. As Justice minister in the early 1990s, Kim Campbell had to drop plans for gun control laws after Conservative backbenchers made it clear they would not support them in the House. More than a decade later, gun control was once again a major issue in caucus. This time, however, Prime Minister Chrétien declared the vote on supplementary funds for the registry a matter of confidence, and his reluctant backbenchers toed the party line. By then the caucus had become a major problem for the prime minister. Leadership issues were being vented in caucus and the prime minister resorted to pleading and threatening as opposition to the government shifted from the floor of the House of Commons to the caucus room.

In some ways caucus can be a victim of its own success. Caucus secrecy means that political observers are uncertain about how powerful the backbencher actually is. An effective prime minister can often convince private members to go along with government plans, assuring them that the party can ride out any temporary dips in popularity.[25] Of course, an overbearing prime minister can push his or her own members too far. When caucus members feel they are being silenced or ignored, this vehicle no longer serves its primary purpose.[26] In recent years government members have abandoned caucus secrecy and allowed their private views to be given public expression. In the final years of Prime Minister Chrétien's leadership, caucus members challenged his leadership on several occasions, including re-electing as caucus chair MP Stan Keyes, who was committed to Chrétien's rival, Paul Martin. Prime ministers have an impressive array of threats and inducements with which to ply their supporters, but these must be used sparingly and with care to preserve party unity.

COMMITTEES

Most of the business of Parliament is done in committees of MPs and Senators. Committees in the House of Commons are potential assets for government. They can provide politically astute analysis, focus attention on policy initiatives instead of miscues, and give backbenchers a voice without giving them a weapon. The potential of committees lies primarily in their ability to offer detached, and often nonpartisan, assessments of difficult policy issues. But, handled badly, committees can become arenas of protest, undermining government consensus and drawing attention to specific policy shortcomings.

Formally, committees of the House of Commons are expected to perform three tasks: fine-tune legislation, investigate broad policy issues, and scrutinize the government's fiscal policy. Committees comprise representatives from all parties and, with some exceptions, conduct their hearings in public. The present committee system is the product of over three decades of reform, most of it aimed at enhancing the role of private members of Parliament and much of it inspired by the view that Parliament should move from an executive-centred body to one that is more Parliament-centred.

While different governments have tinkered with the committee system, the most comprehensive set of reforms in the past quarter-century were based on recommendations of the McGrath Committee report of 1985. The McGrath report wanted all legislation reviewed by legislative committees, ad hoc committees dedicated to producing technically sound legislation but having no subject-matter specialty and no permanent chair. For the first few years after the McGrath report was tabled, all legislation went to these committees. But as early as 1989, standing committees began to re-assert themselves, arguing that they should receive the legislation because they were familiar with the subject matter. When the Chrétien Liberals came to power in 1993, they reverted to the traditional system of having standing committees review most bills.[27]

Standing committees are organized around subject-matter areas, many of which parallel the responsibilities of government departments. Since the McGrath reforms, these committees have been free to frame their own agendas and study those matters that appeal to them. They did not lose this power when the legislative committees were scrapped in 1993, but they have had to suspend much of this general policy work in order to hear witnesses and scrutinize legislation that has passed second reading in the House of Commons.

With the election of five "officially recognized parties" in 1997, Parliament once again altered the committee system. With all five parties now able to claim at least one representative on every standing committee, the workload of members would inevitably have been stretched beyond capacity. Accordingly, the number of standing committees was reduced from 19 to 16.[28] But, at the same time, accommodating the number of recognized parties meant that the size of these committees had to be increased. In the 35th Parliament (1993–97), most standing committees had 11 members. With New Democrats and Conservatives having representation on committees, and with the governing Liberals needing to increase their cohort to maintain a majority on each committee, the committee size increased to an average of 16 members in the 36th and 37th Parliaments. The small, informal setting that often allowed for some nonpartisan debate has been compromised with a return to fewer, larger committees that study both legislation and broader policy issues.

Governments are ambivalent about the launching of general investigations by parliamentary committees. On the positive side (from the government's point of view), public inquiries give the appearance of action, without the substance. They test the waters of public opinion and ascertain the reactions of interest groups to government proposals without requiring a formal commitment to introduce changes. Most important, they provide a vehicle for public input that would otherwise require a task force or some other public body.[29] Governments have been increasingly tempted to ask committees for their advice. Thus, MPs (particularly government backbenchers) are kept busy and all members are given an opportunity to prove themselves.

On the negative side (again, from the government's point of view), committees eventually present reports, and committee members (including those on the government side), not surprisingly, are usually eager to have their proposals discussed. Moreover, these reports are not always what the government wants to see. Veteran Liberal George Baker (Newfoundland) was chair of the Fisheries Committee in 1997–98 when his committee issued a series of reports on the fishing industry in Canada, suggesting that the government was hardly faultless in the decimation of fishing as a way of life on Canada's coasts. Baker was removed as the chair of the Fisheries Committee for his efforts, reinforcing the reputation Jean Chrétien has developed for not tolerating dissent from within the government ranks.[30]

Should the governing party be able to control the leadership of committees in the House of Commons? For years analysts have argued that they should not; committees, they say, are creatures of Parliament and not extensions of the government. This argument was tacitly dismissed until the fall of 2002, when Liberal backbenchers indicated that they had been dictated to long enough. Claiming that the inability of committees to select their own chairs was indicative of a democratic deficit, they insisted in caucus that committees be given the freedom to choose, even if that meant opposition MPs might occasionally take over. A rather remote aspect of parliamentary practice had suddenly become associated with democracy. Fifty-eight Liberal MPs voted in favour of an opposition motion to allow secret-ballot elections of committee chairs. Parties can still remove their own MPs from committees, but this seemingly minor change in leadership selection has significant implications. Not only are members taking ownership of committees, but government members are willing to publicly challenge their leader to make it happen.

Of course, there is still the matter of committee effectiveness. The government is not compelled to act on committee reports, and while governments must respond to reports, responses do not have to be in writing. Until governments are required to act on committee recommendations, doubts about their effectiveness will remain. Nonetheless, given governments' busy agendas, the role of committees in the legislative process is hardly likely to decrease. And if, as seems likely, more and more legislation is referred to committee *before* second reading, the scope for committee intervention will increase rather than decrease.

PRIVATE MEMBERS' BILLS

Only ministers of the Crown have the constitutional authority to introduce legislation that requires the raising or spending of money. That authority is a powerful weapon that is denied both government backbenchers and opposition MPs. However, all members are permitted to introduce legislation. Most back-bench legislation takes the form of private members' bills.[31] The success rate of private members' bills has not been encouraging for parliamentarians wishing to engage in meaningful public policy initiatives. In the two sessions of the 36th Parliament and the first session of the 37th, an average of over 300 private members' bills were introduced, with an average of only five passed. Far fewer government bills were introduced (an average of 58 per session) but the majority (an average of 44 per session) were passed.

Of course, many private members' bills never see second reading, where they are discussed in detail. Of those that do pass second reading and are referred to a committee, many "die" on the order paper—that is, they are never brought to the floor of the House of Commons for a final vote. Recent changes in the Standing Orders of Parliament (the formal rules that govern the operation of the House of Commons) may reverse this bleak prospect and provide new life to some private members' legislation. Until the 36th Parliament, any legislation that was not passed when the House prorogued (rose and next met with a new Speech from the Throne) effectively died. Even if they received second reading and had been vetted by a standing committee, private members' bills would have to be re-introduced in the next session of Parliament. Just before the House of Commons adjourned for its December 1998 break, however, Parliament amended the Standing Orders to allow private members' bills to live on after the session of Parliament dies. While this will not create a stampede of new private members' legislation, it will force some private members' bills to be voted on in third reading on the floor of the House of Commons. For both government and opposition backbenchers, this is a big step.

THE SENATE (AGAIN)

The Senate, too, has recourse to introducing legislation, and often can do so to embarrass the government into action. Naturally, any legislation that is introduced and then passed in the Senate must also pass the House of Commons before it becomes law. When legislation with broad public support passes the Senate but then is stalled in the House of Commons, the government can look stubborn and unresponsive. The Senate passed just such a bill in 1998. Introduced by Liberal senator Colin Kenny of Ontario, Bill S-13 would have imposed a new tobacco tax on every package of cigarettes sold in Canada. The proceeds would then have been directed toward youth anti-smoking programs. Once passed in the Senate, the cause of the bill was taken up by Liberal backbencher Carolyn Bennett. Immediately upon its introduction, Liberal House Leader Don Boudria rose to challenge the bill, claiming (correctly) that neither the Senate nor private members have the authority to introduce legislation that requires the raising or spending of money.[32] While successful in stopping the legislation, this was hardly the government's finest hour.

The Senate is rarely an initiator of important legislation, but it can stall government legislation, as it did with the Free Trade Act in 1988, effectively forcing then Prime Minister Brian Mulroney to hold an election on the issue. During the 37th Parliament the Senate held extensive hearings on the Clarity Act, legislation designed to spell out the conditions for Quebec separation. While this move caused some concern for members of the Commons, the fact that the Senate treated the act on a nonpartisan basis, heard from more witnesses, and held longer hearings than the

Commons muted much criticism. When the Senate acts as a chamber of sober reflection, it can deflect criticism.

Calls for Senate reform were renewed in 1998, when Ontario senator Andrew Thompson made national headlines following revelations about his attendance record. The fact that Thompson continued to draw a senatorial salary without attending any sittings of the Senate outraged many Canadians. The Senate itself tried to punish him but found itself with few options, as most penalties on senators, such as removal from committees or the denial of speaking rights, are based on the assumption that members actually *want to participate!* Eventually, the Senate found a way to withhold his salary, and Mr. Thompson resigned his seat. Calls for Senate reform have died down in the past decade, largely because of past failures.

One of the most widely known calls for Senate reform, the "Triple E" Senate, had been championed by the Reform Party (now the Canadian Alliance) and was based on the principles of equal provincial representation, elected members, and effective legislative authority to protect provincial interests. While still committed to Senate reform, the Alliance is less vocal about pushing for a Triple E model. Past government attempts at Senate reform have been tied to other institutional changes. The failure of so-called mega-constitutional packages such as Meech Lake and the Charlottetown Accord has soured the taste for change among the public and thus politicians.

The Senate serves a useful and important purpose, so while talk of changing the Senate may be silenced for now, there is little doubt that it will resurface at some point, either through actions of senators or from a political party seeking to capitalize on a renewed public enthusiasm for constitutional reform discussions.

Successive changes to the rules of the House of Commons, especially during the 1980s, have strengthened the role of members of Parliament. MPs are now better able to make a timely contribution to the government's policy agenda, and parliamentarians on both sides of the House have acquired a measure of control over the procedures, personnel, and precincts of Parliament. Developments like these suggest that there is another dimension to responsible government. The responsibility of a vigilant assembly to monitor closely the actions of a government need not be borne exclusively by the united opposition. Others, including the government caucus, standing committees, individual MPs, and even the Senate, can reasonably be expected to share that responsibility. As a result, governments must be prepared to negotiate, not simply bully, their way to political success.

CONCLUSION: PARLIAMENT CAN WORK

Successful governments, we have argued, are those whose actions contribute to support for parliamentary institutions. These governments recognize that Parliament is an adversarial arena but do not use this reality as an excuse to abuse their authority or ignore the demands of either supporters or the opposition. Successful governments behave in ways that encourage policy innovation but promote institutional continuity. In short, they govern with integrity.

None of this means that Parliament itself should remain unchanged. Throughout the 1980s reforms were made to provide members of Parliament with more voice in the policy process. Jean Chrétien's failure to provide his backbenchers with more meaningful roles eventually came to haunt him in his last term. Had he initiated reform of the committee structure, he might not have had it thrust upon him by the opposition and many in his own caucus. The trick for governments is to initiate improvement without compromising the Westminster model's commitment to effective leadership. Reform of Parliament will always pivot on this delicate tradeoff.

What we must not do is permit the diminishing or ignoring of Parliament in the name of reform. In an era of polling, cable TV, and the Internet, it is tempting for governments, under the banner of democracy, to establish direct contact with voters. Parliament is partisan and messy; why not allow citizens to receive and respond directly to the government's message? The answer is simple: Democracy is about deliberation. Scripted encounters via television and the Web are about manipulation. Representation involves the aggregation of interests, not simply the articulation of opinions. Only Parliament can provide a public test of the government's full legislative program in a deliberative setting. Parliament pulls interests together and provides focused critique without depriving governments of the chance to govern.

Each government can adopt an agenda of major policy items on which it intends to be judged. When these items are at variance with the public mood or divide the country on regional lines, Parliament is the place where frustrations can be aired and governments can re-calibrate their choices. Those that decide to plough ahead—the Trudeau government with the National Energy Policy, the Mulroney government with the GST, and the Chrétien government with gun control—do so in the full appreciation of the political price to be paid. They cannot reasonably blame "the system," Parliament, their advisers, the provinces, or even the media. Success is well within the reach of any government that understands its parliamentary responsibilities and acts in a manner that increases confidence in parliamentary institutions.

NOTES

1. Harold Clarke, Jane Jenson, Lawrence LeDuc, and Jon H. Pammett, *Absent Mandate: Canadian Electoral Politics in an Era of Restructuring*, 3rd ed. (Vancouver: Gage Publishing, 1996).

2. Of course, given the regional nature of the BQ, and thus far the inability of Reform to make any advance within Quebec, most ridings in Canada have four major parties vying for victory.

3. It must be acknowledged, however, that failure to keep election promises is one of the most serious breaches of faith that a governing party can make. See the polling results reported in Maureen Mancuso, Michael M. Atkinson, Andre Blais, Ian Greene, and Neil Nevitte, *A Question of Ethics: Canadians Speak Out* (Toronto: Oxford University Press, 1998), chap. 6.

4. For a fuller discussion of executive-centred versus member-centred Parliaments, see C.E.S. Franks, *The Parliament of Canada* (Toronto: University of Toronto Press, 1987), chap. 2.

5. The actual size of the ministry in 2003 was 40. However, included in this group are 12 "secretaries of state" who do not hold departmental responsibilities and are not full members of Cabinet. The Leader of the Government in the Senate is a full member of Cabinet but holds no departmental responsibilities.

6. On the various types of bills and the distinction between private bills and private members' bills, see Robert J. Jackson and Michael M. Atkinson, *The Canadian Legislative System*, 2nd ed. (Toronto: Gage, 1980), pp. 93–108.

7. John B. Stewart, *The Canadian House of Commons: Procedure and Reform* (Montreal/Kingston: McGill-Queen's University Press, 1977), p. 201.

8. Michael M. Atkinson and David C. Docherty, "Moving Right Along: The Roots of Amateurism in the Canadian House of Commons," *Canadian Journal of Political Science* 25 (June 1992): 285–315.

9. Eugene Forsey and Graham Eglinton, "Twenty-Five Fairy Tales about Parliamentary Government," in Paul W. Fox and Graham White, eds., *Politics in Canada*, 6th ed. (Toronto: McGraw-Hill Ryerson, 1987), pp. 507–13.

10. See David Docherty, "It's Awfully Crowded in Here: Adjusting to the Five-Party House of Commons," *Parliamentary Perspective* 2 (October 1998): 17.

11. Franks, *The Parliament of Canada*, p. 260.

12. See the Constitution Act, 1867, section 23.

13. David E. Smith, "The Federal Cabinet in Canadian Politics," in Michael Whittington and Glen Williams, eds., *Canadian Politics in the 1990s*, 4th ed. (Scarborough, ON: Nelson, 1995), p. 396.

14. Janet Ajzenstat, *The Political Thought of Lord Durham* (Montreal/Kingston: McGill-Queen's University Press, 1988).

15. Peter Aucoin, "Responsible Government and Citizen Engagement at the Millennium: Are Political Parties 'Irrelevant'?" paper presented at the annual meeting of the Canadian Study of Parliament Group, Ottawa, October 31, 1998.

16. James R. Mitchell and Sharon Sutherland, "Ministerial Responsibility: The Submission of Politics and Administration to the Electorate," in Martin Westmacott and Hugh P. Mellon, eds., *Public Administration and Policy: Governing in Challenging Times* (Scarborough, ON: Prentice-Hall, 1999), p. 25.

17. For a discussion of political parties in Parliament, see Paul Thomas, "Parliamentary Reform through Political Parties," in John Courtney, ed., *The Canadian House of Commons Observed: Essays in Honour of Norman Ward* (Calgary: University of Calgary Press, 1985). See also Aucoin, "Responsible Government and Citizen Engagement."

18. Stewart, *The Canadian House of Commons*, p. 21.

19. Ghita Ionescu and Isabel de Madariaga, *Opposition* (Harmondsworth: Penguin, 1972), chap. 2.

20. James R. Robertson, "Political Parties and Parliamentary Recognition," Background Paper, Research Branch, Library of Parliament, August 1990 (revised August 1996).

21. For a fuller discussion of the function of opposition parties, see Franks, *The Parliament of Canada*, chap. 1.

22. Ibid., p. 155.

23. The "scrum" is a uniquely Canadian event in which opposition and Cabinet ministers are surrounded by reporters in the halls outside the assembly. Of course, for Cabinet ministers, the scrum is often an unpleasant experience. They are asked to elaborate on responses made in the chamber. For opposition MPs, it is a chance to further spread their message. Regular observers of this daily ritual joke that back-bench MPs often "scrum" reporters, trying to get the media to pay attention to their particular issue. Cabinet ministers do not have that worry.

24. See C.E.S. Franks, "The Problem of 'Debate' and Question Period," in John Courtney, ed., *The Canadian House of Commons Observed: Essays in Honour of Norman Ward* (Calgary: University of Calgary Press, 1985), pp. 1–20.

25. Paul Thomas, "Parties and Regional Representation," in Herman Bakvis, ed., *Representation, Integration and Political Parties in Canada*, vol. 14 of the Report of the Royal Commission on Electoral Reform and Party Financing (Toronto: Dundurn Press, 1991), p. 212.

26. David C. Docherty, *Mr. Smith Goes to Ottawa: Life in the House of Commons* (Vancouver: UBC Press, 1997), p. 169.

27. Paul G. Thomas, "The Influence of Standing Committees of Parliament on Government Legislation," *Legislative Studies Quarterly* 3 (November 1978): 683–704.

28. Docherty, "It's Awfully Crowded in Here," p. 13.

29. Jonathon Malloy, "Reconciling Expectations and Reality in House of Commons Committees: The Case of the 1989 GST Inquiry," *Canadian Public Administration* 39, no. 3 (November 1996): 314–35.

30. See Paul G. Thomas, "Caucus and Representation in Canada, *Parliamentary Perspectives*, Canadian Study of Parliament Group, Issue 1 (May 1998).

31. There are actually two kinds of private members' bills: private members' public bills and private bills. The former, which deal with public policy issues, are those of primary concern to us. The latter deal with specific concerns of individuals and are not considered matters of interest to the broader public.

32. House of Commons, *Debates* (November 18, 1998), p. 10145.

FURTHER READINGS

Atkinson, Michael M., and Paul Thomas. "Studying the Canadian Parliament." *Legislative Studies Quarterly* 18 (August 1993): 423–51.

Docherty, David C. *Mr. Smith Goes to Ottawa: Life in the House of Commons.* Vancouver: UBC Press, 1997.

Franks, C.E.S. *The Parliament of Canada.* Toronto: University of Toronto Press, 1987.

Fraser, John. *The House of Commons at Work.* Montreal: Les Éditions de la Chenelière, 1991.

Mitchell, James R., and Sharon L. Sutherland. "Ministerial Responsibility: The Submission of Politics and Administration to the Electorate." In Martin Westmacott and Hugh Mellon, eds., *Public Administration and Policy: Governing in Challenging Times*, pp. 21–37. Scarborough, ON: Prentice-Hall, 1999.

Robertson, James R. "Political Parties and Parliamentary Recognition." Background Paper, Research Branch, Library of Parliament, August 1990 (Revised August 1996).

Seidle, F. Leslie, and David C. Docherty, eds. *Reforming Parliamentary Government.* Montreal: McGill-Queen's University Press, 2003.

Smith, David E. *The Canadian Senate in Bicameral Perspective.* Toronto: University of Toronto Press, 2003.

Smith, Jennifer. "Democracy and the Canadian House of Commons at the Millennium." *Canadian Public Administration* 42, no. 4 (1999): 398–421.

Thomas, Paul. "Caucus and Representation in Canada." *Parliamentary Perspectives* 1 (May 1998).

Weaver, R. Kent. "Improving Representation in the Canadian House of Commons." *Canadian Journal of Political Science* 30 (September 1997): 473–512.

CHAPTER 2

THE PRIME MINISTER, CABINET, AND EXECUTIVE POWER

Michael S. Whittington

Almost everyone would agree that the most visible and powerful individuals in democratic systems of government are those who occupy positions of executive authority. Indeed, it is prime ministers and presidents who give to periods in history their distinctive character. In Canada we speak of the "Diefenbaker Interlude," the "Trudeau Era," or the "Mulroney Years" because it is the personality and image of the prime minister that we associate with the particular tone or flavour of that political time. It is the goal of this chapter to attempt to explain the nature of executive authority in Canada, and in particular to describe the power of the prime minister in our system of government.

THE CONSTITUTION AND THE EXECUTIVE POWER

THE CROWN AND THE GOVERNOR GENERAL

While section 9 of the Constitution Act of 1867 tells us that "The Executive Government and Authority of and over Canada is hereby declared to continue and be vested in the Queen," this assertion is not all that helpful when it comes to trying to understand how the executive branch in Canada actually operates. Clearly, Her Majesty is a rare visitor to Canada, let alone to the Cabinet chamber on Parliament Hill. Moreover, the visits she does make to our shores are by Canada's invitation only and involve purely ceremonial and symbolic chores. By a combination of formal amendment to the Act of 1867, and the strict adherence to a series of constitutional conventions—some inherited from the United Kingdom and some that evolved on this side of the Atlantic—the Queen's role has been reduced to that of appointing the governor general, and, even then, only on the recommendation of our prime minister.[1]

Although the Queen is still the symbol of executive authority in Canada (hence terms such as Crown land, Crown prosecutor, Crown corporation, and Minister of the Crown), all of the formal powers of the monarch in Canada are now exercised by the governor general (and by lieutenant governors in the provinces). Unfortunately, understanding the *formal* role of the governor general also does not tell us very much about how the executive authority in Canada is actually exercised. The last time a Canadian governor general acted other than on the advice of the prime minister was in 1926,[2] and while aficionados of such things will tell us that there are still circumstances in which a governor general might be forced to take his or her own counsel, in practical terms, the job of the Queen's representative in Canada is to do what the prime minister asks and to behave at all times in an apolitical, diplomatic, and statesmanlike manner. But, given that the terms "prime minister," "premier," and "cabinet" are not even mentioned in the Constitution Act of 1867,[3] we now must ask what then is the constitutional source of prime ministerial power?

THE PRIVY COUNCIL AND CABINET

The first part of the answer to this rhetorical question lies in section 11 of the Constitution Act, 1867, which states that "there shall be a Council to aid and advise in the Government of Canada, to be styled the Queen's Privy Council for Canada" and that the members of the Privy Council are to be appointed (or removed) and sworn in by the governor general. The second part of the answer lies in the Preamble to the 1867 Act, which states that Canada is to have a constitution "similar in principle to that of the United Kingdom." This provision formally incorporates all of the applicable (and unwritten) conventions of the British constitution, of which the most important are the following:

1. *Constitutional monarchy*, whereby the Queen (the governor general in Canada) will always act only in a manner consistent with the wishes of the prime minister.
2. *Party government*, whereby, after an election, the Queen (the governor general in Canada) must ask the leader of the party with the most seats in the House of Commons to form a government—that is, to accept an appointment to the Privy Council, to act as the

prime minister, and to advise the governor general as to whom else to appoint as *ministers.*

3. *Cabinet government,* whereby a committee of the Privy Council, called the *Cabinet,* composed of the prime minister and the current ministers of the government, acts in the name of the Queen's Privy Council for Canada.[4]

4. *Responsible government,* whereby the government of the day can only be the government insofar as it holds the support or *confidence* of a majority of the House of Commons.

Thus, the practical reality of the executive power in parliamentary democracies is that it is exercised largely by the *political executive,* the prime minister, whose executive decisions are formulated and tempered within the crucible of the Cabinet chamber. The power of the prime minister, however, is limited not only by the need for the prime minister to maintain collective solidarity among the members of the Cabinet but also by the need for the *government of the day*[5] to secure and maintain the support of a majority of the members of the House of Commons. These latter requirements for the successful exercise of prime ministerial power tend to be determined largely by factors other than constitutional ones, which will be discussed later. We must now turn to a consideration of what the executive function of government comprises.

THE FUNCTIONS OF THE EXECUTIVE

This section addresses the various functions or "jobs" that the executive branch of government must perform if the system as a whole is to operate effectively. We can identify three main sets of functions performed by the executive: the head of state functions, the chief executive functions, and the policy functions, each of which will be dealt with in turn. The reader should note that while our focus is on Canada at the *federal* level of government, these same functions can be seen in all of the Canadian provinces and territories and in most of the countries throughout the world.

HEAD OF STATE FUNCTIONS

While executive *power* in Canada is exercised for the most part by the prime minister and the Cabinet, the symbolic embodiment of Canadian sovereignty is still the Crown, and the *head of state* function of the executive is vested formally in the Queen and her representative in Canada, the governor general. Even today, many of the formal, ceremonial, and honorific functions of the executive, such as greeting visiting foreign heads of state, investing recipients of the Order of Canada, and hosting an annual New Year's Day "levee" are still performed by the governor general. Indeed, it is useful for the busy prime minister to be able to delegate many minor ceremonial jobs to the Queen's representative, leaving more time to devote to the business of heading up the government.

CHIEF EXECUTIVE FUNCTIONS

While the distinction between the chief executive function and the policy function is somewhat blurred, with one job overlapping and flowing into the other, the essence of the former is the *management* of the day-to-day affairs of the government, and the latter, to be discussed later, is deciding what rules, expressed as laws, will be imposed on Canada and on Canadians.

DIRECTING

Central to the function of management, in the private sector as well as in government, is the provision of leadership to an organization and the directing of its day-to-day operations. The government of Canada is essentially an organization, albeit a very large one. The prime minister is the CEO and the Cabinet is his or her board of directors. Thus, as well as providing *political leadership* to the country as a whole, the PM is also responsible for providing broad direction to the vast apparatus we know as the Government of Canada. The PM is responsible for selecting Cabinet members and assigning individual ministers to specific departments, or *portfolios*. Each department is headed by a minister, who is formally responsible to the PM and ultimately to Parliament itself for the performance of the department and of its officials.

While the day-to-day affairs of government departments are for the most part directed by senior public servants known as deputy ministers, and while most Canadians realize that it is unrealistic to expect a minister in modern government to be aware of all that goes on in the department, it is the minister who must answer for the performance of his or her department before the House of Commons and within Cabinet. This principle of *ministerial responsibility* is not as strict as it once was, with ministers sometimes forced to resign in the face of errors or wrongdoings in the department. However, it is still the minister who must "face the music" if his or her departmental officials make a mistake.

ORGANIZING

Another management function of the executive in Canada is the overall *organizing* of the government. Assisted by and heavily influenced by the professional managers of the bureaucracy, the political executive is responsible for the structure of the system, the allocation of responsibilities among departments and agencies, and the effectiveness of the management regime. Since the 1990s, decisions respecting the structure of government have focused on downsizing, privatization, and deregulation. The executive has been engaged in a process of negative-priority determination, eliminating some departments and agencies entirely, combining others under a single portfolio, and transferring still others to the private sector.

STAFFING

As with any organization, government must ensure that the positions within it are occupied by people who can do the jobs required. This management function of *staffing* the government is for the most part performed by the professional managers of the bureaucracy and overseen by the Public Service Commission, which ensures that employment in the public service is based on merit and not on political patronage. However, while essentially excused from the responsibility for staffing the approximately 500 000 rank-and-file positions in the federal government, the prime minister and Cabinet retain the responsibility for "order-in-council" appointments. These are appointments made formally by the governor general, but at the exclusive discretion of the prime minister, and include federal judges, superior court judges in the provinces, lieutenant governors, senators, deputy ministers, ambassadors, royal commissioners, and the presidents, chairs, and boards of directors of sundry Crown corporations and regulatory agencies. Most such appointments are at least influenced by the political affiliations of the appointee and many of them are blatantly patronage choices to reward the faithful for services rendered to the party in power.

CONTROLLING

The chief executive and policy functions of the executive are most interrelated in the area of financial management and *control* of spending. Clearly, the allocation of financial resources among the various programs of the government sets priorities among existing policies, and such spending decisions can be as important as the decisions leading to the implementation of new legislation. However, the power to spend money in order to give effect to government programs is a necessary component of the effective management of the affairs of the state.

It is a cornerstone of responsible government that the Cabinet may only spend money that is appropriated to it by Parliament, and, moreover, such money must be spent only on the measures specifically identified in the appropriations. However, while Parliament must approve spending proposals before the government can spend any money, only a minister can actually *spend* the money—Parliament does not have the power to spend money itself.[6] Moreover, because the prime minister and the Cabinet are held accountable for all government spending, only ministers (not opposition leaders or back-bench MPs) have the authority to initiate financial measures. Thus, all bills that require the expenditure of public monies and all tax legislation must be introduced by a minister. The operational components of the executive branch's responsibility for the financial affairs of the nation include the preparation and presentation of the *budget,* the preparation of the expenditure *estimates* that form the basis for appropriation acts, and the keeping of the *public accounts* that enable Parliament to scrutinize the government's spending. Finally, it is a convention of our Constitution that if a major financial measure is defeated in the House of Commons, it is normally viewed as a "vote of nonconfidence" requiring the prime minister to tender his or her resignation to the governor general and hold a general election.

POLICY FUNCTIONS

Public policy decisions are those taken *within* government about measures to be given effect *outside* government. In other words, a policy is a declaration of government's intention to implement laws and regulations that will directly affect individuals in our society. A policy, per se, has no legal or binding effect on citizens, because, in a system based on the *rule of law,* our rights, privileges, and obligations can only be altered by legislation, by regulations passed pursuant to legislation, and by the decisions of administrative and enforcement officials entrusted with the responsibility for implementing the laws. However, once a government has taken a firm policy decision, it is almost inevitable that it will eventually be transformed into a legally sanctioned instrument that affects the lives of Canadians.

While determining policy is clearly the most important function of governments, it is difficult to state uncategorically where and by whom such important decisions are taken. Policy, in a world as complex as ours and in a system of government based on liberal democratic principles, is rarely made in a single climactic act or by a single identifiable actor or institution. The "off with their heads" model of policymaking can happen only in a mythical autocracy, where decisions are simple "either/or" ones and where the requirements of representative democracy do not apply. In a modern democracy, policies emerge over time through the complex interaction of the large number of individuals, groups, and institutions that make up the *policy community.*

Policy ideas can be introduced or *initiated* by individual Canadians, by interest groups, by experts and specialists in the bureaucracy, and by the politicians themselves. Policy ideas are fleshed out and *formulated* to a large extent by experts in the bureaucracy, and the ultimate policy proposal must be given legal effect and *legitimized* by our elected representatives in Parliament (or the provincial legislatures). However, it is the political executive—the Cabinet and the prime minister—that is the "policy crucible" or core institution of the policy process in Canada. It is the Cabinet that must set broad policy direction for the country, determining, for instance, that spending must be curbed, more should be left to the private sector, a greater effort must be exerted to improve social programs and health care, and so on. Moreover, it is the Cabinet that must establish priorities for the implementation of existing policies: deciding whether a policy option is worth pursuing at all, determining the order in which approved policies must be given legislative effect, and deciding which agencies should be given the responsibility for formulating the specifics of the legislation. Finally, even though it is Parliament that must give legislative legitimacy to all policies, the Cabinet, because it controls a majority in the House of Commons, has the responsibility for introducing the legislation and for piloting the bill through the legislative process.

THE STRUCTURE OF THE POLITICAL EXECUTIVE

As we have seen, because Canada is, in a strictly legal sense, a *constitutional monarchy,* the Queen is the titular head of state and her powers and responsibilities in Canada are delegated to the governor general. Because Canada is a *federal state,* with sovereignty shared between two orders of government, the authority of the Crown in each of the provinces is delegated to a lieutenant governor. Finally, because Canada is a *parliamentary democracy,* virtually all of the powers and responsibilities of the Crown in

Canada are exercised by the political executive, the Cabinet, at both the federal and provincial levels. Hence, in explaining the institutions of the executive branch in Canada, we must focus on the internal workings of the Cabinet, the Cabinet committee structure, and the nature of the executive support apparatus that assists the Cabinet and the prime minister in carrying out their responsibilities.

THE MINISTRY SYSTEM

There has always been an informal hierarchy among ministers in Cabinet, determined by and reflective of the importance of the portfolio held, membership on key committees, experience and seniority, home province, relationship with the prime minister, and, although cynics might scoff, the intelligence and ability of the individuals involved. While these determinants of ministerial influence in Cabinet still operate today, in 1993 the government of Jean Chrétien made two significant changes in the structure of the Cabinet that have had an impact on the power of individual ministers.[7]

First, by contrast to the large (40 members plus) cabinets of Mulroney and Trudeau, Chrétien reduced the Cabinet to about 30 ministers. Sitting as one of 30 instead of one of 40, each minister has a better opportunity to be heard, and hence a higher relative potential to be influential in Cabinet deliberations. Second, so that representation for various groups and regions could be provided in Cabinet, as in the past, the Chrétien government created the new ministerial rank of "secretary of state" that allowed for the appointment of seven to twelve junior "ministers in training." Secretaries of state are sworn in as Privy Councillors and they are in the *ministry* but not in the Cabinet. Each is assigned to a "full" minister and given an area of responsibility within the minister's portfolio, but a secretary of state is not placed in charge of a government department. Secretaries of state receive about 75 percent of the salary of a minister and are permitted to attend Cabinet meetings only at the invitation of the prime minister.[8]

CABINET COMMITTEES

Until the middle part of the twentieth century the vast majority of executive decisions in Canada were taken by the entire Cabinet, meeting as a *plenary* body chaired by the prime minister.[9] As Cabinets grew in size, meetings of the full, or plenary, body became more and more cumbersome. Moreover, as the number of items appearing on Cabinet agendas grew, it became apparent that there was insufficient time to consider all items adequately in full Cabinet. Hence, the practice of delegating certain matters to committees of cabinet[10] gradually grew until, by the Trudeau years and continuing through the Mulroney period, virtually all decisions were taken in committees and the plenary Cabinet seldom even met. Before we discuss the Chrétien system (see Figure 2-1), which has returned a lot of the power to the plenary Cabinet, it is worth looking at a few of the key departures in the evolution of Cabinet committees.

TREASURY BOARD

"The Board" was established in 1875 by the Financial Administration Act to oversee the expenditure budget and to assist the line departments in the preparation and submission of their annual estimates.[11] In 1967, the Treasury Board was given the further mandate to act as a committee of management for the public service, overseeing all aspects of personnel and financial management in government (except those assigned to the Public Service Commission under the Public Service Employment Act). As well, the Treasury Board became the government "employer" for purposes of collective bargaining. Since 1968 the Board has been chaired by the minister designated President of the Treasury Board and includes five other ministers, one of whom must be the minister of Finance. The Board is supported by a large central agency staffed by bureaucrats called the *Treasury Board Secretariat*, or TBS.

FIGURE 2-1 The Chrétien Ministry in 2003

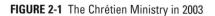

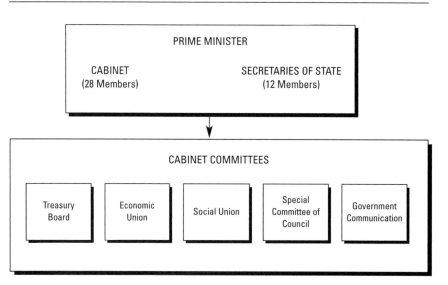

PRIORITIES AND PLANNING

Britain has had a two-tiered cabinet system for a long time, with the key movers and shakers of the government and the most trusted colleagues of the prime minister sitting as members of a de facto committee called the *inner Cabinet.*

Although this type of arrangement emerged briefly in Canada during World War II, when the plenary Cabinet was effectively displaced by the *War Committee* of Mackenzie King's government, it wasn't until Pierre Trudeau's government of 1968 that such a system became a fixture in this country. Trudeau set up a plethora of specialized *standing committees* of Cabinet that dealt with the details of policymaking in the various portfolios of government along with two coordinating committees that choreographed the government's relationships with Parliament (*Legislation and House Planning*) and with the provinces (*Federal–Provincial Relations*). To oversee this complex structure, the Trudeau government established a "mother of all committees," styled the *Cabinet Committee on Priorities and Planning* (P&P), which was, in essence, an "inner Cabinet."[12]

This system, with some minor variations, remained in place throughout the Trudeau and Mulroney years. Mulroney's government added yet another layer to the complexity with the creation of a *Cabinet Committee on Operations* (OPS), which was smaller than Priorities and Planning but included the most important members of P&P and, cumbersome as it may seem, effectively set priorities for the Priorities and Planning Committee. In the final years of the Mulroney era, the executive decision-making process in Canada had become so complex that even the ministers who were part of it could not fully understand it. The only people who seemed to thrive in this multi-layered apparatus were the senior officers in the Privy Council Office. These central agency mandarins acquired disproportionate influence over the policymaking system because only they could follow its many twists and turns. It was this excessive complexity that brought the system to the point of near collapse, and set the stage for the reforms to the Cabinet committee system in 1993.

THE COMMITTEE SYSTEM TODAY

The Cabinet committee system established by the Chrétien government in 1993 bore little resemblance to its predecessor. There is no P&P or OPS, and there are no coordinating committees, the responsibilities of these bodies having been taken over by the plenary Cabinet. The Treasury

Board, because its powers are defined by statute, functions as it did before. Two "policy committees," the *Economic Development Policy Committee* and the *Social Development Policy Committee*—assumed responsibility for the detailed scrutiny of policy proposals previously delegated to the eight to 10 "standing committees" in the Trudeau and Mulroney eras. These two committees are today known simply as the Committee on the *Economic Union* and the Committee on the *Social Union*. The newest Cabinet committee is the Committee on *Government Communications,* which is concerned with the linkages between government and the Canadian people. There is a *Special Committee of Council* that does not deal with policy but takes the responsibility for a number of executive housekeeping chores such as order-in-council appointments. As in the past, the prime minister can establish ad hoc committees at any time to deal with specific problems or projects.

As the Chrétien Cabinet evolved, it became apparent that the workload was not evenly distributed among the policy committees, with the Committee on the Economic Union having a broader range of responsibilities than Social Union. Moreover, it is clear that some individual ministers are more influential than others, their power depending on their portfolio responsibilities, relationship with the prime minister, the region of the country they represent, and so on. Hence, while there is no formal "inner Cabinet," the plenary Cabinet does not make any decisions unless a small coterie of key ministers and the prime minister are in agreement. Thus, the Chrétien Cabinet structure is certainly simpler than that of Trudeau and Mulroney, but, as we shall see, the formal structure tells us only part of the story of how the prime minister and Cabinet actually exercise executive power in Canada.

EXECUTIVE SUPPORT TO CABINET

Before World War I, governments were basically noninterventionist, and the issues of the day were far less complex and technical in nature. Sir John A. Macdonald and Sir Wilfrid Laurier made a lot of policy decisions on their own, tempered with whatever advice they might have chosen to accept from their colleagues in Cabinet. Reliance on large and highly specialized policy units in the bureaucracy was minimal, and the need for executive support staff was limited to secretarial and clerical personnel, a small *Cabinet Secretariat* to keep records of Cabinet deliberations and decisions, and various "gofers" and minor minions who served the personal needs of the ministers.

MINISTERS AND MANDARINS

After the Great Depression and World War II, the policy world became more complex. Prime ministers such as William Lyon Mackenzie King and Louis St. Laurent came to rely heavily on the advice of the senior bureaucracy—the so-called *mandarins*—in making policy decisions. Policy issues had become more technical in nature and the expertise of the bureaucracy gave it significant influence over the policy decisions taken by the basically non-expert Cabinet. The executive support staff of the Cabinet came to include individual ministers' executive assistants and executive secretaries. The Secretariat to the Cabinet, while somewhat larger, was still primarily concerned with the effective keeping of records and facilitating the flow of paper to and from Cabinet.

The 1960s saw an incredible growth in the size and responsibility of executive support units in government, units that came to be called *central agencies*.[13] These agencies expanded in part because the prime minister and Cabinet felt that the power of the mandarins in the bureaucracy could be countered if there were a separate body of experts reporting directly to the prime minister that could filter and interpret the increasingly technical policy documents being considered in Cabinet. The Cabinet Secretariat became the *Privy Council Office (PCO)* and was responsible for the management of the flow of documents from the bureaucracy to the Cabinet. The PCO became an information gatekeeper, filtering, digesting, and interpreting the vast amount of material before Cabinet so that harried ministers might be able to better understand it.

THE PRIVY COUNCIL OFFICE

While the expansion of the central agencies began during the Diefenbaker–Pearson years, the most radical growth in their size and power occurred with the Trudeau government. Certainly it was distrust of the line bureaucracy and the problem of information overload in the policy process that justified PCO growth, but it was also the rationalist philosophy of Pierre Trudeau that spurred this expansion. Trudeau, Canada's "philosopher-king-as-PM," believed that the vast amounts of complex and technical data that had to be read and absorbed for the Cabinet to be able to make informed and effective policy decisions could still be managed. The solution, according to Trudeau, lay in a better central agency apparatus. Moreover, the PCO being under the direct control of the prime minister gave him increased control, not only over the bureaucracy but also over his own ministers. Not surprisingly, when Brian Mulroney became the PM he did not significantly alter the role or structure of the PCO, and in fact it grew during his nine years in office.

To this day, the organization of the PCO reflects the approach of the Trudeau government. Headed by Canada's top public servant, who holds the double-barrelled title of Secretary to the Cabinet and Clerk of the Privy Council, the PCO has a staff of about 500. Its job is to provide coordinative services to the Cabinet and its committees, insuring that agendas are in place for meetings, that the relevant documents are on hand for the ministers to peruse, and that all documentary material is organized, integrated, and summarized in a readily comprehensible form. The PCO forms both a communications link and a "buffer" between the Cabinet and the policy advisers in the line departments of government.

THE PRIME MINISTER'S OFFICE

The Prime Minister's Office (PMO) also expanded rapidly under Trudeau. Just as the substantive and technical components of the policy process could be organized and rationalized by the PCO, so could its political and partisan components be streamlined. In a world of mass communications and public opinion polling, Trudeau realized that "old-fashioned politickin' "—door-to-door canvassing, mainstreeting, baby kissing, and "a chicken in every pot" campaign promises—could no longer win elections. Instead, it was felt that political communication with the electorate should be an ongoing process, with policy decisions taken quite deliberately to find congruence with prevailing public attitudes. Moreover, it was essential that the desired message be sent to Canadians through the media, with the most publicly appealing "spin" or emphasis on the information.

The PMO had a staff of only 40 under Prime Minister Pearson and grew to about 150 under Trudeau. Brian Mulroney, who distrusted the bureaucracy more than Trudeau before him or Chrétien after him, and who hoped to achieve a greater politicization of the policy process, allowed this agency to grow to 300. In 1993, Chrétien vowed that he and his ministers would work more closely with the senior bureaucracy and that he would take a less choreographed and "folksier" personal approach to delivering the partisan message to the country. However, while the PMO is smaller today than it was in 1970, it has grown both in power and size since 1993.

While the PMO may vary in size and influence with successive PMs, it continues to function as the *political technocracy* of government. There is a small unit within the agency responsible for organizing the PM's appointments, itinerary, and day-to-day schedule. There is also a correspondence secretariat that monitors and ensures appropriate action is taken on all mail received by the PM. Under Chrétien, the PMO also includes a number of *regional assistants* who are supposed to keep the PM advised of developments in the hinterland beyond Ottawa. The *Policy and*

Research Branch has senior policy advisers who undertake special projects and maintain ties with the key people in the PCO. Since the PMO reports directly to the prime minister, it also enhances and consolidates his or her power with respect to Cabinet colleagues and the backbenchers in the government caucus.

One of the most important branches of the PMO is responsible for communications. This part of the PMO monitors media reports across the country and gives the PM regular briefings on how he and his government are being perceived. This branch of the PMO also manages the flow of information from government to the media, and hence to the public. Government press releases and press conferences are organized by media relations officers, who also try to maintain close "insider" relationships with members of the press corps in order to influence the "spin" that is placed on news items and announcements of new policy initiatives. However, given the increasingly confrontational relationship between the media and politicians today, "managing the press" becomes more and more difficult for political leaders and their communications mavens alike.

THE PRIME MINISTER AND PARLIAMENT

Prime ministerial power in Canada stems from the fact that by unwritten constitutional convention the PM is the only person with the practical authority to exercise all of the powers of the Crown. The PM can dissolve Parliament and call an election, and the PM decides when to summon, prorogue, or dissolve, Parliament. Only the prime minister can name judges, senators, ambassadors, lieutenant governors, and the governor of the Bank of Canada as well as innumerable lesser "order-in-council" appointees. As well, the prime minister to a large extent controls the agenda of the House of Commons. Because the lion's share of time in the legislature is dedicated to dealing with "government business" and because the PM is the leader of the government, he or she has a great deal of control over the legislative agenda of Parliament. However, the PM's power in Parliament depends on maintaining the support of a majority in the House of Commons, a task that may, from time to time, become troublesome.

MINORITY GOVERNMENT

A *minority government* is one in which the party in power holds fewer than 50 percent of the seats in the House. In this situation, the PM not only must keep his or her own backbenchers in line, but also must win the support of a sufficient number of opposition members to have a majority. Prime ministers in minority situations must be very skillful, setting off an opposition party on the right against a party on the left, promising an opposition party policy concessions in return for its support, and introducing legislation that is popular enough with the public that the opposition cannot risk voting against it. Prime Minister Pearson, from 1963 to 1968, and Trudeau, from 1972 to 1974, demonstrated all of these skills and exercised power effectively in the minority situation. Joe Clark demonstrated virtually none of these skills in 1979–80, stating he would govern "as if he had a majority," and was promptly defeated both in the House and at the polls in the ensuing election. But because minority governments are not the norm in Canada, let us now move to a consideration of how a prime minister leads when the party holds a clear majority in the House of Commons.

MAJORITY GOVERNMENT AND PARTY DISCIPLINE

A *majority government* is one in which the government party holds a clear majority of the seats in the House of Commons. In this situation, all the PM must do to remain in office between elections is to hold the support of his or her own party. For the most part, in Canada, this has not proved to be all that difficult. The reason for this is the conventional mechanism of *party discipline,* whereby the backbenchers, the rank and file of the party's MPs, are always expected to vote with the party leadership. However, backbenchers sometimes disagree with the position taken by their leaders, and in the case of opposition members, such dissidence is often expressed in a vote against the party line in the House. In the case of government backbenchers, such lenience is generally not tolerated because a defeat on a vote in the House could cause the fall of the government and precipitate an election.

Broadly speaking, party discipline does not have to be "enforced" by the government. On the one hand, most MPs run on a party ticket in large measure because they prefer the philosophy and policies of their party over that of the others. Thus, MPs usually vote the party line simply because they agree with it. As well, the prime minister is the democratically elected leader of the party, and in an era of leadership politics, elections are frequently won or lost on the popularity of the party leader. Backbenchers to a large extent owe their electoral success to the fact that they fought campaigns in their own constituencies as members of the party "team," and many are simply swept into office on the coattails of the party and its leader. As a result, they support the prime minister in the House, even when they are not in complete agreement on some issues, if only because "Ya dance wit' da one wot brung ya!"

There are, however, a number of sanctions and inducements that the prime minister has at his or her disposal to force or cajole dissident backbenchers into supporting the government. One inducement is allowing full expression of dissident views within regular meetings of the party *caucus*, with all members of the party, including the PM, in attendance. Caucus is held in camera so that everyone can speak openly. In fact, sometimes the prime minister will listen to caucus and take decisions based on its advice. Because backbenchers do get to air their concerns in caucus, expulsion or the threat of expulsion from caucus can be used as a sanction to discourage habitual "loose cannons" from embarrassing the PM. As an example, John Nunziata, a long-time Liberal backbencher (and an equally long-time loose cannon) was expelled from the government caucus in 1996 for voting against the government on an important bill.

Finally, the prime minister controls a wide range of plums and perks that can be handed out to the faithful and refused to the wayward. The biggest plum of all is a Cabinet post, and hard-working, supportive backbenchers are more likely to get the nod when a vacancy in the ministry occurs. Chairs of Commons standing committees and jobs on the House floor such as whip are also doled out to backbenchers who have served their time in the trenches and toed the party line. Those who are overly outspoken usually miss out on such perks or, as in the case of veteran MP Warren Allmand, have them snatched away as punishment for publicly expressing opposition to a government policy.[14]

Government backbenchers appear to have become more obstreperous in recent years. In part this is because of the very large majorities enjoyed by the Chrétien Liberals for the past decade. There are simply so many competent MPs on the government side of the House that opportunities for advancement to Cabinet are limited, leading to frustration and disgruntlement. However, majority governments in Canada have never had any difficulty in maintaining control, and even if the odd government MP is critical of the party line, the majority is large enough that it doesn't matter very much. The reality is that no majority government has ever been defeated on a recorded vote in Canada's Parliament, and that situation is unlikely to change.

PRIME MINISTERIAL POWER AND LEADERSHIP STYLE

The nature of political leadership in Canada varies a great deal from era to era, and that variation can be explained in part by the circumstances of the times. Two of our greatest prime ministers, Macdonald and Laurier, were "true" leaders in the sense that they were "one-man shows." They led the country and their parties on the strength of their intelligence, political savvy, and the loyalty they earned on the basis of their personal traits. But it can also be argued that the relatively circumscribed character of contemporary politics and political issues made it easier for men such as these to lead. Loyalty could be built and secured through the distribution of perks in the form of patronage, and the central issues of the day were based on such high-minded goals as nation-building, westward expansion, and natural resource development, all of which were difficult to oppose.

THE BROKER

As the issues facing Canada became more complex and more potentially divisive and as the levers of patronage were gradually removed from the hands of our political leaders, leadership by force of personality became more difficult. Mackenzie King, our longest-serving PM, successfully applied a formula for leading the country in the face of economic disaster, global war, and a rising tide of ethnic conflict; he mastered the art of *brokering* compromises and accommodations among opposing interests. King was powerful, in spite of the fact that he lacked all of the outward traits normally associated with leadership—charisma, gregariousness, physical stature, and so on—and, in fact, was downright weird.

However, King's consummate skill was to build coalitions among disparate and often opposing factions, coalitions that held together not because of mutual love for the prime minister, but because he was able to convince the partners to coalesce because it was in their respective best interests to do so. King's ego also allowed him to share the reins of power with those in the Cabinet he deemed most capable. He allowed his lieutenants, such as C.D. Howe and Louis St. Laurent, leeway to assume leadership in their areas of expertise and he didn't even seem to mind if some of the media attention was focused on his cabinet colleagues. Remarkably, his ministers returned his trust with loyalty.

THE CHARISMATIC AND THE COLLEGIAL

John Diefenbaker was the first prime minister to come to power through the medium of television. His political career had been checkered before his election in 1957, with far more political failures than victories. As a Westerner, he was an outsider to the Progressive Conservative Party, the "party of Bay Street." However, Diefenbaker seemed to have a special spark, a certain *charismatic* appeal that bloomed under the glare of the TV cameras. His speeches were characterized by an evangelical zeal, filled with images and symbols that appealed to an electorate that had become dissatisfied with the workmanlike but overly complacent style of previous Liberal governments. In 1958, Diefenbaker led his party to the largest ever electoral landslide, and it appeared that the reins of office might be in his hands for a long time to come.

Unfortunately, however, Diefenbaker's personal flaws were as impressive as his strengths. It soon became apparent to his ministers, particularly those from Central Canada, that his charisma was not backed up with substance and, more damningly, he was unwilling to share any significant decision-making authority with them. As well, he distrusted the bureaucracy and, hence, made complicated decisions without taking advantage of their expertise and experience. Not surprisingly, he made many bad decisions because they were not only uninformed but were often taken in the absence of a consensus in Cabinet. Within five years, Diefenbaker had completely blown his majority and a few years later was dumped by his own party.

Diefenbaker showed us that while electoral success is necessary for becoming prime minister, it is not a sufficient condition for staying in power. By contrast, his archrival from 1958 to 1967, Lester B. Pearson, failed to win a majority government in four tries, but performed effectively through five years of minority government. What Pearson lacked in personal charisma, media appeal, and, hence, electoral success he made up for in terms of brokerage skills and a willingness to share real power with his ministers. His *collegial* style of leadership allowed him not only to hold the loyalty of his Cabinet colleagues and his caucus but also to make the deals and compromises with the opposition parties that kept his government in power even without a majority. Where Diefenbaker viewed those who disagreed with him as disloyal, Pearson encouraged open debate and discussion. Where Diefenbaker could not tolerate any heirs apparent in his Cabinet, Pearson worked harmoniously with his "star" ministers and even actively recruited from private life the man who would be his successor.

HIP, SLICK, AND HICK

The personas of our prime ministers in recent years have been shaped in part by the media and in part by their own self-images. Although Joe Clark, John Turner, and Kim Campbell all made brief "cameo" appearances in the job, none of them was in office long enough to develop or impose their own style of leadership. Hence, in commenting on prime ministerial style and its impact on our system of government, we will focus on the three men who have dominated our political landscape for the past 30 years: Pierre Trudeau, Brian Mulroney, and Jean Chrétien. While all of these men have been successful prime ministers, they each approached the job in a different way and each had a unique impact on the nature of the executive power in our country.

PIERRE TRUDEAU

Trudeau arrived on the political scene "out of nowhere," having little experience in partisan politics and apparently having very limited political ambitions. He was elected not on substance but on image (all he offered us was the slogan, "a just society"). Canadians had become bored with old-style politics and were looking for something different and exciting, and Trudeau offered it. He was "hip," "with it," and "cool," and "Trudeaumania" swept the Liberals to power with a large majority in 1968. While we may have elected him originally on the basis of image alone, it turned out that he was a highly intelligent man. His philosophy of governing was *rationalist*, based on the assumption that if decisions were made in a structured, orderly fashion, with all of the pertinent information taken into account, those decisions would be good ones. Ironically, if Trudeau failed us it was by assuming that all political decisions could be reduced to a clear set of rational choices, that Canadians made their political choices as rational actors. His pursuit of bilingualism, his strong stand against Quebec nationalism, his fight for an entrenched Charter of Rights, and his National Energy Policy were all likely *rational* in terms of Trudeau's perception of the national interest but all were opposed for essentially political reasons in regions such as Quebec and the West. While it was certainly not his intent, Trudeau left us more divided than we were when he was first elected.

In terms of the dynamics of Cabinet decision making, Trudeau certainly set the tone and broad direction of policy. Moreover, for the things that mattered to him personally, such as bilingualism and constitutional reform, he took his own counsel and that of a few close confidants such as Marc Lalonde and Michael Pitfield, with little concern for what his Cabinet might think. However, while Trudeau was certainly not a collegial PM like Pearson, he did not make the mistake of forcing his views on Cabinet in areas where he did not feel strongly. Hence, Trudeau was often content to let Cabinet have its way in, for instance, economic and fiscal decisions and decisions affecting regional economic development. Still, he left the institutional legacy of large central agencies responsible directly to the PM and, hence, enhanced for ever more the power of the office.

BRIAN MULRONEY

Mulroney also came to the political arena from "outside" Parliament, although his Tory credentials were impeccable. Mulroney swept to power less on charisma or image than on a public sense that Canada needed a new style of leadership, one that could not be provided by "yesterday's man," Liberal leader John Turner. Mulroney's public persona always appeared suave, businesslike, and coolly efficient. Unlike Trudeau, who often seemed to be uninterested or unconcerned about what the public thought about him and his policies, Mulroney always seemed to worry about his image. He was concerned about what people and, in particular, the media thought about him.

In decision-making style, Mulroney did not trust the senior bureaucracy, and made certain structural changes designed to leave more power in the hands of the politicians. He increased the size of the PCO, enhanced the influence of the PMO, and greatly increased the size and influence of individual ministerial staff. The Mulroney government also went outside government for technical advice more than previous governments, listening to the captains of industry, conservative economists, and private-sector "think tanks" more than his own public servants. Within Cabinet, some individual ministers, such as Don Mazankowski and Ray Hnatyshyn, were allowed to become powerful forces but only because they were personally loyal to the PM and did not show any inclination to succeed him as party leader or to upstage him in the media limelight.

History will likely be kinder to Brian Mulroney than people would expect. He did preside over Canada in a time of economic difficulties, and his policies of free trade, tax reform, fiscal restraint, and government cutbacks were likely instrumental in turning the economy around. The Chrétien government has continued what Mulroney began and has, perhaps unfairly, taken the lion's share of the credit. Mulroney's downfall, ironically, was precipitated by the public image he was so concerned about cultivating. The concern with his own image began to look self-serving and phony, and the cool, businesslike demeanour that was calculated to inspire public confidence came across as simply "slick" and untrustworthy. With the polls indicating that he was far and away the most unpopular serving prime minister in Canadian history, Mulroney will also be remembered as our only prime minister with a majority government to be pressured into resigning while still in his prime.

JEAN CHRÉTIEN

Jean Chrétien's political career is, if nothing else, a monument to perseverance and longevity. He was first elected in the mid-1960s, served in the cabinets of Pearson and Trudeau, and ran for the leadership of the Liberal Party twice. Eventually, his persistence paid off, and Chrétien was swept to power with a landslide in 1993 and returned, albeit with smaller majorities, in 1997 and 2000. If public opinion polls can be trusted, he had the longest "honeymoon period" of post-election public approval of any PM in history. True, it can be argued that any PM would look good when measured against the "legions of mediocrity" currently sitting in the opposition benches in the House of Commons. Moreover, Chrétien's ascendancy just happened to parallel an upsurge in the Canadian economy, a happy coincidence for which the PM is content to take full credit. However, we often forget that, unlike Mulroney and Trudeau before him, Chrétien has spent his whole life in politics. Above all else, he is a professional politician who knows how to exploit good luck, how to take maximum advantage of a "pat hand" when it is dealt to him.

We forget that Chrétien is a "pro" because he has always downplayed his own political savvy. His public persona is "the little guy from Shawinigan," the simple but honest "hick" from the backwoods of Quebec whom nobody should take very seriously let alone fear. But this public persona is less an image than it is a mask behind which a sophisticated "grownup" hides his significant political acumen. When elected, Chrétien vowed to be a "team leader" in Cabinet, to return to a Pearson-style, "first among equals" approach to Cabinet decision making. His abolition of the complex committee system of cabinet, the reinstatement of the power of the plenary body in priority determination, and the initial reduction in size of the PMO were all seen as indicators of his willingness to follow through on his vow. However, despite the appearances of sharing power with his ministers, Chrétien has, in fact, limited collegiality in decision making to a small coterie of non-elected advisers in the PMO and a small cabal of hand-picked Cabinet colleagues.

Chrétien has also shown little tolerance for dissent among his backbenchers, dumping John Nunziata from caucus entirely and stripping Commons veterans Warren Allmand and George Baker of their committee responsibilities. While it is probably not accurate to go as far as to suggest that Chrétien is a "closet autocrat," he is definitely the "driver of the bus."[15]

Chrétien demonstrated this when, after tolerating his heir apparent, Paul Martin, in the influential Finance portfolio for a number of years, he fired him in the end. A prime minister simply cannot tolerate the sort of insubordination and disloyalty displayed by Martin and his supporters and still maintain credibility within caucus and in the country at large.

Jean Chrétien has been one of the most successful and most popular prime ministers in our history. Most believe that his "swan song" has been too prolonged and that he has become somewhat testy and stubborn in the 18-month "lame duck" period after he announced he was resigning. While perhaps the jury is still out on what the Chrétien legacy will be ultimately, one thing is certain: political opponents and allies alike have had to take this prime minister seriously. Despite his humble protestations to the contrary, history will affirm that the little guy from Shawinigan was no hick.

CONCLUSION

In this, the first decade of a new century, we often hear cries for less concentration of power in the hands of the prime minister and cabinet. While there is no question that Canada has a system that places great power in the hands of the prime minister and Cabinet, our system of government would not work very well if that were not the case.

The Canadian Alliance, in particular, advocates the introduction of devices such as referenda that would put more direct power in the hands of the populace and less in the hands of the government. Some parliamentarians argue that party discipline should be loosened so that individual MPs can vote "according to their conscience" and not necessarily with their party leadership. All of these suggestions are well-meaning, intended to make government more responsive to the people, to be more democratic, but they are also incredibly naive, based on misconceptions about the fundamental nature of our system of government.

Majoritarianism, or majority rule, is the device we employ to make decisions in our legislatures and it is how we elect our members of Parliament.[16] It is how we operationalize democracy, and it is generally a fair system. However, one problem with majoritarianism is that it creates winners and losers, and can result in the tyranny of the majority over minorities. The genius of cabinet government is that it forces the executive to seek compromise and accommodation among competing views and allows the government to minimize the number of "losers" when policy decisions are taken.

The second problem with placing more power directly in the hands of the people or in the hands of backbenchers is that neither has access to expert advice. As we have seen, many modern policy issues are both complex and technical in nature, and effective decisions can only be taken if people with knowledge and expertise are brought into the process. The prime minister and Cabinet have the necessary expertise "on tap" in the policy branches of the various departments in the bureaucracy, and in some ways it is the ability to harness such knowledge and bring it to bear on policy decisions that is the measure of an effective government.

Finally, while the power of the executive branch in Canada is significant, it is not absolute. The prime minister must always heed the advice of his technocrats in the bureaucracy or end up making bad policy decisions. The prime minister must share executive power with provincial premiers and with Cabinet colleagues. The prime minister must constantly deal with views of caucus, must face the public criticism of the opposition in the House of Commons, and must face the people of Canada in a general election at least once every five years. Thus, the democratic checks to prevent abuses of prime ministerial power are in place, but we must remember that Canadian democracy works precisely because the power of the people and the power of Parliament are given expression through the executive function and not directly.

NOTES

1. The Queen also still has the power, on the advice of the governor general (acting, in turn, on the advice of the PM) to appoint up to eight additional senators. This formal power would likely have been transferred to the governor general by amendment to the 1867 Act had it not been assumed to be an unusable provision of the Constitution by convention. Prime Minister Mulroney, however, resurrected the provision in his second term to break what he saw as a deadlock in the upper chamber.

2. Governor General Byng was asked by Prime Minister King to dissolve Parliament and, instead, Byng asked the leader of the opposition, Mr. Meighen, to form a government. This has come to be known as the "King–Byng Affair."

3. In fact, the only mention of the term "prime minister" is in sections 35.1 and 37.1 of the Constitution Act, 1982, requiring the PM to convene constitutional conferences on aboriginal rights. These clauses are now inoperative.

4. Because appointments are for life, the full Privy Council is composed of many individuals, such as ministers of previous governments, who understandably do not get invitations to attend Cabinet meetings. The Privy Council per se never meets as a deliberative body, and it is only the Privy Councillors who are ministers of the government of the day who have the authority to advise the governor general.

5. The terms "Cabinet," "political executive," "the government," and "the government of the day" are all used virtually synonymously. The term "government" is also used

in the broader sense of the "state" or the "political system," but usually can easily be distinguished from the narrower use of "*the* government." Also, while the prime minister is always a member of Cabinet, because of his or her dominant role in that body and because the PM's power is affected by his or her relationship with other ministers, the term "prime minister *and* Cabinet" will sometimes be used in spite of its apparent redundancy.

6. The exception here is with respect to monies required for the day-to-day running of the House of Commons and the Senate. The speakers of the two chambers function in a manner analogous to ministers for purposes of the internal economy of Parliament.

7. Credit must be given here to Kim Campbell, who, in her short term as PM, set the wheels in motion for reforming the structure of Cabinet. She reduced the size and complexity of Cabinet by reducing the number of departments of government and, hence, the number of ministers required to head them up. Chrétien worked from the changes already introduced in instituting his reforms in 1993.

8. It has evolved that secretaries of state are now almost automatically invited to Cabinet committee meetings and often to plenary meetings of the Cabinet as well if a matter being discussed involves their assigned area of responsibility. A few secretaries of state have made the jump to full ministerial status.

9. In fact, both Macdonald and Laurier did set up ad hoc committees of Cabinet to look at specific matters of less urgency than the day-to-day affairs of the government.

10. The first formal Cabinet committees were set up in the hurly-burly of the wartime cabinet room of Borden during World War I.

11. Strictly speaking, the Treasury Board is not a committee of Cabinet but a committee of the Privy Council, which happens to be composed of ministers of the current Cabinet. However, for all practical purposes, the Board functions as a senior Cabinet committee, but with a specialized role and, unlike sister committees, with a statutory mandate.

12. In the brief interregnum of 1979–80, the Clark government actually changed the name of the Priorities and Planning Committee to "inner Cabinet," but without significantly changing the role of the body.

13. The Treasury Board Secretariat is also considered a central agency, but because it serves the Treasury Board specifically we will not deal with it here.

14. Allmand, who was the second-longest-serving MP at the time and who had served in the Trudeau Cabinet, was relieved of his post as chairman of the important Justice Committee in 1995 for publicly disagreeing with the government's spending priorities.

15. *Maclean's* (October 19, 1998).

16. Strictly speaking, an MP is elected if he or she receives a greater number of votes than the other candidates, which may be less than an absolute majority. This is called a single-member *plurality* system of election.

FURTHER READINGS

Aucoin, Peter. "Organizational Change in the Machinery of Government." *Canadian Journal of Political Science* (March 1986): 3–15.

Axworthy, Tom. "Of Secretaries to Princes." *Canadian Public Administration* (Summer 1988): 247–64.

Bakvis, Herman. *Regional Ministers: Power and Influence in the Canadian Cabinet.* Toronto: University of Toronto Press, 1991.

Mancuso, Maureen, R. Price, and R. Wagenberg. *Leaders and Leadership in Canada.* Toronto: Oxford University Press, 1994.

Matheson, William. *The Prime Minister and the Cabinet.* Toronto: Methuen, 1976.

Pal, Leslie, and David Taras. *Prime Ministers and Premiers: Political Leadership and Public Policy in Canada.* Scarborough, ON: Prentice Hall, 1988.

Savoie, Donald. *Governing from the Centre: The Concentration of Power in Canadian Politics.* Toronto: University of Toronto Press, 1999.

Whittington, Michael, and Richard Van Loon. *Canadian Government and Politics: Institutions and Processes.* Toronto: McGraw-Hill Ryerson, 1996.

CHAPTER 3

POLITICS VERSUS ADMINISTRATION: POLITICIANS AND BUREAUCRATS

Reg Whitaker

In liberal democratic states there has always been a certain amount of tension between politicians and bureaucrats over their respective roles in making public policy. No doubt there always will be. The reason for this is straightforward, even if the practice is anything but: it has proved impossible to define decisively the division of responsibilities between ministers and their senior bureaucrats. This relationship is constantly in a state of redefinition and renegotiation, from government to government and from minister to minister in the same government. One thing, however, is sure: while bureaucrats inevitably have an important role in the policy process, it is the politicians who are ultimately responsible to the public.

THE POLITICS/ADMINISTRATION DICHOTOMY

The simple theory of responsible democratic government is that the people choose among competing political parties at election time. Once a government is elected, it has a mandate from the people to enact the policies it has proposed. The bureaucrats are public *servants,* whose task is to execute the will of the people's elected representatives in implementing and administering the government's policies. The problem with this theory is that it is too simple.

In the earlier part of the twentieth century, there was a prevalent theory among students of public administration that reflected this simple approach. This was referred to as the *politics/administration dichotomy.* Politics is politics, and administration is administration. Politics is about setting policy, inevitably a partisan and controversial matter. Administration, on the other hand, is technical and nonpartisan. There is no overlap. This principle was argued both as a statement of fact and as an ethical guide to both politicians and bureaucrats.

No reputable scholar of public administration and public policy would be prepared today to defend the politics/administration dichotomy, at least in its pristine form. As a statement of fact, it is obviously erroneous, as we shall see. As an ethical guide, however, it still informs some of the basic elements of our administrative institutions, such as the *merit principle* in appointment to the public service, and the protection built into the process against *political patronage* in the selection of public servants. It is generally believed to be a good thing that bureaucrats be shielded from undue political interference with their duties. At the same time, the idea that secretive, unaccountable bureaucrats may be shaping public policy behind the scenes is widely viewed as a dangerously undemocratic practice. A popular (and very clever) British TV sitcom—*Yes, Prime Minister*—was premised on the crafty ways in which senior civil servants in Whitehall baffle and manipulate the politicians they are supposed to serve. One might sum up public attitudes as follows: politics and administration *ought to be* separate, watertight compartments, but in fact the bureaucracy is in some degree out of control. Unfortunately, when politicians seek to extend their influence, they are to some extent politicizing administration, and this is just as bad as a bureaucracy out of political control. Obviously, there is no satisfactory "solution" to this dilemma given that the tension is structural. The question is whether this tension can be creative rather than debilitating.

The original impetus for the politics/administration dichotomy came from a desire to banish partisan political influence from the administrative process. This was not surprising considering the prevalence of political patronage in North America in the nineteenth and early twentieth centuries. Especially in the United States, but to a considerable extent in Canada as well, politicians had used patronage appointments to the civil service as a useful political resource (jobs for votes, in effect) and as the most appropriate means of maintaining control over the administration. A strong reaction to the old order came with the progressive reform movements in national and local politics in the early twentieth century. These largely middle-class movements sought to diminish the influence of the political bosses and their machines by, among other things, freeing the administration of government from partisan political control. The creation of nonpartisan boards and commissions, out of the direct reach of politicians, to administer various functions of government was one approach. Another was to replace patronage with a merit system of appointment to the regular civil service. Patronage was associated with corruption and inefficiency. The professionalization of the civil service was seen as a necessary step toward putting government on a more businesslike basis—not to mention offering career avenues for the educated, middle-class people who supported reform.

It is interesting to note that the crucial step toward reducing the patronage system in the federal civil service came when a group of prominent Ontario businessmen put a proposal to the then leader of the opposition, Conservative Robert Borden, during the 1911 election. They offered their support, financial and otherwise, to the Conservative campaign if Borden would pledge himself to a number of policies they had enumerated. Among these was the institution of a merit system of appointment to the civil service. Since they also wanted a stronger role for the federal government in promoting Canadian trade around the world, they obviously saw a merit-based administration as the prerequisite to a more effective government that could act in their interests. Borden did win that election and civil service reform finally came in 1918, when a wartime Union government composed of a coalition of Conservatives and Liberals proved incapable of dividing up the patronage among themselves. The Civil Service Act of 1918 took a good proportion—although not all—of the federal civil service out of the range of patronage and ushered in a new regime of merit selection and promotion, with written examinations for entry and specific qualifications for particular positions. All this was to be guaranteed by the Civil Service Commission (later the Public Service Commission), an appointed and nominally independent body that would act as a watchdog against any recurrence of patronage. Thus was born the modern system of professional administration for the Canadian public service.

Despite some ups and downs over the years, the reforms of 1918 proved irreversible—so much so that a special committee appointed by the federal government reported in 1979 that it had found the likelihood of a return to patronage "about nil."[1] Political patronage continues to exist for a range of senior appointments: judges to federal and provincial superior courts; senators; ambassadors; heads of Crown corporations; and chairs of a host of special boards, commissions, and regulatory agencies. But with the sole exception of deputy ministers (an exception to which we will return shortly), appointments and promotions within the permanent federal public service are on a competitive merit basis and any political interference in these matters is considered quite inappropriate. Thus the institutional structures still tend to reflect the old politics/administration dichotomy. Administrators are supposed to be divorced from politics, and politicians restrained from interfering with administration.

One of the problems with this situation is the ambivalence we display in democratic countries toward "politics." On the one hand, "politics" is often viewed in a dim light as a less than exemplary process typically involving deception, if not downright dishonesty. Not only are politicians held in low social repute, but disdain for politics enters everyday life, as in the term "office politics" to describe manipulative behaviour of fellow workers. On the other hand, "politics" is the means through which the people can assert their public policy preferences, the very mechanism of democracy. Thus political interference with administration is a double-edged sword: the dark side is inefficiency and corruption through the introduction of partisan considerations into the neutral world of administration; the good side is a party with a mandate from the electorate seeking to direct the bureaucrats to fulfill the will of the people. The democratic side of politics can be glimpsed in the public reaction to administrators so insulated from political control that they act autonomously. "Faceless bureaucrats" are denounced for imposing an Orwellian Big Brother state upon the people. It is precisely the lack of direct accountability that leads people to fear unchecked bureaucracy. After all, people can always get back at the politicians in the next election, but the bureaucrats do not have to submit themselves to the direct scrutiny of the electorate.

THE GOLDEN AGE OF THE MANDARINS

The notion of direct political control over the work of government departments focuses on the office of deputy minister. Deputy ministers, the chief executive officers of government departments, are appointed "at pleasure," which means that they do not have security of tenure. Deputy ministers have a double role (some would call it an ambiguous role) in representing the department to the minister and the minister to the department. As such they are the crucial link between the elected politicians and the permanent bureaucracy. It is through the deputy ministers that governments can seek to impose their policy directions on the huge and often unwieldy apparatus of government. Today, deputy ministers are usually career public servants who have moved up the ranks in the bureaucracy based on their ability. While deputy ministers are not often fired by a newly elected government, it is a prime ministerial prerogative to, at any time, move or remove deputy ministers. Appointment of people from outside government to deputy ministerial positions is a prime ministerial prerogative, and is not normally deemed to constitute political patronage. If a deputy minister were unqualified for the post except for partisan political credentials, no doubt a cry would be raised, but this rarely, if ever, happens today. On the other hand, it is a legitimate interest of governments that deputy ministers share their general ideological and policy orientations—or, at least, that they are not actively hostile to them.

When one party remains in office for a long period, there is a tendency for the ministers and the senior civil servants to grow closely together in orientation. But when another party comes to office for the first time, or after long years in opposition, tension is almost inevitable. The Liberals ran Ottawa from 1935 to 1957, an era that has been dubbed in retrospect the "golden age of the civil service mandarins." A small number of deputy ministers became extremely powerful and influential figures in Ottawa, based on the considerable technical knowledge of their departments and their policy fields, and the years of experience accumulated in the Ottawa environment. Indeed, they became the chief source of policy input and ideas to the Liberal governments they served. This relationship became so close, if not symbiotic, that deputy ministers often resigned from the bureaucracy to run as Liberals in a general election. For these reasons, the Liberals of this era have been dubbed the "Government party," and the civil service mandarins were widely seen as "liberals," if not Liberals.

In 1957 this cozy relationship was broken with the unexpected victory at the polls of the Progressive Conservatives under a prairie outsider, John Diefenbaker. Diefenbaker harboured considerable suspicions and misgivings about the Liberal mandarins, but he also grudgingly respected their expertise and experience. Instead of replacing them with a new generation of deputy ministers more attuned to Tory policy directions, Diefenbaker by and large, with a few exceptions, left the incumbents in place. He failed however to utilize them effectively on behalf of his government, due to his innate mistrust of their political tendencies. There was some justification for his mistrust: when the Liberals, under Lester Pearson, returned to national office in 1963, the first Pearson Cabinet was graced with a half-dozen former senior civil servants who had abandoned the bureaucracy for Liberal political careers—including the prime minister himself, who had once been Undersecretary of State for External Affairs.

DECLINE OF THE MANDARINS

Although the Liberals remained in office from 1963 to 1984 (with one nine-month hiatus in 1979–80), there has been no return to the golden age of the mandarinate, Liberal or otherwise. The era of centralization in

Ottawa was coming to a close. With regional tensions on the rise, "province-building" emerged, in the form of competitive provincial state bureaucracies, first in Quebec, then in Ontario and in the wealthier Western provinces as well. The Ottawa public service no longer dominated the field. Moreover, as government became far more extensive and complex in its interventions in the society, as it did in the 1960s and 1970s, the capacity of individual deputy ministers to command all the detail and expertise in their increasingly large and often technically specialized departments became more questionable. Nor could a small number of deputy ministers gain a wide grasp of the business of government as a whole through relatively intimate informal working gatherings of senior colleagues, as in the past. Communication between departments became much more formal and unwieldy as the size and complexity of government grew. Deputy ministers themselves were shuffled from department to department as often as ministers, and were encouraged to move in and out of the public and private sectors to gain wider experience. There was a growth in the number of assistant and associate deputy ministers, resulting in larger senior management teams at the top of departments, but this development failed to re-create the concentration of policy expertise that had once prevailed. In effect, deputy ministers and their assistants and associates were becoming senior administrators whose skills lay in managing large and complex organizations, public or private. Policy expertise, on the other hand, was left to the people hired for their specific technical qualifications.

Even with the relative decline of the once-commanding figure of the deputy minister, questions about the influence of bureaucrats in the policy process persist. Complex interventions by the contemporary state in the private sector require high degrees of technical specialization. This strategically positions the bureaucrats to influence the policy process. One of the weakest links in the politics/administration dichotomy is the idea that victorious parties come out of an election with a clear policy mandate to implement. In the age of professionally packaged image politics, specific policy commitments tend to be avoided, for fear of alienating potential voters. Policy, it is often argued, is too complex to be intelligently discussed during the heat of an election campaign usually run as a personality or image contest. In any event, over the normally four- to five-year mandate of a government, events often move so quickly that policy initiatives are undertaken that were unforeseen during the election campaign. In recent years, four of the most significant policy initiatives of the federal government—the Canada–U.S. Free Trade Agreement, the proposed Meech Lake constitutional accord, the Goods and Services Tax (GST), and the Canada

Health and Social Transfer (CHST)—were not even mentioned in the preceding election campaigns, let alone debated. Although general policy directions may emanate from a ruling party, specific policy is most often worked out by federal and provincial ministers in close conjunction with their bureaucrats and the major interested groups in the society.

The bureaucrats command *information*, a key resource in the policy process—even if that command is now more diffused and less concentrated at the top. Politicians are always at a disadvantage when confronting officials with greater technical knowledge. There is never any question that the elected politicians have the right to set policy directions and that bureaucrats have no business attempting to interpose their own policy preferences—directly, or openly, that is. However, when it comes time to present ministers with detailed policy *options*, the way in which alternative routes to achieving the policy goal are presented can have a powerful effect on how a policy actually takes shape. *Evaluating* the possible effects of a policy change can have similarly dramatic effects on a proposed change. Finally, the way in which a policy is actually *implemented* has a powerful impact on the policy itself, and implementation is a bureaucratic prerogative usually exercised in the relative absence of political attention, that by this time has wandered on to other things.

In each case, it is the permanent officials who normally have greater access to information resources. Ministers, after all, are also MPs and party politicians who spend much of their time giving speeches, travelling, attending political functions, and other activities quite remote from the business of their ministerial portfolios. In many cases, they have no previous training or experience in the policy fields of their departments, little time to gain such knowledge while there, and a relatively short span in one portfolio before moving on (or out). The bureaucracy on the other hand was there before and will be there long after. Moreover, there is a lot of very specialized knowledge that can be marshalled by the organization—that is, after all, what modern complex organizations are supposed to do. But the result is that bureaucrats do have input into the policy process that cannot simply be seen as neutral.

Bureaucratic control over information has, if anything, increased in recent years with the development of what students of interest groups call *policy communities*. Policy communities include all actors with an interest in a policy area sharing a common policy focus and helping shape policy outcomes.[2] Increasingly, such "communities" have grown up around particular policy areas involving bureaucrats from the federal government, their counterparts in the provincial bureaucracies, and the interested private-sector organizations, including companies, trade associations, and pressure groups. For instance, in the energy resource field, the policy community would include officials from the federal Energy department, their counterparts in the energy-producing provinces such as Alberta and British Columbia, the resource corporations, and the various producer groups. In effect, such "communities" expand access to relevant information and establish external bases of potential support for specialized bureaucrats in their policy fields.

Given these kinds of dynamics, no serious student of the policy process would today argue that public policy is not positively affected by both politicians and bureaucrats. Nor would anyone seriously argue that policy could, or should, be entirely divorced from bureaucratic input. To do so would be impracticable, and undesirable. The relative balance of inputs is more debatable. Politicians have become more restive in recent years about the extent of bureaucratic input and have sought various devices to recover ground they believe they have lost. There are a number of reasons for this, and all of them point in the direction of placing greater restrictions and stronger mechanisms of political accountability on the bureaucrats.

THE TRUDEAU ERA, 1968–1984

For the past quarter-century or so, federal governments have shown concern about what politicians have seen as an undue degree of influence exercised by bureaucrats in the policy process. When Pierre Trudeau took over as prime minister in 1968 he indicated a strong desire to establish "counterweights" to the traditional channels of advice from the bureaucracy. One counterweight was sought in a beefed-up Prime Minister's Office (PMO) that would offer *political* policy advice to match the voices offering bureaucratic advice. Although Trudeau took considerable criticism for allegedly "presidentializing" the prime ministership, the PMO never functioned effectively as a policy counterweight to the permanent officialdom. This was not surprising given the lack of expertise, other than political "savvy," among the PMO's often young and relatively inexperienced "politicos" recruited from the party. Nevertheless, the PMO has remained a relatively large and at least sporadically active player in the Ottawa policy process ever since. The PMO functions both as a channel of specifically party-based political input and as an extension of the reach of the prime minister, not only over the policy process generally but over the Cabinet ministers as well.

The main method adopted by Trudeau to counter the bureaucracy was, paradoxically, to use the bureaucracy itself. It was in the Trudeau years, especially the early 1970s, that the role of the *central agencies* in the policy process became a preoccupation of Ottawa decision makers. The central agencies are those parts of the bureaucracy whose leading purpose is to support the decision-making activities of Cabinet. There are three main central agencies, all of which, unlike the PMO, are part of the permanent civil service: the *Privy Council Office (PCO)*, the *Department of Finance*, and the *Treasury Board Secretariat* (TBS).[3]

The PCO is, in effect, the department in charge of the civil service, and the Clerk of the Privy Council is the head of the permanent civil service. The PCO is the official record keeper for Cabinet (the Clerk attends Cabinet meetings and all important Cabinet committee meetings). But above all, the PCO coordinates policy planning within the bureaucracy and keeps watch over the machinery and process of government from the point of view of policy development. Finance, also a department of government with its own functionally specific policy field, exercises general supervision over policy with macroeconomic impact on the Canadian economy, which is to say, virtually all policy that matters. The Finance Department develops the annual federal budget and is responsible for identifying the revenue sources for financing government programs. TBS supports the Treasury Board—a statutory committee of Cabinet—and exercises hands-on intervention on all matters of expenditure control. TBS also personifies government as "management" when it comes to bargaining with organized public servants on matters of pay and conditions of work.

The emergence of the central agencies as key players in the policy process cannot be separated from two other developments in the Trudeau years: an expanded Cabinet committee system and the theory of rational policy management. Regarding the committee structure, it was apparent by the end of the 1960s that the old-style Cabinet, which met as a whole to deliberate and make decisions, could no longer continue. The problem was one of size. Cabinets had grown, from 16 ministers in Diefenbaker's 1957 Cabinet (a number unchanged from the 1920s) to 28 in Trudeau's Cabinet after the 1968 election. This tendency continued to accelerate, reaching 40 ministers, the all-time record for obesity, in Brian Mulroney's 1984 Cabinet.

An elaborate system of Cabinet committees, most devoted to particular policy areas, grew up to replace the then non-functional and largely ceremonial plenary Cabinet. By 1979, the Trudeau Cabinet had five committees on broad policy areas (economic policy, social policy, external affairs, defence, etc.); a number of ad hoc committees struck for specific purposes; and four committees with wide mandates for policy in general:

Priorities and Planning (P&P), Treasury Board, government operations, and legislation and house planning. All these were funnelled into the full Cabinet, but the latter was effectively limited to rubber-stamping matters already decided by the relevant committee (although occasionally when major differences had not been resolved by the various committees, full Cabinet might overturn committee decisions). The central agencies were supportive of the Cabinet committees, but particularly of the four with wide mandates for policy. The P&P committee, supported by the PCO, became particularly influential.

The logical culmination of these developments was the creation in Joe Clark's short-lived government of 1979–80 of a smaller "inner Cabinet" to which the various committees reported. In 1980, the returning Liberals discontinued the inner Cabinet as such (it had attracted much political flack from regions that felt themselves underrepresented in the smaller body). Instead, they simply made the P&P committee the effective inner Cabinet. Later, in the Mulroney years, P&P itself grew so large (19 members at one point) that a yet smaller committee, Government Operations, became the effective "inner" P&P, and the real power centre of Cabinet. This proliferation and differentiation of Cabinet committees required more specialized secretariats within the central agencies to support their activities.

The other factor giving a decisive push to the central agencies in the Trudeau years was the craze for "rational policy planning" that swept Ottawa and other Western capitals in the late 1960s and early 1970s. In this era, characterized by the seemingly inevitable expansion of government, a kind of technocratic approach to policy took hold. In the new age, it was argued, public policy was a matter of *information* and its processing. If all the relevant data could be loaded into policy machinery scientifically designed for processing, the "right" answer would appear at the other end. Trudeau himself was somewhat obsessive about the application of rationality to government (he had adopted as his personal slogan "reason over passion"). Various management fads, tagged with a bewildering variety of acronyms, were applied to the bureaucratic process in successive attempts to rationally organize the technical and intellectual resources of the federal bureaucracy. None of these schemes achieved much success before being abandoned for a newer fad with a trendier acronym. The problem with this rationalist approach was that it tried to assume away politics and to imagine that the policy process in the real world could approximate an abstract technocratic model of inputs and outputs. In the end, a gathering economic and fiscal crisis of the state demonstrated that the model did not work well in the real world. But one of the byproducts of the 1970s was an enhancement of the role of the bureaucrat and an obsession with experimentation with the machinery of government, especially at the level of the central agencies.

Other tendencies in the wider political environment of the 1970s seemed at first to enhance the policy role of the bureaucracy but in the longer run actually served to undermine it. Greater demands for equality in Canadian society and the rise of relatively aggressive equality-seeking groups created new policy constituencies for bureaucrats oriented toward policy innovation. Previously, in the 1960s, francophone demands for equal recognition had fostered bilingualism as a policy goal for the federal government. This had not been limited to the provision of bilingual services to the public but had also necessitated better francophone representation within the public service itself. In the 1970s, feminist demands for gender equality became more insistent. Elements of the bureaucracy tried to co-opt feminist energies by absorbing groups into the administrative apparatus and to encourage new policy initiatives by funding advocacy groups to counter the persistent pressures for restraint and policy conservatism from Finance and the Treasury Board. Multicultural policies followed a similar path.[4]

Although these developments seemed to offer some enhanced capacity to manoeuvre in relatively new policy fields, they had two unanticipated long-term effects. First, there was a great deal of focus by equality-seeking groups on making the bureaucracy more *representative,* to reflect more equally the diversity of Canadian society in terms of language, gender, ethnicity, and so on. An unexceptional objective in itself, representational demands tended to shift attention from achieving difficult policy goals toward the easier goal of bumping up the number of women and minorities in the public service. The extension of representational criteria to the bureaucracy has also had the effect of imposing a whole set of new constraints on appointment and promotion.

A more serious consequence was the political reaction that set in by the end of the 1970s: an anti-bilingual backlash was followed by antifeminist and anti-multicultural backlashes in the 1980s. In an economic climate of recession, inflation, and skyrocketing government deficits, programs designed to meet the needs of specified target groups ran into heavy taxpayer resistance. In fact, few of such programs initiated in the 1970s actually carried overly expensive price tags, but they carried high symbolic significance. It became increasingly difficult to mount new expenditure programs for specially targeted groups. The groups themselves then turned more and more to the courts and to framing their demands in terms of justiciable rights, especially after the enactment of the Canadian Charter of Rights and Freedoms in 1982. The result was that a brief flicker of policy innovation and new initiatives in linking civil society and the state was quickly extinguished. In its place came a determination to cut back public expenditure, pare down the size of the state, and discourage policy innovation as inherently wasteful of tax dollars.

THE MULRONEY CONSERVATIVES, 1984–1993

When the Mulroney Conservatives took over in 1984, there were a number of changes in direction that significantly altered the balance between politicians and bureaucrats. Two in particular require closer examination. First, the suspicion with which the Tories regarded models of bureaucratic rationality translated into a more openly "political" approach to policy and process. Second, the Mulroney Tories, like the contemporary "Thatcherite" Tories in Britain and "Reaganite" Republicans in the U.S., viewed government as inherently inefficient and wasteful and favoured the extension of the scope of the private sector and of the principles of the free market. These two tendencies are, in fact, interrelated.

To the Tories, "bureaucratic rationality" was an oxymoron. Government had grown far too big and far too intrusive in Canadian society. The Trudeau approach of extending bureaucracy to control bureaucracy was little more than a rationalization of out-of-control growth and out-of-control costs. The real way to control government was to downsize it. One of the first things the Tories did upon assuming office was to appoint a special task force of people from the private sector to review government expenditures and programs. This exercise matched similar external reviews by conservative governments in Britain and the United States. In each case, principles of private-sector management were applied to government, with the latter found wanting.

In line with the British Tories and the U.S. Republicans, the Canadian Conservatives also launched programs of privatization and deregulation designed to downsize government and reduce the level of intervention in the private sector. Much of this was consistent with the traditional Conservative emphasis on deficit reduction, at least at the rhetorical level (Tory government performance in deficit reduction was considerably less impressive than the rhetoric). But it also implied that markets were far better regulators of efficiency than bureaucratic mechanisms. This kind of thinking led to a sharp decline in the prestige of senior bureaucrats and a pervasive sense in Tory Ottawa that bureaucratic effectiveness meant reducing the numbers of bureaucrats and limiting their policy influence.

The new conservatism did not necessarily translate into less bureaucracy, just as a rhetorical emphasis on deficit reduction did not necessarily translate into actual deficit reduction. Privatization did proceed apace, as many public enterprises were moved out of the public sector. But deregulation proved difficult to achieve, for the regulatory regime was not reduced, at least as measured by the number of regulatory instruments that continued to be enacted each year. With the Mulroney governments, restraint became a consistent watchword and leading standard to be applied to the evaluation of bureaucratic performance, even if the mechanisms for putting this standard into practice were elusive.

One of the results of restraint-mindedness was that the machinery for central control of bureaucratic activity built up by the previous Trudeau governments found a new life under the Tories. Among the central agencies, Finance and the Treasury Board in particular retained important influence over the line departments in overseeing expenditure control and checking the all-important economic implications of policy. The PCO, as the "department of the public service," also retained a leading role in coordinating the downsizing and reorganization of government along more businesslike lines. Mulroney's Cabinet committee structure increasingly emphasized expenditure controls, but to do this effectively required effective support from the central agencies. A central paradox of the new conservatism was that the goal of cutting down bureaucracy itself required more bureaucracy to do the job. For politicians dedicated to restraint, this presented a real problem. The Tories felt that they had a mandate to reduce bureaucracy, but could the bureaucrats not, in effect, swallow up the politicians even while talking the new line?

It was considerations like these, along with a perhaps understandable suspicion of a bureaucracy that had enjoyed such long and close relations with their Liberal rivals, that led the Mulroney Tories to emphasize a more "political" approach to the relations between ministers and their senior bureaucrats. The Tories instituted "chiefs of staff" for each minister. These were political appointments intended to offer the ministers a political arm in overseeing their departments.[5] The theory was that partisan political input could serve to balance the apolitical advice ministers received from their departments, and that chiefs of staff could offer ministers independent management assistance in running the ministers' offices. Senior bureaucrats were not happy with this innovation. Deputy ministers could not be expected to welcome a political figure interposed between them and their ministers. But the frequency of complaints about inexperience and lack of understanding of the technical details of departmental work on the part of some chiefs of staff suggest that recruitment from the ranks of party service was no guarantee of competence at this high level of policy and administration. By the end of the Mulroney years, resentment of the "politicos" had become a major theme of bureaucratic complaints.

Another ground for friction between politician and bureaucrat lay in the Tory suspicion (not always unfounded, it should be acknowledged) that bureaucrats could use their superior command of information to blunt or undermine the policy directions the ruling party was seeking to impose. To reduce this risk and to stamp their own imprint on the process as firmly as possible, some Tory ministers took to discouraging departments from presenting the kind of detailed policy option papers that the Trudeau government had encouraged. "Don't give us a dozen reasons why we shouldn't do what we want to do," the Tory ministers in effect instructed their departments, "just tell us *how* you intend to do what we want you to do." In one sense, this represented a not unreasonable desire of a democratically elected government to make the unelected bureaucracy fully accountable, to ensure that the civil servants really are *servants* of the peoples' representatives. But there were problems with this approach. Policy options are not always devices for undermining the political will of the politicians. The bureaucrats have the knowledge and experience to point to pitfalls and traps that the politicians have not considered. Bureaucrats pride themselves on keeping their political masters out of trouble, but persistent snubbing of their efforts may create an adversarial situation where one did not previously exist. Moreover, senior and even upper-middle-range bureaucrats in the Mulroney years sometimes felt that their professionalism was being put in question and morale consequently suffered.

Besides threatening to issue bureaucrats with "pink slips and running shoes," the Conservatives also launched more constructive exercises in reorienting the public service. One theme was "let the managers manage." Looking to private-sector analogies, it was argued that senior departmental bureaucrats had become too hemmed in by externally imposed constraints on their authority. *Public Service 2000* was an initiative launched in 1989 that included a series of task forces to investigate various aspects of public service organization. This exercise was intended to enhance flexibility and efficiency in the provision of service to the public by decentralizing authority to senior managers.[6] While this might have been welcomed by those at or near the top of the bureaucracy, the overriding context of fiscal constraint gave the exercise a different twist to the middle and lower ranks. Seen from below, greater managerial flexibility seemed to aggressively impinge on employee prerogatives; labour unrest among the unionized staff increased.

Even from a managerial point of view, the Tory push had a distinct downside. The fashionable conservative paradigm was, and is, "reinventing government,"[7] a concept that rests on trying to make the public sector emulate as fully as possible the private sector. While it is undoubtedly the case, in theory, that government services can be provided more efficiently by units operating in a deregulated and decontrolled environment, the private-sector analogy fails to account for much that is specific to the operations of government. For one thing, the profit motive that drives private-sector enterprise can at best only be artificially applied to most government services, which by their nature cannot be subordinated to profit criteria. Moreover, when the bottom line for government is simply reducing expenditure, payoffs in terms of improved service are dubious. Instead of doing better with less, governments simply do less.

Another point of general significance for the policy role of the bureaucracy is that the reinventing government paradigm focuses almost exclusively on the state's role in service provision, where economic criteria can be applied. Policy innovation in a public-sector context defies private-sector criteria, where product innovation succeeds or fails in the market. There is no "market" to measure public policy innovation. Consequently, the re-orientation of the public service initiated in the Mulroney years (and largely retained, as we shall see, in the post-Mulroney era) has focused on government as a service provider, not a policy initiator. Thus, despite a superficial appeal to the autonomy of the senior bureaucracy, the PS 2000/reinventing government initiatives have had the effect of downgrading the policy role of the mandarins even further. From an active force in shaping Canadian society, the bureaucrats have been reduced to glorified suppliers of nuts and bolts.

DOWNSIZING, 1993

Bureaucrats and Tories were clearly on a collision course that culminated in the summer of 1993, which also happened to be the Conservatives' last days in office. But the course was set at least a year earlier, when Prime Minister Mulroney appointed Glen Shortliffe Clerk of the Privy Council. Shortliffe was widely viewed as a willing instrument for the further politicization of the civil service, a perception already applied to his predecessor, Paul Tellier, who had resigned to join the private sector.[8] Whether this perception was justified or not, the appointment caused consternation, which deepened when it became known that as boss of the civil service, Shortliffe would preside over the most serious overhaul and reorganization of the structure of government ever mounted. In fact, a reorganization project under a Tory Cabinet minister, Robert de Cotret, had called in four former senior civil servants as consultants and already had a preliminary report on the prime minister's desk when the Shortliffe appointment was announced. Pressed politically by the rise of the restraint-minded Reform Party among traditional Tory voters, the Tories wanted finally to radically downsize government. The de Cotret study offered a blueprint, and Shortliffe was to oversee its implementation.

This reorganization involved downsizing not only the bureaucracy but crucially reducing the unwieldy size of Cabinet and the Cabinet committee system. This latter task required some political courage on the part of the prime minister. The Cabinet, and thus the number of ministries, had grown as a result of the rising expectations of regions and of special interest groups in society for ministers, ministries, and programs that "represented" them. Any ruthless cutback of these "representatives" would be sure to run into powerful criticism and thus run political risks. And from within, actual elimination of senior bureaucratic positions, and thus the dismissal of senior civil servants, would inevitably rouse a storm of bureaucratic resistance.

Mulroney, perhaps not too surprisingly, chose not to stir these hornets' nests before his retirement from office. It was thus left to his successor, Kim Campbell, to bite the bullet. This she did when she named her Cabinet in June 1993. It comprised only 25 ministers, a sharp reduction from the Mulroney pattern. She also reduced the number of Cabinet committees from 11 to 5. Under Campbell's plan, which closely reflected the recommendations of the de Cotret group, the number of ministries was reduced from 32 to 23. Many were merged or amalgamated, and overlapping functions eliminated. A small number of "super ministries" (as they were inevitably dubbed by the press) emerged, while other departments either were cut back in importance or in some cases disappeared altogether.

With fewer ministers and a smaller number of Cabinet committees, some observers detected a shift of power back to the bureaucracy, where decisions would more likely be made in the absence of detailed ministerial scrutiny.[9] This perception was at odds with the view that the Tories were "politicizing" the bureaucracy, but in such matters the intended consequences of changes are not always at one with the unintended consequences. Once again, we see the paradox of a government resorting to bureaucratic means to reduce the size of the bureaucracy. Certainly two civil servants in the central agencies—Shortliffe at the PCO and Ian Clark, Secretary of the Treasury Board—now had extremely powerful positions in Ottawa in shepherding the reorganization into place. It was Shortliffe who effectively held the fate of the careers of senior civil servants in his hands. It was essentially on his recommendation that senior civil servants were re-shuffled to fit the new top slots in the reorganized bureaucracy— and in some cases were shuffled right out of the picture.

The seriousness of the situation was made clear little more than a month after the Campbell Cabinet was sworn in. The axe fell on the assistant deputy minister (ADM) level, a category that had risen greatly in Ottawa over recent years to reach 319. These numbers were reduced by 17 percent, for a new total of 266. This left 53 ADMs out of a job; it appears that only about a dozen found alternative government employment. Moreover, normal personnel processes (through the individual departments and the Public Service Commission) were sidetracked in the reorganization. Instead, a small committee of deputy ministers and Glen Shortliffe decided their fates. Those terminated, many of whom had 25 to 30 years of service in government, had no recourse to appeal. This was an unprecedented shakeup of the upper range of the bureaucracy; never before had executive firings on a mass scale been effected in Ottawa. Needless to say, this had severe repercussions on the morale of the civil service as a whole.

Previous Tory governments had shied away from frontal attacks for fear of stirring large conflicts within their own administration. The political situation in the summer of 1993 was such that the "optics" had changed. A press report from Ottawa acknowledged that the "cuts have created a climate of fear within the civil service," but went on to point out that "Ms. Campbell and her ministers are primarily concerned with the political signal they hope the cuts will send—a picture of the bureaucrats in Ottawa experiencing some of the same pain that people in the private sector have felt during the recession."[10] With the Reform Party snapping at Tory heels, and an election pledge to eliminate the deficit in five years without raising taxes, the Tories had reached the point where they not only wanted to reduce and restrain the public sector, but wanted to be *seen* to be doing so—at whatever cost to the morale of their administrators.

THE CHRÉTIEN LIBERAL ERA

It is difficult to evaluate what effect, if any, the Tory adversarial stance against the bureaucracy had on the election of 1993. The Conservatives were not only swept out of power but were virtually eliminated as an active force in Parliament. Reform, with its strong anti-government, pro–free market principles, replaced the Conservatives as the main opposition party in English-speaking Canada and, after the 1997 election, Reform became the Official Opposition. The Bloc Québécois, which formed the Official Opposition from 1993 to 1997, had a sole raison d'être (the sovereignty of Quebec) that, if successful, would cause the most wrenching turbulence in the bureaucracy, especially among francophone civil servants. The spectacular emergence of these two new parties in the opposition benches presaged future storm clouds over the relationship between politicians and bureaucrats.

More immediately significant, however, was the return of the Liberals to office with a majority government, repeated twice more in 1997 and 2000. The Liberals made it clear at the outset that they wished to avoid an adversarial relationship with their bureaucrats, and set a priority on rebuilding morale among the senior civil service. David Zussman, a former senior bureaucrat turned academic who had written sympathetically of the problems of morale in public-sector management,[11] was made head of the Liberal transition team. The Tory innovation of ministerial chiefs of staff was scrapped. Under Chrétien, ministers are allowed to hire a maximum of five officers and seven ministerial support staff, with a capped budget. Interestingly, lobbyists reacted to these changes by switching their attention away from ministerial staff to the bureaucrats.[12]

A former Clerk of the Privy Council, Marcel Massé, who had resigned in protest over what he deemed the politicization of the civil service under the Tories, resurfaced as a star Liberal candidate and, following the 1993 election, as the minister for federal–provincial relations. Massé delivered a speech to the Public Service Alliance that was reassuring to the bureaucracy. "Good government requires a close and congenial relationship between public servants of every level and politicians," Massé said, calling for a new partnership. He criticized the Tory reorganization not only for creating "uncertainty and destabilization" but for putting reduction in size before an appraisal of what the role of government should be and what services it should provide: "How can you decide the shape and size of the instrument without deciding what you want it to do?"[13]

This may have sounded like music to the ears of long-suffering mandarins, but the Liberals have not reversed the main thrust of the reorganization initiated under the Tories. Prime Minister Jean Chrétien's first Cabinet was even smaller, at 23 members, than Kim Campbell's had been, the smallest in three decades. However, in order to meet pressures for regional representation, the Chrétien administration enlarged the ministry to include several Secretaries of State who are not members of Cabinet and who do not oversee a government department. In 2003 the size of the Chrétien cabinet has crept up to 28 full ministers and 12 Secretaries of

State. The standing Cabinet committees were initially reduced from Campbell's simplified structure from five to four, but in 2003 there are again five. The combined effect of these changes has actually been to further enhance centralization of control in the hands of the prime minister and the central agencies, a tendency that now seems almost inevitable, whatever the professed goals of administrative reformers may be.

The Liberals, who had sometimes in previous eras taken (or stolen) policy ideas from the left-of-centre NDP, now took their fiscal policy cues largely from the right-of-centre Reform Party. Having assumed deficit elimination as the commanding priority of their first term, the Liberals did within four years what their Conservative predecessors had only talked about for nine years: the federal government's books were moved into the black. This was an outstanding achievement, but the single-minded way in which this goal was pursued had serious implications for the federal public service. Despite rhetoric about "renewal," the objective of the Liberals in regard to the bureaucracy was saving money primarily through drastic staff reductions. The Liberals enunciated a series of tests to be applied to a program-review exercise carried out within the departments under the direction of Massé. Such tests were strongly oriented toward forcing departments to demonstrate why they, rather than the private or voluntary sectors or the provinces, should be doing what they were doing—or indeed why some things should be done at all. The bottom-line test was the "affordability" test. Under the Liberals, close to 56 000 federal public-service jobs were eliminated from 1993 to 1998. From 1995 to 1998, in the three years following Finance Minister Paul Martin's key budget that promised major reductions, the size of the federal work force declined by 17 percent. To help accomplish this, the government offered buyouts and enriched early retirement packages that together accounted for 43 percent of the departures from 1995 to 1998. Another 18.9 percent of departures were accounted for by devolution of functions to other levels of government or by privatization.[14]

The same budget contained another key initiative that had serious implications for federal government policy. The Canada Health and Social Transfer (CHST) signalled the offloading of the costs of deficit elimination onto the provinces. It also marked the end of the era in which the federal government, through the use of the federal spending power, took the lead in national policy innovation in a number of key areas. It was the use of the spending power that had allowed Liberal governments in the 1960s to enact medicare and the Canada Pension Plan. The Chrétien government has generally declined to use the spending power as a device to coax or coerce provinces into line with federal policy objectives.

The Social Union Framework Agreement (1999)—not including Quebec—formalizes this reduction of the federal presence in the social policy field. The Romanow Commission on health care recommended a directing role for Ottawa in sustaining the public medical care system, but federal–provincial negotiations have already watered down this thrust. The federal government under Chrétien has in practice taken few domestic policy initiatives in areas where provincial jurisdiction intervenes. A notable exception is in the area of postsecondary education and research, where a series of innovations—the Millennium Scholarship Fund, graduate studies scholarships, Canada Research Chairs, beefed-up research and infrastructure funding, etc.—have asserted a stronger federal presence in an area under provincial jurisdiction. Yet even these initiatives tend toward transfers of money with the federal government acting as broker.

Aversion to policy innovation has been further enhanced by an oppositional culture that stresses cost control and searches obsessively for evidence of waste and corruption in government, to the neglect of more complicated, but less sexy, policy issues. This tendency is reinforced by "gotcha" journalism that since the Watergate affair in the 1970s has devoted considerable resources to unearthing potential scandals. An increasingly adversarial and confrontational approach adopted by the Auditor General further focuses opposition attention on mishandling of taxpayer dollars. The inevitable effect on government has been a risk-avoidance culture, in which defence tends to trump offence. Bureaucrats are prized by politicians above all for their skills as "goalkeepers," blocking opposition shots that threaten Cabinet ministers. Ironically, two of the major political embarrassments that have dogged the Chrétien governments—alleged overspending by Human Resources Development Canada and the ballooning of the costs of the National Firearm Registry to a billion dollars—may be partially attributed to downsizing. One of the first functions to be cut back has been internal accounting, leading to vulnerability to overspending and misspending.

In a dispiriting context of years of cutbacks, relentless denigration of the value of the public sector and of the value of public servants, and a dwindling agenda for positive action and policy innovation, it is hardly surprising that morale has suffered. The lower ranks feel threatened in their job security, pressured to perform better with fewer resources, and underappreciated, with few opportunities for advancement.[15] But the senior ranks have demonstrated their discontent in striking fashion—by leaving voluntarily. Their depleted numbers are not generally being filled by new blood from outside the public service, but by reassignment of existing employees.[16] What is particularly insidious about the Chrétien government's program of buyouts and enriched early retirements is that it is precisely the "best and the brightest" who tend to seize these opportunities because they can command attractive offers from the private sector or move into private consultancies. The result is a cumulative impoverishment of talent in the senior public service and further decline of morale. The former Clerk of the Privy Council, Jocelyne Bourgon, was blunt in a report to the prime minister on what she called a "quiet crisis" in the public service:

> It was becoming difficult to retain, motivate and attract people essential to the work of the public service. This was the result of years of downsizing and pay freezes, criticism, insufficient recruitment, and the premature departure of experienced public servants. It was a quiet crisis because few people were willing to talk about it and even fewer were doing something about it.[17]

Before her retirement in late 1998, Bourgon launched an initiative she called "La Relève" to revivify morale in a post-downsizing era. There is, however, little reason to foresee any break in this vicious cycle until the federal government decides to actively re-assert its presence as a leading force in the shaping of Canadian society.

The story is not unmixed. The catastrophic terrorist attacks on the United States on September 11, 2001, posed a serious challenge to the federal state to respond to the threat of further such attacks, potentially including Canada as a target, and to assure the U.S. that Canada was maintaining sufficiently high security along the world's longest undefended border to avoid economically costly border delays and backlogs. Faced with an external challenge of gravity comparable to the Cold War that began in the late 1940s, the federal government demonstrated a relatively supple capacity to reorder priorities, re-allocate resources, and restructure its administrative architecture to meet the challenge. Political leadership was key, with a special cabinet committee chaired by John Manley functioning for a time as a virtual inner or war cabinet. But the bureaucrats responded well to the new security agenda.[18] Pressures on Ottawa from the U.S., but also from a powerful business lobby in Canada, along with many premiers, the official opposition in Parliament, and influential sections of the media, were driving the federal government toward greater continental integration along the lines of a European-style "security perimeter" around North America—which would likely come at a considerable cost in terms of lost sovereignty. The Liberal government adroitly avoided such an outcome, while providing security assurances sufficient to keeping cross-border movement of goods and people relatively free-flowing—even under the stress of Canada's refusal to join in the U.S. invasion of Iraq in 2003. While the post–September 11th experience is transitory, it did leave a mark on the federal public service. Government, however briefly, was re-infused with a sense of mission, and of cooperation between politicians and bureaucrats.

The Clerk of the Privy Council, Mel Cappe, wrote to the prime minister in early 2002:

> As you know, Canadian public servants acted swiftly and skilfully to assist our American friends and to ensure the safety and security of Canadians and the Canadian economy. Our ability to mobilize and perform in times of crisis, as well as in times of calm, reveals the strength of our professional, non-partisan public service. On September 11th, there was no time to consult the rule books. Decisions were needed quickly. Actions were by necessity instinctive and so they were guided by the underlying values of the Public Service of Canada. [19]

Cappe nonetheless went on to admit that the current regime in the public service, "designed to reflect the realities of another time, has become cumbersome and counter-productive." We need, he suggested pointedly, a "competent, non-partisan public service able to speak truth to power." Unfortunately, "the merit *process* we have has developed in a way which undermines the merit *principle.*" Less than year later, the government enacted bill C-25, *The Public Service Modernization Act,* to Parliament. C-25 overhauls all the major legislation governing the public service. Among the central reforms is a modification of the merit process in appointments to permit wider discretion for managers to hire with fewer controls by the Public Service Commission.[20] C-25 would also loosen previous restrictions upon political activities on the part of public servants. Despite the misgivings of some critics about a return to patronage, or to the politicization of the public service, these changes are likely positive, signalling a commitment to a more effective, up-to-date public service.

CHRÉTIEN'S LONG GOODBYE AND POLICY LEGACY

When Jean Chrétien won a third consecutive majority government in 2001, there was every reason to believe that the trends evident in his first two governments would be continued. There was a great deal of criticism concerning one-party domination, heavy-handed control of government by the prime minister and the central agencies acting on his behalf, and the further decline of Parliament. Some even went so far as to refer to the Liberals as the "friendly dictatorship."[21] Yet in 2002, what the most influential student of the centralization of power in the Liberal government had written would be "unthinkable"[22] happened: a powerful prime minister with an unparalleled record of three consecutive majority governments and a fragmented and ineffectual opposition, was forced by his own party to announce his retirement. To be sure, the retirement constituted a "long goodbye," 18 months, to be finalized only in early 2004, months after a successor is to be chosen by the Liberal Party. But the circumstances that led to Chrétien's forced departure, as well as the circumstances surrounding his prolonged leave-taking, have dramatically transformed the policy agenda in Ottawa and have shifted the relationship between politicians and bureaucrats.

Chrétien wished to use the last year and a half of his tenure to establish a legacy in policy innovation. The year 2003 was marked by a flurry of sometimes bold initiatives, a number of them based on ideas he had requested from a special task force of senior public servants following his retirement decision. Some proved controversial indeed. With the ratification by Parliament of the Kyoto Accord on climate change, he not only faced down bitter opposition from Premier Ralph Klein of Alberta but imposed upon a federal bureaucracy that seemed ill prepared a set of ambitious and demanding requirements for implementation. With the Liberal leadership convention looming in the fall, he introduced a radical election financing bill that would virtually ban contributions from corporations and trade unions, and a bill to decriminalize possession of small amounts of marijuana, despite threats from the United States to retaliate if Canada deviated from American punitive practice. Since the latter followed the decision not to support the U.S. and U.K. in the invasion of Iraq, a decision popular at home but a source of strain in Canada–U.S. relations, Chrétien's reputation as lacking vision and avoiding controversy seemed no longer secure. Instead, there was a renewed willingness to use the federal government as a positive instrument to achieve change. The bureaucrats were being called upon once again to help devise a relatively ambitious policy agenda.

The situation in Parliament and in the governing Liberal caucus has been unprecedented since the Chrétien–Paul Martin split boiled over into Martin's departure from Cabinet in 2002. Chrétien's timetable for retirement has only accelerated the divisions. Criticism of government policy has come from within the ruling Liberal Party as much as, or in some cases more than, from across the floor. For example, the political financing bill found its most vocal opponents among Liberal MPs and party organizers, including the party president, who initially characterized the concept of the bill as "dumb as a bag of hammers." As heir apparent, Martin has kept his distance from some of the Chrétien initiatives, and in one case—the controversial First Nations governance bill—he openly stated his intention to dump the idea.

From the standpoint of the senior bureaucrats, this unusual situation presents novel challenges. Already sensitive to the dangers of becoming too closely identified with the politics of the government party in the eyes of a potential alternative government across the aisle in Parliament, the bureaucrats now have to worry about the dangers of being caught up by the warring factions within the government. When Alex Himelfarb was appointed the new Clerk of the Privy Council in June 2002, the first Cabinet meeting he attended was the famous meeting in which Chrétien delivered an ultimatum to Martin, precipitating the latter's departure a few days later, and the events that were to lead to the prime minister's forced resignation. Himelfarb took due note and instructed senior officials to begin a parallel process of preparing the policy agenda for the PM and another transition plan for the new Martin team that could be expected some time in the near future.[23] What will be the relationship between the politicians and the bureaucrats after Martin, as expected, takes over in February 2004, if not earlier, is anybody's guess. But it would seem that we are now entering uncharted waters. Once again, strong policy directions are emanating from the politicians—even if these come in competing versions.

POLITICIANS AND BUREAUCRATS IN THE TWENTY-FIRST CENTURY

The conditions under which governments operate at the beginning of the twenty-first century have changed drastically, as has the relationship between politics and administration. Even with the end of budgetary deficits, governments continue to face powerful constraints on positive government activity. In an era of globalization, all governments, whether of the right, the centre, or the moderate left, are expected to conform to common standards of a neoliberalism that demands less government and greater international competitiveness. Bureaucrats face severe structural limitations on their actions; politicians, whatever their ideology and whatever their basic attitudes toward bureaucrats, will seek to tightly control the bureaucracy, out of motives of political self-preservation if nothing else. At the same time, other expectations are being imposed on bureaucrats, who are supposed to make themselves more representative of the diversity of their societies, to recognize in their practices a wide range of rights in the citizenry that only rarely impinged on their performance in the past, and to make themselves answerable to a wide range of critics.

We are now in an age when the very definition of the boundaries between the public and the private sectors is in fundamental question, and the role of government is constantly being re-defined in the face of such factors as economic globalization and new challenges to the legitimacy of the state. In the former case, the toolbox of economic policy available to national governments has been depleted, leaving citizens angry and dissatisfied about the apparent impotence of their policymakers. In the latter case, a pervasive new populism that has swept through Western democracies (dramatically exemplified in Canada by Reform/Canadian Alliance but hardly limited to that party) demands greater accountability of the political elites to the people. This insistence on political accountability forces politicians to tighten the reins on their bureaucrats and will probably, before the movement has run its course, force previously insulated and secretive areas of administration under more direct public scrutiny. After all, as bureaucracy has penetrated civil society (the growth of complex interventions in and regulations of "private" behaviour, and the emergence of embedded policy communities), it should hardly be surprising that demands for greater transparency of the state should emerge from the society.

To this point, the best that politicians seem able to devise is to "reinvent government" according to rules that govern the private sector. By that standard, politicians and bureaucrats alike will always be found wanting. Until politicians re-discover that citizens are much more than clients and consumers, and that government's mission is different from that of the private sector, but just as important, bureaucrats in particular will bear the brunt of societal distrust and incomprehension, and their relations with their political masters will continue to be strained.

NOTES

1. Guy D'Avignon, *Report of the Special Committee on the Review of Personnel Management and the Merit Principle* (Ottawa, 1979).

2. Definition drawn from William D. Coleman and Grace Skogstad, "Policy Communities and Policy Networks: A Structural Approach," in Coleman and Skogstad, eds., *Policy Communities and Public Policies in Canada: A Structural Approach* (Toronto: Copp Clark Pitman, 1990), p. 26.

3. Federal–Provincial Relations was from the 1970s to 1993 a fourth separate central agency. It was then reintegrated into the Privy Council Office.

4. See Leslie A. Pal, *Interests of State: The Politics of Language, Multiculturalism and Feminism in Canada* (Montreal/Kingston: McGill-Queen's University Press, 1993).

5. The chief of staff was precisely the opposite of the British institution of the private secretary to ministers. In the British case, private secretaries are permanent civil servants who are appointed to head each minister's private office. It has often been argued that this offers the bureaucrats a window on the ministers; the Canadian Tory chief of staff, on the other hand, was designed to offer the ministers a window on the bureaucrats.

6. See Leslie A. Pal, "The Federal Bureaucracy: Reinventing the Links between State and Society," in Michael S. Whittington and Glen Williams, eds., *Canadian Politics in the 1990s*, 4th ed. (Scarborough, ON: Nelson Canada, 1994), pp. 276–91.

7. David Osborne and Ted Gaebler, *Reinventing Government: How the Entrepreneurial Spirit Is Transforming the Public Sector* (Reading, MA: Addison-Wesley, 1992).

8. In fairness to the Tories, the politicization of the office of Clerk of the Privy Council was widely perceived to have begun with Trudeau's appointment of Michael Pitfield, who was dismissed by Joe Clark in 1979 and then reinstated following Trudeau's return to office in 1980. But Shortliffe had gained particular notoriety in 1991 when he engineered what many regarded as the offloading of blame from politicians onto senior civil servants in the Al Mashat scandal at External Affairs (Al Mashat was an Iraqi diplomat given political asylum, an action that caused great political embarrassment).

9. See for instance, Hugh Winsor, "Slim Cabinet Fattens Mandarins," *The Globe and Mail*, July 5, 1993.

10. Hugh Winsor, "Axe to Fall on More Top Bureaucrats," *The Globe and Mail*, August 6, 1993.

11. See David Zussman and Jak Jabes, *The Vertical Solitude: Managing in the Public Sector* (Halifax: Institute for Research on Public Policy, 1989).

12. Rand Dyck, *Canadian Politics: Critical Approaches*, 2nd ed. (Toronto: Nelson Canada, 1996), p. 512.

13. Hugh Winsor, "Liberals Seeking to Improve Relations with Civil Servants," *The Globe and Mail*, October 29, 1993.

14. Treasury Board of Canada Secretariat, *Employment Statistics for the Federal Public Service, April 1 1996–March 31 1997, April 1 1997–March 31 1998*.

15. A 1998 report by independent consultants on morale in one government department indicated "widespread pessimism among employees and a deep mistrust of management ... The study paints a picture of a federal agency stung by a lengthy wage freeze, shrinking resources, and heavy workloads ... Almost two-thirds said they would leave for a higher salary elsewhere." Jim Bronskill, "Bureaucrats Dispirited, Distrustful, Study Finds," *National Post*, November 11, 1998.

16. Data on voluntary departures from the EX (executive) category can be found in Michael S. Whittington and Richard J. Van Loon, *Canadian Government and Politics: Institutions and Processes* (Toronto: McGraw-Hill Ryerson, 1996), pp. 674–75.

17. Jocelyne Bourgon, Clerk of the Privy Council and Secretary to the Cabinet, *Fifth Annual Report to the Prime Minister of Canada on the Public Service of Canada*, Part III (March 31, 1998).

18. Reg Whitaker, "More or Less Than Meets the Eye? The New National Security Agenda," in G. Bruce Doern, ed., *How Ottawa Spends 2003–2004—Regime Change and Policy Shift* (Don Mills: Oxford University Press, 2003)

POLITICS VERSUS ADMINISTRATION   83

19. Mel Cappe, *9th Annual Report to the Prime Minister on the Public Service of Canada, Letter to the Prime Minister,* March 27, 2002.

20. Library of Parliament, Legislative Summary of Bill C-25, prepared by Margaret Smith, 13 March 2003.

21. Jeffrey Simpson, *The Friendly Dictatorship* (Toronto: McClelland & Stewart, 2001).

22. Donald J. Savoie, *Governing from the Centre: the Concentration of Power in Canadian Politics* (Toronto: University of Toronto Press, 1999), p. 362.

23. Bill Curry, "Bureaucrat began plans for new PM last June," *National Post,* May 21, 2003.

FURTHER READINGS

Aucoin, Peter, and Herman Bakvis. *The Centralization–Decentralization Conundrum: Organization and Management in the Canadian Government.* Halifax: Institute for Research on Public Policy, 1988.

Bourgon, Jocelyne, Clerk of the Privy Council and Secretary to the Cabinet. *Fifth Annual Report to the Prime Minister of Canada on the Public Service of Canada,* March 31, 1998.

Canada, Privy Council. *First Progress Report on La Relève: A Commitment to Action.* Presented by Departments, Functional Communities and Federal Regional Councils to the Clerk of the Privy Council and Secretary of the Cabinet. Ottawa: The Privy Council, 1998, 2 v.

Canada, Public Service 2000. *The Renewal of the Public Service of Canada.* Ottawa: Government of Canada, 1990.

French, Richard D., and Richard Van Loon. *How Ottawa Decides: Planning and Industrial Policy Making, 1968–1984.* 2nd ed. Toronto: Lorimer, 1984.

How Ottawa Spends. Annual volumes from 1983, various editors.

Kernaghan, Kenneth, and David Siegel. *Public Administration in Canada: A Text.* 3rd ed. Scarborough: Nelson Canada, 1995.

Osbaldeston, Gordon F. *Keeping Deputy Ministers Accountable.* Toronto: McGraw-Hill Ryerson, 1989.

Osborne, David, and Ted Gaebler. *Reinventing Government: How the Entrepreneurial Spirit Is Transforming the Public Sector.* Reading, Mass.: Addison-Wesley, 1992.

Pal, Leslie A. "The Federal Bureaucracy: Reinventing the Links Between State and Society." In Michael S. Whittington and Glen Williams, eds., *Canadian Politics in the 1990s.* Toronto: Nelson Canada, 1994, 276–91.

Savoie, Donald J. *Governing from the Centre: The Concentration of Power in Canadian Politics.* Toronto: University of Toronto Press, 1999.

Simpson, Jeffrey. *The Friendly Dictatorship.* Toronto: McClelland & Stewart, 2001.

Sutherland, S. L., and G. Bruce Doern. *Bureaucracy in Canada: Control and Reform.* Toronto: University of Toronto Press, 1985.

Zussman, David, and Jak Jabes. *The Vertical Solitude: Managing in the Public Sector.* Halifax: Institute for Research on Public Policy, 1989.

CHAPTER 4

FEDERALISM AND INTERGOVERNMENTAL RELATIONS

Garth Stevenson

Federalism is one of the most obvious characteristics of the Canadian political system, and federal–provincial controversy seems to pervade most aspects of Canadian life. The joke about the Canadian who was asked to write an essay on the elephant and who chose to explore whether the animal fell under federal or provincial jurisdiction is now almost 40 years old. The efforts to modify Canada's formal constitution from the 1960s through the early 1990s directed attention to the politics of federalism, even more than in earlier periods of Canadian history. Although John A. Macdonald hoped, and some twentieth-century social scientists also predicted, that preoccupation with federalism, regionalism, and provincialism would decline in the course of economic and political modernization, this prediction has proved erroneous in the Canadian case, at least up to the present.

Federal–provincial relations in Canada are by no means confined to the politics of constitutional change. In fact, modern federalism wherever it exists seems inevitably to produce a complex pattern of intergovernmental relations involving many aspects of public policy. It would be fair to say, however, that in the most successful and stable federations, such as Australia, Germany, Switzerland, or the United States, intergovernmental relations are less conspicuous, less conflictual, and less controversial than in Canada.

FEDERALISM IN THEORY AND PRACTICE

The importance of intergovernmental relations in federations may seem paradoxical, because formal definitions of federalism suggest that the two levels of government have totally distinct and mutually exclusive areas of responsibility, so that little or no interaction between them should logically be required. In fact, a celebrated judicial interpretation of Canada's constitution once referred to the "watertight compartments" that supposedly confined the federal and provincial governments within their separate fields of jurisdiction.[1] From this perspective it might seem that, given a suitable distribution of responsibilities, each level of government could act unilaterally within its own sphere and ignore the activities of the other level. At most they might require a supreme court with authority to interpret the constitution so as to prevent any government from trespassing on the jurisdictional turf of the other level and to settle interjurisdictional disputes.

This is not, of course, how Canadian federalism really works, but to a large extent the Constitution Act of 1867 did attempt to follow this model. Parallel institutions of government were established, insofar as they did not already exist, at the federal and provincial levels. Each was given access to certain sources of revenue. The types of laws that could be made by Parliament and the provincial legislatures were listed in exhaustive detail, with no less than 48 enumerated categories. All but 3 of the 48 were assigned exclusively to one level of government or the other. According to the Colonial Laws Validity Act of 1865, neither Parliament nor the legislatures could legislate contrary to the terms of any imperial statute applying to them, and since the BNA Act was an imperial statute, this meant in practice that the Judicial Committee of the Privy Council would act as an arbiter in cases of disputed jurisdiction.

Insofar as the Constitution of 1867 deviated from this model, it did so by enabling the federal government to exercise power over the provincial ones, even if the latter remained within their own fields of jurisdiction. Thus the federal government appoints the judges to provincial superior and county courts and also appoints the lieutenant governor, who is formally the chief executive officer at the provincial level. In the early days of Canadian federalism, lieutenant governors exercised real power: sometimes dismissing their ministerial advisers, refusing their assent to acts of the legislature, or reserving such acts for a final decision by the federal government on whether they would be allowed to come into operation. In addition, the federal government can disallow any provincial act within a year of its adoption, although this power was used very rarely after 1911 and has not been used at all since 1943. Parliament can unilaterally assume jurisdiction over "works and undertakings" within a province, although this power also has fallen into disuse. The federal government can interfere in the provincial jurisdiction over education to protect the rights of certain minorities, but the one attempt to exercise this power in 1896 probably demonstrated that it was unusable in practice.

These admitted departures from the pure theory of federalism have little importance for modern intergovernmental relations. The powers of disallowance and reservation are unlikely ever again to be used. While provincial governments certainly complain loudly and frequently about federal "intrusions" into what they regard as their spheres of authority, it is usually the federal government's economic and fiscal policies that give offence, not the appointment of judges and lieutenant governors. Moreover, and in complete contrast to the centralist preferences of the Fathers of Confederation, the provincial governments themselves now possess impressive means of complicating, frustrating, and interfering with policymaking at the federal level.

THE RISE OF PROVINCIAL POWER

The highly centralized version of federalism that John A. Macdonald envisaged in fact lasted for little more than a decade after Confederation. By the 1880s, provincial leaders like Oliver Mowat of Ontario were successfully challenging Macdonald's vision and a type of federalism emerged in which power was quite evenly distributed between the two levels of government. Mowat's view that the two levels of government were roughly equal in importance and that each was sovereign in its own sphere of jurisdiction was ironically similar to the American model, which Macdonald had rejected. Nonetheless it was endorsed by the Judicial Committee of the Privy Council, the highest tribunal of the British Empire, in *Hodge v. The Queen* and later in *Liquidators of Maritime Bank v. Attorney General of New Brunswick*.[2]

The economic crisis brought on by the Great Depression of the 1930s persuaded many Canadians that Macdonald had been right after all, and that a more centralized regime was needed to protect Canadians against unemployment, poverty, and insecurity. The Judicial Committee of the Privy Council thought otherwise, and a number of federal statutes designed to deal with the crisis were struck down on the grounds that they intruded on the provincial jurisdiction over "property and civil rights in the province." Nonetheless, World War II greatly strengthened the central government at the expense of the provinces. In the postwar years Ottawa used its enhanced power to manage the economy, with apparent success, and to provide Canadians with unemployment insurance, family allowances, universal old age pensions, and hospital insurance. Federal revenues and spending far surpassed those of all the provincial governments combined, the BNA Act was amended in 1940 and 1951 to give Parliament power to enact unemployment insurance and pensions respectively, and the Judicial Committee lost its power to decide Canadian cases in 1949. By the 1950s it seemed that Canada, like most other modern states, was destined for an indefinite, and perhaps permanent, era of centralization.

Since 1960, however, this prognosis has proved to be totally mistaken. Admittedly, the federal government has won some recent victories in the courts, notably with regard to jurisdiction over the environment, competition policy, and communications.[3] However, most of the recent evolution of Canadian federalism has been in the direction of increasing the power and importance of provincial governments. Indeed, the larger provinces now exercise powers that would be the envy of many sovereign members of the United Nations. The growth of the state has been a ubiquitous phenomenon in the modern world, at least until recently, but Canada is unusual, and perhaps unique, in the extent to which that growth has taken place at the sub-national level. Economic development and foreign relations, the state functions that were considered most important in 1867 and probably still are today, were originally placed for the most part beyond the reach of provincial jurisdiction. Nowadays the provincial governments routinely seek to influence federal policies in these areas and, with even greater determination, to conduct economic and foreign policies of their own. Provincial revenues, excluding grants, increased from 5.9 percent of GNP in 1960 to 19.3 percent in 2000. Federal revenues, 16.5 per cent of GNP in 1960, increased only slightly to 19.0 per cent of GNP in the same period.[4]

Provincialists, especially in Quebec, will respond that the changes made by the Constitution Act of 1982 weakened the provinces vis-à-vis the federal government. In fact, the impact of those changes on federal–provincial relations was limited and somewhat ambiguous. The Charter of Rights and Freedoms restricted the powers of both levels of government, while increasing the influence and importance of the judiciary. At the same time it gave both levels the power to override most parts of the Charter, a power that has been exercised in two provinces but never at the federal level. The amending formula entrenched what was already accepted practice, namely the involvement of the provincial governments in the amending process. It also includes a uniquely Canadian provision: amendments transferring provincial powers to the federal level will apply only to those provinces that explicitly give their consent. Provincial powers over natural resources were increased to some extent, and the poorer provinces secured constitutional entrenchment of equalization payments, which they had actually received from the federal government since 1957. These changes were less important than the non-constitutional developments that transformed Canadian federalism in the last four decades of the twentieth century. The causes of those developments must now be explored.

CAUSES OF DECENTRALIZATION

Although John A. Macdonald's hope that the provincial governments would dwindle away into insignificance was shown to be fallacious within a decade after Confederation, it is only since about 1960 that the growth of provincial powers and the relatively limited capacity, or willingness, of the central government to act unilaterally in most areas of public policy have appeared to distinguish Canada from other modern states. During that time various Canadian political scientists have attempted to explain these phenomena, although no real consensus has been achieved. Some observers, particularly in Quebec, continue to deny that the Canadian central government is weaker than those of other federal countries. Even among those who recognize that it is, opinions differ as to which are the most significant reasons why this is so. Probably few would argue that any single explanation is adequate. The main categories of explanatory factors that have been suggested are summarized below.

INSTITUTIONS

Some observers attach primary importance to certain features of Canada's federal constitution as explanations for the growth of provincial power, even though the Fathers of Confederation apparently designed it with quite a different intention. There are a number of specific explanations within this category. The adoption of British parliamentary government and an appointed upper house, rather than institutions on the American pattern, limited the ability of the central government to accommodate provincial interests and thus encouraged the growth of strong provincial governments to speak for such interests. The explicit enumeration of provincial legislative powers, although designed to limit them, actually facilitated their expansion in practice by provincial governments and the judiciary, particularly since they included such broad categories as "property and civil rights." The very fact of having provincial governments at all facilitated "province building" and the development of separate identities. Provincial ownership of natural resources, although considered insignificant in 1867, strengthened provincial governments, most obviously in Alberta but in other provinces as well. Health, education, and welfare, all entrusted to some extent to the provincial governments, proved to be more important areas of public policy than had been anticipated in 1867.

GEOGRAPHY

Mackenzie King once observed that Canada has "too much geography."[5] Although sometimes taken for granted, Canada's vast physical extent, small and scattered population, and geographical barriers such as the Laurentian shield, the Rocky Mountains, and the Gulf of St. Lawrence tend to weaken national integration and perhaps to encourage emphasis on the provincial level of government as a supplier of services. The relatively small number of provinces in contrast to the 50 American states, the extremely large size of Quebec and Ontario, whose populations exceed those of most European countries, and the absence of metropolitan areas (apart from Ottawa-Hull) that spill across provincial boundaries may also be significant.

CULTURAL DIVERSITY

Particularly in recent years, the literature on Canadian federalism has tended to emphasize, and often to celebrate, the allegedly distinctive cultural "identities" of Canadians in the different provinces. It is said that Canadians in different provinces are objectively different in terms of such categories as ethnicity and religion, and also that they are subjectively different in that they feel attachments to their respective provinces or "regions" more strongly than to Canada as a whole. According to this view, the provincial governments are strong in Canada because Canadians have distinctive needs and interests that cannot be accommodated within a single national government, and also because Canadians actually want strong provincial governments and a relatively weak federal one. This belief is often used as an explanation for the present state of Canadian federalism, but also as an argument for further weakening the central government through formal constitutional change.

In his classic analysis of Canadian society, *The Vertical Mosaic*, John Porter described the belief that the provinces had distinctive cultures as "hallowed nonsense" unsupported by any evidence, except perhaps in the case of Quebec.[6] Even if it were true, it would not necessarily explain the power exercised by provincial governments. American states are at least as culturally distinctive as Canadian provinces, but American federalism has evolved in quite a different direction.

QUEBEC NATIONALISM

Unlike other North American provinces or states, Quebec has most of the characteristics of a distinct nation. In particular, it is the only part of North America where French is the predominant language. The legal system, the schools, and even financial institutions in Quebec are quite different from elsewhere. Although there are important ethnic minorities in Montreal, the far north, and the Outaouais, most Québécois are descended from French settlers who came to the province during the reign of Louis XIV, and the overwhelming majority of persons born in Quebec remain there throughout their lives. Quebec nationalism has grown more intense since Confederation, partly in response to the ungenerous treatment of francophone minorities in the other provinces and more recently out of resentment against the anglophone domination of Quebec's economy. Since the Quiet Revolution of the 1960s, Quebec has acquired the administrative and institutional capacity to function as a sovereign state. Public opinion polls consistently show more support in Quebec than elsewhere for the view that provincial powers should be increased. The referendum of 1995 suggested that nearly half of the population of Quebec were inclined to support political independence, if economic ties with Canada could be retained.

Apart from the impact of Quebec nationalism on Quebec itself, it has strengthened the centrifugal forces of Canadian federalism in three ways. First, Quebec's example has encouraged other provinces to challenge federal authority, using some of the same arguments and tactics developed by Quebec. In addition, federal efforts to undermine Quebec nationalism by promoting bilingualism and appointing more francophones to positions of influence have sparked an anti-federal and anti-Quebec backlash, which provincial politicians outside of Quebec can use to their own advantage. Finally, and most ominously, recent federal governments have tried to appease Quebec nationalism by transferring federal powers and responsibilities not just to Quebec, but to all of the provinces. Thus some observers believe that the existence of Quebec is a sufficient explanation for Canada's unusually decentralized form of federalism. The fact that the centrifugal tendency in Canadian federalism became most apparent after 1960, when

Quebec was undergoing a process of social and political change known as the Quiet Revolution, gives some credence to the argument.

THE PARTY SYSTEM

While it may be more a symptom than a cause of the difficulties of Canadian federalism, the peculiar character of the party system seems to be associated with them. Parties in a federal system are supposed to accommodate all the divergent interests of the provinces and regions, but Canadian parties have considerable difficulty in doing so. The Conservative Party has not contested a Quebec election since 1935 and the Alberta Liberals have not held office since 1921. Exclusively provincial parties, like Social Credit in British Columbia or the Parti Québécois in Quebec, have sometimes been strong enough to win office. In several provinces the provincial and federal wings of the Liberal Party are completely separate from one another. Quebec's former Liberal premier Robert Bourassa even gave tacit support to the Progressive Conservatives in the federal election of 1988. The weak links between federal and provincial politics have the consequence that very few politicians with provincial experience seek election to the House of Commons. Federal and provincial politicians live throughout their careers in separate environments, interacting only in the formal, and usually conflictual, setting of a federal–provincial conference.

Another aspect of Canada's fragmented party system is the fact that the strength of the federal parties is very unevenly distributed across the country. The Liberals have been weak in the West since the rise of John Diefenbaker more than 40 years ago. The Conservatives were weak in Quebec for most of the twentieth century, although their fortunes there dramatically improved under Brian Mulroney. The federal election of 1993 left the Liberal Party as the only major national party in existence, and even its support was very unevenly distributed. The pro-sovereignty Bloc Québécois gained the role of official opposition although it had presented no candidates outside of Quebec. The Reform Party, with support heavily concentrated in Alberta and British Columbia, was in third place. The 1997 and 2000 elections in which Reform (now known as the Canadian Alliance) won second place while its seats were still overwhelmingly concentrated in Alberta and British Columbia, suggested that the fragmented party system might be a long-term phenomenon. Such voting behaviour both reflects and contributes to regional discontent. A federal government with little support in a province may lack legitimacy there and may even have difficulty in giving that province its usual quota of representation in the Cabinet. This in turn gives credence to claims by the provincial government that only it can speak for provincial interests. Some observers have suggested that proportional representation, either in the House of Commons or in an elected Senate, might overcome this problem.

UNEVEN ECONOMIC DEVELOPMENT

Many features of Canadian economic development might help to account for the relative weakness of the federal level of government and the corresponding strength of the provincial level. Mainly for natural reasons, but perhaps partly because of federal economic policies, the provinces differ considerably from one another in the structure of their economies, the predominance of particular industries, and the nature and extent of their trading and investment ties with foreign countries. Business interests concentrated in a particular province may encourage the strengthening of that province's government and the weakening of the federal government. Interprovincial disparities of wealth and income are very pronounced, and the rank ordering of the provinces in this regard has changed very little since the 1920s. The importance of mining, petroleum, and forestry in the Canadian economy reinforces the provincial level of government, which owns and controls these resources in accordance with the Constitution. The relatively slow and limited development of secondary manufacturing has restricted the mobility of population and thus reinforced provincialist sentiments. The dominant influence exercised by the United States over the Canadian economy, reinforced by the recent trend of globalization, has weakened the effectiveness of the federal government. The domination of Quebec's economy by anglophones, at least until the 1960s and 1970s, stimulated Quebec nationalism and caused resentment to be directed against the federal government. The influence exercised over the federal government by financial, mercantile, and transportation interests caused businesspeople associated with other industries to prefer the provincial level of government. Social and economic changes in Quebec and Alberta have produced new and powerful classes in those provinces dedicated to strengthening the provincial level of government at the expense of the federal. Finally, the North American Free Trade Agreement (NAFTA) prohibits many types of economic initiatives at the federal level but has less impact on the provinces.

All of these types of explanations are of some value, although all have their weaknesses. The institutional and geopolitical explanations fail to explain why Canadian federalism has developed so differently since 1960 from the way it operated previously. The sociocultural explanation is undermined by the important diversities that exist within the provinces and by the increasingly homogeneous character of Canadian society, including, to some extent, even Quebec. Finally, the economic explanations are sometimes guilty of circular reasoning or of surreptitiously borrowing arguments from the other explanations.

In any event, and regardless of which explanations are preferred, the provincial level of government is strong enough to ensure that there will be no uncontested supremacy by the central government, even within many of the fields of jurisdiction assigned to the latter under the Constitution. The federal government apparently cannot disregard the provincial governments and must bargain with them almost continuously in order to achieve its own objectives. The curious expression "the eleven senior governments," which has recently found its way into Canadian political discourse, is symptomatic of this factual equality of bargaining power, whatever the Constitution may say to the contrary. The remaining sections of this chapter will describe the actual, as opposed to formal, division of responsibilities between the two levels, the areas of conflict, and the mechanisms of interaction, before turning to an evaluation and critique of the system.

JURISDICTIONAL CONFLICT

As an aid to understanding how responsibilities are actually divided between the two levels of government, the Constitution Act of 1867, with its detailed and seemingly precise division of jurisdictions, is of very limited value. The categories overlap considerably, many subjects that preoccupy governments in the latter part of the twentieth century are not listed at all, and both levels of government have expanded their activities without much regard for the constitution.

The fields of public policy can be classified into three groups: those occupied exclusively by one level of government with little or no objection by the other, those where both levels of government are active but apparently without much conflict, and those that give rise to federal–provincial conflict. The last category includes some areas that the Constitution Act of 1867 assigns primarily to the federal level, some that it assigns primarily to the provincial level, and some that it does not assign at all because they were insignificant or unknown at the time of Confederation. Naturally the extent to which particular subjects are shared or give rise to conflict changes over time: emphasis will be placed here mainly on the situation at the time of writing.

An examination of the names of departments in the federal and provincial governments suggests what further investigation confirms: very few areas of policy are now occupied exclusively by one level of government. The only exclusively federal areas are military defence, veterans' affairs, postal service, and monetary policy. The only exclusively provincial areas appear to be municipal institutions, lands and forests, roads, liquor licensing, and elementary and secondary education.

Some fields of jurisdiction are partially occupied by both levels of government but are not areas of serious conflict, at least for the moment. These include agriculture and immigration, both areas where the Constitution says either level can legislate, and pensions, which were placed in the same position by subsequent amendments. (An important difference is that federal law is paramount over provincial law with respect to agriculture and immigration, but provincial law is paramount with respect to pensions.) Both immigration and pensions were the source of serious conflicts between the federal and Quebec governments in the not-too-distant past, but these conflicts seem now to have been resolved. Other areas of more or less harmoniously shared jurisdiction, not mentioned explicitly in the federal Constitution, include scientific research, cultural and recreational activities, tourism, and protection of the environment.

A number of areas assigned to federal jurisdiction have become sources of federal–provincial controversy, either because provincial governments have succeeded in becoming involved in them or because some of them are dissatisfied with federal policies and would like to do so. A good example of the latter category is the field of fisheries. Newfoundland, supported by Nova Scotia, demanded as early as 1978 that it be transferred to provincial jurisdiction. In 1987 the ill-fated Meech Lake Accord, in order to secure the support of those two provinces, promised that this demand would be considered at the earliest opportunity after Quebec's concerns had been dealt with. More recently British Columbia has challenged federal authority over fisheries in a particularly strident manner. Admittedly federal management of the fisheries in the 1990s has not been a resounding success, but the subject has international implications that were the rationale for placing it under federal authority in the first place. It also provides much of the basis for federal environmental policy.

Another example is unemployment insurance, which was placed under federal authority by a constitutional amendment in 1940 with the unanimous consent of the nine (at that time) provincial governments. Nonetheless, two constitutional committees of the Quebec Liberal Party, the Langlois Committee in 1980 and the Allaire Committee in 1991, recommended that the subject be transferred to provincial jurisdiction.

When then federal Minister of Finance Paul Martin proposed in 1998 that the surplus in the unemployment insurance account be used for other purposes, his provincial counterparts in Ontario and Alberta protested vigorously, demanding that the surplus be eliminated by reducing premiums instead.[7] Apparently the federal government cannot expect to perform even its "exclusive" responsibilities without provincial interference.

Trade and commerce, including the external aspects of commercial policy, is another field of federal jurisdiction that has seen increasing provincial involvement and intergovernmental controversy. Alberta has complained periodically about the control of grain exports by the Canadian Wheat Board, and in 1996 challenged its validity through the courts. Provinces have tried to become involved in foreign trade policy by influencing the federal government or even, on occasion, by direct dealings with foreign governments. In 1986, when the Mulroney government began to negotiate a comprehensive free trade agreement with the United States, several provincial governments expressed concern that the agreement might affect areas of provincial jurisdiction. Most withdrew their objections because of their support for the general aims of the negotiations, and because the federal government was careful to keep them informed as the negotiations progressed. The Ontario government, both before and after the agreement was concluded, suggested on various occasions that the federal government might lack the legal authority to conclude an agreement that would bind the province. These remarks caused some concern in Washington, but Ontario did not actually do anything to block the agreement, perhaps because its legal case was weak and perhaps because the Ontario business community generally supported free trade with the United States.

Interprovincial, as well as international, trade has been a source of controversy among Canada's governments. The federal government has argued for years that various provincial policies, such as discriminating against out-of-province enterprises in the purchase of goods and services, hurt the Canadian economy by creating barriers to interprovincial trade. Ontario, whose business enterprises sell much of their output to other parts of Canada, has often supported the federal position, and even Quebec has shown some sympathy at times. Other provinces were more hostile because their manufacturing and service industries were relatively weak and seemed to need protection, while their more dynamic sectors relied on international rather than interprovincial trade. After years of discussion an Agreement on Internal Trade was signed by all governments in July 1994 and came into effect a year later, despite obvious reluctance on the part of British Columbia and Newfoundland. Its provisions are fairly minimal and its long-term effect remains to be seen.[8]

The provinces have become interested in macroeconomic policy, particularly since the temporary imposition of wage controls by the Trudeau government in 1975. Although that initiative was supported by the provincial governments, which cooperated by limiting wage increases in their own public sectors, the price of their acquiescence was a federal commitment to convene first ministers' conferences on the management of the economy, a useless practice that continued long after its original justification had disappeared. On these occasions, which were annual between 1984 and 1989, provincial premiers could be counted on to seek easy popularity by irresponsible demands for lower interest rates. They could offer this unsolicited advice knowing that it would probably not be adopted and that, even if it were, the resulting inflation would be the federal government's problem.

Some intergovernmental conflict involves clashes between fields of federal and provincial jurisdiction. Federal responsibilities for the aboriginal peoples, and for trade and commerce in sources of energy, may conflict with provincial ownership and control of public lands and natural resources within their borders. The interests of the fisheries, under federal jurisdiction, may conflict with those of the forest industry, under provincial jurisdiction. The administration of justice, a responsibility that the constitution divides between the two levels of government, has led to conflict over federal efforts to prosecute offences under the Narcotics Control Act, the Combines Investigation Act, and the Food and Drugs Act. The provinces, which have traditionally prosecuted ordinary criminal offences, argued that the federal government was trespassing on their jurisdiction, but the Supreme Court ruled that it was not.[9]

Fields of jurisdiction that were not envisaged in 1867 may be difficult to categorize as either federal or provincial. For example, is upgrading the skills of the labour force part of provincial jurisdiction over education or of federal jurisdiction over unemployment insurance? Responsibility for it has in practice been shared between the two levels since 1942, only two years after unemployment insurance was added to the list of federal legislative powers. The subject has gained prominence in recent years because of growing concern about the international competitiveness of Canadian industry, and because the traditional Keynesian belief that full employment can be secured by increasing the level of aggregate demand in the economy has been largely discredited. While many Canadians believe that the federal government should implement a national training strategy, like the central governments in some European countries, Quebec has grown increasingly strident in its claim that the subject falls under provincial jurisdiction. (The claim is not entirely new, since Premier Adélard Godbout, who had agreed to the unemployment insurance amendment, protested against federal involvement in labour training during World War II.)[10]

The ill-fated Charlottetown Accord of 1992 would have formally transferred "labour market development and training" to provincial jurisdiction. Although Canadians rejected the accord, Prime Minister Kim Campbell agreed in 1993 to transfer responsibility for training to Quebec, without a formal constitutional amendment; the agreement drew criticism from anglophone Canadians, and particularly from the then premier of Ontario. Campbell's defeat at the polls in the 1993 election delayed, but did not prevent, the implementation of her suggestion. When polls immediately prior to the 1995 Quebec referendum suggested a possible victory for the sovereigntists, Prime Minister Jean Chrétien promised that Quebec would be rewarded with a transfer of control over training programs and the funds to provide them if its people voted for federalism. Following the referendum a similar offer was made to all of the provinces. The first transfer agreement, with Alberta, was signed in December 1996. Quebec followed in April 1997, the fifth province to sign. Within a year all had accepted their new responsibility except Ontario, which was still haggling over the size of the financial settlement. Ironically, a poll conducted in the summer of 1998 showed that only one-third of Quebeckers were even aware of the federal concession that their political elites had demanded, and that this level of awareness was the lowest in the country.[11]

FISCAL CONFLICT

A particularly important area of intergovernmental conflict, and one that exists to some extent in all federal countries, is that of finance and taxation. Since both levels of government rely on the same taxpayers, the need for coordination and the scope for conflict are obvious. Apart from its obvious purpose of providing revenue, taxation is used by governments as a tool for manipulating, regulating, and stimulating the economy. Moreover, tax concessions to both individuals and corporations are important means of winning and keeping political support. Thus the stakes in financial negotiations are high.

In the early years the financial needs of the state were modest. The federal government, with exclusive authority to impose "indirect" taxes on goods and commodities, relied mainly on excise taxes and the customs tariff. The provinces imposed "direct" taxes on incomes or property and received small federal subsidies. During World War II the federal government monopolized personal and corporation income taxes and paid the provinces an additional subsidy for "renting" their authority to impose these taxes. It would have liked to continue this system after the war, as Australia actually did, so that it could use fiscal policy to control the amount of demand in the economy. However, pressure from Quebec and Ontario, particularly after Quebec imposed its own income tax in 1954, forced the Canadian government to retreat. It reduced its own taxes in a series of stages and agreed to collect income and corporation taxes on behalf of any province that wished it to do so and remit the revenue to the province concerned. The provinces could set their own rates of taxation, whether or not they signed a tax collection agreement. Equalization payments from the federal government, instituted in 1957 and required by the constitution after 1982, ensured that provinces with below-average incomes would not have to raise their rates of taxation to prohibitive levels.

Every province except Quebec chose to have the federal government collect its personal income tax. Only Quebec and Ontario, later joined by Alberta, preferred to collect their own corporate taxes. The agreements are renewed every five years, at which time adjustments are also made in the equalization formula, which has grown increasingly generous over the years. (Equalization payments to seven provinces total about $9 billion each year.) The larger provinces occasionally threaten not to renew the tax collection agreements, which in response have been made increasingly flexible, allowing all sorts of credits, exemptions, deductions, and surtaxes that vary from province to province. There are 10 different versions of the federal income tax return form, one for each province. (Quebec residents also file a separate form for their provincial tax.) An additional source of friction is the fact that provincial personal income tax rates, apart from that of Quebec, are expressed as percentages of the federal rate. This means that if the federal government reduces its rate, to win political favour or to stimulate the economy, provincial revenues will decrease also. Of course a province may counteract this by raising its own rate to a higher percentage of the federal tax, but this is not likely to make the provincial government more popular.

Further conflict erupted over the federal Goods and Services Tax, which replaced the old Manufacturers Sales Tax in 1991. Some provinces appeared to believe that sales taxes should be exclusively provincial while Alberta, as a legacy of its Social Credit past, is ideologically opposed to any tax on consumption. The federal government hoped that provinces would harmonize their own sales taxes with the federal tax but only Quebec, where popular hostility to the GST was much less than elsewhere, made any effort to do so.[12] (Alberta, with no sales tax, obviously could not do so.) In 1996 the Liberal federal government, whose members had opposed the GST when in opposition, persuaded New Brunswick, Newfoundland, and Nova Scotia to abolish their sales taxes in return for sharing the proceeds of a 15 percent GST, which compares with the 7 percent rate paid in other provinces. The three also received "adjustment assistance" of nearly a billion dollars over four years. Critics in other provinces charged that this financial settlement was too generous, but voters in the three provinces were apparently not impressed. In the 1997 election Liberal support in all three fell to the lowest levels since Confederation.

The most important source of intergovernmental controversy for the last decade has been federal spending in the areas of health, education, and welfare. Although these matters have mainly been provincial responsibilities, most Canadians, except perhaps in Quebec, regard "social programs" as part of the Canadian identity and expect "national standards." The federal government initially offered to share the costs of these programs in an effort to encourage provinces to establish them. After the programs were established, and as their costs began to escalate, the federal government would try to impose a ceiling on its own expenditure or even to withdraw from the field altogether. Provincial governments argued that these conditional grants put pressure on them to alter their spending priorities (which was precisely the federal government's intention), that the terms and conditions of federal support prevented them from designing programs that fitted their own needs, and that subsequent federal efforts to restrict federal spending placed an unfair burden on the provinces.

These issues have become increasingly complex over the years and have become entangled with the issues of tax sharing as discussed above. In 1965 Quebec was allowed to "opt out" of certain programs, meaning that federal grants and federal taxes were both reduced, allowing Quebec to increase its own taxes and run the programs without federal interference. In 1977 all provinces were given a combination of cash payments and additional tax room in place of the payments previously received in support of health insurance and postsecondary education, an innovation known as Established Programs Financing (EPF). In 1984 the Canada Health Act re-imposed strict federal conditions regarding the design of health insurance programs. Although it was supported by all three parties that were then represented in Parliament, most provincial governments resented this measure.

Between 1984 and 1997 the fiscal crisis of the Canadian state, described in Chapter 10 of this book, cast a long shadow over federal–

provincial fiscal relations. The Mulroney government responded to its fiscal crisis by cutting back its expenditures, including payments to the provinces. British Columbia, supported by Alberta and Ontario, took the federal government to court after the 1990 budget imposed a "cap" to limit the increases in Canada Assistance Plan welfare payments to the three richest provinces. The Supreme Court ruled in 1991 that Parliament had the authority to control federal spending, regardless of any agreement with the provinces.[13] In 1995 Liberal Finance Minister Paul Martin announced further cutbacks in his second budget. Beginning in the 1996–97 fiscal year, the Canada Assistance Plan would be abolished. EPF was replaced by a Canada Health and Social Transfer (CHST), which was supposed to represent the federal share of welfare costs as well as health care and postsecondary education. The CHST amounted to substantially less than the two grants that it replaced, and a further reduction of almost $2 billion was promised for 1997–98.

These events inspired the premiers of the two richest provinces, Alberta and Ontario, to proclaim at the annual premiers' conference in August 1995 that the federal government should play no part in the definition of social programs. Quebec was boycotting the conference and the other premiers who were present did not support this extreme position. Following the Quebec referendum the federal government offered to discuss with the provinces new guidelines for managing the Canadian welfare state, which it called the "social union." Quebec refused to participate but discussions nonetheless reached an impasse by the summer of 1998. Later that year all 10 provincial premiers proclaimed at their annual conference (which Quebec had rejoined) that the federal government should cease imposing financial penalties under the Canada Health Act and should introduce no new social programs without provincial consent. In February 1999 the federal government and nine provinces arrived at a Social Union Framework Agreement by which the federal government promised not to launch new programs involving grants to provinces unless a majority of provinces consented, and to give advance notice of any major changes in funding. However Quebec refused to sign the document since it explicitly recognized, and endorsed, the federal spending power and since it gave Quebec neither a veto nor the automatic right to opt out of new programs.

In resisting or opposing federal initiatives, provincial governments make use of a variety of arguments. Sometimes they say that the provincial level of government is "closer to the people" and better able to understand their needs; sometimes that the federal government is seeking to impose "bureaucracy," centralization, and excessive spending; sometimes that their province's allegedly distinctive "way of life" is in danger; and sometimes (more rarely in recent years) that the terms of the constitution are being violated. Western provincial governments often argue that federal policies discriminate in favour of Ontario and Quebec while Quebec governments argue that federal policies discriminate in favour of Ontario and the West. As the great economic historian Harold Innis commented in 1946:

> The hatreds between regions in Canada have become important vested interests. Montreal exploits the hatred of Toronto and Regina that of Winnipeg and so one might go through the list. A native of Ontario may appear restive at being charged with exploitation by those who systematically exploit him with their charges of exploitation, but even the right to complain is denied to him.[14]

Behind the rhetoric, the interests at stake are often more specific than appears at first sight. Provincial politicians may try to deflect attention away from their own policies (or absence thereof) by making "Ottawa" the scapegoat for the province's problems. Provincial officials may want to expand the budget and clientele of their own "shop" by excluding the federal government from a contested field of policy. Interests in the private sector are also influential. Ontario is sensitive to the needs of manufacturing and service industries that are based there, as British Columbia is to lumber and fishing, Saskatchewan to wheat farming, or Alberta to oil and gas. When they oppose federal economic initiatives, the provinces tend to reflect the interests of those sectors of the economy. Federalism provides regionally concentrated interests with a powerful defence against the possibility of being overridden by a national majority. It also gives such interests a powerful incentive to use their influence on behalf of the provincial level of government.

The intensity of federal–provincial conflict of course varies over time, and from province to province. Newly elected federal governments sometimes enjoy a "honeymoon" in their relations with the provinces, but after four or five years in office relations typically deteriorate. The parliamentary opposition then blames the federal government for the situation and promises to do better, but when the opposition party eventually wins office the same cycle repeats itself. Heads of government also differ in their preferred approach to federal–provincial relations. Prime Minister Trudeau favoured a more formal and structured approach while Prime Minister Mulroney preferred to make "deals" with political allies such as Robert Bourassa of Quebec or Grant Devine of Saskatchewan. The provinces themselves may vary in their behaviour over time, depending on economic conditions, partisanship, and even the personality of the premier. On the other hand there are certain continuities in their behaviour.

Quebec is always the most sensitive to any restrictions on its autonomy, with Alberta not far behind. Some of the smaller provinces are traditionally quite passive and accommodating in their dealings with the federal government.

INTERGOVERNMENTAL MECHANISMS

Because of the many ways in which the two levels of government affect one another's freedom of action, a variety of mechanisms and processes have developed for coordinating policies and resolving conflicts. A common characteristic of these mechanisms and processes is that none of them is provided for in the constitution. Those institutions that were provided for, the lieutenant governors and the Senate, have proved to be insignificant as means of facilitating the operation of the federal system.

JUDICIAL REVIEW

As in most other federations, the judiciary is an important mechanism for resolving questions of jurisdiction. Established in 1875, the Supreme Court of Canada did not actually become the highest court of appeal until 1949, when Parliament abolished the right of appeal to the Judicial Committee of the Imperial Privy Council in London. The Judicial Committee's interpretations of Canada's constitution, as noted above, had tended to restrict the powers of the central government and to enhance the status of the provinces, and were thus deplored by Canadian nationalists. For two decades after the abolition of appeals, the Supreme Court did not strike down any federal statutes and it was also quite permissive in regard to provincial statutes, so that it attracted little controversy. After Bora Laskin became chief justice in 1973, the Supreme Court was much more in the limelight as it struck down provincial statutes in relation to agricultural marketing, taxation, management of natural resources, and Quebec's efforts to regulate cable television.[15] Critics in Quebec and the prairie provinces charged that the Court had a "centralist" bias, perhaps because its members were appointed by the federal government. The critics however ignored the fact that the Supreme Court struck down a number of federal statutes in the same period.[16] In 1979 it also ruled that the reform of the Senate involved provincial rights and was thus not within the powers of Parliament.[17] In playing a more active role the judges may have wished to give the Supreme Court itself a higher profile, but they were not biased against either level of government.

The Supreme Court's interpretations of the Constitution may arise out of litigation in which an individual or a corporation challenges the constitutionality of a federal or provincial statute. Until the Charter of Rights and Freedoms was enacted in 1982, such a challenge could only be made on the grounds that the statute trespassed on the powers of the other level of government. Judicial interpretations may also arise out of reference cases, in which a government seeks an advisory opinion on a question of constitutional law. A government may do this either to forestall litigation directed against its own legislation, as a means of challenging another government's legislation, or simply to clarify an uncertain situation. The federal government can submit reference cases directly to the Supreme Court. Provincial governments can submit them to their own superior courts, whose decisions can be appealed to the Supreme Court of Canada. Governments that are not directly involved frequently intervene in important constitutional cases, whether these arise as references or as ordinary litigation.

COOPERATIVE FEDERALISM

Politicians generally prefer political solutions, in which they can split the difference and provide partial satisfaction to both sides, to the clear-cut, "either-or" decisions produced by the judicial process. For some provincial politicians, this preference is reinforced by the belief, as noted above, that the Supreme Court has a centralist bias. In fact, a great variety of informal political mechanisms for arriving at solutions are available. Federal and provincial governments interact at a number of different levels; bilateral contacts between the federal government and one provincial government are a part of the process, and there are also interprovincial relations not involving the federal government.

During the two decades that followed World War II, as the two levels of government began to have a greater and greater impact on one another's activities, there was a rapid development of collaborative relationships, including semiformal and semi-permanent committees with representatives of both levels. Most of these involved officials, sometimes of relatively junior rank. Most were concerned with a few functional areas of policy in which there was a large amount of intergovernmental interaction: finance, health, welfare, agriculture, renewable resources, and statistics. This pattern of intergovernmental relations came to be designated by the term "cooperative federalism." In many cases it was related to programs that were jointly financed by the two levels of government, though primarily administered by the provincial. It was characterized by a fragmentation of intergovernmental relations within each government, since departments with specific responsibilities were given a largely free hand to conduct their own relations with counterpart departments in other governments. Most of the officials involved were more concerned with resolving problems and running effective programs than they were with scoring points for their level of government in relation to the other level. In fact it is not easy to be certain, even in retrospect, whether cooperative federalism was centralizing or decentralizing in its overall impact. At the time, no one much cared.

EXECUTIVE FEDERALISM

Beginning in the 1960s, this pattern of intergovernmental relations was transformed into a new pattern for which the term "executive federalism," rather than "cooperative federalism," is more appropriate. Conditional grants, in which the federal government pays a fixed percentage of the cost of provincially administered programs that meet federally determined criteria, became unpopular as both levels of government sought to tighten control over their expenditures. Central agencies such as the Privy Council Office and its offshoot, the Federal–Provincial Relations Office, began to play a greater role in intergovernmental relations, riding herd on the activities of the functional departments. Political leaders, as opposed to appointed officials, also played an increasingly prominent role. For all of these reasons there was an increasing tendency, among both federal and provincial participants, to assign the prestige and power of "their" level of government a higher priority than the resolution of conflicts or the success of programs in delivering services to the public.

These changes were partly associated with the growth of the sovereignty movement in Quebec and with the energy crisis, developments that led to more conflict and less collaboration in federal–provincial relations. They were also encouraged by the popularity of "rational" approaches to decision making, which were based on the premise that each government could and should arrange its priorities in a centralized fashion and exercise a tight grip over its expenditures. Central agencies and elected politicians are more inclined than specialists in health, welfare, or resource development to think in terms of maximizing their government's power in relation to other governments.

FIRST MINISTERS' CONFERENCES

A characteristically Canadian institution that has assumed great prominence is the first ministers' conference, which brings together the federal prime minister and the 10 premiers, assisted by numerous officials. Until the 1960s, first ministers' conferences occurred only occasionally, usually in connection with proposed amendments to the Constitution or major changes in fiscal arrangements between the two levels of government. Since 1963 there has been at least one such meeting in most years. The Meech Lake Accord of 1987 would have made an annual first ministers' conference obligatory, in the same way that the constitution now requires an annual session of Parliament. More recently, enthusiasm for this peculiar institution seems to have cooled to some extent. Quebec has boycotted some of the meetings, and the federal government has recognized that bilateral meetings with individual provinces may be more fruitful. The public has also become disillusioned, with many Canadians questioning whether "11 white men in suits" should be allowed to make decisions of fundamental importance.

These misgivings are justified, for the record of first ministers' conferences in reaching agreements or solving problems is poor. In fact it would be difficult to devise a worse way to carry on the nation's business. Provincial premiers often have no strong incentive to reach an agreement and may even gain popularity by being as unreasonable and intransigent as possible. The federal prime minister, on the other hand, is expected both to defend the national interest and to satisfy the demands of all the provincial governments, two objectives that may be totally incompatible. He or she, rather than the premiers, will be blamed if an agreement is not concluded, and the temptation is therefore strong to sacrifice the national interest to provincial demands.

A majority vote at a first ministers' conference would have little meaning, because the prime minister represents Canadians in every province and should logically have as many votes as all of the premiers combined. The premiers themselves are not equal except in a formal sense. Ontario's population is 80 times that of Prince Edward Island and almost equal to the total of all the Western and Atlantic provinces combined. Only Alberta can cut off the nation's supply of oil and gas, and only Quebec can plausibly threaten to secede from Canada and become a sovereign state. All of the Atlantic provinces depend on federal grants to maintain even a semblance of provincial status. Thus agreement must be on a basis of consensus or, at the very least, include the federal government and the four largest provinces. (Some constitutional amendments can be made by seven provinces, including either Ontario or Quebec, but the provinces that did not agree would have the right to opt out if the amendment affected any of their "rights or privileges".)[18] Consensus, whether on constitutional amendments or on more mundane matters, is not easily achieved among governments representing different regions, political parties, and jurisdictional interests. If it is achieved, it will probably be because the prime minister has given the premiers everything they asked for. Parliament, not to mention the provincial legislatures, will then be told that it must give automatic approval to the agreement or else run the risk of a dire threat to national unity. This of course makes a mockery of responsible government. In any event, opposition parties in the House of Commons are often reluctant to criticize intergovernmental agreements involving premiers with whom they share a party label, or agreements popular in a province where they hope to win votes.

While first ministers' conferences, particularly those dealing with the constitution, are the most publicized aspect of executive federalism, there are also frequent meetings at the ministerial level, which involve almost every field of public policy. Other meetings include non-elected officials, rather than politicians, and may be designed either to prepare for the executive sessions or to implement agreements concluded by the politicians, or simply to exchange information.

The provincial premiers also hold an annual summer meeting without the prime minister, after which they issue a communiqué that usually criticizes an assortment of federal policies and initiatives. The first such meeting was actually in 1887, but the second was not until 1960, when Premier Jean Lesage of Quebec revived the practice in an effort to gain allies in his battles against the federal government. Subsequently it became a regular event, with the provinces taking turns to play host. From 1980 to 1984, when no provincial government had the same party label as the federal government, the communiqués issued by these meetings were exceptionally strident and hostile in tone. More typically, they are toned down in deference to the sentiments of premiers who may be political allies of the prime minister.

CONCLUSION

While Canada's problems are less severe than those of many other countries, and while the federal state has survived a number of decades in which its future appeared less than assured, there is real cause for concern about its present situation and prospects. The picture that Canada presents to the outside world is that of a collection of semi-sovereign provinces, with a central government unable or unwilling to exercise much control over the economy or to carry out coherent policies even within its own fields of jurisdiction. Compared with almost any other modern state, or with Canada itself as recently as the 1950s, the extent of provincial power and the weakness of the central government are remarkable. The effort that the central government must devote to bargaining with the provinces lessens its ability to function effectively and undermines its authority in the eyes of the public. First ministers' conferences resemble a meeting of a medieval king with his feudal barons more than the government of a modern state. The implicit assumption that regional divisions and interests are the most significant ones in Canada, and that only the provincial governments are capable of representing them, calls into question the authority and usefulness of Parliament, which must often rubber-stamp the results of intergovernmental agreements and which is prevented from legislating even in the areas assigned to its jurisdiction without interference by the provinces.

Particularly but not only in Quebec, some persons continue to propagate what former federal cabinet minister Jim Fleming once called "the myth of the power-hungry centralizers" and to argue that the provincial governments need more influence over federal policies and more freedom to pursue their own.[19] The reality is that Canada is already the most decentralized country in the industrialized world. Only in Canada is the central government barred from any role in setting educational standards. Only in Canada are the provinces free to borrow money overseas without regard for the balance of payments. Only in Canada does a province (Quebec) have a minister of international relations. Only in Canada do national labour laws and standards cover less than 10 percent of the labour force. Only in Canada is there no single national agency to regulate the trading in securities, even though the stockbrokers and stock exchanges would welcome the convenience of having one.[20]

Prime Minister Jean Chrétien left a mixed legacy to Canadian federalism. For several years after taking office in 1993, his government was preoccupied with the need to reduce the deficit and thus was cautious about taking new initiatives that might involve significant spending. Once the deficit had been eliminated, it became somewhat more inclined to launch new programs and to assert federal leadership but less so than Liberal governments in the past. Perhaps for this reason, its relationships with the provinces, apart from Quebec, have been relatively harmonious. Mr. Chrétien's most dramatic initiative with regard to federal–provincial relations was the so-called Clarity Act adopted in 2000, which purports to set out rigid rules and conditions for any possible negotiations with Quebec should that province attempt to secede from Canada. Although the Quebec government naturally resented this measure, public opinion in Quebec appeared to take it in stride.

Although there is no immediate prospect of another referendum on sovereignty, an independent Quebec remains a real possibility in the twenty-first century, for the nationalist feelings of Quebeckers are deep and genuine. Most Canadians outside Quebec seem extremely reluctant to contemplate any solution that would give Quebec more formal powers than the other provinces, and this creates a temptation to give all the provinces the degree of autonomy that Quebec seeks, and to reduce the federal government's role and status to the lowest possible level. Nonetheless, the gradual dismantling of the federal government without the consent of the Canadian people would be the worst possible solution. Canada could survive the secession of Quebec, as the United Kingdom survived the secession of Ireland and as France survived that of Algeria. It could not long survive a so-called renewed federalism like that envisaged by the Quebec Liberal Party's Allaire Committee, which would leave the central government with little more than symbolic powers.[21]

Canada is a medium-sized country in a world where most of its competitors are larger, stronger, and more centralized. If it is to survive in this environment and to overcome the divisive effects of its geographical barriers and its closeness to the United States, it may require a stronger central government than it has enjoyed in recent years, and a corresponding reduction in the powers of provincial governments. Moreover, a lessening of the Canadian obsession with provincial interests and jurisdictional controversies might direct attention to more significant issues, such as industrial productivity, the environment, the long-term decline of the Canadian dollar in relation to other currencies, and the unequal distribution of wealth, power, and opportunity among the population.

NOTES

1. Lord Atkin in *A.G. Canada v. A.G. Ontario* [1937] A.C. 327.

2. (1883) 9 App. Cases 117; [1892] A.C. 427.

3. *The Queen v. Crown Zellerbach Canada Ltd.* [1988] 1 S.C.R. 401; *General Motors of Canada v. City National Leasing* [1989] 1 S.C.R. 641; *Alberta Government Telephones v. Canada* [1989] 2 S.C.R. 225; *Telephone Guevremont v. Quebec* [1994] 1 S.C.R. 878.

4. Karin Treff and David B. Perry, *Finances of the Nation 2001* (Toronto: Canadian Tax Foundation, 2001), Table B.3, pp. B:6–7.

5. Canada, *House of Commons Debates,* Session 1936, p. 3868.

6. John Porter, *The Vertical Mosaic: An Analysis of Social Class and Power in Canada* (Toronto: University of Toronto Press, 1965), p. 382.

7. "Trouble is brewing for Martin's UI scheme," *The Globe and Mail,* September 26, 1998.

8. For two detailed assessments of the agreement see Harvey Lazar (ed.), *Canada: The State of the Federation 1997: Non-Constitutional Renewal* (Kingston: Institute of Intergovernmental Relations, 1998), chapters 5 and 6.

9. *The Queen v. Hauser* [1979] 1 S.C.R. 984; *A.G. Canada v. CN and CP Transport* [1983] 2 S.C.R. 206; *The Queen v. Wetmore* [1983] 2 S.C.R. 284.

10. Jean-Guy Genest, *Godbout* (Sillery: Septentrion 1996), pp. 246–47.

11. "Quebeckers unaware of power transfer," *The Globe and Mail,* August 13, 1998.

12. Prince Edward Island and Saskatchewan took tentative steps towards harmonization in 1990, but reversed them a year later.

13. *Reference re. Canada Assistance Plan* [1991] 2 S.C.R. 525.

14. Harold A. Innis, *Political Economy in the Modern State* (Toronto: Ryerson 1946), p. xi.

15. *Burns Foods Ltd. v. A.G. Manitoba* [1975] 1 S.C.R. 494; *CIGOL v. Saskatchewan* [1978] 2 S.C.R. 545; *Central Canada Potash v. Saskatchewan* [1979] 1 S.C.R. 42; *Dionne v. Public Service Board of Quebec* [1978] 2 S.C.R. 191.

16. *MacDonald v. Vapor Canada* [1977] 2 S.C.R. 134; *Dominion Stores v. The Queen* [1980] 1 S.C.R. 844; *Labatt Breweries v. A.G. Canada* [1980] 1 S.C.R. 914.

17. *Reference re. Legal authority of Parliament to alter or replace the Senate* [1980] 1 S.C.R. 54.

18. *Constitution Act,* 1982, section 38.

19. Jim Fleming, "The Myth of the Power-Hungry Centralizers," address to the Empire Club, Toronto, February 19, 1981, in *The Empire Club Addresses 1980–81* (Toronto: Empire Club, 1981) pp. 247–62.

20. "Canada's securities markets: Thirteen into one won't go," *The Economist,* July 13, 2002.

21. See the Allaire Committee's report, *A Quebec Free to Choose,* released on January 28, 1991.

FURTHER READINGS

Bakvis, Herman, and Grace Skogstad. *Canadian Federalism: Performance, Effectiveness, and Legitimacy.* Toronto: Oxford University Press, 2000.

Banting, Keith G. *The Welfare State and Canadian Federalism.* 2nd ed. Montreal: McGill-Queen's University Press, 1987.

Cairns, Alan C. *Constitution, Government and Society in Canada: Selected Essays.* Toronto: McClelland & Stewart, 1988.

Lazar, Harvey, ed. *Canada: The State of the Federation 1999/2000, Toward a New Mission Statement for Canadian Fiscal Federalism.* Kingston: Institute of Intergovernmental Relations, 2000.

Leslie, Peter. *Federal State, National Economy.* Toronto: University of Toronto Press, 1987.

Monahan, Patrick J. *Constitutional Law.* 2nd ed. Toronto: Irwin Law, 2002.

Rocher, François, and Miriam Smith, eds. *New Trends in Canadian Federalism.* 2nd ed. Peterborough: Broadview, 2003.

Saywell, John T. *The Lawmakers: Judicial Power and the Shaping of Canadian Federalism.* Toronto: University of Toronto Press, 2002.

Simeon, Richard, and Ian Robinson. *State, Society, and the Development of Canadian Federalism.* Toronto: University of Toronto Press in co-operation with the Royal Commission on the Economic Union and Development Prospects for Canada, 1990.

Stevenson, Garth. *Unfulfilled Union: Canadian Federalism and National Unity.* 3rd ed. Toronto: Gage, 1989.

CHAPTER 5

ABORIGINAL
SELF-GOVERNMENT

Michael S. Whittington

With the coming into common parlance of terms such as "inherent right," "third order of government," and "aboriginal self-government," the last two decades have seen an expansion of the already arcane vocabulary of constitutional debate in Canada. This phenomenon is the outcome of a series of failed attempts, from 1983 to 1992, to effect a package of constitutional reforms that would meet the demands of the aboriginal peoples of Canada for self-government. The first step in attempting to deal with these demands of the aboriginal peoples of Canada was to establish a separate constitutional process to deal with aboriginal issues. In an attempt to provide self-government rights through an amendment to section 35 of the 1982 Constitution Act (*Rights of the Aboriginal Peoples of Canada*—see Appendix I), a series of conferences that included the first ministers, the premiers of the two northern territories, and representatives of four national aboriginal organizations were held from 1983 to 1987.

This "aboriginal round" of constitutional negotiations foundered in 1987 for three main reasons. First, the provinces of Alberta, British Columbia, Newfoundland, and Saskatchewan could not agree to a package of self-government provisions because, even after three and a half years of discussion, they still felt that they didn't know what self-government meant. Second, on the other side of the table, the Assembly of First Nations was not ready to agree to the package because it did not include an explicit recognition that self-government was an existing or "inherent" aboriginal right. Finally, it was clear that both the Quebec government and Brian Mulroney wanted desperately to get on with the "Quebec round" of talks.

Thus, having made a "reasonable effort" to deal with aboriginal concerns, the prime minister and the premiers immediately embarked on a series of conferences that ultimately produced the ill-fated Meech Lake Accord. This round of constitutional talks excluded the territorial governments and the national aboriginal organizations, and, while there are many variables that contributed to the demise of the accord, the failure to deal with aboriginal issues was perhaps *the* fatal flaw. Elijah Harper's lonely stand in the Manitoba legislature, which ultimately scuttled the Meech Lake agreement, clearly would not have happened had aboriginal self-government provisions been part of the package.

The next paroxysm of constitutionalizing featured another series of conferences in 1991–92, culminating in what has come to be known as the Charlottetown Accord. But, the lesson of Meech having been learned, this set of negotiations included not only the first ministers but the premiers of the Yukon and NWT, as well as four national aboriginal organizations. That the astonishing and unprecedented achievement—a consensus among 17 parties at the negotiating table—was nullified in a national referendum is now simply an artifact of history. What has changed forever is that in future such constitutional processes will likely have to include territorial governments and aboriginal leaders. And in the unlikely event that an agreement is reached, that agreement will have to pass muster in a national referendum before the Constitution can be amended by the legislatures.

What has also changed forever is that the argot of constitutionalese, featuring terms such as "Triple E" Senate, "distinct society," and "Canada clause," has been enriched with the vocabulary of aboriginal self-government. When the Chrétien government was first elected in 1993, it was made clear that there would be a moratorium on constitutional reform. Nonetheless, the Chrétien government committed itself to dealing immediately and fairly with the outstanding grievances of Canada's aboriginal peoples, and in particular to negotiating self-government agreements.

ABORIGINAL RIGHTS IN CANADA

The aboriginal people of Canada are the descendants of the people who were living on this continent when European explorers "discovered" it (although the aboriginal people continue to insist that they "knew it was here all along"). Canadian aboriginals include Indians, Inuit, and Métis and make up 4–5 percent of the Canadian population.[1] While we tend to speak of aboriginal people as a discrete and identifiable segment of the

Canadian population, in fact there is a very wide diversity of language, culture, and history among the various groups across Canada. What allows us to continue to use the general term is the fact that they have shared a common and usually unhappy historical relationship with non-Natives and governments.

Aboriginal rights are those rights that aboriginal people possess today because they had them before contact with non-Native settlers. These rights continue to exist despite the fact that the continent has come to be populated by large numbers of "newcomers." According to the Canadian courts, aboriginal rights can only be extinguished by conquest, by treaty, or by explicit act of the Parliament of Canada. Moreover, even Parliament may not frivolously or casually enact legislation that affects aboriginal rights and must consult the people affected, minimize the impact, and provide compensation for any abrogation of those rights.

Aboriginal rights were originally incorporated into the Constitution through the British Proclamation of 1763, which recognized the rights of the Indian nations and provided that their rights could not be taken away except in accordance with the principles of British justice—in effect, by negotiated treaty. The obligations under this proclamation were automatically transferred to the Government of Canada by the British North America Act (Constitution Act, 1867), section 91(24), which stipulates that only the *federal* government has the legislative authority to affect the rights of aboriginal peoples. The Constitution Act, 1982, recognizes and affirms "the existing aboriginal and treaty rights of the aboriginal peoples of Canada," while section 25 of the Charter of Rights and Freedoms provides that the Charter cannot be construed so as to abrogate aboriginal or treaty rights. Hence, although the Constitution of Canada explicitly recognizes the existence of aboriginal rights and provides protection for those rights, it does not tell us what those rights are or whether they might have been surrendered or extinguished at some time in the past.

One way to come to grips with the nature and extent of aboriginal rights is to establish what the traditional or precolonial patterns of use and occupancy of the land were. Indeed, because traditional aboriginal societies were largely based on hunting and gathering (in some cases supplemented by agriculture), the land is the foundation of aboriginal economy, culture, and society. But the aboriginal concept of land is very different from the European one. Where the European system is based on the notion of private *ownership,* aboriginal societies base their system on the notion of *shared use* of the land. The land belongs to everyone living today and to the unborn generations of the future. Although there may have been informal understandings among communities or tribal groups that recognized each other's more or less exclusive use of certain territories for purposes of hunting and fishing, the land was owned only by the Creator, who put it there for the use of *all* people.

Thus, aboriginal rights have not been exhaustively defined by the Constitution, statutes, or the common law. However, it is generally agreed that such rights include, at a minimum, the right to hunt and fish and to harvest plants, and the necessary rights of access and occupancy on the land upon which such activities are done. Moreover, while aboriginal land rights are not the equivalent of the *fee simple title* under which Canadians normally own a residential property, the courts have recognized that aboriginal rights include *aboriginal title* to lands not explicitly surrendered to the Crown through treaties or land claims.[2] The significance of this is that unless there has been an explicit surrender of land rights through a previous treaty or land claim agreement in a given area, governments, both federal and provincial, must protect aboriginal interests before they can sell or otherwise grant interests in public lands to individuals or corporations.[3] The thrust of the comprehensive claims process today is to eliminate the uncertainty with respect to lands burdened by unextinguished aboriginal rights and titles by negotiating a surrender of those rights in exchange for a set of rights defined in a "modern treaty," that is, a land claim agreement.

It is clear that aboriginal rights include at least a set of rights associated with the use and occupancy of the land, including title, and that these rights remain alive and in effect until such time as they have been surrendered. The question that has not been answered by the courts is whether there is an aboriginal right to self-government.

THE RIGHT TO SELF-GOVERNMENT

Aboriginal people, as citizens of Canada, currently do participate in the governmental process. Despite being denied the right to vote in the past, and despite structural impediments to meaningful participation in the political process—such as lower levels of political, educational, and financial resources available to be spent on political involvement—aboriginal Canadians today enjoy the same political rights of all Canadians. Aboriginal individuals vote, run as candidates, get elected as federal, provincial, and territorial legislators, and become members of cabinet at all levels of government.

Unfortunately, this has not always been the case. When the European settlers came, they brought with them not only their culture, language, and religion but they also imported political institutions such as parliamentary democracy. While these institutions, by most measures, provide a fairly good system of governance, even parliamentary democracy only works for groups or individuals who are included in the citizenry.

The aboriginal people of Canada were, from the outset, *subjects* of governmental policy and a *matter* of legislative jurisdiction, but never fully enfranchised citizens. "Indians," from the beginning (and the Inuit considerably later), were simply another political problem or issue, and were part of the governmental process only as "subjects" of Her Majesty and "wards of the state." And, as wards of the state, in a little more than a century aboriginal people were deprived of their traditional means of livelihood, their cultures and languages were wiped out, and their communities became socially dysfunctional. Aboriginal people point out that they governed themselves long before Europeans arrived in North America and, by all accounts, they did a fairly good job of it. In the aboriginals' view, the "white man's government" has messed up their lives for the past hundred years or so, and the First Nations are now saying, "Give us a crack at it— we certainly can't do any worse!"

AN INHERENT RIGHT?

While they do not reject Canadian democracy, it is clear that the aboriginal people of Canada want the right to govern themselves in a manner more consistent with their traditional ways. In essence, they want to incorporate aboriginal modes of political decision making into their own governments while retaining the rights and freedoms that they possess as Canadians. Aboriginal people argue that the right to self-government *is* an existing aboriginal right under section 35 of the Constitution Act of 1982, and they may be correct. However, the problem has been how to get the federal and provincial governments to recognize such an *inherent* right and to negotiate self-government agreements based on that recognition.

Given their past experience in dealing with governments, it is not surprising that the aboriginal people of Canada would prefer an explicit recognition in the Constitution that their right to self-government is one of the *existing* aboriginal rights affirmed in section 35 of the Constitution Act of 1982. However, there are a number of barriers to achieving this. First, while the government of Canada has stated as a matter of policy that it recognizes the inherent right to self-government, it has steadfastly refused to reopen any constitutional negotiations. Second, a number of provinces still refuse to recognize an inherent right at all and would certainly never agree to recognize it constitutionally.

Finally, the recognition that self-government is an existing aboriginal right raises a serious concern for aboriginal people who already have entered into treaties with the Crown. All of these treaties feature an "extinguishment clause" whereby the aboriginal people surrender their "aboriginal rights, titles, and interests" in exchange for explicit treaty rights. If such a surrender includes the aboriginal right of Native people to govern themselves, the groups with treaties would not have the inherent right enjoyed by groups in, for instance, British Columbia, the Yukon, and parts of the Northwest Territories, where there are no treaties. On the other hand, although the courts have not rendered any specific decisions on this issue, it can be argued that because the surrenders in the treaties were "in and to the land" only, the aboriginal right to self-government is still intact. Governance involves authority with respect to people or citizens, and while most governmental jurisdiction is limited territorially, "land" per se is not what is "governed." These issues, however, may have become moot. In stating that their approach to negotiating self-government with aboriginal people would be to start with the recognition of an inherent right to self-government, the Chrétien government also stated that this would apply to all aboriginal peoples in Canada.

In sum, while we are unlikely to see a constitutional affirmation of the inherent right to self-government, the federal government has affirmed it will proceed to negotiate self-government agreements with aboriginal people who desire to do so. Moreover, although some provinces are not particularly enthusiastic, most have agreed to participate in this process. As long as it is clear that negotiated self-government agreements are without prejudice to the question of an inherent right to self-government, the aboriginal people have little to lose and a lot to gain by coming to the negotiating table.

A THIRD ORDER OF GOVERNMENT

Having established that aboriginal peoples should have the right to govern themselves, we have still addressed only a part of the issue before us. Whether that right is inherent, constitutionally affirmed, or merely created by statute, the practical reality is that the relationships between First Nations governments and the federal, provincial, and territorial governments that are already in place have to be defined through negotiations. This is because, with a very few exceptions, the aboriginal peoples of Canada wish to remain Canadians and wish their governments to exist within the context of and under the protection of the Constitution of

Canada. However, aboriginal communities also want to be able to deal with other levels of government, not as petitioners, supplicants, or interest groups, but on a government-to-government basis.

Most Native communities realize that it is unnecessary and impractical for them to attempt to take control of all the responsibilities of modern government in order to achieve their objectives. In order to take control of their lives, it is essential to have legislative authority over matters such as their lands and resources; social, community, and health services; education; economic development; and many aspects of the criminal justice system. For the most part, they neither need nor want responsibility for matters such as national defence, navigation and shipping, banking and currency, bankruptcy, patents, and so forth. These are powers exercised by the federal government and involve matters that can generally be dealt with more effectively at the national level.

However, in the areas currently under provincial control where the aboriginal nations will want to assume responsibility, there will be a need to work out the relationship between the aboriginal regimes and the affected province or territory. For example, while the aboriginal people will likely wish to take over matters such as community health services, in the case of most aboriginal communities it will be impractical to provide separate acute-care facilities—hospitals—for their people. In other areas such as municipal services, in cases where the Native community is adjacent to a municipality, it may make financial sense to share the cost of a single fire department or sewage system—aboriginal sewage being pretty much indistinguishable from any other.

Finally, very few aboriginal communities today possess the economic base or the fiscal resources to be able to take over complete responsibility for the programs currently being delivered by other governments. In a perfect world, the financing of aboriginal governments would be achieved totally by their own taxation regimes. The aboriginal government would finance its own programs and services and would bear the same burden of fiscal responsibility in its spending practices as any other government. However, this level of self-sufficiency is unattainable for many provincial governments today. As is the case with the poorer provinces and the northern territories, the aboriginal governments have to be supported by intergovernmental transfer payments until they can develop the economic base that will allow them to pay their own bills with their own tax revenues.

Thus, there is a clear need for negotiated agreements between the First Nations[4] and existing governments in order to give practical effect to the right to self-government and to define the new intergovernmental relationships that will evolve. These agreements, however, need not be exceedingly lengthy or detailed. Clearly, matters of exclusive First Nations legislative authority have to be explicitly enumerated, and the location of paramountcy in the case of conflict between First Nations laws and those of other levels of government has to be specified. However, a large portion of the agreement will define *processes* for intergovernmental coordination, cost sharing, fiscal transfers, and the resolution of interjurisdictional disputes. Before returning to a discussion of some of the issues surrounding the contents of self-government agreements, we must look at the broader question of the legal and constitutional status of such agreements once they are put in place.

THE CONSTITUTIONAL STATUS OF SELF-GOVERNMENT AGREEMENTS

The constitutional status of self-government agreements is a matter of great concern to aboriginal peoples. One issue involves the question of which governments should be party to the agreements. While their experience with the federal government has never been particularly happy, most First Nations would prefer to deal with the "devil they know" than to get into three-party negotiations that include the provinces or territories. However, while section 91(24) of the Constitution Act, 1867, gives the federal government exclusive jurisdiction over Indians and lands reserved for Indians, many non-status Indians, Métis, and Inuit in provinces such as Quebec and Newfoundland and Labrador are subject to the provincial laws of general application. Hence, even if other things were equal, strictly bilateral federal–aboriginal agreements would potentially exclude over half of Canada's aboriginal people. Moreover, other things are *not* equal.

Most significantly, the lion's share of the governmental powers that the First Nations wish to assume are those currently in the provincial or territorial sphere. In the absence of provincial or territorial participation in the agreements, there would be a high risk of creating many situations of conflict of law and overlapping enforcement and program delivery regimes.

As well, for reasons of efficiency and economies of scale, there will be many situations in which the aboriginal community and the provincial government will find it mutually beneficial to establish joint or shared-cost programs. Moreover, in a number of jurisdictions, many of the services to aboriginal people off reserves (even status Indians) are delivered currently by the province or territory, with the costs recoverable from the federal government through a "charge-back" mechanism.

The key point is that the provinces and territories are already involved in a political relationship with aboriginal people, and it simply would not work "on the ground," whatever the constitutional niceties, to exclude this order of government from the table. Besides, the current political reality in Canada is that the federal government, as a matter of policy, is unwilling to risk the ire of the provinces and territories on this question when they need their cooperation in so many other areas of national concern.

The second and perhaps more troublesome concern about the status of the agreements is whether and how they will be given protection once they have been negotiated. The Indian Act has long provided for limited local government on reserves through a system of elected band councils. Through this system, the band has bylaw powers that are municipal in nature but not even as extensive as those enjoyed by most municipalities. While this system is flawed by a too narrow range of powers, the more important problem is that the powers are only *delegated* to the band council. The Minister of Indian Affairs can veto all bylaws and band council resolutions, and the department can replace the band council with an appointed administrator if it is felt that the affairs of the band are not being well managed. Obviously this won't cut it with First Nations, and, moreover, the provisions do not apply to Inuit communities, none of which have reserves.[5]

The Mulroney government recognized the aboriginal concern with constitutional protection and took the formal position that negotiated self-government agreements should be given protection as "treaties" or land claim agreements under section 35 of the Constitution Act of 1982 (Rights of the Aboriginal Peoples of Canada). The Charlottetown Accord went still further and stated that the First Nations governments were to constitute a "third order of government," implying that their status would be constitutionally equivalent to that of the provinces.

However, while the Conservative government took this brave position at the constitutional table, ultimately it was unwilling to deliver on its promise. The original four self-government agreements completed and ratified in the Yukon in 1993 as part of the land claims process were kept separate from the land claims agreements ratified at the same time. The land claims agreements are section 35 treaties, and despite the urging of the Council of Yukon Indians (CYI) and the government of the Yukon, Canada insisted that the self-government agreements could be given effect only through ordinary statute. To be credible, self-government agreements must be treated as solemn covenants among three orders of government and must be amendable only with the consent of the parties that negotiated them. This can be achieved only through granting them constitutional protection.

The Chrétien government has agreed to allow certain aspects of self-government agreements to become treaties, and the recently concluded Nisga'a Final Agreement includes a broad package of self-government provisions that will be protected as part of the section 35 treaty. The negotiation of the Labrador Inuit Association (LIA) claim has also proceeded with the understanding that the self-government provisions will form part of the final agreement. Agreement has now been reached by all three parties to constitutionally protect self-government provisions along with the LIA final agreement. Since the Liberal government announced its new approach to constitutional protection of self-government provisions, the Council for Yukon First Nations has been negotiating with the federal and territorial governments to "retrofit" its self-government agreements so they can be constitutionally protected. But, unfortunately, after almost 10 years, the parties have still not been able to reach agreement. As well, the 2002–2003 First Nations Governance Bill, while improving considerably on the Indian Act band council regime, does not provide for constitutional protection.

COMPREHENSIVE LAND CLAIMS AND SELF-GOVERNMENT

Since 1973, the Yukon First Nations[6] have been engaged almost constantly in the negotiation of comprehensive land claims agreements with the governments of Canada and the Yukon. In 1984, an agreement in principle was successfully negotiated but was subsequently rejected by the Yukon First Nations. Although the 1984 agreement failed, it did form a starting point for the subsequent successful negotiation of four Yukon First Nations final agreements, which were ratified by all parties by May 1993. Negotiations have continued with the remaining 10 Yukon First Nations, the majority of which have now concluded final agreements.

The Mulroney government was adamant that the Yukon self-government agreements themselves could not be section 35 treaties. However, it did bow to pressure from the CYI and the NDP government of the Yukon and allowed self-government provisions to be negotiated simultaneously with the land claim process. The government of Canada also agreed that a "commitment to negotiate" self-government agreements with the Yukon First Nations, along with guidelines for such negotiations, could be included as a chapter in the Final Agreement. Hence, the principle of self-government was given constitutional protection but the details of the self-government agreements were included in a separate statute.

Thus, First Nations self-government agreements in the Yukon have been ratified through the same process as the Final Agreements; they come into effect at the same time, and in practical if not legal terms, they are completely interdependent. The First Nations institution that bears responsibility for taking on the obligations under the land claim is not a corporation, as in previous claim settlements, but the First Nations government. It is also the First Nations government that must manage and administer all of the rights and benefits of its citizens under the land claim. This integrated process of negotiations—self-government and comprehensive claims at the same table—became the template for such negotiations elsewhere in Canada. Moreover, while the Yukon First Nations are still struggling to have their self-government agreements given constitutional protection, the federal policy has relaxed and aboriginal groups such as the Nisga'a and the LIA will have constitutionally protected self-government provisions.

NUNAVUT

Before moving to a discussion of the substantive provisions of self-government agreements in Canada, it is appropriate to speak briefly about the Tungavik Federation of Nunavut (TFN) claim and the Territory of Nunavut. Almost from the outset of negotiations in 1975, the Inuit of Canada's eastern Arctic have made the establishment of their own territory a non-negotiable condition for the settlement of their land claim. Both the federal government and the government of the Northwest Territories generally accepted the principle of separating the NWT into two territories. However, the federal government was strongly opposed to placing such a provision in a section 35 treaty. The compromise that allowed for the ratification of the TFN agreement in 1992 was a commitment in the final agreement to attempt to negotiate a side deal—an accord—that would provide the guidelines for the establishment of the new territory of Nunavut through separate federal legislation. That agreement was successfully negotiated, and the territory of Nunavut came into existence on April 1, 1999.

While Nunavut is viewed as an Inuit homeland, it is not aboriginal self-government per se. Rather, Nunavut is a territorial government, similar in form and legal status to the governments of the Yukon and the Northwest Territories. In the parlance of Indian Affairs, Nunavut is a "public government," meaning that all residents of Nunavut who are Canadian citizens—Inuit, and non-Inuit alike—have equal political rights under the new government. Non-Inuit can run for all territorial offices and can vote in all Nunavut elections. Moreover, all citizens of Nunavut have equal rights before the law and equal access to social services, health care, education, and other government programs. The Inuit are happy with this arrangement because they are confident that, making up 85 percent of the 30 000 residents of Nunavut, they will be able to control their own destiny well into the future.

SELF-GOVERNMENT AGREEMENTS: SUBSTANTIVE PROVISIONS

As mentioned above, the Yukon process established the basic rules for the negotiation of subsequent self-government agreements. As well, the substantive provisions of the Yukon self-government agreements have, in many ways, provided a guideline for what is negotiable and what is not. Previous agreements such as the Sechelt Agreement in British Columbia; the Cree-Naskapi Act, which sets up a local government regime in the James Bay region of Quebec; and the Nunavut Accord mentioned above are idiosyncratic and unique to those specific situations. Although the Yukon self-government model is far from everything the aboriginal people would like, it did break some important new ground and went much further in the direction of meeting the needs of the aboriginal people of Canada than any self-government arrangements negotiated previously. While some federal officials, particularly in departments such as Indian Affairs, Finance, and Justice, and many provincial governments still believe the Yukon model goes too far, it has become a kind of high-water mark for other negotiations.

Recent land claim settlements with the Tetlit Gwitchin, the Sahtu, and the Dogribs of the Northwest Territories include a commitment to negotiate self-government in the future, but those negotiations have not commenced. The Nisga'a Final Agreement contains extensive self-government provisions, most of which are similar to those in the Yukon but with some differences, which we shall discuss below. Finally, while the final details are as yet unavailable, Canada, Newfoundland, and the Labrador Inuit Association have reached an agreement in principle that contains extensive self-government provisions. Again, many of these provisions reflect precedents established in the Yukon and in Nisga'a, but there are some differences.

All of these self-government agreements share a number of general provisions couched in "boilerplate" legalese. These include clauses about the processes for ratification, amendment, and dispute resolution, and about the rules of interpretation. As well, all agreements deal with the applicability of the Charter of Rights to the aboriginal governments, legal remedies and the legal status of the aboriginal governments, and the relationship between the land claim agreement and the self-government provisions. However, there are six key sets of substantive provisions in each agreement that define the status of the aboriginal governments vis-à-vis the federal, provincial, and territorial regimes. Each of these requires some elaboration.

CONSTITUTIONS

The agreements provide that the aboriginal government must have a constitution and that the constitution must contain a definition of citizenship, an amending formula, a system of financial accountability to citizens, and provisions recognizing the rights and freedoms of individual citizens. As well, the constitution must establish the basic institutions of government. However, the agreements do not require that the constitution be approved by the federal and the provincial or territorial government, and essentially leave it to the aboriginal community to define their own internal rules and regulations of governance. In this sense, the First Nations constitutions in the Yukon, the Nisga'a Constitution, and the Labrador Inuit Constitution are freestanding and reflective only of the political values and traditions of the First Nations.

There was no explicit requirement that Yukon First Nations be subject to the Charter of Rights, because the Yukon agreements were to be implemented by federal statute and, hence, would automatically be subject to the provisions of the Charter. However, it is now the policy of the federal government that there must be a clear statement that the Charter applies to aboriginal governments that are to be given section 35 protection. Generally, aboriginal communities accept this requirement; if they have any reluctance, it is because they would prefer to have their own charter in their own constitutions, which in most cases would go beyond the Canadian Charter in protecting civil liberties. Aboriginal people, it seems, have had long and, for the most part, unhappy experience with governments, and the strong protection of individual rights in their own constitutions tells us that they simply don't trust governments—even their own.

While they do have to make their governments accountable to their citizens and while all groups have, in fact, opted for democratic elections, the Yukon First Nations constitutions do not have to provide for elections.

Although there was significant opposition from federal departmental offi-cials to giving such free reign to the First Nations, the First Nations con-stitutions are, if anything, more democratic than Canada's (for instance, none of them has opted for a hereditary monarch as head of state). For the most part, aboriginal political traditions are based on consensus rather than majority rule and, as such, the First Nations constitutions in the Yukon require important decisions to be taken by more than a simple majority. The Nisga'a Constitution will guarantee an electoral system for certain institutions, and the draft LIA agreement states that the Labrador Inuit Constitution must provide for democratic accountability, but not necessarily in the form of European-style elections.[7]

CITIZENSHIP

For some reason, federal policy requires that all aboriginal constitutions contain a citizenship code, despite the fact that the Canadian Constitution itself doesn't have one. This unusual requirement did not meet with any significant opposition either in the Yukon or for the Nisga'a. The LIA are not happy with the requirement, preferring to deal with questions of citi-zenship through their own statutory citizenship act. Generally, however, First Nation citizenship is automatic for individuals who are beneficiaries under the comprehensive land claim and all members of a pre-land claim "Indian Act band." As well, any other individuals who are deemed (usually by the community elders) to have a long-standing involvement with the community are eligible to be citizens of that First Nation. Hence, what is created is a unique form of dual citizenship that is *internal* to Canada—individuals affected enjoy the benefits of both First Nations and Canadian citizenship. The agreements also provide that any First Nation citizen may renounce his or her First Nation citizenship at any time.

It is also stated explicitly in all land claim final agreements that nothing in the agreements can be construed to take away any of the rights an individual enjoys as a Canadian citizen. However, the agreements also provide that First Nation citizens who receive program benefits from the First Nations cannot demand benefits from similar or equivalent programs of territorial or provincial governments. This is merely a practical provision to prevent enterprising First Nations citizens from "double-dipping."

RIGHTS OF NON-ABORIGINALS

The self-government agreements in the Yukon do not contain much in the way of specific provisions dealing with the rights of people who are not

First Nations citizens. There are very few reserves in the Yukon and most reserve lands are not currently occupied; hence, the question of the rights of non-Native residents on reserves was not at issue. Moreover, the First Nations are not permitted to select land as "settlement land" if it is privately owned. Where there are third-party interests (other than outright ownership) on settlement lands, these are "grandfathered" and cannot be unreasonably taken away or significantly altered by the First Nations. However, all individuals who are on settlement land are subject to First Nations laws dealing with hunting, fishing, environmental control, and land management, but all people subject to these laws are guaranteed equal protection and equal access to mechanisms of redress.

Most communities in the Yukon already had municipal institutions, and these remain in place, as do the rights of the non-First Nations citizens in these communities. The self-government agreements also provide consultative mechanisms whereby cooperative arrangements can be worked out between the First Nations and the municipal government in areas such as shared municipal services, public works, and zoning.

When their final agreement was negotiated, the Nisga'a already had a certain amount of reserve lands that were subject to Indian Act band government. Non-Nisga'a who resided on the reserves did not have any special rights, and there were no municipal institutions in Nisga'a communities when the final agreement was signed. Hence, the Nisga'a agreement simply provides that the Nisga'a government must consult with non-Nisga'a who reside on Nisga'a lands if decisions are to be taken that significantly affect them. As well, the Nisga'a government must provide for some sort of direct participation for non-Nisga'a in Nisga'a public institutions such as school boards, hospital boards, police commissions, and so on, but there is no provision for direct non-Nisga'a participation in the Nisga'a government itself. As in the Yukon, non-Nisga'a who enjoy rights of access to Nisga'a lands are subject to Nisga'a laws while they are on those lands.

In Labrador, the Inuit do not have any reserves, and the five Inuit communities in the Labrador Inuit Settlement Area all have standard municipal governments. While the details are still being worked out, the self-government provisions in the LIA agreement provide for the complete dismantling of the existing municipal governments. These are to be replaced by Inuit community governments that will have jurisdiction over Inuit and non-Inuit alike. Long-term residents of these communities will be given guaranteed representation in the community governments. As with the other agreements, non-Inuit are subject to Inuit laws when they are on Inuit lands.

FIRST NATIONS JURISDICTION

The legislative authority of Yukon First Nations falls into three basic categories. First, the agreements provide for *exclusive* jurisdiction over all internal administrative matters and over all rights and obligations of the First Nations pursuant to the land claim agreements.

A second category includes virtually comprehensive power to enact laws on First Nations land ("settlement land" under the land claim). The only significant limit to the exercise of these powers by the First Nations on their own territory is that the laws must be of a "local or private nature" and not encroach upon federal jurisdiction in areas such as the Criminal Code and public health and safety. As mentioned above, it is important to note that First Nations laws will apply to all people on First Nations land and not just to First Nations citizens.

The third category of First Nations jurisdiction includes an extensive list of provincial-type powers such as health and social services, child welfare and adoption, education and training, solemnization of marriage, and, in general, the provision of a wide range of services to citizens. What is unique about this category of legislative jurisdiction is that it extends to First Nations citizens anywhere in the Yukon and not just on settlement land. This was a completely untried experiment and it has proven to be difficult to implement, requiring close cooperation between the government of the Yukon and the First Nations governments. However, if it does prove workable in the long run, it may help to point the way to a solution to the problem of providing self-government rights to aboriginal people who lack an extensive land base, such as the Métis in parts of western Canada.

The governments of British Columbia and Newfoundland have not been willing to go as far as the government of the Yukon with respect to First Nations jurisdiction. Moreover, federal officials have tried to "claw back" some of the provisions of the Yukon agreements that they felt went too far. For example, unlike in the Yukon agreements, there are no "exclusive powers" granted to either the Inuit of Labrador or the Nisga'a of British Columbia. Instead, there are a few categories of jurisdiction generally dealing with internal First Nations government affairs and cultural matters, where the aboriginal laws prevail in the case of a direct conflict with federal or provincial laws. As well, neither British Columbia nor Newfoundland has been willing to go as far as the Yukon with respect to First Nations jurisdiction over citizens when they are off settlement land. Nevertheless, Nisga'a laws and Inuit laws respecting matters such as certain social services, adoption, and education apply throughout their respective provinces, with the proviso that the federal or provincial laws will prevail in the event of a conflict. Jurisdiction on or respecting Nisga'a or Inuit lands is very similar to that granted to the Yukon First Nations.

A few areas of First Nations jurisdiction are dealt with as special cases because of their complexity and because of the need to carefully integrate First Nations laws with the laws of general application. First, while the aboriginal governments will have extensive powers to raise money by direct taxation, their tax systems will have to be integrated with the federal and provincial or territorial systems. As well, collection agreements have to be worked out with Canada and the province or territory where a tax field is being shared by the aboriginal government. Second, while the First Nations must have the power to enforce their laws, the responsibility for policing, administering justice, and particularly for providing judicial remedies must be coordinated with the Canadian justice system. Hence, all of the agreements provide for a delay in the coming into effect of these powers to allow for a negotiated set of arrangements.

Finally, it is important to recognize that while the Yukon First Nations, the Nisga'a, and the Labrador Inuit are able to exercise a wide range of legislative powers, they are in no way forced to assume any responsibilities until they are ready. This model provides that all the laws of general application and all government programs and services being delivered to First Nations citizens continue unchanged until the aboriginal government "occupies the field" by enacting its own legislation. When the First Nations law is given effect, the general law of the province or territory ceases to apply to the extent that it is inconsistent with the new First Nations law.

The beauty of this sort of "phasing-in" arrangement is that the new aboriginal governments are not rushed to take on all the responsibilities of government immediately for their citizens. Moreover, the fact that the general laws apply until explicitly superseded by a First Nations law means that there will be no hiatus in the transitional period—that is, no period when *no* law is in effect in a given area. The end result of employing a model such as this is that the First Nations may decide *never* to occupy many areas of jurisdiction, instead utilizing their limited resources on matters that are culturally sensitive or affordable within the limited economies of scale of the First Nations communities.

FINANCING FIRST NATIONS GOVERNMENTS

As stated earlier, one of the main obstacles to effective aboriginal self-government in virtually all situations across Canada is the lack of a stable tax base. Clearly, the ultimate goal for aboriginal governments is that they be financially self-sufficient, financing their programs with their own revenue sources. Indeed, the agreements provide that the aboriginal governments must make a serious effort to raise their own revenues and to govern as efficiently as possible. However, the reality is that very few aboriginal communities have the economic base to support their governments without assistance from the other two orders of government.

Thus, the agreements provide for the negotiation of a system of transfer payments from the senior governments to the aboriginal governments. These arrangements have to be worked out, taking into account, among other things, fiscal need, the ability of the First Nations to raise their own revenues, and the costs associated with diseconomies of scale. Also factored in are the net savings to governments as a result of the First Nations taking over programs that are currently being delivered to First Nations citizens by federal and provincial or territorial governments. These agreements on fiscal arrangements must be negotiated on a multiyear basis, and be contractual only and not constitutionally protected.

INTERGOVERNMENTAL RELATIONS

As we have seen, all self-government agreements have anticipated that the transition from the status quo to full aboriginal governance will be gradual and driven by the initiative of the aboriginal government. They are not forced to take on all of the burdens of modern government at a single moment, but will assume responsibilities as they feel ready and able to do so. As a consequence, there are many provisions in the agreements that identify processes for ongoing negotiation, consultation, and coordination among the First Nations, Canada, and the province or territory. There is also a recognition that some programs can be delivered jointly; some existing programs can be made compatible with aboriginal interests by including First Nations representatives in their adaptation and development; and some program responsibilities may be taken over by the First Nations only in part. While the aboriginal governments have the power to "go it alone" in many areas of jurisdiction, they and the other levels of government can see a mutual benefit in the sharing of expensive program responsibilities.

Finally, both the Nisga'a and the Labrador Inuit have "two-tier" or federal-type governmental arrangements. The Nisga'a Lisims Government is the government of the Nisga'a Nation and it shares jurisdiction with a Nisga'a Village Government in each of the communities. Similarly, a central Inuit Government will have broad jurisdiction over Inuit and Inuit lands in the settlement area in Labrador, while Inuit Community Governments will have more local jurisdiction within the five communities on the north coast. Because the Yukon agreements were negotiated one at a time, there are no provisions for a Yukon-wide First Nations government. Moreover, unlike the Nisga'a and the Labrador Inuit, who view themselves as a single people, the Yukon Indians comprise five separate language groups with significant cultural differences and a range of distinct political agendas. However, the Yukon agreements do allow for and even encourage the First Nations to delegate their powers to regional or Yukon-wide aboriginal bodies. Certainly, by providing some programs and services on a regional or territorial level, there can be greater economies and efficiencies as well as higher-quality service to citizens.

CONCLUSION

None of the existing self-government agreements are by any means perfect, and, in recognition of this fact, they include opportunities for the First Nations to renegotiate some provisions if the policies vis-à-vis self-government are made more favourable to aboriginal interests in the future. In other words, for example, the Yukon First Nations are not penalized for having taken a lead role and they are permitted to "top up" their agreements by incorporating new rights and benefits that may emerge elsewhere in Canada through constitutional change or aboriginal policy developments in the future. On the other hand, there are many features in the Yukon agreements that have set precedents for the negotiation of aboriginal self-government arrangements elsewhere in Canada. The Nisga'a and the LIA agreements, while building on the Yukon model, have themselves set new precedents and developed new approaches that provide useful guidelines for negotiations elsewhere.

What is required now is for the federal and provincial governments to build on these positive steps and to extend the opportunity for aboriginal self-government across the country. While no government seems eager to return to the constitutional fray to deal with aboriginal concerns, there appears to be at least limited political will to move ahead on the *negotiation* of self-government in other provinces as well. At the political level, the major difficulty in dealing effectively with demands for self-government is the cost. There is absolutely no way to disguise the reality that a third order of government is going to be extremely expensive, and while nobody "does democracy" because it is cheap or efficient, large annual deficits and the fiscal burden of national and provincial debts cannot be ignored. At a minimum, however, there is no reason governments cannot begin to transfer at least the resources they currently expend on aboriginal people to the First Nations themselves.

As for the non-financial obstacles to effective aboriginal self-government, some provincial governments are still uneasy giving negotiated self-government agreements section 35 "treaty" status. At the federal level, while there is an explicit policy of recognizing the inherent right to self-government, there is also a seemingly contradictory policy that the existence of that inherent right cannot be affirmed in the negotiated self-government agreements. It is to be hoped that some federal minister in the future will be struck by this anomaly and remedy it.

There are also new approaches being developed that would allow for negotiated self-government agreements for First Nations that do not have a comprehensive land claim. Following an extensive multi-year process of task forces and consultations between the Department of Indian Affairs and aboriginal groups, the government of Canada introduced the First Nations Governance bill in 2002 and launched an extensive process of consultation. This legislation aimed to replace the existing Indian Act provisions and enable First Nations to set up their own political institutions. While the First Nations Governance bill is a big improvement on the Indian Act band council arrangements, and includes provisions for a more regularized system of fiscal transfer payments, the Assembly of First Nations (AFN) has come out strongly against it. One obvious flaw in the Governance bill is that the First Nations governments so established would not be protected constitutionally. The aboriginal people feel, understandably, that their governments must have more than statutory protection because statutes can be changed at the whim of the legislature that passed them.

As well, the aboriginal groups argue that the fiscal arrangements provisions set out accountability requirements that would leave First Nations governments still largely under the control of the Minister of Indian Affairs. The AFN, through its National Chief, has argued that the new legislation does not reflect what was agreed to in the lengthy process of consultations and that the current minister, Robert Nault, has reneged on some of the concessions the First Nations thought they had negotiated. While the First Nations Governance Act may still be pushed through Parliament in the coming months, it has created a deep rift between the federal government and the largest aboriginal organization in Canada. Such a situation, in the short run, does not augur well for the new Act's acceptance in the Native community. Perhaps more interesting is that Paul Martin, Liberal heir apparent, has said he will not implement the First Nations Governance Act if he becomes prime minister!

To conclude on a more optimistic note, despite the obstacles and the oft-stated concern of politicians and bureaucrats that "we still don't know what we are getting into," progress has been made in the past 15 years. New precedents have been established that have gone a long way to clarifying the issues surrounding aboriginal self-government, and there are now models in place that can form a template for those of the future. Certainly, there is no going back at this point, and the demands for aboriginal self-government will continue to increase in the coming years. Doing the "right" thing instead of the "safe" thing (that is, nothing) has required a modicum of political courage on the part of federal, territorial, and provincial politicians, and there is reason to be cautiously optimistic. The ultimate measure will be to see how well existing and future aboriginal governments stand the test of time.

NOTES

1. It is difficult to establish a firm estimate of aboriginal populations because aboriginal governments define them according to status under the Indian Act. Only about three-quarters of a million Indians have such status.

2. See *Delgamuukw*, SCC, 1997.

3. The courts have generally held that aboriginal rights have been extinguished on privately owned land. However, since the 1982 affirmation of existing aboriginal rights, the government cannot dispose of Crown land that is burdened by underlying aboriginal rights unless the aboriginal people are accommodated or compensated.

4. While the Inuit do not generally refer to themselves as a "First Nation," for ease of expression the term is used in this paper to include the Labrador Inuit. Hence, "First Nations government" would include "Inuit government" in Labrador.

5. Another possible means of protection is through specific legislation for each self-government agreement. The Sechelt Band in the lower mainland of British Columbia has such a regime in place, and while most First Nations today would find that the actual provisions of the agreement do not go far enough, the generic problem is that the legislation giving effect to the deal could be amended unilaterally at any time.

6. The Council for Yukon Indians became the Council For Yukon First Nations after the 1993 ratification of the first four Final Agreements. While individual First Nations must negotiate their own final agreements, the CYI/CYFN often negotiates Yukon-wide issues with the agreement of the First Nations.

7. In fact, it is likely that the LIA will opt for a simple system of elections for most public institutions.

FURTHER READINGS

Boldt, Menno. *Surviving as Indians: The Challenge of Self-Government*. Toronto: University of Toronto Press, 1993.

Canada. *Report of the Royal Commission on Aboriginal Peoples*. Volumes 1, 2, and 5. Ottawa: DSS, 1996.

Cassidy, Frank, and R.L. Bish. *Indian Government: Its Meaning in Practice.* Halifax: IRPP, 1989.

Smith, Dan. *The Seventh Fire: The Struggle for Aboriginal Government.* Toronto: Key Porter, 1993.

Stasiulis, Daiva, and Nira Yuval Davis, eds. *Unsettling Settler Societies.* London, UK: Sage Public Education, 1995.

STATE AND SOCIETY

STATE AND SOCIETY

The seven chapters of Part II focus on the relationship between the state and the "real people" in Canadian society. The state–society relationship is a reciprocal one in which social forces have an impact on government decisions, which in turn effect changes in society. Government agendas are drawn directly out of this relationship as politicians, bureaucrats, and judges seek to mediate and adjudicate societal conflicts. Through the making of foreign and macroeconomic policy, the state also responds to tensions in the external environment while at the same time addressing various domestic audiences.

In a chapter that questions whether a twenty-first-century "globalized" Canada still makes sense as a country, Williams sets the stage for Part II's discussion of state–society relations. Positing that Canada may best be seen as a northernmost region of the United States, he explores how our North American location has shaped Canada's regionalism/federalism, its economy, its defence and foreign relations, as well as its political culture. Continental spatial structures, he suggests in Chapter 6, present unique challenges to the Canadian state system in managing major policy issues that have both domestic and bilateral dimensions, issues such as the environment, the economy, social welfare, labour, and regional development.

Political parties and the electoral process link the society to the state by allowing the citizenry to select political leaders and to register approval or disapproval of the present government and its policies. Alexandra Dobrowolsky's Chapter 7 describes the evolution of the party system while at the same time decrying the "dumbing down" of modern politics. This is related, in part, to the emergence of a multi-party system and in part to the increased complexity of policy issues. However, the trivialization of substantive issues at the beginning of the twenty-first century has been made possible, above all, by the emergence of the mass media as the principal link between politicians and voters. Television election campaigns allow politicians either to grossly oversimplify issues or to ignore them completely by emphasizing symbols and leadership images. Because TV is a one-way communication system, voters cannot challenge the politicians in the same way they could in old-fashioned, face-to-face, door-to-door campaigns.

In Chapter 8, Jon Pammett confirms this trend by analyzing recent election results to discover what determines the choices of Canadian voters. His chapter on the electoral system supplies answers to questions about whether voters make their choices on the basis of the election issues, party loyalty, or the appeal of individual candidates. Pammett also explains the decline of traditional parties, the emergence of new parties, and the apparent stability of a five-party system in the House of Commons.

Interest groups and social movements also pressure the country's political leadership to make policy choices that will satisfy the political claims of the Canadians they represent. In Chapter 9, Miriam Smith describes the evolution of social movements and organized interests and explains how social power can be transformed into political power, profoundly influencing both the agenda of political discourse and the policy choices of governments.

Government policies, given effect through legislation, are the mechanism through which the Canadian state "governs" society. Among the most important policy areas for governments at the beginning of the twenty-first century are the management of the national economy and the ongoing definition and re-definition of Canada's role in the global context. Hence, two of the chapters in Part II deal with macroeconomic policy frameworks and Canada's external relations.

Neil Bradford's Chapter 10 describes how macroeconomic policy in Canada has been dominated by two "governing policy paradigms" since the 1930s. The first, Keynesianism, prevailed until the 1970s and featured extensive government intervention in the marketplace and the development of a welfare state. The second, neoliberalism, emerged in the 1980s and has been characterized by reductions in government social policy expenditures, deregulation of the market, and the pursuit of balanced budgets. At the beginning of the twenty-first century, and with budget surpluses to be allocated, Bradford concludes that neoliberalism may itself be replaced by a new paradigm whereby governments will spend money to build Canada's "social capital" and intervene in the marketplace to foster technological development and build Canada's "knowledge-based" assets.

A key link between the state and society can be found in the Charter of Rights and Freedoms. The Charter defines and sets limits on the rights of Canadians vis-à-vis the Canadian state. Through interpreting the Charter, the courts tell the state which of its laws are constitutionally acceptable and which are not. Here, the line between the right of the state to govern and the democratic rights of groups and individuals to act in Canadian society is ultimately drawn.

Radha Jhappan's Chapter 11 explains the structure of the Charter and highlights its key provisions by analyzing the significance of landmark judicial decisions arising out of court challenges to legislation. Critics of the Charter come from all over the political spectrum. Some say the Charter doesn't go far enough in fostering social rights, such as equality in society, because it is focused for the most part on individual rights. It guarantees freedoms from some things but not the rights to such items as a fair wage, a reasonable standard of social services, or a certain quality of life. Others criticize the Charter because it goes too far, preventing the government, for instance, from effectively dealing with pornography, limiting third-party advertising at election time, or combating crime.

Jhappan also highlights the growing debate over whether the Charter has given too much power to the courts. Some people argue that it is "undemocratic" for a non-elected body to overrule decisions taken by a sovereign Parliament or legislature. On the other hand, others contend that the principle of an independent judiciary is itself a cornerstone of our Constitution because it puts in place an adjudicative process that is above and unbiased by the partisan political fray.

In Chapter 12, Laura Macdonald observes that the process of economic globalization has gone hand in hand with increasing regionalism. Given Canada's location within North America, these two trends have posed particular challenges to Canadian sovereignty. Canada's traditional self-image as a "middle power" may no longer be appropriate in the face of the emergence of the United States as an international "hyper-power" and Canada's increasing economic integration with the United States. In the wake of the end of the Cold War and the September 11, 2001, attacks on New York and Washington, a newly assertive U.S. foreign and defence policy stance has made it increasingly difficult for Canada to cling to its traditional multilateralism in the face of the unilateralism of its powerful southern neighbour.

CHAPTER 6

REGIONS WITHIN REGION: CANADA IN THE CONTINENT

Glen Williams

An atlas portrays an uncomplicated image of the lines that divide northern North America: two colours, two nationalities, on one side of the border 49 states, on the other 10 provinces and 3 territories. This seeming clarity obscures one of the most complex bilateral relationships in the world. In the twentieth century, the informal development of Canada's continental role in relation to the United States paralleled along a number of important dimensions the formal incorporation of the Canadian colonies into the French and British Empires during the seventeenth to nineteenth centuries. Just as the evolution of modern Canada has been marked by the development of a dense system of interregional relations, so too have Canada's regions developed in relation to specific, often geographically adjacent, local areas in the United States. And, insofar as Canada is more than simply the sum of its southward-facing parts, over time the country as a whole took on many of the properties of a northernmost region of the United States.

Central to the definition of Canada as a northernmost region of the United States were a relatively small number of nation-building policies directed by the federal government in Ottawa. These included the building of east–west transcontinental transportation and communications systems, the promotion of a national economy rooted in a domestic manufacturing sector, and the establishment of national social welfare programs such as medicare financed through fiscal transfers from the richer to the poorer Canadian provinces. For reasons to be explored later, the federal government has been cutting back on these nation-building policies for at least the last two decades and no replacement policies have yet been found to take their place. This raises the question of whether a political void has been created by the relative weakness of Ottawa as a national "command and control" policy centre promoting a separate political nationality in northern North America and whether this political void could eventually lead to demands for new forms of North American regional governance or even for political annexation to the United States.

In order to consider this question, we need to reflect on some of the continental spatial structures that give meaning to Canada's North American regional identity. These structures have been most readily visible within Canadian economic life: when investment, production, and trade are considered, the Canadian economy appears more like a politically sovereign *zone* within the American economy than a distinct national economy. And, that zone is itself fractured both by Canada's system of federal political institutions and by extremely robust, continentally organized, regional economic formations that fly over the formally demarcated border between the United States and Canada.

Canadians and Americans currently each hold about $200 billion in direct investments in the economies of each other. However, because of the considerably smaller size of the Canadian economy, U.S. direct investment since World War II has held a near dominant share of Canada's most modern and productive manufacturing and mining sectors. Canada and the United States are each other's largest trading partners. Canada buys nearly one-quarter of total U.S. exports while the U.S. purchases over four-fifths of total Canadian exports.[1] Exports are critical to Canada's economy, representing more than two-fifths of GDP compared to exports being only 11 percent of U.S. GDP.[2] Not surprisingly, there is a direct link between American and Canadian direct investment and trade between the two countries. According to Industry Canada, "the 50 largest Canadian-owned multinationals in the U.S. and U.S. subsidiaries in Canada account for 90 percent of all two-way foreign direct investment (FDI) and well over 70 percent of all bilateral trade."[3]

Overall, the Canadian provinces ship a substantially greater proportion of their goods outside the country (mainly to the United States) than to each other. They also import more from outside the country—again, mainly the United States—than from each other.[4] Further, as Table 6.1 demonstrates, each of Canada's five geographic regions has developed its own intensive, deeply pervasive, north-south trading relationship with its closest American regional neighbour or neighbours. On the American side, Canada is the leading export market for 38 of the 50 states.[5] Direct borderland trade is a commercial anchor for many provinces: for example, over two-fifths of New Brunswick's U.S. exports are sold to Massachusetts and Maine; one-fifth of Quebec's U.S. exports go to New York and

TABLE 6.1 Trade of Canadian Regions with United States Census Regions* They Directly Border, 1992, 2001 (percentage of total trade with the U.S. for each Canadian region)

	Exports		Imports	
	1992	*2001*	*1992*	*2001*
Atlantic	78	79	51	45
Quebec	63	53	59	57
Ontario	77	78	58	79
Prairies	58	52	49	47
British Columbia	53	60	54	55

Bordering U.S. census regions are Atlantic, Midwest, Mountain, and Pacific.

Source: Calculated from Canada, Statistics Canada, Merchandise Trade, *Exports* and *Imports*, 1992, 2001.

Vermont; one-half of Ontario's U.S. exports go to Michigan, Ohio, and New York; one-fifth of Manitoba's U.S. exports are shipped to Minnesota and North Dakota; and over one-quarter of British Columbia's U.S. exports are destined for Washington.

Canada's regional identity/identities within its continental space is not only visible from these economic indicators but is also manifested at the focal points of Canadian politics, society, and culture. This can be illustrated by an overview of the historical development of Canada's federal political structures, its economic growth policies concerning trade and investment, and its foreign and security policies.

NORTHERNMOST REGION: FEDERAL POLITICAL INSTITUTIONS

Canada and the United States were formed in direct relation to the same European power, Great Britain, and out of the same process of conquest and settlement of the American New World that began with the Spanish and Portuguese in the 1500s. The late-eighteenth-century revolutionary upheaval that created the United States divided northeastern North America into two parts—one loyal to its station within a hegemonic worldwide empire and the other animated by a vision of constructing a unique republican political identity for North America. The revolutionary Continental Congress was rebuffed in its 1774 appeal to Nova Scotia and

Quebec to "unite with us in one social compact formed on the generous principles of equal liberty." Following success in the War of Independence, cession of Nova Scotia to the United States was one of the secondary negotiating goals of the Americans in the peace talks with Britain.

Based on growing cross-border migration, trade, and communications, extensive borderland communities quickly grew up that remained vibrant and connected even through the British–American hostilities during the War of 1812. Throughout the nineteenth century, informed American opinion had faith that a historical convergence, based on shared Anglo-Saxon cultural and political values, would lead in time to the annexation of the British North American colonies. In this regard, because of its French and Roman Catholic culture, Quebec was obviously viewed somewhat more skeptically.[6]

Shared political values did not lead in time to political union, but they did contribute to the choice made by the political elites of both countries to construct a federal political structure in order to manage the regional conflict inherent in governing a geographically vast and diverse polity. In North America, federalism is also rooted in liberal democratic notions of limiting the power of the state by dividing and separating its power between branches and levels. In fragmenting state power, its capacity to interfere with individual freedom is to be minimized.

While concerned with the management of regional conflict, the framers of both federal constitutions also worried about the dangers of too much decentralization. The terms of the Constitution of the United States of America (1788) and the British North America Act (1867) both reflect this fact. In the U.S.'s case, the impracticality for national governance of the post-revolutionary, confederal Articles of Confederation (1777) had led to demands for a new constitutional order along the lines set out in the Federalist Papers (1787–88). Accordingly, while "state's rights" were still privileged in the 1788 U.S. Constitution, American sovereignty was now unquestionably shared between Washington and the states.

Eight decades later, the Canadian framers of the 1867 British North America Act were greatly concerned that the U.S. Constitution had given the sub-national states too much power and that this had created centrifugal forces that had resulted in the American Civil War between the states (1861–65). Many of the Canadian framers would have preferred a unitary form of government as in Britain. But the political realities imposed by the need to reconcile the interests of the previously organized British Colonies that were being incorporated as provinces into Canada plus the desire to accommodate important and distinct linguistic and religious communities dictated a federal arrangement. Nonetheless, the balance was weighted heavily against the provinces and in favour of the national government in Ottawa—so much so that some scholars have argued that in 1867 Canada was only a quasi-federation.

In 1867, the federal Parliament was given an expansive general mandate to make laws promoting Canada's "peace, order and good government." This was intended to include all the important nation-building powers (trade and commerce, banking, currency, transportation, patents); all the important taxing and borrowing powers; jurisdiction over the military and defence, criminal law and superior courts; the ability to declare "local works and undertakings" to be "for the general advantage of Canada" and to take them under federal control; the ability to intervene in provincially administered education if it considered that the rights of religious minorities were not being upheld; and the power necessary to carry out Canada's international obligations even if the matter was otherwise in provincial jurisdiction. In contrast, the provincial legislatures were given powers that fitted into two categories: (1) matters where the colonial legal traditions of the provinces had traditionally differed; and (2) matters that had previously been the concerns of the local colonial administrations such as education, hospitals, Crown lands and natural resources, and municipal institutions. As a final form of insurance for the federal power in Ottawa in its dealings with the sub-national governments, it was given the power of disallowance over all provincial laws.

Today no one in Canada imagines that Ottawa rules a "quasi-federation" of subordinate local legislatures. In fact, it has frequently been suggested that Canada is currently the most decentralized federation in the world—even more decentralized than a United States that has now become far more Washington-centred than its constitutional framers could have ever imagined in 1787. How and why did these changes in the federal balance of power in Canada and the United States take place? Significantly, in the case of both countries, it was not primarily through the route of constitutional amendment—their present written constitutions are almost identical to their original eighteenth- and nineteenth-century versions in respect to federalism. Instead, a mix of judicial review and long traditions of freely negotiated interjurisdictional arrangements between the national and sub-national governments have over the decades created substantially changed federal realities in the two countries.

These negotiated changes have taken place partly in direct response to long-term centrifugal and centripetal political/ideological/economic pressures and movements generated within the two North American civil societies and also partly in answer to exceptional disturbances in the political environment like wars and economic booms and depressions. During the twentieth century in Canada and the United States, the pendulum of federal power swung back and forth at least three times. In the early decades of that century, the national governments were relatively small in size and lacked policy vigour and initiative. The two World Wars, the Great Depression, and the Cold War ushered in the era of unprecedented relative ascendancy in Ottawa and Washington grounded in war economics and the building of the welfare state. This period of national government primacy was brought to a close in the 1980s as a result of fiscal crisis and the rise of a neoliberal ideology hostile to social welfare spending and favourable to cutting taxes. In Canada in particular, the federal government became a shadow of its former self while in relative terms the significance of the provinces to their citizens grew dramatically.

This process, whereby negotiated agreements within the federation rather than formal constitutional amendments have facilitated historic and dramatic shifts in the federal balance of power, is known in Canada as *executive federalism*. It has depended on national and sub-national political and administrative elites taking a shared view of the constitution as a flexible instrument to solve policy problems rather than a rigid written doctrine determining absolutely the limits of state authority.

Four British provinces in North America were joined together in federal Canada in 1867—Ontario, Quebec, Nova Scotia, and New Brunswick. But Canada actually acquired most of its present land area from Britain through purchase and cession of most of the northern half of the continent comprising the lands of the Hudson's Bay Company (in 1870) and the Arctic Archipelago (in 1880). Although three other British colonies later decided to join Canada—British Columbia (1871), Prince Edward Island (1873), and Newfoundland and Labrador (1949)—all the remaining provinces and territories were subsequently carved out of the northern territories. In addition, both Ontario and Quebec more than doubled their size by sharing in the northern Hudson's Bay lands that were contiguous to their Confederation boundaries.

As in many other federations, the present-day boundaries of Canada's provinces and federally-administered territories catalyze important internal political cleavages. As Table 6.2 displays, just two of the 10 provinces, Ontario and Quebec, have together over three-fifths of Canada's population, GDP, and Commons seats along with just under one-half of total Senate seats. The four Atlantic Provinces have together only 7.7 percent of the national population and produce just 5.7 percent of the total GDP but have over 10 percent of Commons representation and over 25 percent of total Senate seats. Alberta and British Columbia have together somewhat less than one-quarter of Canada's population and

GDP but only have about one-fifth of the total Commons representation and one-tenth of Senate seats. The three northern federal territories together make up 40 percent of Canada's area but have only 0.3 percent of Canada's population and contribute 0.45 percent of Canada's GNP.

These dramatic asymmetries are reflected in the differing capacities of larger/richer and smaller/poorer provinces to finance the delivery of state services, especially social and health services that are primarily in their constitutional jurisdictions. One of the principal tasks undertaken by Ottawa at the apogee of the Canadian welfare state (roughly 1950s–1980s) was to lead social policy development in the provinces though its ability to tax citizens of the wealthier provinces and redistribute this income in the form of equalization grants and conditional grants to induce policy harmonization from province to province. Since the rise of neoliberalism in the 1980s with its distaste for social-policy spending, and the increasing need to harmonize Canadian taxes with the lower rates prevalent in contiguous U.S. regions, the federal government has been pulling back on its redistributive spending. The resulting fiscal crisis has caused richer provinces to question why the taxes of their citizens, now more than ever needed to pay for hospitals and schools at home, are being diverted by the federal government to less wealthy provinces. On the other hand, the

TABLE 6.2 The Territorial Configuration of the Canadian Federation, 2001

	% Canada Population	% Canada GDP	% Commons	% Senate	% Canada Territory
Provinces					
Newfoundland & Labrador	1.7	1.3	2.3	5.7	4.1
Prince Edward Island	0.5	0.3	1.3	3.8	0.1
Nova Scotia	3.0	2.3	3.7	9.5	0.6
New Brunswick	2.4	1.8	3.3	9.5	0.7
Quebec	24.1	21.1	24.9	22.9	15.4
Ontario	38.0	42.1	34.2	22.9	10.8
Manitoba	3.7	3.3	4.7	5.7	6.5
Saskatchewan	3.3	3.0	4.7	5.7	6.5
Alberta	9.9	12.1	8.6	5.7	6.6
British Columbia	13.0	12.3	11.3	5.7	9.5
Federal Territories					
Yukon	0.10	0.11	0.3	1.0	4.8
Northwest Territories	0.12	0.27	0.3	1.0	13.5
Nunavut	0.09	0.09	.3	1.0	21.0

poorer provinces are embittered by the need to raise their local taxes to higher levels that make them ever more uncompetitive in relation to more prosperous U.S. and Canadian regions in order to pay for their citizens' basic social services. Needless to say, both rich and poor provinces are disillusioned with Ottawa and increasingly question its policy leadership role.

The waning legitimacy of the federal government has spilled over spectacularly into the national political party system. The last three elected Parliaments have featured acrimonious quarrelling between three regionally based party blocs. Further eroding Ottawa's standing, the bitter partisan intensity of these confrontations is in marked contrast to the previous Canadian pattern of managing regional conflicts through executive federalism.

Although the electoral franchise became nearly universal in Canada during the early twentieth century, any tradition of populist democratic participation was considerably circumscribed by relatively high deference to the country's social, economic, political, and bureaucratic elites by the mass of the population. Accommodation within and between elites was characteristic of Canada's governance. Regular elections ensured some level of public oversight over policy outputs but these elections most often centred on political style rather than substance with about half of the voting population making their choice on the basis of party or leader image. This led to great stability in the federal system. One party, the Liberal Party, was so dominant in Ottawa that Liberals were only out of power for about one-third of the twentieth century. *Elite accommodation* according to generally agreed rules and norms underpinned the process of executive federalism in Canada as described above.

While populist participation in federal politics has, nonetheless, had an important impact on Canadian federalism in recent decades, it has generally acted as a destabilizing force. During the 1970s and 1980s two contending populist movements emerged that were strongly rooted in two distinct Canadian regions. On the one side were nationalist and separatist forces in Quebec who held that the special place properly given to their province as one of Canada's two "founding nations" within federal elite accommodation was breaking down. On the other side, particularly centred in the western provinces of Canada, was the neoliberal view that Canada's traditional form of elite accommodation had unfairly privileged Ontario and Quebec and that Ottawa should treat all citizens and provinces equally.

Both populist movements sought constitutional reform of Canada's federal architecture in order to achieve their goals. Nationalists and separatists in Quebec each touted their own versions of power-sharing arrangements with "English Canada" under slogans such as "sovereignty-association" and "distinct society." Power-sharing between Quebec and Ontario had been tried from 1841 to 1867 and had foundered on complaints about the undemocratic representational balance between the two united provinces of Canada East and Canada West. The 1987 Meech Lake constitutional accord, supported overwhelmingly by Canada's elite accommodationist political classes, projected this failed mid-nineteenth-century idea of power-sharing into the late twentieth century when only 24 percent of Canadians were Quebeckers. Unsurprisingly, Meech met a wall of popular hostility outside of Quebec. This rebuff served to stiffen the spine of now "humiliated" Quebec nationalists and separatists.

British Columbians and Albertans together also make up 24 percent of Canadians, with nowhere near the influence of Quebec in federal politics. Many believed that this was because of the way in which elite accommodation between Ontario and Quebec politicians had set the agenda for national policymaking. Beginning in the 1980s, the provincial government of Alberta spearheaded a proposal for the creation of a "Triple E" federal Senate[7] designed to increase regional power in relation to central Canada.

Following the 1992 defeat in a national referendum of the Charlottetown Accord, which attempted to enshrine "distinct society" status for Quebec in the Constitution, the 1993 federal election proved to be a watershed. The confrontation between the two regionally based visions of Quebec and the West has led to what has so far proved to be a decade-long crisis of legitimacy for the national party system. The Reform/Alliance has held sway in British Columbia and Alberta, the Liberals in Ontario, and the Bloc Québécois in Quebec, making inter-party brokerage and elite accommodation impossible. Compounding this situation has been the fact that the separatist Parti Québécois formed the provincial government in Quebec during all these years and nearly won a referendum on sovereignty in 1995. In the face of this, the coping strategy of the federal Liberal government has been to keep a tight lid on any discussion of constitutional reform. Our analysis would suggest, however, that demands for regional rebalancing of federal power are to some extent structurally based in the rise of the West and the relative decline of Quebec and so are likely to re-emerge. The 2003 electoral victory of the Liberal Party in Quebec over the Parti Québécois may prove to be the catalyst, as the provincial Liberals are pledged to begin discussions with the federal government on a demand for constitutional recognition of Quebec's "specificity"—a formula that they propose will have the same legal weight as "distinct society."

NORTHERNMOST REGION: THE POLITICS OF CONTINENTAL ECONOMIC INTEGRATION

Countries reliant on natural resource production are more vulnerable to upheavals in the world economy than manufacturing countries because resource products suffer from irregular cycles of demand and competitors can easily replace traditional suppliers. Historically, Canada's response to these marketplace uncertainties has been to seek special concessionary trading relationships with its largest customers. Until the latter half of the nineteenth century, Canadian fish, fur, lumber, and agricultural products found shelter in Great Britain behind a system of Empire tariff preferences. When this privileged access was lost, many important Canadian business leaders signed a petition to annex Canada to the United States. The Reciprocity Treaty of 1854, allowing relatively open American market access for resource products from the British North American colonies, was an attempt to forestall growth in annexationist sentiment.

Although the Reciprocity Treaty was only in effect from 1854 to 1866, these years were subsequently romanticized by Canadian merchants and resource producers as "golden years" of prosperity. For many decades after the abrogation of reciprocity by the Americans, its memory was honoured in widespread and persistent calls for the renegotiation of a free trade arrangement with the U.S. Continental trade expanded with and without reciprocity. The growing sophistication of American industry became in part predicated on ready access to Canada's new staple resources: pulp and paper, minerals, and energy. And it is hardly surprising that U.S. direct investment in Canadian resource industries sought to secure this access. As early as 1926, Americans owned one-third of Canadian mining and smelting. By 1963, they owned one-half.

After World War II, U.S. investment flowed into Canadian resource industries that were complementary to its own manufacturing sector. Through investment and trade in Canadian natural resources, a continental division of labour was forged in which Canada's role became that of "a specialized (resource producing) adjunct to the American political economy."[8] The logic of profitability guided individual business decisions by private firms that cumulatively promoted the development of Canada's continental role as a resource storehouse. These decisions were also made within a supportive atmosphere fostered by government officials on both sides of the border who sought to establish resource security for the "free world" in the context of the Cold War of the 1940s and 1950s. Furthermore, Canadian politicians and bureaucrats were eager to promote an economic formula that had stimulated, in their view, the post-war economic boom.

Canadian producers of industrial raw materials enjoyed remarkable success within the continental marketplace. Resource companies dominated the list of Canada's top exporters and at the end of the twentieth century supplied more than one-third of U.S. imports of copper, one-half of its imported nickel, three-fifths of its imported zinc, and nearly three-quarters of its imported aluminum. Canada also supplied all of the American imports of electricity and almost all of its imports of natural gas. Exports of Canadian forestry commodities supplied four-fifths or more of U.S. imports of paper and paperboard, simply worked wood, and pulp and wastepaper.[9]

Cast as ancillary to staples resource extraction, Canada's manufacturing industries also developed as regional extensions of American production. We can identify four periods, each with its own distinct production pattern. The industrial strategy employed by late-nineteenth–early-twentieth-century Canadian manufacturers was import substitution industrialization (ISI). It was characterized by unchallenged technological dependence through the use of foreign machinery and production processes and a disinterest in production for anything but Canadian domestic consumption. Ottawa played an indispensable role in ISI through setting tariff levels high enough to make feasible the domestic production of goods that would otherwise be imported. Canadian manufacturers, seeking a cheap and effective shortcut, licensed American industrial processes rather than developing their own. In contrast to more aggressive industrialists in other countries who initially borrowed technology and then assimilated, adapted, and innovated from this knowledge base, the use of foreign machinery and production processes became a permanent part of the early Canadian industrial pattern, thus tying it in an important structural way to the evolution of industry in the United States.

With geographic proximity to the northeastern American industrial heartland, a tariff-protected domestic market, and concessionary tariff privileges within the British Empire, south-central Canada was an obvious location for the establishment of U.S. branch plants. Through takeovers of existing Canadian manufacturing firms (often already linked to them through licensing arrangements), and the establishment of new subsidiaries, American industrialists consolidated a place of prominence in Canada's most dynamic industrial sectors by the 1920s. The second period, from the 1920s to the late 1940s, consolidated the worst features of the ISI behaviour of the Canadian-owned industries that dominated the first period. U.S. firms established a Canadian presence in order to gain access to a tariff-protected market for products they would otherwise have shipped from their southern factories. There was no provision in their Canadian branch plants for the development of distinct product lines for world markets save for the transfer of some export business from their U.S. operations to take advantage of the preferential tariff access that Canada enjoyed in Great Britain and the other Dominions.

The third period, from the late 1940s to the mid-1970s, further institutionalized the import substitution model and, with it, Canada's industrial role in the continent. With the collapse of Empire preferences, Canadian branch plants ceased even this limited export role. Increasingly, U.S. firms viewed the Canadian market as part of their *domestic* operations. Typically, an administrative division of the North American market would establish a Canadian *satellite* plant to satisfy regional demand in this country, just as, say, a Chicago plant would fill demand in the U.S. Midwest, while research and development as well as exports were centred in the U.S. parent plant.

Production in the contemporary period, roughly the late 1970s to the present, continues to be organized on a continental basis. Instead of satellite plants that produce a large range of miniature-replica lines for a limited territory, however, North American plants have now become *rationalized*. Following the lead of the automotive industry in the successful U.S.–Canada Auto Pact trade model of the 1960s, this means specialization in the production of a limited range of lines for the entire continent. Falling Canada–U.S. tariffs under the multilateral General Agreement on Tariffs and Trade (GATT) made rationalization possible, and increasing international competitive pressure made it necessary.

Continuing investment in Canadian plant locations was made attractive by a radical program of currency devaluation that by 2002 had chopped a full 35 percent from the value of Canada's 1976 dollar. Devaluation created a marked Canadian labour cost advantage over American plant locations in certain key industries like automobiles. Nevertheless, it is important to recognize that continental rationalization did not fundamentally change the rules of the game. Most American-owned Canadian factories were no closer to becoming highly efficient and technologically advanced plants capable of autonomously generating world-competitive products. In both the miniature-replica satellite and continentally rationalized production models, managerial authority, research and development, and export marketing all remain the prerogatives of the U.S. parent firms.

The Canadian political climate remained favourable to continentally organized production during the ongoing process that fashioned Canada's resource and manufacturing industries as regional extensions of the U.S. economy. In some measure, this was due to the growing ability of foreign investors to reward or punish Canadian politicians. This could be accomplished directly through the provision of funding for political parties and corporate directorships for retired politicians or indirectly through manipulating the levers of economic expansion or contraction. Politicians became understandably loath to threaten what they believed to be the motor of the economic growth on which their electoral fortunes depended.

Ultimately more decisive than the considerable power of foreign investors to promote or protect their own interests in the Canadian political system, however, has been the simple fact that Canada's economic, political, bureaucratic, and academic elites, along with the population as a whole, have all generally favoured an extensive measure of continental economic integration. Debate, when it has occurred, has been restricted to the terms of this integration. *Continentalists* have favoured the elimination of trade and investment barriers between Canada and the United States while *nationalists* have preferred to use the Canadian state system to lever favourable deals from U.S. firms and to promote Canadian entrepreneurs.

Because they do not want to tie the hands of Ottawa in its negotiations with the Americans, the nationalists have strongly resisted formal moves to liberalize economic access between the two countries. Laurier's Liberals discovered this fact in the 1911 federal election when their moderate trade "Reciprocity" agreement with the U.S. fell to cries of "no truck nor trade with the Yankees." Nationalist opponents of Reciprocity successfully mounted an emotional campaign based on claims that Canada was signing away its unique British cultural identity and would ultimately become vulnerable to annexation by the Americans.

For decades after the spectacular failure of the 1911 Canada–U.S. Reciprocity Agreement, Canadian politicians avoided dealing so openly again with an issue obviously bonded to the electorate's fears of territorial surrender and/or loss of sociocultural distinctiveness. W.L.M. King established a pattern, in the mid-1930s, of depoliticizing continental commercial relations by presenting movement toward Canada–U.S. tariff liberalization as a disjointed series of technical, bureaucratic adjustments to tariff schedules. Under the post–World War II General Agreement on Tariffs and Trade (GATT), this bureaucratic process of tariff reduction continued. Particularly through the 1967 Kennedy and 1979 Tokyo Rounds of GATT negotiations, something very close to de facto Canada–U.S. free trade was established. By 1987, 95 percent of Canadian goods were to enter the U.S. with duties of 5 percent or less, and 91 percent of U.S. exports to the Canadian market were to be in an equivalent position.

From being a deeply buried public issue for at least half a century, Canada–U.S. free trade was catapulted by the Mulroney government to the head of Canada's political agenda through a 1985 announcement that it would begin free trade negotiations with the Americans. Considering the already existing liberalized continental tariff regime under the GATT, two main factors seem to have been responsible for the surprising reentry of the potentially explosive free trade question into the Canadian political atmosphere: (1) the rise of an American protectionism that threatened to disrupt, through the use of non-tariff barriers, regional Canadian resource and manufacturing production systems that by the mid-1980s had become largely based on assumed low-tariff access to U.S. markets; and (2) the increasing partisan appeal of Canada–U.S. free trade, long favoured by most Canadians as an abstract concept, among important Conservative Party constituencies within the neoliberal right, Quebec nationalists, and populist Westerners.

In the end, the 1987 Canada–U.S. Free Trade Agreement (CUFTA), although it removed remaining tariffs between the two countries, left standing the non-tariff barriers that had initially prompted Canadian business to press the Tories for the negotiations. Chapter 19 of the CUFTA established that each country will retain its domestic anti-dumping and countervailing duty laws, although appeals on whether these laws have been properly applied can be made to binational panels. Of far more import than tariff matters was the way in which the CUFTA politically hobbled Canadian economic nationalism. Articles 105, 1402, and 1602 prohibited discrimination between foreign and Canadian firms in regard to establishment, investment, operations, and sale. Pertaining to manufacturing, Article 1603 proscribed performance requirements such as export quotas or domestic sourcing for foreign firms. Pertaining to resources, Articles 408 and 409 forbade export taxes and export restrictions, and Articles 903 and 904 restated these prohibitions with specific reference to the energy sector. At the conclusion of the negotiations, then Deputy Prime Minister Donald Mazankowski described the energy provisions to Calgary oil executives as "insurance against your own government" by preventing nationalist policies from being introduced.[10]

The 1988 election was a direct confrontation over ratification of the CUFTA between forces carrying nationalist and continentalist banners. The remarkable strength of the nationalists in the free trade debate stood in sharp contrast to their historically weaker position within Canadian political culture. Indeed, right up to the vote, public opinion was running against the agreement. The nationalist forces skillfully evoked the same emotional symbols employed by opponents of the 1911 Reciprocity Agreement: protection of Canadian territory from American annexation and maintaining the distinctiveness of Canada's sociocultural milieu. In regard to territory, the nationalists repeatedly warned the public that Canada's political independence was at stake and Canada was about to become the fifty-first state. One of the campaign's most effective television advertisements purported to show the CUFTA negotiators taking an eraser to the Canada–U.S. border on a map of North America. In regard to national identity, the nationalists argued effectively that traditional Canadian cultural and social values were in jeopardy from direct threats posed by the CUFTA to Canada's social welfare programs as well as regional and cultural subsidies. So powerful were these nationalist arguments that the continentalist forces led by Mulroney's Conservatives could not simply respond by stressing what they believed were the considerable economic benefits of the CUFTA. In order simply to hold their own, they were forced to protest vigorously that the nationalists were "liars"; extravagantly promise that Canada's distinct social, cultural, and regional programs would not be endangered by the CUFTA; and air their own television advertisements that pointedly re-drew the Canada–U.S. border on a map of North America.

In the years immediately following the 1988 election, Canada's strained economic circumstances appeared to confirm the nationalist case against the CUFTA. During this period, an international economic recession hit Canada earlier, harder, and lasted longer than was the case in most other developed countries. Many Canadian factories, both foreign- and domestically owned, closed their doors and some even moved their operations to the United States. Employment in Canadian manufacturing was devastated, with 340,000 jobs lost between 1989 and 1992.[11]

Since tariffs between Canada and the U.S. had already been largely liberalized under the Auto Pact and GATT *before* the CUFTA was implemented, nationalist claims that Canada's early-1990s economic woes embodied toxic CUFTA fallout were greatly overblown. In fact, Canada's post-CUFTA economic reverses were only indirectly related to the trade policies of the Mulroney Conservatives. Driven by an excess of rigid monetarist ideological zeal, and to the betrayed horror of the same business allies who had backed their 1988 re-election, the Tories forced the value of the Canadian dollar spectacularly upwards by approximately 20 percent between 1987 and 1992. This revaluation had the immediate effect of making Canadian products far less competitive in U.S. markets already shrunk by the force of a major economic recession. Ironically, the Tories' high-interest-rate/high-dollar policies worked at cross-purposes with the CUFTA by seriously undermining one of Canada's principal locational advantages in the rationalization of continental production.

Given the intensity of the emotions that had been stirred in the rancorous free trade debate, nationalist arguments that Canada's economic problems stemmed from CUFTA resonated with many ordinary Canadians for several years following its ratification. As late as the summer of 1993, a plurality remained opposed to it.[12] As it gradually became apparent that the nationalist electoral rhetoric had been overblown—that Canada's territorial borders were by no means about to disappear and that the nation's sociocultural distinctiveness had been retained—the emotional sting was removed from the 1988 nationalist crusade. When CUFTA became understood as an economic management issue, rather than as a threat to Canada's geographic or sociocultural existence, it lost its salience.[13] This is because unlike the jealous manner in which Canadians have guarded the borderlines of their region's geographic or sociocultural territory within North America, the consensus view has historically favoured an extensive measure of continental economic integration.

Beginning after 1992, a turnaround of Canadian opinion on free trade occurred in spite of the opening of negotiations to include Mexico within the CUFTA framework in a North American Free Trade Agreement (NAFTA). As in the CUFTA, market access through tariff reduction was not the principal question. Mexico had already abandoned its highly nationalist investment and trade policies when it signed on to the GATT during the 1980s. Nonetheless, important elements within U.S. and Canadian business judged Mexico to be an important complement to the CUFTA regime. Formally incorporating its low-wage economy into the CUFTA zone could offer significant competitive advantages in the contemporary era of global manufacturing and international trade rivalry. Some even dreamt of a regional trading bloc composed of the nations of North and South America that could surpass the economic successes of the European Community. Canada's economic and political elites wanted to be stakeholders in this visionary enterprise and feared the consequences of being left as spectators on the sidelines. They also saw NAFTA, and its possible South American extensions, in the light of the traditional Canadian foreign policy objective of filtering Canada's bilateral relationship with the United States through multilateral screens.

With their 1988 momentum long abated, Canada's nationalist forces tried to regroup to fight NAFTA during the 1993 federal election. However, only the hapless NDP championed their cause. Going into the

1993 election, polls showed that three-fifths of Canadians were against the ratification of NAFTA. Still, the nationalists were not able to replay the successes of their 1988 campaign. Mexico, unlike the United States, could hardly be argued to present a tangible threat to Canada's geographic or sociocultural territory. Left to fight on the far less emotionally volatile terrain of economic nationalism, the nationalists' rhetorical assault against NAFTA was met by the public with polite, fatigued resignation. At present, nearly three-quarters of Canadians favour continental free trade. Only one-half of Americans and Mexicans share this view. Nearly two-thirds of Canadians (and Americans) think that residents of Canada and the United States should enjoy the right to work in each others' country. Nearly half of Canadians would be willing to surrender the Canadian dollar in favour of a continental currency like the Euro or simply to adopt the U.S. dollar in Canada.[14]

NORTHERNMOST REGION: IDENTITY AND INTERNATIONAL RELATIONS

It was after World War II that Canadians were first warned that their nation had moved from "colony to nation to colony."[15] Similar sentiments are still being expressed, although it is hard today either to picture clearly our British colonial past or to understand fully the significance of this often repeated figure of speech. It is, however, helpful to realize that in the earliest part of the twentieth century, Canadians, especially English Canadians, were privileged members of the world's most powerful empire, and their identity and sense of "nationalism" grew out of that association. Colonial, rather than indigenous, symbols and institutions defined both Canadians' view of themselves and Canada's position on the international stage. For example, it was not until 1993 that Canada inaugurated its first ministry of *Foreign* Affairs. When its venerable predecessor, the Department of *External* Affairs, was created in 1909, it was the supremacy of the British Colonial Office in the conduct of our imperial and foreign relations that first designated Canada's international business as "external" rather than "foreign."

Just as most Canadians were content through the nineteenth and early twentieth centuries to accept the primacy of Britain in defining the boundaries of imperial foreign and military policy, so now the United States is usually given the lead. This transition was facilitated by the foreswearing of armed conflict between the British and the Americans in North America following the inconclusive result of the War of 1812. All-important here as well was the fact that Canada fell increasingly under the protective, largely benign, security blanket of the powerful U.S. military. The 1823 Monroe Doctrine of the United States permanently safeguarded Canada from invasion by any hostile European power, and the 1940 Ogdensburg Agreement established a Permanent Joint Board on Defence that still meets biannually. In 1958, NORAD (North American Aerospace Defence Command) was established with a joint military command, and in 1956 the Defence Development and Defence Production Sharing Arrangements were instituted to rationalize Canada–U.S. military production and procurement. In all, Canada and the U.S. currently manage their complex security relationship through some 80 bilateral defence treaty agreements, 250 memoranda of understanding, and 145 discussion forums.[16]

Deference, of course, is not to be confused with the abrogation of national sovereignty. If there was any cause for doubt on this question, periodic disengaged moments in the conduct of Canada's foreign policy serve to demonstrate to both American and Canadian audiences that Canada retains the capacity to be something more than a U.S. satellite. A list of such episodes would include Canada's maintenance of trade ties with China and Cuba during the Diefenbaker years, Prime Minister Pearson's 1965 call for a pause in the U.S. bombing of North Vietnam, the "Third Option" of the early 1970s that called for reducing Canada's dependence on the U.S. by expanding its relations with other countries, Canada providing development aid to Nicaragua during the Reagan presidency of the 1980s, and Canada's refusal to join the American-led invasion of Iraq in 2003.

Canadians realize that volunteering to be an extension of the American political economy carries with it certain costs to national independence in world affairs. However, this sense of realism and deference to U.S. leadership in the world does not carry over to the expression of what are perceived to be Canadian *regional* issues within North America. Here, autonomy is jealously guarded. As we discovered in reviewing the Reciprocity and CUFTA debates, territory is an outstanding example of a subject where Canadian national sensibilities will readily engage American interests. Whether the issue is Northwest Passage access, Georges Bank fishing rights, the southward diversion of fresh water from Canada's lakes and rivers, or acid rain originating in the bordering American states, Canadians display uncharacteristic enthusiasm in tracing the physical border between the two countries with some measure of precision.[17] Canadians are map-nationalists. Less than 13 percent would favour Canada becoming a part of the U.S. or their province joining the U.S., and only 17 percent think that within a generation Canadians will form a single country with the U.S. and elect politicians in Washington. When asked in 1964 and again in 2002 if Canada–U.S. union was inevitable, three-fifths disagreed.[18]

National identity as manifested through the preservation of images of distinctiveness in social culture or lifestyle is another no-go area. An important cultural legacy of the British colonial past has been the quiet conviction of many Canadians that they are more civilized than the avaricious and quarrelsome republicans to the south. However pronounced the similarity of the two national cultures in a world perspective, Canadians want very much to believe that they are different. And so, two-thirds of Canadians reported in 1990 that they judged the Canadian way of life had been influenced too much by the United States.[19] In 2002, two-thirds of Canadians disagreed that "Canadians and Americans have the same basic values." Only one in 10 Canadians wanted Canada to become more like the U.S.[20] Based on this view, Canadians continually define and measure (at least rhetorically) their social practices and policies against what is frequently perceived to be a negative American yardstick. So in addition to territory, the Canadian region currently draws its sociocultural frontier by characterizing itself as possessing higher levels of societal order and urban cleanliness as well as a greater willingness to deliver goods and services collectively through the state.[21] In 2002, 87 percent of Canadians opposed harmonizing Canada–U.S. health care policies in order to remove trade barriers between the two countries, and 75 percent, unfazed by Ontario's standing as one of North America's top three polluters, opposed harmonizing environmental policies. Convinced almost to a person of their happy state of sociocultural transcendence, 89 percent of Canadians in 2003 held that Canada enjoyed a better quality of life than the U.S.[22]

Living comfortably (for the most part) under the roof of U.S. foreign and defence policy while still asserting sovereignty is a position fraught with contradictions. One 1975 survey of some 300 members of Canada's foreign policy elites showed that nearly two-thirds saw the United States as Canada's best friend and one-half defined Canada as a "partner" in North America, suggesting that on most issues in international affairs Canadian and American interests are essentially the same. Even so, 52 percent also felt that the continentally organized economy "significantly limited" Canadian autonomy in domestic affairs and only 28 percent believed that, compared to most other countries, Canada acted independently in international relations.[23]

Elite opinions and mass opinions on this subject closely coincide. Seventy percent of Canadians in the 1980s viewed the United States as Canada's best friend, and one-half expressed "very great" or "considerable" confidence in the ability of the Americans to deal wisely with world problems.[24] When asked in the mid-1970s and again in the mid-1980s, only one-quarter of Canadians were prepared to agree that we should withdraw from NATO and our defence agreements with the U.S. and adopt a policy of neutrality.[25] At least a plurality of Canadian public opinion backs the U.S. in almost all its overseas military campaigns.[26] For example, even though it lacked United Nations blessing, the U.S.-led air campaign against Serbia in 1999 was supported by two-thirds of Canadians, and three-fifths would have supported sending ground troops to Kosovo.[27] In 2002, four-fifths of Canadians wanted either the same level of closeness or closer in military relations between the two countries, while only one-fifth wanted less close relations. An identical survey question posed 17 years earlier had virtually the same result.[28] In a poll taken in the immediate wake of the September 11, 2001, terrorist attacks on New York and Washington, three-fifths of Canadians felt that Canada should become more aligned or a lot more aligned with the United States in world affairs, while one-third wanted no change or less alignment.[29]

Even so, and reflecting the ambiguous approach of the state elite to this subject, two-thirds of Canadians in the mid-1980s believed that their government's views on international affairs were "unduly affected" by another country and three-fifths identified the United States as that country.[30] In the mid-1990s, a majority of Canadians wanted both a more independent foreign policy for Canada and closer military cooperation with the United States.[31] In 2002, two-thirds of Canadians felt that the U.S. had "no business telling Canadians to increase defence spending or to support U.S. foreign policy as these are sovereign issues for Canada," while one-third felt that such requests were "reasonable" and "we are risking our own interests" by ignoring them.[32]

An excellent illustration of the contradiction in asserting sovereignty while sharing the American security umbrella can be found in the reactions of Canadians to the two American-led Persian Gulf wars against Iraq in 1991 and 2003. In 1990, 52 percent of Canadians believed that U.S. President George H.W. Bush (the elder) had too much influence on Prime Minister Brian Mulroney. Yet, 58 percent favoured Canadian participation in the American-led 1991 Persian Gulf War against Saddam Hussein's Iraq and 57 percent approved of Mulroney's handling of Canada's involvement in that war.[33]

Based on the analysis presented to this point as well as the 1991 precedent, one might have reasonably predicted that Canadians would also support the U.S. in its 2003 war against the Iraqi Ba'athists and Saddam Hussein, but this did not turn out to be the case. As previously recorded, on the heels of the September 11, 2001, terrorist attacks, Canadian public opinion became even more pro-American as well as decidedly hawkish. By a margin of 52 percent to 37 percent, Canadians agreed with U.S. President George W. Bush's (the younger) "Axis of Evil"

State of the Union address in January 2002 in which he characterized Iraq, Iran, and North Korean as allies of terrorism and a "grave and growing danger" that must be checked. Almost seven in 10 Canadians blamed Saddam Hussein as being a main contributor to the Arab–Israeli conflict.[34] In this context, it is not surprising that 51 percent of Canadians favoured American military action against Iraq in February 2002 while 44 percent were opposed.[35]

Prime Minister Jean Chrétien's Liberal government, however, was unsettled by Bush's "Axis of Evil" speech. In a February 2002 European swing that included bilateral meetings in Germany and Russia as well as attendance at the "Progressive Governance" Summit of 11 countries in Stockholm, Chrétien began to distance Canada from any "unilateral" American military action against Iraq. William Graham, the Canadian foreign minister, told the Commons that it was necessary to work through "international mechanisms to constrain Iraq" so that "world peace" would not be "destabilized by this man [Hussein] or by any action that might be taken against him either."[36] This attempt to seize the moral high ground through a balanced approach was undermined by some of the previously held positions of the Chrétien government. In 1998, Chretien had argued that a fresh UN Security Council resolution for new military action to enforce Iraqi disarmament by the U.S., Great Britain, and Canada was unnecessary because "...we are acting under a valid resolution which has existed since 1991. When Saddam Hussein broke the agreement of ceasefire he gave us the authority to have the resolution of 1991 respected by him."[37] And, in 1999, Chrétien had excused on pragmatic grounds NATO's failure to secure UN approval for its military campaign against Serbia by pointing out that "the reality is that both Russia and China have a veto at the Security Council and we cannot move."[38]

Notwithstanding the contradictions, the Liberal attack on the American policy on Iraq became ever sharper and more insistent in the ensuing months. It was suggested that Bush's approach was illegal, unreasonable, and dangerous. Graham, for example, held that "in Canada we prefer to work through multilateral international institutions which will enable us to guarantee the peace and security of the world, and that we must be very careful that we do not start unilateral actions which in fact will destabilize, because they may be copied by other regimes that may choose to use the same actions against us, which could be very dangerous."[39] Powerfully reinforcing this line was a subtle appeal to the traditional Canadian nationalist conviction, dating from our British colonial past, of moral superiority. Defence Minister McCallum contrasted Canada's putative adherence to international law and multilaterism with the Bush administration's advocacy of a "unilateral, power-based system, which kind of means the law of the jungle." Graham pompously advanced that "to those who call upon us to follow blindly whenever and wherever the United States would lead, even if such actions would threaten the multilateral system we have built together with our American partners so painstakingly over the past 50 years, we say, true friends talk straight to each other..."[40]

Several Liberal backbenchers were less delicate in turning the anti-Republican, anti-American screw. For example, one observed that "the truth is that the President of the United States was elected by only 200 well-placed votes in Florida. The United States is going into congressional and senate elections and needs an external evil to rally Republican voters to go to the polls. The Democrats in the United States have expressed these concerns, and if they dare challenge the President of the United States they are called unpatriotic. What irony. The same is practised by Saddam Hussein, who calls unpatriotic all his citizens who dare argue with him. He goes one step farther. He exterminates them..."[41] Another admitted, "Very frankly that I find the triumvirate of President George W. Bush, Vice President Dick Cheney and Secretary of Defence Rumsfeld scary and frightening for world peace. They give the impression of a war-happy trio, anxious to pull the trigger at all costs, looking for the excuse and the self-justification to let the B-52 bombers and the small [sic] bombs loose. President Bush gives the impression of someone involved on a personal vendetta, on a crusade, determined no matter what the odds to complete the task left uncompleted by his presidential father. Somehow this has become a Bush fixation: let us fire the torpedoes and somehow the world will be a better and safer place...."[42] Another Liberal backbencher questioned the patriotism of Canadians who supported the U.S. position on Iraq: "...after listening to the hon. member for Calgary Southeast, what bothers me is that he demonstrates absolutely no self-respect as a Canadian. I would think that the man from Calgary would stand up and exhibit some pride in Canada and instead of being a clone of Americans and a clone of their policy, that he would want some independent thought from Canadian policy-makers. No, just throw our lot in completely with the Americans."[43]

By December 2002, Chrétien had polished his nationalist argument that UN-sanctioned multilateralism was a traditional, required element for the foreign commitment of Canadian forces, even to the point of revising the history of the 1999 Kosovo intervention. He claimed to CBC's *The National* that "we always moved with the approval of the UN, when we went to Kosovo, when we went to any other situation of peacekeeping. But

Kosovo was a war. The planes were used against the Serbs and we did 10 percent of the sorties of the military. It was under NATO but approved by the UN. That is the system. We believe in multilateral organization... It's very important for countries like Canada to be great promoters of multilateral organizations. We have only one superpower, it happens to be a friend of ours, but to maintain the equilibrium in the world it is very important that we have these multilateral organizations like the UN or others."[44]

Some have tried to explain the antiwar stand of the Chrétien government by contending that it was dictated by Canadian public opinion.[45] In fact, the evidence points us in the opposite direction: the Liberals campaigned for several months to bring public opinion around to their side. In early 2002, a slight majority of Canadians favoured attacking Iraq. From late February to early December 2002, the public was fairly evenly split with slightly more against than for Canadian participation in an American-led Iraq war. But in January and February 2002, the scenery dramatically changed, with two-thirds of Canadians disapproving of U.S. "unilateral" military action against Iraq and three-fifths saying that Canada should intervene militarily only with UN approval.[46] While echoes from the growing strength of the antiwar movement in Europe and the United States also played a role here, the Chrétien government's framing of this issue as a nationalist defence of Canada's sovereignty and an expression of our sociocultural/moral superiority over the Americans appealed to the same powerful symbols that were mobilized so successfully in the 1988 CUFTA and 1911 Reciprocity elections. And emotions ran very high: in December 2002, 38 percent of Canadians believed that George W. Bush was a greater threat to world peace than Saddam Hussein.[47] After the war actually began, more traditional opinion patterns regarding security re-emerged, with 51 percent in favour of Canada offering help to the U.S.-led coalition and 46 percent opposed.[48]

CONCLUSION: MANAGING THE CONTINENTAL RELATIONSHIP

As a regional extension of a larger and more powerful political economy, the Canadian social formation faces special problems in self-management. The politics of issues such as the environment, economic expansion, social welfare, labour, and regional development have by necessity both a domestic and a bilateral dimension. This duality creates a basic instability in the economic management capacity of the Canadian political economy, an instability that is further exaggerated by the spatial dispersal of power within a federal structure of government. In the context of this instability, then, the Canadian state system is called upon to play the role of a point of balance by focusing, mediating, protecting, and developing the regional position of the Canadian social formation within the continental political economy.

The management of regional relations within the continent is far from easy. For one thing, the point of balance must continually shift to take account of the continuing changes that result from economic expansion and transformation. For another, finding balance within the political environment is also difficult with the fortunes of regionally defined political ideas and parties that articulate them constantly on the rise and fall. Finally, there are underlying centripetal and centrifugal forces at play in the Canadian federation with respect to continentalism. In recent decades, these challenges have played out in the CUFTA/NAFTA debates; the rise of neoliberalism and the retreat of the social welfare state; the Meech Lake and Charlottetown constitutional battles; the breakdown of elite accommodation and executive federalism; and replacement of the federal party system by antithetically opposed, region-based party blocs.

With its nation-building leadership role in promoting Canada-wide transportation and communications policies, economic development policies, and social welfare policies, the federal government has traditionally been the key balancing institution. But during the last decade, Ottawa has found it increasingly difficult to define a national role for itself in the face of the many centrifugal stresses that confront it domestically. Curiously, foreign affairs remains as one policy area where the federal government still asserts a unique sovereign role and identity for itself through working to contain and restrain U.S. power within multilateral institutions.[49]

The faltering federal capacity to act as a point of continental balance through offering nation-building leadership raises important questions. Have provincial elites been left free to pursue Balkanizing regional economic development strategies without having to measure them against any national programs developed by the federal government? Is there now a political void at Canada's political centre that will lead in time to demands for new forms of North American regional governance or even for political annexation to the United States?[50] These questions emerge at a time when Canadian provincial economies have been strengthening their already remarkably pronounced southward orientations. Ontario, once considered the centralizing bulwark of coast-to-coast Confederation, has become re-centred within the Great Lakes basin. In 2001, exports accounted for 46 percent of Ontario's GDP. Ninety-three percent of Ontario's exports are destined for the U.S. market and the province is the third largest trading partner of the U.S. after Canada and Mexico. Ontario exports more per capita than Japan, Germany, France, and Great Britain.[51] Ontario, and other provinces, may increasingly find that political decisions taken in Washington have as much, or even more, relevance for their local economies as decisions taken in Ottawa.

Before concluding that the Canadian federal state system is on the way out, a number of additional factors need to be considered. To begin, direct political representation in the U.S. political system would not necessarily be more effective than the current "special relationship." Without exception, the population of each of Canada's five regions is only a small fraction of the population of their contiguous American counterparts. Representation in the U.S. Congress would be correspondingly small: Ontario, for example, would go from having more than one-third of the seats in the Canadian House of Commons to fewer than one-twentieth of the "representation by population" districts in the U.S. Congress. Further, Canada's state system has given considerable advantage to Canadian elites over regional elites elsewhere in the continental economy both by bringing Canadian elites together to recognize their joint interests and by providing them with a common vehicle for promoting these interests. Although the Canadian social formation is not electorally represented in the U.S. political system, Canada's state system has developed considerable means for the "external" political expression of its regional interests to the U.S. Canada can have an influence on the American political executive, Congress, and state governments through diplomacy, treaty, and the advocacy of private Canadian interest groups. Private advocacy is primarily energized by American businesses fostering and protecting their Canadian investments but may also include strategic alliances with indigenous forces within U.S. politics whose issue positions are similar to Canadian ones.[52]

When it is remembered that all of Canada's regions share common interests in resource production and export to U.S. markets, sometimes shipping the same products, the further utility of constructing a common Canadian position through a separate and sovereign federal order is clear. It should also be remembered that the burden of providing the highly expensive transportation infrastructure necessary for resource export has traditionally been shared by all of Canada's regions through the federal state. As well, while equalization payments and social transfers may be shrinking in relative importance, weaker Canadian regions have historically employed the federal state to capture some of the benefits of the uneven development of the continental economy from the stronger Canadian regions. Similarly, although its relative importance is shrinking, the national market provided by trade between the Canadian regions will likely remain a factor of some significance for all the provinces. On this point, because of the exceptionally strong emotional commitment of Canadians to the integrity of their geographic territory, any province like Quebec that considered leaving the federation would have to consider the almost certain prospect of stiff retaliatory measures from the remaining provinces. These would likely include economic exclusion not only from the Canadian market but also from NAFTA.[53]

Four-fifths of Canada's business leaders currently disapprove of a U.S.–Canada political union primarily because Canadian values, culture, and beliefs are "too different."[54] For some primary opinion-leading and agenda-setting sectors, such as the Canadian communications/media industries, the Canadian cultural and federal political elites, as well as academics who study Canada, a protected national market is key, and they could be counted on to oppose any siren call to annexation as if their livelihoods depended on it. Finally, and perhaps essentially, the maintenance of a federal state allows ordinary Canadians a means to affirm symbolically their autonomous national self-definition through preserving their territorial and sociocultural distinctiveness within the continent.

NOTES

1. Canada, Department of Foreign Affairs and International Trade, Economic and Trade Analysis Division, *Third Annual Report on Canada's State of Trade*, May 2002.

2. Ontario, Ministry of Enterprise, Opportunity and Innovation, Ontario Economic Development, *Ontario Facts: Economic Structure—International Trade*, June 2002. <http://txt.2ontario.com/facts/txt_fact04.cfm>.

3. Canada, Industry Canada, *International Investment Policy*, December 16, 2002. <http://strategis.ic.gc.ca/epic/internet/inii-ii.nsf/vwGeneratedInterE/ii18414e.html>.

4. In 1988, 31 percent of provincial goods were exported while 22 percent were sent to other provinces. Imports were the source of 32 percent of provincial goods while 22 percent came from other provinces. Calculated from Canada, Statistics Canada, *The Daily*, April 29, 1992, p. 6. In 1996, interprovincial exports represented 54 percent of the value of international exports while interprovincial imports represented 60 percent of the value of international imports. Calculated from Canada, Statistics Canada, *The Daily*, May 16, 1997.

5. Canada, Department of Foreign Affairs and International Trade, Embassy of Canada to the United States, *The United States-Canada: The World's Largest Trading Relationship*, August 2001.

6. R. Stuart, *United States Expansionism and British North America, 1775–1871* (Chapel Hill: University of North Carolina Press, 1988), pp. 11, 14–15, 25, 58, 65–66, Chapter 4, 163–66.

7. Triple E: *Equal* representation for each province; members *Elected* to represent the province by popular vote; *Effective* in relation to the federal House of Commons with the right of veto.

8. M. Clark-Jones, *A Staple State: Canadian Industrial Resources in Cold War* (Toronto: University of Toronto Press, 1987), p. 11.

9. Calculated from United States, National Trade Data Bank, International Trade Administration, *U.S. Foreign Trade Highlights*; and Canada, *Summary of External Trade*, December 1992.

10. *The Globe and Mail*, October 17, 1987: A4. For an extensive treatment of the idea that CUFTA was a "supraconstitution" to constrain nationalist policy initiatives, see S. Clarkson, *Uncle Sam and Us* (Toronto: University of Toronto Press, 2002).

11. Statistics Canada, *Historical Labour Force Statistics*, 1992, p. 158.

12. Canadian Institute of Public Opinion, *The Gallup Report*, August 31, 1993.

13. By 2001, Compas found that more Canadians disagreed than agreed—37 percent vs. 43 percent—with the statement, "Free trade is bad because countries such as Canada and their governments lose power and sovereignty." Compas concluded that "limited public concern about threats to sovereignty may present a strong barrier to growth in support for Canadian nationalist positions on trade." Compas Inc., *Strong Majority Support for Free Trade for Pragmatic Reasons*, April 16, 2001.

14. EKOS, *EKOS/PPF Symposium, Rethinking North America. Part II: North American Economic Dimensions*, June 18, 2002.

15. H. A. Innis, "Great Britain, the United States and Canada," in *Essays in Canadian Economic History* (Toronto: University of Toronto Press, 1956), p. 405.

16. Canada, Department of National Defence, Key Documents and Major Reports, *Canada–United States Defence Relations*, December 6, 2001. <http://www.dnd.ca/site/Reports/budget01/Canada-US_b_e.htm>.

17. For a discussion of how Canadian territorial consciousness has been manifested in the conduct of Canada–U.S. environmental relations, see my "Greening the New Canadian Political Economy," *Studies in Political Economy*, Spring 1992.

18. Canadian Institute of Public Opinion, *The Gallup Report*, November 15, 1988, and June 7, 1990; Compas Inc., *President Bush, Missile Defense, The Environment and US–Canada Relations*, June 18, 2001; and Centre for Research and Information on Canada, *Most Canadians Remain Confident of their Independence*, October 28, 2002.

19. Ibid., June 7, 1990. In a 1993 Gallup survey, just over one-third of Canadians identified themselves as "great, passive, friendly, or reserved," while a similar number identified Americans as "self-centred, pushy, patriotic, ignorant or rude" (February 11, 1993).

20. Centre for Research and Information on Canada, *Canadians Are Protective of Their Way of Life and Consider Their Values Distinct from Those of Their US Neighbours*, October 28, 2002.

21. See S.M. Lipset, "Canada and the United States: The Cultural Dimension," in *Canada and the United States: Enduring Friendship, Persistent Stress*, C. Doran and J. Sigler, eds. (New Jersey: Prentice-Hall, 1985); and D. Bell, *The Roots of Disunity: A Study of Canadian Political Culture*, rev. ed. (Toronto: Oxford University Press, 1992).

22. Centre for Research and Information on Canada, *Canadians Are Protective of Their Way of Life and Consider Their Values Distinct from Those of Their US Neighbours*, October 28, 2002; "Canadians think Canada's No. 1, even if the U.N. doesn't," *The Edmonton Journal*, July 6, 2003.

23. P.V. Lyon and B.W. Tomlin, *Canada as an International Actor* (Toronto: Macmillan, 1979), p. 85.

24. Canadian Institute of Public Opinion, *The Gallup Report*, July 4, 1985, and March 6, 1986.

25. Ibid., June 19, 1976, and May 26, 1986.

26. A vivid illustration of this phenomenon occurred when, during their 1987–88 confrontation with Iran in the Persian Gulf, the American military mistakenly downed an

Iranian passenger plane, with the loss of 290 lives. Concerning this tragic event, 49 percent of Canadians believed that "the U.S. acted in good faith to protect an American naval ship and lives," while only 31 percent felt that the U.S. military presence in the area made such an event "inevitable." Ibid., July 21, 1988.

27. Angus Reid Group, *Nato Action in Yugoslavia*, April 11, 1999.

28. Centre for Research and Information on Canada, *Canadians Favour Close Military Ties with US*, September 9, 2002.

29. Compas Inc., *Canadians' Anti-Terrorist Mindset: Foreign Policy after the World Trade Center Calamity*, September 19, 2001.

30. Canadian Institute of Public Opinion, *The Gallup Report*, November 27, 1986.

31. Canada, Department of Foreign Affairs and International Trade, Department of National Defence, Canadian International Development Agency, *Canadian Opinions on Canadian Foreign Policy, Defence Policy and International Development Assistance (1995)*, July 10, 1998. <http://w3.acdi-cida.gc.ca/cida_ind.nsf/8949395286e4d3a58525641300568be1/bd197a6c9ddc9b54852563ff0049f7f3?OpenDocument#sec7>.

32. EKOS, *Canada–US Relations*, December 6, 2002.

33. Canadian Institute of Public Opinion, *The Gallup Report*, October 4, 1990, February 22, 1991, and June 28, 1991.

34. Compas Inc., *Axis of Evil*, March 17, 2002.

35. Ipsos-Reid, *Canadians Split on Expanding 'War on Terrorism' to Take down Iraq President Saddam Hussein*, February 22, 2002. A January 2002 poll had similarly found 52 percent in favour of an Iraq attack with only 26 percent opposed. *The Toronto Star*, September 9, 2002.

36. Canada, House of Commons, *Debates*, February 19, 2002.

37. Commons, *Debates*, February 10, 1998.

38. Commons, *Debates*, April 12, 1999.

39. Commons, *Debates*, June 19, 2002.

40. Commons, *Debates*, October 1, 2002.

41. Ibid., (Jim Karygiannis).

42. Commons, *Debates*, October 2, 2002 (Clifford Lincoln).

43. Commons, *Debates*, October 1, 2002 (John Harvard).

44. CBC News Online, Adam Segal and Erik Missio, *Canada's Position*, August 20, 2002, and April 7, 2003. <http://www.cbc.ca/news/iraq/players/canada_role.html>.

45. For example, former Prime Minister Brian Mulroney criticized the Liberal's Iraq policy as "a classic example of followership, not leadership." *The Toronto Star*, March 24, 2003.

46. EKOS, *EKOS/CBC/SCR/Toronto Star/La Press Poll*, 21 Feb. 2003; and Ipsos-Reid, *Almost Seven in Ten (67%) Disapprove of United States Taking Unilateral Military Action Against Iraq*, February 7, 2003.

47. EKOS, *Canada–US Relations*, December 6, 2002.

48. Ipsos-Reid, *Canada and the Iraq War: Two Solitudes Emerge*, April 6, 2003.

49. But Ottawa may be, at least for the moment, becalmed here too. Together, the fall of Communism and the 9/11 terror attacks appear to have crystallized a newly unipolar moment in international relations based on an overwhelming U.S. hegemony. Gone is the stability and predictability of the Cold War blocs in organizing the international order. Unipolarity does not necessarily favour the kind of "you scratch my back, I'll scratch yours" Canada–U.S. relationship characteristic of the Cold War period and depicted by Adam Chapnick as "unequal co-dependency." Chapnick traces the way in which Canada, while generally supportive of American foreign policy goals in promoting democracy and the rule of law, enjoyed historic success in persuading the U.S. to seek multilateral cover

because "international forces cloak United States military choices in a degree of moral and political credibility that is unattainable unilaterally." (See Adam Chapnick, "Collaborative Independence: Canadian–American Relations in Afghanistan," *International Journal*, Summer 2002.) In the 2003 Iraq war, Canada, flying its traditional flag of UN and Western alliance multilateralism, found itself unable to constrain an America determined to pre-empt a rogue state capable of arming terror groups with weapons of mass destruction. Even partnered with Germany, France, and Russia, Canada lacked any influence with the Americans and spent the early weeks of the war trying to decide whether it was safe to say that it wanted the U.S. to win and the Ba'athists to lose. In the more fluid post–Cold War environment, the U.S. faced little difficulty in employing its influence to create an ad hoc "coalition of the willing" to provide a measure of legitimizing "credibility." Canada's support was no longer required.

50. On this question see R. Inglehart, N. Nevitte, and M. Basanez, *The North American Trajectory* (New York: Aldine De Gruyter, 1996).

51. Ontario, Ministry of Enterprise, Opportunity and Innovation, Ontario Economic Development, *Ontario Facts: Economic Structure – International Trade*, June 2002. <http://txt.2ontario.com/facts/txt_fact04.cfm>.

52. For example, the 2003 support of the U.S. National Association of Home Builders for removal of softwood lumber duties against Canadian lumber arguing that they added $1000 U.S. to the price of a new home. National Association of Home Builders, *Home Builders Support Senate Resolution Calling for Free Trade of Canadian Lumber,* March 14, 2003. <http://www.nahb.org/news_details.aspx?newsID=326>. See also the U.S.–Canada Partnership for Growth, <http://www.partnershipforgrowth.org>. Similarly, Canadian interests ally with private American groups to influence the policy process in Canada. In the softwood lumber trade sector, see Benjamin Cashore, "An Examination of Why a Long-term Resolution to the Canada–US Softwood Lumber Dispute Eludes Policy Makers," Working Paper 98.02, Canadian Forest Service, December 1998. <http://warehouse.pfc.forestry.ca/pfc/5247.pdf>.

53. Article 2204 of NAFTA gives Canada, Mexico, and the United States a veto on the accession of new member states.

54. Compas Inc., *Most Oppose Can-Am Union Because of Different Values While Large Minority Believes U.S. Would Want Union,* January 27, 2003.

FURTHER READINGS

Bothwell, Robert. *Canada and the United States: The Politics of Partnership.* Toronto: University of Toronto Press, 1992.

Clark-Jones, Melissa. *A Staple State: Canadian Industrial Resources in Cold War.* Toronto: University of Toronto Press, 1987.

Clarkson, Stephen. *Uncle Sam and Us: Globalization, Neoconservatism, and the Canadian State.* Toronto: University of Toronto Press, 2002.

Clement, Wallace, and Glen Williams. *The New Canadian Political Economy.* Montreal: McGill-Queen's University Press, 1989.

Courchene, Thomas J. *From Heartland to North American Region States: An Interpretative Essay on the Fiscal, Social and Federal Evolution of Ontario.* University of Toronto: Centre for Public Management, 1998.

Doern, G. Bruce, and Brian Tomlin. *Faith and Fear: The Free Trade Story.* Toronto: Stoddart, 1991.

Inglehart, Ronald. F., Neil Nevitte, and Miguel Basanez. *The North American Trajectory: Growing Cultural, Economic, and Political Ties among the United States, Canada, and Mexico.* New York: Aldine De Gruyter, 1996.

Lipset, Seymour Martin. *Continental Divide: The Values and Institutions of the United States and Canada.* New York: Routledge, 1990.

Meinig, D.W. *The Shaping of America: A Geographical Perspective on 500 Years of History.* Vols. 1–3. New Haven: Yale University Press, 1986, 1993, 1998.

Thompson, John Herd, and Stephen J. Randall. *Canada and the United States: Ambivalent Allies.* 3rd ed. Montreal: McGill-Queen's University Press, 2002.

Williams, Glen. *Not For Export: The International Competitiveness of Canadian Manufacturing.* 3rd ed. Toronto: McClelland & Stewart, 1994.

CHAPTER 7

POLITICAL PARTIES: TELETUBBY POLITICS, THE THIRD WAY, AND DEMOCRATIC CHALLENGE(R)S

Alexandra Dobrowolsky

Teletubbies are cute, cuddly, fluorescent-coloured, plush-toy-like characters who converse in high-pitched inanities on a British television program for tiny tots. The phrase "Teletubby politics" depicts the "dumbing down" of politics and the ascendancy of image over substance for easy media and public consumption. The Third Way, another British import, represents Labour Prime Minister Tony Blair's quest for an alternative to the free-market neoliberalism of Thatcher and Reagan on one hand, and socialism on the other. Blair calls it a "new alliance between progress and justice," marking a route between the "new right" and the "old left."[1]

Why begin a chapter on Canadian political parties with Teletubbies and the Third Way? The answer lies in the impact of globalization. To be sure, long before the term *globalization* was conceived, Canada was under the sway of first Britain and then the United States. But globalization has deepened Canada's relations of interdependence and integration in international culture (e.g., Teletubbies), politics (e.g., parties' policy visions), economics (e.g., trade), and technology (e.g., the Internet). Cultural globalization explains the popularity of Teletubbies at home and abroad. Political globalization "refers to the intensification and expansion of political interrelations across the globe."[2]

What follows is that, on the plane of politics, there is a growing trend of policy convergence in which ideas (like the Third Way), programs, and platforms grow more alike, across countries and between political parties. In this context, there is a danger of decreased policy thinking, a reliance not only on similar slogans but parallel political directives, and, in turn, a thriving Teletubby politics. This is highly problematic because political parties are meant to be representative vehicles that link civil society with the state and engage in activities critical to a healthy democracy, including the articulation of distinctive ideas and the aggregation of diverse interests and identities.

PARTIES, GLOBALIZATION, AND CONVERGENCE

Globalization does not explain everything—we will see later in this chapter that parties remain strong, historically rooted institutions with considerable capacity to make choices. Nonetheless, globalization has made it more difficult for individual states to act independently, and it has also served to constrain political parties. With economic globalization and, for example, efforts at integration through trading arrangements like the North American Free Trade Agreement (NAFTA) or within the European Union (EU), the degree of differentiation among the programs of governments across state boundaries has diminished. This also translates into less flexibility for political parties as the ideological space between them shrinks.

CONVERGENCE, NEOLIBERALISM, AND THE THIRD WAY

In the face of globalization's universalizing imperatives, developing distinctive platforms and charting new and different political courses becomes a greater challenge. In Canada, themes of deficit, debt management, and tax breaks ran through every political party in the 1990s. Then, given the severity of budget cuts, all the parties also had to grapple with the critical state of health services and scandalous levels of poverty. Although there are marginal variations among parties, there is a startling amount of convergence, and it is important to flag this growing contemporary phenomenon.

Of course, some would argue that political parties in Canada have never been that ideologically distinguishable in the first place.[3] The lack of content epitomized in Teletubby politics and the compromises that characterize the Third Way are no great stretch for Canadian parties that have long-standing experience with brokerage politics. In Canada, parties historically have fought for the middle ground through the accommodation of many diverse interests. In their eager pursuit of electoral success, brokerage parties have shunned long-term, ideologically based commitments in favour of seeking strategic positions that would gain them the most electoral votes.[4]

On the other hand, it has also been the Canadian experience that in times of socioeconomic upheaval new parties have arisen to challenge old-style parties and their brokerage practices. In the first decades of the twentieth century, as the country urbanized and industrialized, a variety of socialist and labour parties formed, and parties spawned by the farm-based Progressive movement-party burgeoned. Similarly, the 1930s Depression gave rise to both the populist Social Credit Party and the socialist Co-operative Commonwealth Federation (CCF), a precursor to the modern New Democratic Party (NDP).

In more recent years, the political and economic turbulence of the 1980s and the early 1990s saw the establishment of the Reform Party and Bloc Québécois (BQ). However, these new challengers, unlike their forebears who contested the organizational form of disciplined parliamentary parties, have not constituted a radical departure from the conventional brokerage-style parties in either their form or their substance. Rather, we have witnessed more sameness than difference. It seems possible that the increased intersection of transnational concerns has had an impact on parties by not only influencing their policy priorities but reducing their policy options.

The sweeping socioeconomic changes of the last few decades have left their mark on political parties in Canada. The early 1980s recession shaped the dying days of the welfare state and propagated a new "neoliberal" approach characterized by market-oriented policies. The Trudeau Liberal government's Macdonald Commission planted the seeds of change and the Mulroney Conservative government cultivated them by promoting free trade, promising deficit reduction, and proposing a streamlined, less activist state. However, it was not until the Liberals returned to power under Chrétien in 1993 that the neoliberal crop was harvested.

Canada's neoliberal growth was nourished by the fact that similar policy priorities were being vigorously implemented in Britain, by Prime Ministers Thatcher and Major, and in the United States, by Presidents Reagan and Bush. Although there were somewhat different emphases in Canada, as opposed to those in Britain and the United States, there was, nevertheless, an overall consensus on the outlines of neoliberal policies. The welfare state had to be checked: there had to be cuts to the state bureaucracy and to social programs because government deficits and debts had to be controlled (see Chapter 10).

While there have been some significant and evolving departures in recent years, neoliberal imperatives continue to be present in the policies of the liberal and leftist governments that succeeded the conservative regimes of the 1980s in Canada, Britain, and the United States.[5] Both

Clinton's Democrats and even New Labour under Tony Blair have trod a fiscally conservative course and toned down their respective liberalism and socialism. In Canada, the lack of deviation was even more dramatic, as the neoliberal words of Mulroney's Conservatives became deeds under the Chrétien Liberals. While the Progressive Conservatives talked about making drastic cuts to the public service and reducing the deficit, the Liberals acted on these issues and actually advanced more rapidly toward these goals.

In the light of the devastating social repercussions of this neoliberal agenda, which has seen the gap between rich and poor dramatically widen, there has been a budding popular sense that the cuts may have gone too far. What is more, a swelling budgetary surplus, compounded by departing Prime Minister Chrétien's desire for a legacy, meant that the government would begin to spend again. However, as was the case in Britain, expenditures would be cautious, strategic, and future-oriented.[6] New spending is explained in neoliberal terms as supporting the knowledge economy and sponsoring employability efforts. Here Canada's discourse perfectly mimics Blair's Third Way–speak.[7] The only difference is that Chrétien dubs this the "Canadian way" and our "innovation strategy." [8]

CONVERGENCE AND THE PARTY SYSTEM

It could be observed that the current extent of convergence is not unlike the 1930s Depression era and the post–World War II period, when there was also a certain degree of policy consensus. During the Depression, Canadian Conservative Prime Minister Bennett went down to defeat despite his last-ditch plan to combat extreme social disparity, modelled on U.S. President Roosevelt's "New Deal." Upon Bennett's defeat, Liberal Prime Minister King borrowed from New Deal notions, from the CCF's appeal for universal social programs, and from the views of progressive state bureaucrats.[9] The latter were swayed by the ideas of British economist John Maynard Keynes. It was these and other influences that combined to style the Canadian welfare state. While it was tailored to our specific context, the welfare state in Canada was still in line with initiatives that took place elsewhere. Moreover, there was certainly a level of agreement across the parties in Canada that the federal government should become more interventionist.

One important difference between the welfare state era and the early twenty-first century is that it is now more difficult to distinguish between Canadian party platforms, despite the fact that there are many more of them.[10] Our party system, once described as a two-and-a-half party system made up of the Conservatives, Liberals, and CCF/NDP, was transformed into a true multiparty system with the electoral success of the Reform Party (founded in 1987 and, since 2000, called the Canadian Reform Conservative Alliance) and the Bloc Québécois (founded in 1990). Nevertheless, familiar neoliberal refrains echo in the rhetoric of all five of our leading political parties. In the 1990s, the Liberal Party promoted fiscal restraint, as did the Conservatives, Reform, and the BQ. The Liberals, in power for most of the 1990s, were self-satisfied in their elimination of the deficit, something the Conservatives tried and failed to do for most of the 1980s. While the Reform and PC parties were the most vocal in their calls for debt reduction and decreased taxes, even the NDP began to call for tax breaks, advocating a lowering of the GST by 1 percent and pointing to its provincial government counterparts to lend legitimacy to its claim to be a deficit buster. It is no wonder that polls taken around the 1997 election campaign indicated that citizens were not able to pinpoint which party stood for reduced taxes.[11]

By the 2000 election, the Liberals were promoting their "balanced" approach, which, in effect, meant neoliberalism with a Third Way inflection; that is, it involved paying down the debt and reducing taxes, but also "investing" for the future in health care, education, innovation, children, and the environment. Devolution and "partnerships" with the provinces along with the private and third (voluntary) sectors were also the rage. These were all catch phrases in Britain, where, for example, New Labour promoted "investment" and forged "partnerships" with national assemblies and local government as well as business and voluntary organizations.

Given its sovereigntist aspirations, it is not surprising that the BQ would be all for devolution, but what is more striking is that other elements of its 2000 election platform had a familiar neoliberal/Third Way ring to them. For instance, Bloquistes proposed $7.3 billion in tax cuts, but also promised more bang for the buck when it came to health care, increased funding for education, and social programs. Youth and sustainable development were also identified as "winning" by voting Bloc.[12] The Alliance chimed in, sounding as if it were singing a Liberal, "Canadian way" jingle, rather than a typical Reform party ditty. Although devolution also hit the right note for the Alliance, what seemed more discordant was its crooning about all Canadians having "access to quality health care regardless of their financial situation." "Quality post-secondary education and training," the Alliance intoned, "are essential to Canada's future in the knowledge based economy of the 21st century, where life long learning will be required." It pledged, "We will cooperate with the provinces…in the development of strong partnerships with organizations that have a stake in the quality of training, education and research."[13] The Conservatives tried to squeeze between the Liberals and the Alliance, while the NDP also joined the chorus on health care, but sang more of a one-note tune with its stress on homecare and pharmacare.

The 1990s were lean times for the Progressive Conservatives. From the electoral highs of 1984 and 1988, the party suffered staggering lows in 1993 and experienced only a minimal recovery in the 1997 federal election. As Brian Mulroney's appeal plummeted through the 1980s and into the 1990s, the party tried to regroup under Kim Campbell. In replacing Mulroney, Campbell became Canada's first female prime minister, but only for a whirlwind 133 days. She was still strongly associated with the Mulroney years, and this, combined with her inexperience and a certain degree of intra-party backstabbing, contributed to the party's free fall in the 1993 election. The Tories were humiliated, securing only two seats. Jean Charest held on to one of them and in time managed to regain some ground for the party in his role as Campbell's successor. In 1998, a well-seasoned Joe Clark headed the party once more, having been, at a more tender age during the late 1970s and early 1980s, PC leader for seven years and prime minister for nine months.

In the 1990s, the Tory platform contained familiar neoliberal refrains left over from the 1980s. By the start of the new millennium, however, some softening in the PCs' neoliberal stance could be found with, for instance, its proposal to establish a "Canadian Covenant" to maintain national standards on health care and postsecondary education. This mellowing, in part, could be attributed to Joe Clark, who was known as a "Red Tory," but it also reflected PC Party efforts to woo more moderate social conservatives and Alliance supporters, as well as those seeking an alternative to the Liberals. Clark attacked the Alliance for espousing too extreme an ideological viewpoint that would not appeal to all Canadians and thus tried to re-assert the PC's brokerage party claim.[14] As a result, the Conservatives would sound increasingly like the Liberals. This was apparent in the 2000 election, when the PC Party's analysis of the country's troubles centred on "healthcare, education, particularly the brain drain; rising taxes: [and] safe communities."[15] Thus, the Tories were not particularly distinguishable from their major opponents on either the right or left.

The ease and speed with which the Grits shifted ideological gears in their 1990s neoliberal drive was breathtaking. After all, this was the party that had forged Canada's Keynesian consensus in the first place, with

Mackenzie King's state interventionism being expanded and refined under Pearson and Trudeau. Granted, the party also displayed conservative orientations in the St. Laurent years and some cautious tendencies in the Trudeau era, but still, the Liberals were very much associated with the welfare state. This was the case even though much of their social reform legislation was appropriated from CCF/NDP platforms. From the party's centralist thrust in the 1970s and early 1980s to the downsizing, devolution, and dismantling of social programs that became the norm in the 1990s, the Liberal Party took a sharp turn to the right.

The Liberals of the 1990s, led by Jean Chrétien, who was meant to be the compromise candidate between welfare-oriented Liberals (such as Sheila Copps) and those with a pro-business slant (like Paul Martin),[16] promoted bigger and grander international trade deals, often with countries with suspect human rights records. Liberal Finance Minister Paul Martin tackled the deficit and debt with abandon, tearing asunder Canada's social safety net in the process. In short, a once middle-ground party leapt nimbly onto the neoliberal bandwagon. When this picked up too much speed, and when a substantial budgetary surplus accrued, however, more of a Third Way path was taken. The prime minister called this a balanced approach that entailed "allocating half our surpluses to tax and debt reduction, and the other half to social and economic investments."[17]

The 2003 federal budget of Paul Martin's successor as Finance minister, John Manley, epitomized this "balance." While there was notable spending, $25 billion, Finance officials were careful to point out that expenditures did not rise dramatically "when measured against the size of the economy—a key benchmark of affordability."[18] Although the budget was couched as an "investment," there was new support for social policy spending on health care, education, and children (in particular, the child benefit and childcare). In future, with business Liberal Martin as the heir apparent to Chrétien as prime minister, we are likely to see this "balance" weighted more toward neoliberal fiscal priorities than social policy "investments."

At first blush, it would seem that the Reform/Alliance Party counters this convergence argument most convincingly, since it has been represented as a new and even "postmodern" force in the Canadian party system that rejects the "old" ideologies and brokerage political parties.[19] However, since its establishment in 1987, the Reform Party has demonstrated many sides, from initially being the Party of the West, to positioning itself as the Party of the Hinterland, while at the same time adeptly portraying itself as both the Party of the Right and the Party of the People.[20] In these ways, it scooped up both Conservative and NDP defectors. Its degree of "difference," postmodern or otherwise, is questionable given that its initial expression of Western protest and its populism harkened back to earlier Western-based movements and parties like the Social Credit. Furthermore, the Reform Party's platform did little to detract from, but rather has reinforced, prevailing neoliberal ideals. Although it promoted itself as an alternative to the old-style parties, the policies it pursued merely buttressed dominant socioeconomic and political priorities.[21]

As Reform morphed into the Alliance, it again softened its approach and image. This has been described as the "metamorphosis of a Western, grassroots, mass-based extraparliamentary party into the shell of a more traditional brokerage party."[22] In typical brokerage party fashion, the greater the Reform/Alliance's potential for electoral success, the more its "alternative" and controversial positions were watered down. While Reform was depicted by its supporters as representing "English-speaking Canada" and by its critics as being anti-Quebec (it denounced official bilingualism and fought against any distinct status for Quebec), the new Alliance party accepted bilingualism and its first leader, Stockwell Day, worked on improving his French. Reform decried multiculturalism, but Alliance began actively recruiting "visible minority" candidates. Lastly, in its desperate press for electoral success, the Alliance left many of Reform's populist policies behind. The party's penchant for petitioning and referenda was questioned when the comedy show *This Hour Has 22 Minutes* initiated a wildly popular e-mail campaign to gather the requisite support to have Stockwell Day's name changed to Doris! According to Faron Ellis, the Alliance's policies in 2000, overall, appeared "anemic" compared with its "harder edged" platforms of 1993 and 1997.[23] Like a classic brokerage party, the Alliance focused on its leader and his image. This backfired, for Stockwell Day's promised strengths became less apparent as his publicity stunts grew more outrageous, including a painfully inappropriate photo of the leader in a wet suit on a Jet Ski.

By succumbing to various brokerage tendencies, and behaving antithetically to Reform's raison d'être, the Alliance appeared to be "little more than a collection of factions loosely bound together by a party organization where the parliamentary caucus, not the membership base, [was] the most cohesive element and the driving force."[24] Its claim to distinctiveness dissipated as many Reform policy preferences were take up by the Liberals. For instance, given substantial Liberal backtracking on issues such as multiculturalism, immigration, and refugee policy, some have observed that the Liberals tried to "out-reform" the Reform Party.[25] After Stockwell Day's less-than-stellar 2000 election performance, he stepped down; but even with a new leader, Stephen Harper, the party appears to be at a standstill. The Alliance is caught between a neoliberal/neoconservative rock and a brokerage party hard place. With the Reform–Alliance transition, the party appears even more like all the rest.

Policy convergence has affected the left as well. From the CCF's Regina Manifesto (1933), which announced it would work to eradicate capitalism, by way of the tamer Winnipeg Declaration that promoted greater social equality and led to the formation of the NDP in 1961, through more recent electoral appeals to "ordinary" and "average" Canadians, the party has certainly come a long way. There is also no denying that it has diluted many of its leftist principles. Once considered the most ideological and programmatically innovative contributor to our party system, as compared with the pragmatic policy flip-flops demonstrated by the Liberals and Conservatives, many would now question this distinction. Some would even go so far as to say that the NDP currently brokers and compromises its principles with the best of them.[26] While this is most explicit at the provincial level, where the NDP actually wins elections (e.g., Manitoba's NDP marketed itself as "Today's NDP," i.e., the new NDP not the old, like New Labour not old Labour), such tendencies are also evident at the federal level.

A study of activists at political party conventions discovered that the differences between activists in the NDP and those in the Liberal Party are greater than the differences between the Liberal and Conservative activists on a range of issues. It concluded that the NDP is clearly on the ideological left, the Liberals are in the centre, and the Progressive Conservatives are on the right.[27] However, this assessment is based on surveys of the attitudes of delegates at party conventions, not those of decision makers at the party core. Rank-and-file party activists may have more ideologically based positions than the parliamentary leadership, but these ideas do not necessarily filter up to the party's leadership cadre.

Moreover, if ideological concerns of the party grassroots do become adopted within a policy platform when the party is in opposition, these positions are often bypassed if it forms a government. Since the NDP has never led a federal government, we do not know how much policy distinctiveness would actually occur were it in power. We do know that when the NDP moved closer to this goal, it tended to backtrack. For instance, when Ed Broadbent received higher approval ratings before the 1988 election than either the Conservative Prime Minister Mulroney or the Liberal Opposition Leader John Turner, the NDP came up with its most innocuous, middle-of-the-road platform ever. Not only did it eschew a class-based rallying cry, something that the NDP has always avoided, but it even moved away from championing substantive social equality with a wishy-washy appeal to "fairness" for "average Canadians and their fami-lies." No wonder the NDP was accused of succumbing to "contentless pop-ulism" and "flirt[ing]" with the brokerage model."[28]

Although the NDP reached a peak in popularity in the 1988 election, winning 43 seats, Broadbent stepped down with the disappointment of not winning the election. Support for the NDP tumbled with his successor, Audrey McLaughlin, the first woman to lead a federal party in Canada. In fact, the 1993 election went down as a particularly bad one for women, as both women "firsts," Campbell and McLaughlin, led their parties into the political wilderness with the NDP winning only nine parliamentary seats.

After McLaughlin, Alexa McDonough tried to rebuild the party. Her popularity in the Maritimes helped to bring unexpected gains, 21 seats, in the June 1997 election. Eight of these NDP seats were in Atlantic Canada, with an unprecedented six seats from Nova Scotia and two seats from New Brunswick. This reflected approval in the East for the NDP critique of the Chrétien government's handling of unemployment and its dwindling financial commitment to the provinces. While the NDP continued to act as a critical conscience in this respect, it also became a party of balanced budgets and tax cuts. Here provincial NDP governments' conduct had an impact. For instance, the Saskatchewan NDP government engaged in severe spending cuts to balance the budget and make peace with business. Then, to hold on to power, it resorted to forming a coalition with the provincial Liberal Party.

In its pursuit of electoral gains, the federal NDP looked not only to the provinces but to the international successes of social democratic parties in Europe, and British Labour in particular. Thus, the Third Way became a serious consideration. McDonough caused a swirl of controversy with her decision to court business and her talk of creating new partnerships. Whereas unions used to be seen as a conservative influence on the party, the Canadian Labour Congress (CLC) took on the role of the radical critic voicing opposition to this new option, and reproachfully commented that with the Liberals in power and Reform/Alliance in opposition, the country did not need more politicians to represent the interests of business!

While the NDP still characterizes itself as a party of social democ-racy, especially in its support for an active role for the state and quality social programs, the tension between such social democratic passions and more electorally opportunistic Third Way prospects is apparent. For example, in the party's January 2003 leadership race, the long-serving NDP MP and leadership hopeful Lorne Nystrom represented the latter, advocating fiscal responsibility and encouraging the party to stake out the middle of the political spectrum. Even the eventual winner, Jack Layton, who represented a more critical, urban, pro-environment left (and thus obtained the backing of alternative forces associated with the New Politics Initiative), argued that it was possible to be on the left and be progressive, as well as be pragmatic and pursue balanced budgets.[29]

The Bloc Québécois also has demonstrated slightly left-of-centre policy preferences and advocates an activist role for the state—but for Quebec, not the federal government. In this way, the BQ underscores the fact that it is truly different from all the rest. Somewhat paradoxically then, given that on the face of it, Reform/Alliance, the NDP, and the BQ would appear to be the most dissimilar, all three have been jostling for the same "alternative party" title meant to distance them from the emblematic brokerage Liberal and Conservative parties.

The BQ is exceptional in that its main goal is to make Quebec a sovereign country within a Canada–Quebec union.[30] Before achieving this goal, however, the party has worked to ensure that Quebec has the powers it needs to decide its own social, political, and cultural priorities. Despite some left-leaning tendencies, because the party is a nationalist amalgam of Conservatives, Liberals, and Parti Québécois supporters, it has not always been easy to pinpoint the BQ's policies as either categorically on the left or on the right. Underlining its social democratic affinities, the BQ, like the NDP, has pushed for job creation and other initiatives that would improve citizens' quality of life, especially for those who experience economic hardship. Paradoxically, the BQ also falls into the neoliberal camp in calling for cutbacks in public spending by billions of dollars and for tax reduction.[31] In the run-up to the 2000 election, two Bloc MPs even jumped ship to run for the Alliance in Quebec. These ideological tensions are to be expected from a party that was first led by a former member of Mulroney's Conservative cabinet, Lucien Bouchard, and is now headed by a past Communist Workers' Party (Marxist-Leninist) activist, Gilles Duceppe. Still, its consensus lies in its basic objective: sovereignty. Notably, however, this is now portrayed as consisting of a "new partnership (*partenariat*) between Quebec and its neighbours."[32] In 2001, the party marked a muted tenth anniversary, for its longevity merely underscores the Bloc's failure to realize its goal. It is meant to pull out of, not prop up, federal politics. Then the Parti Québécois government's defeat in the spring of 2003 made the BQ's existence even harder, given the two sovereigntist parties' symbiotic relationship. Consequently, the options presented by the Bloc are becoming more limited and its combination of tax cuts and strategic social spending and partnerships is now familiar Third Way fare.

Historically, policy innovation has come from parties beyond the two traditional brokerage powerhouses. The Liberals and Conservatives, in fact, both raided policy ideas from the Progressives and from the CCF/NDP. More recently, the Liberals have taken on board Reform initiatives. But now, a more subdued, less reactionary Alliance Party mostly mirrors a brokering centre-right consensus. It is also increasingly difficult to distinguish the Alliance from the Liberal or the Conservative Party. While both the BQ and NDP do consider other policy options and certainly have demonstrated social democratic inclinations, neither has achieved electoral success on the federal level, nor is this likely to occur. The BQ has benefited from Canada's first-past-the-post electoral system in which regionally concentrated party votes are rewarded. Still, the BQ's seats are confined to Quebec alone, and it has no interest in working as a national, as opposed to a nationalist, party. Conversely, the NDP is disadvantaged by an electoral system that penalizes parties with weak, dispersed support. But even if the NDP did somehow win big, radical departures seem doubtful given its bow to fiscal responsibility at the provincial level and its flirtation with the Third Way and greater pragmatism at the federal level.

To reiterate, policy convergence has translated into less room for political alternatives and political choice. Although Canada has more parties, we are not witnessing an increase in policy differentiation. Similar platforms across states, as well as across parties, have been highlighted. While to some extent this has always taken place in Canada, our current socioeconomic context has exacerbated and expedited these tendencies. The problem is that people are then constrained to choose from among few options, and the political conversation becomes quite closed. It thus becomes more difficult to open up the debate to new ideas and approaches.

PARTIES: DECLINING OR DISINTERESTED?

Having made the case that globalization and the socioeconomic environment exert influence on political parties, with a particular effect on policy convergence, we must not overstate it. Indeed, it has become too easy to invoke these factors as scapegoats or excuses for parties not incorporating different dimensions or forging ahead in new directions. Even in an era of global interdependence, driven by markets and new technologies, governments can make choices. The same can be said for political parties.

Obviously, distinctive policy delivery becomes more difficult, but not impossible. For example, there has been a role for strong leaders guiding parties onto new ground, and recently, leaders have become, if anything, even more dominant.[33] In Britain, Thatcher's neoliberal/neoconservative mandate altered the Conservative Party, and Blair consolidated New Labour and its Third Way approach. In Canada, through the governing Liberal Party, Trudeau pushed to formalize his Canadian nationalist liberal ideals in patriating the Constitution and establishing a Charter of Rights and Freedoms. Mulroney's embrace of neoliberalism constituted a deliberate reversal for the Conservatives. The party once opposed to liberal individualism and free markets became their champion. Again, broader structural influences are implicated, and our current global context facilitates this, but party leaders and parties as institutions are not debilitated. They can take major or minor parts in these interrelated socioeconomic and political dramas, just as they can be more or less directive.

Parties, as with all political institutions, have relative strengths and weaknesses. It could be argued that the policy convergence outlined above merely provides an indication of parties' waning powers and even their decreasing political relevance. In a classic article, John Meisel listed a number of rationalizations for what he described as the "party decline" phenomenon in Canada.[34] Some factors, such as the rise of the bureaucratic state, are no longer as compelling as they were when the piece was first written in the 1980s, given the "downsizing" of the public sector in the 1990s. Nonetheless, the inordinate powers of central agencies such as the Prime Ministers' Office (PMO) continue to be of concern.[35] Meisel's discussion of the effects of corporatism on party decline also may appear to be less relevant, due to the fluctuating strength of unions in Canada and abroad. But other contentions still hold sway. In light of the above, Meisel's identification of the heightened significance of economic interests is pivotal. In addition, he directs our attention to the centrality of federal–provincial diplomacy, the proliferation of interest groups, and the rise of media technologies. All of these matters continue to have implications for political parties' strengths and/or weaknesses.

PARTIES AND CONTEMPORARY FEDERAL–PROVINCIAL DIPLOMACY

The current practices of federal–provincial diplomacy are a serious concern. Federal–provincial diplomacy, or executive federalism, describes processes that arise from Canada's unique political amalgam of a highly executive-controlled Parliament combined with a federal system. To accommodate both aspects, the prime minister, the premiers, and their key staff meet to hammer out federal–provincial arrangements and even constitutional agreements. These negotiations bypass partisan politics and, as well, discourage any meaningful citizen involvement. This is the theory, although in practice the situation is often more complicated.

Now the whole justification for brokerage parties in Canada is that they are meant to aggregate the diverse cleavages in our complex society and thereby operate as instruments of national integration. Along with this, parties are supposed to act as vehicles that link citizen with state. They are meant to accommodate different political discourses, as well as to introduce policies that reflect these debates and deliberations. Canada's seemingly perpetual state of constitutional crisis attests to the fact that parties are not performing in these areas. The elitist side of the executive federalist spectrum was highlighted in the Meech Lake saga, whereas the Charlottetown round of constitutional struggle contained greater opportunities for citizen participation via task forces, committees, commissions, conferences, and ultimately a referendum on the agreement. In both instances, on the surface at least, there was near all-party consensus. It is true that there were battles behind the scenes, but despite their reservations, in the end, all the traditional national federal parties supported both the 1987 Meech Lake and 1992 Charlottetown Accords. The only exceptions were Reform in 1987 and Reform and the Bloc in 1992.

It was left to other collective political actors—such as elements of the women's movement, aboriginal organizations, and groups based on race, ethnicity, ability, and sexual orientation—to voice concerns, provide critique, and demand redress or revisions, not the political parties. In fact, it was primarily these social movements that delegitimized the executive federalist ways and means of Meech Lake and worked to open up the process in Charlottetown, adding more actors and issues to the mix.[36] Thus, many of these groups engaged in alliance building, aggregated diverse interests and identities, and provided substantial policy thinking—that is, exactly the activities that were sorely lacking on the part of the parties. The social movements, not the parties, were the innovators.[37]

Largely due to the lack of creativity on the part of political parties, and also as a reaction against the gains made by other collective actors, more inclusive constitutional reform projects have taken a back seat of late. State officials have determined that it is too difficult or too ambitious to try to hear from many people and include numerous issues when it comes to our constitutional future. Instead, statements of so-called good will, such as the Calgary Declaration, or issue-specific negotiations, including devolving job training to the provinces, are arrived at through closed consultations with limited numbers. This is not just incremental reformism; it is constitutional change by stealth. The fact that constitutional adjustments are at stake is denied, and thus executive federalist processes proceed with impunity. Nonetheless, the issues involved, as with the 1999 Social Union Framework Agreement (SUFA) regarding intergovernmental cooperation on social policy, for example, have tremendous constitutional implications. It is precisely the concerns that are now up for discussion in executive federalist forums that collective actors were so worried about in the larger constitutional packages of Meech and Charlottetown. Both parties *and* social movements have an even smaller role to play in this context, despite the language of "partnerships" contained in federal–provincial agreements like SUFA.[38]

According to the party decline thesis, other collective actors, especially interest groups, are often viewed as party competitors. Meisel wrote that the influence of interest groups with resources and lobbying capacities had grown. While these groups have clout within their specific areas or sectors of activity, parties that aggregate the "general" interest receive scant attention. However, parties have failed to articulate this "general" interest, and other collective actors, promoting many interests and identities, have been compelled to step into the breach. This will be considered at length below. For now, it must be acknowledged that while the proliferation of interest groups and the presence of diverse social movements are an issue for political parties, it is not because they have the potential to wipe out parties but because they have challenged them. Parties remain instruments of public participation, although interest groups and social movements raise justifiable questions about their effectiveness and cast aspersions on their legitimacy in our current socioeconomic and political conjuncture. Put simply, interest groups and social movements highlight the parties' democratic flaws and imperfections.

Certainly there are some tasks that parties execute more or less effectively. In countering Meisel's decline-of-party thesis, Ron Landes writes, "As organizations the parties are, on the whole, organizationally sound, financially solvent and pragmatically vibrant elements of the Canadian pattern of representative democracy."[39] Parties have grown in sophistication. As electoral machines, they continue to structure the vote, mobilize the citizenry, especially at election time, as well as recruit leaders and organize government. Meisel acknowledges these realities and, in turn, has modified his arguments of late, admitting that parties are not in decline, but, rather, have a series of "dysfunctions."[40] Others concur that parties may not necessarily be in decline but have certainly been "transformed."[41] However, there is little disagreement with the fact that parties' faculty for policy thinking, their capability to connect citizen with state, and their integration of various interests and identities are in disrepute. As a result, the well-being of representative democracy in Canada is at risk. A lot depends on how parties deal with these contemporary circumstances and whether the parties really want to address their own defects.

PARTIES AND THE NEW ERA OF INFORMATION AND COMMUNICATION TECHNOLOGY

The rise of multiple forms of media, especially television, and the growth of polling and new information and communication technologies have also had an impact on party behaviour. While some observers recount how these technological advances have accentuated party weaknesses, others consider these developments to be indications of party strength.[42] As a result of polling and the new technologies, parties are not withering away, but they have grown in sophistication and are flourishing. Polling, for instance, can establish greater contact between parties and citizens and encourage a more active citizenship. Yet, as the lessons of Britain's New Labour suggest, such mechanisms can also be a means of consolidating the power of the leader and circumventing the party channels thereby creating a "partyless democracy."[43]

The growth of glitzy, expensive campaigns and the reliance on fancy polling and marketing techniques are also a cause for concern because this slick professionalism and manipulation of new technologies can contribute to even greater emphasis on image and leadership. Given that parties rely on media, especially television, the image of the leader can be more important than his or her party's principles. More than ever before, parties have on board a whole crew of professionals: speech writers, media experts, groomers, spin doctors, pollsters, and now even computer systems specialists. The very real danger here is a surge of Teletubby politics. Because of this dependence on assorted media and technology consultants, politicians more easily slip into hyperbole, catch phrases, and simplified messages. With this emphasis on "sound bites," how can citizens learn about policy positions? The media and new technologies tend to reinforce the pragmatic, opportunistic side of parties as electoral machines, as opposed to their programmatic, principled, and educative dimensions.

More optimistically, the media and the new information and communication technologies can be harnessed to strengthen parties and enhance their democratic capacities. The Internet, for example, has the potential to provide greater access to the parties. Citizens can avail themselves of the detailed party policy positions lacking in image-driven television portrayals. Realistically, these new technologies have incredible implications with respect to both time as well as space, and there are positive and negative sides to both. The speed of communications has accelerated phenomenally. This means that citizens can be provided with all kinds of timely, up-to-the-minute information on political parties. The flip side is that people may be bombarded with empty rhetoric, misinformation, or unreliable data.

Furthermore, new technologies can both contract and expand political space. They can contract space in that political connections can be made locally and globally with the click of a mouse. This has the potential to create new forums for political interaction. But the quality of this political space is up for discussion, as are questions of access. Does the individualized focus detract from community involvement and collective action? Who has access to the computers and the computer skills? What about the nature of the information—does it just constitute party propaganda? And where do the materials come from—the parliamentary party or the extra-parliamentary party, from party headquarters or constituency offices, from the top or the bottom? The risk here is that party organizations can become more centralized and party power brokers can become further distanced from the citizenry.

Parties have powers, and they have options as to how they can use them. With respect to the Internet, parties can manipulate websites or feign an interest in feedback and then proceed to ignore it. Data can be gathered in ways and for uses reminiscent of "Big Brother" rather than out of a desire for participatory democracy.[44] Nevertheless, instead of reflecting, shaping, or, worse, distorting political realities from above, political actors and policy dynamics can be re-positioned through information and communication technologies. Parties can work to decentralize, to provide spaces to receive input from below, and to actually vocalize and act on people's concerns. They can use new technologies to enhance their performance of the articulation and aggregation functions and to initiate consultative projects that engage in substantive debates. There can be moves to develop a "'wired democracy' ... [by] using television, the video, the telephone and the personal computer, the 'electronic town hall' can be created " with meetings between parties and the public, where people and ideas interact.[45] Parties can use these tools to educate and inform, and to become educated and informed. This, in turn, could contribute to more long-term policy consideration. Citizens could use these technologies to ensure that parties are held accountable for their actions and committed to their projects. Admittedly, the new technologies are not a panacea. The citizenry must have the resources to learn the skills and to access facilities. Concomitantly, parties have to be advocates for these innovative possibilities for collective interaction. This is a big catch: Parties have to want to make these progressive changes. Parties need to have the desire to democratize and reform themselves.

PARTY POWERS: PROMISES OR PITFALLS?

In 1991, the report of the Royal Commission on Electoral Reform and Party Financing (RCERPF), or the Lortie Commission, provided a detailed account of how Canadian political parties had been transformed, outlining their failings and offering concrete, workable suggestions as to how the parties could address them. However, the Lortie Commission's report fell between two stools. It was ignored by those who wished to expand democracy for not being transformative enough and it was seen as too radical for the political parties, which considered the Commission's findings threatening.[46] In delegitimizing other political actors beyond parties, as will be discussed below, clearly the Commission made critical errors. While it can also be argued that its scope could have been widened (to consider proportional representation, for example) and that some of its suggestions for reform were flawed, its recommendations still merited careful attention by the parties. Unfortunately, many were ignored and even overridden.

An early, direct response to all this research was Bill C-114, which followed the release of the RCERPF report.[47] The bill received all-party support, which is not surprising because it dealt with only a few of the smaller issues raised in the report. The legislation avoided the larger problems, such as representational reform, and made minor changes, such as extending the franchise to certain groups. It also banned the publication of polls just before election day and called for some weak restrictions on third-party spending. These reforms were a halfhearted response to RCERPF recommendations for more fair, just, and equitable electoral procedures. What is worse, some of its provisions actually worked against the spirit of Lortie, by making it more difficult for smaller and newer political parties. For instance, candidates would now have to submit a $1000 (up from $200) deposit, of which only half would be returned if the candidate won less than 15 percent of the vote in his or her constituency. Furthermore, it deemed that if a registered party failed to nominate 50 candidates during an election campaign, its assets would be liquidated. This had a devastating effect on the Communist Party of Canada (CPC) in the 1993 election, because it only ran eight candidates and was subsequently de-registered.

As the parties drag their heels on electoral reform, increasingly the courts are making strides in this area. From the banning of the publication of opinion polls just before an election to limits on third-party spending, various electoral issues are being tested against the Charter of Rights and Freedoms. In 2002, the Supreme Court heard the *Figueroa* case that argued on behalf of the leader of the CPC that Bill C-114's 50-candidate threshold infringes the Charter rights of small parties. Also in 2002, the Supreme Court struck down the law that barred some but not all prisoners from voting in federal elections. Currently, the highest court's final decision on third-party spending is pending.

This is not to say that change by and to the parties is impossible. Almost 10 years after Lortie, a new Elections Act, Bill C-2, came into effect, and tempered some of the provisions of Bill C-114. In 2003, the Liberals' Bill C-24, *An Act to Amend the Canada Elections Act and the Income Tax Act (political financing)*, gained considerable notoriety, exposing deep rifts in the governing party. Its controversial provisions included banning corporations and unions from contributing to parties, and capping their donations to individual politicians. Advocates hoped that this would not only limit business and union donations but also their influence. Many women applauded other aspects of the bill, such as the spending limits on nomination campaigns, an area identified as a major deterrent to more women seeking nominations. Critics have pointed out that the prime minister pushed through this legislation with little party consultation. Cynics note the hypocrisy involved: after 40 years of free-wheeling fundraising, Chrétien was making life more difficult for his successors. Predictably, the Alliance underscored that public monies will have to cover the shortfall and taxpayers will pay the tab here. The NDP acknowledged that the legislation will have a major impact on its relationship with organized labour.

The transformation of the leadership selection process is another example of the parties reforming themselves. Here efforts have been made to use new techniques to implement more direct democracy. Previously, through party conventions, selections were made in questionable circumstances often within strategically packed gatherings with dubious representational emphases. Increasingly, parties are changing their leadership contests to try to open up the process to more party activists. Clearly there are risks involved with these "neo-conventions," and it is fair to say that such moves toward direct democracy provide a double-edged sword.[48] Still, the shift does demonstrate that parties can choose to make changes to try to reform themselves.

All in all, while parties are not likely to fall off the political scale, this is not to say that they are in top shape. To the contrary, substantial concerns arise when one evaluates political parties, especially on issues of long-term policy planning and their participatory potential. At the same time, parties clearly have adapted to the new environment and have demonstrated a capacity for change. The question is whether they choose to use their powers in reformative ways or remain indifferent to their representational and democratic shortfalls. The parties are able, but are they willing?

As a caution, this argument should not be pushed to an extreme where parties are seen as omnipotent. Parties respond to a changing socioeconomic environment and to ideas that are prevalent at particular moments. They may work to shape discourses and have the power to modify their actions, but there are also limits placed on these efforts. For example, many of the Lortie Commission's recommendations required regulations and expenditures—for example, rewarding parties for redressing representational disparities through reimbursements or creating institutions to enhance parties' policy thinking. This necessitates state funding and involves the collection of more revenues. Given the recent consensus with respect to decreasing, not increasing, taxes, or the Alliance's opposition to Bill C-24 reforming party financing, for example, more public funding for such initiatives seems doubtful. As the first part of this chapter attests, parties are influenced by overarching structural considerations like the ascendancy of neoliberalism in relation to globalization.

Additionally, parties are challenged by mobilization from below, and this is the thrust of the last part of this chapter. In accounts that stress the leading role of parties in defining the political agenda, there is often not enough credit given to other political actors in and beyond the parties.[49] Parties have been pushed and prodded by various collective identities, and while progress has been slow and often erratic, changes have occurred. Because various forms of identity politics and ideas that stem from social movements have prevailed upon political parties in the past and in the present, they must also be examined.

PARTIES AND THE INFLUENCE OF IDEAS AND IDENTITY POLITICS

Beyond the preeminence of neoliberalism over the last two decades and now the Third Way, other forceful ideas have left their impression on Canadian political parties. While some ideas derive from key individuals— Keynesian influence on the welfare state, for example—others originate in social movements. This section examines the relations among ideas, movements, and political parties. Here it will be stressed that, contrary to popular portrayal, social movements and identity politics are not new phenomena plaguing political parties. Rather, they have rich histories and intricate relationships with parties. Most importantly, it is argued that these alternative representational forms provide a boost in democratic participation rather than the opposite. Social Gospel ideas, rooted in a religious movement that formed as early as the 1880s, are revealing in these respects.

A response to the upheavals created by industrialization and urbanization, Social Gospel went beyond a commitment to Christian principles and practices to promote social justice causes that challenged the status quo. Movement followers not only preached and set up missions to raise awareness of the plight of the poor, they also worked for a collective moral, social, and economic system, one in which workers had the right to decent wages and working conditions. In fact, it has been argued that Social Gospel was the "single most important factor in the growth of democratic socialism in Canada."[50]

Social Gospel was committed to maintaining better relations between the classes; and in not prioritizing class over gender, it had more room for women in its ranks than did the materialist socialists.[51] The movement became influential in the first decades of the twentieth century and had a major effect on political parties, especially the CCF/NDP. Central figures in the party were adherents of the Social Gospel, such as J.S. Woodsworth, the CCF's first leader, and Tommy Douglas, the first CCF premier of Saskatchewan and then the first national leader of the NDP. This movement and its ideas helped to shape the early CCF/NDP's commitment to egalitarianism, its critique of privilege, and its work to respond to the ravages of industrial capitalism in Canada.

The complex and shifting relations that develop between party leaders, party members, and their respective movement support bases mean that ideas can be channelled in different directions. This is quite apparent if one considers the wide spectrum of both populist and nationalist ideas and their disparate uses. In the 1930s, right-wing populism fermented in the Bible study groups that formed the basis of the Social Credit Party in Alberta. Under the tutelage of William "Bible Bill" Aberhart, and drawing on the ideas of Major C.H. Douglas, the party proceeded to criticize the centrally based financial interests that controlled the banking system. In contrast, the CCF's left-wing populism, born out of farmers' and labour movements, contained a critique of capitalism and had affinities with class-based Marxism.

Contestation among party leaders, members, and movements has helped shape Canadian democracy. In the first decades of the twentieth century the Progressive movement-party advocated direct delegate democracy, whereas in the 1930s and 1940s, Social Credit in Alberta and the populist and nationalist Union Nationale (UN) in Quebec displayed some fundamentally anti-democratic tendencies. Later, unlike the UN, the populist and nationalist Parti Québécois, especially in its early phases, promoted a social democratic vision. In the 1990s, the PQ entertained notions of difference, whereas the inverse is apparent with the nationalism and populism of other Canadian political parties. The Reform Party, for example, fashioned populist appeals that advocated assimilation. Reform/Alliance calls for sameness across the board: equal treatment for all provinces and equal treatment of all citizens, undifferentiated by gender, race, ethnicity, sexual orientation, and so on.

Ideas and the nature of collective actors that bring them forward can change over time. Consider the many forms of nationalism that have spurred Quebec parties. Whereas the nationalism of the UN took on a very conservative, retrogressive hue, there were marked changes in the nationalism of parties like the Rassemblement pour l'indépendence nationale (RIN) and the PQ of the 1960s. Moreover, the nationalism of the later PQ changed substantially, moving toward an increasingly economic orientation and affirming greater recognition of other identities beyond Quebec nationalist ones—those of women, gays and lesbians, ethnic and racial minorities, and aboriginal people. In each instance, as the composition of the collective actors that reinforced the party changed, so too did the party's nationalist rhetoric. The UN was bolstered by devotees of the Catholic Church, whereas the PQ was supported by a "new middle class" and then, increasingly, by elements of "Quebec Inc.," the francophone business elite, counterbalanced by an array of social movement activists.

Ideas championed by movements can also be appropriated by parties and be used in ways that are unanticipated or unintended, with contradictory results. For instance, while the women's movement broke ground in promoting equality rights, now the Reform/Alliance Party uses the movement's equality discourse to work against feminism and affirmative action of all kinds. While these types of reversals are always a danger, there is no denying that in generating these ideas and often raising levels of awareness to them, social movements have a bearing on political parties in Canada.

PARTIES AND IDENTITY POLITICS

Identity politics are not a new phenomenon for Canadian political parties. Since their inception, political parties in this country have had to deal with multiple dimensions of identity, including territorial and non-territorial identity claims and their various combinations and permutations. What is more, the parties' success in doing so has been in question almost from the start. The feat of creating two parties, the Conservatives and Liberals, and achieving a fully functioning two-party system in the 1800s, was achieved through the accommodation of territorial, ethnic, linguistic, and religious identities from Canada East/Quebec and Canada West/Ontario. After Confederation, it was not long before the alliances formed within the Conservative and Liberal parties became unhinged. Therefore, in the first decades of the twentieth century, regional, rural, class, and even gender-based unrest contributed to the rise of a series of so-called third parties.

Initially, the West's complicated amalgam of territorial and non-territorial identities, ranging from those based on region to farmers' and workers' identities, sustained new partisan contenders that constituted a threat to the Liberals and Conservatives. However, these challengers to the leading parties were not restricted to the West. For example, Social Credit not only prospered in Alberta and British Columbia, provincially, but also in Quebec on the federal level. While Atlantic Canada is not notorious for its "third parties," examples can be cited at the provincial level, such as the United Newfoundland Party. In New Brunswick, the Parti Acadien and the Confederation of Regions Party (CoR) provide a study in contrasts, for the former promoted Acadian interests and identities in the early 1970s, whereas the latter came to prominence in the early 1990s on a plat-form based on a reaction against official bilingualism and linguistic equality. In addition, the recent NDP breakthrough in the Maritimes can also be viewed as a form of regional protest. More generally, the fact that we continue to have "regional" parties even at the federal level, like the Reform/Alliance Party or the BQ, attests to the fact that the Liberals and Conservatives still have difficulty brokering territorially based identities.

Collective actors, and those that are not necessarily territorially identified, have affected party politics in the past and continue to do so. The women's movement is a prime example, for its relationships with political parties have been sustained, complex, and challenging. Women have worked both outside and inside the parties to bring about change. As a reaction to women's successful campaign to secure the vote at the start of the twentieth century, the Liberals and Conservatives set up separate women's auxiliaries. Conservative clubs for women were founded in the big cities by the 1920s, and the Women's Liberal Federation was established in 1928. Under the pretence of easing women into conventional politics, these auxiliaries essentially prevented women's participation in the parties' main-stream. Women tended not to have meaningful and/or powerful positions in political parties; rather, they were considered to be the "perennial menials." As a result, mobilization continued outside of the parties. Women's activism went beyond the so-called first wave of the women's movement and created the groundswell of contemporary feminism.

Consequently, there is now much more awareness of the gendered nature of political parties and a recognition of their structured inequalities. Women in and outside the parties ensured that auxiliaries were disbanded, and, in their stead, groups geared toward recruiting women and promoting them within the party ranks were created. The NDP established its Participation of Women Committee (POW) in 1969; from the 1960s onward, the Liberal Party formed a series of federations, the latest being the National Women's Liberal Commission; and in the early 1980s, the Conservatives created a National Progressive Conservative Women's Federation and a Women's Bureau at party headquarters. These initiatives inside the parties were bolstered by efforts on the outside as women formed groups such as Women for Political Action (WPA) and the Committee for 94 with the express intent of increasing women's numbers in conventional politics.[52] Throughout, the women's movement and feminist activists continued to work on changing broader discourses and practices in both partisan and nonpartisan political domains.

In spite of the energy expended by women, the parties have been slow to redress their numerical imbalances. The Reform/Alliance has taken the most unabashed anti-affirmative-action stance. It argues that measures to address underrepresentation constitute special treatment and create inequalities by treating people differently; thus, "gender and other ascriptive characteristics should not be acknowledged by party or public policy."[53] By advocating equal treatment for unequals, the Reform/Alliance Party ignores systemic discrimination and obscures precisely the issues feminists and other equality seekers have worked to expose and address.

This is not to say that there has been no improvement in the parties' treatment of women and no progress on issues of diversity. Ironically, even the Alliance has employed feminist-inspired discourse, e.g., gender equality, to veil its intentions. There have been some more noteworthy changes as well. Recent studies show that many of the obstacles to women's partisan participation are declining.[54] For instance, it used to be that women were the "sacrificial lambs," typically positioned to run in lost-cause ridings. While more men are nominated in safe seats than are women, the gap is closing. Furthermore, most parties have come to recognize the financial barriers that women face when they try to run for office, and thus the Liberals, Conservatives, and NDP all have established special funds for women.

There also have been efforts to situate women in areas of influence. The Liberal Party ensures that its strategic national committees have women as co-chairs and that the party leader has the power to be able to choose candidates where a local association fails to nominate a woman or visible-minority candidate. The NDP has gone to the greatest lengths in passing affirmative-action resolutions and setting targets not only for members on its federal executive and council but for its candidates. Again, this came as a result of pressure in and outside of the party. The NDP's POW, for instance, campaigned hard for mandatory provisions from within, and this was certainly bolstered by movement activism from without.[55]

Although the numbers of women have grown, and there have been incremental gains in the percentage of other underrepresented groups in the parties, there is no guarantee that the trend will continue,[56] that the numbers will increase or even remain at their present levels. Patterns such as "the higher the fewer" women, are hard to break. Further, the case has been made that numerical representation has not translated into substantive representation and, in fact, the reverse may be true.[57] With more women in the parties, feminist gains seem to be more at risk. It is also true that the Canadian women's movement appears to be at a low ebb. With cutbacks and hard economic times, its resources have been strained, and this has affected its ability to put pressure on the parties to ensure that decisions made do not work to women's detriment.

The lesson here is that without any identity politics mobilization, without the work from within and without, advancement of the democratic agenda is not likely to occur at all. Parties' representational capacities have been challenged. Because parties at first failed to integrate and aggregate diverse territorial and non-territorial identities, collective actors within and outside the parties mobilized and, in turn, helped to change political parties' discourses and some of their practices.

In some cases, parties appeared so intransigent that, historically, certain forms of collective action directed toward them was deemed practically futile. Mobilization around the issue of sexual orientation is revealing in this respect.[58] Given the fact that there were only a couple of uncloseted gay men serving in federal party politics in Canada, it is no wonder that gays, lesbians, and bisexuals have been skeptical about the inroads that can be made in partisan politics. And so, lesbian and gay activism has primarily revolved around community-oriented and extra-parliamentary politics. Nonetheless, because parties do affect political debates and directions, activists began engaging in social movement organizing geared toward gaining party support.

Although the Trudeau Liberals partially decriminalized homosexual activity in 1969, the 1976 Canadian Human Rights Act did not include sexual orientation, nor did the 1982 Charter of Rights and Freedoms. However, persistent mobilization outside the parties kept the issue alive and gained some sympathetic party insiders. Through the 1980s and into the 1990s, lesbians and gays worked in their communities, lobbied politicians, and used the Charter and the courts to turn the situation around.[59] The group EGALE, Equality for Gays and Lesbians Everywhere, formed in the mid-1980s and worked in coalition with feminists, disability organizations, the Canadian Labour Congress, and the United Church of Canada to push for legal and legislative change provincially and federally. Eventually, this extensive mobilization would have an impact. While key court cases such as *Vriend* and *M. v. H.* would provide the spur, the governing party would have to take the kick. In 1996, the Liberals introduced Bill C-33, amending the Human Rights Act and adding sexual orientation to all provisions except affirmative action. That same year, they extended certain benefits, such as health and relocation benefits, to same-sex federal government employees, including survivor benefits in 1999. By 2000, 68 statutes were amended to ensure that common-law relationships (both opposite- and same-sex) would have similar rights and responsibilities as heterosexual married couples. The next year, common-law partners, including same-sex partners, were considered as part of the family class category when it came to immigration policy, and the census asked for the first time whether citizens were living in common-law relationships that included same-sex relationships.[60] And, of course, there has been movement recently in the Liberal Party on the same-sex marriage issue. Certainly, times have changed for the better, when one of the contenders in the 2003 Conservative leadership race did not consider it necessary to conceal the fact that he was gay.

As with feminist concerns, the response of political parties to the issue of sexual orientation has been slow and the activism required was strenuous. Nevertheless, due to collective mobilization, there has been change. Gains are typically limited, are often contradictory, and can be revoked. Still, the purpose of this discussion is to emphasize the long and diverse histories of social movement interaction with political parties and to stress the fact that various forms of identity politics have been influential.

Some studies contend that old-style party politics has been replaced by a new politics that values personal autonomy and identity.[61] The growth of social movements, they say, has contributed to a "new" citizens' revolution, which has led to party decline. But the purpose of this chapter is to show that just as long as there have been political parties in Canada, there have also been other forms of collective mobilization. In fact, various movements have helped to establish new parties. Collective action gave rise to various leftist parties and regional protest parties, along with populist and nationalist parties. We have also witnessed combinatory movement-parties in Canada from the Progressives in the first decades of the twentieth century to the Feminist Party or the Green Party in more recent decades.

While Meisel and the writers of the Lortie Commission's final report state that these alternative representational forms compete with parties and contribute to their weaknesses, Susan Phillips illustrates that interest groups and social movements are, more accurately, "complementing" and "connecting."[62] In many instances, the lines between representational forms are even blurred. These intricate relationships do not thwart democracy but help it to thrive. Since parties have been criticized for their lack of policy thinking, interest groups and social movements can fill this gap. The latter will continue to disseminate different ideas and, ideally, to foster innovation and propagate progressive, critical discourses. They should not be disparaged but, rather, encouraged to act in these capacities.

CONCLUSION

This chapter has addressed past and present trends within political parties in Canada. It has examined the diverse influences that have affected parties without losing sight of the fact that political parties have their own powers that they can wield. We have seen how the socioeconomic context helps shape party agendas and, increasingly, how globalization has encouraged a disturbing degree of policy convergence across parties. At the same time, parties have proven to be adaptive and are subject to various balancing forces, not just structural ones. Movement-based ideas and identities have also left their mark on Canadian political parties. Nonetheless, the parties continue to display profoundly problematic tendencies in their lack of policy thinking, in the ways they have succumbed to Teletubby politics, and in their continuing representational shortcomings.

Because of their flexibility, political parties will not disappear, but their lack of responsiveness means that their potential in promoting an active, democratic citizenship has not been realized. Here, alternative representational forms have taken the lead. However, redressing democratic deficiencies cannot be achieved by validating one representational form (the political party) and delegitimizing others (interest groups and social movements). While it is true that social movements have highlighted the parties' lapses, this is not such a bad thing. The goal should be to expand all representational routes and even to encourage their overlap for mutual enhancement. Rather than imitating the "Third Way," Canadian political parties could look to their own experiences and consider multiple paths that crisscross with other representational forms so that democracy in Canada flourishes.

NOTES

The author wishes to thank her SSHRC research project team, and notably Jane Jenson and Denis Saint-Martin, for their work on the consolidation of the social investment state, and a LEGO model which encapsulates Third Way priorities. See Jane Jenson and Denis Saint-Martin, "Building Blocks for a New Welfare Architecture: Is LEGO™ the model for an active society?" a paper prepared for the 4th International Research conference on Social Security, Antwerp, Belgium, May 4–7, 2003. For other papers in the project see <http://www.fas. umontreal.ca/pol/cohesionsociale>.

    1. Tony Blair, "What the Third Way Stands for: Tony Blair," *The Globe and Mail,* September 21, 1998: A23. See also Anthony Giddens, *The Third Way: The Renewal of Social Democracy* (Cambridge: Polity Press, 1998); Stuart White, "The Ambiguities of the Third Way," in Stuart White, ed., *New Labour: The Progressive Future?* (London: Palgrave Press, 2001), pp. 3–17.

    2. Manfred B. Steger, *Globalization: A Very Short Introduction* (New York: Oxford, 2003), p. 56.

    3. In fact, this observation was made at the turn of the twentieth century by the French sociologist André Siegfried. André Siegfried, *The Race Question in Canada* (London: E. Nash, 1907).

    4. Harold Clark, Lawrence Leduc, Jon H. Pammett, and Jane Jenson, *Absent Mandate: Canadian Electoral Politics in an Era of Restructuring* (Toronto: Gage, 1991).

    5. Sylvia Bashevkin, *Welfare Hot Buttons: Women, Work and Social Policy Reform* (Toronto: University of Toronto Press, 2003).

    6. Alexandra Dobrowolsky and Denis Saint-Martin. "Agency, Actors and Change in a Child-Focused Future: Problematizing Path Dependency's Past and Statist Parameters," paper prepared for the American Political Science Association Annual Meeting, Boston, August 29–September 1, 2002.

    7. Alexandra Dobrowolsky, "Rhetoric versus Reality: The Figure of the Child and New Labour's 'Social Investment State,' " *Studies in Political Economy* 69 (Autumn 2002): 43–73.

    8. Canada, *Knowledge Matters, Skills and Learning for Canadians* (Ottawa: HRDC, 2002).

    9. Reg Whitaker, *The Government Party: Organizing and Financing the Liberal Party of Canada, 1930–1958* (Toronto: University of Toronto Press, 1977).

    10. This chapter provides an alternative interpretation to the view of Carty, Cross, and Young, who write: "Not only do they [voters] have more parties to choose from, but the parties are also increasingly staking out distinctive policy positions." See R.K. Carty, William Cross, and Lisa Young, *Rebuilding Canadian Party Politics* (Vancouver: University of British Columbia Press, 2000), p. 8. It is more in line with the counterargument of Clarkson, who writes, for example, that Carty et al.'s "fourth party system is more similar to than different from the third." Stephen Clarkson, "The Liberal Threepeat: The Multi-System Party in the Multi-Party Stystem," in Jon H. Pammett and Christopher Dornan, eds., *The Canadian General Election of 2000* (Toronto: Dundern Press, 2001), p. 15.

    11. André Blais, Elisabeth Gidengil, Richard Nadeau, and Neil Nevitte, "The Fickle Finger of Folk," *The Globe and Mail,* June 7, 1997, D1, 9. They also examine the PC's and Reform's concerted focus on tax cuts in Neil Nevitte, André Blais, Elisabeth Gidengil, and Richard Nadeau, *Unsteady State: The 1997 Canadian Federal Election* (Toronto: Oxford University Press, 2000), p. 130.

    12. Bloc Québécois, *Le Québec gagne à voter Bloc* (BQ: 2000), p. 9.

13. Alliance, *Declaration of Policy* (Alliance: January 2000), p. 7.

14. David Stewart and Miriam Koene, "Canadian Parties in the New Century," in Janine Brodie and Linda Trimble, eds., *Reinventing Canada: Politics of the 21st Century* (Toronto: Prentice Hall, 2003), p. 267.

15. Peter Wooolstencraft, "Some Battles Won, War Lost: The Campaign of the Progressive Conservative Party," in Jon H. Pammett and Christopher Dornan, eds., *The Canadian General Election of 2000* (Toronto: Dundern Press, 2001), p. 98.

16. This welfare and business liberal distinction is made by Colin Campbell and William Christian, *Parties, Leaders and Ideologies in Canada* (Toronto: McGraw-Hill Ryerson, 1996).

17. Prime Minister Chrétien, Foreword, in *Opportunity for All: The Liberal Plan for the Future of Canada* (Ottawa: Liberal Party of Canada, 2000), p. 3.

18. "PM's successor will be left to pay for his legacy or renege on it," *The Globe and Mail,* February 19, 2003: A8.

19. Richard Sigurdson, "Preston Manning and the Politics of Postmodernism in Canada," *Canadian Journal of Political Science* 27, no. 2 (June 1994): 252.

20. Tom Flanagan, *Waiting for the Wave: The Reform Party and Preston Manning* (Don Mills, ON: Stoddart, 1995).

21. Steve Patten, "Preston Manning's Populism: Constructing the Common Sense of the Common People," *Studies in Political Economy* 50 (Summer 1996): 103. See also David Laycock, *The New Right and Democracy in Canada: Understanding Reform and the Canadian Alliance* (Toronto: Oxford University Press, 2002).

22. Faron Ellis, "The More Things Change … The Alliance Campaign," in Jon H. Pammett and Christopher Dornan, eds., *The Canadian General Election of 2000* (Toronto: Dundern, 2001), p. 84. Nevitte et al. predicted that Reform or its successor may "look more and more like a traditional brokerage party" as, they noted, "There is perhaps no more striking testimony to the compelling logic of brokerage politics than Preston Manning's attempts, however unsuccessful to date, to reach out to Quebec nationalists." See Nevitte, Blais, Gidengil, and Nadeau, p. 102.

23. Ellis, p. 76.

24. Ibid., p. 84.

25. Della Kirkham, "The Reform Party of Canada: A Discourse on Race, Ethnicity and Equality," in Vic Satzewich, ed., *Racism and Social Inequality in Canada* (Toronto: Thompson Educational Publishing, 1998), p. 265. See also, Yasmeen Abu-Laban and Christina Gabriel, *Selling Diversity, Immigration, Multiculturalism, Employment Equity and Globalization* (Peterborough, ON: Broadview Press, 2002), chapters 2–4; and Yasmeen Abu-Laban, "Liberalism, Multiculturalism and the Problem of Essentialism," *Citizenship Studies* 6:4 (2002): 459–82.

26. A. Brian Tanguay, "Canadian Party Ideologies in the Electronic Age," in R.K. Carty, ed., *Canadian Political Party Systems: A Reader* (Peterborough, ON: Broadview Press, 1992), p. 484.

27. Keith Archer and Alan Whitehorn, *Political Activists: The NDP in Convention* (Toronto: Oxford University Press, 1997), pp. 26–27.

28. Neil Bradford and Jane Jenson, "Facing Economic Restructuring and Constitutional Renewal: Social Democracy Adrift in Canada," in Frances Fox Piven, ed., *Labour Parties in Postindustrial Societies* (New York: Oxford University Press, 1992), pp. 209–11; and Nevitte, Blais, Gidengil, and Nadeau, p. 133.

29. Jeffrey Simpson, "If there's pizzaz, it must be Jack Layton," *The Globe and Mail,* September 28, 2002: A25.

30. André Bernard, "The Bloc Québécois," in Alan Frizzell and Jon H. Pammett, eds., *The Canadian General Election of 1997* (Toronto: Dundurn Press, 1997), p. 142.

31. Jean Crête and Guy Lachappelle, "The Bloc Québécois," in Hugh G. Thorburn, ed., *Party Politics in Canada*, 7th ed. (Scarborough, ON: Prentice Hall, 1996), p. 424.

32. André Bernard, "Bloc Québécois," in Jon H. Pammett and Christopher Dornan, eds., *The Canadian General Election of 2000* (Toronto: Dundern Press, 2001), p. 144.

33. John Courtney, *Do Conventions Matter?* (Montreal & Kingston: McGill-Queen's University Press, 1995).

34. John Meisel, "The Decline of Party in Canada," in Hugh G. Thorburn, ed., *Party Politics in Canada*, 5th ed. (Scarborough, ON: Prentice Hall, 1985).

35. Donald Savoie, *Governing from the Centre: The Concentration of Power in Canadian Politics* (Toronto: University of Toronto Press, 1999).

36. Alexandra Dobrowolsky, "Of 'Special Interest': Interest, Identity and Feminist Constitutional Activism," *Canadian Journal of Political Science* 31, no. 4 (December 1998), and *The Politics of Pragmatism: Women, Representation and Constitutionalism in Canada* (Toronto: Oxford, 2000).

37. Here the Quebec Liberal Party's Allaire Report provides a significant exception.

38. Susan D. Phillips, "SUFA and Citizen Engagement: Fake or Genuine Masterpiece?" *Policy Matters* 2:7 (2001).

39. Ron Landes, "In Defence of Canadian Political Parties," in Mark Charlton and Paul Barker, eds., *Crosscurrents: Contemporary Political Issues* (Scarborough, ON: Nelson, 1991), p. 268.

40. John Meisel, "The Dysfunctions of Canadian Parties: An Exploratory Mapping," in Alain G. Gagnon and A. Brian Tanguay, eds., *Democracy with Justice* (Ottawa: Carleton University Press, 1992), pp. 407–31.

41. A. Brian Tanguay, "Reflections on Political Marketing and Party 'Decline' in Canada ... or, A Funny Thing Happened on the Way to the 1988 Election," in Alain G. Gagnon and A. Brian Tanguay, eds., *Democracy with Justice* (Ottawa: Carleton University Press, 1992), p. 403.

42. Khayyam Z. Paltiel, "Political Marketing, Party Finance and the Decline of Canadian Parties," in Alain G. Gagnon and A. Brian Tanguay, eds., *Canadian Parties in Transition: Discourse, Organization, Representation* (Scarborough, ON: Nelson, 1989), pp. 348–49.

43. Peter Mair, "Partyless Democracy: Solving the Paradox of New Labour?" *New Left Review* 2 (March/April 2001): 21–35.

44. Cynthia J. Alexander, "Plugging Into New Currents: The Use of New Information and Communication Technologies in Party Politics," in Hugh G. Thorburn, ed., *Party Politics in Canada*, 7th ed. (Scarborough, ON: Prentice Hall, 1996), 597–99. See also Cynthia J. Alexander, "Digital Leviathan: The Emergence of E-politics in Canada," in Hugh G. Thorburn and Alan Whitehorn, eds., *Party Politics in Canada*, 8th ed. (Scarborough, ON: Prentice Hall, 2001), pp. 460–76.

45. Patrick Seyd, "In Praise of Party," *Parliamentary Affairs* 51, no. 2 (April 1998): 200.

46. Alexandra Dobrowolsky and Jane Jenson, "Reforming the Parties: Prescriptions for Democracy," in Susan D. Phillips, ed., *How Ottawa Spends: A More Democratic Canada?* (Ottawa: Carleton University Press, 1993), pp. 43–81.

47. Louis Massicote, "Electoral Reform in the Charter Era," in Alan Frizzel and Jon H. Pammett, eds., *The Canadian General Election of 1997* (Toronto: Dundurn, 1997), pp. 173–75.

48. Leonard Preyra, "From Conventions to Closed Primaries? New Politics and Recent Change in National Party Leadership Selection in Canada," in Hugh G. Thorburn and Alan Whitehorn, eds., *Party Politics in Canada*, 8th ed. (Scarborough, ON: Prentice Hall, 2001), pp. 443–59.

49. Janine Brodie and Jane Jenson, "Piercing the Smokescreen: Brokerage Parties and Class Politics," in Alain G. Gagnon and A. Brian Tanguay, eds., *Canadian Parties in Transition: Discourse, Organization, Representation* (Scarborough, ON: Nelson, 1989).

50. Colin Campbell and William Christian, *Parties, Leaders and Ideologies in Canada* (Toronto: McGraw-Hill Ryerson, 1996), p. 112.

51. Linda Kealey, *Enlisting Women for the Cause: Women, Labour and the Left in Canada, 1890–1929* (Toronto: University of Toronto Press, 1998), pp. 90, 109–10.

52. Lisa Young, "The Canadian Women's Movement and Political Parties, 1970–1993," in Manon Tremblay and Caroline Andrew, eds., *Women and Political Representation in Canada* (Ottawa: University of Ottawa Press, 1998), pp. 197–98, 201. See also Lisa Young, *Feminists and Party Politics* (Vancouver: University of British Columbia Press, 2000).

53. Lisa Young and William Cross, "Women's Involvement in Canadian Political Parties," in Manon Tremblay and Linda Trimble, eds., *Women and Electoral Politics in Canada* (Toronto: Oxford University Press, 2003), p. 106.

54. Ibid., p. 107.

55. Jocelyn Praud, "Affirmative Action and Women's Representation in the Ontario New Democratic Party," in Manon Tremblay and Caroline Andrew, eds., *Women and Political Representation in Canada* (Ottawa: University of Ottawa Press, 1998), p. 173.

56. Daiva K. Stasiulis and Yasmeen Abu-Laban, "The House the Parties Built: (Re)constructing Ethnic Representation in Canadian Politics," in Kathy Megyery, ed., *Ethno-Cultural Groups and Visible Minorities in Canadian Politics: The Question of Access* (Toronto: Dundurn, 1991). See also Jerome H. Black, "Differences That Matter: Minority Women MPs, 1993–2003," in Manon Tremblay and Linda Trimble, eds., *Women and Electoral Politics in Canada* (Toronto: Oxford University Press, 2003), p. 59.

57. Lise Gotell and Janine Brodie, "Women and Parties in the 1990s: Less Than Ever an Issue of Numbers," in Hugh G. Thorburn, ed., *Party Politics in Canada*, 7th ed. (Scarborough, ON: Prentice Hall, 1996), pp. 54–71.

58. David Rayside, *On the Fringe: Gays and Lesbians in Politics* (Ithaca, NY: Cornell University Press, 1998), pp. 105–39.

59. Miriam Smith, "Social Movements and Equality Seeking: The Case of Gay Liberation in Canada," *Canadian Journal of Political Science* 31, no. 2 (June 1998): 285–309; Miriam Smith, *Lesbian and Gay Rights in Canada: Social Movements and Equality Seeking, 1971–1995* (Toronto: University of Toronto Press, 1999); Didi Herman, "The Good, the Bad and the Smugly: Sexual Orientation and Perspectives on the Charter," in David Schneiderman and Kate Sutherland, eds., *Charting the Consequences: The Impact of Charter Rights on Canadian Law and Politics* (Toronto: University of Toronto Press, 1997), pp. 200–217; Gloria Filax and Debra Shogan, "Sexual Minorities in Canada," in Janine Brodie and Linda Trimble, eds., *Reinventing Canada: Politics of the 21st Century* (Toronto: Prentice Hall, 2003), pp. 164–74.

60. "Quest for Rights. Milestones for gays and lesbians in Canada," *The Globe and Mail*, May 2, 2003: A4.

61. Grant Jordan, "Politics without Parties: A Growing Trend?" *Parliamentary Affairs* 51, no. 3 (1998): 314.

62. Susan D. Phillips, "Competing, Connecting and Complementing: Parties, Interest Groups and Social Movements," in A. Brian Tanguay and Alain G. Gagnon, eds., *Canadian Parties in Transition*, 2nd ed. (Scarborough, ON: Nelson, 1996), pp. 440–62.

FURTHER READINGS

Archer, Keith, and Alan Whitehorn. *Political Activists: The NDP in Convention.* Toronto: Oxford University Press, 1997.

Bashevkin, Sylvia. *Toeing the Lines: Women and Party Politics in English Canada,* 2nd ed. Toronto: Oxford University Press, 1993.

Bashevkin, Sylvia. *Welfare Hot Buttons: Women, Work and Social Policy Reform.* Toronto: University of Toronto Press, 2002.

Bickerton, James, Alain G. Gagnon, and Patrick J. Smith. *Ties That Bind: Parties and Voters in Canada.* Toronto: Oxford University Press, 1999.

Brodie, Janine, and Jane Jenson. *Crisis, Challenge and Change: Party and Class in Canada Revisited.* Toronto: Methuen, 1988.

Campbell, Colin, and William Christian. *Parties, Leaders, and Ideologies in Canada.* Toronto: McGraw-Hill Ryerson, 1996.

Carty, R.K., William Cross, and Lisa Young. *Rebuilding Canadian Party Politics.* Vancouver: University of British Columbia Press, 2000.

Clarke, Howard, Jane Jenson, Lawrence Leduc, and Jon H. Pammett. *Absent Mandate: Canadian Electoral Politics in an Era of Restructuring,* 3rd ed. Toronto: Gage, 1996.

Cross, William, ed., *Political Parties, Representation and Electoral Democracy in Canada.* Toronto: Oxford University Press, 2002.

Dobrowolsky, Alexandra. "Rhetoric versus Reality: The Figure of the Child and New Labour's 'Social Investment' State." *Studies in Political Economy* 69 (2002): 43–73.

Driver, Stephen, and Luke Martell. *Blair's Britain.* Cambridge, U.K.: Polity, 2002.

Flanagan, Tom. *Waiting for the Wave: The Reform Party and Preston Manning.* Don Mills: Stoddart, 1995.

Laycock, David. *The New Right and Democracy in Canada: Understanding Reform and the Canadian Alliance.* Toronto: Oxford University Press, 2002.

Nevitte, Neil, André Blais, Elisabeth Gidengil, and Richard Nadeau. *Unsteady State: The 1997 Canadian Federal Election.* Toronto: Oxford University Press, 2000.

Pammett, Jon H., and Christopher Dornan, eds. *The Canadian General Election of 2000.* Toronto: Dundurn Press, 2001.

Simpson, Jeffrey. *The Friendly Dictatorship.* Toronto: McClelland & Stewart, 2001.

Tanguay, A. Brian, and Alain G. Gagnon, eds. *Canadian Parties in Transition.* Toronto: Nelson, 1996.

Thorburn, Hugh, and Alan Whitehorn, eds. *Party Politics in Canada,* 8th ed. Scarborough, ON: Prentice Hall, 2001.

Tremblay, Manon, and Linda Trimble, eds. *Women and Electoral Politics in Canada.* Toronto: Oxford University Press, 2003.

Webb, Paul, David Farrell, and Ian Holliday, eds. *Political Parties in Advanced Industrial Democracies.* Oxford: Oxford University Press, 2002.

White, Stuart. *New Labour: The Progressive Future?* London, U.K.: Palgrave Press, 2001.

Young, Lisa. *Feminists and Party Politics.* Vancouver: University of British Columbia Press, 2000.

Young, Lisa, and Keith Archer, eds. *Regionalism and Party Politics in Canada.* Toronto: Oxford University Press, 2002.

CHAPTER 8

ELECTIONS

Jon H. Pammett

Although the concept of universal suffrage is a product of recent times, the notion that leaders should be chosen by voting is an ancient one. In the Athens of 500 B.C., an assembly of citizens elected generals and voted on numerous policy questions. Republican Rome operated an elaborate system of voting assemblies that elected consuls, tribunes, and many other officials. The Roman Catholic Church began electing its pope by assembling the cardinals in a special conclave at the end of the thirteenth century. Medieval city-states such as Florence and Venice developed very complex structures of government in which officials were chosen by a combination of election and selection by lot.[1]

One of humanity's most ancient political institutions, elections have become virtually omnipresent in the nations of the modern world. They are so popular because they serve a multiplicity of functions for almost everybody connected with them, as well as for the political system that sponsors them. Whatever complaints are registered about the time they take, the expense they involve, the choices they present, or the results they produce, elections are vital to the image that almost every country wishes to present to the rest of the world. Whether they are perceived to be "meaningful" or not, few would truthfully wish to do away with them altogether.

Impressive catalogues of functions performed by elections may be compiled on all levels of analysis. For the *political system,* elections fulfill at the outset a recruitment function by providing an orderly way of choosing the rulers or elites that govern the society. By facilitating grouping within the political system, elections participate in the creation and maintenance of political parties. We have already mentioned that elections operate as symbols through which a country signals to the rest of the world its democratic nature. This legitimation function is also important within the bounds of the political system in that elections generate support for that system (providing the result is seen as having been fairly arrived at) as well as a certain amount of legitimacy for the resulting government. Elections also perform an important political socialization function by focusing attention on the political system and thereby providing citizens with opportunities to learn about it. An election is one of the few genuine communal experiences shared by people in a diverse country, and simple participation in the same activity can be integrative for the system as a whole.

Political parties, for their part, are served by elections, which provide a ready-made occasion for a party to build or renew its internal organization. In some cases, elections may perform the function of allowing competing party elites to resolve internal power relationships and strategic conflicts within the party.[2] Elections can also provide the parties with policy guidelines or parameters, depending on how politicians interpret the impact of particular issues on the election result. The messages to be gleaned from elections range from very specific policies that were accepted or rejected along with the party, to more general philosophical or ideological approaches to governing. Finally, the result of an election legitimizes the status of a party, whether it be that of victor, official opposition, major, or minor party.

For individuals, elections serve the function of forging a link between them and the political system. This connection can foster a sense of support for the system or a sense of voter efficacy, a belief in the potential of provoking a response of the system to personal or group demands. It has been suggested that elections protect individuals by giving them control over those in power and a "voice in their own affairs."[3] Elections facilitate the socialization function by educating and informing individuals about politics, as well as by affecting the partisanship they hold. Elections can also give individuals an opportunity to make a political statement, and to boost their egos by impressing others with their political knowledge or cynicism. Finally, political participation, stimulated by the election context, may advance a variety of functions, ranging from direct personal gain and advancement to satisfaction derived from working with other people.

In keeping with the foregoing division of the functions of elections, analysis by political scientists takes place at both the level of the individual and the level of the political system, and includes as well a considerable number of studies of the internal operations of political parties. The individual-level analysis attempts to explain voting behaviour, or, more precisely, how individuals arrive at their decision to support one party or another at a particular time. Researchers in this field have carried out numerous surveys in order to amass the data they need to test their theories. The less common system-level studies are generally of two types. The first involves intensive study of the "context" of a particular election—the party platforms and activities, the media coverage, the events of the campaign, the patterns of the results, and so on.[4] The second involves the use of survey data to explain the outcomes of particular elections. We will explore this subject further after examining some aspects of individual voting behaviour in Canada.

VOTING BEHAVIOUR IN CANADA

The fact that elections perform a variety of functions for the individuals who vote in them would lead us to expect considerable diversity in their reasons for casting ballots in any given election. All indications we have from the National Election Studies, surveys conducted after Canadian federal elections, are that this expectation is easily met. The evidence from these studies (which can be consulted in more detail in several of the books mentioned in the Further Readings section at the end of this chapter) shows that virtually any shorthand explanation of why Canadians vote is bound to be correct for only a portion of the electorate. Thus, one should be highly suspicious of the generality implied by such interpretations as, "Canadians provided a mandate for free trade in 1988"; "Voters rejected traditional politics in 1993"; "Regionalism dominated the 1997 election"; or "Stockwell Day lost the 2000 election for the Alliance." None of the factors underlying each of these interpretations produced the election result by itself, or even came close to doing so.

Rather than being some monolithic entity, the Canadian electorate is composed of subgroups of people who vote for many different reasons. Some people say they are voting for the party as a whole, because of either long-standing loyalty or a newfound conviction that it is time to give a new lot of politicians a chance to run the country. To another set of voters, the comparative evaluation of the leaders is a major factor in their decision to vote; for some others it is the local candidate from their riding who makes the difference. A wide variety of different issues are cited, some of long-standing concern (like the problems of unemployment and economic growth) and others specific to certain elections (free trade in 1988 but not 1993.)

The question of the importance of issues to individual voting decisions has long interested political scientists. Because the electoral process involves decisions made by most of the public, and therefore by many people who score low in political information or interest, there has always been scope for charges that voting decisions are not being taken for the "right reasons." Voters are accused of deciding on the basis of personality or image, or unthinking party loyalty, rather than on "the issues." This kind of debate often includes questions about the extent of "rational voting," that is, voting on the basis of a reasoned consideration of the issues important to the voter.

The extent to which voting choice in Canada is motivated by issue concerns can be seen more clearly if we look at how voters rank four factors—leaders, candidates, parties, and issues—in terms of their importance to their voting decisions. To avoid setting up a direct choice between issues and these other factors in people's minds (we felt that the number citing issues might be artificially high since voting on the issues is a more socially approved answer), survey respondents were asked to choose among the three factors of party, leader, or candidate, and then asked whether or not there was an issue basis to their choice. The percentage of people ranking the four factors important in the last eight federal elections is shown in Table 8.1.

As the table indicates, the party as a whole emerges as the most important factor in all elections. Interestingly, choice of this factor is increasing with time, while the party leader factor has become less important to voting choice in recent years. The importance of party leader to voting choice was much greater during the Trudeau years, when it rivalled the party factor for top spot. There is a certain amount of variation

TABLE 8.1 Most Important Factors in Voting, 1974–2000 (percentage citing issue basis in parentheses)

Election	Party Leaders	Local Candidates	Party as a Whole
2000	22% (60)	21 (58)	58 (46)
1997	20% (71)	22 (58)	58 (57)
1993	22% (62)	21 (52)	57 (54)
1988	20% (71)	27 (57)	53 (57)
1984	30% (56)	21 (46)	49 (37)
1980	36% (53)	20 (40)	44 (43)
1979	37% (54)	23 (43)	40 (45)
1974	33% (58)	27 (48)	40 (43)

Sources: 1974–84 Canadian National Election Studies; 1988 re-interview of 1984 CNES; 1993 Insight Canada Research Post Election survey; 1997 and 2000 Pollara Perspectives Canada survey.

between elections, as well, in the number of people who declared there was an issue basis to their choice of party. While less than half of those citing party as the most important factor in their voting choice declared there was an issue basis to this choice in 1984, greater numbers have done so since 1988. This reflects the enhanced importance of issues in recent elections, particularly free trade in 1988, job creation and deficit reduction in 1993 and 1997, and the provision of health care in 2000. Similarly, the number of people reporting an issue basis to choice of leader or candidate as most important to them rose substantially in 1988, and has stayed high ever since. In Canadian elections, a majority of the electorate now reports an issue basis for their voting decision, a finding that refutes assertions that elections are just popularity contests among the leaders.

Academic surveys on voting behaviour show that a large proportion of reasons for voting are distinctly short-term in nature. Leaders and candidates are subject to frequent change. There were four new leaders of major parties in 1993, two in 1997, and two more in 2000. A large number of elected MPs are new to the House of Commons after each election. The importance and nature of issues can also vary greatly from one election to the next. Although Canadians are by no means bereft of general images of, and loyalties to, the political parties, a majority claim to make up their minds at each election on the basis of short-term factors operative at the time.

This picture of the Canadian electorate is supported by research findings on the nature of partisanship in this country. A majority of voters develop party loyalties that are either weak, changeable over time, or different at the two levels of the federal system. All of these factors contribute to the *flexible* partisanship that characterizes the link between about 60 percent of Canadian voters and the federal political parties. Thus, the question, "To which party do you feel closest?" may elicit different answers from the same respondent if repeated at various intervals over a period of time.[5]

Several facets of the political culture contribute to the flexibility of voter ties to political parties. The basic one is that Canadian political culture is relatively apolitical. While Canadians are moderately interested in politics, this interest does not translate for most into substantial political involvement. The amount of detailed political information possessed by the average Canadian is low. Studies of children's political learning, or socialization, show a relatively weak transference of preference for a political party from parent to child. Such transmission of enduring partisan ties from generation to generation is not the norm because these feelings may not be strongly or persistently held in the adult "socializer." As a result, children are less likely to develop such feelings for themselves, and, in turn, a culture is perpetuated in which partisanship is weakly held or is changeable.

Canadians are not often content with being apolitical; in many cases they are downright anti-political. In particular, the public feels negatively about political parties and politicians; ratings of them after recent elections were lower across the board than at any time since such surveys began. People believe that parties spend their time quarrelling rather than solving the real problems facing the country; that they confuse the issues rather than provide a real choice; that MPs lose touch with their constituents once elected; and that, once elected, politicians pay little attention to their electoral promises.[6] Given such an atmosphere, it is no wonder that large numbers of people are unwilling to stick with "their party" in perpetuity. When those people who change their partisanship are asked their reasons for doing so, more talked of the negative qualities of the party they are changing from than mentioned the positive qualities of the party they are changing to.[7] It was not hard to foresee that when the 1993 and 1997 elections presented opportunities to choose new parties, many voters would do so.

Because of the conflicts and regional loyalties associated with its founding and development as a nation, Canada is governed by an extremely complex federal system. As we enter the new millennium it is clear that a complete understanding of our system of government requires information about, and orientations toward, national and provincial political systems, as well as sophisticated notions about their interrelationships. While most people have a basic understanding of the constitutionally established functions performed by the various actors of the federal system, it would be unrealistic to expect detailed knowledge of intergovernmental relations on the part of the mass public. Lack of knowledge begets lack of interest. Further, the image of conflict surrounding the Canadian federal system contributes to the general public mood of exasperation with, and cynicism about, the political process.

Those whose ties to political parties are flexible are more likely to shift their votes from one election to the next, though only a minority of them do so in normal times. The factors that influence such partisans, particularly those who switch their votes, are predominantly short-term in nature—liking a political party at a particular time, positive (or negative) feelings toward a leader or candidate, concern about a particular issue, or some combination of these factors. We can pinpoint further types of flexible partisans who will be influenced by different factors if we subdivide them on the basis of their political interest. About one-third of the electorate are flexible partisans who have a low degree of interest in politics, while just over a quarter of the electorate are flexible partisans with a high degree of political interest. It is this flexible higher-interest group that gives relatively heavy weight to political issues in determining their voting choice; the parties aim to appeal to this group with their issue-oriented campaigns. The flexible lower-interest group, on the other hand, pays less attention to issues and more to general images of leaders and parties; the personal appeal of leaders tends to influence this group.

The flexibility of partisanship in Canada and the tendency for voting decisions to be determined by short-term considerations relating to parties, issues, leaders, and candidates active at any given time has meant that the social cleavages sometimes thought to form enduring loyalties in the population have little influence over how people vote. One of these cleavages—religion—can still be discerned in voting patterns (for example, in the tendency of Roman Catholics, particularly those outside Quebec, to vote Liberal). Overall, however, analysts see the relationship between religion and voting decisions as weak (and continuing to decline) or as impossibly difficult to explain in modern circumstances.[8] Studies have consistently found that another important cleavage—social class—has very little relationship to voting choice in Canadian federal elections, though currently there is a tendency for lower-income voters to favour the NDP and the Bloc Québécois.[9] Finally, although male and female voters have demonstrated differences in their choice of party and issues, these have not been substantial or consistent enough to provide convincing evidence for a Canadian "gender gap."[10] The votes of Canadians, then, are not heavily "preordained" by social or demographic factors, just as they are not predetermined by durable party loyalties.

One major consequence of this situation is that election campaigns can be of major importance in affecting election outcomes. Over half the electorate claims to arrive at a voting decision during the campaign period, while about one-fifth say they decide during the last week of the campaign or on election day itself. Given the short-term nature of the factors that influence many voting decisions, and the potential impact of the campaign and its events, the Canadian electorate is highly volatile. The potential for dramatic swings in election results is always present. However, it takes a particular constellation of factors to make them occur; it is to this subject that we now turn our attention.

ELECTION OUTCOMES

It may seem anomalous that a political system in which the electorate is characterized by such volatility appears so stable at the aggregate level of federal election results that it has at times been referred to as a one-party dominant system. The Liberal Party, or "Government Party" as it has been called, was in power for much of the twentieth century, with the Conservatives forming governments only under Borden (1911–20, part of which was a wartime Unionist government), Meighen (1926), Bennett (1930–35), Diefenbaker (1957–63), Clark (1979–80), and Mulroney (1984–93). With the collapse of the Conservative Party in 1993, some observers see a Liberal dynasty stretching well into the twenty-first century.

The resolution of the apparent paradox between individual volatility and aggregate stability lies in our ability to differentiate between the effects of electoral conversion and electoral replacement, and to plot the patterns of the "vote flows" related to them. *Conversion* involves the extent of vote switching among those who are members of the "permanent electorate," that is, people who are already eligible voters and who can be counted on to vote every time. All parties, through their campaign appeals, try to persuade those who voted for some other party in the previous election to switch their allegiance in this one. We have seen that the potential for such conversion is high, since the incidence of durable party loyalty is relatively low. *Replacement*, in contrast, is the impact on the result that is brought to bear by newly eligible voters, as well as by "transient" voters who do not turn out in every election. The impact of the transient vote will be determined by the difference in behaviour between those leaving the electorate and those returning to the electorate from a past abstention. The overall success of the federal Liberal Party has been achieved in part because, whatever the patterns of conversion in any given election, the party has usually gained through the process of electoral replacement.

Canadian elections held in the last two decades illustrate how conversion and replacement frequently operated to the Liberals' benefit.[11] In 1974, the Liberals were able to increase their overall popular vote from 1972 and win enough seats to form the majority government that had eluded them two years earlier. However, if the process of conversion had been the only one operating, the result of the 1974 election would actually have been *worse* for the Liberals than 1972. This is because vote switching from 1972 to 1974 among members of the permanent electorate favoured the Conservatives. The process of electoral replacement, however, worked quite differently from 1972 to 1974. The Liberals won the bulk of the young voters who became newly eligible in 1974, and also the majority of support from transient voters who had not gone to the polls in 1972. Thus, because those who did not vote in the previous election, either through choice or through lack of eligibility, favoured the Liberal party by wide margins, the party's losses through vote switching were more than offset.

In determining the outcome of the 1979 election, in which the Conservatives came close to forming a majority government, conversion and replacement again operated differently. There was substantial vote switching of 1974 Liberals away from that party toward the Conservatives. In addition, the Conservatives gained slightly from switches between their party and the NDP, a better performance than they had managed in 1974. Once again, however, electoral replacement was the Conservatives' Achilles' heel. They did manage to win a slight plurality of the transient vote, important because of the high turnout in 1979. Newly eligible voters, on the other hand, still favoured the Liberals by a substantial margin, and this new-voter group was particularly large in 1979 because of the five-year interval since the previous election. Because of the effects of the high post–World War II birthrate, almost 2.5 million new voters had come of age since the previous election. The Liberals' ability to retain their appeal to this group, therefore, reduced the magnitude of their 1979 defeat; conversely, the Conservatives' unpopularity with the same group denied that party not only majority-government status but also the opportunity to renew their support among the young.

In the 1980 election held a scant few months later, the processes of conversion and replacement worked in the same direction, favouring the Liberals. The Liberals showed a net benefit in vote switching with the PCs and the NDP, and also regained their edge among transient voters moving into the electorate from a non-voting stance in 1979. Similarly, since voting turnout in 1980 was down from 1979, it is relevant to note that the Conservatives suffered disproportionately from the 1980 abstention of voters who favoured them a year earlier.

By 1984, voter dissatisfaction with the Trudeau and Turner regimes finally caught up with the Liberal Party. The factors of electoral conversion and replacement both operated strongly in the same direction, away from that party. The proportion of the total electorate switching to the Conservatives from a 1980 Liberal vote was almost as high as that remaining with the Liberals. Similarly, transient voters entering the electorate from a 1980 abstention favoured the Conservatives by a wide margin, as did newly eligible voters by a narrower margin. The resulting landslide gave the Conservative Party one of its few solid majority governments in the twentieth century.

The 1988 election reflects a different scenario. As happens frequently to parties in power, vote switching went against the Conservative government. Although the differences between those abandoning the Tories and those attracted to them were not overwhelming, they were consistent. The Tories lost voters to the Liberals, the NDP, and the new Reform Party. The

Conservatives managed to win the 1988 election because their margin of victory in 1984 had been so overwhelming that they could afford to lose votes through electoral conversion and still survive comfortably. Second, however, the PCs were able to win a plurality of transient and newly eligible voters, suggesting a tendency for these groups to support incumbent governments unless the overall electorate is in a mood for massive change.

The 1993 election saw over 40 percent of the total electorate change their votes from the previous election. Conservatives who stayed with their party from 1988 to 1993 were fewer in number than former Tories who switched to the Liberals or those who opted for a Reform vote. A further substantial percentage of voters changed from the Conservatives to the Bloc Québécois. The NDP lost slightly more of its 1988 voters to the Liberals than they retained for themselves and gave up another important group to the Reform Party. Overall, the strong showing of the Bloc and Reform parties meant that the number of voters changing their behaviour between 1988 and 1993 was likely the largest in Canadian history. The reduced voter turnout in 1993 also affected the result. Previous Conservative and NDP voters who decided not to vote in 1993 were more numerous than 1988 Liberal voters who did the same. Finally, the Liberals gained substantially from the voting choices made by newly eligible, mostly young, voters in 1993. More new voters went to the Liberals than to all the other parties put together.

In the 1997 election, the Liberal Party barely succeeded in retaining majority-government status. Almost two-thirds of those who had voted Liberal in 1993 chose that party again, a higher rate than for either of the other two "old-line parties." However, the Reform Party and the Bloc Québécois managed to hold on to 80 percent of their previous support. Offsetting patterns of electoral conversion were therefore not favourable to the Liberals between 1993 and 1997, and hence the party's vote dropped to an all-time Canadian low (38 percent) for any party that went on to form a majority government at the federal level. The Liberals were also hurt in 1997 by disproportionate losses of their former supporters who decided not to vote at all. Once again, however, the Liberals were the beneficiaries of votes from first-time voters. With a regionally divided opposition and a number of three-way races, particularly in Ontario, the "Government Party" found itself still in power.

The 2000 Canadian federal election bears a number of similarities to its two immediate predecessors. The Liberals increased their proportion of the overall vote somewhat, to just over 40 percent. Once again, the party benefited from a divided opposition. This time, however, the increase of the Alliance vote over previous support totals for the Reform Party allowed it to gain enough seats to form the official opposition and to provide the major challenge to the Liberals in Ontario. But voters overall were not energized by this Alliance challenge, and furthermore turned away from the Conservatives and New Democrats, leaving these parties scrambling to elect enough members to retain official party status in the House of Commons.

The big story from the 2000 federal election was the continuing decline in the turnout rate. From a postwar high of 75 percent of eligible voters, the 1993 turnout dipped to 70 percent, the 1997 voting rate to 67 percent, and the 2000 rate to just over 61 percent of registered voters. The most disturbing characteristic of this decline in electoral participation is the fact that it is occurring predominantly among the youngest sectors of the electorate, to the point where a recent study finds that barely one-quarter of those under 25 years of age voted in 2000.[12]

There are three main reasons for these turnout declines. First, people express disinterest in the election, as they find the electoral situation non-competitive and their votes relatively meaningless. Second, the public negativity we have referred to earlier means that people are less likely to find the candidates, parties, leaders and issues attractive or meaningful to them. Finally, a group of personal or administrative factors deters prospective voters, things like being "too busy", away from their constituency or not on the voters' list. The marginal nature of the voting act for many people, especially the young, means that these factors, while not difficult to overcome in themselves, represent a significant deterrent to voting.

CONCLUSION

If we return to consider some of the major functions of elections referred to at the beginning of this chapter, it is apparent that federal elections in Canada perform some of these functions much better than others. Recruitment, for example, is reasonably well served; each election produces the requisite number of leaders to operate the ministries. However, the fact that the strength of the parties is often highly variable across regions can affect their performance of another function—namely, creating support for the political system and legitimizing it in the eyes of its citizens. Election results since 1993 leave the federal government open to charges that it represents certain parts of the country at the expense of others. Those who supported the Alliance/Reform Party in the West, the Bloc Québécois in Quebec, and the NDP and the Conservatives in the Atlantic region were not all protesting either the operations of the federal system or the viability of the country; however, there is no doubt that the elections allowed many negative sentiments to be expressed about both. Those concerned about the survival of Canada as a federal country sometimes find it difficult to summon up the act of faith that allows them to argue that the continuity implied in the simple conduct of federal elections is more important than the pattern of particular results.

We have also noted that elections perform functions for the political parties themselves. They give parties opportunities to revive and re-establish their organizations; since many of them exist primarily for the purpose of contesting elections, these events are a sine qua non. With regard to the proposed function of setting policy parameters for the parties, or sorting out the specific policies they will have a mandate to enact, the Canadian election system does not perform very well. This is partly because parties often seek to avoid specific policy stands during election campaigns, for these positions usually alienate as many voters as they attract. Even if specific policies are proposed, recent Canadian history shows that parties rarely feel bound by them. During the 1974 campaign, for example, the Liberals fought strenuously against the idea of wage and price controls, and then promptly introduced them once re-elected. On free trade, the Mulroney government turned from opponents to proponents in the 1984–88 period, and one of the first acts of the new Liberal government in 1993 was to accept the free trade legislation it had battled so fiercely a short time before. Advocates of a gradualist approach to budget cutting in the 1993 campaign, the Liberals moved quickly to balance the budget once in power, acting much as Reform would have done. Those who promised to save public health care in 2000 are the ones who put it in danger in the first place. These campaign tactics mean that elections provide little opportunity for the public to affect policy; they damage the credibility of politicians and increase political cynicism among the population, now at an all-time high.

Most Canadians are not confident that they understand or can influence the political system, and many are skeptical about the possibility of producing any significant change through elections. This situation may be mitigated somewhat by the feeling on the part of most Canadians that neither their general well-being nor their standard of living is greatly affected by government. Thus, the feeling that elections accomplish little sometimes manifests itself not in political protest but rather in a bemused detachment from the whole political process—a symptom of the apolitical political culture we noted earlier. Some observers have argued that this situation is, on balance, beneficial in that elites are free to govern and to implement policies that might have been more vigorously opposed in a more politicized society. That may be true, but in a country that depends heavily on politics to negotiate solutions to its numerous problems there are also inherent dangers in having a public so divorced from, and cynical about, the political process.

NOTES

1. These and other examples of ancient elections are discussed in Jon H. Pammett, "A Framework for the Comparative Analysis of Elections across Time and Space," *Electoral Studies* 7, no. 2 (1988): 125–42.

2. Primary elections in the United States are an obvious example of this; however, it also takes place in other contexts. See Jane Jenson, "Strategic Divisions within the French Left: The Case of the First Elections to the European Parliament," *Revue d'integration européene/Journal of European Integration* (September 1980).

3. Norman D. Palmer, *Elections and Political Development* (Durham, NC: Duke University Press, 1975), p. 87.

4. See Jon H. Pammett and Christopher Dornan, eds., *The Canadian General Election of 2000* (Toronto: Dundurn, 2001). For an influential early study, see John Meisel, *The Canadian General Election of 1957* (Toronto: University of Toronto Press, 1962).

5. See Harold D. Clarke, Jane Jenson, Lawrence LeDuc, and Jon H. Pammett, *Political Choice in Canada* (Toronto: McGraw-Hill Ryerson, 1979); and *Absent Mandate: Canadian Electoral Politics in an Era of Restructuring* (Toronto: Gage, 1996).

6. Clarke et al., *Absent Mandate*, p. 181; and André Blais and Elisabeth Gidengil, *Making Representative Democracy Work: The Views of Canadians* (Toronto: Dundurn, 1991), p. 42.

7. Clarke et al., *Political Choice in Canada*, p. 150.

8. See William Irvine, "Explaining the Religious Basis of Partisanship in Canada," *Canadian Journal of Political Science* 7 (1974): 560–63; John Meisel, "Bizarre Aspects of a Vanishing Act: The Religious Cleavage and Voting in Canada," in John Meisel, *Working Papers in Canadian Politics*, 2nd rev. ed. (Montreal/Kingston: McGill-Queen's University Press, 1975), pp. 253–84; Richard Johnston, "The Reproduction of the Religious Cleavage in Canadian Elections," *Canadian Journal of Political Science* 18 (1985): 99–114.

9. See Jon Pammett, "The Voters Decide," chap. 12 of *The Canadian General Election of 1997*, p. 244. For a more general analysis of the relationship between social class and voting, including an extensive bibliography, see Jon H. Pammett, "Class Voting and Class Consciousness in Canada," *Canadian Review of Sociology and Anthropology* 24, no. 2 (1987): 269–90.

10. In Canadian federal politics, women have traditionally been somewhat less likely than men to support the Conservative and NDP parties. Recently, however, women have become somewhat more likely than men to support these parties, particularly the NDP, which has chosen two recent female leaders. Currently, women are less likely to vote for the Alliance than are men; if this difference is sustained in upcoming elections, it has the potential to form a real "gender gap."

11. More complete analyses of the voting patterns in these elections may be found in Clarke et al., *Political Choice in Canada*, and various editions of *Absent Mandate* by the same authors.

12. Jon H. Pammett and Lawrence LeDuc, *Explaining the Turnout Decline in Canadian Federal Elections: A New Survey of Non-voters* (Ottawa: Elections Canada, 2003), p. 20.

FURTHER READINGS

Beck, Murray J. *Pendulum of Power.* Toronto: Prentice-Hall, 1968. Gives accounts of Canadian election campaigns to 1968.

Blais, André, Elisabeth Gidengil, Richard Nadeau, and Neil Nevitte. *Anatomy of a Liberal Victory.* Peterborough: Broadview, 2002. Uses Canadian Election Study data to explain the Liberal victory in the 2000 federal election.

Clarke, Harold D., Jane Jenson, Lawrence LeDuc, and Jon H. Pammett. *Political Choice in Canada.* Toronto: McGraw-Hill Ryerson, 1979, and abridged edition, 1980. An extensive treatment of Canadian voting behaviour and partisanship.

————. *Absent Mandate: Canadian Electoral Politics in an Era of Restructuring.* Toronto: Gage, 1996. An analysis of voting behaviour and election outcomes through 1993.

Gidengil, Elisabeth. "Canada Votes: A Quarter Century of Canadian Election Studies." *Canadian Journal of Political Science* 25, no. 2 (1992): 219–48. A thorough and balanced review of the use of election surveys in Canada. Numerous references make it very useful for students.

Johnston, Richard, André Blais, Henry E. Brady, and Jean Crête. *Letting the People Decide: Dynamics of a Canadian Election.* Montreal/Kingston: McGill-Queen's University Press, 1992. A detailed study of the 1988 election that focuses on the campaign dynamics.

LeDuc, Lawrence, Richard G. Niemi, and Pippa Norris, eds. *Comparing Democracies 2: New Challenges in the Study of Elections and Voting.* Thousand Oaks, CA: Sage, 2002. The second edition of this popular comparative book on elections provides an international context for Canadian elections.

Milner, Henry, ed. *Making Every Vote Count: Reassessing Canada's Electoral System.* Peterborough: Broadview, 1999. A recent collection of articles proposing reform of the first-past-the-post electoral system.

Pammett, Jon H., and Christopher Dornan, eds. *The Canadian General Election of 2000.* Toronto: Dundurn, 2001. Analyses of party strategy, media coverage, and voting behaviour in the 2000 election. Companion volumes on previous elections are also available in this series.

Royal Commission on Electoral Reform and Party Financing. *Reforming Electoral Democracy.* This 1991 report provides an extensive analysis of various recommended initiatives to strengthen the party system and ensure fairness in election campaigns. It was accompanied by 24 volumes of research studies on a wide variety of subjects relating to parties and elections.

Tremblay, Manon, and Linda Trimble, eds. *Women and Electoral Politics in Canada.* Don Mills, ON: Oxford, 2003. Articles examine women's representation in Parliament, political parties, and the media during election campaigns.

CHAPTER 9

INTEREST GROUPS AND SOCIAL MOVEMENTS

Miriam Smith

Perhaps the most visible signs of citizen protest in early 2003 as the Chrétien government entered its final months in office were the large anti-Iraq-war demonstrations taking place in Canada's cities. These protests followed in the wake of major demonstrations in 2001 organized by the burgeoning anti-globalization movement at the Quebec City Summit of the Americas. In Montreal, Ottawa, Toronto, and Vancouver, antipoverty protestors occupied vacant property, establishing "squats" to challenge government social and housing policies. In Ottawa, gun control opponents burned their firearm registration cards in a demonstration against the new gun registry. Canadian farmers led a campaign to influence federal policies on the rules governing agricultural trade before the World Trade Organization (WTO) and protested new tariffs imposed by the U.S. The Canadian Council of Chief Executives, a business lobby group, argued for Canadian–U.S. security cooperation at the border after the 9/11 terrorist attacks. Parents in Ontario schools took the provincial government to court, after the province implemented funding cuts by circumventing the elected school board. Trade unions, appearing before the Romanow Commission on Health Care in 2002, argued for the preservation of public medicare. While these groups differed in the means by which they exercised influence—some protested in the streets while others wrote letters to the prime minister—in all of these cases, the interests involved were defined by non-territorial political cleavages: antiwar, anti-globalization, and antipoverty protestors; gun owners; farmers; business; parents; and labour.

Groups and social movements have traditionally been viewed as key links between citizens and government. While the electoral system provides for the territorial representation of citizens, groups and movements organize citizens according to non-territorial interests and identities. In the electoral system, voters choose a representative of the geographical area in which they live; in group politics, citizens join together with like-minded citizens to form a group or movement that reflects political cleavages such as economic interests, gender, language, race, or simply political opinions.

Group and movement organizations allow for the articulation of political opinions that are much more specific than those that can be expressed through voting periodically in a federal or provincial election or even by actively participating in party politics. Some citizens may feel that none of the parties represents their views on issues that are important to them. Environmentalists, for example, might feel that party politics is a waste of time and that their political activism would be more effectively channelled through participation in the environmental movement. Canadians who support the pro-life side of the abortion debate may join a pro-life organization that reflects their specific viewpoint. Many Canadians belong to religious and cultural organizations; although these organizations do not exist primarily to influence government, they may from time to time involve themselves in politics and aim to influence government policy. Some citizens may feel that government is not serving their interests and may organize in their own communities to provide services that they feel are needed. Many women's organizations, such as rape crisis lines and battered women's shelters, started out as community-based organizations that were intended to fill gaps in public services.

In recent years, a public discourse has developed in Canadian politics that views group politics as reflecting so-called special interests. In this view, advocacy groups are depicted as reflecting minority points of view and as pushing their extreme views on an unwilling silent majority. Such a perspective does not bear close scrutiny. Group politics in Canada includes organizations ranging from the left to the right of the political spectrum, from groups opposed to gun control to feminists, from trade unions and farmers' organizations to high-powered business groups such as the Canadian Bankers' Association. Group politics also comes in a large number of organizational forms ranging from tightly organized mass membership organizations to movements composed of networked activists with little formal organization.

Group politics is not a level playing field. Some groups have more power in the Canadian political system than others. Ironically, it is the traditionally marginalized groups such as welfare recipients, women, and people of colour who are usually labelled "special interests." Such a public discourse ignores the privileged position of business in a capitalist market economy such as Canada's. It also ignores the long-recognized fact that a lively and active group politics is one of the essential preconditions for a democratic political system. In newly democratizing societies such as the countries of the former communist bloc, much attention has been paid to the task of building "civil society," that is, non-state organizations that bring citizens with common interests and identities together. And so, far from allowing the minority to override the majority, a rich and diverse associational system is a vital characteristic of democratic political life.

THEORETICAL PERSPECTIVES ON GROUP POLITICS

Political scientists have developed a number of different perspectives to explain the role of groups in the political process. Each of these makes different assumptions about what groups are and about how they exercise political influence. There is a broad range of such theories and this chapter will briefly discuss several of the most important: pluralism, neo-pluralism, structural approaches, and social movement theory.

For many decades, the dominant view in most empirical studies of group politics in Canada has been pluralism. The pluralists view society as divided by multiple lines of political cleavage. Each individual citizen has a diverse set of interests and preferences, any one of which can form the basis for participation in a group that seeks to influence government. In Canadian society, for example, language, religion, region, socioeconomic status, gender, and ethnicity might all be considered important lines of political cleavage. Groups form when like-minded individuals join together in pursuit of their common interests and pressure or lobby government for policies that will favour their group. Pluralists usually describe such groups as "interest groups" or "pressure groups."

Because there are many potential political cleavages in complex societies, pluralist theory argues that no one group will ever dominate politics for long. If one group becomes too powerful, another group will arise to counterbalance its power. In this view, public policy is a reflection of the struggle between groups. State actors such as politicians and bureaucrats are not seen as playing an independent role in the development of public policy. Pluralist theory suggests that all is well in democratic societies because there are multiple access points to the political system for all citizens through group politics. Even if one group wins a particular conflict over public policy, the same group is unlikely to win all the time.

In the 1960s and after, pluralist theory was found wanting on several fronts. The social conflicts of this era suggested that not everyone has access to the political system. Some groups may be permanently marginalized and some groups may indeed have more power than others. The government itself may play a key role in shaping the public agenda. In response to these criticisms, the pluralists developed a new perspective, often called neo-pluralism.[1] The neo-pluralists conceded two important points to critics of the original pluralist theory. First of all, they acknowledged that democratic capitalist societies such as Canada might be characterized by persistent social inequality that would create barriers to the formation and influence of interest groups. For example, poor people are unlikely to have the economic and social resources to form effective interest groups, and their interests will not be reflected in the political system. The political system itself may "mobilize bias"; that is, certain types of political issues may be mobilized out of political consideration and debate. For example, until recently, the idea that Canadian society might be characterized by a pervasive racism was not a subject of political debate. The issue of racism was simply ignored or denied by governments and by powerful groups in the political system. Political debate was biased against consideration of the problem of racism in Canadian society and of how public policies could be designed to deal with it. Second, the neo-pluralists recognized that governments themselves could play an important role in the development of public policy. Governments were not simply carrying out the wishes of the strongest group. Politicians and bureaucrats were actively involved in the development of public policy and often used groups to communicate with particular constituencies of citizens and to legitimate their policies. Groups might advocate their interests to government but the bureaucracy might also develop institutionalized links with key groups and consult them regularly on the formation of policy.

In contrast to pluralism and neo-pluralism, structural theories of the role of social forces in the political process stress that the power relations are not the result of individual choices but of socially patterned behaviour, collective action, and institutional and organizational configurations. Individual choices are overwhelmed by the structural forces that shape behaviour. The pattern of group formation is affected by factors such as economic and social inequality, which create systematic obstacles for marginalized groups in the political system. There are a number of such structural theories, including Marxism and neo-Marxism as well as approaches that emphasize the role of gender and race in shaping the organization and mobilization of social forces in politics.

The most elaborated structural theory is Marxism and its neo-Marxist variants. Unlike the pluralists and neo-pluralists who see social forces as organized into "groups" or "interest groups," for Marxists social forces are organized into classes. Classes are not merely socioeconomic groupings such as "middle class" or "lower class" but are specifically defined by their relationship to the means of production. For Marxists, the economic organization of society determines class relationships. In a capitalist economic system such as Canada's in which property is privately owned, the means of production (land, labour, and capital) are owned by the capitalist class or the bourgeoisie, and the working class or proletariat, which does not own the means of production, is forced to work in order to live. The capitalist class attempts to extract as much value from the labour of the working class as possible and the working class, in turn, struggles to resist this exploitation. The conflict between capitalists and workers in a capitalist economy is termed *the class struggle*.

In the Marxist view, political conflict centres on the class struggle between workers and capitalists.[2] This structural perspective constitutes a profound critique of the pluralist and neo-pluralist perspective on the role of interest groups. It suggests that the main cleavages in society are not based on multiple group membership but on economic divisions rooted in the capitalist economic system. All groups in society do not have access to the political system; rather, the system is profoundly unequal and the subordinated classes face structural barriers to political influence and participation. There is no tendency toward equilibrium between groups in a capitalist society. Instead, the system is characterized by the contested domination of one class.

Aside from Marxism, there are a number of other structural approaches to understanding the role of social forces in politics. The rise of the women's movement has highlighted the role of patriarchy as a social structure in shaping the discourse and practice of politics. A structural feminist approach to understanding group and movement behaviour in Canadian politics would emphasize the extent to which such activities are gendered. Women and men face very different opportunities for social, economic, and political participation and much of the discourse of mainstream politics defines such activities as inherently male, mobilizing women's interests and identities out of the political arena.

Historically, political participation in Canada, including group and movement activity, has been shaped by gender. Men have led and participated in group and movement activity. There are no data on the extent to which the universe of group and movement activity in Canadian politics today reflects this gendered participation in politics, a finding that in itself demonstrates the ways in which our definition of politics has been based in the assumptions of patriarchy. While women's organizations such as the National Action Committee on the Status of Women (NAC) have consistently challenged patriarchal assumptions, they have faced a backlash from antifeminist groups. Much of the leadership of the English-speaking women's movement in Canada is characterized by what Jill Vickers calls "radical liberalism," a view that is relatively optimistic about the possibilities for policy gains for women from the Canadian state,[3] but other feminists challenge this view. As Sandra Burt describes in Chapter 14, radical feminists would argue that it is only through the thorough transformation of social, economic, and political institutions that patriarchal social relations can be fundamentally altered.

Another structural approach to understanding group politics in Canada focuses on the role of racism in shaping group and movement political activity. As Daiva Stasiulis and Yasmeen Abu-Laban argue in Chapter 15, Canadian political science has traditionally ignored race and racism. Yet it is undeniable that most group and movement activity in Canadian politics is dominated by members of the British and French groups and that Canadian politics itself has usually been defined as being about the British–French cleavage. This dominant discourse has marginalized the participation and concerns of non-British, non-French groups in Canadian society. A structural approach to understanding the role of racism in group and movement politics in Canada focuses on the ways in which group and movement activity are shaped by power relationships between ethnic and racial groups that systematically operate to the benefit of some at the expense of others. Such power relationships are based on the legacies of colonialism and imperialism in Canadian society.

Social movement theory describes yet another approach to understanding group activity in politics. In part, it is based on the experiences of the 1960s when a number of new movements arose that posed profound challenges to the status quo. The women's movement, the environmental movement, the gay liberation movement, the peace movement, the student movement, and the civil rights movement suggested that all was not well with capitalist democracies. *New left* movements, as they were sometimes termed, engaged in mass protests and demonstrations and generated a culture of transformative and liberatory politics. These spontaneous mass protests seemed to be fundamentally different from the well-organized and institutionalized interest groups of pluralist theory and from the class politics of neo-Marxist theories.

What is a social movement? The broadest definition is offered by Manuel Castells: "purposive collective actions whose outcome, in victory as in defeat, transforms the values and institutions of society."[4] The typical depiction of social movements suggests that such movements have certain features that distinguish them from other forms of group politics. For example, the social movements of the 1960s and later challenged the traditional boundary between state and society, public and private. In pluralist and neo-pluralist theory, there is a clear distinction between state and society. Groups form in society and attempt to influence the state, and although groups may develop institutionalized links to government, there is still a clear distinction between public and private.

Social movements challenge this distinction, arguing that "the personal is political," and bring issues that were once defined as private into the sphere of public debate and discussion. For example, violence within the family was once an issue that was not discussed in public debate. The women's movement politicized the issue of violence against women in general and violence in the family in particular. Social movements may also challenge the public–private divide by demonstrating how the private sphere is imbued with power relationships or politics. The gay liberation movement challenged the heterosexual assumption of the public presentation of sexuality. The women's movement pointed to power relationships within the family and within relationships as profoundly political. The environmental and animal rights movements have challenged human dominance over the natural world and animals, recasting economic issues as environmental concerns and injecting completely new issues such as animal testing into public consciousness.

Social movements may also emphasize the creation and reinforcement of identity and the promotion of certain values over the pursuit of material interests. As such, social movement goals may be primarily aimed at society rather than the state. The second wave of the women's movement often engaged in consciousness-raising, in which small groups of women would meet to share their experiences. In the process, women realized that their problems and experiences were not unique, that many women had had similar experiences, and that their problems had social and political causes. In this way, a common bond of solidarity was created among feminist women and a new identity was formed which, in turn, provided the base for women's mobilizing. Many of the goals of the women's movement, such as ending violence against women, are aimed at changing the definition of socially acceptable behaviour or, as Alberto Melucci has put it, challenging the dominant "codes" of society.[5] Although state policies may also be targeted, state policy alone cannot effect changes in social behaviour. Similarly, the environmental movement encourages people to "reduce, reuse, recycle," thus targeting the dominant cultural codes and social practices of consumerism.

Social movements may engage in strategies and tactics that are more radical than those used by interest groups. While interest groups may attempt to influence government policy through the conventional means of lobbying politicians or bureaucrats in one form or another, social movements often engage in direct action tactics. For example, the environmental movement has often chosen to confront its opponents directly rather than to work with government. The dispute over clear-cut logging is an example. Environmentalists have spiked trees and chained themselves to trees to prevent clear-cut logging. Such direct action tactics are often particularly useful to social movements because they create dramatic media footage that can be used to promote the values of the movement. Large-scale disruptive demonstrations and protests may also be used to force government action and to capture media attention.

Social movements may also have a more decentralized and democratic organization than interest groups. Social movements often form as loose networks of activists with little formal organization, and even where formal organizations exist, they are often highly decentralized. The new left, for example, explicitly rejected bureaucratization and majority rule as oppressive, and often operated by direct democracy, task rotation, and consensus decision making, in which each member of the group could veto group decisions and in which leadership tasks were rotated among members.

In reality, social movements may not conform to any ideal, typical picture. Some social movements have been quite well organized, at least during certain periods, and may seek to influence government through participation in consultative exercises or policy communities. Unlike traditional interest groups, social movements usually form networks of smaller groups rather than well-organized and hegemonic organizations. In the environmental field, for example, it has been estimated that there are at least 1800 individual environmental groups in Canada. Rather than conforming to the ideal type description of social movement political behaviour, many movements may follow a dual strategy of influencing the state and influencing society. Environmental groups may lobby government while engaging in activities that are designed to influence public opinion and to change social attitudes. In practice then, social movements pursue diverse strategies.[6]

Why do social movements arise? There are two views on this question. Some feel that social movements mobilize preexisting grievances. It is not the grievances that are new but the resources that movements can bring to bear to press their demands.[7] Others argue that social movements are increasingly a feature of the developed capitalist democracies as the older class-based politics has declined. According to this view, the developed democracies are increasingly post-materialist, that is, their political cultures are increasingly oriented around non-material political issues such as identities and values. Post-materialist values emphasize issues such as quality of life and political participation rather than the material questions of who gets what, when, where, and how. This political cultural change sets the stage for the rise of movements that stress identity and non-material goals.[8]

While pluralism, neo-pluralism, and structural approaches to understanding the role of organized interests in politics offer different perspectives on power relations in society, social movement theory is best understood as describing a specific type of group activity. Unlike the pluralists or the Marxists, social movement theorists do not have a unified or coherent view of power relationships in society. Some studies of social movements follow a structural approach while others reduce social movement organizations to the status of pressure groups competing with other groups for the attention of governments, not unlike classical pluralist theory.

METHODS OF INFLUENCE

In the Canadian classic *Group Politics and Public Policy*, A. Paul Pross describes a number of ways in which collective actors may seek to influence society and government, including influencing bureaucracy, influencing politicians and elections, influencing the courts, and influencing the media.[9] To this list, we may also add the ways in which collective actors in Canadian politics are increasingly forming alliances across borders and engaging in activism that is primarily aimed outside of Canada.

INFLUENCING POLITICIANS

In Canada's Westminster-style political system, the governing party usually has a majority government. Because of party discipline, it is unlikely that MPs for the governing party will vote against their own government, and opposition MPs do not have the numbers to stop government legislative initiatives or to pass their own proposals in the legislature. For collective actors seeking to influence government policy, then, targeting individual members of the legislature, whether on the governing or opposition side, is not a fruitful strategy.[10]

Under certain circumstances, however, individual members of the legislature may play a role in determining the outcome of political battles. The leadership of the governing party must retain the loyalty of its MPs and, although the leadership has many carrots and sticks to force MPs into line, there have been several occasions in recent years when the leadership has been faced with revolts in its own caucus over the direction of government policies. For example, in the 1980s, the Mulroney government faced a major controversy within its own caucus on the issue of abortion. The government proposed a compromise bill that satisfied neither the pro-choice nor the pro-life sides, and pressure from within the party created an opportunity for groups on both sides of the question to lobby MPs and even senators. The bill was finally defeated in the Senate on a tie vote after a furious lobbying effort by both pro-life and pro-choice sides.[11] Similarly, the Chrétien government has faced divisive debates about gun control and lesbian and gay rights. Organized interests can play a key role in such battles both by mobilizing public opinion to create pressure on MPs and by seizing the opportunities created by caucus rifts to change the direction of government policy.

Another method by which collective actors may seek to influence politicians is by intervening in elections, by supporting certain parties or candidates and opposing others. It has been estimated that in the 1988 federal election campaign, third parties spent $4.7 million, most of it on the free trade issue.[12] While spending by parties and candidates is regulated under the Election Expenses Act, it has proved difficult to check campaign spending by third parties. On two occasions, the federal government has passed legislation to limit spending by advocacy groups in election campaigns and, on two occasions, this legislation has been challenged successfully by the National Citizens' Coalition.

The question of permitting groups to advocate their points of view during election campaigns was considered extensively by the Royal Commission on Electoral Reform and Party Financing (the Lortie Commission), which reported in 1991. The commission recommended a limit on third-party spending, arguing that third parties should not be able to influence election outcomes through expenditure. Such spending would privilege groups and individuals that have money, allowing them disproportionate influence in election campaigns. On the other hand, groups such as the National Citizens' Coalition argue that limiting election spending by groups is an unreasonable abrogation of the right of free expression. From this perspective, it seems undemocratic to limit the expression of political views during election campaigns when groups have the right to spend in support of their views at other times. Based on studies of the 1988 election in which pro– and anti–free trade groups spent considerable sums attempting to influence the campaign, it is not clear that third-party spending significantly influenced the outcome of the campaign.[13]

INFLUENCING BUREAUCRACY

One of the fruits of the neo-pluralist approach to understanding the role of groups in Canadian politics has been the emphasis on institutionalized and regularized linkages between bureaucracy and groups. These institutionalized linkages between the bureaucracy and collective actors are often termed policy communities. The policy community is composed of advocacy groups with an interest or "stake" in a particular area of public policy and the relevant government departments or agencies that are involved in the same area of policy. In the policy community, the links between the bureaucracy and the stakeholder groups are regularized; bureaucrats routinely consult groups over the general and specific direction of policy. For groups, this means regular access to bureaucratic decision makers who are developing the policies and policy choices that may ultimately be either routinely approved by the minister or presented to Cabinet. Because of the growth of government during the twentieth century and the increasing complexity of policy development, many routine policy decisions are now made in the bureaucracy. Even when the bureaucracy is developing policy options rather than making policy decisions, its influence in the general direction of policy development is substantial. This influence results from the concentration of expertise in departmental policy branches and the fact that the Cabinet is essentially a non-expert body.

The policy community works best for groups that meet several criteria. In order to interact with government, groups must be relatively well organized and institutionalized, with regular membership, a secure financial base, and policy expertise. The group's claim to represent a certain constituency is key to the influence it can exercise. Some groups may represent a large number of members and may thus claim to speak for a certain social group. For example, NAC has over 500 member groups. Other organizations, such as the Canadian Council of Chief Executives or the Canadian Bankers' Association, may have only a few large and influential members (corporations and banks, respectively). Furthermore, the group must have relatively narrow policy goals that can fit within the ambit of existing government policies. Groups whose goals are too broad or that are at odds with the stated principles and direction of government policy will be unlikely to obtain a foothold in the policy community. To participate in the policy community, groups must have a certain degree of knowledge about government and its workings as well as specialized knowledge about the particular policy area.

The bureaucracy may have several reasons for seeking to bring organized groups into the policy process. For government, it may be cheaper to obtain some types of information from groups than to seek out the information directly. Groups may have information that is useful to government, such as information about the views of their own members or information about policy options and implementation. For example, if government wants to know what farmers think about the implications of World Trade Organization (WTO) agreements on agriculture, one of the fastest and cheapest ways to find out is to ask farmers' groups. Groups can also provide feedback on the effects of existing policies and on the feasibility of policy alternatives, based on their own experience and expertise.

Aside from information, the bureaucracy may also be seeking the legitimacy that group support can provide for government policies. Certain groups play a key role, especially through the media, in legitimating government policy. While the views of opposition parties in Parliament may receive some media play in coverage of the government's policies or legislative initiatives, opposition parties are expected to oppose the government of the day and the public may discount their views to a certain extent. In contrast, the opinions of groups that do not appear to be associated with the governing party may be more legitimate in the public eye. The annual release of the federal budget is a good example of a time when the media seeks out groups to approve or disapprove of the government's course of action. Predictably, budget reaction starts off with the views of the opposition parties and then moves on to reaction from business and labour as well as from farmers, consumers, small business, and antipoverty groups. In this manner, governments gain legitimacy from group support as well as information about the views of group members and about policy effects and options.

The state itself plays a key role in shaping policy communities, with the structure of government in part determining their role and organization. In Canada, a relatively decentralized federal system means that organized interests must often participate at both levels of government and may themselves develop a decentralized organization with strong regional blocs that may inhibit concerted action. The government may directly encourage the formation of organized interests to represent particular sectors by providing core or occasional funding to organizations.[14] Government policies may further shape the nature of the policy community by providing incentives for alliances among groups or by privileging some types of groups at the expense of others. Because of these differences, policy communities vary greatly across policy areas. Some policy communities contain one dominant group that represents most of the interests in the sector. Other policy communities are highly pluralistic, with a large number of competing groups. In some policy communities the state is able to play the lead role, while in others, the state itself is fragmented and particular departments and agencies may depend on the groups themselves for information and policy expertise but also as allies in interdepartmental competition.[15]

INFLUENCING THE COURTS

In recent years, there has been an increase in the use of the courts by groups to further their policy objectives. The entrenchment of the Charter of Rights and Freedoms in the Constitution in 1982 has enhanced the possibilities for groups to use courts to advance their goals. Entrenched human rights protections have increased the opportunities for litigation by equality-seeking groups. The Charter regulates the relationship between governments and citizens by laying out basic rights that governments may not infringe. For example, under section 15 of the Charter, governments may not discriminate on the basis of sex, race, and other grounds. This has resulted in an increase in human rights cases reaching the courts. Strong protections for official language minority rights in the Charter have also resulted in a large number of court cases. In some cases, groups have either brought complaints to the courts or intervened as third parties in court cases.

Another reason for the increase in group involvement in litigation arises from changes in the Supreme Court's rules on intervention by third parties in court cases and on standing to bring cases. The Court has loosened up its rules to permit greater access to litigation by third parties that wish to present their views to the court in particular cases.[16] A broad range of groups has litigated under the Charter. Litigation—or even the threat of litigation—has become a common weapon in the arsenal of group politics. For example, lesbian and gay rights organizations used litigation to shape public policy on same-sex relationships recognition at the provincial and federal levels. Gun control opponents challenged the 1995 Firearms Act as a violation of Charter rights and an infringement of provincial jurisdiction. Ethnocultural organizations have intervened in cases involving racial profiling and fairness in jury selection for people of colour.

Group involvement with litigation should not be exaggerated, however. Many collective actors used litigation as a tactic prior to the Charter.[17] Aboriginal people used the courts to force recognition of land claims in the Calder case in the early 1970s. Manitoba francophones litigated to protect the education and language rights that had been guaranteed to them by the terms of Manitoba's entry into Confederation in 1870. In the Persons Case, five Canadian women litigated for the right to be recognized as "persons" for the purpose of appointment to the Senate. While litigation was a political weapon in the Canadian political system prior to the Charter, the Charter has certainly created new openings for such litigation. In the first 10 years after the Charter's entrenchment, the most common type of Charter challenge occurred in the area of criminal law.

Business has also been in the forefront of the use of the Charter, especially on issues such as freedom of expression (e.g., business's right to direct advertising at children).[18]

INFLUENCING THE MEDIA

The success of collective actors in challenging government policy or seeking to influence social norms and values may be greatly enhanced through the skillful use of the media. In particular, when groups seek to influence politicians and elections, the media provide a vehicle for drawing public attention to the group's point of view. In the cases of gun control, abortion, and lesbian and gay rights, supporters and opponents on each issue attempted to capture the media's attention as a way of bringing pressure to bear on MPs. Because media such as television tend to focus on dramatic conflicts within a limited time frame, groups that can successfully produce quick sound bites tend to receive more attention than collective actors who are attempting to call attention to the structural forces that shape government policy or societal norms.

In the case of environmentalism, for example, there are a wide variety of "deep ecology" perspectives that emphasize how economic development in many parts of the world threatens humanity's survival. However, complex scientific and philosophical arguments about deep ecology are unlikely to produce the quick media clips that television demands. Hence, successful environmental groups have often sought to dramatize environmental issues in ways that can be captured easily for global media consumption. As Stephen Dale has pointed out, Greenpeace is a master of media tactics. By capturing media attention, a tiny band of Greenpeace protesters were able to draw worldwide media attention to a U.S. nuclear test in the Aleutian Islands in 1971 by sailing into the test site. This was Greenpeace's start as an environmental organization. From a few protesters in an old fishing boat, Greenpeace grew into an international organization with a budget of U.S.$28.3 million in 1994.[19]

TRANSNATIONAL CONNECTIONS

Globalization has had important effects for group mobilization in Canadian politics. More than ever, public policy is subject to pressures from beyond Canada's borders. Enhanced communications technology facilitates links between groups across borders. International organizations ranging from the World Trade Organization (WTO) to the United Nations (UN) play an increased role in the making of policy decisions.

Trade agreements such as the North American Free Trade Agreement (NAFTA) limit the range of policy choices that are open to government. This process of "decentring" the state, as Magnusson has termed it, has been characterized by a marked increase in transnational group activity in recent years.[20] These increased transnational and global connections can be divided into several ideal types; in practice, transnational organizing will often overlap these categories. First, organized social forces in Canadian politics may appeal to international organizations to pressure the Canadian state. This may occur in cases in which groups have failed in their efforts to achieve positive results through domestic strategies alone. As Radha Jhappan has argued, Canada's aboriginal peoples have increasingly sought to use international organizations such as the UN to bring pressure to bear on Canadian governments. The Lubicons in Alberta appealed to the UN in their dispute with logging companies and the Alberta government. The UN Human Rights Committee ruled that Canada had violated the International Covenant on Civil and Political Rights in its treatment of the Lubicons.[21]

Second, organized groups in Canada may form alliances with other groups outside of Canada. In the last 20 years, First Nations in Canada have developed links with indigenous peoples around the world, especially through the World Council of Indigenous Peoples. Another example of transnational linkage is the campaign against the Free Trade Agreement of the Americas (FTAA), which organized huge protests at the Quebec City Summit of the Americas in April 2001. A broad range of groups from across the Americas protested the expansion of neoliberal hemispheric free trade agreements. Such linkages are in part the product of the trade agreements themselves; for example, as Gabriel and Macdonald have demonstrated with regard to NAFTA, linkages are developing between feminist activists in Canada and Mexico as women attempt to deal with the economic, social, and political consequences of North American economic restructuring.[22]

Third, groups within Canada may mobilize to influence politics elsewhere in the world, targeting foreign states or international organizations in an effort to influence the behaviour, policies, and practices of foreign states and international actors. The 2002 movement against war in Iraq is one such example. Another is the student-led protest at the University of British Columbia in 1997 that targeted the APEC (Asia-Pacific Economic Cooperation) leaders' summit. The protesters argued that China and Indonesia's leaders were responsible for extensive human rights violations and that the effects of APEC were "massive job losses, environmental degradation, the commodification of culture, the displacement and genocide of indigenous peoples, greater disparities in wealth, the trafficking of women and children, human rights violations, less and less local democracy and greater corporate control."[23] The student protesters were mainly concerned about the effect of APEC for peoples outside of Canada.

In many cases, the boundaries between these types of activities overlap. For example, Canadian women have been active at several different levels on the issue of the problems facing refugees and, in particular, refugee women. Canadian activists have participated with activists from other countries in the International NGO Working Group on Refugee Women that has consistently advocated for more protection for refugee women from the United Nations High Commission on Refugees. Activists have pressured the Canadian government to change its requirements for refugee status for admission to Canada to recognize gender persecution. In addition, feminists have worked to directly assist refugee women both in refugee camps and in gaining admission to Canada. In this case, women's activism in the area of refugees has focused on pressuring both international organizations and the Canadian government as well as on providing direct services to refugee women and capturing media attention to the gender-specific problems and experiences of refugee women. This activism has been channelled through a network of NGOs, some Canadian, some transnational in their membership and scope.[24] This is an excellent example of the ways in which transnationalism overlaps with domestic politics.

FUTURE DIRECTIONS

Traditional political science theories of the role of groups and movements have tended to focus on the relationships between these forces and domestic states. Yet the state itself is in relative decline, as evidenced by the Canadian government's decreased autonomy in areas such as economic policy. The advent of increased levels of globalization in finance and communications and the larger role played by international institutions such as the WTO and the OECD (Organization for Economic Cooperation and Development) and by trade agreements such as NAFTA and the FTAA have changed the space in which politics occurs. Increasingly, the arenas of politics are transnational, global, and international rather than domestic. As the evidence on increased transnational connections between social movements and NGOs makes clear, the boundaries between domestic and international group activity are blurring. Domestic governments have become one target among many in group politics rather than the preeminent target of group activity that they were even a decade ago. This does not mean that governments are irrelevant; it merely means that their relative authority and autonomy have declined and that there are other institutional levers for the exercise of group influence. As this development occurs, students of group politics in Canada will increasingly have to look beyond the domestic context to understand the full parameters and spaces of group political life.

NOTES

1. For a survey of pluralism and neo-pluralism, see Stephen Lukes, *Power: A Radical View* (London: Macmillan, 1974). For a Canadian discussion, see A. Paul Pross, *Group Politics and Public Policy*, 2nd ed. (Toronto: Oxford University Press, 1992), pp. 230–43.

2. For a Canadian survey of Marxist approaches, see Leo Panitch, "Elites, Classes, and Power in Canada," in Michael S. Whittington and Glen Williams, eds., *Canadian Politics in the 1990s* (Toronto: Nelson, 1995), pp. 152–75.

3. Jill Vickers, "The Intellectual Origins of the Women's Movement in Canada," in Constance Backhouse and David Flaherty, eds., *Challenging Times: The Women's Movement in Canada and the United States* (Montreal: McGill-Queen's University Press, 1992).

4. Manuel Castells, *The Power of Identity* (Oxford: Blackwell, 1997), p. 3.

5. Alberto Melucci, *Challenging Codes: Collective Action in the Information Age* (Cambridge: Cambridge University Press, 1996).

6. On environmental groups, see Jeremy Wilson, "Green Lobbies: Pressure Groups and Environmental Policy," in Robert Boardman, ed., *Canadian Environmental Policy: Ecosystems, Politics and Process* (Toronto: Oxford University Press, 1992), pp. 109–25.

7. J. Craig Jenkins, "Resource Mobilization Theory and the Study of Social Movements," *American Review of Sociology* 9 (1993): 527–53.

8. Claus Offe, "New Social Movements: Challenging the Boundaries of Institutional Politics," *Social Research* 53: 4 (1985). On post-materialism, see Ronald Inglehart, *Modernization and Postmodernization: Cultural, Economic and Political Change in 43 Societies* (Princeton: Princeton University Press, 1997).

9. Pross, pp. 140–86.

10. For a survey of the literature on advocacy in Parliament, see F. Leslie Seidle, "Interest Advocacy through Parliamentary Channels: Representation and Accommodation," in F. Leslie Seidle, ed., *Equity and Community: The Charter, Interest Advocacy and Representation* (Montreal: Institute for Research on Public Policy, 1993), pp. 189–223.

11. Janine Brodie, Shelley A.M. Gavigan, and Jane Jenson, *The Politics of Abortion* (Toronto: Oxford University Press, 1992).

12. Janet Hiebert, "Fair Elections and Freedom of Expression under the Charter," *Journal of Canadian Studies* 24 (Winter 1989): 23.

13. William Cross, "Regulating Independent Expenditures in Federal Elections," *Canadian Public Policy* 20, no. 3 (1994): 253–64.

14. Leslie A. Pal, *Interests of State: The Politics of Language, Multiculturalism and Feminism in Canada* (Montreal: McGill-Queen's University Press, 1993).

15. William D. Coleman and Grace Skogstad, "Policy Communities and Policy Networks: An Integrated Approach," in William D. Coleman and Grace Skogstad, eds.,

Policy Communities and Public Policy in Canada: A Structural Approach (Mississauga: Copp Clark Pitman, 1990), pp. 14–33.

16. Sharon Levine, "Advocating Values: Public Interest Intervention in Charter Litigation," *National Journal of Constitutional Law* 2 (1993): 27–62.

17. Kent Roach, "The Role of Litigation and the Charter in Interest Advocacy," in F. Leslie Seidle, ed., *Equity and Community: The Charter, Interest Advocacy and Representation* (Montreal: Institute for Research on Public Policy, 1993), pp. 159–88.

18. Richard W. Bauman, "Business, Economic Rights, and the Charter," in David Schneiderman and Kate Sutherland, eds., *Charting the Consequences: The Impact of Charter Rights on Canadian Law and Politics* (Toronto: University of Toronto Press, 1997), pp. 58–108.

19. Stephen Dale, *McLuhan's Children: The Greenpeace Message and the Media* (Toronto: Between the Lines, 1996), pp. 4, 15ff.

20. Warren Magnusson, "Decentring the State," in James Bickerton and Alain-G. Gagnon, eds., *Canadian Politics* (Peterborough: Broadview Press, 1994).

21. C. Radha Jhappan, "Global Community?: Supranational Strategies of Canada's Aboriginal Peoples," *Journal of Indigenous Studies* 3, no. 1 (Winter 1992): 64–68.

22. Christina Gabriel and Laura Macdonald, "NAFTA, Women and Organising in Canada and Mexico: Forging a Feminist Internationality?" *Millennium* 23, no. 3 (Winter 1994): 535–62.

23. University of British Columbia, APEC Alert, "What the hell is APEC?" <www.cs.ubc.ca/spider/fuller/apec_alert/propoganda/what_the_hell.html>.

24. Ruth Roach Pierson, "Global Issues," in Ruth Roach Pierson and Marjorie Cohen, eds., *Canadian Women's Issues, Volume II: Bold Visions: Twenty-five Years of Women's Activism in English Canada* (Toronto: James Lorimer, 1995), pp. 385–93.

FURTHER READINGS

Agnew, Vijay. *Resisting Discrimination: Women from Asia, Africa and the Caribbean and the Women's Movement in Canada.* Toronto: University of Toronto Press, 1996.

Ayres, Jeffrey. *Defying Conventional Wisdom: Political Movements and Popular Contention Against Free Trade.* Toronto: University of Toronto Press, 1998.

Cameron, David, and Fraser Valentine, eds. *Disability and Federalism: Comparing Different Approaches to Full Participation.* Montreal: McGill-Queen's University Press, 2001.

Carroll, William K., ed. *Organizing Dissent: Contemporary Social Movements in Theory and Practice.* 2nd ed. Toronto: Garamond Press, 1997.

Dobrowolsky, Alexandra. *The Politics of Pragmatism: Women, Representation, and Constitutionalism in Canada.* Don Mills: Oxford University Press, 2000.

McKenzie, Judith. *Environmental Politics in Canada: Managing the Commons into the Twenty-First Century.* Don Mills: Oxford University Press, 2002.

Rayside, David. *On the Fringe: Lesbians and Gays in Politics.* Ithaca and London: Cornell University Press, 1998.

Robinson, Ian. "The International Dimension of Labour Federation Economic Strategy in Canada and United States, 1947–2000." In Robert O'Brien and Jeffrey Harrod, eds., *Global Unions? Theory and Strategy of Organized Labour in the Global Political Economy,* pp. 115–29. London: Routledge, 2002.

Smith, Miriam. "Ghosts of the JCPC: Group Politics and Charter Litigation in Canadian Political Science." *Canadian Journal of Political Science* 35, no. 1 (March 2002): 3–29.

Stanbury, William. *Business–Government Relations in Canada.* Scarborough: Nelson, 1993.

CHAPTER 10

GOVERNING THE CANADIAN ECONOMY: IDEAS AND POLITICS

Neil Bradford

In 2003, Finance Minister John Manley rose in Parliament to announce the federal government's sixth consecutive balanced budget. After nearly 50 years of having been confined by the imperative of restraint, the boundaries of Canadian macroeconomic policymaking have now expanded to include debates about how to allocate annual budgetary surpluses. Are they to be used for program spending, tax reduction, or debt repayment? Indeed, the new "politics of the surplus" has reopened fundamental questions about Ottawa's proper role and responsibilities in relation to the economy, society, the provinces, and the international community.

For citizens and governments alike, much is at stake in the struggle to re-define Canadian macroeconomic policy. Decisions about expenditure, taxation, and the money supply directly affect the public issues that people care most about in their daily lives: the availability of jobs, the stability of prices, the cost of borrowing, the amount of disposable income, and the quality of health care. Moreover, Ottawa's "spending and cutting" choices reverberate across the country's critical political fault lines, shaping conceptions of social citizenship, national identity, federal–provincial relations, and public security. Simply put, macroeconomic policy is central to modern governance. In complexity and breadth, it is truly a policy field "unlike the others."

This chapter analyzes the dynamics of federal budgeting, tracing developments from the dawn of modern macroeconomic policy in the Great Depression of the 1930s to the present day. The historical narrative is structured by the concept of the governing policy paradigm, an analytical device that captures the crucial interplay over time between ideas and politics in macroeconomic policy. This field is both politically charged and technically complex. Governments rely on the advice of professional economists, who devise sophisticated models to understand the economy and forecast its direction. As such, governing macroeconomic paradigms are coherent policy doctrines that acquire for a time substantial influence in the expert community, the political system, and departments of state.

We will see that Canadian macroeconomic policy has been governed by two such paradigms. Keynesian economic theory organized federal policy for nearly three decades after World War II, and neoliberalism assumed a similar dominance in the 1980s and 1990s. Today Canada approaches another macroeconomic crossroads, with the prevailing neoliberal paradigm under stress as a series of economic shocks and geopolitical crises challenge its premises. No clear alternative has yet crystallized to underpin either a re-formulated expert consensus or political realignment. The chapter closes with consideration of the emerging lines of conflict over the best macroeconomic route for the early twenty-first century.

BASIC DEFINITIONS AND KEY CONCEPTS

Macroeconomic policy manages the "whole" economy through *fiscal policies* of aggregate spending and taxing and *monetary policies* for setting the money supply, interest rates, and the value of the dollar. Since the "Keynesian revolution" of the 1930s and 1940s, four basic objectives have been central to this process: economic growth, full employment, price stability, and balance-of-payments equilibrium. Controversy arises as governments set priorities among these objectives and give particular meanings to each. For example, basic judgments must be made about whether low unemployment or low inflation will be the key goal. Similarly, governments may re-define full employment to be when the unemployment rate is lower than 6 percent. Choices are also made about whether economic growth will be tempered by concerns about ecological sustainability, regional balance, or income distribution.

THE BUDGET

Government thinking in these matters is elaborated in the annual budget statement read by the Finance minister in Parliament. It details the government's expenditure and revenue plans, announces new programs or tax changes, and forecasts the budgetary deficit or surplus. Through budgets, governments communicate to the private sector and the public their economic priorities, ranking of macroeconomic objectives, and official definitions of optimal growth, employment, inflation, and trade balance. Internally, the budget is the key "framework document" for governing. Its allocations establish parameters and expectations around program initiatives for a host of state departments and their constituencies.

Four principal sets of actors influence federal budget making and therefore Canadian macroeconomic policy: the Department of Finance, the Bank of Canada, international financial markets, and provincial governments. In fiscal policy, the federal Cabinet, empowered constitutionally to introduce money bills into Parliament and equipped with general spending and revenue-raising capacity, is formally the central actor. More precisely, the Department of Finance dominates Ottawa's taxing and spending decisions. In monetary policy, the Bank of Canada is the major player, regulating the interest rate for borrowing money and the total amount of currency in circulation. While appointed by and accountable to the federal minister of Finance, the Bank's governor operates with substantial independence. (Finance ministers are generally unwilling to risk the turbulence in financial markets that could flow from public disputes between fiscal and monetary authorities.)

The next important player in macroeconomic policy is the international financial community, on which national governments increasingly depend for their borrowing. The power of these markets is indirect but significant. Monitoring the macroeconomic choices of governments, they impose penalties in the form of credit-rating downgrades or even national "currency runs" for what they deem irresponsible fiscal or monetary behaviour. The final principal actors in federal macroeconomic decision making, equally subject to the scrutiny of international money markets, are provincial governments. They are independent fiscal authorities responsible for about one-half of the total budget for the aggregate Canadian public sector. While control over the main fiscal, monetary, and exchange rate instruments is concentrated at the federal level, macroeconomic policy is characterized by extensive interdependence. Federal decisions about the use of its spending power in areas of provincial jurisdiction, or equally, about offloading strategies for its deficit reduction, have large consequences for provincial budget making.

Secondary players influencing federal macroeconomic policy include opposition political parties, organized interests and social movements, the media, and policy experts outside the state. In particular, business representatives command influence as corporate investment decisions condition the efficacy of spending and taxing instruments. Moreover, they often align themselves with international financial markets in linking "irresponsible" macroeconomic policy to threats of domestic capital flight. While other organizations—for example, those representing workers or the poor—do not enjoy the power of business, they may, by mobilizing their constituencies, gain representation in bureaucratic agencies that pressure the Department of Finance for specific expenditures. Finally, outside policy experts such as academics in universities or researchers in private-sector think tanks or financial institutions can shape choices by generating new and different analytical perspectives on macroeconomic objectives. Injected into public debates and official deliberations, these frameworks can shift perceptions of feasible policy options or priorities.

IDEAS AND POLITICS: GOVERNING PARADIGMS

The substantial role of experts in shaping macroeconomic policy underscores the importance of ideas in policy fields that are highly technical and that rely on theories and data generated by social scientific research.[1] In macroeconomic policy, these ideas take the form of well-developed policy paradigms that interpret past performance and project future trends. They define for governments the broad goals behind policy and the problems that must be solved to attain these goals. As such, policy paradigms address both "philosophical" matters about the legitimate role of the state in the economy and "technical" concerns about causal relationships among objectives and the likely effectiveness of potential instruments. Macroeconomic paradigms thus contain fundamental judgments about whether government intervention is needed to correct any alleged market shortcomings. They establish conceptual parameters for the annual budgeting process that, in turn, define programmatic possibilities in formally distinct policy fields including health, welfare, education, and technology.

Policy paradigms can be said to be *governing* when their public philosophies and technical models channel thought and behaviour in two key contexts: expert ideas and sociopolitical interests. In the former, social scientists coalesce behind certain theoretical suppositions and devote scholarly resources to applying this knowledge to society's problems. Disciplinary "mainstreams" (like those in economics) evolve socialization processes for professional recruitment and advancement that reinforce the intellectual power of the dominant paradigm. In the case of the political system, a similar dynamic can be observed as the influence of a policy paradigm spreads across institutional settings. Political parties invent symbols and rhetoric appropriate to the paradigm's definition of the public interest and the economic role of government. Societal actors make peace with the paradigm—

some on terms to their own liking, others coming only reluctantly to an accommodation. Civil servants develop new data sets, operating procedures, and administrative capacities to implement programs consistent with the paradigm. Finally, international financial markets incorporate new criteria for judging the performance of domestic governments.

In sum, when a governing paradigm is embedded in state and society there is a *match between the technical and political dimensions of public policy.* Controversy may persist but it will be confined to debates about the particulars of putting into practice widely accepted goals. Policy adjustments are incremental and political conflict is bounded by larger agreement. However, history reveals that such periods of consensus and accommodation are punctuated by episodes of breakdown, as "anomalies" emerge that cannot be managed, even understood, within the existing paradigm. At these critical junctures, intellectual debate and political struggle are especially intense. Research communities revisit first principles and causal theories. Partisan alignments and social alliances come apart. From this upheaval, a new governing paradigm reconnecting ideas, politics, and administration may emerge.

CANADA'S KEYNESIAN REVOLUTION: FROM THE 1940S TO THE 1970S

KEYNESIAN IDEAS

When the Great Depression savaged Canada in the 1930s, the federal government had virtually no recognizable macroeconomic policy. Guided by the nostrum of "sound finance," Conservative and Liberal cabinets had by tradition set a relatively limited role for the state in the economy. Unemployment, bankruptcy, foreclosure, and poverty were all understood to be individual and private matters, with families, churches, charities, and municipalities being the primary lines of defence. This narrow conception of the state's responsibilities reflected the prevailing laissez-faire philosophy of the period. As well, there was no analytical framework to inform an expanded government role. Public finance was more akin to accounting than economic management with its priority to ensure an annual balance between expenditures and revenues. Not yet considered was the state's potential role in maintaining not simply short-term, sound finance, but also, over the longer term, a sound economy.

The Depression provided the intellectual–political context for the Keynesian breakthrough in the second half of the 1930s. Keynesian economic theory proved "revolutionary" in a number of respects, but most obviously it provided a theoretical critique of economic orthodoxy about the self-correcting market. The capitalist economy, Keynes and his followers argued, was inherently subject to wild fluctuations rooted in the vagaries of business and consumer confidence. Even when interest rates were very low, private investment and expenditure could stagnate, leaving the economy in equilibrium at high levels of unemployment. The key problem was the lack of aggregate demand for goods and services, and this was not something natural or unalterable. For Keynesians, aggregate demand became a variable that was subject to conscious manipulation by governments through fiscal policy. Maintaining stability in investment and employment required adjusting expenditures over the full business cycle of boom and bust—stimulating demand through deficit financing in hard times and cooling inflationary pressures by running surpluses during booms.

Keynes saw public finance as no mere bookkeeping exercise. Reconceptualizing the economy as a field of strategic action where economists could offer their new knowledge to the "positive state," he enabled politicians to take responsibility for growth and employment. Conceived at the height of the Great Depression and emphasizing an active role for government, Keynesian macroeconomics privileged the employment objective over price stability and fiscal policy over monetary policy. Demand management, supported by low interest rates, encouraged private investment while reducing debt repayment charges. With this technical reconstruction in place, Keynesian theory's full political import came into focus. New policy tools were invented to address the major economic problem of the day—unemployment—and, further, governments were tutored on the details of their operation. Keynesian ideas mapped political ground beyond the polarized extremes of laissez-faire and centralized planning. Politicians could now take pragmatic but purposeful policy action to correct market failures.

Canada's Keynesian revolution was notable both because the policy transformations came late in comparison with breakthroughs in many other countries and because it was not driven by visionary politicians taking bold action in the face of the economic crisis. While workers and farmers devastated by the Great Depression created new parties to protest the economic orthodoxy, these new movements stalled electorally and remained marginal to official policy debates. In the end, senior civil servants pushed and pulled a reluctant federal Cabinet toward macroeconomic experimentation. Only the emergency of financing World War II moved Canadian policymakers to apply the economic innovations that the policy experts had produced in the 1930s through their work on various public inquiries, most importantly the National Employment Commission and the Royal Commission on Dominion–Provincial Relations (the Rowell-Sirois Commission). [2]

Emerging through techno-bureaucratic processes rather than in the public light of ideological competition between political parties, Canadian Keynesian theory proved more circumscribed and tentative than that evolving in countries where explicit political commitments were made to full employment, public investment in economic infrastructure, and labour force development. Such grand ideas were dismissed by the technocrats behind Canada's Keynesian paradigm as "impractical and illusory schemes for which there was neither the know-how nor a demonstrated need."[3] In place of structural reforms to capitalism, it was believed that government policy experts could stabilize the environment for private investment and restore confidence in the future. It followed that the institutional changes required to implement Canada's form of Keynesian theory were comparatively limited. Arrangements to centralize fiscal capacity within the federation were linked to renovation of Ottawa's administrative and statistical expertise in priming the pump of an essentially sound economy and then fine-tuning its operation. Canada's Keynesian countercyclical instruments of choice were corporate tax cuts and automatic social stabilizers such as unemployment insurance payments, which compensated for market fluctuations but limited government intervention.

Thus, in the early postwar years, economic experts moving between the departments of government and academia formalized the relationship between the "smart state" and Keynesian doctrine. National income analysis was anchored in economic models and forecasting techniques of increasing sophistication, expressing the shared expectations of public- and private-sector decision makers about the economy and public policy. The paradigm was housed in key bureaucratic locales such as the Finance and Reconstruction departments, and the Bank of Canada. Related support came from the Dominion Bureau of Statistics, which gathered the necessary data, and other federal line departments in health, welfare, and employment policy, which administered specific stabilization programs in partnership with the provinces. Further buttressing the domestic consensus were new international agreements and institutions mandated by national governments to stabilize and regulate financial and trade flows across borders, such as the General Agreement on Tariffs and Trade (GATT). Officials from Canada's Department of External Affairs also played a significant role in creating the facilitative international context for national implementation of Keynesian policy.

KEYNESIAN POLITICS

Canada's technical consensus eventually found its match in a political accommodation that encompassed party and interest-group systems and intergovernmental relations. In fact, the bureaucratic form of Keynesian theory proved well suited to the dynamics of Canada's party system. "Brokerage politics," pioneered by the Mackenzie King Liberals, emphasized political caution, policy vagueness, and balancing of multiple, often competing interests. Pressured by the leftist Co-operative Commonwealth Federation (CCF), the government found it useful in the late 1930s to defer the challenges of economic policy innovation to nonpartisan experts, and, in the mid-1940s, to re-fashion a partisan identity around the discourse of managerial efficiency and technocratic problem solving generated by Canada's Keynesians. As the Liberals made these shifts, the Conservatives also adjusted to the new paradigm: they embraced the positive state, added Progressive to their name, and chose John Bracken, a strong advocate of Keynesian theory, as leader. By 1945, both governing brokerage parties had created new space for their progressive factions: social Liberals and red Tories. Even the CCF moderated its earlier calls for the replacement of capitalism and embraced a form of "social Keynesianism" that questioned only specific aspects of the governing paradigm. Indeed, the depth and breadth of the Keynesian accommodation in the postwar federal party system led some observers to question its implications for democratic debate and policy accountability.[4]

Within the institutions of federalism, Ottawa linked its Keynesian fiscal and social measures to a new "centralism" constructed around the twin pillars of national standards and regional equalization. While Quebec remained at best a limited partner to the accommodation, the other provinces accepted the new paradigm and acknowledged Ottawa's leadership role. Keynesian economic theory supplied the terms for cooperative federalism expressed in official-level negotiation of fiscal arrangements for social programs and coordinated budgeting to counter business cycles. Meanwhile, regional conflicts among first ministers were muted as debate shifted to provincial claims on an expanding economic pie.

After the war, business, labour, and agricultural interests, like political parties, remained "policy takers," deferring to experts in matters of macroeconomic management. Both labour and agriculture had reasons to contest the limited form of Canadian Keynesian theory but lacked the national organizational capacity, not to mention the political clout, to advance alternatives. Consequently, they reacted to bureaucratic initiatives and accepted expert judgments about feasible options. Gaining political legitimacy and certain rights within the overall Keynesian philosophy, workers and farmers turned their attention to securing further protections through collective bargaining, agricultural marketing, and price support programs. For business, the Keynesian accommodation was smoothed by the technocratic emphasis on arm's-length government fine-tuning of private investment and capital formation. Moreover, business representatives were offered an ongoing voice in shaping the terms of Keynesian practice, as information about their investment intentions became critical in budget decisions and forecasts.

For the first three decades of the postwar period, Keynesian theory was a governing macroeconomic paradigm in Canada, underpinning both a robust technical consensus and a broad political accommodation. In these years, the economy achieved success across all four objectives: high employment, price stability, economic growth, and international balance. Ironically, however, as many observers have noted, federal budgeting in these years exhibited no consistent Keynesian countercyclical pattern in the face of mild economic cycles.[5] In fact, by the 1950s, the chief Keynesian goal of high employment came to be seen to depend more on international demand than domestic economic management. Continental integration through natural resource exporting and foreign direct investment became the effective national economic strategy. And in the 1960s, concerns were increasingly raised about problems of a non-Keynesian sort: high foreign ownership, inadequately skilled workers, regional underdevelopment, and lagging productivity and technological innovation. By the early 1970s, these new concerns intersected with old problems thought to be banished by Keynesian fine-tuning: rising inflation *and* unemployment.

BREAKDOWN: THE 1970S

In the 1970s, economic conditions suddenly changed for the worse in ways that confounded the Keynesian paradigm. Increased internationalization of investment raised the spectre of "deindustrialization" as transnational corporations rationalized production globally. Stagflation—the combination of high inflation and high unemployment—defied the most basic Keynesian tradeoff between price stability and jobs. Deepening the confusion was the dissolution of the postwar international financial regime premised on fixed exchange rates to create space for domestic Keynesianism. The onset of floating currencies imposed powerful constraints on government fiscal activism.

Bewildered by these pressures, the federal government groped for direction. Initially following an expansionary course featuring large corporate tax cuts to entice productivity-enhancing investment, the government soon changed to a deflationary focus. In 1975, it imposed mandatory wage and price controls, without the support of either business or labour, following an election campaign that promised the opposite. The Bank of Canada began to restrain the growth of the money supply, suggesting a commitment to low inflation over other macroeconomic objectives such as job creation. Meanwhile, within the bureaucracy, planning began on a longer-run national industrial strategy to solve Canada's productivity and innovation problems. Rather than concentrating on deflation and restraint, this strategy contemplated new government-directed spending and a regulatory regime to transform the branch-plant, commodity-dependent economy.[6]

Canadian macroeconomic policy in the 1970s has been aptly characterized as "'ad hocism' practiced with a vengeance."[7] Inflation more than tripled in the first half of the decade, and unemployment doubled in the second half. Large federal expenditures on tax incentives and cuts, combined with increased pressure on automatic stabilizers caused by deteriorating economic conditions, created another problem: persistent, growing annual budget deficits. Further, the severity of the deficit difficulties for the Department of Finance was exacerbated by the Bank of Canada's success in combating inflation and defending the value of the Canadian dollar through higher interest rates. In short, Keynesian instruments were either failing or working at cross-purposes.

The governing paradigm was in crisis. Policy experts pursued numerous, and often mutually exclusive, "post-Keynesian" lines of thought: monetarism, corporatist productivity bargaining, nationalist megaprojects, continental integration, and social welfare reform. The collapse of the existing technical consensus was paralleled by new political mobilization against the old Keynesian accommodation. In the party system, social Liberals and red Tories found themselves on the defensive as new factions sponsored business-based conceptions of the public good that celebrated free markets, not smart states. Within federalism, the provinces increasingly contested Ottawa's macroeconomic dominance in both its fiscal and social policy dimensions: province-building premiers asserted new claims for control over regional economic development and joined Quebec in resisting the imposition of federal social priorities, especially when federal contributions to shared-cost programs began to decline. In society, latent class conflict resurfaced. Business and labour fought Ottawa and each other over wage and price controls, and each elaborated divergent post-Keynesian macroeconomic paradigms. Labour advanced an interventionist and nationalist full-employment strategy premised on greater worker voice in productivity—enhancing public investments in technology and workplace reorganization. Business went on the offensive with a market-based, inflation-fighting, continentalist restructuring thrust valuing, above all else, corporate flexibility.

If the 1970s were years of inconclusive macroeconomic experimentation, the 1980s would be the decade of paradigm shift. Neoliberal ideas became a new orthodoxy among economists and a critical ingredient in the major realignment of sociopolitical forces in the party, state, and intergovernmental systems.

CANADA'S NEOLIBERAL RESTORATION: FROM THE 1980S TO THE 1990S

NEOLIBERAL IDEAS

As with Keynesian philosophy a generation earlier, the creation of the neoliberal governing paradigm was anchored in theoretical reconstruction by professional economists, notably Milton Friedman from the University of Chicago. Deep-seated assumptions about accountability for the economy's performance were overturned. Governments, not markets, were prone to failure; individuals were responsible for their own labour market circumstances and well-being. Left alone, the private economy supplied the incentives and disciplines for optimizing behaviour by workers, firms, and communities. The great risk was intervention by state managers who not only lacked the knowledge for corrective action but were motivated to compound, over the long run, any short-term dislocations generated by free markets. Keynesian theory institutionalized all manner of inefficiency: "rent-seeking" behaviour by interest groups securing special benefits and expenditures; workers and companies insulated from new realities and therefore avoiding adjustments; and politicians and bureaucrats seeking to advance their own careers through various kinds of "pork barrelling." Neoliberalism thus unveiled a new public philosophy whose goal was to substitute impersonal market rules for government discretion based on Keynesian expertise.

This philosophical critique was given concrete macroeconomic meaning through the interrelated policy doctrines of monetarism and the non-accelerating inflationary rate of unemployment (NAIRU). The NAIRU disputed the assumed tradeoff between employment and inflation that had been central to Keynesian theory. The NAIRU stated that there was no necessary relationship between higher inflation and lower unemployment because of the way Keynesian social policy structured the choices of workers. Expansionary demand management measures that traded short-term inflation for longer-term employment were undermined as individuals responded to changing work and pay incentives. Seeing their real earnings diminished by inflation, the argument ran, rational workers would either press for higher wages or quit to take advantage of social benefits. The result would be not simply higher inflation but higher unemployment; domestic workers either priced themselves above the global competition or voluntarily left their jobs.

The NAIRU's implications for social policy were evident: all assistance and support should be recast through "active" labour market strategy to force worker adjustment to market dictates. Structural reforms to remove impediments to change included rolling back minimum wages, trade union rights, unemployment insurance, and welfare benefits. Savings realized from deep cuts in Keynesian stabilization programs could be diverted to skills upgrading or labour mobility. Ideally, such adjustment responsibilities would be privatized: worker training was a management prerogative exercised in relation to market signals, or a matter of individual choice as workers invested in their own human capital.

Neoliberal theory typically set the NAIRU in the range of 8 percent, a level unthinkably high for Keynesians, and set a target of zero inflation for monetary policy, incomprehensibly low from a Keynesian perspective, in which monetary policy was in the service of countercyclical fiscal activism. Neoliberals sought to return Canadian unemployment to its "natural" level, where workers would neither demand higher wages nor substitute social programs for paid work. Consequently, neoliberalism recast unemployment as a necessary component in macroeconomic strategy to eliminate inflation. The break with Keynesian theory was complete: price stability became the overriding objective, monetary policy the principal instrument, and central banks with independence from politicians the governing authority.

This neoliberal technical consensus was expressed in a variety of expert policy forums in the 1980s. Think tanks and research institutes such as the Economic Council of Canada, the C.D. Howe Institute, and the Fraser Institute all offered their own specialized contributions to the emerging paradigm. Business leaders, in a marked departure from the postwar pattern of deference to bureaucratic expertise, created an umbrella organization, the Business Council on National Issues (BCNI), and gave it the resources to disseminate sophisticated neoliberal policy analysis and advice.

The Royal Commission on the Economic Union and Development Prospects in Canada (the Macdonald Commission) was a galvanizing process for neoliberal economic ideas and business interests. Issued in the midst of protracted economic problems and policy confusion, the Commission's 1985 report fully endorsed the economists' theoretical case for the inherent superiority of markets to other modes of resource allocation such as corporatist negotiation or statist planning. It devised an integrated neoliberal policy package advocating continental free trade, "natural" unemployment rates, and social welfare retrenchment. The commission delivered a full-blown statement of a new economic paradigm in a fashion reminiscent of the pathbreaking contributions to Canadian Keynesian theory made by the Rowell-Sirois Commission of the 1930s. Advocates of industrial strategies, defenders of Keynesian ideas, and critics of the NAIRU found no space in the report's description of Canada's "new reality." By the mid-1980s, dissenters from the neoliberal technical consensus were marginalized.

NEOLIBERAL POLITICS

In the wake of the Macdonald Commission report, the neoliberal technical consensus was matched by a new political accommodation as the paradigm gathered support in the state, party, and interest-group systems. Among parties, support for neoliberalism was signalled by changes in the leadership of both the Progressive Conservatives and the Liberals. Conservative Brian Mulroney and Liberal John Turner each arrived with strong ties to the business community and proclaimed their general opposition to the post-Keynesian interventionism and nationalism that had informed the final Trudeau government of the early 1980s. The Mulroney government was elected with a massive majority in 1984 but stumbled badly in its first year without apparent economic or social policy direction. In 1985, despite the Mulroney campaign's statements against welfare retrenchment and continental free trade, the government suddenly embraced just such a neoliberal "adjustment agenda."

This structural reform package was reinforced by macroeconomic policy. Expenditure restraint achieved through cuts in unemployment insurance, social assistance, and provincial transfers became near-permanent features of Mulroney government budgets. The Conservative Finance minister also backed the unprecedented commitment made by the Bank of Canada to the goal of zero inflation. Indeed, in its constitutional proposals of the early 1990s, the government proposed making price stability the sole objective of the Bank and federal monetary policy. One consequence of the pursuit of this extreme anti-inflationary goal was to greatly increase the costs of public debt servicing. In practice, the

Finance Department's fiscal restraint was undermined by the Bank's monetary restraint. Interest payments on the debt consumed a growing proportion of federal revenues, amounting to nearly one-third of every expenditure dollar when the Conservatives left office in 1993. The annual budget deficit was $42 billion, or 6 percent of gross domestic product. Interestingly, another consequence of this effective disjunction between fiscal and monetary policy was to buttress political support for neoliberalism. The mistaken perception that deficits and debt problems were caused by excessive and rising social spending hardened into received wisdom, reinforcing calls in the media and among politicians and business interests for more cuts.

In relation to all this, the Liberals re-positioned themselves to compete for the same economic policy space as the Conservatives and the emerging Reform Party. Moreover, the New Democratic Party fell into line, at least in the critical "free trade" election of 1988, when it opted to avoid economic policy discussion altogether and campaign in classic brokerage fashion on the basis of an appealing leader and myriad specific promises to social movement constituencies. By the time of the 1993 election, neoliberalism defined the political terms for a governing macroeconomic consensus. Conservative Kim Campbell told the voters as much when she declared that governments, regardless of partisan stripe, could do nothing to reduce unemployment.

While the Liberals campaigned on a "Red Book" offering a Keynesian-style alternative to Campbell's unvarnished neoliberalism, the Chrétien government's post-election conversion to deficit and debt reduction confirmed the paradigm's power. Retaining the goods and services tax, cutting unemployment insurance and federal transfer payments, the Liberals made continuity not change the hallmark of their macroeconomics. Between 1993 and 1998, total federal program spending as a percentage of the economy declined by 3.9 percent, falling to 12.7 percent, its lowest point since 1949–50.[8] During the years of Conservative government, the Bank of Canada took the lead and the Department of Finance moved in step. Under the Liberals, the Department of Finance and Paul Martin moved centre-stage with unprecedented spending cuts, supported by central agencies orchestrating equally sweeping program and expenditure management reviews to shrink the role and size of the federal public sector. The process culminated in the 1995 budget, which in the depth and breadth of its cuts and downsizing led more than one observer to announce the "end of Canada as we know it."[9]

In intergovernmental relations, a new accommodation, albeit one marked by considerable controversy, reversed the centralism of Canadian

Keynesian theory. Guided by the NAIRU and monetarism, the federal government's use of its spending power in areas of provincial jurisdiction for national purposes declined precipitously. Decentralization and provincialism captured the political and fiscal dynamics of Canadian federalism reframed by Ottawa's neoliberal macroeconomic paradigm. In the means used to offload their deficit problems, there were, nonetheless, important differences between the Conservative and Liberal governments. The Conservatives proceeded incrementally through expenditure freezes, benefit de-indexation, and regressive tax burden shifts. They were criticized for this "stealth" approach to change that carried huge implications for the country's identity and the workings of the federation.

By contrast, the Liberals in their 1995 budget addressed matters openly and all at once, through fundamental institutional change in federal–provincial relations. The Canadian Health and Social Transfer created a new fiscal regime for social policy that reduced the flow of federal dollars by about $6 billion while providing greater discretion to the provinces in allocation. In this case, critics argued that the Liberals had used macroeconomic decisions to effect a major constitutional restructuring of the postwar federal social bargain. Regardless of the preferred implementation style, it was clear that the neoliberal paradigm in its intergovernmental guise spoke persuasively to the economic and national unity agendas of both the Mulroney and Chrétien governments. Ottawa could reduce its deficit while offering more autonomy to the provinces.

Meanwhile, the business community, through the research and mobilization of the BCNI, actively supported the paradigm. Under its leadership, regional and sectoral tensions within Canadian business over macroeconomic policy were replaced by a unity of purpose defined by neoliberal restraint and liberalization. The BCNI found ample space for its ideas in influential policy development locales such as the Macdonald Commission, think tanks, and the media. At the same time, the sociopolitical accommodation never included representatives of workers or the social movements comprising the "popular sector." These groups contested neoliberal claims about natural rates of unemployment or incentive-distorting social programs even as federal governing parties and many premiers embraced them. Yet this social coalition remained on the defensive with its constituencies reeling from the combined impact of neoliberal policies and wrenching economic restructuring that stripped away resources for political mobilization.

The new Canadian domestic consensus and accommodation found its international counterpart. Continental free trade, floating exchange rates, and financial deregulation were all seen by neoliberal advocates to further discipline domestic states and societies to conform to market imperatives. In fact, the global policy constraint argument followed a logic similar to the domestic policy constraint case based on the NAIRU. Expansionary fiscal policy would lead international money traders to sell national currencies, effectively forcing the government to raise interest rates to defend the currency's value, with deleterious impacts on domestic investment and employment. As with the NAIRU, Keynesian policymakers would only worsen the very problems they originally set about to correct.

Thus, in the 1980s and 1990s, neoliberalism was embedded in the state and society as Canada's new governing macroeconomic paradigm. While the technical consensus behind neoliberal ideas re-defined the mainstream of the economics profession away from Keynesian philosophy, the political accommodation remained more tenuous. Challenges persisted along a number of policy lines. Would federal retrenchment lead to a patchwork "social Canada" distinguished by interprovincial discrepancies in standards and services? Were Canadians equipped with the requisite skills to meet the challenges of economic globalization and knowledge-based competition? In the early 2000s, such questioning of the neoliberal paradigm acquired much wider currency as the fiscal circumstances of the federal government dramatically improved, and the events of September 11, 2001, suddenly re-focused attention on the powers and capacities of national governments to provide security for their citizens.

THE POLITICS OF THE SURPLUS: A NEW GOVERNING PARADIGM?

After struggling through weak growth for most of the 1990s, the Canadian economy recovered strongly at the decade's end. Years of growing public deficits were abruptly replaced by large budgetary surpluses. By the early 2000s, Canada emerged as a leader within the OECD in economic growth, and for four consecutive years its economic performance surpassed that of the United States. Federal tax revenues soared, growing by 54 percent between 1993–94 and 2000–2001. In 2003, the new Liberal Finance minister, John Manley, introduced the government's sixth consecutive balanced budget, estimating surpluses rising to $10.7 billion by mid-decade. In five years, the federal debt had been reduced by $47.6 billion, and with the Bank of Canada setting interest rates at their lowest levels since the 1960s, the government's debt repayment burden lightened significantly.

In these altered conditions, a new consensus is taking shape in the Canadian macroeconomic policy community that rejects key elements of each of the established twentieth-century macroeconomic paradigms. On the one hand, Keynesian demand management through deficit financing has been taken off the table, but equally, there is little support for a neo-liberal monetary policy preoccupied with eliminating inflation. Within these broad parameters, strong differences are now emerging over how precisely to allocate the "fiscal dividend" among competing purposes, focused on three options: program spending, debt repayment, and tax reduction. In relation to these choices, the alignment of opinion is following a pattern long familiar to students of Canadian politics. On both the left and right of the political spectrum, coalitions of political parties, social interests, and policy intellectuals have clearly staked out their ground, while the governing Liberals span an amorphous political centre, claiming a balanced approach that brokers the "extremes" of left and right.

On the left, a *social reinvestment alliance,* comprised of organized labour, social activists, the New Democratic Party, some members of the Bloc Québécois, and economists outside the profession's neo-classical mainstream, is networking through the Canadian Centre for Policy Alternatives (CCPA) to produce annual "alternative" federal budgets. The analytical departure point is that the "fiscal successes of the Chrétien years were accompanied by a huge social debt."[10] At issue is the failure of federal economic and social policy to compensate for the growing market-based income inequality resulting from the rising unemployment, underemployment, and declining real wages of the 1980s and 1990s. By dismantling national social programs such as the Canada Assistance Plan and Unemployment Insurance, the federal government deprived an increasing number of Canadian families of income support just as "good jobs" were also disappearing in both the private and public sectors. In what the social reinvestment alliance views as two "lost decades," the results were evident: a shrinking middle class, increased child poverty, and the appearance of homelessness and food banks in many cities and communities.[11] Despite the growth of the 2000s, the rising tide was unlikely to lift all boats. Major new federal investments in basic income support and labour force development were required to ensure full participation in the so-called new economy, with its increasingly knowledge-intensive demands.

On the right, a *tax reduction and debt repayment alliance,* encompassing the corporate sector, business-oriented think tanks such as the C.D. Howe Institute and the Fraser Institute, and the Canadian Alliance Party, offered an entirely different perspective on post-deficit politics.[12] State intervention created barriers to competitive adjustment by people on both sides of the social and economic divide. For the less well-off, comprehensive social programs were disincentives to labour market upgrading and mobility. For the elite, with many options in the global economy, their potential "flight" to avoid the rising tax bills to pay for such social assistance threatened a

Canadian brain drain. From this perspective, then, new investments in the knowledge infrastructure were crucial for Canada's long-term competitiveness, but they remained private rather than government responsibilities. Individuals in free markets will maximize their own human capital if provided with the appropriate incentives and educational choices. Competitive firms will create innovations if guaranteed intellectual property rights and low tax rates. Unified in its opposition to new social spending, the tax and debt reduction alliance remained somewhat divided in its ranking of priorities. Some spokespersons called for debt repayment above all, while others advocated immediate across-the-board tax cuts. Another group, influential in Ontario and British Columbia governing circles, audaciously claimed taxes and deficits could be simultaneously reduced, provided spending cuts were sufficiently deep and sustained.

Faced with these bold and polarizing projects, the Liberals have charted a fiscal course bridging the policy differences and straddling the political fence. During both the 1997 and 2000 federal election campaigns, Prime Minister Chrétien promised that future budgetary surpluses would be allocated according to a "balanced approach."[13] Half the surplus would be reinvested in social and economic priorities for health care, poverty reduction, education, and research and development. The other half would be dedicated to maintaining a sound fiscal climate, through the reduction of federal taxes and the repayment of federal debt. Although the prime minister never committed to dividing the surplus in half in each fiscal year, the "50:50" framework was supposed to guide the government's evolving budgetary choices over its full mandate. In 2002, Finance Minister John Manley looked back on the five years of surplus budgeting and observed that the government's record was "about 55:45," favouring debt repayment and tax reduction over program spending.[14] Certainly, the preference for tax reduction was amply demonstrated in the October 2000 pre-election mini-budget when the Liberals announced "the largest tax cut in Canadian history" totalling $100 billion over five years.[15] Similarly, debt repayment has been rapidly advanced through various novel budgetary techniques.[16] The most prominent of these is the annual $3 billion "contingency and prudence fund" available, in principle, to the Finance minister for meeting emergencies but, in practice, routinely applied to debt repayment.

Close observers of the government's overall approach to budgeting in the era of surpluses have described the process as *thematic incrementalism*.[17] Since 1997–98, when the federal books were brought back into balance, Liberal Finance ministers have emphasized two broad policy themes to organize new spending: *economic innovation* and *social inclusion*.[18] In relation to these big policy ideas, discrete programs have been introduced in successive budgets to be implemented in step-by-step installments in a multi-year time frame. The innovation theme is targeted primarily at business and technology leaders: investments have been made in basic and applied research, the commercialization of scientific and engineering breakthroughs, and the micro-electronic infrastructure for high technology clusters. The inclusion theme addresses the needs of families, workers, and students: investments have been made in literacy, education and skills, measures to help families exit poverty, and programs for early childhood development. Beginning in 2001, in the aftermath of the events of September 11th, a third organizing theme has been incorporated into the framework: national security, involving initial expenditures of $7.7 billion for defence, intelligence, and border-crossing modernization.

For the Liberals, this middle course, combining an ambitious vision of the future with a cautious plan for its realization, offers a number of benefits. In policy terms, it affords considerable flexibility for Finance ministers to adjust expenditures to accommodate unforeseen short-term pressures while minimizing the risk of deficits. As well, the multi-year rollout of the innovation and inclusion agenda affords the time necessary for complex intergovernmental negotiations in the many areas of shared jurisdiction. From a political perspective, the strategy has helped Chrétien to manage the competing factions of social liberals and business liberals in his cabinet and caucus, not to mention effectively insulating his government for the better part of a decade from meaningful partisan challenge on the left or right. Moreover, the incrementalist approach also conforms to the prime minister's own pragmatic leadership style, famous for its avoidance of the mega-policy breakthroughs pursued by his recent predecessors.[19]

Of course, the reactions to the 2003 "Chrétien legacy budget" (expected to be the last under the prime minister's watch) underscore the ongoing, deep-seated differences regarding the meaning and consequences of the Liberals' claims of a balanced, cautious approach. This budget shifted the emphasis to program spending away from the previously dominant tax reduction and debt repayment priorities. Long-term commitments were outlined in many social policy areas, including health care, childcare, foreign aid, the environment, and aboriginal communities. The result was a $14.3 billion rise in program spending from the previous budget, an 11.5 percent increase.

Not surprisingly, the tax reduction and debt repayment alliance saw in the 2003 budget evidence of a "spending binge."[20] The C.D. Howe Institute feared the federal government was "hooked on spending" and destined to return to deficits.[21] For its part, the social reinvestment alliance, notwithstanding the legacy budget's spending spike, judged the

Liberal six-year record in allocating the fiscal dividend as neither balanced nor incremental. On the contrary, the CCPA's budgetary analysis suggests the breakdown was closer to 90:10 in favour of debt repayment and tax reduction over program spending.[22] Only by consistently understating the size of the surplus and counting various tax credits as program spending could the government credibly claim to be guided by its 50:50 election promises. From the left, then, the budget represented "an appropriately weak legacy" for a prime minister who will exit "with Canada's social challenges unmet."[23]

MACROECONOMIC POLICY AT THE CROSSROADS

As controversy swirls around the politics of the surplus, it is apparent that Canadian macroeconomic policy stands at another historic crossroads. Today's economic policy environment is more uncertain and complex than in previous decades. In the early 2000s, a series of challenges revealed the limits of both the Keynesian and neoliberal paradigms. On the one hand, a rapid succession of short-term economic shocks and geopolitical crises—ranging from the 9/11 attacks and the ensuing war on terror and Iraq, to the unexpected downturn of the U.S. economy and rapid "dot-com" meltdown, to the SARS (severe acute respiratory syndrome) public health crisis—have dramatically altered much of the economic policy terrain, introducing new policy priorities while tightening old constraints. On the other hand, underlying structural changes in global production and markets have accelerated, forcing governments everywhere to search for policy combinations to ensure that the new economy's prosperity is shared fairly among all citizens.

In tackling these challenges, it is also clear that federal policymakers face new and different dynamics in their relations with three other governments central to Canadian economic governance. First, in the United States, the Bush administration is implementing an astonishing $3 trillion tax cut on personal income and investment dividends, at the same time that it is pressing for far greater expenditure on international and continental security.[24] Assessing the implications for the Canadian economy and budgetary choices of this unprecedented U.S. fiscal direction is now a major preoccupation for Canada's Finance Department officials. Second, provincial governments are justifiably wary of any renewed federal policy activism in their jurisdiction. In this regard, Ottawa is confronting the legacy of mistrust and resentment built over two decades of unilateral financial cutbacks and program retrenchment. Third, municipal governments are finding a stronger economic policy voice, not only as representatives for the 80 percent of Canadians who now live in urban areas, but also as spokespersons for localized networks widely recognized as the crucial engines of growth and creativity in the knowledge-based economy. Yet, despite this growing activism, municipal leaders rightly protest the "culture of non-recognition and neglect" that continues to define their interactions with federal officials.[25]

Governing the Canadian economy at the start of the twenty-first century remains a significant technical, political, and institutional challenge. Federal budgetary surpluses afford the opportunity to approach problems with imagination and purpose. Thus far, a broad policy direction has been set. Innovation and inclusion are laudable themes, suggestive of a powerful macroeconomic paradigm matched to the challenges of the new economy. Further progress now depends on committing sufficient resources to get on with the job, and forging collaborative relations with governing partners in the provinces and municipalities. But progress is also likely to require considerable policy creativity and political will in resisting continental pressures to emulate the U.S. model of minimal public investment in the vital social infrastructure of the new economy.

NOTES

1. For insightful discussions of policy paradigms, see Peter A. Hall, "Policy Paradigms, Experts, and the State: The Case of Macroeconomic Policy in Britain," in Stephen Brooks and Alain-G. Gagnon, eds., *Social Scientists, Policy, and the State* (New York: Praeger, 1990), pp. 53–79; and Margaret Weir, *Politics and Jobs: The Boundaries of Employment Policy in the United States* (Princeton: Princeton University Press, 1992).

2. Neil Bradford, *Commissioning Ideas: Canadian National Policy Innovation in Comparative Perspective* (Toronto: Oxford University Press, 1998), chap. 2.

3. W.A. Mackintosh, "The White Paper on Employment and Income in Its 1945 Setting," in S.F. Kaliski, ed., *Canadian Economic Policy Since the War* (Ottawa: Carleton University Press, 1965), p. 19.

4. Eugene Forsey, "Parliament Is Endangered by Mr. King's Principle," *Saturday Night* (October 9, 1948): 10.

5. Robert Campbell, *Grand Illusions: The Politics of the Keynesian Experience in Canada, 1945–1975* (Peterborough, ON: Broadview Press, 1987); David A. Wolfe, "The Rise and Demise of the Keynesian Era in Canada: Economic Policy, 1930–82," in M. Cross and G. Kealey, eds., *Modern Canada: Readings in Canadian Social History* (Toronto: McClelland & Stewart, 1984).

6. Glen Williams, *Not for Export: The International Competitiveness of Canadian Manufacturing*, 3rd ed. (Toronto: McClelland & Stewart, 1994), chap. 6.

7. G. Bruce Doern and Richard Phidd, *Canadian Public Policy: Ideas, Structure, Process* (Toronto: Methuen, 1983), p. 409.

8. Canada, Department of Finance, *Government Announces First Budget Surplus in 28 Years* (October 14, 1998).

9. Former Ontario premier Bob Rae and former federal deputy minister Arthur Kroeger each used this expression to describe the impact of the 1995 budget.

10. Bruce Campbell and Todd Scarth, "The Real Chretien Legacy Budget," Canadian Centre for Policy Alternatives (February 18, 2003), p. 2.

11. For detailed analysis of these trends, see Andrew Jackson, David Robinson with Bob Baldwin and Cindy Wiggins, *Falling Behind: The State of Working in Canada, 2000* (Ottawa: Canadian Center for Policy Alternatives, 2000); and Keith Banting, Andrew Sharpe, and Frances St-Hilaire, eds. *The Review of Economic and Social Progress: The Longest Decade: Canada in the 1990s* (Montreal: Institute for Research on Public Policy and Centre for the Study of Living Standards, 2001).

12. William B.P. Robson, *Hooked on Spending? The 2003 Budget Will Show Whether Ottawa Can Hold the Line Against Unsustainable Expenditures* (Toronto: C.D. Howe Institute, 2003).

13. Liberal Party of Canada, *Opportunity for All: The Liberal Plan for the Future of Canada* (Ottawa: Liberal Party of Canada, 2000), p. 3.

14. Canadian Centre for Policy Alternatives, *A Funny Way of Sharing: Revisiting the Liberal Government's "50:50" Promise* (Ottawa: Canadian Centre for Policy Alternatives, 2003), p. 1.

15. "Reaping the Rewards," *The Globe and Mail*, February 19, 2003.

16. Geoffrey E. Hale, "Innovation and Inclusion: Budgetary Policy, the Skills Agenda, and the Politics of the New Economy," in G. Bruce Doern, ed., *How Ottawa Spends, 2002–2003: The Security Aftermath and National Priorities* (Toronto: Oxford University Press, 2002), p. 40.

17. This interpretation is presented in various chapters in G. Bruce Doern, ed., *How Ottawa Spends, 2002–2003*. In particular, see Geoffrey E. Hale, "Innovation and Inclusion," and Michael Prince, "The Return of Directed Incrementalism: Innovating Social Policy the Canadian Way."

18. For an elaboration of the two policy themes, see Canada, *Achieving Excellence: Investing in People, Knowledge and Opportunity* (Ottawa: Industry Canada, 2003); and Canada, *Knowledge Matter: Skills and Learning for Canadians* (Ottawa: Human Resources Development Canada, 2003). Both publications are available electronically at <http://www.innovationstrategy.gc.ca.>

19. Michael Prince, "The Return of Directed Incrementalism," p. 192.

20. "Economists give Finance Minister mediocre marks," *National Post*, February 19, 2003.

21. William B.P. Robson, "Hooked on Spending," p. 1.

22. Canadian Centre for Policy Alternatives, "A Funny Way of Sharing."

23. Bruce Campbell and Todd Scarth, "The Real Chretien Legacy Budget," p. 2.

24. "Bush's Growth Gamble," *Business Week* (February 17, 2003).

25. Federation of Canadian Municipalities, *Brief to the Prime Minister's Caucus Task Force on Urban Issues* (Ottawa: Federation of Canadian Municipalities, 2001). For a broad discussion of Canada's emerging urban policy agenda, see Neil Bradford, *Why Cities Matter: Policy Research Perspectives for Canada* (Ottawa: Canadian Policy Research Networks, 2002).

FURTHER READINGS

Banting, Keith, Andrew Sharpe, and Frances St-Hilaire, eds. *The Review of Economic and Social Progress: The Longest Decade: Canada in the 1990s.* Montreal: Institute for Research on Public Policy and Centre for the Study of Living Standards, 2001.

Bradford, Neil. *Commissioning Ideas: Canadian National Policy Innovation in Comparative Perspective.* Toronto: Oxford University Press, 1998.

Campbell, Robert. *Grand Illusions: The Politics of the Keynesian Experience in Canada, 1945–1975.* Peterborough: Broadview Press, 1987.

Doern, G. Bruce, ed. *How Ottawa Spends, 2002-2003: The Security Aftermath and National Priorities.* Toronto: Oxford University Press, 2002.

Hale, Geoffrey. *The Politics of Taxation in Canada.* Peterborough: Broadview Press, 2001.

Lewis, Timothy. *In the Long Run We're All Dead: The Canadian Turn to Fiscal Restraint.* Vancouver: University of British Columbia Press, 2003.

Rice, James J., and Michael J. Prince. *Changing Politics of Canadian Social Policy.* Toronto: University of Toronto Press, 2000.

CHAPTER 11

CHARTER POLITICS AND THE JUDICIARY

Radha Jhappan

It has been over twenty years since the Canadian Charter of Rights and Freedoms was enacted, yet curiously, Canadians may still be more familiar with the constitutional rights of their American neighbours than with their own. Given the domination of Canadian television and cinemas by U.S. productions, it is perhaps not surprising that many Canadians believe that the U.S. Bill of Rights applies to them. They imagine, for example, that arresting officers must inform suspects that they have the right to remain silent, when in fact police in this country are not constitutionally bound to do so.[1] It is common for Canadians to invoke the U.S. protection against self-incrimination by "taking the fifth," but invoking the fifth article of our Charter of Rights means calling upon Parliament and each provincial legislature to sit at least once every 12 months.

This chapter examines the Canadian Charter of Rights and Freedoms with a view to distinguishing it both from the U.S. Bill of Rights and from Canada's previous constitutional arrangements. Many have argued that the addition of the Charter to the Canadian Constitution in 1982 was the single most important event in our political development since 1867. The Charter has expanded the rights and liberties of citizens, as well as the power of judges, at the expense of governments, and hence it has changed the manner in which we conduct politics. Some regard these developments as healthy and progressive, while others worry that the Charter has done more damage than good.

The discussion that follows seeks to explain these conflicting views of the Charter's impact on Canadian politics. As the Charter's significance cannot be measured without an understanding of what came before it, the chapter begins with a brief overview of the courts' treatment of civil rights under the British North America (BNA) Act, 1867, and the 1960 Canadian Bill of Rights. After examining some of the changes implied by the adoption of entrenched civil and political rights, the chapter outlines the key provisions of the Charter, distinguishing between negative liberties and positive rights, and between individual and collective rights. This is followed by a short survey of major Charter decisions issued by the higher courts in a variety of policy fields, including new challenges for Charter rights implied by post–September 11, 2001, anti-terrorism measures and new technological developments such as genetic engineering. Finally, the chapter outlines the main debates that have developed among left- and right-wing critics, as well as feminist and First Nations activists and scholars, about the nature of Charter rights and the enhanced role of the courts in public policymaking.

CIVIL RIGHTS FROM THE BNA ACT TO THE CANADIAN BILL OF RIGHTS

Before the enactment of the Charter of Rights in 1982, the civil and political rights of Canadians were not entrenched as the fundamental law of the land. This may help to explain why they were seldom discussed by political scientists, whose analysis of the constitutional system focused on federalism and the BNA Act (now the Constitution Act, 1867). In fact, as Alan Cairns observed, and as generations of students of Canadian politics can confirm, the BNA Act is "a document of monumental dullness which enshrines no eternal principles and is devoid of inspirational content."[2] In contrast, almost a century before the act became the cornerstone of Canada's constitutional system, our closest neighbours had drawn up the U.S. Declaration of Independence (1776), which begins with the heady statement,

> We hold these truths to be self-evident, that all men are created equal, that they are endowed by their Creator with certain unalienable Rights, that among these are Life, Liberty, and the pursuit of Happiness. That to secure these rights, Governments are instituted among Men, deriving their just powers from the consent of the governed.

The Declaration was rather a sham, of course, since the only men treated as equal at the time were white men, while indigenous, African, and Asian men and women were variously the targets of state-sponsored genocides and/or were dispossessed, enslaved, and excluded from social, economic and political power.[3] They did not enjoy the rights to "Life, Liberty, and the pursuit of Happiness," and although they were subjects of coercive government power, their consent was neither required nor possible given their exclusion from the franchise, in most cases until well into the twentieth century.[4] The federal system adopted ostensibly to prevent the tyranny of the majority of the central over the state governments (or of national majorities over local minorities) echoed the overall design of the political system that ensured the tyranny of the minority—the enfranchised, white, male portion of the population. The same was true in Canada, though it is equally impossible to discern this from the written provisions of the BNA Act.[5]

The BNA Act made no attempt to embellish with ringing concepts (such as rights, equality, liberty, or happiness) the reality of Canada's colonial status or the subjugation of indigenous nations, those of African or Asian descent, and women of all ethnicities. The act began with a less-than-arresting preamble declaring the creation of the Dominion "with a Constitution similar in principle to that of the United Kingdom." The union of Canada, Nova Scotia, and New Brunswick would "conduce to the Welfare of the Provinces and promote the Interests of the British Empire." Thus, whereas the Americans (at least rhetorically) put the welfare and interests of citizens above all else, the BNA Act was wholly concerned with the interests of the Empire and of the federal and provincial governments. Indeed, section 91(24) authorized the continued internal colonization and dispossession of the indigenous nations (dubbed "Indians" following Columbus's mistake) and their lands by granting exclusive legislative jurisdiction over them to the federal government rather than to their own governments, which were subsequently dismantled under successive Indian Acts.

As for non-Natives, the BNA Act lacked not just impassioned lyricism, but also any mention of citizens or their relationship to the governments whose compositions, legislative organs, powers, and jurisdictions are meticulously laid out. No lofty principles grace the 50 pages of the act. Of its 147 articles, only one—section 93—mentions the rights of citizens vis-à-vis governments. The section allows provinces to make laws in respect to education subject to "any Right or Privilege to Denominational Schools which any Class of Persons have by Law in the Province at the Union." The only other section that comes close to acknowledging a "right" is section 133, which declares that either English or French may be used in Parliament, the Quebec Legislature, and the courts, and provides that legislative acts and records be kept in both languages. Though they did not express a set of civil and political rights likely to arouse the sort of ideological and patriotic fervour inspired by the U.S. Constitution, sections 93 and 133 privileged two

European languages and the Christian religion of the colonizers over the many others that existed in the territories that became Canada. In this and other ways, the Constitution sanctioned the exclusive "two nations" construction of Canada that has never described its sociological reality.

Instead of spelling out the relationship between the governors and the governed, the BNA Act described the major political institutions and laid out the respective powers of the federal and provincial governments. The imported parliamentary system was founded squarely on the doctrine of parliamentary supremacy, or the unlimited power of the legislature to enact laws. The doctrine holds that current statutes always take precedence over older statutes, Cabinet orders, common law, and hence common-law rights. It was tempered in the Canadian context only by federalism, which constrained each level of government to legislate solely within the areas of jurisdiction assigned exclusively to it under sections 91 or 92 of the BNA Act.

The division of powers and the idea of legislative supremacy meant that the courts were entrusted with a relatively modest duty in the constitutional sphere: they would be asked only whether a government, in enacting a law, was acting within its proper jurisdiction. An ultra vires (beyond jurisdictional competence) ruling against one level of government meant only that the loser could not legislate in a given policy field, but the other level of government could. This form of judicial review, *federalism review*, was only concerned with the proper allocation of power; virtually any law with any content could be passed, as long as it was passed by the *right* level of government. Without an entrenched bill of rights, the courts did not have to consider the wisdom, morality, justice, or impact of legislation. This is not to say that Canadians had no rights, however.

Before the enactment of the Charter, the civil rights of Canadians were ostensibly protected by the body of common-law rights established over several centuries by the judiciaries of Britain, Canada, and the other Commonwealth countries. However, beyond freedom of religion and speech and legal rights such as *habeas corpus*, few civil liberties were actively protected by Canadian courts. Indeed, Canadian courts could not boast a particularly distinguished record with respect to individual liberties.

A series of court decisions made in the nineteenth century and the first half of the twentieth century upheld racial segregation or exclusion in theatres, restaurants, and taverns as the acceptable exercise of the private rights of the owners.[6] On those rare occasions when the courts found in favour of a plaintiff, it was on some tangential ground. The *Sparrow v. Johnson* decision (1899) is a case in point: when a black couple were refused the right to take their reserved theatre seats because of their race, the court refused to decide the case on the grounds of racism, but awarded damages for breach of contract.[7] In the vast majority of cases, however, governments were able to enact racist laws with impunity. For example, in 1903 a British Columbia statute that disqualified people of Chinese, Japanese, or Indian descent from voting was upheld, as was a 1914 Saskatchewan law that prohibited Chinese men from employing white women.[8] Chief Justice Duff remarked that although the legislation may have affected the civil rights of "Chinamen," it was only incidental to the main aim of protecting women and children (though he did not say from what).[9] The Supreme Court of Canada went even further in a 1939 case involving a black man who was refused service in a Montreal tavern, holding that racial discrimination was not "contrary to good morals or public order."[10] Taken together, such decisions in effect told racists within and outside government that racist or discriminatory laws were constitutional if they were promulgated by the proper level of government and legal if practised by "private" actors.

In fact, up to 1982, Canadian courts had customarily deferred to parliamentary supremacy. Only occasionally had they ranked civil liberties above that doctrine, and then only vis-à-vis provincial governments. In 1938, for example, the Supreme Court struck down a number of Social Credit laws in Alberta that, among other things, impinged upon freedom of the press.[11] Chief Justice Duff argued that there was an "implied bill of rights" in Canada, although the idea was not taken up by the majority of the Court (and presumably did not extend as far as "Chinamen"). Nevertheless, in the 1950s, on a variety of grounds, the Court struck down a series of Quebec laws aimed at suppressing the activities of Jehovah's Witnesses and Communists, though the judgments were based as much on violations of the division of powers as on freedom of religion or a right to equal application of the law.[12]

In part because of such unsatisfactory outcomes, by 1960 there was a feeling in some quarters that Canada ought to have a domestic bill of rights in keeping with the increasing post–World War II international concern for civil liberties, as exemplified by the United Nations Universal Declaration of Human Rights (1948). This was the commitment of the Prairie populist prime minister, John Diefenbaker. His Progressive Conservative government enacted the Canadian Bill of Rights, which substantially resembled the first bill of its kind in any Canadian jurisdiction, the Saskatchewan Bill of Rights (1947). The Canadian Bill of Rights represented a codification of the various common-law and statutory rights that had developed over the years, from the English Magna Carta to its American counterparts. Of the Canadian bill's two substantive articles, the first promised fundamental freedoms (life, liberty, religion, speech, assembly, association, property, the press, equality before the law, equal protection of the law, and security of the person). These freedoms were to be enjoyed without discrimination by reason of race, national origin, colour, religion, or sex. The second substantive article provided that laws of Canada should not be construed so as to abrogate legal rights such as *habeas corpus*; immunity from cruel and unusual punishment; and the rights to a fair trial, counsel, bail, and the presumption of innocence.

Unfortunately, although the Canadian Bill of Rights opened up the area of civil liberties for the courts, it was disarmed by conditional provisions. In the first place, it was an ordinary federal statute rather than the fundamental law of the land. As a result, it was subject to easy amendment, repeal, or simple override through use of its "notwithstanding" clause. Second, as a federal statute, it applied only to federal legislation; the provinces were free to continue to pass laws within their jurisdictions without any particular concern for their effects on civil liberties.

These limitations may help to explain why the courts did not use the 1960 Bill of Rights to become human-rights crusaders correcting the violations committed by legislatures. Indeed, between 1960 and 1982, of the 34 Bill of Rights cases decided by the Supreme Court of Canada, the rights claimant won in only five cases, a success rate of under 15 percent. Moreover, the Court was able to bring itself to defy parliamentary supremacy and actually strike down a law in only one case. The *Drybones* decision of 1970 was the sole instance in which the Supreme Court's application of the Canadian Bill of Rights rendered a discriminatory section of a statute void. The case involved a registered "Indian," Drybones, who had been found intoxicated off a reserve, contrary to an Indian Act provision that prohibited Indians from possessing or manufacturing intoxicants, or being intoxicated off a reserve, on pain of a $10 to $50 fine or three months in prison. As non-Indians were not subjected to such prohibitions, five of the six judges found that Indians, because of their race, were being denied equality before the law in section 1 of the Bill of Rights.[13]

While the line of reasoning in *Drybones* seems the only logical one, the Supreme Court retreated to its traditional judicial passivism in the 1974 *Lavell* case.[14] This case also involved the Indian Act, section 12(1)(b) of which provided that an Indian woman who married a non-Indian man would lose her status under the Act, as would any children of the union; hence, she and her children could not live in the reserve community and would forfeit all other benefits associated with Indian Act status. On the other hand, if an Indian man married a non-Indian woman, not only would he *not* lose his status, but his wife and their children would gain Indian status. In a perplexing decision, five of the nine Supreme Court justices found that the section did not violate equality before the law, since all Indian women who married non-Indian men were being treated in the same way. In doing so, they were taking the "formal equality" approach, according to which there can be no inequality as long as everyone in a given ascribed category is treated in the same fashion. This approach would not identify the appropriate reference group as non-Indians or even Indian men, but rather as other Indian women; hence, it would tend to allow almost all forms of legislative discrimination.

As Justice McIntyre noted 15 years later in the *Andrews* case, the formal equality approach would justify Hitler's Nuremberg laws because "similar treatment was contemplated for all Jews."[15] The same sort of reasoning was nevertheless repeated in the *Bliss* case of 1979. This case involved a section of the Unemployment Insurance Act that stipulated a longer qualifying period for pregnant women than for others. Again, the Court found that there was no gender or other discrimination, curiously attributing the difference in treatment to nature (which has determined that only women carry children), rather than to a policy choice on the part of legislators.[16]

All in all, the Canadian Bill of Rights turned out to be disappointing. Its inherent limitations, together with the traditionally circumscribed role of the courts, made for some rather questionable results. In the end, the only right the courts were willing to protect under it was the right to be drunk regardless of one's race, which hardly ranks as a cardinal civil right, especially in light of the role alcohol has played historically in disempowering aboriginal communities and individuals. On the other hand, blatant examples of racism, sexism, and other forms of discrimination, in the Indian Act as well as in many other laws, were all but endorsed by the courts.

WHAT THE CHARTER CHANGED

Given the courts' deference to legislatures prior to 1982, the Charter of Rights represented a watershed in terms of the power of citizens and courts vis-à-vis the power of governments. First and foremost, the Charter explicitly rejects the timeworn doctrine of parliamentary supremacy by declaring in section 52 that "the Constitution of Canada is the supreme law of Canada, and any law that is inconsistent with the provisions of the constitution is, to the extent of the inconsistency, of no force or effect." This means that governments can no longer enact virtually any legislation they like on any matter within their respective jurisdictions. Instead, the Charter requires that their legislative and policy actions not violate the

rights and freedoms enshrined in it. Hence, the Charter manacles governments in a manner unprecedented in Canadian constitutional history.

A second major change wrought by the Constitution Act, 1982, concerns the much wider scope of judicial review. Under federalism review, a
government on the wrong side of an ultra vires ruling may well find the
other level of government simply exercising the power instead. In contrast,
if a law is struck down as unconstitutional under the Charter, neither level
of government can enact it. Moreover, Charter review is much broader in
scope than federalism review because for the first time in Canadian history
the federal spending power and indeed all executive actions are subject to
judicial review.

A third and critical consequence of the 1982 reform is the fact that
the Charter made it easier for some 30 million citizens to initiate constitutional review. Section 24 of the Charter grants a very broad right of
standing to individuals in providing that "[a]nyone whose rights or freedoms, as granted by this Charter, have been infringed or denied may apply
to a court of competent jurisdiction to obtain such remedy as the court
considers appropriate and just in the circumstances." In fact, this clause
empowers both citizens and judges, since any court may declare a statute
or other executive act invalid, although, of course, Supreme Court decisions have the final authority. Because specific acts can be disputed one by
one, in a sense governments are more explicitly accountable to the people
than they ever were under the traditional mechanism of periodic elections.

Finally, while some Canadians mistakenly believe that the Charter
covers abuses of their rights by private parties, the Charter did not change
this aspect of the constitutional system. In fact, it applies only to executive
actions or laws passed by federal or provincial governments and not to
individual or group relations in the private sector. Rights or discrimination disputes between individuals and non-governmental parties such as
corporations, vendors, landlords, employers, neighbours, or retailers must
still be routed through provincial or territorial human rights codes.

CHARTER PROVISIONS

Although the Charter of Rights and Freedoms was itself a novel addition
to Canada's Constitution, its provisions represent a collage of rights bun-
dled together from various sources. In some cases, the phraseology is taken
directly from other documents: rights such as those against "unreasonable
search" and "cruel and unusual punishment" or to "due process of law" are
found in the U.S. Bill of Rights, and the majority of Charter rights are

found in more or less the same form in the 1960 Canadian Bill of Rights. What is new about the Charter, then, is not so much that it creates wholly new rights but that it codifies and enshrines the rights of people vis-à-vis both levels of government.

The Charter of Rights and Freedoms consists of the first 34 clauses of the Constitution Act, 1982, though not all of them contain substantive rights. There are two critical distinctions to be made among different kinds of rights included in the Charter. First, true to Canadian tradition, the document contains a mixture of individual and collective rights. In fact, all of the substantive rights or freedoms up to section 23 are granted to "every individual," "every citizen," "everyone," "any member of the public," or "any person"—in other words, they are rights individuals can assert against the federal and provincial governments. In contrast to these individual rights, at least two sections refer to rights that are claimable only by virtue of one's membership in a group. Section 23 grants collective minority language education rights to "Citizens of Canada" who belong to the English or French minority population in the province in which they reside. Section 25 states that the provisions of the Charter cannot be construed so as to abrogate the aboriginal and treaty rights of the aboriginal peoples of Canada.

The second important distinction among the rights protected by the Charter is that between negative liberties and positive rights. Generally speaking, a negative liberty can be understood as freedom from interference by the state. Examples of negative liberties include freedom of conscience, religion, or association, where all that is required is that governments refrain from interfering with the exercise of certain facilities. On the other hand, a positive right involves a claim against another party who in turn has a duty to provide or contribute something so that the right might be exercised. In other words, a positive right is an entitlement. Examples of positive rights would include the right to legal counsel or to state-funded education. Obviously, the key difference between negative liberties and positive rights is that the former are in infinite supply (their observance is costless), whereas the latter are in finite supply to the extent that resources are scarce.

Although the Charter contains, as its title suggests, both rights and freedoms, the majority of its provisions recognize negative liberties rather than extend positive entitlements. Perhaps the most important of these negative liberties are found in section 2—the "fundamental freedoms" clause—which, along with freedom of the press, guarantees everyone freedom of conscience, religion, thought, belief, opinion, expression, peaceful assembly, and association. Considered essential to democracy, these liberties are complemented in section 3 by democratic rights, defined in Charter terms as the right of citizens to vote in elections for federal and provincial legislatures and to be qualified for membership in either. As governments assume the costs of holding elections, section 3 might be interpreted as a positive right, since the state must provide the physical requisites by which the right is to be exercised. On the other hand, the mobility provisions in section 6 guarantee citizens the right to free movement, including the right to enter, remain in, or leave Canada, and the right to move to and gain a livelihood in any province. However, governments have no obligation to guarantee citizens either the financial means of moving or their livelihoods. On the contrary, subsection 3(b) actually enables provincial governments to limit the receipt of publicly funded social services to those who meet certain residency requirements.

Sections 7 to 14 of the Charter provide for legal rights, most of which are derived from common-law practice or from statutes such as the Criminal Code, and almost all of which are negative liberties. They include the rights to life, liberty, and security of the person; to security against unreasonable search and seizure; to be free from arbitrary detention or imprisonment; to *habeas corpus;* to be presumed innocent until proved guilty; not to be subjected to any cruel and unusual treatment or punishment; not to be tried or punished for an offence more than once; and not to be compelled to be a witness in proceedings against oneself. On the other hand, in the mix of rights and freedoms, a few provisions in sections 7 to 14 imply some positive rights; for example, the authorities must provide for a fair and public hearing by an independent and impartial tribunal; a trial by jury if the maximum punishment for the offence is five or more years; and an interpreter for witnesses who are deaf or who do not understand the language in which a legal proceeding is being conducted. By granting these three rights, the state clearly assumes financial burdens. Finally, a more ambiguous right is found in section 10(b), which declares that everyone has the right on arrest or detention to retain and instruct counsel. It is not entirely clear whether this section grants a constitutional right to state-funded legal services. In practice, however, all provinces and territories provide legal aid on a means-tested basis so that no one charged with a criminal offence has gone without legal services.

The equality rights section of the Charter has been heralded by many as the most important and far-reaching equality guarantee in any modern democratic constitution. As section 15(1) states,

> Every individual is equal before and under the law and has the right
> to the equal protection and equal benefit of the law without discrim-
> ination and, in particular, without discrimination based on race,

national or ethnic origin, colour, religion, sex, age or mental or physical disability.

It must be noted, however, that these guarantees do not fit easily into the negative liberties/positive rights distinction. At a general level, they may be understood as negative liberties, because they do not enjoin governments to ensure equality of outcomes, but merely forbid governments to discriminate among groups on the listed grounds. Section 15 does not mean that laws cannot make distinctions and treat people differently for different purposes, but it does mean that governments may not impose burdens on people on the basis of irrelevant criteria. Indeed, section 15(2) allows for *affirmative action* programs aimed at ameliorating the conditions of individuals or groups who are disadvantaged because of the listed attributes. However, although it insulates such programs from charges of reverse discrimination, it does not in any sense require them; in this respect, section 15(2) is a negative liberty for governments.

The most unambiguous positive rights in the Charter are undoubtedly those in sections 16 to 23. Apart from entrenching official bilingualism by declaring English and French the two official languages of Canada and enshrining the negative liberties to their use in all of the institutions of the Parliament and government of Canada (and New Brunswick), these sections require that statutes, records, and journals of Parliament be printed and published in both English and French. Further, section 20 stipulates that the government of Canada must provide services in both of the official languages in any head or central office, or in local offices, where numbers warrant. Similarly, section 23 grants citizens the right to have their children receive primary- and secondary-school education in the language of the English or French linguistic minority population of a province (subject to several conditions and where numbers warrant).

The remaining articles of the Charter are largely general interpretive principles or non-derogation clauses. Section 25, for example, insulates aboriginal, treaty, and land rights from certain Charter rights; section 27 provides that the Charter be interpreted "in a manner consistent with the preservation and enhancement of the multicultural heritage of Canadians"; and section 28 guarantees Charter rights and freedoms equally to male and female persons.

Finally, it must be noted that Charter rights are not absolute. The framers of the Charter attempted to accommodate the fact that rights occasionally clash with one another, as well as the possibility that governments might have legitimate policy objectives that could justify overriding some individual rights. Hence, there are three important sources of limitation in the Charter. First, some clauses contain internal or built-in qualifications. For example, as noted above, section 6 allows provincial governments to impose residency requirements for the receipt of social services. Even section 7—the right to life, liberty, and security of the person—is not absolute, as it goes on to suggest that one can be deprived of these things as long as it is "in accordance with the principles of fundamental justice."

The second vital limit on Charter rights is section 33, the *notwithstanding* or override clause. The section allows the federal and provincial governments to exempt legislation from sections 2 and 7 to 15 of the Charter for a five-year renewable period. Thus far, the section has been applied successfully in three high-profile contexts: by the Parti Québécois government up to 1987 to exempt all Quebec legislation from what was seen by that party as the illegitimate post-1982 constitutional regime; by Premier Robert Bourassa in 1988 after the Supreme Court struck down Quebec's French-only sign law as a violation of freedom of expression; and by the Saskatchewan government in 1986 to force striking public servants back to work. In fact, apart from Quebec's omnibus invocation of the section, it has been applied to 16 different pieces of legislation (7 of which are still in force), although as Kahana points out, they largely dealt with complicated policy matters that were not on the public agenda and thus attracted little public attention.[17]

Despite its relatively infrequent use, many have called for the repeal of section 33. If the Charter is to mean anything, critics argue, it should not grant rights with one hand and take them away with the other. Moreover, the section in effect creates a hierarchy of rights in which some are considered so important that governments are not allowed to override them, while others are treated as contingent and dispensable. Although it is possible to think of valid grounds for legislatures to suspend certain rights, it is not immediately apparent why equality rights and fundamental freedoms, which can be overridden, are any less important than language, mobility, or democratic rights, which cannot.

The third and pivotal limit on Charter rights is section 1, which states that the Charter "guarantees the rights and freedoms set out in it subject only to such reasonable limits prescribed by law as can be demonstrably justified in a free and democratic society." This clause allows governments to infringe *any* Charter right, as long as they can come up with a justification that is satisfactory to the courts. It involves a two-step process in which a claimant must first show that a Charter right has been impaired by a law before the onus shifts to the government to justify the infringement. In one of its most important decisions to date, in 1986 the Supreme Court of Canada laid out what came to be called the "Oakes test."[18] Peter

Hogg points out that "this judgment has taken on some of the character of holy writ,"[19] in that it is routinely used in almost all Charter cases where a rights violation has been found. The two-part Oakes test holds that if a government is to limit a right, its objective must be pressing and substantial, and the means employed must be proportional to that objective. In other words, there must be a rational connection between the objective and the limit; the right must be impaired as little as possible to achieve the valid objective; and the costs of impairing the right must be proportional to the benefits.

As David Beatty argues, "section 1, not the substantive sections in which the rights and freedoms are entrenched, is where all of the action takes place,"[20] precisely because, through it, governments can negate any and all Charter rights. The higher courts have applied section 1 and the Oakes test with varying results, sometimes upholding legislation as meeting a pressing and substantial objective, sometimes striking down laws as unreasonable limits on Charter rights. Nevertheless, sections 1 and 33 re-introduce legislative supremacy to the constitutional system by in a sense giving governments the right to conduct legislative review of judicial review. If the courts strike down a law that violates fundamental freedoms, legal rights, or equality rights, the government can simply invoke section 33 and re-introduce the legislation. Alternatively, through section 1, governments can willfully violate any Charter right under the guise of wider objectives (as long as they can persuade the courts of their importance).

MAJOR CHARTER DECISIONS

The Supreme Court of Canada decided approximately 100 Charter cases between 1984 and 1989. On average, Charter cases accounted for just under a quarter of the Court's annual post-1982 caseload. Whereas rights claimants had only a 15 percent success rate under the Canadian Bill of Rights, in the first two years of Supreme Court Charter decisions, claimants enjoyed a success rate of 67 percent. This rate declined significantly over the ensuing years, however, to between 27 percent and 32 percent from 1988 to 1992.[21] A subsequent analysis of the first 352 Supreme Court Charter decisions from 1984 to 1997 shows that, in general, Charter claimants won 117 cases (or 33 percent) and lost 218 (or 62 percent), while 17 (or 5 percent) were inconclusive. The highest success rates were for language and minority language education rights claims (41 percent, or 7 out of 17 cases), followed by legal rights (31 percent, or 83 of 264 cases), fundamental freedoms (26 percent, or 14 of 53 cases), equality rights (22 percent, or 8 of 36 cases), democratic rights (20 percent, or 1 of 5 cases), and mobility rights (17 percent, or 1 of 6 cases), while claimants in each of two cases brought under the multiculturalism and gender equality sections (27 and 28) were unsuccessful.[22]

The decline in Charter success rates may be explained partly by a shift in the Court's view of its role after the initial burst of activism, partly by changes in the Court's composition, and partly by the fact that over time the courts come to settle certain legal and constitutional questions as well as the principles and tests by which they adjudicate them. Yet whatever the success rates for litigants, higher-court decisions clearly have had far-reaching effects on public policy, governments' spheres of decision making, and individual and group rights.

Since 1982, the Supreme Court has made important Charter decisions on a wide range of issues, including abortion, fetal rights, mandatory retirement, strikes and secondary picketing, welfare rights, Sunday shopping, advertising aimed at children, cigarette advertising, prostitution, minority language education rights, French-only signs, official bilingualism, extradition, drunk driving, narcotics, breathalyzer tests, sexual assault, nuclear weapons, assisted suicide, pornography, hate literature, political rights of public servants, constituency boundaries, and the rights of lesbians and gays, people with disabilities, dangerous offenders, battered women, prisoners, and refugees, to name but a few.

These issues have been decided under a variety of Charter provisions. Because only a limited number of categories is provided, many different issues will be argued in court under a single Charter provision. Freedom of expression, as a case in point, has incorporated very diverse issues, with the Supreme Court sometimes upholding and sometimes invalidating statutes. For example, the Court has upheld freedom of expression by striking down the French-only signs provision of Quebec's Bill 101,[23] supporting federal public servants' right to participate in election campaigns on behalf of a party or candidate,[24] and striking down a federal law that banned cigarette advertising.[25] On the other hand, the court has found reasonable limits to freedom of expression in cases involving violent, "degrading and dehumanizing" pornography,[26] child pornography,[27] the dissemination of hate literature,[28] communicating for the purpose of prostitution,[29] advertising aimed at children,[30] and bans on publishing the names of victims of sexual assault.[31]

Because the Charter is silent on some issues, litigants must sometimes squeeze round pegs into square holes. For example, because the Charter accords unions no express collective rights, they have been forced to defend rights previously won by political struggle over many decades by means of section 2(d), "freedom of association." In 1987, the Supreme Court released the so-called labour trilogy of cases in which it found that freedom of association was not infringed by three separate laws denying public-sector employees the right to strike, ordering striking dairy workers back to work, and imposing caps on future wage increases of public-sector employees.[32] The Court further found that while section 2(d) of the Charter includes employees' right to form a union, it is a right possessed by individuals not associations. Freedom of association does not, according to the Supreme Court of Canada, include a right of trade unions to strike. In fact, it took 20 years of Charter jurisprudence for the Supreme Court finally to uphold certain union rights in its most recent labour trilogy. In *Dunmore,* it rejected the attempt of the Progressive Conservative government of Ontario to take away the right of agricultural workers to form unions, and listed other union rights as including the freedoms to organize, to assemble, to participate in lawful activities of the association, to make representations to the employer, and to be free from interference, coercion, or discrimination in the exercise of those freedoms.[33] In *Pepsi-Cola,* the Court effectively legalized secondary picketing by allowing striking employees to picket a retail outlet selling their employer's goods.[34] Finally, it held that a law requiring construction workers in Quebec to belong to a union did not violate their freedom of association right.[35] As such, this decision was consistent with the only other major Supreme Court decision to have favoured a union, in which a community college employee who objected to his union's use of compulsory dues to contribute to political parties lost his case to establish a right not to associate.[36]

Because the Charter is silent on economic and property rights, the business sector, buoyed by the courts' willingness to define corporations as legal persons, has been creative in its use of various Charter rights to fend off government regulation. In the *Big M Drug Mart* case for instance, under the guise of the section 2(a) right to religious freedom, a corporation managed to persuade the Supreme Court of Canada to strike down the federal Lord's Day Act, which prohibited commercial activity on Sunday. The Court found that the act infringed religious freedom since its purpose was "to compel the observance of the Christian Sabbath."[37] It is doubtful, however, whether the corporation's true interest was in religious freedom rather than the right to conduct business seven days a week. Other Charter rights successfully deployed by business include the section 8 right against unreasonable search and seizure, which frustrated a combines inquiry into Southam newspapers,[38] and the section 2(b) right to freedom of expression to invalidate sections of the Quebec Charter of the

French language requiring French-only commercial signs,[39] to strike down federal restrictions on tobacco advertising,[40] and to dismantle Ontario regulations on the media and content of advertising by dentists.[41] Such successes led Richard Bauman to conclude that on balance, business interests "have so far been well served in the course of Charter history."[42]

Again, because Charter provisions are both few in number and very much open to interpretation, at times the same clause has been invoked to support two utterly opposing claims. Section 7, for example, was used by Henry Morgentaler to argue that a woman's life, liberty, and security of the person included her right to abort an unwanted fetus in the landmark Supreme Court decision that struck down the abortion law in 1988.[43] Joe Borowski also appealed to section 7, though he argued (unsuccessfully) that it was not the woman's but the fetus's right to life, liberty, and security of the person that should prevail.[44]

Section 7 has also been invoked to support a medley of other causes. In the *Rodriguez* case, for example, the Supreme Court upheld the Criminal Code's prohibition of assisted suicide against a dying woman's claim that her right to life, liberty, and security of the person included her right to a doctor-assisted suicide without the imposition of criminal penalties on her assistant.[45] The section was invoked, also to no avail, by a coalition of groups who wanted to ban the testing of American cruise missiles in Canada by arguing that the increased chances of accidents and of nuclear war that would result from the testing would violate Canadians' rights to life, liberty, and security of the person.[46] On the other hand, the *Singh* case of 1985 was an important exception, in which the "security of the person" and "fundamental justice" aspects of section 7 required that the government provide an oral hearing for refugee claimants whose lives could be in danger if they were deported to their countries of origin.[47] This decision was supplemented recently in *Suresh* when the Court found a violation of the procedural safeguards of section 7 regarding the deportation of a suspected member of a "terrorist organization" who may have been at risk of persecution upon return to Sri Lanka.[48]

A final observation about the fate of certain Charter provisions over the last decade concerns the fact that some have not provided much relief to the groups they were ostensibly intended to assist. Section 15(1), for example, extends to "every individual" equality before and under the law as well as equal protection and equal benefit of the law "without discrimination based on race, national or ethnic origin, colour, religion, sex, age, or mental or physical disability." It was initially expected that the section would be the instrument through which traditionally oppressed groups such as women, ethnocultural minorities, the elderly, and people with disabilities could challenge systemic inequalities. Section 15 was quickly conscripted, however, by an unlikely troop of individuals who claimed their equality rights were being violated: criminals wanting to be tried by a judge instead of a jury; drunk drivers seeking acquittals because of variations in provincial laws; drivers protesting mandatory seatbelt laws; academics opposing mandatory retirement; men trying to get access to the few benefits available to women (such as welfare benefits for single mothers, maternity benefits for adoptive parents) or contesting affiliation and child-support orders being applied only against men; and miscellaneous offenders challenging rape-shield laws, criminal procedures, sentencing, prison, and release policies.[49]

Moreover, as the statistics on Charter success rates cited above show, the expected beneficiaries of section 15 seem to have lost most of the few claims they have made. The Supreme Court has allowed several forms of age discrimination to prevail, ruling, for example, that mandatory retirement is a reasonable limit on equality rights.[50] At the other end of the scale, in *Gosselin*, a majority of the Court recently rejected a claim of age discrimination and a violation of security of the person in a case involving Quebec's policy of reducing welfare benefits for individuals under 30 who were not participating in training or work experience employment.[51] The finding was consistent with the Court's unwillingness to date to elevate social entitlement claims of economically disadvantaged groups to the status of constitutional rights.

Several disability rights cases have likewise failed, including an equality rights claim by the parents of a 12-year-old girl with cerebral palsy against a school board's placement of their daughter in a special education class rather than a regular class.[52] And while corporations won their claim in *Big M* (discussed above) that religious freedom should enable them to ply their trade on Sundays, claims by members of minority religions have typically failed,[53] including one made by two members of the Salish First Nation charged with hunting deer without a licence and out of season. Though it agreed the deer had been killed for the purpose of a religious ceremony, the non-aboriginal court insisted that there was no reason why frozen deer meat could not be used, thus presuming to amend a Native religious rite to conform to provincial game policy.[54] And while lesbians and gays have won about half the cases they have initiated in the lower courts (usually appealing to provincial human rights codes), it was not until 1998 that the Supreme Court of Canada upheld an equality claim based on sexual orientation.[55]

As far as sex equality is concerned, women have been neither the chief initiators nor the predetermined beneficiaries of sex equality claims.

Kathleen Lahey's oft-cited study showed that as early as two years after section 15 came into effect, male complainants were making and winning 10 times as many equality claims as women.[56] Two years later, in an analysis of 591 reported and unreported decisions from all levels of court between 1985 and 1989, Gwen Brodsky and Shelagh Day noted that of 44 sex equality cases, 35 (or 79 percent) had been made by or on behalf of men, with only 9 made by or on behalf of women. The authors note that these figures represent only those explicitly framed as sex equality issues; the picture would look much worse for women if many other cases framed in different ways but still having serious impacts on sex equality were included (for example, men's challenges to sexual assault laws and to women's reproductive freedom via "fetal rights" claims).[57] Unfortunately, no follow-up study comparable to that by Brodsky and Day has been conducted, so we cannot know what the data since 1989 might show. More recent data focus on ultimate resolutions of cases at the Supreme Court level, thus accounting for only a small proportion of the cases decided in the lower courts.

At the Supreme Court level, women have suffered some substantial losses, among them the now infamous *Seaboyer* decision, which struck down the rape-shield law that had prevented accused rapists from using their alleged victims' past sexual history to imply consent;[58] the *Thibaudeau* decision, which upheld the Income Tax Act in allowing non-custodial parents (98 percent of whom are men) to deduct child-support payments from their taxable income while custodial parents were taxed on both their own portion of child support and that of the non-custodial parent;[59] the *O'Connor* decision, which allowed a Catholic bishop accused of raping a number of young First Nations students of a residential school in the 1960s access to their therapeutic records;[60] and the *Daviault* decision, in which extreme intoxication was accepted as a defence for rape.[61]

On the other hand, some Supreme Court decisions have delivered substantial gains to women in general or to some classes of women, although they have not all been decided on section 15 grounds. Among those that were "successful" according to the claimant involved and to many feminist litigators are the 1988 *Morgentaler* decision, which decriminalized abortion (creating a negative liberty though not a positive right to abortion);[62] *Daigle*, in which the Supreme Court declared that the fetus has no right to life under current Canadian laws and that there is no paternal veto over a woman's right to choose an abortion;[63] *Brooks*, which found the exclusion of pregnant women from the employee group health insurance plan to be sex discrimination, thus overturning the *Bliss* decision (discussed above);[64] *Janzen*, which recognized sexual harassment as sex discrimination;[65] *Butler,* in which the Supreme Court of Canada upheld the obscenity provisions of the Criminal Code on the grounds that degrading and dehumanizing pornography offends women's equality rights;[66] *Shewchuck,* which upheld allegedly discriminatory child-support and paternity determinations as they served to place the financial burden of care for children on fathers rather than the state;[67] and the key equality rights case to date, *Andrews,* in which the Court held that equality should be understood as a substantive rather than merely a procedural right.[68]

The case record shows, therefore, that section 15 has been used by a wide range of litigants with vastly different, even conflicting, purposes. Yet it is not the only section affecting equality rights: issues such as abortion, pornography, prostitution, and past sexual history evidence, each decided under a different clause, have had just as much (if not more) impact on the equality rights of various groups. In fact, the selection of an appropriate section may be the key strategic decision in Charter litigation.

CHARTER DEBATES

Although the courts have produced a mixed bag of results over the last decade, there is no question that the Canadian public has embraced the Charter of Rights.[69] Some have even argued that it has become a key symbol of national unity, an inviolate set of values that is now fundamental to Canadians' understanding of what it means to be Canadian. The same is not necessarily true of academic and legal circles, however. No chorus of hosannas was heard in the hallways of the courts and universities when the Charter was first proclaimed, although some were generally in favour of it. But two decades' worth of mixed results have tempered the accolades of even Charter enthusiasts. Debates continue between those who take the position that, on balance, the Charter is an improvement over the previous regime of legislative supremacy that had permitted such flagrant violations of civil rights, and those who believe that the Charter has done us much more harm than good.

In the pro-Charter camp we might include the various groups and individuals who wish to use the Charter to pursue their interests, together with many liberal and progressive academics and legal practitioners. These individuals and groups generally take the position that the Charter has expanded democracy by giving "the people" the chance to challenge government actions that they feel infringe their rights and interests. At last there is a check on the potential excesses of majoritarian governments, and at last Canadians can enjoy a sense of national unity, secure in the knowledge that they have fundamental rights no matter where they live. Rights are good insofar as they build fences around individuals and protect us from unlimited state power. Moreover, entrenched rights can offer historically and currently oppressed minorities not just relief from discrimination, but affirmative action, and all of this can only enhance democracy as citizens are acknowledged and empowered by the Charter.

On the other hand, a number of scholars, activists, lawyers, and others have become increasingly skeptical about the Charter and its impact on Canadian society. Oddly enough, quite similar critiques issue from those on the left and right of the ideological spectrum, though representatives of each are motivated by very different underlying concerns. They tend to focus on two major issues: first, the nature of the Charter itself and the kinds of rights it enshrines; and second, the enhanced role of the judiciary in policymaking. Yet while this left/right debate has absorbed much attention in the universities, strong critiques of the Charter have been offered by feminist and First Nations scholars and activists, each highlighting the gendered and cultured nature of the Charter and the courts. The following discussion seeks to convey the flavour of these various critiques in general terms, stressing the points of convergence and divergence between them.[70]

THE NATURE OF CHARTER RIGHTS

To begin, both left- and right-wing critics worry that the Charter has led to the Americanization of our legal and political systems, as well as of our political culture. Early on, there was a concern that Canadian courts would use U.S. precedents and approaches to rights claims, although the Supreme Court of Canada soon rejected the idea of relying on American precedents.[71] A second fear was that Canadians would become litigation-loving libertines, more concerned with our individual interests and pleasures than with collective values and goods. Hence, like the Americans, we would be more apt to sue not only governments, but one another because rights-thinking is atomistic, conducive not to a sense of community but to rampant self-interest. Of course, the sense of community and values to be lost differs according to the ideological persuasion of the critic. Nevertheless, it is self-evident that the Americans' unbridled individualism has torn the social fabric asunder, and the same fate awaits us if we encourage such self-oriented thinking. Now that we have entered our third decade of Charter litigation, however, this apprehension seems to have been somewhat overdrawn.

Still, for different reasons, both right- and left-wing critics maintain that the Charter is a profoundly anti-democratic document. There is considerable anxiety that "special interests" are now able to use the Charter to win through the courts what they could not achieve by lobbying elected representatives in the normal political process. Right-wingers such as Knopff and Morton believe that the courts have fallen under the influence of a so-called court party comprising liberal or progressive groups such as women's, gay, ethnic, and other identity-based organizations, academics, and bureaucratic and media elites.[72] As we have seen above, these groups have, among other things, used the courts to strike down the abortion law, deny the fetus human status, allow girls to play hockey in teams with boys,[73] prohibit violent and degrading pornography, and recognize aboriginal rights,[74] all in direct opposition to the policy choices of our elected representatives. By appealing to Charter rights, then, the "court party" has subverted the idea of representative democracy and the electoral process.

On the other hand, leftists, who also criticize interest groups' new-found ability to circumvent democratic decision making, worry about an entirely different set of "special interests," namely private corporations, the wealthy, and the privileged. As shown above, these interests have used the courts to roll back hard-won union rights, to deny workers a day of rest by allowing Sunday shopping, to win "equality" rights for otherwise privileged, non-citizen lawyers, to override the principle of "one person one vote,"[75] and to protect free speech for white supremacists who claim that the Holocaust is a hoax concocted by international Jewish conspirators.[76] Leftists argue that the Charter is in fact the instrument of the advantaged—business, the wealthy, private interests, and professionals—and that the real losers must be the poor, ethnic minorities, women, workers, the unemployed, and other disadvantaged groups.[77]

Leftists point out that the Charter basically enshrines negative liberties (it protects individuals from state interference) rather than positive rights to employment, income, education, social services, health care, and so on.[78] Hence, it does not contribute to substantive equality, but at best provides only limited guarantees of equality of opportunity, and then only insofar as individual–government relations are concerned. Protection against discrimination by governments will not produce real equality, because it is in the so-called private spheres of the workplace, housing, the family, and other social and economic spaces where sexism, racism, homophobia, ableism, and other forms of discrimination and disadvantage flourish. Furthermore, whereas right-wingers fret, for example, that equality rights decisions extending spousal benefits to same-sex couples will force governments to spend more and more on expensive social programs, the left is perturbed by quite the opposite prospect. As Andrew Petter argues, the Charter is "a 19th century document let loose on a 20th century welfare state," and the rights enshrined in it "are founded on the belief that the main enemies of freedom are not disparities in wealth nor concentrations of private power, but the state."[79] Thus, he fears, private and business interests will use the courts to attack redistributive taxation and equalization policies, social services, and state regulation.

Whereas leftists value equality over liberty, right-wing critics take the opposite tack. For them, the Charter is a dangerous document because it includes certain rights at the expense of others. They worry that it sacrifices liberty for equality: it is a misguided attempt at "social engineering" that denies natural differences among individuals, and that will ultimately stifle the creativity and individual initiative a healthy (capitalist) economy requires. Human rights codes and Charter provisions to guarantee not just equal opportunity but equality of result will curtail freedom, which surely must be the fundamental aim of society.[80] This problem is compounded, it is argued, by the fact that there is no balancing mechanism in the Charter in the form of property rights, which means that individuals cannot control the disposition of their property against encroachments or regulation by the state. The twin facts that property rights have always been respected by the common law and that private interests have managed to use different Charter provisions to protect themselves against regulation do not seem to satisfy such critics.

THE ROLE OF THE JUDICIARY

Apart from the nature of Charter rights, the second major prong of the anti-Charter assault concerns the augmented role of the judiciary. It is generally accepted that in a democracy in which elected politicians make the law through the executive, and civil servants administer it, there must be some ultimate check at the operational stage. In theory, even a parliamentary system has some checks and balances in the policy process, as the House of Commons, the Senate, interest groups, and others assume certain roles in policy formulation. But after a policy or law is passed, some body must be able to ensure that it is properly implemented and that it does not penalize some members of society unfairly. It is also generally accepted that a strong, independent judiciary is essential to the functioning of a democracy for several reasons. First, statutes passed by the elected representatives normally codify broad rules and principles, and hence their texts are open to interpretation. No matter how well written, statutes contain ambiguous language; they cannot cover all contingencies, nor can they guarantee impartial application by the various departments and agencies responsible for implementing them. Second, in a federal system such as Canada's, jurisdictional disputes between the two levels of government need to be adjudicated by a neutral body susceptible to neither bribe nor threat. Third, in states that have bills of rights enshrining the basic rights and freedoms of citizens, the courts play a critical role in determining whether government actions are respectful of those rights and fundamental values such as freedom and equality.

According to anti-Charter factions, however, the Charter of Rights has inflated the role and importance of judges beyond the legitimate functions of yesteryear. It has judicialized or "legalized" politics so that instead of being decided in an open political process by elected representatives, policy issues are now transformed into technical questions to be settled by lawyers in a closed legal process.[81] Furthermore, if the Charter has "legalized" politics, it has politicized the law in equal measure. To the extent that judges have the power to uphold or strike down laws they consider inconsistent with the Charter, they are in effect making and breaking policy. Moreover, because legal language in general and constitutional provisions in particular tend to be imprecise, judges' interpretations (which may vary considerably depending on the individual judge) can either create new rights or negate rights the framers of the Constitution intended to include. Thus, according to Knopff and Morton, judges have become "politicians in robes." They can be as activist or as deferential to Parliament as they choose, but in the meantime politicians can hide behind those spacious robes to dodge their decision-making responsibilities regarding controversial issues.

Charter skeptics do not believe that judges are competent in these new spheres. For a start, they are unelected. They are appointed by the federal government in a closed process because of their training as lawyers, not because they have any particular expertise regarding complex social, moral, economic, or political problems. It is not immediately apparent why lawyers should have ultimate decision-making authority over anyone else. In addition, there is the question of accountability. Superior court judges have tenure until the age of 75, a measure to ensure that neither politicians nor popular pressures can compromise their judgments.[82] Protecting judges from bullying, however, also means rendering them unaccountable, either to those who appoint them (elected representatives) or to the public, the consumers of their decisions. All of this was fine when judges merely enforced the law and umpired federalism, but now that they are more significantly engaged—making and breaking public policy, deciding tricky issues, constructing fences around the individual, and putting up "no-trespassing" signs against governments—their lack of accountability is at least questionable.

Leftist scholars have pointed out that judges as policymakers are not only unaccountable, they are relatively inaccessible as well. Because litigation is extremely expensive and legal aid is only automatically available for criminal matters, individuals and groups with non-criminal causes can be shut out of the courts for want of money. Whereas governments and wealthy private interests have virtually unlimited resources, time, and personnel to fight cases through trials and appeals, the "oppressed and disempowered groups who are the supposed beneficiaries of progressive Charter litigation will, because of their lack of resources, be the least likely to have genuine access to the Courts."[83] Moreover, the Charter has also forced such groups to take defensive actions against privileged parties who are using the courts to promote their interests at the expense of others, and hence they must divert their precious resources from other activities to the black hole of litigation.

Apart from the question of access, there is also concern that judges' ideological biases might further limit the policy options of governments. The fact is, the law moves slowly over time, and one legal decision based on the particular ideological interpretation of incumbent judges can handcuff elected representatives for a very long time, despite changes in social and economic needs. Not surprisingly, while right-wing skeptics are convinced that the legal elite is dominated by left-wing intellectuals, leftist critics argue that "legalized politics is the quintessential conservative politics."[84] This is because judges are unrepresentative of the Canadian population, and their world-views cannot help being informed, if not biased, by their privileged backgrounds.

In an earlier age, when Canada's political culture was perhaps more deferential to the authority of various elites, we were more apt to accept the mystique of the judge as an eminence who had no particular identity or self-interest, but symbolized something larger than himself—justice. He (as it was always a he) was a luminary who dispensed justice from a legal pulpit in a spirit of omniscient, anonymous, and fair-minded detachment, and the exercise of his powers could be questioned by none but more senior members of the same priesthood. In contemporary Canadian politics, however, judicial objectivity, far from assumed, is considered all but impossible.

Charter critics frequently observe that Canadian judges are not representative of a cross section of Canadian society in terms of characteristics such as class, gender, ethnicity, age, religion, marital status, and political experience. In fact, when judges make decisions involving discretion, they often apply the "average reasonable person" standard. The problem, however, is that "the 'average reasonable person,' as seen through the eyes of a typical judge, is likely to be a high-achieving male of British or French origin adhering to one of the mainline religions, approaching 60 years of age, living in a comfortable middle-class or upper-class environment, and active in a political party."[85] In fact, as of 1997, of 2500 judges in Canada, only 263 (or 10.5 percent) were women, and only 2 percent were so-called visible minorities.[86] Quite apart from the constricted rules of evidence that present extremely partial accounts of those who appear before the courts, judges with the foregoing characteristics cannot possibly appreciate the life circumstances of the disadvantaged. Because of their backgrounds, and because of a legal culture that is itself inherently conservative, it is argued, judges' decisions must be infused with conscious and unconscious biases.

In fact, several studies have shown that individual judges have different ideological leanings that lend some degree of predictability to their rulings in certain kinds of cases.[87] For example, a study of 4000 Supreme Court decisions from 1949 to 1992 concluded that "[t]here's no suggestion that the underdog always loses—it's just that they tend to lose, on balance over the long run," and that "rather than acting as a check on the rich and powerful, [the courts] have privilege-reinforcing tendencies."[88] Moreover, the fact that the federal government instituted a policy in 1989 "to improve the representation of traditionally under-represented groups in the judiciary," particularly "aboriginal peoples, francophones, persons with disabilities, racial minorities, and women,"[89] suggests that it is aware of a problem, either of systemic bias within the legal system, or at least of legitimacy in the public eye.

The question of judicial bias has been the subject of many studies and publications and has become one of the key critiques of the legal system offered by feminist and ethnocultural minority activists and scholars.[90] Feminist scholars have pointed out that gender-biased or sexist decisions are not necessarily products of the pathologies of individual judges or their deliberate intention to favour those of their own gender, ethnocultural group, or class (although those factors may apply). Rather, the law itself, in a sense, has a gender; designed by men largely to serve male interests, it is deeply informed by male points of view, assumptions, experiences, behavioural patterns, and approaches to justice. It assumes a universal subject that is somehow genderless (as well as raceless, classless, etc.) and claims impartiality, even as it enshrines the general interests of men over those of women, as evidenced by a wide range of laws that have discriminated against women. If we add to the "maleness" of the law itself the fact that the overwhelming majority of the personnel of the legal system, from police officers to lawyers to judges, have been male, it would only be surprising if we did not get gender-biased decisions.

Aboriginal scholars and women of colour have similarly pointed out that the law in general and the Charter in particular have a culture. As noted above, the Charter, like the BNA Act before it, privileges certain ethnocultural groups over others by enshrining the European languages and religions of the two main colonizers (the English and the French), and by insulating the hierarchy thus entrenched by means of the principle that one part of the Constitution cannot be invoked to invalidate another. This means that excluded groups cannot invoke equality rights to make claims on the public purse for schooling in their languages or religions, for example. But, further, as Mary Ellen Turpel points out, the Charter is an instrument of cultural hegemony that reinforces "troubling hegemonic delusions like the one about the two founding nations, or the concept of multiculturalism within a bilingual (French and English) context." The Charter is infused with Anglo-European cultural values, both in the text and in the interpretive jurisprudence it has fostered, from the adversarial model of litigation—rather than the consensus decision-making and mediatory traditions of First Nations; to the abstract, liberal, individual rights paradigm—rather than a collectivist and responsibilities-oriented one; to the "authority which one culture is seen to possess to create law and legal language to resolve disputes involving other cultures." Noting that the elitist and Euro-Canadian judges write and interpret the law from "a conceptual framework of rights derived from the theory of a natural right to private property," Turpel is profoundly skeptical that Canadian courts can comprehend, let alone accommodate, cultural difference, and she ultimately rejects the application of the Charter to First Nations.[91]

Finally, despite the fact that numerous Euro-Canadian judges have exhibited all manner of biases from sexism to heterosexism to racism, as Canada's first and only Asian-Canadian woman judge, Maryka Omatsu, has pointed out, it is extraordinary that the few judges who have actually been investigated for gender or racial bias have been women and/or ethnic minority judges. In her discussion of a range of U.S. and Canadian cases, Judge Omatsu highlights the assumptions that women judges cannot fairly judge cases involving sex discrimination (presumably only men can be "impartial" in this area), and that judges from racial/ethnocultural minorities cannot be unbiased in cases in which race is an issue (presumably only white judges and juries can be "impartial" about racial discrimination).[92] In fact, the first Supreme Court case in which racial bias on the part of a judge was at issue involved a decision by Nova Scotia's first African-Canadian judge in a case involving a black youth charged with assaulting an officer while trying to prevent his friend's arrest. In her oral reasons for her credibility finding in favour of the youth, Her Honour Judge Corrine Sparks remarked (in response to a rhetorical question by the Crown) that police officers had been known to mislead the court in the past, and that they had been known to overreact, particularly with "non-white" groups. The Crown's appeal on the grounds of reasonable apprehension of bias was upheld by the Nova Scotia Court of Appeal, and Judge Sparks was "disciplined" by the chief justice of the province. The Supreme Court of Canada overturned the appellate court's decision, however, and developed, for the first time, a test for judicial bias.[93] The case is significant, however, in that in all of Canada's history of racist and sexist decisions, Judge Sparks's integrity was impugned because she dared to acknowledge a social context of racism (in a province in which the Donald Marshall, Jr., inquiry had admitted systemic racism against First Nations people and had led to policy changes) and to pull back the veil of neutrality in the administration of justice.

In view of the varied criticisms outlined above, it is important to remember that despite the socio-demographic profile of the Canadian judiciary, some important legal decisions have favoured disadvantaged claimants. On the other hand, those who fear the influence of the "court party" cannot easily explain decisions that have favoured privileged interests. In the end, both left- and right-wing skeptics are asking us to rely on elected representatives to make our public policies when they are not necessarily more "representative" than judges. Politicians too tend to be male, white, of British or French origin, Protestant or Catholic, middle-aged, trained in law or business, living in a comfortable middle-class or upper-class environment, and of course, active in a political party. The assumption that they will somehow make better policy choices than judges when they are responsible for passing the discriminatory laws that are subsequently challenged under the Charter is suspect. In addition, the argument that at least the policymaking process is democratic is also questionable, given the concentration of power in the hands of political executives and senior (unelected) bureaucrats at the expense of ordinary elected MPs. Besides, the role of the court is precisely to protect the rights of the casualties of majoritarian politics. This is perhaps why feminists, lesbians and gays, and people with disabilities have been rather less hostile to Charter politics than have male scholars from the ideological left and right.[94]

CONCLUSION

The Canadian Charter of Rights and Freedoms has undoubtedly had a significant impact on Canadian politics. But must it mean the end of democracy as we have known it, as Charter skeptics maintain? In fact, after 20 years of experience, it is clear that the critics have overestimated the political, social, and economic impacts of the Charter and of the expanded role of judges. Certainly, some higher-court Charter decisions have had serious repercussions. For example, the Supreme Court decision that struck down the French-only sign law as a violation of freedom of expression led the government of Quebec to invoke the notwithstanding clause so that it could reenact the law. The premier of Manitoba, in turn, stopped discussion of the Meech Lake Accord in the legislature, an action that ultimately led to the unravelling of an agreement that might have satisfied Quebec's constitutional demands. Yet even so, if Quebec should decide to separate from the federation in the future, no one could seriously blame the Supreme Court. The legal decision is merely one link in a chain of complex historical events that might take an entirely different course at any time.

The anxiety among both left- and right-wing critics that the courts have been captured by the other side is also somewhat overblown. In fact, the behaviour of the courts is inconvenient to both, precisely because they do not consistently favour the advantaged over the disadvantaged or vice versa. Although there are legitimate questions to be asked about the expanded role of the courts in the Charter era, given that legal decisions rendered by non-elected, non-accountable judges can overrule decisions made by our democratically elected representatives, a number of factors suggest that the Charter has not given courts unlimited power over legislatures.

First, the fact that the Charter has three built-in sources of limitation, including sections 1 and 33, recognizes the policymaking authority of legislatures even if their policies violate Charter guarantees. Second, legal decisions cannot be considered the final and definitive pronouncements on issues. The fact of the matter is that courts must interpret the law as it stands. But if legislatures do not like court decisions, they can change the law, or, ultimately, they can change the Constitution they imposed on themselves. For these reasons, legislatures are still very much in control of the policy process, with the courts acting as reviewers to ensure that policy is consistent with the fundamental values the legislatures have enshrined in the Constitution.

Third, after an initial burst of activism in the early 1980s, the success rate of Charter claims has declined dramatically. There is no reason to expect that it will suddenly shoot up again, for the simple reason that many of the issues avoided by legislatures have now been settled by the courts. After two decades, legislatures have cleaned up their acts, as it were, and are now more careful to frame legislation that will not violate the Charter.

The new century has undoubtedly brought new challenges for the Charter and the courts charged with its interpretation. Technological developments such as new reproductive technologies and genetic engineering will give rise to a host of challenges to government attempts at regulation of such matters as cloning, germline genetic alteration, xenotransplantation, the creation of animal–human hybrids, sex selection, and health and other risks associated with agricultural biotechnology.[95] Corporate interests, infertile couples, people with various maladies, organizations such as the Raelians (promoters of human cloning), public interest groups, and others can be expected to mobilize Charter rights to life, liberty and security of the person, freedom of expression and belief, and even equality to get the courts to invalidate measures banning or restricting the use of these and other technologies in ways that will challenge the very ethical foundations of Canadian society.

Finally, the culture of security foisted upon us in the wake of September 11, 2001, will surely pose a range of fresh challenges to the constitutional rights of Canadians and non-citizens alike. In particular, while the government took pains to declare the Anti-Terrorism Act of 2001 to be consistent with the Charter (and it was certainly drafted to provide for many Charter rights explicitly in the text), some of its provisions will surely be vulnerable to Charter claims. For example, legal rights in sections 7–14 will probably be invoked regarding the broad definition of terrorist activity, preventive detentions, the allowance for investigative hearings that compel testimony from witnesses before any charges have been laid, rules regarding the financing and seizing of property of alleged terrorist organizations, the potential for racial profiling of suspects, and the criminalization of religious and political motives.[96] It is likely, but not a foregone conclusion, that government appeals to section 1 justifications will reach sympathetic judicial ears in view of the real or perceived threats posed by terrorism, though if the Supreme Court's decisions in *Suresh* and in the *U.S. v. Burns* case are anything to go by, the standard of justification for rights infringements, even of accused terrorists, will remain high.[97]

Does the Charter of Rights, in the end, threaten or enhance Canadian democracy? It could be argued that international trade agreements that manacle domestic policymakers, technological revolutions, increasing concentration of wealth in the hands of a small elite, the degradation of the environment, and the ascendancy of a mercenary capitalism known as globalization are all far greater threats to Canadian democracy as we know it than is the Charter of Rights. Although the Charter and the courts will undoubtedly continue to affect Canadian politics in the twenty-first century, the chances are that they will become less rather than more controversial over time as greater forces transform our material, social, economic, and discursive ways of life. Indeed, the Charter and the courts may well prove to be a bulwark against some of those forces in the years to come.

NOTES

1. The U.S. Supreme Court found that the Fifth Amendment required this caution in the 1966 case *Miranda v. Arizona* (1966) 384 U.S. 436. In Canada, however, even though it has been a common-law right, there is no constitutional provision to that effect. In practice, Canadian police, after informing the accused of a Criminal Code charge, advise him or her of the right to retain and instruct counsel without delay and the right to legal assistance without charge. But whereas the "Miranda card" refers to the *right* to remain silent, the procedure in Canada is for the officer to offer a less direct caution: "You need not say anything. You have nothing to hope from any promise or favour and nothing to fear from any threat whether or not you say anything. Anything you do say may be used as evidence." In fact, the old common-law right of an accused person to refuse to answer any question on the grounds that the answer might tend to incriminate her or him has been abolished in Canada. It has been replaced by section 13 of the Charter, which provides only that the incriminating answer cannot be used against the witness in any other proceedings.

2. A.C. Cairns, "The Living Canadian Constitution," in D.E. Williams, ed., *Constitution, Government and Society in Canada: Selected Essays by Alan C. Cairns* (Toronto: McClelland & Stewart, 1988), p. 27.

3. See David Stannard, *American Holocaust: The Conquest of the New World* (New York: Oxford University Press, 1992); or Ward Churchill, *A Little Matter of Genocide: Holocaust and Denial in the Americas, 1492 to the Present* (San Francisco: City Light Books, 1997).

4. See, for example, Joe R. Feagin and Clairece Booher Feagin, *Racial and Ethnic Relations*, 4th ed. (Englewood Cliffs, NJ: Prentice Hall, 1993), p. 236.

5. See Daiva Stasiulis and Radha Jhappan, "The Fractious Politics of a Settler Society: Canada," in Daiva Stasiulis and Nira Yuval-Davis, eds., *Unsettling Settler Societies: Articulations of Gender, Race, Ethnicity, and Class* (London: Sage, 1995), pp. 95–131.

6. Ian Greene describes these and other early civil rights cases in *The Charter of Rights* (Toronto: James Lorimer, 1989), pp. 17–23.

7. Cited in Noel A. Kinsella, "Tomorrow's Rights in the Mirror of History," in G.L. Gall, ed., *Civil Liberties in Canada: Entering the 1980s* (Toronto: Butterworths, 1982), p. 32.

8. For excellent in-depth analyses of major race discrimination cases, see Constance Backhouse, *Colour-Coded: A Legal History of Racism in Canada, 1900–1950* (Toronto: University of Toronto Press, 1999); and James W. St. G. Walker, *"Race," Rights and the Law in the Supreme Court of Canada* (Waterloo: Wilfrid Laurier University Press, 1997).

9. *Quong-Wing v. R.* [1914] 49 S.C.R. 440. See M.L. Berlin and W.F. Pentney, eds., *Human Rights and Freedoms in Canada: Cases, Notes and Materials* (Toronto: Butterworths, 1987), p. 12.

10. Quoted in D.A. Schmeiser, *Civil Liberties in Canada* (Toronto: Oxford University Press, 1965), p. 264.

11. Reference re Alberta Statutes [1938] 2 S.C.R. 100.

12. For example, in *Saumur v. Quebec* [1953] 2 S.C.R. 299, the Supreme Court found the Quebec government's requirement that Jehovah's Witnesses obtain a permit to distribute their literature in the street a violation of an implied freedom of religion. In the famous *Roncarelli v. Duplessis* case [1959] S.C.R. 121, the Court held that the principle of equal application of the law had been infringed when the Quebec government cancelled the liquor licence of a wealthy Montreal restaurateur who habitually posted bail for Jehovah's Witnesses arrested for distributing their literature. On the other hand, in *Switzman v. Elbling* [1957] S.C.R. 285, the Court struck down Quebec's 1937 Padlock Act (under which any premises used to produce or distribute communist literature could be locked up) because it violated the federal government's jurisdiction over criminal law.

13. *R. v. Drybones* [1970] S.C.R. 282. It is interesting to note, however, that it was not until 1985 that the offence of being drunk on a reserve was repealed.

14. *Lavell v. A.G. Canada* [1974] S.C.R. 1349.

15. *Andrews v. Law Society of British Columbia* [1989] 1 S.C.R. 143.

16. *Bliss v. A.G. Canada* [1979] 1 S.C.R. 183.

17. Tsvi Kahana, "The Notwithstanding Mechanism and Public Discussion: Lessons from the Ignored Practice of s. 33 of the Charter," *Canadian Public Administration* 44, no. 3 (2001).

18. *R. v. Oakes* [1986]1 S.C.R. 103.

19. Peter Hogg, *Constitutional Law of Canada*, 3rd ed. (Toronto: Carswell, 1992), p. 866.

20. David Beatty, *Talking Heads and the Supremes: The Canadian Production of Constitutional Review* (Toronto: Carswell, 1990), p. vii.

21. F.L. Morton, P.H. Russell, and M.J. Withey, "The Supreme Court's First One Hundred Charter of Rights Decisions: A Statistical Analysis," *Osgoode Hall Law Journal* 30, no. 1 (1992): 8–9.

22. James B. Kelly, "The Charter of Rights and Freedoms and the Rebalancing of Liberal Constitutionalism in Canada, 1982–1997," *Osgoode Hall Law Journal* 37 (1999): 641. These statistical analyses should be read with caution for the following reasons: (1) they focus exclusively on cases definitively resolved by the Supreme Court of Canada and do not include the decisions of lower courts, human rights boards, or administrative tribunals or cases not appealed (for any number of reasons), which therefore stand as precedents; (2) they do not include decisions on applications for leave to appeal, which, if unsuccessful, decide the issue by preserving the appellate court result; and (3) they exclude cases decided without reasons, cases decided together with others raising similar issues, those decided on the basis of non-entrenched rights (for example, through the Canadian Bill of Rights, 1960), cases dealing with non-Charter constitutional rights (from the Constitution Act, 1867, or aboriginal rights in the Constitution Act, 1982), and cases ultimately decided on non-Charter grounds (such as the division of powers). The statistics therefore exclude thousands of decisions whose inclusion would change the picture radically. See Morton, Russell, and Withey, "The Supreme Court's First One Hundred Charter of Rights Decisions," pp. 50–52.

23. *Ford v. Quebec (Attorney General)* [1988] 2 S.C.R. 712.

24. *Osborne v. Canada* [1991] 2 S.C.R. 69.

25. *R.J.R. MacDonald Inc. v. Canada (A.G.)* [1995] 3 S.C.R. 199.

26. *R. v. Butler* [1992] 1 S.C.R. 452.

27. *R. v. Sharpe* [2001] 1 S.C.R. 45. In one of its most controversial recent decisions, the majority of the Supreme Court substantially upheld the child pornography sections of the Criminal Code, while allowing exceptions for "artistic merit" and for materials held exclusively for personal use.

28. *R. v. Keegstra* [1990] 3 S.C.R. 697; *Taylor and the Western Guard Party v. Canadian Human Rights Commission and A.G. Canada* [1990] 3 S.C.R. 892.

29. *Re ss. 193 and 195(1) of Criminal Code (Prostitution Reference)* [1990] 1 S.C.R. 1123.

30. *Irwin Toy Ltd. v. Quebec (Attorney General)* [1989] 1 S.C.R. 232.

31. *Canadian Newspapers Co. v. Canada (Attorney General)* [1988] 2 S.C.R. 122.

32. The three cases were, respectively: *Re Public Service Employees Relations Act* [1987] 1 S.C.R. 313; *RWDSU v. Saskatchewan* [1987] 1 S.C.R. 460; and *PSAC v. Canada* [1987] 1 S.C.R. 424.

33. *Dunmore v. Ontario (A.G.)* [2001] 3 S.C.R. 1016. For an analysis of the modesty of this win for labour, see Diane Pothier, "Twenty Years of Labour Law and the Charter," *Osgoode Hall Law Journal* 40 (2002): 369–400.

34. *R.W.D.S.U. Local 558 v. Pepsi-Cola Canada Beverages West (Ltd.)* [2002] 1 S.C.R. 156

35. *R. v. Advance Cutting and Coring Ltd.* [2001] 3 S.C.R. 209.

36. *Lavigne v. Ontario Public Service Employees Union* [1991] 2 S.C.R. 211.

37. *R. v. Big M Drug Mart* [1985] 1 S.C.R. 351. However, in *R. v. Edwards Books and Art* [1986] 2 S.C.R. the Court upheld Ontario's Retail Business Holidays Act on the grounds that the purpose of the act was the secular one of providing for a common day of rest.

38. *Hunter v. Southam* [1984] 2 S.C.R. 145.

39. *Ford v. Quebec (Attorney General)* [1988] 2 S.C.R. 712.

40. *R.J.R. MacDonald Inc. v. Canada (A.G.)* [1995] 3 S.C.R. 199.

41. *Rocket v. Royal College of Dental Surgeons of Ontario* [1990] 2 S.C.R. 232.

42. Richard W. Bauman, "Business, Economic Rights, and the Charter," in David Schneiderman and Kate Sutherland, eds., *Charting the Consequences* (Toronto: University of Toronto Press, 1997), p. 59.

43. *Morgentaler v. the Queen* [1988] 1 S.C.R. 30. The Supreme Court of Canada struck down s. 251 of the Criminal Code on procedural grounds: that is, the therapeutic abortion committee requirement and the fact that not all hospitals had such committees or provided abortion services meant unnecessary delays and unequal access to abortion across the country. As a result of the *Morgentaler* decision, abortion reverted back to a negative liberty but certainly did not become a positive right.

44. *Borowski v. Canada (Attorney General)* [1989] 1 S.C.R. 342. The case was moot as the Supreme Court had recently struck down s. 251 of the Criminal Code in *Morgentaler*. Subsequent cases have held that the fetus does not have a right to life and is not a legal person possessing rights under current Canadian law. These include *Daigle v. Tremblay* [1989] 2 S.C.R. 530, in which the Supreme Court of Canada dismissed a civil (non-Charter) action brought by a biological father to prevent his ex-fiancée from having an abortion claiming a fetal right to life as well as a paternal right to veto a woman's decision to have an abortion; and *Winnipeg Child and Family Services v. D.F.G.* [1997] 3 S.C.R. 928, in which the Court found a violation of the rights of a woman addicted to glue-sniffing who had been ordered detained and treated against her will by a superior court judge in the interests of preventing harm to the unborn child.

45. *Rodriguez v. British Columbia (Attorney General)* [1993] 3 S.C.R. 519.

46. *Operation Dismantle Inc. v. the Queen* [1985] 1 S.C.R. 441. The Court found the argument hypothetical and purely speculative since the group could not prove the projected outcome.

47. *Singh v. the Minister of Employment and Immigration* [1985] 1 S.C.R. 177. It was in this case that the Supreme Court found that everyone physically present in Canada enjoys Charter rights (except those that expressly require citizenship).

48. *Suresh v. Canada (Minister of Citizenship and Immigration)* [2002] 1 S.C.R. 3.

49. Gwen Brodsky and Shelagh Day, eds., *Canadian Charter Equality Rights for Women: One Step Forward or Two Steps Back?* (Ottawa: Canadian Advisory Council on the Status of Women, 1989), chap. 5, *passim*.

50. *McKinney v. University of Guelph* [1990] 3 S.C.R. 229. On the other hand, the Court overruled the age discrimination in the Unemployment Insurance Act, which denied benefits to persons over 65 in *Tetreault-Gadoury v. Canada* [1991] 2 S.C.R. 22.

51. *Gosselin v. Quebec (A.G.)* [2002] S.C.J. No. 85.

52. *Eaton v. Brant County Board of Education* [1997] 1 S.C.R. 241.

53. See, for example, *R.B. v. Children's Aid Society of Metro Toronto* [1995] 1 S.C.R. 315. The Supreme Court dismissed the appeal by the parents of a premature infant who had had a blood transfusion (authorized by the Children's Aid Society, which was granted temporary wardship over the child for the purpose) against their wishes as Jehovah's Witnesses. The Court held that the child's section 7 rights to life and security of the person could not be overridden by her parents' religious freedom rights under section 2 of the Charter.

54. *Jack and Charlie v. R.* [1985] 2 S.C.R. 332.

55. *Vriend v. Alberta (A.G.)* [1998] 1 S.C.R. 493. The Court ruled that Alberta's Individual Rights Protection Act violated the Charter and Delwin Vriend's equality rights because it did not include sexual orientation as a prohibited ground of discrimination.

56. Kathleen Lahey, "Feminist Theories of (In)Equality," in S.L. Martin and K. Mahoney, eds., *Equality and Judicial Neutrality* (Toronto: Carswell, 1987), p. 82.

57. Brodsky and Day, *Canadian Charter Equality Rights for Women*, p. 49. Similarly, in "Legitimizing Sexual Inequality: Three Early Charter Cases," *McGill Law Journal* 34 (1989): 360–62, Andrew Petter notes that of the first 35 sex discrimination cases, 25 (70 percent) had been brought by men, and of 11 successful cases, 7 (65 percent) involved male litigants.

58. *R. v. Seaboyer* [1991] 2 S.C.R. 577.

59. *Thibaudeau v. Canada* [1995] 2 S.C.R. 627.

60. *O'Connor v. the Queen* [1995] 4 S.C.R. 411.

61. *R. v. Daviault* [1994] 3 S.C.R. 63.

62. *R. v. Morgentaler* [1988] 1 S.C.R. 30.

63. *Tremblay v. Daigle* [1989] 62 D.L.R. (4th) 634.

64. *Brooks v. Canada Safeway Ltd.* [1987] 1 S.C.R. 1219.

65. *Janzen v. Platy Enterprises* [1989] 1 S.C.R. 1252.

66. *R. v. Butler* [1992] 70 C.C.C. (3d) 129.

67. *Re Shewchuck v. Ricard* [1986] 28 D.L.R. (4th) 429.

68. *Andrews v. the Law Society of British Columbia* [1989] 1 S.C.R. 143. The Court found that the B.C. Law Society's exclusion of non-citizens from the bar violated the equality rights of otherwise qualified non-citizens, in this case, a landed immigrant from Britain who had passed his bar exams in the province. As many have observed, it is ironic that the first significant section 15 case should have upheld the equality rights of a healthy, potentially wealthy male of British origin, rather than a member of a group that has been

historically oppressed. It is also ironic that the decision has not been applied by the courts to other non-citizens (such as foreign domestic workers) who suffer serious "disadvantage" in the sense that they are excluded from labour code provisions governing health and safety, hours of work, minimum wages, unionization rights, and the like.

69. The Parti Québécois government of René Lévesque refused to sign the Constitution Act, 1982, and it has frequently been assumed in the rest of Canada that the Charter is regarded as illegitimate in Quebec. However, Andrew Heard has shown that residents of Quebec have used the Charter for a wide range of claims, much like residents of other provinces, and that Quebec courts have been willing to accept Charter claims roughly as often as courts in other provinces. See Andrew Heard, "Quebec Courts and the Canadian Charter of Rights," *International Journal of Canadian Studies* 7–8 (Spring–Fall 1993): 153–66.

70. For an excellent, in-depth discussion of the ideological debate, see Richard Sigurdson, "Left- and Right-Wing Charterphobia in Canada: A Critique of the Critics," *International Journal of Canadian Studies* 7–8 (1993): 95–115.

71. Beatty, *Talking Heads and the Supremes,* p. 19.

72. Rainer Knopff and F.L. Morton, *Charter Politics* (Scarborough, ON: Nelson, 1992), p. 79.

73. *Blainey v. Ontario Hockey Association* [1986] 54 O.R. (2d) 513 (C.A.).

74. For an analysis of major Supreme Court of Canada decisions on aboriginal rights, see Patrick Macklem, *Indigenous Difference and the Constitution of Canada* (Toronto: University of Toronto Press, 2001).

75. *Re Provincial Electoral Boundaries (Saskatchewan)* [1991] 2 S.C.R. 158. The Supreme Court upheld Saskatchewan's electoral boundaries law that allowed a 25 percent variation in constituency size (from a rural district with 6309 voters to an urban riding of 10 147), resulting in the overrepresentation of rural voters.

76. *R. v. Zundel* [1987] 58 O.R. (2d) 129 (C.A.). In 1987, the Ontario Court of Appeal upheld Ernst Zundel's conviction for the Criminal Code offence of spreading false news via his claim that the Holocaust was a hoax invented by Jews in an international conspiracy. However, the Supreme Court of Canada struck down the Criminal Code provision in 1992 on the grounds that freedom of expression in s. 2(b) of the Charter protects even falsehoods if there is a defence of honest belief.

77. Michael Mandel, *The Charter of Rights and the Legalization of Politics in Canada,* rev. ed. (Toronto: Thompson Educational Publishing Inc., 1994). Similar left positions can be found in two articles by Andrew Petter and Allan Hutchinson, "Rights in Conflict: The Dilemma of Charter Legitimacy," *UBC Law Review* 23, no. 3 (1989): 531; and "Private Rights/Public Wrongs: The Liberal Lie of the Charter," *University of Toronto Law Journal* 38 (1988): 278. See also Judy Fudge and Harry Glasbeek, "The Politics of Rights: A Politics with Little Class," *Social and Legal Studies* 1 (1992): 45.

78. Section 36 of the Constitution Act, 1982 (which is not part of the Charter, incidentally) commits the federal and provincial governments to "(a) promoting equal opportunities for the well-being of Canadians; (b) furthering economic development to reduce disparity in opportunities; and (c) providing essential public services of reasonable quality to all Canadians." It also commits the federal government to equalization payments to the provinces. However, the section is a commitment in principle rather than an actionable or justiciable clause.

79. Andrew Petter, "Immaculate Deception: The Charter's Hidden Agenda," *The Advocate* 45 (1987): 857.

80. For articulations of this view, see, for example, Rainer Knopff, *Human Rights and Social Technology: The New War on Discrimination* (Ottawa: Carleton University Press, 1989).

81. See Peter Russell, "The Political Purposes of the Canadian Charter of Rights and Freedoms," *Canadian Bar Review* 61 (1983): 30–54.

82. Peter McCormick and Ian Greene describe the terms, conditions, functions, socioeconomic backgrounds, and attitudes of Canadian judges in *Judges and Judging: Inside the Canadian Judicial System* (Toronto: James Lorimer and Company, 1990).

83. Joel Bakan, "Constitutional Interpretation and Social Change: You Can't Always Get What You Want (Nor What You Need)," in R. Devlin, ed., *Canadian Perspectives on Legal Theory* (Toronto: Emond Montgomery, 1991), pp. 449–50. On the other hand, the Court Challenges Program was instituted in 1985 to fund test-case litigation on equality rights, multiculturalism, and language issues. The program was cut in the 1991 federal budget, however, which left many groups stranded, though it was eventually reinstated. Nevertheless, the point is that funding depends on the government's willingness to provide funding to disadvantaged groups; it is not automatic, has been continuously scaled back, and unlike wealthy interests, claimant groups must submit themselves to rigorous bureaucratic evaluation processes.

84. Mandel, *The Charter of Rights and the Legalization of Politics in Canada*, p. 4.

85. McCormick and Greene, *Judges and Judging*, p. 79.

86. Maryka Omatsu, "The Fiction of Judicial Impartiality," *Canadian Journal of Women and the Law* 9, no. 1 (1997): 4.

87. See Andrew Heard, "The Charter in the Supreme Court of Canada: The Importance of Which Judges Hear an Appeal," *Canadian Journal of Political Science* 24, no. 2 (1991): 289.

88. Study by Peter McCormick reported in *The Globe and Mail*, November 6, 1993: A1.

89. Omatsu, "The Fiction of Judicial Impartiality," p. 2.

90. See, for example, the collection of essays in Joan Brockman and Dorothy Chunn, eds., *Investigating Gender Bias: Law, Courts and the Legal Profession* (Toronto: Thompson Educational Publishing, 1993).

91. Mary Ellen Turpel, "Aboriginal Peoples and the Canadian Charter: Interpretive Monopolies, Cultural Differences," in Devlin, ed., *Canadian Perspectives on Legal Theory*, pp. 503, 506, 513.

92. Omatsu, "The Fiction of Judicial Impartiality," pp. 9–15.

93. *R. v. R.D.S.* [1997] 3 S.C.R. 484.

94. For more detailed critiques of the legal left's position, see Sheila McIntyre, "Feminist Movement in Law: Beyond Privileged and Privileging Theory," and Radha Jhappan, "Introduction: Problems and Possibilities of Feminist Engagement with Law," in Radha Jhappan, ed., *Women's Legal Strategies in Canada* (Toronto: University of Toronto Press, 2002). See also Richard Sigurdson, "The Left-Legal Critique of the Charter: A Critical Assessment," *Windsor Yearbook of Access to Justice* (1993): 116.

95. At the time of writing (spring 2003), the majority federal Liberal government's Bill C-13, the Assisted Human Reproduction Act, has passed first and second readings and the report stage, and is expected to be passed into law before the end of the current Parliamentary session. The Supreme Court's recent decision (*Harvard College v. Canada (Commissioner for Patents)* [2002] S.C.J. No. 77) denying a patent for the Harvard "onco-mouse" on the grounds that a higher life form is not an invention even if it is genetically altered, was not based on a Charter challenge.

96. See Kent Roach, "Did September 11 Change Everything? Struggling to Preserve Canadian Values in the Face of Terrorism," *McGill Law Journal* 47 (2002): 893–947; Jeremy Millard, "Investigative Hearings under the Anti-Terrorism Act," *University of Toronto Faculty of Law Review* 60 (2002): 79–87; and Alexandra Dostal, "Casting the Net Too Broadly: The Definition of 'Terrorist Activity' in Bill C-36," *University of Toronto Faculty of Law Review* 60 (2002): 69–72.

97. *U.S. v. Burns* [2001] 1 S.C.R. 283. Effectively overturning its earlier decision in *Kindler v. Canada (Min. of Justice)* [1991] 2 S.C.R. 779, the Supreme Court found a breach of s. 7 in the Minister's discretionary decision under the Extradition Act to extradite two accused murderers to the United States without seeking assurances that the death penalty would not be imposed.

FURTHER READINGS

Bakan, Joel. *Just Words: Constitutional Rights and Social Wrongs.* Toronto: University of Toronto Press, 1997.

Brodsky, Gwen, and Shelagh Day, eds. *Canadian Charter Equality Rights for Women: One Step Forward or Two Steps Back?* Ottawa: Canadian Advisory Council on the Status of Women, 1989.

Hiebert, Janet L. *Charter Conflicts: What Is Parliament's Role?* Montreal and Kingston: McGill-Queen's University Press, 2002.

Howe, Paul, and Peter H. Russell, eds. *Judicial Power and Canadian Democracy.* Kingston: Queen's University Press, 2001.

Jhappan, Radha, ed. *Women's Legal Strategies in Canada.* Toronto: University of Toronto Press, 2002.

MacDougall, Bruce. *Queer Judgments: Homosexuality, Expression and the Courts in Canada.* Toronto: University of Toronto Press, 2000.

Mandel, Michael. *The Charter of Rights and the Legalization of Politics in Canada,* 2nd ed. Toronto: Wall and Thompson, 1993.

Morton, F.L. and Rainer Knopff. *The Charter Revolution and the Court Party.* Peterborough: Broadview, 2000.

Schneiderman, David, and Kate Sutherland, eds. *Charting the Consequences: The Impact of the Charter of Rights on Canadian Law and Politics.* Toronto: University of Toronto Press, 1997.

Women's Legal Education and Action Fund. *Equality and the Charter: Ten Years of Feminist Advocacy before the Supreme Court of Canada.* Toronto: Emond Montgomery, 1996.

CHAPTER 12

IN THE SHADOW OF THE HYPERPOWER: BEYOND CANADA'S MIDDLE-POWER IMAGE

Laura Macdonald

The terrorist attacks against the World Trade Center in New York and the Pentagon in Washington, D.C., on September 11, 2001, now look like a watershed in global politics. The U.S. response to these attacks—the "war on terror," the wars in Afghanistan and Iraq, and the redesign of U.S. security policy—oblige us to rethink the way the world works, and Canada's role within it.

Canada's ranking in the international system has been debated for decades by scholars and policymakers. The most popular view portrays Canada as a *middle power*—not a superpower, but big enough to make a significant difference in the world, particularly when operating within multilateral institutions like the United Nations (UN) or the North Atlantic Treaty Organization (NATO). This image has been popular not only among academics but also among successive generations of Canadian foreign policy decision makers. Competing perspectives have slotted Canada into the category of either *principal power*—a rising contender on the global stage—or *peripheral power*—weakened by its long-standing and growing dependence on the United States.[1]

These approaches to understanding Canada's role in global politics are products of the structure of world order during the Cold War. The fall of the Berlin Wall in 1989 ended the Cold War, but many of the institutions and ways of thinking that had sprung up during the Cold War survived, as the nature of the new global order remained unclear. The shocking attacks of September 11, 2001, and the response of the United States to them, have led to greater clarity about the nature of power, conflict, and transformation in the "new world order." Two features of our contemporary era are particularly important. One (which existed prior to

September 11th but which is especially clear since) is the overwhelming character of U.S. military power. A second feature, somewhat paradoxically, is that for almost the first time in its history, the United States now feels vulnerable to attacks on its soil. John Lewis Geddis notes that even while insecurities existed during the Cold War, Americans always felt that threats were vague and distant, and lay *outside* their country. Now, argues Geddis, "Americans have entered a new stage in their history in which they can no longer take security for granted." [2]

Dramatic world events have to some extent distracted the public from an equally important change already far advanced before September 11th—globalization. Taken together, the end of the Cold War, globalization, and the rise of terrorism have left analysts, accustomed to the relative stability of the past era of the Cold War and Keynesian economics, confused about how rapid changes in the international environment have affected states' ability to act. This has been particularly true for students of Canada's international behaviour. Given Canada's shaky self-image in the light of internal pressures toward fragmentation and the overshadowing influence of the United States, attempts to slot Canada into a single spot on a stable hierarchy of world order have been even more difficult.

Moreover, some aspects of Canada's experience defy analysis based on the simple state-centric assumptions of classical foreign policy analysis—the idea that the world is best understood as made up of distinct, autonomous units called states. Canada's gradual economic and cultural integration over the past several decades with the United States suggests that while the country does retain the capacity to act independently in some spheres, in other respects we are better understood as part of a broader North American economic region (Chapter 6). This chapter will begin by outlining Canada's position from the end of World War II to the mid-1980s, first by contrasting our apparent middle-power status in the international ranking of world states with our gradual economic integration with the United States. The following section looks at how globalization and the emergence of U.S. unipolarity have affected this status.

"MIDDLEPOWERMANSHIP" IN THE OLD WORLD ORDER

Canada's position in the "old world order" during the Cold War led to the construction of an extraordinarily durable national consensus around the doctrine of "middle-power internationalism." The concept of middle power has traditionally been used to refer not just to a country's intermediate power and status but also to a certain style of foreign policy committed to a cooperative international regime centred in international law and international institutions. Since Canada was clearly not a superpower, Canadian policymakers attempted to differentiate themselves from less wealthy and influential countries by carving out a role for "middle powers" in the international system. Despite the fact that Canadian foreign policy did not always conform to the ideals of "middlepowermanship," this self-image continued to shape the views of both supporters and critics of Canadian foreign policy throughout the Cold War period. It is doubtful, however, whether the "middle power" notion can survive the recent dramatic changes in the world.

The image of Canada as a middle power emerged in response to the country's situation after World War II. Before the war, Canada retained preferential treatment within the British empire as a "white" Dominion. This special status, combined with the country's geographic distance from European conflicts, meant that most Canadians, like most Americans, favoured a policy of international isolationism. Canada's external relations were concentrated on managing its growing relationship with the United States and its declining colonial links with England. It is important to note, however, that while Canada was at the forefront of struggle for autonomy in foreign policy matters within the British Empire, that struggle was waged on behalf of the "white" Dominions only, not of the "non-white" colonies.

The events of World War II convinced the Canadian foreign policy elite as well as the general public that isolationism was no longer a viable option. Both Canada and the United States were drawn into World War II, although Canada entered much earlier because of its historic ties to Britain.[3] The United States emerged as the hegemonic power after World War II, with the economic, military, political, and ideological weight necessary to exercise preponderant influence in the shaping of the postwar order.

The new international order was based on principles of economic liberalism and multilateralism, with the establishment of political and economic institutions designed to promote international peace and the opening of markets. This version of multilateralism, however, originally excluded most of the less developed parts of the world, which were still under colonial control. Only 46 states were present at the signing of the Charter of the United Nations on June 26, 1945. As well, despite its openness to all existing nation-states, effective control of the UN remained in the hands of the great powers. The United States, the Soviet Union, England, France, and China were granted permanent seats on the Security Council and the right of veto over all its decisions.

Leaving behind its previous dependent status, Canada emerged from World War II in a relatively strong position, with a new commitment to international activism. According to John Holmes, "Canada went through a remarkably swift transition from the status of a wartime junior partner in 1945 to that of a sure-footed middle power with an acknowledged and applauded role in world affairs ten years later."[4] Canada had made an important contribution to the war effort, both in military and economic terms, and expected to be rewarded with an important position in the fledgling international organizations of the postwar order. The Canadian approach to these issues came to be known as *functionalism*—the argument that authority in international affairs should neither rest with the great powers only nor be distributed on an equal basis to all participants in the system, but rather that representation be awarded on a functional basis, with countries that are able to make a substantial contribution to the issue in question receiving disproportionate power.

For example, on the design of the United Nations Relief and Rehabilitation Agency (UNRRA), which was seen as a prototype for the new international organizations, Mackenzie King stated,

> While experience between the wars has shown the great practical difficulties of applying to membership in international bodies the legal concept of the equality of states, we are confident that no workable international system can be based on the concentration of influence and authority wholly in bodies composed of a few great powers to the exclusion of all the rest. It is not always the largest powers that have the greatest contribution to make to the work of these bodies or the greatest stake in their success. In international economic organizations such as the Relief Administration representation on such bodies can often be determined on a functional basis and in our view this principle should be applied wherever it is feasible.[5]

As a rich country with high levels of education and ample physical resources, Canada could be expected to do well if these became the rules of the game. Canada's eagerness to define a role for itself as a middle power was thus partly an attempt to maintain a relatively privileged position within a hierarchical system of world power. While Canada was clearly not a superpower, the policy was designed to explain to the world that "Canadians were of greater consequence than the Panamanians."[6] On the other hand, Canadian representatives at the United Nations and in External Affairs were clearly committed to the idea that stronger international organizations served the world community as a whole, and were not just a means of promoting Canadian national interests.

As the international system evolved, some of Canada's early hopes about the character of the postwar order dimmed. In particular, the escalation of conflict between the U.S.S.R. and the United States eliminated early hopes that the United Nations could create an effective system of collective security.[7] During the Cold War, the potential power of the Security Council was paralyzed by the ability of either of the superpowers to veto any decision. With the intensification of the Cold War, the middle-power role shifted away from the corridors of international organizations toward the relationship between the superpowers. The term "middle power" is perhaps misleading in this context, since it seems to indicate that Canada sat as a neutral body halfway between the two contending powers. Instead, Canada was clearly aligned with the United States, and Canadian leaders shared their ally's anti-communist ideology. The rigid constraints imposed by the bipolar alignment of global forces left the so-called middle powers little room in which to manoeuvre. Canada's attempts at international mediation were designed not just to maintain global peace and stability, but also to curry favour in Washington. Canada's role as "middle power" was thus closely linked to its position in the Cold War alignment of forces and to its "special relationship" with the United States.

Canada had been increasingly integrated into U.S. plans for continental defence as early as the Ogdensburg Agreement of August 1940. Canada's postwar defence commitments were also partly based on geopolitical realities, particularly because if the U.S.S.R. launched its long-range strategic bombers they would necessarily fly over Canadian territory. The continental defence arrangements eventually led to the establishment in 1958 of the bilateral North American Aerospace Defence Command (NORAD) and the Defence Production Sharing Agreement (DPSA), which integrated continental defence production.

As we have already seen, it was Canada's desire to avoid total U.S. domination of the continental relationship, together with frustration at the inability of the United Nations to promote collective security, that had led to the search for multilateral alternatives. Canada thus strongly supported the creation of the North Atlantic Treaty Organization (NATO) in 1949 on the grounds that it would ensure against a U.S. return to isolationism, commit the United States to the defence of Europe, and, finally, balance the U.S. preponderance in the continental relationship.

Canada's continued claim to middle-power status thus did not rest on an equidistant position between the two superpowers. Rather, the country took on the role of mediator and "helpful fixer" not from a position of neutrality, but as a committed member of the Western alliance. Canada's mediation efforts were usually made with the approval of the

United States, which recognized that unrestrained competition between the superpowers could be dangerously destructive. For example, during the Reagan presidency of the 1980s, when the United States was actively hostile toward many multilateral organizations like the United Nations, Canada's attempts to bolster those organizations were probably in the United States' long-term interests in terms of international cooperation and stability. Canada was a good candidate for this role, since its lack of participation in direct colonial rule made its mediation more acceptable to the newly independent countries of the Third World, which were increasingly important theatres of superpower conflict. Thus, as peacekeeper and truce supervisor (participating in all UN-sponsored peacekeeping operations), Canada made a modest but significant contribution to maintaining international order in the perilous years of the Cold War.

In addition to its roles in peacekeeping, the United Nations, and NATO, Canada also participated actively in establishing and maintaining the organizations of the international financial system, the Commonwealth, La Francophonie, and a host of smaller international organizations. Canada thus became the international "joiner" par excellence out of a general philosophical commitment to multilateral organizations and the continued hope of offsetting U.S. power in North America with a diverse set of international linkages.

All of these decisions were strongly influenced by the limitations and opportunities presented to Canada by the Cold War context and its close geographic, political, military, and economic relationship with the United States. Canada's international role after World War II cannot be adequately appreciated, however, without an understanding of its economic position in the North American continent.

CANADA AND THE NORTH AMERICAN REGION

Part of the appeal of the middle-power concept for Canadian government officials was undoubtedly the fact that it emphasized the country's autonomy from Washington. Yet, as we have seen above, foreign policy practice was, in fact, strongly curtailed by the country's growing military and economic integration with the United States. Conventional rankings of countries' foreign policy status, which rely on such relatively static factors as size, population, resources, military power, and so on, have difficulty taking into account the impact of economic relations among states. Yet those critics who emphasize Canada's economic relations with the United

States often commit the opposite mistake of concluding that Canada is a weak and peripheral power, comparable to a Third World state.

Another perspective suggests that Canada can less and less be considered a distinct space as delineated on a map and increasingly must be analyzed as an integral part of a North American regional space. As Williams notes in Chapter 6 of this volume, "[W]hen investment, production, and trade are considered, the Canadian economy appears more like a politically sovereign *zone* within the American economy than a distinct national economy." Similarly, recent anthropological and sociological work on borders and borderlands "has moved away from the concept of national cultures as territorially contained units, and now attempts to reconceptualize culture from the perspective of a deterritorialized world."[8] Given its pattern of intensive settlement near the forty-ninth parallel, Canada can be seen as a borderland state, defined more than any other industrialized country by its intensive interaction with another, more powerful, economy and society.

This emphasis on the permeability of national boundaries does not mean that borders had entirely lost their relevance or that Canada had completely yielded its foreign policy autonomy to the United States. A series of episodes—for example, Canada's decision to maintain trade ties with China and Cuba during the Diefenbaker years, Lester B. Pearson's 1965 criticism of the U.S. bombing of North Vietnam, the refusal to support U.S. policy in Central America during the 1980s, and the recent refusal to join the U.S.-led coalition of forces in the invasion of Iraq—display that Canada has and will continue to dissent from U.S. foreign policy. As well, Canadian domestic policy retains features distinctive from those of the United States because of the maintenance of independent political institutions[9] and a distinct political culture. Nevertheless, over the last several decades, the main trend in Canada's informal international relations has been the construction of a durable web of economic, political, and cultural ties with our neighbour to the south.

Canadian economic history has largely been characterized by a series of attempts to manage economic integration with the United States. Two contending perspectives on how to manage this relationship vied for influence between the 1960s and 1980s. One perspective, *continentalism,* argued that increased economic interaction with the United States, based on the elimination of tariffs and investment barriers between the two countries, would allow Canadians to prosper. *Nationalists,* on the other hand, while not rejecting continental ties, feared the effects of unfettered integration on Canadian values and sovereignty. Proponents of this view argued for greater state intervention in the economy to promote Canadian ownership and technological development among Canadian-owned companies that would make the country more competitive on the world stage. Nationalist strategies also advocated greater diversification of trading partners and the movement away from a resource-based economy. While Canada maintained formal autonomy, and policymakers resisted formal economic integration with the United States until the Canada–U.S. Free Trade Agreement (FTA) of 1988, each step in informal integration limited the potential for the formation of a nationalist economic alternative, and bound the country more tightly to the continentalist option.

Isolated from European trade, Canada moved away from its earlier ties to Britain toward closer economic linkages with the United States during World War II. For two decades after the war, the continentalist option was dominant in both elite and popular Canadian opinion. During this period, the booming U.S. economy expanded abroad, and American companies turned to Canada as an additional market for U.S. goods when their own market had become saturated, and as a source of raw materials for U.S. industry. By 1963, U.S. companies owned half of the Canadian mining and smelting industries. Canada and the United States also became each other's most important trading partners.

A major defining step in economic relations between the two countries was the 1965 Canada–U.S. Auto Pact, which integrated production by the Big Three U.S. car producers on a continental basis. Continental economic integration was also promoted by the liberalization of the global trading system that occurred under the sponsorship of the General Agreement on Tariffs and Trade (GATT). In particular, the Tokyo Round of the GATT during the 1970s led to a substantial reduction in Canada's tariff barriers, resulting in a gradual abandonment of the protectionist strategy of import-substituting industrialization that Canada had pursued since Confederation.[10] For Canada, given the pattern of integration with the United States that had already been established, the liberalization of trade on a multilateral basis under the GATT led not to a diversification of trading partners but to an intensification of its ties to the United States.

The "special relationship" that Canada had established with the United States began to unravel, however, as the United States' economic hegemony began to be challenged in the late 1960s and early 1970s by the rise of the European Community and Japan. A symbolic turning point was U.S. President Nixon's unilateral decision to abandon the gold standard in 1971 and impose a 10 percent surtax on imports, including imports from Canada. As well, by the 1960s, concerns began to spread in Canada about the overwhelming predominance of American control in the Canadian economy. During the 1970s and 1980s, economic nationalist perspectives gained popular ground and even had some influence with the Trudeau Liberals. Nationalist legislation in the form of the Foreign Investment Review Agency (FIRA), which screened new foreign investment in Canada, and the National Energy Program (NEP), which increased Canadian control over the energy industry, was eventually enacted. The Canadian government also tried, unsuccessfully, to expand Canada's trade relations with states other than the United States, such as the European Community and Japan. The NEP and FIRA were viewed with outrage by U.S. companies, and after the election of Ronald Reagan to the presidency in 1980 on a more aggressive foreign policy platform, Washington threatened retaliatory measures unless Canada withdrew these programs.[11]

By the mid-1980s, then, Canadian policymakers were at a crossroads. The mild version of economic nationalism that had been pursued by the Trudeau government had met with hostility in Washington, and the Liberals lacked the political will to hold out in defiance of U.S. trade retaliation. As we will see below, changes in the international economic environment, as well as domestic political changes, led succeeding governments to pursue the continentalist path that had already been established by preceding administrations, further consolidating Canada's integration into the North American economy. At the same time, however, changes were occurring in the international political and military environment that further unsettled traditional conceptions of Canada's place in the world.

AFTER THE COLD WAR: THE UNIPOLAR MOMENT?

Since the fall of the Berlin Wall and the end of the Cold War, policymakers, academics, and concerned citizens alike have been squinting at the horizon, attempting to glimpse the shape of the emerging structures of a transformed world order. During the Cold War, international security issues had centred on the hostility between the two superpowers and on their constant one-upmanship, whether in the form of an arms buildup or in the "proxy wars" between countries identified with one superpower or the other. This situation tended to confirm the view of the nation-state as the main actor in the international system.

The end of the Cold War has, however, brought about the disintegration of many states and led to the outbreak of a series of deadly intrastate conflicts based on competing ethnic or religious identities.[12] While such conflicts are the more negative side of the new international order, the end of the Cold War has also permitted new space for participation in the international system by non-state actors, especially non-governmental organizations (NGOs) devoted to such issues as human rights, democracy, peace building, development, and the environment. The post–Cold War era is thus characterized by the rapid proliferation both of new kinds of security threats and new types of international actors.

On the other hand, states have certainly not gone away, and they continue to compete for prestige and power in the international system. The vision of a "new multilateralism" promoted by NGOs collides with a vision that is more state-centred, exclusive, and anti-democratic. In fact, one way to conceptualize emerging trends is to examine patterns of "inclusion in" or "exclusion from" global structures of power and prestige. While the Cold War period was hardly a phase of egalitarian participation, forces such as decolonization and multilateralism permitted at least the symbolic inclusion of lesser states such as the emerging countries of the Third World. This occurred largely because expanding competition between the superpowers throughout the world increased the geopolitical significance of areas outside the North Atlantic triangle. In contrast, the new world order appears to be characterized by greater concentration of economic, political, military, and ideological power in the hands of a few states and the construction of new international institutions based on the exclusion of the many.[13]

The venerable concept of Canada as a middle power has also not gone away. A 1997 textbook on Canadian foreign policy, for example, after surveying the contending perspectives on Canada's international role, returned to the middle-power framework. While recognizing that the middle-power approach needed to be broadened, the book's author, Andrew Cooper, stated,

> Notwithstanding all the dissent about its claims to authentically represent Canadian foreign policy behaviour, [the middle power] framework remains the consensual champion among the competing conceptual frameworks. Displaying a considerable degree of resilience against criticism, the middle power framework has demonstrated an unremitting ability to remain at the epicentre of dialogue.[14]

Thus, despite rapidly changing circumstances, ideas do not change overnight. For example, under Lloyd Axworthy, Minister of Foreign Affairs from 1996–2000, the concept of "human security" became prominent within Canadian foreign policy. As defined by Axworthy, human security relates to the importance of the safety and well-being of the individual, as opposed to state security. Human security is to be promoted through the promotion of good governance, human rights, the rule of law, and sustainable development.[15] Under this human security agenda, some aspects of recent Canadian foreign policy behaviour, such as its leadership role in the international campaign to ban the use of landmines, may support the impression that the end of the Cold War opened up more space for middle powers like Canada to exercise a leadership role in international forums. The anti-landmine campaign in particular reveals how countries like Canada, in alliance with other like-minded states and a newly prominent and accepted array of transnational NGOs, can play a positive role in some areas.[16]

Nevertheless, it is the contention of this chapter that in the current and foreseeable atmosphere of international economic and political reorganization, the role of the middle power has lost its erstwhile appeal as a source of (moderate) power and prestige. While it was possible, in the period following World War II, for countries like Canada to gain some credibility through claiming middle-power status, the global hierarchies of economic and political power have now fundamentally shifted. In economic terms, U.S. power is impressive. With less than one-twentieth of the world's population, the U.S. economy represents one-third of the world's gross domestic product. U.S. economic power has increased compared with other competitors over the last decade as a result of the stagnation of the Japanese economy and the collapse of the Russian economy. The United States also appears to be in the best position to take advantage of the trends associated with globalization because of its advantages both in the areas of technology and services and in its ability to attract investment and highly skilled workers from around the globe.[17] However, U.S. dominance is most clear in the military domain. At the dawn of the twenty-first century, American defence spending represents over one-third of the military spending among all 190 countries in the world.[18] In 2003, U.S. projected defence spending amounted to more than the next 15 to 20 biggest spenders combined.[19]

In this context, world leaders and analysts of world politics are left grasping for terms and concepts to capture the United States' primacy. The term "superpower" (which gave rise to the concept of "middle power") no longer seems adequate to describe the nature of U.S. military might in the new, unipolar world. French Foreign Minister Hubert Vedrine has coined the term "hyperpower," while others have resurrected the term "empire" to capture the way in which the U.S. surpasses its allies and potential rivals. As Stephen Brooks and William Wohlforth put it, "the United States has no rival in any critical dimension of power. There has never been a system of sovereign states that contained one state with this degree of dominance."[20] Of course, being a hyperpower does *not* mean that the United States is able to achieve whatever it wants on its own and does not need the assistance of its allies or the United Nations on occasion.

Despite the U.S. military and economic predominance, the September 11th attacks evoked a new feeling of vulnerability in the U.S. to "asymmetrical threats" from weapons of mass destruction employed by terror organizations and/or implacably hostile secondary states. This has led to a radical rethinking of U.S. military strategy and the emergence of a new grand strategy within the Bush administration. According to this new strategy, "America is to be less bound to its partners and to global rules and institutions while it steps forward to play a more unilateral and anticipatory role in attacking terrorist threats and confronting rogue states seeking [weapons of mass destruction]."[21]

This new strategy is characterized by several key elements. First, there is a commitment to maintaining a unipolar world in which the United States has no peer competitor. Second, there is a new analysis of global threats in which terrorist groups may acquire highly destructive nuclear, chemical, or biological weapons. Traditional tools of statecraft such as appeasement or deterrence will not deter these fanatical terrorist groups, so they—and the rogue states that may support them—must be eliminated. Third, since deterrence no longer works, the United States has the obligation to adopt the preemptive use of force to take on major threats before they become a problem. This new strategy has serious implications for traditional concepts of sovereignty, and for the institutions of multilateralism such as the United Nations. State sovereignty is not respected if the state involved is perceived as harbouring terrorists or weapons of mass destruction. Traditional allies become less useful, at least in military terms, since a decade of U.S. military spending has left all its allies far behind.[22] However, the United States must struggle not to appear overly unilateral, since there exist a raft of problems, such as the stability of the global economy, migration, drugs, environmental threats, and so on, where it needs the support of other nations.

Some U.S. foreign policy analysts believe that the new grand strategy described above, based on U.S. geopolitical dominance of the global system, is excessively risky and expensive. For example, Benjamin Schwarz and Christopher Layne argue that the lesson of September 11th should be that the supervisory role the United States has assigned itself in the Persian Gulf has made it vulnerable to a backlash. This role, they argue, has resulted not from the U.S.'s need for the oil resources from the Gulf, on which it is much less dependent than Western Europe and Japan, but from its desire to convince these allies that they do not need to increase their own military power to challenge U.S. predominance. The U.S. has adopted the role of "adult supervision" over other potential rivals, and thus draws the ire of state and non-state actors in the rest of the world that resent its policies and that must also incur disproportionate military costs.[23] Charles Kupchan contends that the decline of U.S. unipolarity is inevitable as other large countries develop and resist following U.S. leadership: French and German refusal to back the United States–led war in Iraq is perhaps a sign of this. Instead, he believes the United States should prepare for its decline by "encouraging the emergence of regional unipolarity in each of the world's three areas of industrial and military power—North America, Europe, and East Asia."[24] His system of "benign unipolarity" differs from traditional empires because while both are characterized by a hierarchical structure in which a country at the core establishes a "hub-spoke pattern of influence" over a weaker periphery, a benignly unipolar order emerges from a consensual bargain between core and periphery.[25]

Whatever the outcome—whether continued U.S. primacy or the eventual emergence of regional unipolarity—the implications for smaller countries are rather bleak. Either structure of world order is highly concentrated and excludes the majority of the world's population. For example, mechanisms like the Group of 7/8, representing the richest industrial states, have in some measure superceded more inclusionary bodies like the United Nations. Beginning in the mid-1970s, the political leaders of the G7 began meeting to loosely coordinate macroeconomic policies in order to avoid international economic disorder. Canada was left out of the first meeting in 1975, but was invited by U.S. President Gerald Ford to attend the 1976 meeting. Referring to the summits, Sir Shridath Ramphal, then Secretary-General of the Commonwealth, wrote in 1988 that the global consensus that had emerged in the 1970s about the interdependence of nations and the need for cooperation between weak and strong "has become a casualty in the drift towards dominance and the ascendancy of unilateralism in world affairs." Said Ramphal, "cooperation within a directorate of powerful countries is hardly the answer to the world's needs, the needs of all its nations. In fact, it could well have the result of reinforcing the dominance of the few over the many."[26]

As we have seen, there have been substantial changes in the structure of the world system, the role of international organizations, and the relative position of the United States in the world system. Under the wing of its neighbour to the south, Canada has been an active participant in, and supporter of, all of these trends toward concentration of economic and political power in the new world order. According to John Kirton,

> [Canada's] traditional preoccupation with universalism, or at least ever broadening multilateralism, has been set aside in favour of

plurilateralism, and particularly the plurilateralism of the plutocracy where Canada is grouped along with the great.[27]

However, the changing shape of global order militates against Canada's aspiration to maintain its profile as one of the world's movers and shakers. Whether the United States maintains its current trajectory of global unilateralism or retreats eventually to regional unilateralism within North America, the implications for Canada are quite similar. Under neither scenario is the old construct of "middlepowermanship" viable. Critics of Canadian foreign and military policy who protest that Canada is entering into a period of decline and becoming a "fading power" because of inadequate military and foreign aid spending[28] ignore the changing nature of global power. In the context of the extreme predominance of the United States discussed above, no conceivable increase in Canadian military spending could halt the country's decline from its middle power "Golden Age."

Moreover, the shift in U.S. strategic thinking in the wake of the September 11th attacks implies that Canada figures in the U.S. strategic vision not as an independent state with middle-power aspirations, but as a geopolitical extension of the American homeland. The fact that Americans now feel vulnerable on their own territory means, as discussed earlier, that the North American continent is now the focus of defence thinking in a way almost without precedent in U.S. history. In this new vision, "homeland security" becomes paramount, but it is not clear whether the territorial limits of the "homeland" refer to the United States alone or include all of North America. U.S. Ambassador Paul Cellucci has called for the creation of a "North American security perimeter" to prevent terrorists from entering the United States across either the U.S.–Mexico or U.S.–Canada border. As well, since September 11th the United States has created within its armed forces a new unified command called Northern Command (NORTHCOM). The U.S. NORTHCOM will be assigned responsibility for U.S. homeland security, and the commander of the force will be responsible for coordinating activities of U.S. forces throughout North America. As well, both Canada and Mexico have reached agreements with the United States to adopt "smart border" measures to reduce risks at both borders.[29]

The North American continent thus increasingly resembles Kupchan's description of "benign unipolarity"—indeed unipolarity is stronger here than in other regional formations such as Europe or East Asia because of the United States' continued predominance in economic and military power. The region has been peaceful because the smaller states—Canada and Mexico—have recognized U.S. supremacy, but this relatively undemanding unipolarity means formal institutions of regional governance have not been established: "Instead, U.S. preponderance creates a de facto core and a surrounding periphery. A hub-spoke pattern of intraregional relations has evolved largely through the operation of the market and America's unilateral efforts—including direct and indirect military intervention—to create a security environment to its liking."[30]

GLOBALIZATION AND NORTH AMERICAN ECONOMIC INTEGRATION

The image of Canada as a middle power gained popularity after World War II, a period when most of the world was locked into relatively stable international positions by the Cold War. Although economic interdependence was increasing, the economic role of the nation-state was still protected by a system of "embedded liberalism" in which states were able to play an active role in sheltering weaker social groups through welfare-state policies.[31] The Canadian economy was more integrated with that of the United States than most, but the illusion of state autonomy and independence still held sway. Recent changes in the global and North American economies pose difficult challenges for Canada as a nation.

Globalization has been defined as "processes whereby social relations acquire relatively distanceless and borderless qualities, so that human lives are increasingly played out in the world as a single place." In a globalizing economy, "patterns of production, exchange and consumption become increasingly delinked from a geography of distances and borders" because of the spread of global trade, global finance, and global production.[32] In the context of globalization, ideas and culture also appear to be increasingly shared across national borders, and states are losing many of their traditional powers to protect local culture, local living standards, and local industries. Globalization has resulted from, and has in turn encouraged, the growing worldwide acceptance of a neoliberal economic philosophy promoting the opening of state borders to foreign investment and trade as well as a view of the free market as a panacea for societies' economic problems (Chapter 10). The spread of globalization does not mean, however, that state policies, national cultures, and economics have been completely homogenized and harmonized.

As well, somewhat paradoxically, globalization has gone hand in hand with regionalism, the process of establishing increased informal and formal cooperation, economic exchange, and political interdependence between states that are geographically linked.[33] For Canada, globalization has primarily taken the form of the country's growing incorporation into the North American region. As we saw above, a high level of informal integration had already occurred between the Canadian and U.S. economies since World War II. Thus, the Canada–U.S. Free Trade Agreement of 1988 was, in many ways, merely a reflection of preexisting economic trends. Politically, Prime Minister Brian Mulroney's decision to pursue a free trade agreement with the United States was no "aberration [or] high-risk bilateral exception to the multilateral norm of Canadian trade policy": rather, "when viewed over Canada's 140-year trade policy history, bilateralism is the norm, and multilateralism is the exception."[34]

The decision did require, however, several important actors in Canadian society, including politicians, bureaucrats, and business elites, to drop their earlier resistance to the idea of formal economic integration. A free trade agreement with the United States had earlier been resisted because of politicians' concerns about the implications for Canadian sovereignty and national unity, as well as businesses' fears of being swamped by more competitive U.S. imports. By the mid-1980s, however, tariffs had already come down as a result of the Auto Pact and the GATT, so the FTA seemed less of a threat to Canadian businesses than it had previously. Neoliberal economists had also gained influence in the bureaucracy and in the business community, and argued that free trade would increase the efficiency of Canadian firms and contribute to the long-run competitiveness of Canadian industry in a globalized economy. As well, some of the provinces, particularly Alberta and Quebec, chafed against Ottawa's economic predominance in the federation and argued in favour of the continentalist option.

The most important influence on Canada's decision to pursue a free trade agreement, however, was probably external—namely, the rise in protectionist measures adopted by the U.S. government. Suffering the effects of the recession of the early 1980s, the Reagan administration used antidumping and countervailing duties provisions of its trade legislation to target what were perceived as unfair trading practices by its major trading partners, including Canada. These "unfair trading practices" were blamed for the decline in the United States' trade position. Canada's decision to seek an FTA thus largely represented an attempt to gain secure access to Canada's largest market by receiving shelter from these provisions. Ironically, critics charge that the United States' refusal to include a subsidies code in the agreement meant negotiators failed to achieve this fundamental objective.[35]

This situation was also not satisfactorily addressed when the FTA was expanded to include Mexico in a new North American Free Trade Agreement (NAFTA). As with Canada, Mexico's entry into a formal free trade agreement with the United States represented a new level of institutionalization of the already high levels of economic integration between Mexico and the southern United States. NAFTA was less controversial for Canadians than the FTA because overall levels of Canada–Mexico trade are so much smaller than Canada–U.S. trade. Canada decided to enter into NAFTA primarily to ensure that it did not lose out on the supposed benefits of its secure access to the U.S. economy gained in the FTA. Despite the defensive motives involved in this decision, Canada's membership in NAFTA has involved the country in new trilateral institutions concerning the environment and labour standards. It seems likely that increased levels of economic integration between the three countries will, in the future, require a greater level of institutional development for managing a wide range of issues within the North American region. According to Kupchan, the signing of NAFTA has resulted in a shift from a North American order based on de facto power asymmetries toward a regional formation characterized by benign unipolarity. The trade agreement was thus a result of the attempt by the two weaker countries to "structure and control de facto power asymmetries by design, rather than to let them operate by default."[36]

Canada's economic integration with the United States has profound implications for our place in the international system. The FTA and NAFTA have solidified the trends away from domestic east–west economic and political ties and toward international north–south relations in the new continental space. Thomas Courchene argues that as a result of the forces of globalization and regionalization, Ontario, for example, is now best understood as a "North American region state," shifting from its postwar status as the "heartland of Canada" to a quest to become a "heartland of North America."[37] Courchene observes that while Ontario's exports to the rest of the world and its exports to the other provinces were roughly equal at $40 billion a year in 1981, by 1995 international exports had soared to $140 billion, roughly three times the level of exports to the rest of Canada. Since the 1988 accord with the U.S., Canada's trade dependence on the United States has risen dramatically—more than 85 percent of total Canadian exports are now destined for the U.S. market.[38] Between 1990 and 2000, exports grew from 25.7 percent to 45.6 percent of Canada's gross domestic product, while imports rose from 25.7 percent to 41 percent in the same years.[39]

Despite achieving their prime political goal of the 1980s, the free trade agreement with the United States, Canadian business representatives remain concerned about Canada's economic future in the North American economy. Thomas d'Aquino and David Stewart-Patterson, from the Canadian Council of Chief Executives (CCCE—formerly the Business

Council on National Issues), warn that "Canada is losing the struggle for top workers, for highly skilled work, and, ultimately, its role as home base to successful global enterprises.[40] Canadian business leaders are also worried that U.S. security concerns about its northern border may lead it again to close down the Canada–U.S. border as it did immediately following the September 11th attacks. The Canadian economy's high degree of integration with the U.S. economy means that any slowdown at the border represents a substantial threat. Canadian business leaders like d'Aquino have floated a series of proposals to allay U.S. concerns and further deepen U.S.–Canadian integration. These proposals include the creation of a common market, harmonization of Canadian and U.S. immigration and refugee policies, further Canadian and U.S. intelligence and military cooperation, and the downgrading of the Canada–U.S. border to an "internal checkpoint." [41] Mexico's position within a redefined North America is not clear.

CONCLUSION

Canada, like other states at the dawn of the new millennium, is undergoing a transformation in its identity and international position. Recent dramatic events in global politics require a radical rethinking of how power is organized globally and where Canada fits in. The clear predominance of the U.S. hyperpower at the global level and Canada's increasing economic integration with the United States have profound implications for Canada's position in the world. America's anger after the September 11th events, and its turn toward unilateralism, create clear dilemmas for Canada as a nation that has always preferred multilateralism. While Canada can continue to practice "niche diplomacy" with initiatives like the landmines treaty, its capacity for influence internationally is severely constrained. Globalization has come to Canada principally in the form of the North American Free Trade Agreement and the fundamental realignment of international power that attended the conclusion of the Cold War. Still, none of this means that Canada has today lost its power for independent action on the international stage, as demonstrated by Prime Minister Chrétien's decision not to enter the U.S.-led alliance in the 2003 war on Iraq.

It is time to put to rest the old debate over Canada's international stature—whether as middle, principal, or peripheral power—and get on with a more substantive discussion of the limits to and potential for a constructive global role for both the Canadian state and Canadian non-state actors in a post–September 11th, globalized system.

NOTES

1. For other overviews of these contending images, see Andrew Cooper, *Canadian Foreign Policy: Old Habits and New Directions* (Scarborough, ON: Prentice Hall Allyn & Bacon, 1997); Mark Neufeld and Sandra Whitworth, "Imag(in)ing Canadian Foreign Policy," in Wallace Clement, ed., *Understanding Canada: Building on the New Canadian Political Economy* (Montreal/Kingston: McGill-Queen's University Press, 1997), pp. 197–214; and Laura Macdonald, "Going Global: The Politics of Canada's Foreign Economic Relations," in Clement, ed., *Understanding Canada*, pp. 172–96.

2. John Lewis Gaddis, "And Now This: Lessons from the Old Ear for the New One," in Strobe Talbott and Nayan Chanda, eds., *The Age of Terror: America and the World After September 11* (New York: Basic Books, 2001), pp. 1–22.

3. However, in an exercise of displaying Canada's new autonomy in foreign affairs, Mackenzie King waited 10 days before declaring war on Germany.

4. John W. Holmes, *The Better Part of Valour: Essays on Canadian Diplomacy* (Toronto: McClelland & Stewart, 1970), p. 5.

5. Quoted in Tom Keating, *Canada and World Order: The Multilateralist Tradition in Canadian Foreign Policy* (Toronto: McClelland & Stewart, 1993), pp. 31–32. Reprinted by permission of Oxford University Press, Canada.

6. John Holmes, "Most Safely in the Middle," in J.L. Granatstein, ed., *Towards a New World: Readings in the History of Canadian Foreign Policy* (Mississauga, ON: Copp Clark Pitman, 1992), p. 90.

7. Under a collective security system, all members of the international community agree to respond automatically to violations against the sovereignty of any of them by imposing a set of agreed-upon measures (up to and including the use of force) to punish the aggressor.

8. Robert R. Alvarez, Jr., "The Mexican–US border: The Making of an Anthropology of Borderlands," *Annual Review of Anthropology* 24 (1995): 449.

9. See Keith Banting, George Hoberg, and Richard Simeon, *Degrees of Freedom: Canada and the United States in a Changing World* (Montreal/Kingston: McGill-Queen's University Press, 1997).

10. Glen Williams, *Not For Export: The International Competitiveness of Canadian Manufacturing*, 3rd ed. (Toronto: McClelland & Stewart, 1994), pp. 143–46.

11. Stephen Clarkson, *Canada and the Reagan Challenge* (Toronto: James Lorimer & Company, 1982).

12. Lloyd Axworthy, "Towards a New Multilateralism," in Maxwell A. Cameron, Robert J. Lawson, and Brian W. Tomlin, eds., *To Walk without Fear: The Global Movement to Ban Landmines* (Toronto: Oxford University Press, 1998).

13. For a similar argument focusing on Canada's role in the international economy, see David Black and Claire Turenne Sjolander, "Multilateralism Re-constituted and the Discourse of Canadian Foreign Policy," *Studies in Political Economy* (Spring 1996). See also Miguel de Larrinaga and Claire Turenne Sjolander, "(Re)presenting Landmines from Protector to Enemy: The Discursive Framing of a New Multilateralism," in Cameron et al., *To Walk without Fear*, pp. 364–91.

14. Cooper, *Canadian Foreign Policy*, p. 25.

15. Peter Howard and Reina Neufeldt, "Canada's Constructivist Foreign Policy: Building Norms for Peace," *Canadian Foreign Policy* 8, no. 1 (Fall 2000): 12–13.

16. See Cameron et al., *To Walk without Fear*.

17. Stephen Brooks and William C. Wohlforth, "American Primacy in Perspective," *Foreign Affairs* 81, no. 4 (July/August 2002): 22–23.

18. Paul Kennedy, "Maintaining American Power: From Injury to Recovery," in Talbott and Chanda, eds., *The Age of Terror*, p. 59.

19. Brooks and Wohlforth, "American Primacy in Perspective."

20. Ibid., p. 23.

21. G. John Ikenberry, "America's Imperial Ambition," *Foreign Affairs* (September/October 2002), p. 49.

22. Ibid., pp. 49–55.

23. Benjamin Schwarz and Christopher Layne, "A New Grand Strategy," *The Atlantic Monthly* (January 2002).

24. Charles Kupchan, "After Pax Americana: Benign Power, Regional Integration, and the Sources of a Stable Multipolarity," *International Security* 23, no. 2 (Fall 1998): 42. According to Romano Prodi, the president of the European Commission, one of the chief goals of the European Union is to create "a superpower on the European continent that stands equal to the United States." Charles A. Kupchan, "The End of the West," *Atlantic Monthly* (November 2002): 42.

25. Ibid., p. 42.

26. Quoted in Robert W. Cox, "Multilateralism and World Order," *Review of International Studies* 18 (1992): 161–80.

27. John Kirton, "Further Challenges," in John Holmes and John Kirton, eds., *Canada and the New Internationalism* (Toronto: Canadian Institute of International Affairs, 1988), pp. 141–42.

28. See Maureen Appel Molot and Norman Hillmer, "The Diplomacy of Decline," in Norman Hillmer and Maureen Appel Molot, eds., *Canada Among Nations 2002: A Fading Power* (Don Mills: Oxford University Press, 2002).

29. Christina Gabriel and Laura Macdonald, "Beyond the Continentalist/ Nationalist Divide: Politics in a North America 'without Borders,'" in Wallace Clement and Leah F. Vosko, eds., *Changing Canada: Political Economy as Transformation* (Montreal & Kingston: McGill-Queen's University Press, 2003), pp. 213–240.

30. Kupchan, "After Pax Americana," p. 56.

31. John Ruggie, "International Regimes, Transactions, and Change: Embedded Liberalism in the Post-War Economic Order," *International Organization* 36 (Spring 1982), pp. 379–415.

32. Jan Aart Scholte, "Global Trade and Finance," in John Baylis and Steve Smith, eds., *The Globalization of World Politics: An Introduction to International Relations* (Oxford: Oxford University Press, 1997), p. 484. See also Roland Robertson, *Globalization: Social Theory and Global Culture* (London: Sage, 1992); and Jan Aart Scholte, "Beyond the Buzzword: Towards a Critical Theory of Globalization," in Eleanore Kofman and Gillian Young, eds., *Globalization: Theory and Practice* (London: Pinter, 1996), pp. 43–57.

33. Joseph Nye, cited in Fiona Butler, "Regionalism and Integration," in Baylis and Smith, eds., *The Globalization of World Politics*, p. 410.

34. G. Bruce Doern and Brian W. Tomlin, *Faith and Fear: The Free Trade Story* (Toronto: Stoddart, 1991), pp. 45–46.

35. See Doern and Tomlin, *Faith and Fear*, for an overview of the factors leading up to the decision to pursue an FTA, as well as a description of the negotiation process.

36. Kupchan, "After Pax Americana," p. 56.

37. Thomas J. Courchene, *From Heartland to North American Region State: The Social, Fiscal and Federal Evolution of Ontario* (Toronto: Centre for Public Management, Faculty of Management, University of Toronto, 1998), pp. 276–78.

38. Wendy Dobson, "Trade can brush in a new border," *The Globe and Mail*, January 21, 2003: A15.

39. Michael Hart and William Dymond, "Common Borders, Shared Destinies: Canada, the United States and Deepening Integration" (Ottawa: Centre for Trade Policy and Law, November 2001), p. 3.

40. Thomas Paul d'Aquino and David Stewart-Patterson, *Northern Edge: How Canadians Can Triumph in the Global Economy* (Don Mills, ON: Stoddart, 2001).

41. Christina Gabriel and Laura Macdonald, *Of Borders and Business: Canadian Corporate Proposals for North American "Deep Integration.* Presented to Studies in Political Economy conference, Ottawa, January 2003.

FURTHER READINGS

Cooper, Andrew. *Canadian Foreign Policy: Old Habits and New Directions.* Scarborough, ON: Prentice Hall Allyn & Bacon, 1997.

DePalma, Anthony. *Here: A Biography of the New American Continent.* New York: PublicAffairs, 2001.

English, John, and Norman Hillmer, eds. *Making a Difference? Canada's Foreign Policy in a Changing World Order.* Toronto: Lester Publishing Ltd., 1992.

Gabriel, Christina, and Laura Macdonald. "Beyond the Continentalist/Nationalist Divide: Politics in a North America 'without Borders.'" In Wallace Clement and Leah F. Vosko, eds., *Changing Canada: Political Economy as Transformation*, pp. 213–40. Montreal & Kingston: McGill-Queen's University Press, 2003.

Hoberg, George, ed. *Capacity for Choice: Canada in a New North America.* Toronto: University of Toronto Press, 2003.

Holmes, John. *The Better Part of Valour: Essays on Canadian Diplomacy.* Toronto: McClelland & Stewart, 1970.

Keating, Tom. *Canada and World Order: The Multilateralist Tradition in Canadian Foreign Policy.* Toronto: McClelland & Stewart, 1993.

Langille, Howard Peter. *Changing the Guard: Canada's Defence in a World in Transition.* Toronto: University of Toronto Press, 1990.

Macdonald, Laura. "Going Global: The Politics of Canada's Foreign Economic Relations." In Wallace Clement, ed., *Understanding Canada: Building on the New Canadian Political Economy*, pp. 172–96. Montreal/Kingston: McGill-Queen's University Press, 1997.

Nossal, Kim Richard. *The Politics of Canadian Foreign Policy*, 3rd ed. Scarborough, ON: Prentice-Hall, 1997.

Painchaud, Peter, ed. *From Mackenzie King to Pierre Trudeau: Forty Years of Canadian Diplomacy, 1945–1985.* Québec: Les presses de l'université Laval, 1989.

Pastor, Robert. *Toward a North American Community: Lessons from the Old World for the New.* Washington, D.C.: Institute for International Economics, 2001.

POLITICS, CULTURE, AND SOCIETY

POLITICS, CULTURE, AND SOCIETY

The six chapters of Part III examine the ways in which conflict and cooperation are structured within our political culture. Although they are always evolving, the values and attitudes of Canadians are still deeply rooted in our collective history. One hundred years ago our ideas concerning the limits of political discourse and the subjects of political conflict, our attitudes toward women, and our perceptions of racial and ethnic minorities were very different from those prevailing today. But, as the contributors to Part III make clear, our past is clearly reflected in our present.

Political culture is made up of the aggregate political values and attitudes of a society and of stable subgroups of political values we call ideologies. It is our political culture that defines what is politically acceptable—what our governments can and cannot do. Political culture is reflected not only in people's behaviour but in the operation of our political institutions and in our constitutional documents, such as the Charter of Rights and Freedoms. In Chapter 13, David Bell traces the historical roots of Canada's political culture, which is an amalgam of the ideologies of liberalism, conservatism, and socialism transported here in different waves of immigration. Canadian political culture is at present dominated by the ideology of neoliberalism, a set of values that has had a marked impact on Canadian political life today. As Bell sees it, we enter this century with the Canadian right fragmented, the Canadian left disoriented, and the centre defined almost entirely by neoliberal nostrums.

Canadian state policies and practices regarding gender issues have been responsive to the larger twentieth-century societal debate concerning the proper place of women in "private" (family) and "public" (state, economy) spheres. However, as Sandra Burt tells us in Chapter 14, people's attitudes and government's policies still have a way to go before we can reach the goal of gender equality. Through her review of three policy areas—equality rights, employment laws, and woman abuse—Burt shows that the state has been far more inclined to grant women rights previously granted to men than to listen to feminist claims for a gendered understanding of citizenship. The recent dominance of neoliberal ideas has consolidated this trend and made it even less likely that a gendering of Canadian policies and policy structures can take place in the immediate future.

Racism and ethnocentrism have long been a part of Canada's political culture and were institutionalized in legislation and government policy before Confederation. Aboriginal peoples were viewed as inferior "races" by the English and French mainstream, and French Canadians and aboriginal peoples were marginalized economically. Non-French and non-English immigrant groups—particularly visible minorities from Japan, China, Africa, and the Indian subcontinent—faced a long history of official and societal discrimination. In their Chapter 15 on race and ethnicity, Daiva Stasiulis and Yasmeen Abu-Laban describe the sorry history of Canada's treatment of visible minorities, in particular Asians. Denied the right to vote in most jurisdictions, confronted with "European only" immigration policies, and, in the case of the Japanese, interned in wartime camps as "enemy aliens," such visible minority groups have been consistently denied equal access to the opportunities available to European immigrant groups. Although official discrimination for the most part ended in the 1960s, and although section 15 of the 1982 Charter of Rights and Freedoms prohibits discrimination by governments, Stasiulis and Abu-Laban document the persistent underrepresentation in public office of such groups. As well, section 15 of the Charter can be overridden by the "notwithstanding clause" and does not prevent discrimination by private individuals or companies. Added to the ongoing problem of racial inequality, both governmental and public support for the policy of multiculturalism appears to be in decline as we enter the twenty-first century.

In Chapter 16, Ken McRoberts traces the roots of Quebec nationalism from its origins in colonial times, through the economic and social transformation that led to the Quiet Revolution in the 1960s, to the present-day movement for independence from Canada. His account centres on the economic and social marginalization of French Canadians within Quebec and the political isolation of Quebec governments within Canada. Quebec nationalism today is energized more by past "humiliations" than by current grievances, but the fervour of the separatist movement, in spite of having lost its control of the provincial government in 2003, is unlikely to dissipate soon.

As the principal communicators of political images and messages in Canadian society, the mass media have a central role in constructing a "public space" for defining and debating the agenda of our political life. Throughout the twentieth century, the media provided a vital link between politicians and voters. But Fred Fletcher and Robert Everett explain in Chapter 17 how the combined forces of technology, globalization, and neoliberalism are now influencing the Canadian media system and challenging our viability as a national community. The modern phenomenon of media "convergence"—or integration of telecommunications, computers, television, radio, newspapers, and magazines—is rapidly re-defining the way in which political messages are sent and understood. Complicating this picture even further, Fletcher and Everett argue, is the rise of privately held media conglomerates and the decline of Canadian public broadcasting. All of these trends, they state, add to the difficulties of sustaining Canadian democracy.

CHAPTER 13

POLITICAL CULTURE IN CANADA

David V.J. Bell

THE IMPORTANCE OF POLITICAL CULTURE

Culture is a fundamental component of life because it affects how we understand the world and how we interact with it. Culture provides a set of lenses through which people view the world. Beliefs about the world and individually held values shape both attitudes and actions. Culture also provides a way of doing things, a common stock of knowledge about appropriate and inappropriate behaviour in different social settings. As we are socialized into a culture, we learn to behave in ways that others in the same culture will find acceptable and comfortable. We learn what to wear, what to say, and how to stand. We learn about privacy and community, how to engage in conversation, how to say "hello" and "goodbye," how to maintain appropriate "social distance," how to indicate pleasure or unhappiness, amusement or disgust.[1]

Political life is similarly affected by "*political* culture." Political culture consists of the ideas, assumptions, values, and beliefs that condition political action. It affects the ways we use politics, the kinds of social problems we address, and the solutions we attempt. Political culture serves as a filter or lens through which political actors view the world; it influences how they see the role of the state, and what importance they assign to politics and government. It is also reflected in our political and governmental institutions.

SYMBOLS AND THE LANGUAGE OF POLITICS

Political perception and political action are mediated through language and speech. Political culture is the language of political discourse, the vocabulary and grammar of political controversy and understanding. Frequently, political values, beliefs, and attitudes are crystallized in various symbols. In its simplest sense, a symbol is a kind of shorthand, something that stands for something else. In politics, symbols usually evoke both thoughts and feelings and reflect long-standing traditions to which individuals become strongly attached.

Canadian political culture includes a number of symbols. Some, such as Parliament, the CBC, and Mounties in red coats, have been around for a long time. Others, such as the Charter of Rights and Freedoms, the Meech Lake Accord, "distinct society," NAFTA, and the Free Trade Area of the Americas (FTAA), are much more recent. Political symbols can evoke images of consensus and cooperation—as does the idea of helping the poorer provinces, or furthering Anglo–French partnership. But symbols can also catalyze negative emotions and hatred or distrust—as does the phrase "forcing French down our throats," angry references to Sikhs in turbans, or the bitter symbol of Eastern domination, the National Energy Policy. Symbols often evoke very different responses from different segments of the population, as in the case of "pay equity," "abortion on demand," and most recently, "gay marriage," and "medicinal marijuana."

As a symbol, even the Canadian Constitution is a source of ambivalence. To most Canadians it evokes Canadian independence and political maturity. However, many Quebec nationalists still see it as a symbol of the betrayal of Quebec by the nine other provinces, who accepted the compromise offered by the federal government in an attempt to win support for their project to patriate the Constitution. In Quebec political culture, the date of November 5, 1981, on which this alleged "betrayal" occurred, is immortalized as "the night of the long knives."[2]

Some symbols are nonverbal. As the principal medium through which most Canadians learn about politics, television has produced enduring visual symbols that have galvanized political emotions and values. Consider the images of the free trade protests in Seattle and Quebec City; the World Trade Center towers collapsing on September 11, 2001; the 2003 protests in Vancouver, Toronto, and Montreal against war in Iraq. Earlier images seared into the brain of many Canadians include the unforgettable picture of a Mohawk warrior face to face with a

Canadian soldier during the Oka crisis; Brockville citizens stomping on the Quebec flag; tens of thousands of Canadians swaying on the streets of Montreal holding up a huge Canadian flag just before referendum day; an RCMP officer pepper-spraying student protesters during the APEC meetings in Vancouver; and Paul Henderson scoring the winning goal in the first-ever hockey series between Canada and the Soviet Union.

The variety and richness of political symbols demonstrate that Canadian politics simultaneously features harmony and disunity, conflict and cooperation. Politicians invoke symbols in their speeches in order to rally support for their parties and policies, to quiet discontent, or to inflame feelings of anger directed against their opponents. Political advertisements (especially during election campaigns) involve carefully constructed image manipulations developed on the advice of highly paid image consultants or "spin doctors." Members of the general public, for their part, often appear to need symbolic reassurances, to identify with the symbols that are manipulated in public debate by their political leaders, and to find gratification in the symbolic aspect of politics when more practical and material aspects are less than satisfactory.[3]

Because of its impact on individuals in their capacity as both citizens and subjects, followers and leaders, political culture (including symbols) affects the content and nature of what goes on in the "black box" that we call the political system. It helps transform the inanimate machinery of government into the living organic reality of politics. Cultural inhibitors affect "what are to be considered culturally appropriate areas for political decision."[4] In any political system, the political culture demarcates the zone of appropriate action for government, and sets other areas beyond the realm of the legitimate. Thus, for example, Pierre Trudeau announced soon after his first election as prime minister in 1968 that "the state has no place in the bedrooms of the nation."[5]

Conversely, the political culture provides a range of acceptable values and standards upon which leaders can draw in attempting to justify their policies. Unless a culturally viable justification can be attached to a controversial policy, it will not usually be adopted. Thus, political culture shapes the perception of politically relevant problems, thereby affecting both the recognition of these problems as issues requiring some sort of governmental action and the diagnosis of what sort of action is appropriate. Political culture influences beliefs about who should be assigned responsibility for solving problems and what kind of solutions are likely to work. This aspect of political culture is related to broader notions about the general purposes of government and the kinds of processes and substantive decisions that are seen as acceptable and legitimate.[6]

The political culture also greatly influences political discourse. In effect, political culture serves as the "language," while political discourse constitutes "speech." This language–speech metaphor is very helpful for understanding the day-to-day significance of political culture: in effect, political culture establishes the content of "the universe of political discourse"—defined by one scholar as comprising "beliefs about the ways politics should be conducted, the boundaries of political discussion, and the kinds of conflicts resolvable through political processes."

> The universe of political discourse functions at any single point in time by setting boundaries to political action and by limiting the range of actors that are accorded the status of legitimate participants, the range of issues considered to be included in the realm of meaningful political debate, the policy alternatives feasible for implementation, and the alliance strategies available for achieving change.[7]

POLITICAL CULTURE, POLITICAL PARTIES, AND IDEOLOGIES

When people talk about political issues and problems, they draw on symbols and concepts, embedded in the political culture, that help to define the situation. The political culture privileges or favours one set of definitions over others. It thus helps establish a dominant discourse that, in turn, will favour the interests of particular groups in society. Typically, political parties that support the status quo articulate the dominant discourse. At the same time, parties or groups that wish to achieve significant reform are forced to challenge the dominant discourse and attempt to gain legitimacy for an alternative discourse.

Over the course of its nine years in power (1984–1993) the Mulroney Conservative government largely displaced the neo-Keynesian discourse of the Trudeau Liberals with a neoliberal discourse of monetarism, deregulation, and privatization. Neither of these discourses pays much attention to class conflict and class divisions, matters deemed to be at the very heart of politics by class-based parties of the left. The dominance of neoliberal discourse became so complete that NDP governments elected in subsequent years in the provinces of Ontario and British Columbia were accused of adopting a neoliberal agenda!

The Ontario NDP, for instance, formally lost the support of a number of major unions in retaliation for imposing "social contract" legislation that was considered by many critics to be "anti–working class." After defeating the NDP in 1995, the Mike Harris Conservatives, whose election platform was outlined in a booklet called the "Common Sense

Revolution," showed how much still further right the true neoliberal agenda could lead. At the national level, the election of Jean Chrétien's Liberals in 1993 did not in any significant way transform the dominant neoliberal discourse of the Conservatives. As several observers had predicted, the Liberals followed the same course set out by Mulroney, giving Canadians an "honest, small 'c' conservative government punctuated by populist gestures."[8]

It's not unreasonable to attach the label "ideology" to neoliberalism. Ideologies are more or less coherent and explicit clusters of attitudes, beliefs, and values that tend to be held by people whose political involvement is unusually high. In this sense, ideologies have a programmatic aspect insofar as they provide activists with a diagnosis of the problems facing society and a prescription of solutions for those problems. Ideologies are often derived from, or closely related to, more profound and sophisticated statements set forth in works of political philosophy. Indeed, ideologies in many instances amount to a comprehensive way of viewing the world. However, compared with political philosophies, ideologies are more simplified and less profound; they emphasize action over thought, and may stress emotions rather than carefully reasoned arguments. Most of the great studies on the subject link ideologies to a set of underlying interests and predispositions, often derived from one's class position in society. Thus, one speaks of a ruling-class ideology, a working-class ideology, a bourgeois ideology, and so on. This awareness of the connection between ideology and interests leads inexorably to a concern with "unmasking" ideologies in order to discover their material base in social relations.

Studies have shown that relatively few people have political ideas that are coherent and explicit enough to deserve the designation "ideology." Many individuals lack a clear, consistent set of political views. They react in an ad hoc fashion or simply avoid thinking about politics altogether. They may have low levels of information, hold contradictory opinions, or misunderstand basic concepts.

Enter the concept of political culture! From the outset, political culture was intended as a broader concept with wider application than ideology. Political culture involves the study of all segments of society, including members of the general public whose ideas about politics are insufficiently coherent and programmatic to be called ideological. Moreover, a single political culture could comprise several ideologies. Historically, the Canadian political culture has been described as including the ideologies of conservatism, liberalism, and socialism. New issues, ideas, and political forces are transforming these classical ideologies. The contours of these newly emerging ideologies are difficult to discern.

Concerns about identity (including ethnicity and gender), participation, and quality of life are emerging alongside disenchantment with existing political institutions and leaders.

The composition of the House of Commons following the 1993 federal election reflected these ideological transformations. The traditional parties of the left (NDP) and the right (Progressive Conservative) were reduced to nine and two members respectively, too small even to qualify for official party status. In their place (with over 50 members each) were elected the Western-based Reform Party, which espoused a peculiar mixture of populism and fiscal and social conservatism;[9] and the Quebec-based Bloc Québécois, whose sole ideological commitment is to the dissolution of Canada and the attainment of sovereignty for Quebec. (Shortly after the election, a senior official of the federal government remarked, "The opposition benches are dominated by one party that doesn't believe in government and another that doesn't believe in Canada!")

The 1997 election confirmed the trend toward "de-alignment" of the party system. Again the Liberals were elected (with a reduced majority) and the Bloc and Reform parties were next in size. This time, however, the Reform Party elected enough members to overtake the Bloc and gain Official Opposition status. But the much-hoped-for breakthrough for the Reform Party in Central and Eastern Canada failed to materialize, seeing them elect no members east of Manitoba. The NDP won new seats in the Atlantic region, and the Conservatives picked up seats there and in Quebec, returning a total of 21 members of Parliament.

The strong perception of Reform was that the Liberals had stolen electoral victory by winning ridings where conservative voters split their votes between PC and Reform candidates. The Reform Party felt that if only the "right" could pull together, electoral success could be achieved and the Liberals defeated. A movement to "unite the right" culminated in a weekend "United Alternative" (UA) conference in Ottawa in February 1999. Organized by the Reform Party, the UA conference attracted a few PC supporters (primarily provincial rather than federal activists). Newly elected federal PC leader Joe Clark, and most federal party members, refused to participate, however, dismissing the initiative as an act of desperation on the part of Reformers or, worse still, a clumsy attempt to take over the PC Party.

The UA convention adopted a resolution calling for the formation of a new party, but one political commentator doubted that many Canadians would be fooled by a "new party that looks like the wine of the Reform

Party poured into a new bottle, even with a new label."[10] The next day, the same commentator offered the following assessment:

> The coalition built and sustained by former Conservative prime minister Brian Mulroney still lies in fragments across the Canadian landscape ... One important fragment, the Reform Party, remains just that: an important fragment, incapable as currently configured of cementing other fragments together to challenge the Liberals for power.

Even if the United Alternative convention had resulted in a fusion of the Reformers with the PCs—an outcome described as "unlikely"—the "enlarged fragment" would still "need to cement relationships with many other fragments within the Canadian electorate before it contended seriously for power."[11] Having failed to effect a union with the PC Party, the Reform Party attempted to reinvent itself as the Canadian Alliance. The founder and leader of Reform, Preston Manning, lost the leadership of this new version of the party to Stockwell Day, an Alberta politician who had no federal political experience. Day was unable to defeat Jean Chrétien, who won a third term in the 2000 election, in which the PC party under Joe Clark barely managed to elect the minimum 12 members to continue to exist as an official party. Day soon faced bitter opposition from within his own caucus, and a splinter group even left to join up with the PCs. Day was forced out of the leadership in a convention that elected Stephen Harper and most of the dissidents returned to the fold.

Meanwhile the federal NDP seemed to have lost its focus. Perhaps the most articulate ideologist of the left, former NDP premier of Ontario Bob Rae published a book urging the party to reconcile itself to the reality of global capitalism, abandon any atavistic hopes for achieving some sort of socialist transformation, and concentrate instead on "humanizing" the new reality. Inspired in part by the success in Britain of Tony Blair's "New Labour," Rae declared that "the issue in the modern world is not between capitalism and socialism, it is about the kind of capitalism we want to have."[12] But to the extent that Rae's analysis is correct, one journalist argued that it completely cuts the ground from under the NDP as a viable party:

> There already is a Blairist party in Canada, one willing to embrace capitalism, shift its policies in line with the public mood and do anything to get elected. It is called the Liberal Party. If Rae is right, the most sensible thing for the New Democrats to do would be to wind up their interesting 67-year experiment and join Jean Chrétien.[13]

Under the leadership of Alexa McDonough, the NDP did get more seats than the PC Party in the 2000 election, but were still well behind the Alliance and the Bloc Québécois. When McDonough stepped down as leader, the NDP chose a charismatic Toronto municipal councillor, Jack Layton, as party leader. A few months later, the PCs replaced Joe Clark with Peter MacKay. Meanwhile, a leadership race was well underway to select a successor to Jean Chrétien, who in August 2002 bowed to pressure from the supporters of front-runner Paul Martin and announced that he would retire in February 2004.

So, at the beginning of the twenty-first century, with new leaders taking the helm of nearly every political party, the picture of political ideologies in Canada shows a fragmented right, a disoriented left, and a "centre" party emerging from 10 years of deficit-fighting and downsizing with a fiscal surplus and a legacy of neoliberal policies. As we shall see, such ideological flux reflected important changes in Canada's political culture.

APPROACHES TO THE STUDY OF POLITICAL CULTURE

Political culture is invisibly interwoven into all aspects of politics and government. While one can isolate the cultural variable for the purposes of analysis, to do so requires a sensitive appreciation of the techniques that can render the often hidden assumptions, values, and beliefs visible and comprehensible. The study of political culture can, therefore, remain rather general and abstract, encompassing the broadly stated political values at their highest level, or it can be made more specific and focused on beliefs and values related to particular issues, policies, or political figures.

Most students of political culture seem to agree on one point: culture is a collective phenomenon, the attribute of a group, not an individual. An individual cannot make or possess a culture. However, she or he can learn a culture. For this reason, the components of a political culture—values, beliefs, and attitudes, among others—can be observed in the individual. Thus, one might refer to X's religious values or Y's attitudes to abortion as aspects of a culture. But what does it mean to talk about a *group* value or attitude? Is a group merely the sum of those individuals who are part of it, and its culture the median beliefs of its membership? Or is culture something different again from majority opinion or a statistical mean? In grappling with these questions, social scientists tend to fall into one of two camps: some opt for an individualistic approach or "methodological individualism," while others insist on a "holistic" approach.

INDIVIDUALISTIC APPROACH

The individualistic approach to political culture assumes that values and beliefs exist only in specific individuals, who may or may not resemble one another. To generalize about the values of a group of people requires reliable information obtained from a large sample of individuals who are representative of the population as a whole. These data are almost always obtained by survey research. Once these individual-level survey data have been gathered, the problem of how to aggregate them in order to make judgments about the entire population involves the use of various statistical techniques to assess the reliability of the findings and to identify "modal" characteristics. The term "mode" refers to that point along a continuum where a large concentration of attitudes is found.

The first and most prominent example of the individualistic approach to political culture is Gabriel Almond and Sidney Verba's study of five countries: the United States, Britain, Mexico, Germany, and Italy.[14] The authors selected a sample of respondents from each country and administered a long questionnaire designed to elicit attitudes to the political system in general, and to the role of the individual as both a citizen (i.e., a participant in the decision-making process) and a subject (i.e., someone on the receiving end of the laws and regulations enforced by the system).[15] In analyzing their data, Almond and Verba introduced several categories that allowed them to generalize about the "modal" characteristics of each of the societies they studied. For example, they planned to use results of "citizen efficacy" and "subject competence" questions, together with questions about orientations to the system as a whole, to locate societies along a continuum, ranging from "parochial" political cultures, in which there is little awareness of the existence of the nation-state or of the individual's role in the national political system; through "subject" cultures, in which the individual responds positively to the system's outputs but has a low sense of personal citizen efficacy; to the most advanced "participant" cultures, which display high measures of both efficacy and competence.

Almond and Verba's survey results proved somewhat disappointing. The neat distinctions they hoped to find between participant, subject, and parochial political cultures did not materialize. Instead, Almond and Verba found a mixture of attitudes encompassing elements from all three categories. Consequently, they used the term "civic culture" to denote the hybrid mixture of attitudes and values—some "modern," others premodern—found in what they believed to be the most highly developed democratic political system in their study: the United States.[16]

Although Almond and Verba did not include Canada in their five-nation study, virtually every major academic survey conducted in Canada since 1965 has included one or more items from the civic culture survey. Researchers have emphasized, in particular, the questions on "efficacy" and "trust."

While these and similar survey results are clearly interesting and illuminating, they also have important limitations. Surveys provide a *direct* measure of political culture and have the advantage of forcing people to make explicit what may otherwise be obscure or implicit. In doing so, however, these measures sometimes distort or twist reality in subtle ways. We cannot be sure that survey responses validly reflect what people really believe or value, and whether these responses accurately reflect the way people actually behave. Furthermore, surveys have only been carried out in Canada since about 1950, and obviously cannot be used to help us understand the earlier periods of history that some scholars think contain important clues to the development of political culture.[17]

Useful supplements to interviews and surveys are the *indirect approaches*, which are particularly important for historical research. A number of techniques, usually involving some form of content analysis, allow researchers to extract from written documents or speeches the values and beliefs that are implicit in them. In the case of the political values of the elite, a highly specialized "operational code" approach has been used to reconstruct the outlook and assumptions of key individuals.[18]

Biographies and autobiographies shed light not only on cognitive beliefs and values, but also on life experiences that reflect how important those values are for behaviour. Indeed, by studying the behaviour of individuals, or the collective behaviour of institutions (i.e., their adoption of various policies), skillful students of political culture can excavate latent assumptions about politics and thus create an inductive picture of the political culture of both the present and the past.

HOLISTIC APPROACH

The latter kind of indirect approach often accompanies a "holistic" conception of political culture. In one form of holistic approach, political culture is viewed as a kind of "ethos" that envelops and conditions a society.[19] According to this view, certain values and predispositions are, figuratively speaking, "in the air," and thus one can speak of a "climate" of opinion. Like climate, values influence behaviour invisibly but nonetheless effectively. The individual born into a particular cultural ethos absorbs it through a kind of osmosis. Though people may vary in the degree to which they absorb the culture, everyone is exposed to cultural values. An individual's departure from the prevailing ethos (often defined as "social deviance") in no way disproves the existence of the culture, because socialization is never complete.

Descriptions of the ethos of Canadian political culture are many and varied. Sometimes geography has been credited with having produced a distinctive Canadian ethos. Two years after Confederation, for example, in a lecture about Canadian "national spirit" delivered to the Montreal Literary Club, Robert Grant Haliburton stressed the formative influence of Canada's "northern" geography and climate: "[M]ay not our snow and frost give us what is of more value than gold or silver, a healthy, hardy, virtuous dominant race? [For Canada] must ever be ... a Northern country inhabited by the descendants of Northern races."[20] Haliburton regarded the superiority of northerners as a fundamental axiom of politics. Rhetorically he asked, "If climate has not had the effect of moulding races, how is it that the southern nations have almost invariably been inferior to and subjugated by the men of the north?" From the felicitous marriage of racial inheritance and northern environmentalism, there would emerge a Canadian people worthy of the ideals of "the true north, strong and free."

Fortunately not all efforts to define a Canadian ethos are infected by the virus of racial nationalism. Nor do they necessarily emphasize the formative impact of geography. Seymour Martin Lipset explicitly posits the existence of a national ethos in the following passage: "[V]alue differences between the United States and Canada suggest that they stem in large part from two disparate founding ethos."[21] But for Lipset (as we will see below), historical events rather than geographical factors account for the cultural differences between the two countries.

The approach presented in this chapter draws on both individualism and holism. We are interested in the pattern of individually held values and beliefs, and thus examine relevant survey results. But the individualistic approach alone is insufficient. To appreciate the importance of the larger whole within which individuals operate (without, however, arguing that values and beliefs are somehow preserved in an invisible ethos, a kind of social formaldehyde) requires attention to certain distinctively Canadian political institutions, such as Parliament, the Constitution, federal–provincial relations, the CBC, elements of popular culture (novels, poetry, songs, television sitcoms, films, etc.), that form part of Canada's political personality and illuminate the character of Canadian politics. In important respects, these institutions exist independent of the modal attitudes and values of individuals living in Canada at any particular moment in time.

Some institutions present themselves to the outside world as quintessentially Canadian, frequently with explicit authorization to speak or act on behalf of Canada. Notwithstanding the wide range of possible variation within the country, there are times and places where a single voice speaks, and it calls itself Canadian.[22] In these settings, the individual or group that presumes to speak for the collectivity, insofar as it is effective, becomes the collectivity. Individuals who hold a different outlook become irrelevant, at least until they are able to project a dissenting voice or image. The world, in short, contains significant "institutional facts" that exist apart from the individuals who surround and inhabit them. Whatever their individual conceptions of value and purpose, Canadians live and breathe to some extent in a common political space dominated by institutions whose very design and functioning evolves from, and gives shape to, the complexities of Canadian political culture. Thus, it is useful to examine the values promoted by, and embodied in, these institutions. Of particular interest are institutions that explicitly undertake a role in political socialization and that therefore may be described as helping build the "foundations of political culture."

POLITICAL SOCIALIZATION: THE LEARNING OF POLITICAL CULTURE

Political socialization is the process of transmitting political values and attitudes through time and across space. Agencies involved in the process include families, peer groups, schools, churches, political parties, and, perhaps most importantly, the mass media. These and similar institutions consciously attempt to inculcate certain values and foster particular attitudes toward politics. Political socialization is especially effective during the "formative stage" in the development of the individual's values and orientations (the early teen years), but political socialization can continue beyond adolescence.[23]

Socialization and learning are not perfectly congruent. Socialization suggests a planned, controllable, linear pattern of acquiring knowledge and values. But people learn more than they are "socialized" to learn. They learn from unpredictable events in both the natural and the social environment. A flood can serve as a fundamental learning experience, as can a war, a movie, a hockey game, or even a federal election. People learn from introspection and self-education, often despite what their socializers would like them to learn instead. They learn as well from individuals and groups whose values run counter to the prevailing political culture. In short, learning, unlike socialization, is a dialectical process full of contradictions and unpredictable outcomes.

Furthermore, socialization is not always a benign process. The attempt to preserve and transmit a culture can have a nasty side. Although the following observation might appear to exaggerate the extent to which coercion is used to "socialize" people in our society, it would not seem particularly outlandish to an aboriginal person who had gone through the residential school system. It serves to remind us that cultural continuity should never be taken for granted:

> To maintain and transmit a value system, human beings are punched, bullied, sent to jail, thrown into concentration camps, cajoled, made into heroes, encouraged to read newspapers, stood up against a wall and shot and sometimes even taught sociology. To speak of cultural inertia is to overlook the concrete interests and privileges that are served by indoctrination, education, and the entire complicated process of transmitting a culture from one generation to the next.[24]

SOCIETAL ORIGINS OF POLITICAL CULTURE: FOUR VIEWS

We may surmise, therefore, that an individual acquires political culture traits through a learning process, part of which is controlled by various socializing agencies. But where do the political culture traits embraced by these socializing agencies come from in the first place? In attempting to answer this question, students of political culture have adopted differing interpretations. One theorist, Louis Hartz, argues that societies such as Canada and the United States, which were founded by immigrants from Europe, have developed a political culture that reflects the values and beliefs of the groups that were dominant during the "founding period." Hartz contends that the "founders" are able to shape the political culture of a "new society" by setting up institutions and myths that imbue their values and beliefs with a nationalistic flavour, thus making membership in the nation contingent on accepting the dominant ideology.[25]

Thus, new societies, "fragments of Europe transported to the New World," tend to have a political culture that conserves and preserves the values, beliefs, and attitudes of the founders of that society. This "fragment theory" was first applied to the United States. Hartz describes the political culture of the United States as "bourgeois," and points to its origins in seventeenth- and eighteenth-century British society. Applying the fragment theory to Canada is complicated by the fact that ours is a "two-fragment" society. La Nouvelle France was founded by seventeenth- and eighteenth-century emigrants from feudal France. English-speaking Canada was founded largely by Loyalist refugees from the American Revolution, who, Hartz argues, were largely bourgeois in outlook. According to fragment theory, much of the present-day difference between Canadian anglophones and francophones can be traced back to the cultural differences between these two founding groups or "fragments."

Seymour Martin Lipset disagrees with Hartz's view that societies bear forever the cultural marks of their birth. In his view, cultural inheritance is less significant than the experiences that society undergoes. Lipset suggests that one can identify certain "formative events" in the history of a country that help mould or shape its values and consequently make a lasting impression on its cultural and institutional practices.[26] When he applies his formative-events notion to English-speaking Canada, however, the differences between him and Hartz shrink. For Lipset, the most important formative event in Canada's history—the "counter-revolution" and subsequent migration north of the Loyalists—is the obverse of that in the United States; this event, he believes, affected Canada's political culture as significantly as the American Revolution moulded the United States.

Thus, both Hartz's fragment theory and Lipset's formative-events notion focus attention on the Loyalist experience as a major source of English-speaking Canada's political culture. Yet the cultural consequences of the Loyalist migration are a subject of considerable controversy among historians and social scientists. Much of the debate has turned on defining the ideological outlook of the Loyalists. One key issue has been a disagreement over the extent to which the Loyalists presented an "organic conservative" alternative to the "individualistic liberal" world-view of the revolutionaries who expelled them and shaped the political institutions and culture of the new United States. Lipset himself speaks of the Loyalists as "counter-revolutionaries" who helped make Canada more elitist, ascriptive, and particularistic (with greater emphasis on the collectivity) than the United States. To substantiate his claims, he examines not only survey results but also data comparing crime rates, educational practices, economic policies, popular culture, fiction, and even religious traditions in the two countries.

A number of scholars have criticized Lipset's interpretation of these data, particularly his failure to distinguish anglophones from francophones. Clearly, the two groups had different cultural origins and experienced different formative events. The French Canadians were relatively unaffected by the American Revolution. For them, the major formative event was undoubtedly the Conquest (described in their history books as the *Cession,* a term that reveals their profound sense of betrayal by France). French-language history books used in schools in the 1960s, for example, typically depicted the events leading up to 1763 as a "catastrophe," and devoted half of their space to the "golden age" that preceded it.

One advantage of Hartz's fragment theory is that it highlights the cultural uniqueness of the anglophone and francophone fragments. But despite a general consensus about the political culture of the francophone fragment, followers of Hartz have disagreed even among themselves about the impact of the Loyalists. Some have seen the Loyalists as primarily a bourgeois fragment, albeit "tinged with Toryism." Others have insisted that we not dismiss the "Tory touch," which is deemed to have had an important influence on both policies and institutions.[27]

While both perspectives on the Loyalists (i.e., the "liberal" interpretation and the "conservative" view) contribute important insights, they tend to ignore effects of the Loyalist migration that go beyond the usual categories of European ideology. Although Canada's unique brand of "conservative liberalism" probably can be traced back to our Loyalist origins, so too can our profound identity crisis, our fascination with the mosaic, and our willingness to use the state for "interventionist" purposes that most Americans would reject. Furthermore, one can regard the Loyalist experience as having produced an "anti-fragment" insofar as it encouraged a prolongation of emotional and cultural ties to Britain instead of leading to the kind of cultural isolation that is a precondition to the "freezing" of the fragment culture. Consequently, English-speaking Canada found no difficulty importing British-style parliamentary socialism in the twentieth century, whereas both Quebec and the United States rejected it as "alien."

Although the fragment theory, enriched by the introduction of Lipset's formative-events notion, illuminates the otherwise baffling history of ideologies and political parties in Canada, political culture studies need not be confined by the categories of analysis that derive from the European ideologies of conservatism, liberalism, and socialism. Much of the experience of the New World lies beyond these categories, and, in any event, the study of political culture can and should embrace other aspects of political practice. Similarly, Almond and Verba's concern with efficacy and trust is too limiting. They chose to focus on those aspects of political culture because they were primarily interested in the problem of democracy. But the problem of democracy is not the central political problem in Canada. Therefore, there is no reason to stick with their concepts and concerns either. Instead, as students of the Canadian experience, we need to examine values, attitudes, and beliefs that relate to more fundamental and pressing problems, such as language, gender, and environment, not merely to the problem of democracy or the problem of class and ideology that animated the work of those who pioneered in the use of political culture.

Furthermore, we need to supplement Hartz's and Lipset's rather idealistic approaches to political culture with approaches that have a much firmer appreciation of the structural bases of culture. For culture never exists in a vacuum, nor does it have an all-determining effect on politics. Rather, culture and its structural underpinnings are interrelated and interdependent. To understand this aspect of culture and trace it back to its societal origins, we need to examine the work of two additional theorists, Harold Innis and Karl Marx.

Although he did not consider himself a student of political culture, Harold Innis offers important insights into the process of cultural transmission.[28] Unlike Hartz and Lipset, who seem to treat values and beliefs as determinants of social and political structures, Innis reverses the causal arrow by arguing that it is not culture that shapes society. On the contrary, for Innis, cultures are heavily affected by the *technology of production and distribution of ideas*. Hence the culture of society is transformed when new developments take place in the technology of communication. The invention of the printing press revolutionized Western culture, according to Innis. Recent "revolutionary" developments in communications technology include the discovery of radio and television, the introduction of inexpensive copying machines, the VCR, the technology of the microchip, fibre optics, satellite relays, electronic mail, fax, two-way video communication, and the Internet, or "information highway."[29] In the near future, the second generation of wireless communication will fully integrate cellular technology with the World Wide Web, pushing technological integration to new levels.

Of course, Innis died before most of these innovations had become widespread, and thus he did not live to see how they have affected Canadian political culture. However, his insights concerning the importance to culture of the underlying structures and technologies of communication help illuminate some aspects of the Canadian identity crisis in the twentieth century. Clearly, ownership and control of the means of distribution of culture (including popular culture) are important determinants of what ideas get transmitted to the general public. Canada, unlike virtually any other country in the world, has a cultural-transmission system that is very largely in the hands of foreigners. Most Canadian children pass into adulthood without, for example, ever seeing a Canadian feature-length film. They watch American television and even read school textbooks that are produced and written in the United States. They listen to

American music and eat food produced by mass-distribution food outlets based in the United States. They see American commercials and read American advertising. Little wonder then that they grow up with a very shaky sense of Canadian identity and relatively little knowledge about their own country and political institutions, much less any sense of what might constitute Canadian culture in the mass media, the arts, music, and letters. So extreme has been the domination of our cultural networks that, in a document prepared in 1977 to provide new directions for the Canadian Broadcasting Corporation, the then CBC president, Albert Johnson, commented, "Canada today faces its greatest crisis in history: the combination of national life-threatening arguments over our nationhood and the relentless American cultural penetration."[30]

Whether this cultural domination leads to economic domination— or the reverse—is perhaps immaterial. The massive U.S. presence on the Canadian cultural scene is matched by an equally dominant U.S. presence in our economy, fully reinforced by the Free Trade Agreement and later consolidated under NAFTA. Recent North American trade disputes involving split-run magazine publication, satellite broadcasting, media content classifications, and film distribution reinforce this unequal relationship. This leads us directly to Marxist and neo-Marxist analyses of the Canadian dilemma.

According to Karl Marx, the material conditions under which a society produces its wealth are major factors in determining the nature of the political culture. In his view, there are relatively few "modes of production": primitive, feudal, capitalist, and socialist. Each limits the kind of political structures and culture that can exist. Within a given mode of production, however, variations will occur as a result of different patterns of external trade relations and internal control of production and distribution. Students of contemporary Canadian politics who have applied Marxist concepts to Canada emphasize the effect on our political culture of Canada's major economic structures. The fact that we are a capitalist country with a long history of economic dependence on foreign capital has had a huge impact on Canada's political development.

Within the dominant capitalist class are various "fractions" that have different perceptions of their interests and different orientations toward the economic system. Some neo-Marxists distinguish in particular between a mercantile-financial class fraction, which makes profits on the circulation rather than the production of goods and services, and a more entrepreneurial industrial-capitalist fraction, which is focused on industrial development and expansion. Particularly in the crucial period of the late nineteenth century, the interests of these two class fractions were opposed. The mercantilists did not favour the development of an indigenous heavy industry in Canada, but instead sought to profit on the exchange of staple products from the hinterland for manufactured goods imported from the imperial centre (i.e., Britain and, at a later point, the United States). According to these neo-Marxists, the political culture of colonialism and imperial dependency was consciously fostered by the mercantile class fraction to support its own economic interests. As the dominant element of Canada's capitalist class, members of this group did not see themselves as rulers of a strong, independent nation-state. Supporters of a colonial mentality, they opposed any efforts to develop a true Canadian nationalism.[31]

Each of the above approaches to political culture sheds light on the social origins and development of culture. A comprehensive historical analysis must therefore take account of the following:

1. the "cultural genes" implanted by the founding groups (Hartz);
2. the kinds of formative events that affect cultural values and institutions (Lipset);
3. the nature of the technology of communication (Innis); and
4. the material conditions and economic infrastructure of society (Marx).

These four perspectives complement one another. Any one of them alone is insufficient, yet together they illuminate the complexity and richness of a political culture. It is possible to analyze the development of Canadian political culture in more detail using the four approaches.

From the Hartzian perspective, we realize that Canadian political culture developed from the cultural genes implanted by the two major founding groups, the English and the French. These two groups embodied contrasting ideologies that would never easily mix together. The cultural uniqueness of the French fragment generated the commitment to *la survivance* that today underlies much of Quebec nationalism, including reference to *pure laine* Québécois and the insistence on recognition as a "distinct society."

The anglophones, for their part, were a very strange mixture of elements. Irrespective of how important the Tory touch was, the anglophone bourgeois culture had the ironic and paradoxical characteristic of being simultaneously liberal and anti-American. Because the United States had adopted liberalism as its national culture, the anglophones were prevented from doing so; hence the origin of Canada's never-ending identity crisis and the peculiar combination of celebration of the British connection and antipathy toward a culture that was ideologically very similar to that of English Canada. Furthermore, because of the failure to nationalize the political culture of the anglophones, and because of the pattern of settlement that led to a direct importation into the Canadian West of new "founding groups" from Europe that did not become socialized to either English- or French-Canadian culture before settling there, the Canadian West featured what some have called a process of "subfragmentation": new groups brought with them ideologies that reflected their European origin and that were much more progressive than those of the older fragments. Thus socialism arose in Saskatchewan.

The Alberta subfragmentation reflected the influence of the United States, from which many of Alberta's founding settlers came. In general, the political culture of the Canadian West has shown noticeable differences from that of the older parts of the country and earlier in the century featured the appearance of at least two ideological variants not found in much strength elsewhere: socialism and social credit. More recently, of course, the West gave birth to the Reform Party.

The Lipset notion of formative events is similarly revealing. Canada had no single great nationalizing formative event. The significant events in our history show the strong influence of the colonial powers, because in almost every instance these events were the outcome of struggles taking place between England and France or England and the United States: the Conquest of New France in 1763, the American Revolution in 1776, and the War of 1812. Two other significant events that bear more of a homegrown imprint were the uprisings in 1837 and the passage of the British North America Act in 1867. But even the latter event took place in England as a statute of the British Parliament, a fact that continued to bedevil attempts to patriate the Constitution until 1982.

A second insight from the formative-events notion is that different regions and different cultural fragments have each had a unique perspective on these formative events and, in effect, a different kind of history. Provincial control of education has militated against the production of a common national history curriculum even among the English-speaking provinces, which have emphasized the peculiarities of their own brand of regional/provincial history.

The Innis approach suggests how important it is to have a national communications network capable of binding the community together. This system would serve to offset cultural fragmentation between anglophones and francophones and the enormous cultural influences from south of the border. But in several respects we have failed to accomplish this task successfully. Despite the setting up of a national broadcasting network in the 1930s, the CBC has proved incapable of bringing together francophones and anglophones or of offsetting infusions of American culture. As already mentioned, responsibility for education was assigned to the provinces, and political party organizations developed into quasi-autonomous provincial organizations with a very loose federal alliance at the top. Thus, two of the most critical socializing agencies have been under provincial control and have contributed to the development of provincial or regional political cultures, in some cases at the expense of a national culture. In the early 1990s, Canada was facing a severe crisis over the control of new communications systems such as Cablevision, pay-TV, and satellite broadcasts. The provinces, aware of the potential of the communications system to influence the "thoughts and minds" of the public, fought against letting this control pass to the federal government.

Finally, from the Marxist perspective, we see immediately the important impact on our political culture of foreign dependency and the different alignment of capitalist groups around the dominant capitalist forces in the country. We see as well the effect that geographically uneven economic development has had on the country in fostering regionalism and leading to the growth of regional economic interests and regional perspectives. Paradoxically, however, class divisions (supposedly the major determinants of political culture in a modern society) have had only a minor effect on Canadian politics, in part because the party system and the electoral system enhance horizontal rather than vertical cleavages.

TRANSFORMATION OF CANADIAN POLITICAL CULTURE

Many critics argue that insofar as political culture is assumed to be an unchanging feature of the political system, the political culture approach ignores change. But, clearly, political culture itself changes over time. To understand how and why it changes, we need to revisit the theoretical approaches that we invoked to explain the origins of political culture. As well, additional factors need to be introduced.

One obviously important influence on political culture is immigration and emigration. This insight follows clearly from the fragment theory and from other approaches that recognize that infusions of new groups of people with different values will have an effect on the societal value systems of the countries they enter or leave.

In addition to the French- and English-speaking immigrants who came to what is now Canada in the seventeenth, eighteenth, and early nineteenth centuries and who are often referred to (erroneously, given the pre-existence here of many aboriginal groups that were the true "first nations") as the "two founding peoples," Canada has attracted scores of other immigrant groups from all parts of the world. The rich contributions these groups have made to Canadian culture were officially recognized by the Royal Commission established in the early 1960s to inquire into bilingualism and biculturalism. The commission felt obliged to publish a separate volume of its report on "The Contribution of the Other Ethnic Groups." Shortly thereafter, the Canadian government introduced an official policy of multiculturalism. In 1961, 90 percent of Canadian immigrants came from the "traditional" source locations of Europe, the United States, and Australasia. Over the next 30 years, a dramatic shift occurred in the pattern of immigration to Canada so that by 1991, nearly 70 percent of immigrants came from countries in Africa, Asia, Latin America, and the Caribbean. While little systematic research has been done to measure the impacts of these new groups on Canadian political culture, their presence has certainly transformed the face—and the voice—of Canadian society and has made the "Canadian mosaic" much more interesting and colourful.[32]

Political culture might also undergo a transformation in response to a formative event such as a revolution, major war, or other cataclysmic activity. Since the continuity of culture depends on political socialization, however, any interruption or transformation of the socialization process could have a transformative impact on political culture. Thus, new ideas about child rearing, or the introduction of new technologies of communication such as television, can change political culture.

A parallel hypothesis was developed around Karl Deutsch's concept of social mobilization.[33] According to Deutsch, changes in values (particularly in developing countries) would come about through a combination of social changes that he called the "subprocesses of social mobilization"; these included education, urbanization, industrialization, increased literacy, growing wealth, and exposure to mass media. Deutsch hypothesized that social mobilization was the central engine of modernization. Although his theory gave the impression that once countries had passed certain thresholds, the mobilization effects diminished or disappeared, his insights draw attention to the relationship between a shift in values and changing aspects of the social structure of a society.

Each new generation presents a challenge for political socialization and to some extent experiences a world different from the preceding one. A number of students of political culture have used "age cohort analysis" to look at intergenerational differences in fundamental values and orientations. This is precisely the approach underlying Ronald Inglehart's seminal work on the changes he associates with the transition from materialist to postmaterialist values. In his first work in this area, entitled *The Silent Revolution*, Inglehart argued that the values of Western publics have been shifting from an over-whelming emphasis on material well-being and physical security toward greater emphasis on the quality of life. The causes and impli-cations of this shift are complex, but the basic principle may be stated very simply: people tend to be more concerned with immediate needs and threats than with things that seem remote or non-threatening.[34]

Inglehart's approach assumed that as the material conditions of advanced industrial societies improved, public attention would shift to non-material values. Even despite the economic difficulties that beset all indus-trial societies in the early 1980s and again at the start of the 1990s, Inglehart continued to argue that the shift from materialist to postmaterialist values was a profound and irreversible change. His second major book, *Culture Shift*, presents considerable support for this hypothesis.

Karl Deutsch thought he could explain the dynamics of moderniza-tion. Scholars today are trying to understand the cultural and structural dynamics of the countries once thought to be fully "modernized," and have introduced the term *postmodernization* to describe these changes. The social structures of advanced industrial societies are currently being trans-formed by forces of globalization in the economic sphere; new technology in communications and information transfer; shifting political identities and affiliations; and major developments in education and religion. This structural transformation has been accompanied by radical cultural changes involving values, attitudes, and beliefs in all of the "late industrial" societies, including Canada.

Ronald Inglehart and his colleagues have undertaken the most com-prehensive and ambitious comparative study of political culture ever—the world values survey (WVS), which involves extensive surveys conducted in 43 countries, including Canada. A book about Canada based on the survey—Neil Nevitte's *The Decline of Deference*—provides a comparative perspective on recent changes in Canada's political culture. Despite the uniqueness of specific challenges Canada faced in the 1980s (the "decade of turmoil"), many of the same patterns of value change took place in nearly all the "late industrial" countries, and WVS allows us to track these changes. The main trends include weakening support for mainstream political parties, an increase in interest and participation in politics, and a loss of confidence in political leaders, government institutions, and non-governmental institutions. These trends show marked intergenerational differences and are directly related to an increase in postmaterialist values particularly evident in the younger age cohorts.[35]

Recent research by Michael Adams has shown that through the 1990s, the pattern of value change in Canada began to diverge from that of the United States. While Canada has followed a trajectory (similar to many European countries) toward more postmaterialist values featuring "idealism and autonomy," Americans appear to be "retrenching" and "seem inclined to latch on to traditional institutional practices, beliefs and norms as anchors in a national environment that is more intensely competitive, chaotic, and even violent."[36]

Central to the changing cultural outlook that emerged in the latter part of the twentieth century was a new perspective on the environment, one that represents a paradigm shift as profound as the change that occurred at the dawn of the modern age.[37] Nature was then viewed as fully explainable and controllable by human science and technology—as a rich storehouse of virtually limitless resources to be harvested or exploited for the benefit of humans, and an inexhaustible "sink" into which we could pour the wastes generated by our profligate lifestyle. This outlook minimized or ignored at least two problems: the possibility of exhausting nature's "storehouse" and the danger of doing irreparable and irreversible environmental damage by overflowing the "sinks" and polluting the biosphere. Though some spoke out to warn of these dangers, their cries went largely unheeded until the last 40 years.

The discovery by scientists and others that ecological systems are fragile and threatened by human incursions has reverberated throughout modern society, resulting in a re-evaluation of policies at all levels. Legislation and new agencies devoted to "environmental protection" have brought a new range of considerations and additional levels of complexity to the policymaking process of both government and industry. Environmental degradation has profound consequences for human health. Changed consumer behaviour and preferences have transformed the marketing of products as well as the techniques for producing them. Concerns about pollution and the deteriorating quality of the basic resources of air, land, and water have led to new sub-fields and journals in various academic disciplines, new industries concerned with environmental technology, and new social movements and political parties.

What began as a concern for the environment has broadened into a more comprehensive focus on *sustainable development*. This concept, which proposes a new paradigm for decision making in the public and private sectors, as well as in our personal lives, was introduced into the lexicon through the work of the World Commission on Environment and Development, chaired by the then Norwegian Prime Minister Gro Harlem Brundtland. The commission's report, entitled *Our Common Future*, defined sustainable development as "development that meets the need of the present generation without compromising the ability of future generations to meet their own needs." Canada responded to the Brundtland Commission by setting in motion a series of new policies and institutions, including the Green Plan and the creation of roundtables on the environment and economy. This culminated in the 1996 establishment of a federal Commissioner of the Environment and Sustainable Development (CESD) and the requirement that all federal departments and agencies incorporate the new paradigm of sustainability into all aspects of their policies and practices.[38] Canada renewed its commitment to sustainable development at the 2002 World Summit for Sustainable Development. Nevertheless, the Commissioner maintains that Canada's environmental and sustainable development deficit continues to grow, and the political will required to power positive change remains elusive.[39]

A driving force behind the new perspective on the environment has been the environmental movement, which is but one of several new social movements (see Chapter 9) that deliberately set out to change fundamental attitudes in such areas as gender, sexual orientation, disability, and ethnicity. In many respects, these social movements have captivated public attention and added to the political agenda a whole new range of concerns and issues that are themselves evidence of transformations occurring in our political culture and political discourse. Canadian political discourse features a vocabulary uncontemplated 20 or 30 years ago, with concerns like aboriginal self-government, gay rights, the Kyoto Accord, and identity politics well placed in the vocabulary and high on the political agenda.

CONCLUSION

Political culture consists of individually held values, attitudes, and beliefs concerning politics; symbols that catalyze sentiments and beliefs about politics and political action; politically relevant knowledge and perceptions, including perceptions of historical experiences and notions of identity; and, finally, ideologies as aggregations of values and beliefs that have coherence and internal cohesion. Political culture serves as an important filter that affects political action by narrowing perceptions about politics, notions of what constitute political problems, and prescriptions for resolving these problems.

Political culture is historically derived. It is affected by the cultural baggage brought to a society by immigrants, especially first settlers. It is also moulded by the formative events a society undergoes in the course of its modernization. It is conditioned by such structural underpinnings as class relations, trade patterns, the flow of transportation, and communications. It changes as a result of many dynamics, including structural transformation, new technologies, and contact with other cultures.

Political culture can be seen as the "language" of politics. Political discourse is its "speech." Through political discourse, contending groups in society attempt to shape both public perceptions and governmental responses. They proffer competing conceptions of problems that embody their interests and preferences and privilege the outcomes they wish to see achieved. In effect, these conceptions entail both a diagnosis of the nature of the problem and a prescription concerning the appropriate response to it. Political discourse is not always manipulated in such a conscious, deliberate manner. Sometimes the discourse reflects assumptions and values that are no longer obvious or explicit—historical viewpoints that have sunk beneath the surface of conscious awareness but that are potent forces nonetheless. To achieve social change, these implicit conceptions may have to be "excavated" and made apparent.

NOTES

1. Cf. Clyde Kluckhohn, *Culture and Behavior* (New York: Free Press, 1962), p. 42: "Culture is—among other things—a set of ready-made definitions of the situation that each participant only slightly re-tailors in his idiomatic way." (Cf. also Clifford Geertz's definition of culture as "an historically transmitted pattern of meanings embodied in symbols, a system of inherited conceptions expressed in symbolic forms by means of which men communicate, perpetuate, and develop their knowledge about and attitudes toward life." *The Interpretation of Culture* (New York: Basic Books, 1973), p. 89. Quoted in S.M. Lipset, *Continental Divide: The Values and Institutions of the United States and Canada* (New York: Routledge, 1990), p. 8.

2. According to then premier of Alberta Peter Lougheed, the "night of the long knives" was a "myth." He offers as proof an exchange of letters he had with Quebec premier René Lévesque. See his book, *Constitutional Patriation: The Lougheed-Lévesque Correspondence* (Kingston: Queen's University, 1999).

3. For a discussion of symbolism in politics, see the several books by Murray Edelman, including *The Symbolic Uses of Politics* (Urbana: University of Illinois Press, 1964); and Lowell Dittmer, "Political Symbolism and Political Culture: Toward a Theoretical Synthesis," *World Politics* 30 (1977).

4. David Easton, *A Systems Analysis of Political Life* (New York: John Wiley and Sons, 1965), p. 101.

5. The boundaries of legitimate political activity, like other elements of the political, can and do change over time. Responding in part to the growth of neoliberalism in Britain and the United States, and in part to a homegrown concern that government had become too big and too interventionist, the Mulroney government began to "privatize" a number of Crown corporations and to "deregulate" some aspects of the Canadian economy. The Mike Harris Conservatives in Ontario were very committed to what some critics have called "3D" government: deregulation, downsizing, and devolution. For a general discussion, see Susan Strange, *The Retreat of the State* (Cambridge: Cambridge University Press, 1996).

6. See, among others, David V.J. Bell, "The Political Culture of Problem-Solving and Public Policy," in David Shugarman and Reg Whitaker, eds., *Federalism and Political Community* (Peterborough, ON: Broadview Press, 1989).

7. Jane Jenson, "Changing Discourse, Changing Agenda: Political Rights and Reproductive Policies in France," in Mary F. Katzenstein et al., eds., *The Women's Movement of the United States and Western Europe: Consciousness, Political Opportunity and Public Policy* (Philadelphia: Temple University Press, 1987).

8. James Laxer, "A Healthy Dose of Heresy for Unbending Orthodoxy," *The Toronto Star,* January 2, 1994. For a theoretical discussion of these issues, see contributions by Janine Brodie, Jane Jenson, Neil Bradford, and Duncan Cameron to Alain Gagnon and A. Brian Tanguay, eds., *Canadian Parties in Transition: Discourse, Organization, and Representation* (Scarborough, ON: Nelson Canada, 1988).

9. For a discussion of the origins and ideological orientation of the Reform Party, see Tom Flanagan, *Waiting for the Wave: The Reform Party and Preston Manning* (Toronto: Stoddart, 1995); and Trevor Harrison, *Of Passionate Intensity: Right-Wing Populism and the Reform Party of Canada* (Toronto: University of Toronto Press, 1995).

10. Jeffrey Simpson, "Old Reform Wine in New Bottle Won't Sell," *The Globe and Mail,* February 22, 1999.

11. "Message for Reform: Fragments Do Not Govern," *The Globe and Mail,* February 23, 1999.

12. Bob Rae, *The Three Questions: Prosperity and the Public Good* (Toronto: Viking, 1998).

13. Thomas Walkom, "If It Walks Like a Duck ..." *The Toronto Star,* February 28, 1999: D25.

14. Gabriel Almond and Sidney Verba, *The Civic Culture* (Princeton: Princeton University Press, 1963).

15. The distinction between citizen and subject was first discussed by Jean Jacques Rousseau in *The Social Contract,* trans. W. Kendall (Chicago: Henry Regnery, 1954). Rousseau says: "The members of a body politic call it 'the state' when it is passive, 'the sovereign' when it is active, and 'a power' when they compare it with others of its kind. Collectively they use the title 'people' and they refer to one another individually as 'citizens' when speaking of their participation in the authority of the sovereign, and as 'subjects' when speaking of their subordination to the laws of the state" (p. 21).

16. Carole Pateman and many other scholars sharply criticized Almond and Verba's interpretation of their results. Faced with evidence that large numbers of Americans were apathetic, and that apathy correlated highly with low socioeconomic status, Almond and Verba counselled complacency, apparently in the belief that modern democracy requires apathy to ensure stability. This viewpoint left Almond and Verba (and others who shared their outlook) unprepared for the "participation explosion" that erupted in the United States in the late 1960s. See Pateman's "Political Culture, Political Structure and Political Change," *British Journal of Political Science* 1, no. 3 (July 1971): 291–306.

17. For an insightful, constructive critique of the use of polling and surveys, see F.J. Fletcher, "Polling and Political Communication: Lessons from the Canadian Case," conference paper available from *International Association for Mass Communication Research,* 1990.

18. See, among others, Ole Holsti, "The 'Operational Code' Approach to the Study of Political Leaders: John Foster Dulles's Philosophical Beliefs," *Canadian Journal of Political Science* 3 (1971).

19. For a discussion of "ethos theory," see Edward Banfield and James Q. Wilson, *City Politics* (New York: Vintage Books, 1963).

20. Quoted by Carl Berger, "The True North Strong and Free," in Peter Russell, ed., *Nationalism in Canada* (Toronto: McGraw-Hill, 1966), p. 6.

21. S.M. Lipset, *Revolution and Counterrevolution* (New York: Anchor Books, 1970), p. 55.

22. By the same token, however, a number of important institutions are provincial, and they help foster and maintain a provincial outlook.

23. For a discussion on a related theme, see Jon Pammett and Jean-Luc Pepin, eds., *Political Education In Canada* (Montreal: Institute for Research on Public Policy, 1988).

24. Barrington Moore, *Social Origins of Dictatorship and Democracy* (Boston: Beacon Press, 1966), p. 486. To validate Moore's point, one need only review the history of cultural contact between whites and aboriginals in Canada. The coercion that sometimes accompanies political socialization indeed proves, as Moore argues, that cultural inertia is not inevitable. But it also shows how difficult it is to engineer cultural change. This difficulty complicated attempts to inculcate the "official" political culture in countries such as Poland and Czechoslovakia, where values from an earlier era continue to dominate. See Archie Brown and Jack Gray, eds., *Political Culture and Political Change in Communist States* (London, U.K.: Macmillan, 1977). To some extent, the collapse of communist regimes in the former Soviet Union and Eastern Europe is testimony to the strength of national political cultures, even in the face of determined policies of cultural transformation pursued relentlessly by the communist governments that controlled these countries for decades.

25. Louis Hartz et al., *The Founding of New Societies* (New York: Harcourt Brace, 1964). Hartz is well aware that the so-called founding groups in all cases impose themselves on a society already in place. His work discusses the interaction between the "fragments" and aboriginal groups that truly constitute the "first nations."

26. Lipset, *Revolution and Counterrevolution*. See also Lipset, *Continental Divide*.

27. See especially Gad Horowitz, *Canadian Labour in Politics* (Toronto: University of Toronto Press, 1967).

28. See, for example, the following works by Harold Innis: *Canadian Economic History* (Toronto: University of Toronto Press, 1956); *The Fur Trade in Canada*, rev. ed. (Toronto: University of Toronto Press, 1970); and *Empire and Communications*, rev. by Mary Q. Innis (Toronto: University of Toronto Press, 1972). See also James W. Carey, "Harold Adams Innis and Marshall McLuhan," *Antioch Review* (Spring 1967); William H. Melody et al., eds., *Culture, Communication and Dependency: The Tradition of H.A. Innis* (New Jersey: Ablex Publishing, 1981); and Daniel Drache, ed., *Staples, Markets and Cultural Change* (Montreal/Kingston: McGill-Queen's University Press, 1995).

29. See David V.J. Bell, "Global Communications, Culture and Values: Implications for Global Security," in David Dewitt and John Kirton, eds., *Building a New Global Order* (Toronto: Oxford University Press, 1993).

30. Albert Johnson, *Touchstone for the CBC* (mimeo, 1977), p. 2. See also T.H.B. Symons, Commission on Canadian Studies, *The Symons Report* ([Toronto] Book and Periodical Development Council: distributed by McClelland & Stewart, 1978); John Redekop, "Continentalism: The Key to Canadian Politics," in John H. Redekop, ed., *Approaches to Canadian Politics*, 2nd ed. (Scarborough, ON: Prentice-Hall, 1983); and Keith Acheson and Christopher Maule, *Much Ado About Culture: North American Trade Disputes*, Studies in International Economics, Robert M. Stern, ed. (Ann Arbor: University of Michigan Press, 1999). Twenty-two years later, little has changed despite a revision to the Broadcasting Act (1991) that removed mention of "contributing to the development of national unity" from the CBC's mandate, and cutbacks in funding that have threatened the

CBC's viability as an agency of cultural public policy. For a discussion of these issues, see Colin Haskins and Stuart McFadyen, "The Mandate, Structure and Financing of the CBC," *Canadian Public Policy* 18 (1992); and Marc Raboy, *Missed Opportunities: The Story of Canadian Broadcasting Policy* (Montreal/Kingston: McGill-Queen's University Press, 1990). Despite the weakening of the cultural underpinnings of Canadian distinctiveness noted above, Michael Adams has analyzed survey research conducted over the past 10 years and found that Canadians and Americans exhibit significant value differences, and that these differences appear to be increasing. See Michael Adams, *Fire and Ice: The United States, Canada, and the Myth of Converging Values* (Toronto: Penguin, 2003).

31. Gary Teeple, ed., *Capitalism and the National Question* (Toronto: University of Toronto Press, 1972). For a critique, see Glen Williams, "The National Policy Tariffs: Industrial Underdevelopment through Import Substitution," *Canadian Journal of Political Science* 12 (June 1979).

32. See Neil Nevitte, *The Decline of Deference* (Peterborough: Broadview Press, 1996), pp. 15–18. The 2001 census showed the extent to which immigration continues to transform Canada. Over a fifth of the Canadian population is foreign born. In the major urban centres where most immigrants settle, the proportion is much higher. In Toronto it is nearly half (about the same as the proportion of non-whites).

33. Karl W. Deutsch, "Social Mobilization and Political Development," *American Political Science Review* 55, no. 3 (September 1961).

34. Ronald Inglehart, *The Silent Revolution: Changing Values and Political Styles among Western Publics* (Princeton, NJ: Princeton University Press, 1977), p. 3. See also Ronald Inglehart, *Modernization and Postmodernization: Cultural, Economic, and Political Change in 43 Societies* (Princeton, NJ: Princeton University Press, 1997).

35. See Nevitte, *The Decline of Deference,* particularly chaps. 3 and 9. See also Michael Adams, *Sex in the Snow: Canadian Social Values at the End of the Millennium* (Toronto: Penguin Books, 1998): "[Canadians are a] people who are assuming more personal control over their own lives and are no longer relying on others (their parents, their spouse, their boss, or the corporate, political and religious establishments) to take care of them and lead them into the future" (p. 197).

36. See Michael Adams, *Fire and Ice,* p. 52. Note also Michael Moore's striking movie, *Bowling for Columbine.*

37. An image made possible by space exploration may have contributed to this transformation. The opening paragraph of the report of the World Commission on Environment and Economy (the Brundtland Commission) reads: "In the middle of the 20th century, we saw our planet from space for the first time. Historians may eventually find that this vision had a greater impact on thought than did the Copernican revolution of the 16th century, which upset the human self-image by revealing that the Earth is not the centre of the universe. From space, we see a small and fragile ball dominated not by human activity and edifice but by a pattern of clouds, oceans, greenery and soils. Humanity's inability to fit its doings into that pattern is changing planetary systems, fundamentally. Many such changes are accompanied by life-threatening hazards. This new reality, from which there is no escape, must be recognized—and managed." *Our Common Future* (New York: Oxford University Press, 1987), p.1.

38. The sustainability paradigm may be the last best hope for the continued survival of humankind beyond the next millennium. If it is to take hold, this paradigm will require the establishment of a supportive "culture of sustainability" in all parts of the world. The blueprint for the promotion of sustainability is a 40-chapter document called *Agenda 21,*

which was approved at the Earth Summit held in Rio de Janeiro in 1992. This was the largest gathering of heads of state that has ever taken place.

39. The reference to these assertions can be found at the Commissioner of the Environment and Sustainable Development website, <http://www.oag-bvg.gc.ca/domino/cesd_cedd.nsf/html/menu2_e.html>.

FURTHER READINGS

Adams, Michael. *Fire and Ice: The United States, Canada, and the Myth of Converging Values.* (Toronto: Penguin, 2003).

Bell, David V.J. *The Roots of Disunity. A Study of Canadian Political Culture.* Toronto: Oxford University Press, 1992.

Carroll, William K., ed. *Organizing Dissent: Contemporary Social Movements in Theory and Practice.* Toronto: Garamond Press, 1992.

Clarke, Harold, and Alan Kornburg. *Citizens and Community: Political Support in a Representative Democracy.* New York: Cambridge University Press, 1992.

Drache, Daniel, ed. *The Market or the Public Domain? Global Governance and the Asymmetry of Power.* London and New York: Routledge, 2001.

Gagnon, Alain, and A. Brian Tanguay, eds. *Canadian Parties in Transition: Discourse, Organization, and Representation.* Scarborough, ON: Nelson Canada, 1988.

Hartz, Louis, et al. *The Founding of New Societies.* New York: Harcourt Brace, 1964.

Inglehart, Ronald. *Culture Shift in Advanced Industrial Society.* Princeton, NJ: Princeton University Press, 1990.

———. *Modernization and Postmodernization: Cultural, Economic, and Political Change in 43 Societies.* Princeton, NJ: Princeton University Press, 1997.

Lipset, Seymour Martin. *Continental Divide: The Values and Institutions of the United States and Canada.* New York: Routledge, 1990.

Merelman, Richard M. *Partial Visions: Culture and Politics in Britain, Canada, and the United States.* Madison, WI: University of Wisconsin Press, 1991.

Nevitte, Neil. *The Decline of Deference.* Peterborough, ON: Broadview Press, 1996.

CHAPTER 14

WOMEN AND CANADIAN POLITICS: TAKING (SOME) WOMEN'S INTERESTS INTO ACCOUNT

Sandra Burt

INTRODUCTION

Until the 1950s it was generally taken for granted by legislators that women's place was in the home—that is, women should restrict their work to caring for their families. Early laws reflected this understanding and generally placed barriers in front of those women who opted for political activity or paid employment outside the home. But by 1956, when the federal government passed a law guaranteeing women equal pay for equal work in those industries that were within its jurisdiction, the possibility that women could be useful members of the paid labour force was beginning to gain some credence. This transformation in government's perceptions was a slow one—in part at least because, both historically and today, relatively few women sit in either federal or provincial legislatures. For some years following that historic 1956 equal pay law, the federal government set up departments specifically charged with considering women's interests; enacted provisions for equal pay for work of equal value; undertook initiatives to end woman abuse; provided funding to women's groups; and constitutionally entrenched women's equality rights as well as the principle of affirmative action.

In spite of these various initiatives, women's status in Canadian society remains well below that of men on several measures. The problems are particularly acute for aboriginal women, for women who are lone parents, and for immigrant women. Furthermore, even those measures that have been enacted since the 1950s to improve women's status are in danger of being overturned by governments committed less and less to a women's agenda. In addition, many of the reforms enacted in the past 50 years have failed to take into account the differences among women because of their race, socioeconomic status, age, geographic location, and sexual orientation. It is not possible in this brief overview to explore the significance of all of these differences, but it is argued that we need to recognize that people living and working within the Canadian state are differentiated in their claims in part by their gender, racial, and other locations (see Chapter 15). Equally important, we need to recognize that policymakers' understanding of needs and selection of priorities are affected also by their various sociopolitical and historical locations.

This chapter reviews women's claims on their political system as they have emerged in recent history, and compares these claims with policymakers' responses. The review is illuminated by a closer look at three policy areas that have been significant for women's lives: equality rights, employment laws, and policy responses to woman abuse. Each of these areas offers particular insights into the gendered state of Canadian politics. When considered together, they reveal some of the patterns in Canadian politics. The review begins with a consideration of some of the various ways in which women's political interests have been conceptualized.

DEFINING WOMEN'S INTERESTS

The nature of the policies made for women will take on the shape of policymakers' understanding of women's needs. To some extent that understanding is framed by taken-for-granted assumptions about appropriate gender roles. Over the years, these assumptions have been challenged by a variety of factors, including women's political activism and changes in the shape of the female universe in Canada. Some aspects of that universe have not altered much over the years but have until recently remained invisible to policymakers. For example, aboriginal women have always been part of that universe, but have not been acknowledged politically in the past and continue to struggle for recognition. At a recent roundtable discussion sponsored by Status of Women Canada, aboriginal women expressed again their frustration with the federal government's failure to acknowledge their organizations as legitimate and equal to other national organizations.[1]

Historically, women's claims on the political system were made by women's groups that formed in one wave in the late nineteenth and early twentieth centuries, and in a second wave in the mid-1900s. The nature and number of these groups have changed significantly over the years. The earliest groups were primarily religious organizations dedicated to issues of public health and safety. By the 1960s, these and newer groups had shifted to an economic platform. For the next decade the national women's groups in Canada, such as the National Action Committee on the Status of Women (NAC) and the National Council of Women of Canada (NCWC), focused primarily on economic equality claims. But by the end of the 1970s, the emphasis had shifted once again, to broader claims for publicly funded childcare, peace, aboriginal women's rights, improved social services for single parents, reproductive freedom, and measures to end rape and domestic violence. When the Liberal government ended public funding for women's groups in the 1990s, the voices of these organizations became more muted and their presence became much less apparent in federal policymaking circles. Other factors, including the increasing diversity of Canadian women, also contributed to the declining strength of some of the national organizations. Women's groups today are much more fragmented, and also more diverse in their goals.

However, while the power of the women's lobby has been in decline in recent years, support among women for publicly funded social programs has remained strong. By the late 1980s, "polls showed a consistent [gender] gap whereby females were more supportive of social welfare spending, less inclined to endorse the use of military force, and less approving of free trade policies."[2] More recently, Joanna Everitt has found that responses to the 1997 Canadian Election Study indicate that "next to a strong sympathy for the welfare state, gender is one of the most important variables influencing the level of priority given to social welfare issues." For example, in that 1997 survey 29 percent of women, compared to only 10 percent of men, selected social issues as the most important ones in the campaign.[3] However, as Canada became firmly committed to a neoliberal agenda in the 1980s, policymakers were moving away from social programs and losing their commitment to women's programs.

POLICY FRAMES

Governments are continually making choices among competing options, and the resulting policy decisions reflect their particular understanding, or representation, of an issue. As Carol Bacchi notes, this can have important policy consequences. For example, "describing racism as the product of individual prejudice provides little leverage to challenge structural discrimination."[4] Constructing the problem of women's inequality as a need to create a situation where women will have working conditions equal to those of men (the federal government's construction of the issue), is quite different from thinking about the problems of women's equality as one of challenging the underlying structures of current employment situations (many women's understanding of the issue).

In the 1970s when the federal government began to take note of what it termed "women's issues," it worked on the assumption that women should be given greater opportunity to achieve formal equality with men. It set up a complex network of government agencies charged in various ways with the responsibility to "equalize opportunities and ensure progress through a series of specific changes to government legislation, policies, and programs."[5] In this early period, the federal government was interested only in extending formal legal equality to women. For example, in 1979 the Liberal federal government issued its first formal plan of action for women following the release in 1970 of the Report of the Royal Commission on the Status of Women. The authors of that plan wrote generally about the need to help women achieve economic independence and targeted five specific areas of policy concern: rape, wife battering, sexual harassment, women in the media, and pensions.[6]

Missing from the list were other demands of women's groups that would move the government into the area of *substantive equality* (an understanding of equality that would take women's differences into account). These other demands included affirmative-action strategies for the labour force, pay equity, and accessible, affordable childcare (for without a safe place to leave one's children during working hours, economic independence could not become a reality for most Canadian women). Also neglected was the problem of the "feminization of poverty," already well underway in 1979, in which the incomes of women heads of households are disproportionately below the poverty line.

The federal government limited most of its policy initiatives to obtaining formal *legal equality* for women. The chronology of developments prepared at the beginning of its 1983 plan of action, *Towards Equality for Women,* lists the legal barriers broken by Canadian women in the period leading up to the publication of that report. For example, the authors noted that in 1929 the British Privy Council declared that women were "persons" in the legal sense and therefore eligible for appointment to the Canadian Senate. In 1955, marriage restrictions on women working in the federal public service were removed, and in 1961 the federal Parliament passed the Canadian Bill of Rights, which included a provision guaranteeing the equal application of laws to Canadian women and men.

These changes were introduced by governments committed to the principle that women should have equal access to the paid labour force and to political participation. Such an approach is embedded in an understanding of women's interests that draws on the already established norms and patterns that have taken hold in Western liberal democratic societies during and after the Industrial Revolution. These norms and practices have been variously called paternal, patriarchal, or fraternal.[7] They are based on the concept of *separate spheres*, where the public sphere of paid labour and politics is the exclusive preserve of men, and women are restricted to the private sphere of the family. It was always an unequal relationship, since the laws generally reinforced men's financial and legal power over women, even in the private sphere, since men alone could own property and exercise legal authority in the household.

When capitalism emerged in the seventeenth century, the liberal political theorists who began to write about the capitalist state developed a set of guidelines for the new liberal states that took for granted, first, that employment "was a means through which able-bodied men would gain their livelihood"[8] and, second, that state–citizen relations should adhere to Aristotelian principles that assign women to the private, and men to the public, sphere. This has meant that when women were admitted gradually to the public sphere, most visibly since the 1970s and later, their new rights were simply added on to a set of norms and practices designed for and by men. We can see the long-term effect of this framing of gender relations in, for example, the structures of legislative assemblies. In a recent study of female legislators in Ontario, the women interviewed referred to the physical inadequacies of the legislative assembly, including too few washrooms and desks that were too large. Some commented as well on the confrontational style of parliamentary discussion, noting that sexist language, noisy debates, and the hurling of insults made it difficult for them to function effectively in the legislature.[9]

When the Liberal government of Pierre Trudeau first took office federally in 1968, it appeared to offer the promise of a different framing of policy, one that moved away from the notion of equality as sameness to equality as rewarding people equally even when they have different attributes and skills. The Liberals' creation in the 1970s of a Ministry Responsible for the Status of Women, with the bureaucratic support of Status of Women Canada, offered the possibility that the federal government would begin to take women's interests into account from new perspectives developed by and for women. Status of Women was only part of a fairly extensive network of senior advisers that included an Advisory Council, as well as a Women's Program[10] whose responsibility was to make policy recommendations to the government on so-called women's issues. Despite the fact that some of the women working in this network were feminists who had strong links with women's movement activism, for the most part this network had little impact and the promise of difference was not realized. This has been the case in other countries as well, where women who tried to work within the state have concluded that feminists who have tried to alter existing state practices and patterns of policy were themselves absorbed into the dominant male culture.[11]

Certainly this network of women's advisers failed to deter governments elected in the 1980s from adopting the politics of neoliberalism, a philosophical approach that is at odds with most of the claims advanced by women. Since 1984, the ideological context within which women's interests have been constructed by the Canadian state, whether by women or men in legislatures, has been one of deficit cutting, efficiency, privatization, deregulation, globalization, free trade, and self-reliance (see Chapter 10).

Since the mid-1980s federal governments have been pulling back from social programs, transferring more responsibilities and fewer dollars to the provinces, and focusing increasingly on deficit reduction. One of the most significant developments for women in the 1990s was the demise in 1995 of the Canada Assistance Plan (CAP), which had provided funding dollars for women's movement claims throughout the 1990s. But the federal Liberal government cancelled CAP in 1996 and replaced it with a Canada Health and Social Transfer (CHST) that gives the provinces much more flexibility to decide how the now reduced federal transfer payments will be spent. This has resulted in the erosion of national standards for health and welfare and the removal of programs such as stable funding for women's shelters. Also disadvantaged by the CHST are women with disabilities, who are finding that they have reduced access to home-care services and community hospitals, as well as experiencing staff and program cuts in institutional settings.[12]

Successive federal governments' emphasis on economic growth through self-reliance, individual initiative, and productive jobs has contributed to the view (at least within government rhetoric) that Canadians should embrace the concept of economic citizenship—that is, the necessity to obtain and keep a "good" (that is, a technologically mature and productive) form of employment in order to be a full citizen. Yet, at the same time, the government has pulled back from child-care initiatives, funding for job training, and affirmative-action programs. These policy choices have worked against the interests of many Canadian women, and have occurred in spite of the government's adoption in 1995 of what it calls a gender-based strategy for policy development. The government claims that it has committed itself to the use of gender-sensitive language, gender-disaggregated data (when appropriate), the development of progress indicators, and training of its bureaucrats to carry out gender-based analysis.[13]

Gender-based analysis (GBA) has some potential to uncover the different impact of policies on women and men. The Women's Bureau developed a *Gender-Based Analysis Guide* in 1997, and some departments (Justice, the Canadian International Development Agency, Indian Affairs and Northern Development) have created sector-specific guidelines for applying GBA to policy development. GBA is intended to bring the particular needs of women directly into mainstream policy discussions at an early stage. However, the implementation of GBA has been hindered by a variety of factors. The emphasis continues to be on research rather than action, and there are few signs that the gender lens has made much of a difference to the policy frames adopted by the federal government. One of the difficulties is that the federal bureaucracy continues to be dominated by men. Although 52 percent of federal public servants in 2003 are women, only 23 percent of senior officers are women (still a big improvement from less than 1 percent in 1967). While a gender perspective that takes women into account is not an exclusive female preserve, there is evidence that a traditional male approach that is based on a competitive management style is still predominant.[14]

Nevertheless, there have been some GBA successes as well. The Department of Justice and Health Canada have been the most proactive, and Justice now uses GBA in policy development and program evaluation. In 2000, GBA was applied to the revised (1994) employment insurance guidelines, to make the program more accessible to women. The new regulations also make it possible for parents to work part-time while they claim some benefits.[15] Statistics Canada reports that the new guidelines for parental leave, which allow either parent to claim paid leave for up to one year, have had a significant social impact. In 2000, only 3 percent of fathers claimed this leave, but by 2001 the proportion had increased dramatically to 10 percent. The future success of GBA is heavily dependent on the ability of government departments to understand and implement the guidelines. And it must be remembered the GBA always operates within the general blueprint of government policy. As long as that blueprint is focused on neoliberal values, many of the planks of a women's agenda will remain outside the policy cycle.

THE POLICYMAKERS

Even since the 1970s and the emergence of the second wave of Canadian women's movements, there have been few women, and even fewer feminist women, making policy decisions in government. This is significant, for recent research has shown that there are gendered connections between policymakers and policy content that extend beyond the ideological flavour of the party in power. Linda Trimble and Jane Arscott review the successes and failures of women's participation in electoral politics in Canada, and they conclude that women remain seriously underrepresented in top legislative jobs. "These social facts present a public policy problem because they provide consistent and damning evidence of a gendered democratic deficit that reproduces systemic bias...."[16]

We know that feminist women in legislative assemblies can make a difference. Even in the first half of the twentieth century when women regularly constituted less than 1 percent of the elected federal members, those isolated few often articulated a politics of difference in legislative debates.[17] More recently, women in legislatures have pressured for a different style of representation: less confrontation in legislative debates, more streamlined committees, the removal of discriminatory language in parliamentary discourse, and greater concern for consensus-building among legislators. But with a glass ceiling of about 20 percent of women in the governing party at the federal level, it is difficult to imagine a future in which women's views are counted in.

In the 2000 federal election, 39 female Liberals were elected, or 23 percent of their total elected members. Historically, the conventional wisdom suggested that electing 23 percent of women was a critical mass, sufficient for making a difference in a party's agenda. But as Lisa Young notes, 1993 marked a turning away of the Liberal Party from women's issues, and even the presence of a so-called critical mass could not halt this process. It occurred in part because there was a general shift to the right in national party politics, with the NDP and Conservatives losing ground. Reform, later the Canadian Alliance, with its antifeminist agenda, took up their space on the political spectrum. At the same time, women's groups were increasingly turning away from electoral politics. Although the Liberals appealed to women voters in the 2000 campaign, with a specific reference to a pro-choice stance, the party has not followed through with action on issues that are significant for Canadian women.[18]

It should be noted as well that female legislators' positions on policy issues are mediated by factors such as personal beliefs, particularly their views of feminism; party allegiance; the strength of party competition in the legislature; the support they receive from women outside the legislature; and the overarching framework for policy decisions at the time of their election. For example, Kim Campbell, a self-proclaimed feminist, a Cabinet member in the Progressive Conservative government of Brian Mulroney, and, for a short time in 1993, the prime minister, did little to advance women's interests because her feminism was embedded in a neoliberal political agenda, because she had little support from women's movements across the country, and because she was surrounded by antifeminist forces within her own party.

Nevertheless, studies of legislative changes have revealed that women sitting in legislative positions can make a difference. Federally, for example, even the "pro-family" stance of the ruling Progressive Conservative Party could not keep Barbara McDougall from speaking out in the House of Commons in support of freedom of choice on the abortion question. She called on women's individual intellect and spirit in the struggle to deal with the abortion question, arguing that "women make the right choice, a far better choice than you or I or all the pageantry of institutions that have been invented."[19] Much earlier, women like Agnes Macphail and Grace MacInnis helped to break down existing stereotypes of women's appropriate roles. Grace MacInnis was particularly instrumental in winning maternity leave legislation for women in 1970, and in pressuring the minority Liberal government of Lester Pearson to set up the Royal Commission on the Status of Women.

Provincially, the record of female legislators is just as impressive. Irene Parlby, representing the United Farmers of Alberta in the government they formed in 1921, worked in the Alberta legislature to obtain a minimum wage for women, property rights for married women, and mothers' allowances.[20] A recent study of the significance of female legislators in contemporary Alberta politics concludes that women have been more likely to engage in debates on the basis of their issue positions than on their partisan identification in the legislature. Opposition women in particular are prepared to work across party lines.[21]

For the most part, however, determining women's interests still remains the prerogative of men in Canada's legislative assemblies. Federally, for example, although women's presence in the House of Commons has increased over time, from one woman (Agnes Macphail, in the 1921 legislature) to 21 percent in 2000, there is evidence that the numbers are no longer increasing. Provincially, women's representation currently ranges from 5 percent in Nunavut to 25 percent in Manitoba. And as Linda Trimble and Jane Arscott note, "Most Canadian political parties assume that more representation for women—up to 25 per cent of candidates and seats—is good enough."[22]

TAKING WOMEN'S INTERESTS INTO ACCOUNT

A consideration of three policy areas—employment laws, woman abuse, and equality rights—illustrates how governments have configured women's interests, both historically and today, and brings some of the points noted above into sharper focus.

EMPLOYMENT LAWS

Women have always worked, but that work had no public "value" until it became something that could be counted into economic productivity and measured by a wage. Even today, women in dual-income households where there are young children spend about 72 percent more time on childcare than their male partners.[23] But this work that women do in the home is not taken into account when the country evaluates its national productivity and its place in the international economic order.

The issue here is one of difference. Since the onset of the Industrial Revolution, women and men have had different working lives. The difference was most pronounced in the nineteenth century, when women were theoretically if not always in reality restricted to childbearing, child rearing, and caring for their husbands. The difference worked its way into women's lives in the first half of the twentieth century, when the exigencies of running wartime economies convinced legislators that women were needed in the public world of commerce and industrial labour. The practice of segregating jobs by sex was well entrenched by the time women moved in large numbers into the paid labour force. Newspapers published separate help wanted ads for women and men, and it was generally assumed that women's paid employment was a temporary phenomenon in their lives. By 1928 women were earning on average only 39 percent of what men were earning and, at least until the end of World War II, the popular image of the contented housewife framed governments' labour policies.

By the end of World War I, organizations representing women engaged in waged labour began to challenge this perception of women as primarily domestic workers. They demanded equal access for women into the world of waged labour. Without the pressure exerted by strong women's groups such as the Federation of Women Teachers or the Young Women's Christian Association, it is unlikely that governments in Canada would have introduced, beginning in 1956, a series of legislative measures intended to reduce, if not remove, the practice of segregating the labour force.

The first legislative initiative was narrow in focus, for it guaranteed women equal pay for carrying out the same work as men. The story of how that first equal-pay law was implemented underlines the limits of the government's early commitment to change. Marion Royce, appointed in 1954 as the first director of the Women's Bureau in the Department of Labour, was asked to chair a committee to investigate the issue of equal pay for women. Her committee recommended that the federal government undertake an inquiry to determine why women were earning less than men. The government refused and, ignoring the committee's report, set up a new committee with a different chair and passed its limited legislation guaranteeing equal pay for the same work.

Subsequently, the government moved slowly to expand its position. By 1971, the equal-pay provision was moved to the Canada Labour Code, a provision was added to the Unemployment Insurance Act to prohibit discrimination on the grounds of sex and marital status when referring a worker seeking employment, and the Unemployment Insurance Act was amended to include 15 weeks of benefits to women in the event of maternity. One year later, the government amended the Canada Labour Code to prohibit discrimination on the grounds of sex, marital status, or age.

Thus, two principles were slowly emerging in the legislative initiatives of Canadian governments in the 1970s: equal access to waged labour and equal pay. Equal-access strategies were first labelled "affirmative action" and later "employment equity." Affirmative-action policies at both federal and provincial levels have called for the removal of structural obstacles that could restrict women's access to the public sphere, and, throughout the 1980s, both levels of government passed some affirmative-action laws. These laws fall short of establishing quotas but do encourage the hiring or promotion of female candidates who have the same qualifications as male applicants.

Federal policy initiatives have also included some limited and voluntary affirmative-action measures for the federal public service and large companies doing business with the federal government. In 1986, the federal government passed the Employment Equity Act and the Federal Contractors Program, both of which were revised in 1995. These laws require employers covered by the legislation to report data on the representativeness of their work force with respect to women, aboriginal persons, people with disabilities, and racial minorities. "Employers are subject to compliance audits, and the reports of employers covered under the Act are available to the public and to the Canadian Human Rights Commission, which has the power to file and adjudicate complaints of systemic discrimination."[24]

However, the results of such initiatives have been disappointing, particularly for women who are aboriginal, or disabled, or members of racial minorities. The laws contain no compliance mechanisms, only reporting requirements. Also, while legislation can address systemic discrimination, it is difficult to change discriminatory popular attitudes. One study that examined the situation of aboriginal people working in the 370 federally regulated companies covered by the Employment Equity Act found that in 1987, members of the four designated groups made up 49 percent of the work force in those companies. By 1995, this proportion had increased to only 57 percent.[25]

There is also evidence that employers are trying to move away from employment equity strategies. Shortly after its election in 1995, the

Conservative government of Mike Harris in Ontario quickly removed the 1993 legislation of its NDP predecessor, which had imposed tougher employment equity measures (but still fell far short of imposing hiring quotas) on provincially regulated employers. Both public- and private-sector employers have increasingly been using the language of "managing diversity" rather than employment equity in their workplace strategies. From a gendered perspective, managing diversity is a step backward for it incorrectly assumes that gender segregation in the labour force has already been removed.

Pay equity laws, based on the principle of similar rewards for work of similar value, have also become more common, with five provinces (Manitoba, Ontario, Nova Scotia, Prince Edward Island, and New Brunswick) passing different versions of such laws between 1985 and 1989. These laws differ from earlier equal-pay provisions in two important respects. First, they place the responsibility for ensuring equal pay for women on the employer rather than on the female employee. This is particularly important in view of women's historical record of insecurity in the labour market. Second, they take into account the fact that women and men are not always in the same or similar occupations but may be carrying out equally valuable jobs. And, finally, while the federal government has reduced its commitment to providing affordable, accessible childcare (in particular between 1986 and 1993 when privatization and family values highlighted the federal Conservative agenda), new union agreements in the automobile industry suggest that unions may take more responsibility for this issue in the future. Pay equity legislation means that, for the first time, women's jobs are compared with men's in the same establishment on the basis of criteria such as qualifications required, responsibilities involved, and the nature of the duties performed. Only female job classes (that is, jobs in which 60 to 70 percent of the holders are female) qualify for assessment.

Although the Ontario Conservative government has reduced the amount of money available for pay equity settlements for public employees, that province's pay equity legislation is still the most progressive, since it applies to both private and public employees. Ontario "permits a job class to contain only one person, while Manitoba's, Nova Scotia's, and New Brunswick's legislations require that there be ten people before a group of positions can be a job class, and thus qualify to be involved in the pay equity exercise."[26] However, even Ontario's legislation reveals the limits of state action on issues affecting women. Sue Findlay, a former consultant to the Pay Equity Commission in Ontario observes that almost one-half of the women in workplaces covered by the act cannot

claim pay equity adjustments under it. Women for whom there is no comparative male group in the same workplace are excluded, and although
special provision was made for women in this situation in the early
drafting of the Ontario law, subsequent policy directives have not cor-
rected the problem. Section 33 of the Ontario legislation includes the proviso that the Pay Equity Office conduct a study of the problem and make
recommendations within one year of the commencement of the program.
Findlay concludes that institutional and structural constraints have
retarded action:

> In the struggle to define ways for women in predominantly female
> establishments to achieve pay equity adjustments, it was clear that our
> reforms were shaped in three major ways: one, by the balance of
> power at the political level where public issues are translated into
> political commitments; two, by the presentation of our interests in the
> policy-making processes of the state bureaucracy where the imple-
> mentation of these commitments is organized; and three, by the insti-
> tutionalization of our own political practices as we participated in
> these processes.[27]

Other observers have also concluded that the Ontario legislation will
do little to reduce the wage gap between women and men. Indeed, in 1991,
Ontario women working full-time for a full year were still earning only
69.8 percent of what men were earning. Furthermore, women who see
their wages increase minimally as a result of the legislation "will be told
that they now have 'pay equity' and will, therefore, have no recourse but to
engage in undoubtedly lengthy and expensive litigation over the issue of
gender neutrality."[28]

Furthermore, there are indications that in the 1990s governments
began pulling away from pay equity strategies. In 1998 the Canadian
Human Rights Tribunal ruled that the federal government had been
paying too little to 200 000 employees working in female-dominated jobs
for the previous 13 years. The federal government balked at the $4 billion
cost involved in compliance with the ruling and unsuccessfully appealed
the decision to the Federal Court. Even more serious problems arise when
governments adopt economic strategies such as free trade that obviously
fail to take women's needs into account. In 1993 the Ontario NDP government prepared a study of the impact of the North American Free Trade
Agreement (NAFTA) on women. The authors of the study note women's
vulnerability to the effects of NAFTA and conclude that "the cumulative
and indirect effects of the agreement will likely result in greater economic
inequality for women."[29] They estimate that the earlier (1989) Free Trade

Agreement contributed to the loss of 55 000 jobs for women in the manufacturing sector, and that the disproportionate effect of NAFTA on women will be even greater.[30]

Today we have a much better sense of what is needed to create a fairer world for women, even within the context of the equal-opportunity principle. Women's labour-force participation patterns demonstrate clearly the areas of need for women seeking access to, or appropriate remuneration for, participation in the work world. Since 1951, when the Women's Bureau in the federal Department of Labour first began publishing its annual report on women in the labour force, women's participation rate had jumped from 24 percent to 53.4 percent in 1988. Even more dramatic is the increase in the proportion of "working wives": from 11 percent in 1951 to 59 percent in 1988. And in 1988, "about two-thirds (65.9 percent) of women whose children were under 13 years of age participated in the labour force."[31] In spite of affirmative-action programs at both levels of government, women remain concentrated in five occupational groups: clerical, medical health, teaching, social sciences, and service.[32] The barriers facing immigrant and visible-minority women are even more severe.

The work force is still highly segregated by gender, although participation rates in 2002 were similar (61 percent for women and 73 percent for men). In addition, while women's participation in full-time employment has increased, so too has their involvement in the part-time economy. In 2003, 28 percent of women in the paid labour force were working part-time, compared to 11 percent of men. The percentage of women in the unemployed work force has also increased, to 46 percent in 1989 (although at the time women made up only 44 percent of the total labour force).[33] One comprehensive review of the special problems of immigrant women concludes that for essentially "unskilled and dead-end" jobs these women "must have a variety of general, interchangeable skills that they have developed from housekeeping and childrearing." The jobs are short-term and insecure, with irregular and long working hours, and few labour standard protections.[34]

WOMAN ABUSE

At the same time as governments have been moving away from strategies that take women's interests into account in the public sphere, they have also been retreating from programs that could assist in the resolution of problems in the home. A review of government policies on woman abuse makes this clear. Woman abuse has always been a problem and one that has been located primarily within the private sphere of the home, although its causes and effects are certainly linked to the public sphere. While woman abuse in the past was generally not considered by legislators to be part of their policy agenda, in the 1970s women active in the second wave of women's movements in Canada began to urge governments to take action. In particular, they wanted financial support for women's shelters. The federal government did provide some money for such shelters beginning in 1973, through project funding administered by the Women's Program in the Secretary of State. By 1979 there were 71 shelters across Canada, many of which relied on per diem funding from provincial governments, as well as building, counselling, and special project funding from the federal government. The system wasn't perfect, but it did provide basic shelter and emotional support for some abused women. By 1984 the federal government also had a mandatory charging policy for persons accused of domestic abuse.

At about this time, the federal government shifted its focus from wife abuse to family violence, and set up a National Clearinghouse on Family Violence, located within the Department of Health and Welfare. In 1988, it launched a four-year Family Violence Initiative that was to act as a coordinating unit to bring together the various federal departments concerned with issues of family violence. In response to the December 6, 1989, murder of 14 women at the Université de Montréal's École Polytechnique, the federal Conservative government designated December 6 as a national day of mourning. It also set up five new research centres, each of which would receive an annual operating grant of $100 000 for five years to research violence against women and children.

These initiatives were criticized by frontline workers in women's shelters as minimalist strategies that failed to deal with the systemic bases of violence against women. They argued for an integrated approach that would both provide help for women already in difficulty and develop economic initiatives to remove the cycle of violence. This would include economic programs to help further women's financial independence, as well as counselling and treatment programs that would take abused women's race, age, and geographic location into account.

However, in the early years of the twenty-first century, governments have moved toward a law-and-order strategy of punishing current offenders. Recent initiatives have included gun control legislation, strengthening of anti-stalking laws, and stronger legal procedures to deal with dangerous offenders. The federal operating grants for the research centres ended in 1996; the Family Violence Initiative in Health Canada lives from year to year on a significantly reduced budget ($7 million in 1997); and federal funding for shelters has almost disappeared with the demise of the Canada Assistance Plan.[35]

In 1993 Statistics Canada surveyed 12 300 women, 18 years and older, in the first national survey on violence against women. These women were asked about their experiences of physical and sexual violence since the age of 16. On the basis of the survey findings, the authors concluded that 29 percent of Canadian women who have been married to or have lived with a man have been physically assaulted by that man. The most prevalent forms of physical assault were pushing, grabbing, and shoving, followed by threats, slapping, throwing objects, kicking, biting, and hitting with fists. In addition, 35 percent of the women interviewed reported emotional abuse from a partner.[36]

The research contains several tentative conclusions. First, woman abuse is widespread, and has different causes than violence against children, men, and older people. Also, women are at greater risk of abuse than are men. Second, a crime control strategy is ineffective, in part because few women are prepared to report their partners to the police for many reasons, including fear of further violence. Third, services must be maintained for women who have been abused. Finally, a community-based strategy of prevention is essential for reducing the problem. Unfortunately, none of these conclusions informs current federal or provincial policies on woman abuse.

EQUALITY RIGHTS

While governments have clearly been pulling back from legislative initiatives first introduced in the late 1970s and early 1980s that had, within the limits of equal opportunity, improved women's prospects for safety in the home and enhanced their employment prospects, the federal government has not yet pulled away so dramatically from what we might call equality rights (although it includes human rights issues as well). This is due primarily to the power of the 1982 Charter of Rights and Freedoms, and the influence of the courts.

In many important respects the legal status of women in Canada has changed significantly since the start of the twentieth century, and in particular since the report of the Royal Commission on the Status of Women was tabled in Parliament in 1970. The most dramatic improvement came from sections 15 and 28 of the Canadian Charter of Rights and Freedoms. According to the Charter, Canadian women and men are equal before and under the law. The Charter equality guarantees replaced the 1960 provision in the Canadian Bill of Rights that simply instructed the courts to apply all Canadian laws equally to women and men without imposing any restrictions on discriminatory provisions within such laws. The 1982 provisions, included in response to women's strong lobbying efforts in 1980 and 1981, have had a profound impact on some women's lives (see Chapter 11).

In 1981, when the federal Liberal government introduced its Constitution Bill in an ongoing effort to patriate the British North America Act and provide Canadians with constitutionally entrenched rights, Canadian feminists who were part of the organized women's movement became mobilized around the equal-rights issue for the first time in their history. Before 1981 they had concentrated on winning specific legislative reforms such as equal pay for work of equal value, affordable and accessible childcare, abortion on demand, and improved access to all sectors of the labour market. But the possibility of a constitutionally entrenched declaration of rights that might exclude women mobilized some of the older groups, and gave rise to the creation of some new ones, to ensure that women were well represented at the bargaining table.

After a mass rally of women on Parliament Hill in 1981, members of the newly created Ad Hoc Committee on the Constitution and the somewhat older (1974) National Association of Women and the Law (NAWL) negotiated with Jean Chrétien, then Minister of Justice in the Liberal government of Pierre Trudeau, for meaningful legal equality clauses in the Charter. Women's demands were based on the resolutions passed at that 1981 rally. Most of the women who participated in the lobbying process were elated with their successes. They were convinced that the revised Charter would improve women's access to substantive equality with men, allow for the creation of affirmative-action programs as necessary, and make it impossible for provincial governments to override the sex-equality provisions. One activist expressed her enthusiastic response to the process in these terms: "This process has strengthened the idea that women can move and they can be heard. They can be taken seriously. Women's groups feel that they are more powerful now, they are bolder and more confident. The government has recognized that women are a significant force."[37]

The constitutional entrenchment of equality rights for women resulted in the creation in 1985 of another new group, the Women's Legal Education and Action Fund (LEAF), composed primarily of feminist lawyers and human rights professionals. LEAF sponsors selected cases involving women's rights and at the same time engages in the process of legal education and legislative lobbying.[38] LEAF's emergence marked a new reliance by some women's groups (in particular the National Action Committee on the Status of Women and the Canadian Abortion Rights Action League) on advice from feminist legal experts. In the tradition of the wording of the sex-equality clause in the Charter, LEAF has tried to pressure the courts to think in terms of substantive rather than formal equality. Beverley Baines summarizes the distinction between these two interpretations of equality rights this way:

"Formal equality" is simply another name for the Aristotelian theory of equality, the theory that assumes equality is achieved when the law treats likes alike. Sometimes it is appropriate for the law to treat women and men as alike or formally equal—the right to vote being a prime example. However, since women and men are not identically situated much of the time, mostly "the formal equality model breaks down; in fact, it is inherently discriminatory." Formal equality is inadequate because it fails to encompass or even to acknowledge that "Women's conditions are worse than men's: they are disadvantaged, exploited, degraded, and brutalized."[39]

LEAF's second and related goal has been to convince the courts to listen to women's stories—to develop a contextual understanding of court cases as they relate to women, and place women's equality claims within the context of their past experiences as a subjugated group.

The equality provisions of the Charter did not take effect until 1985. A 1989 review of the first three years of Charter litigation concluded that the Charter had not been of much help to women because the courts were basing their decisions on a formal rather than a substantive interpretation of equality rights. As well, equal-rights provisions were used more frequently by men than by women, and primarily in child custody cases. In other words, the equal-rights clause in the Charter was working against rather than for women's interests, with the result that more men than ever were winning child custody cases. The problem lay in the fact that the courts were treating women and men as if they were "the same" and failing to take into account women's historical and current social and economic disadvantages.[40]

Throughout the 1990s the Supreme Court showed some signs that it was prepared to adopt a broader definition of equality rights in its rulings, whether or not the Charter was involved. There may be cause for qualified optimism about the potential for more decisions based on a vision of substantive equality in some Supreme Court decisions that have not been based on the Charter. In the *Brooks* case of 1989, the Supreme Court took the position that discrimination on the basis of pregnancy could be sex discrimination, and thus recognized that one of the characteristics that makes women different from men (pregnancy) could impose unfair costs on women only. In the *Lavallee* case of 1990, the Court was willing to take into account a woman's history of battering when assessing her action of shooting her partner in the back. But optimism about the legal possibilities of court action must be tempered by the observation that "in the context of the Charter it is impossible to ignore the Supreme Court's record of avoidance when the sex-equality provisions are invoked."[41]

In some cases, the courts and the legislatures have influenced each other. In 1991, the Supreme Court nullified section 276 of the Criminal

Code, which had removed the right of an accused rapist to introduce the alleged victim's sexual history as evidence in the case. Then, in 1995, the Court allowed the use of complainants' personal records in two cases of alleged sexual assault. Once again, in 1997, in the case of Nick Carosella, the judges declared (by a 5–4 margin) that "Carosella was denied a fair trial because the rape crisis centre where the complainant in the case sought advice had shredded the interview notes."[42] Parliament responded by introducing a measure to limit the use of counselling records in cases of sexual assault. In *R. v. Daviault* (1994), the Supreme Court ruled that extreme drunkenness could be a defence in a case of sexual assault. Parliament responded quickly by introducing 1995 legislation to limit extreme drunkenness as a defence in violent crimes.

But in the case of gay and lesbian rights, Parliament has been less quick to respond. In 1985, a parliamentary subcommittee of the Mulroney Progressive Conservative government recommended that the government include sexual orientation in its human rights laws as a prohibited ground of discrimination. By 1993, when the Liberals came to office, no action had been taken. Finally, in 1996 the Liberals held a free vote on a Senate-initiated bill to amend the Canadian Human Rights Act to include sexual orientation. The amendment passed 153 to 76.[43] But the government took a minimalist position, and was willing to protect against only the most obvious forms of discrimination. Indeed, the Liberal government was unwilling to legislate on the issue of same-sex benefits. At one point, Alan Rock, the Minister of Justice, remarked, "We'll have to see what the courts and tribunals decide."[44]

Meanwhile, the courts were becoming much more activist in their decisions and have taken the lead on same-sex benefits. One study has shown that court decisions, combined with rulings of the Canadian Human Rights Tribunal, led the federal government to extend same-sex benefits to its employees. "Like their Tory predecessors, the Liberals would prefer to shield themselves from public controversy on lesbian and gay rights by either implementing policy changes incrementally, without high profile legislative change, or by passing the political hot potato to the courts."[45] And the courts have led the way on issues of human rights for gays and lesbians, and the delivery of some same-sex benefits. In other words, on politically sensitive issues the federal government has preferred to turn to the courts for reforms even when the possibilities for changes have been less certain.

The gender composition of the bench has been a factor in court decisions. Madame Justice Bertha Wilson was the first female appointee to the Supreme Court of Canada, sitting on the bench from 1982 to 1991. Madame Justice Claire L'Heureux-Dubé, a self-described feminist, was appointed in 1987, and Madame Justice Beverley McLachlin in 1989. While a gender split has not been apparent in all decisions, it was Madame Justice Wilson who articulated the issue of substantive equality rights in 1985 in *Operation Dismantle v. The Queen*. In that case she raised the question of "whether fundamental justice is entirely procedural in nature or whether it has a substantive impact as well."[46] In 1988, Madame Justice Wilson invoked the concept of substantive equality when the Supreme Court struck down Canada's abortion law. She argued that "the more recent struggle for women's rights has been a struggle to eliminate discrimination, to achieve a place for women in a man's world, to develop a set of legislative reforms in order to place women in the same position as men."[47] In the 1993 judgment on the eligibility of child-care expenses as a business deduction (*Symes v. Canada*), the two women on the bench dissented from the majority opinion and supported the request of a woman partner of a law firm who wished to deduct wages she paid to a nanny in her income tax return.

Finally, it must be noted that success in the courts does not always translate into improved conditions for the majority of those affected by the legal decisions. For example, the Supreme Court's decision in 1988 to render invalid the 1969 provision of the Criminal Code (section 251) that set out specific conditions for legal abortions was hailed by many women as a victory for choice. Section 251 restricted abortions to women who, in the view of a therapeutic abortion committee of at least three physicians, were at risk for their health through the continuation of the pregnancy. In this decision (*R. v. Morgentaler*) the Court drew on section 7 of the Charter, which guarantees "life, liberty and security of the person and the right not to be deprived thereof except in accordance with principles of fundamental justice." Because the therapeutic abortion committees required by section 251 were not available in all communities, the Court ruled that this posed a restriction on some women's right to security. In the judgment, Justice Brian Dickson wrote,

> Section 251 clearly interferes with a woman's bodily integrity in both a physical and emotional sense. Forcing a woman, by threat of criminal sanction, to carry a foetus to term unless she meets certain criteria unrelated to her own priorities and aspirations, is a profound interference with a woman's body and thus a violation of security of the person.[48]

A victory for women? One commentator draws on the American experience in sounding a note of caution. In the United States, the landmark decision in *Roe v. Wade* opened the door to legal abortions, but that decision placed no responsibility on the state "to provide safe and accessible abortions, to curb the growth of private abortion clinics whose interest is profit, to provide counselling, or pre-natal education and nutrition, and child-care after the birth of a continued pregnancy."[49] In Canada, as well, there is no evidence that the favourable court decision has resulted in greater access to abortion for those women living in remote northern or rural communities, or in cities where the majority of the physicians in residence are not prepared to offer the service. Although Prince Edward Island is the only province with no abortion services, the other provinces are not legally obliged to provide this procedure. Even in the provinces that do provide abortions, rural women are often poorly served. For example, in Alberta in 1996, 94 percent of all abortions were performed in either Calgary or Edmonton.[50]

CONCLUSION

For at least the past 30 years, feminists have been learning the difference between the process of numerically counting women into existing structures, and *gendering* those structures by re-fashioning them with women's interests in mind. The difference is one of substance as well as of process. When women are numerically counted into policies, we get programs such as affirmative action, designed to improve women's abilities to compete with men for previously defined positions in the paid labour force. Or we get woman abuse strategies that try to incarcerate offenders or provide shelter to those who have been abused. Gendering structures requires a fundamental rethinking of the meaning of work and the nature of occupations. It results in anti-violence strategies that seek to rebuild communities where violence can become anomalous rather than the norm.

Ironically, as feminists have become clearer about the need to gender Canadian politics, governments have been moving away from even counting women in numerically. In spite of the federal government's apparent commitment in 1995 to a gender-lens strategy of policy development, women today are counted in less and less often when governments are making policy choices. This is due in part to the fact that the category of "woman" has become increasingly problematic, as previously existing but historically unrecognized racial, geographic, and age differences among women are becoming more apparent. It is due as well to the fact that governments are retreating from welfare state policies, of which women have historically been the major consumers. But it is due fundamentally to the ever-increasing commitment of Canadian governments to economic citizenship and to the associated values of individual initiative and self-reliance. Within the context of this neoliberal social order, Canadian women are beginning a new century within a policy agenda that makes it increasingly unlikely that their governments will want to take their interests into account.

NOTES

1. Canada, Status of Women, *Aboriginal Women's Roundtable on Gender Equality, Roundtable Report* (Ottawa: Supply and Services, 2000), p. 8.

2. Joanna Everitt, "Gender Gaps on Social Welfare Issues: Why Do Women Care?" in Joanna Everitt and Brenda O'Neill, eds., *Citizen Politics: Research and Theory in Canadian Political Behaviour* (Don Mills: Oxford Univ. Press, 2002), p. 111.

3. Ibid., p. 114.

4. Carol Lee Bacchi, *Women, Policy and Politics: The Construction of Policy Problems* (London: Sage Publications, 1999), p. 7.

5. Canada, Status of Women, *Towards Equality for Women* (Ottawa: Minister of Supply and Services, 1983), p. 9.

6. Canada, Status of Women, *National Plan of Action for Women* (Ottawa: Supply and Services, 1983).

7. See, for example, Rosemary Pringle and Sophie Watson, "Fathers, Brothers, Mates: The Fraternal State in Australia," in Sophie Watson, ed., *Playing the State* (London: Verso, 1988), pp. 229–43.

8. Carole Pateman, "A Comment on Johnson's 'Does Capitalism Really Need Patriarchy?'" *Women's Studies International Forum* 19, no. 3 (1996): 204.

9. Sandra Burt, Alison Horton, and Kathy Martin, "Women in the Ontario New Democratic Government: Revisiting the Concept of Critical Mass," *International Review of Women and Leadership* 6, no. 1 (July 2000), pp. 1–12.

10. For more discussion of these various state instruments, see Sue Findlay, "Facing the State: The Politics of the Women's Movement Reconsidered," in Heather Jon Maroney and Meg Luxton, eds., *Feminism and Political Economy: Women's Work, Women's Struggles* (Toronto: Methuen, 1987), pp. 31–50.

11. For an excellent discussion of the literature on women and the state, see Kathy Teghtsoonian, "Gendering Policy Analysis: Women's Policy Offices and the 'Gender Lens' Strategy in British Columbia and New Zealand," paper presented at the Annual Meeting of the Canadian Political Science Association, St. John's, Newfoundland, June 8–10, 1996.

12. Shirley Masuda, "The Impact of Block Funding on Women with Disabilities," Status of Women Canada <http://www.swc-cfc.gc.ca/pubs/066263473X/index_e.html>.

13. The government's understanding of gender-based analysis is presented in Canada, Status of Women, *Setting the Stage for the Next Century: The Federal Plan for Gender Equality* (Ottawa, August 1995).

14. Gregory J. Inwood, *Understanding Canadian Public Administration*, 2nd ed. (Toronto: Pearson, Prentice Hall, 2003), pp. 280, 282.

15. For a longer discussion of the successes and failures of GBA, see Sandra Burt and Sonya Lynn Hardman, "The Case of Disappearing Targets: The Liberals and Gender Equality," in Leslie A. Pal, ed., *How Ottawa Spends 2001–2002* (Don Mills: Oxford Univ. Press, 2001), pp. 201–22.

16. Linda Trimble and Jane Arscott, *Still Counting: Women in Politics Across Canada* (Peterborough: Broadview, 2003), pp. 161–62.

17. Agnes Macphail was the first woman to be elected to the House of Commons in 1921. She represented the Co-operative Commonwealth Federation of Canada (CCF). The term "politics of difference" is the subject of an excellent book by Iris Marion Young, *Justice and the Politics of Difference* (Princeton: Princeton University Press, 1990).

18. Lisa Young, "Can Feminists Transform Party Politics? The Canadian Experience," in Manon Tremblay and Linda Trimble, eds., *Women and Electoral Politics in Canada* (Don Mills: Oxford University Press, 2003), pp. 76–90.

19. Barbara McDougall, as quoted in Janine Brodie, Shelley A.M. Gavigan, and Jane Jenson, *The Politics of Abortion* (Toronto: Oxford University Press, 1992), p. 76.

20. Alison Prentice et al., *Canadian Women: A History* (Toronto: Harcourt Brace Jovanovich, 1988), pp. 281–82.

21. Linda Trimble, "A Few Good Women: Female Legislators in Alberta 1972–1991," in Randi Warne and Cathy Cavanaugh, eds., *Standing on New Ground: Women in Alberta* (Edmonton: University of Alberta Press, 1993), pp. 87–118.

22. Linda Trimble and Jane Arscott, *Still Counting: Women in Politics Across Canada*, p. 63.

23. Warren Clark, "Economic Gender Equality Indicators 2000," Status of Women Canada, <http://www.swc-cfc.gc.ca/pubs/egei2000/index_e.html>.

24. Carol Agócs and Catherine Burr, "Employment Equity, Affirmative Action and Managing Diversity: Assessing the Differences," *International Journal of Manpower* 17, no. 4/5 (1996): 34.

25. Cora Voyageur, "Employment Equity and Aboriginal Peoples in Canada," unpublished Ph.D. dissertation, Department of Sociology, University of Alberta, 1997, p. 106.

26. Patricia McDermott, "Pay Equity in Canada: Assessing the Commitment to Reducing the Wage Gap," in Judy Fudge and Patricia McDermott, eds., *Just Wages: A Feminist Assessment of Pay Equity* (Toronto: University of Toronto Press, 1991), p. 23.

27. Sue Findlay, "Making Sense of Pay Equity: Issues for a Feminist Political Practice," in Fudge and McDermott, eds., *Just Wages*, p. 104.

28. Patricia McDermott, "Pay Equity in Canada," p. 28.

29. Ontario Women's Directorate, *The North American Free Trade Agreement: Implications for Women* (Toronto, 1993), p. 7.

30. Ibid., p. 2.

31. Canada, Department of Labour, Women's Bureau, *Adapting to a Changing Work Force*, prepared by Judith L. MacBride-King (Ottawa: Supply and Services, 1992), p. 3.

32. Canada, Department of Labour, Women's Bureau, *Women in the Labour Force* (Ottawa: Supply and Services, 1990/91), pp. 3–7.

33. National Action Committee on the Status of Women, *Our Lives: Excerpts from the Review of the Situation of Women in Canada, 1993* (Toronto, 1993).

34. Roxana Ng, "Racism, Sexism and Immigrant Women," in Sandra Burt, Lorraine Code, and Lindsay Dorney, eds., *Changing Patterns: Women in Canada*, 2nd ed. (Toronto: McClelland & Stewart, 1993), p. 289.

35. For a more complete discussion of past initiatives and current strategies, see Sandra Burt and Christine Mitchell, "What's in a Name? From Sheltering Women to Protecting Communities," in Leslie Pal, ed., *How Ottawa Spends: 1998–99* (Toronto: Oxford University Press, 1998), pp. 271–92.

36. Karen Rodgers, "Wife Assault: The Findings of a National Survey," *Juristat* 14, no. 9 (March 1994).

37. Interview with member of the Ad Hoc Committee on the Constitution, March 10, 1983.

38. For a good review of the origins and operation of LEAF, see Sherene Razack, *Canadian Feminism and the Law* (Toronto: Second Story Press, 1991).

39. Beverley Baines, "Law, Gender, Equality," in Burt et al., eds., *Changing Patterns,* p. 269, with quotations from Gwen Brodsky and Shelagh Day, *Canadian Charter Equality Rights for Women: One Step Forward or Two Steps Back?* (Ottawa: Canadian Advisory Council on the Status of Women, 1989), p. 148. Reprinted by permission of Oxford University Press Canada.

40. Brodsky and Day, eds., *Canadian Charter Equality Rights for Women.*

41. Ibid., p. 272.

42. Sylvia Bashevkin, *Women on the Defensive: Living through Conservative Times* (Toronto: University of Toronto Press, 1998), p. 227.

43. For a full discussion of the Liberal government's various positions on lesbian and gay rights, see Miriam Smith, "Reluctant Recognition: The Liberal Government and Lesbian and Gay Rights," in Pal, ed., *How Ottawa Spends,* pp. 293–314.

44. Quoted in Ibid., p. 302.

45. Ibid., p. 309.

46. *Operation Dismantle Inc. v. The Queen* (1985), Supreme Court Reports, 49–51, as quoted in A. Wayne Mackay, "Fairness after the Charter: A Rose by Any Other Name?" *Queen's Law Journal* 10 (1985): 301.

47. *R. v. Morgentaler* (1988), Supreme Court Report 30, p. 172.

48. *R. v. Morgentaler,* Reasons for Judgment by the Rt. Hon. Brian Dickson, p. 16.

49. W.A. Bogart, *Courts and Country: The Limits of Litigation and the Social and Political Life of Canada* (Toronto: Oxford University Press, 1994). In Chapter 5, Bogart discusses the relationship between women and the courts.

50. Childbirth by Choice Trust, *Abortion in Canada Today: The Situation Province by Province.*

FURTHER READINGS

Bashevkin, Sylvia. *Women on the Defensive: Living Through Conservative Times.* Toronto: University of Toronto Press, 1998.

Canada, Status of Women. *Setting the Stage for the Next Century: The Federal Plan for Gender Equality.* Ottawa, 1995.

Everitt, Joanna, and Brenda O'Neill, eds. *Citizen Politics: Research and Theory in Canadian Political Behavior.* Don Mills: Oxford, 2002.

Tremblay, Manon, and Linda Trimble, eds. *Women and Electoral Politics in Canada.* Don Mills: Oxford University Press, 2003.

Vickers, Jill. *Reinventing Political Science: A Feminist Approach.* Halifax: Fernwood Books, 1997.

Waring, Marilyn. *Three Masquerades: Essays on Equality, Work and Hu(man) Rights.* Toronto: University of Toronto Press, 1996.

CHAPTER 15

UNEQUAL RELATIONS AND THE STRUGGLE FOR EQUALITY: RACE AND ETHNICITY IN CANADIAN POLITICS

Daiva Stasiulis and
Yasmeen Abu-Laban

On the heels of the 9/11 terror attacks on New York and Washington, many editorials in Canada's newspapers endorsed the use of ethnic and racial profiling. For example, the *National Post* boasted one entitled "Racial Profiling? Yes Please," the *Ottawa Citizen* featured an editorial called "Profiling is No Crime," and *The Vancouver Sun* printed one headlined "Racial Profiling is a Proper Weapon Against Terrorism."[1] In the post–September 11th environment, the term "profiling" entered the everyday parlance of Canadians as not only some newspapers, but also some public officials and academics began to endorse the idea that both Canadian citizens and non-citizens who are Arab or Muslim, or "look" Arab or Muslim, should be subjected to greater scrutiny by law enforcement and immigration officials and airport security personnel.[2]

Of course, these security-based arguments endorsing discriminatory treatment on the basis of race, ethnicity, or religion have also been highly controversial in Canada. This is because they are in direct conflict with the equality that is implied in the country's liberal democratic as well as multicultural traditions. Canadian political philosopher Charles Taylor has observed that in culturally diverse immigrant-receiving societies like Canada the "politics of equal recognition" involves struggles to achieve two seemingly contradictory principles: *universalism* and *difference*.[3] *Universalism* relates to individual rights which to be fully actualized require "blindness" to ethnic, racial, gender, and other differences amongst citizens. *Difference* on the other hand recognizes and values in a positive, as opposed to discriminatory, way distinct ethnic and other cultural identities among citizens. Canada's federal policy of multiculturalism, adopted in 1971, might be an example of the principle of difference. The debate around profiling, and the challenges such a practice poses both to individual rights and to valuing difference, draws our attention to how issues of immigration, race, and ethnicity are infusing political and policy discussions in Canada in the early years of the twenty-first century.

In this chapter, we argue that the study of Canadian politics must be able to address such developments. Yet Canadian political scientists traditionally have not paid a lot of attention to questions of race and ethnicity, with the notable exception of the French–English cleavage.[4] As a result, the Canadian political science literature most often presents politics as being shaped by regional, class, or federal–provincial relations.[5] Consequently, there has been a problematic silence on a number of formative and dynamic features of Canadian government and politics, including the increasingly heterogeneous ethnic and racial character of Canada's population.

Beginning in the 1970s and accelerating since the 1990s, Canadian immigration and demographic trends have brought about an absolute decline in Canadians of European origin and an increase in the population of people with origins in the Caribbean, Central and South America, Africa, the Middle East, and, especially, Asia. Whereas prior to 1961 some 90 percent of immigrants to Canada were of European origin, between 1991 and 2001 only 11 percent of incoming immigrants to Canada came from Europe, while 58 percent of immigrants came from countries of Asia including the Middle East. Some 94 percent of immigrants who arrived during the 1990s settled in urban centres, with nearly three-quarters settling in Toronto, Vancouver, and Montreal.[6]

The growing diversity of urban Canada should command the attention of those interested in politics because it raises in a dramatic fashion a number of questions about cultural and racial pluralism. How have race and ethnicity been represented in Canadian state institutions and policies, and in the visions and practices of those who govern? What success have ethnocultural groups had in enlisting the state in support of particular projects? How accessible have Canadian political institutions been to ethnic and racial minority groups and their concerns? For their part, what role have ethnic minorities played in Canadian politics? To what extent should Canadian public institutions accommodate ethnocultural and racial diversity?

In addressing these questions, this chapter takes a fivefold approach. In the first section, the concepts of "race" and "ethnicity" are considered in relation to political power in Canada. This is followed by a discussion of the history of representation of ethnic groups in state and party politics. The contemporary activities of ethnic minorities in legislative and party politics are addressed in the third section. Alternative (non-electoral) forms of political participation are then examined. We conclude with a discussion of contemporary state policies regulating diversity and equity.

DEFINING RELATIONS: RACE, ETHNICITY, GENDER, AND CLASS

Social scientists are often uneasy about referring to "race" when the concept has no scientific or biological validity. There are no objectively identifiable "races," for "there is much genetic variation within so-called races that are superficially similar in physical appearance."[7] As a result, we, and most social scientists today, say that the belief that there are inherent biologically based differences between distinct "races" of humankind is not based on fact, but rather is socially constructed outside of an objectively identifiable physical reality.

To say that "race" is socially constructed does not mean that scholars do not appreciate the importance of the commonplace belief that there are races, or the reality of social processes like racism and racial discrimination. We are mindful that the very belief in the objective existence of "race" spawned the eugenics policies of the Nazis. The fear that actively using the term *race* could legitimate new racist policies has led to one convention of placing the term in quotation marks. Similarly, public policymakers in Canada have invented the euphemism "visible minorities" to refer to peoples who are "non-Caucasian in race or nonwhite in colour," thus escaping accusations that public authorities are perpetuating racism by continually making reference to the discredited notion of race.[8]

Like race, the notions of "ethnicity" and "ethnic group" or "ethnocultural group" are contested and elusive concepts among scholars and in society at large. According to the original meaning of the term "ethnicity," derived from the Greek *ethnos* (people or nation), all Canadians can be said to be "ethnic." In its popular contemporary usage, however, ethnicity is typically ascribed only to non-dominant immigrants and their descendants—Canadians who are perceived to deviate from an assumed norm (white, English- or French-speaking, northern or western European). Thus, British and French Canadians are misleadingly assumed not to be "ethnic," whereas Canadians either born or with origins in Italy, China, Jamaica, and the Ukraine are considered as such.

Some anthropologists and sociologists have defined ethnicity as a "primordial" phenomenon, as something given or ascribed at birth and associated with a number of "givens" such as kinship ties, "being born into a particular religious community, speaking a particular language ... and following particular social practices."[9] Ethnic groups are shaped historically through the emergence of a sense of common origin and feelings of loyalty toward members of the ethnic collectivity. Individuals' identification with their ethnic group or community is facilitated by a number of common features such as ancestry, distinct language, religious beliefs, and cultural and political traditions. However, some authors argue that the cultural resources of ethnic groups are less significant than the external forces that construct and activate ethnic sentiments and solidarity, as well as produce particular "ethnic traits."[10]

State institutions play a central role in drawing the external boundaries of ethnic groups through population censuses that ask (or fail to ask) questions about ethnic origins, through state funding of ethnic community organizations, and through other forms of official sanction (or suppression) of ethnic organizations.[11] When state authorities wish to downplay the political importance of ethnic or racial divisions, official census-taking may simply omit questions about ethnicity or race. The politics of constructing the ethnic categories for the census question on ethnic origin also involves lobbying on the part of particular groups in order to bolster official recognition of their distinctness, numerical weight, and potential political significance.[12] Indeed, just prior to the 2001 census, there was a very passionate debate about whether to even ask the ethnic origin question, although in the end this question was retained.

A definitional issue that has sparked heated debate is whether there is a clear distinction to be made between the concepts of "race" and "ethnicity." The view that there is a significant difference between what in Canada have been referred to as "visible minorities" and "invisible (or white) minorities" is based on the assumption that discrimination and exclusion are exclusively linked to "non-white" skin colour. Unlike the liabilities of "invisible-minority" immigrants (for example those who lack fluency in official languages), which can disappear over time, the physical differences of visible minorities from the white majority continue to define them as "other" and inferior across many generations. This distinction is built into recent public policies meant to ameliorate inequalities. Employment equity policies, for example, have existed for visible but not invisible minorities in the federal government since 1986.[13] As elaborated below, the view that visible minorities face greater discrimination than white ethnic minorities in Canadian politics wins some support insofar as the non-Anglo, non-French groups best represented in political parties and Parliament are white, northern and eastern European groups that migrated early to Canada.[14]

One need not deny the unique histories of racism experienced by Canadian blacks, Asians, and other visible minorities in order to argue that racism can also be directed against groups that share the same (white) skin colour as the dominant racial/ethnic group. Different racisms have developed as waves of European and non-European migrations have brought to Canada people who do not conform to Anglo-Saxon culture and physical appearance. Language, religion, and other cultural markers have made diverse groups targets of racist scorn, intolerance, and unequal treatment—groups including the Catholic Irish in the nineteenth century, the European Jews who unsuccessfully sought refuge in Canada from the Holocaust in the 1930s, and southern Italians who migrated to postwar Toronto. For example, a 1941 Anglican Church report opposed the immigration to Canada of southern Italians on the grounds that they were "'amenable to the fallacies of dictatorship,' 'less versed' in democratic traditions and better suited for the hot climate of 'fragile' political structures of Latin American nations."[15]

Moreover, for racial minority groups, it is not skin colour per se that produces racism, but rather the historical legacy of the social and economic denigration and exploitation of non-white peoples that is responsible. This is true, for example, for Jamaican Canadians and more recently for Somali refugees in Canada. What is more important than their black skin is the residue of a historical vision of Canada as a white country, as well as the contemporary portrayal of these groups by the media and politicians as criminals and welfare frauds.

Whether it is anti-aboriginal, anti-black, anti-Italian, or anti-French, each racism can be viewed as having a specific genealogy that arises from a particular set of historical, material, and cultural circumstances, and that is reproduced through systemic, institutional, and ideological mechanisms. But each type of racism is also positioned in relation to other racisms. Thus, while French Canadians and aboriginal peoples in Quebec can both be said to have had histories of colonization and economic marginalization at the hands of British and English Canadians, the particular nature of anti-French and anti-aboriginal racism situates these groups differently within Canadian society. As part of the white settler groups who viewed aboriginal peoples as "uncivilized" and without legitimate claim to territory or self-government, French Quebeckers have been placed in a dominant position vis-à-vis aboriginal peoples. Thus, Daniel Salée observes that the standoff in 1990 between the Mohawk and town officials of the village of Oka, Quebec, created an "ironic twist" when "Quebecers, who have ... long been cast in the role of oppressed but courageous victims of historical circumstances, appeared ... as the intolerant and unsympathetic oppressors."[16] This illustration conveys a sense of the importance of understanding the different and fluid positions of different racisms with respect to one another, in place of the more commonplace racial ranking.[17]

Feminists have drawn attention to how all forms of social relations, whether based on global inequities, class, race, or ethnicity, are also gendered. This gendered aspect of racism was a critical dimension of the historical project to build a "white Canada" from the mid-nineteenth century to the 1960s, a project that relied on immigration as well as the marginalization of aboriginal peoples. Although political elites wished to limit the entry of Asians and blacks through restrictive immigration laws, business actively recruited cheap migrant labour from Asia. Thus, legislation was introduced to prevent migrants from these groups from bringing in and establishing their families in Canada. Today, the disempowerment of many immigrant women who currently enter the country as part of the "family class" category of immigrants is accomplished through assigning female immigrants inferior entry status as dependants of husbands. In conjunction with the rules governing entitlement to other state policies such as government-assistance schemes and official language and job training, a dependent immigration status has relegated many immigrant women to vulnerable, low-paid, and dead-end positions in the service sector, or in highly competitive industries such as the garment trades. Differences among racial/ethnic groups in terms of their political concerns and actions have been shaped by such historical patterns of state-led discrimination in immigration as well as by other policies that reflect an intersection of racial/ethnic, gender, and class relations.

CANADA'S HISTORY OF RACIAL AND ETHNIC HIERARCHIES IN STATE POLICIES

Canada's position within the British Empire meant that two sets of conflicting principles were played out in the formation of policies such as immigration, foreign affairs, and governance of aboriginal peoples. On the one hand, the imperial philosophy of a non-racial empire, influenced by nineteenth-century liberal humanitarianism, proclaimed that all subjects were equal before the law, regardless of race, creed, or colour. On the other hand, a sense of the racial superiority of all things Anglo-Saxon, including the special capacity for political self-governance through a constitutional system, led to the impulse among British settlers to build a country that was as white and as British as possible.[18] These two contradictory principles were played out in the policy debates among Canadian politicians over the immigration and citizenship rights of Asian and black immigrants, who were perceived as being inherently incapable of assimilation to British-Canadian culture, and therefore a threat to British civilization.

The idea that only certain "kindred races" can successfully intermingle was rooted in the supposedly "scientific" race theories popular in Europe during the nineteenth century. In 1885, Canada's first prime minister, Sir John A. Macdonald, elaborated this view as he introduced legislation to deny the federal franchise to persons of Chinese descent:

> [A]ll natural history, all ethnology, shows that while the crosses of the Aryan races are successful—while the mixture of all those races which are known or believed to spring from common origins is more or less successful—they will amalgamate. If you look around the world you will see that the Aryan races will not wholesomely amalgamate with the Africans or the Asiatics. It is not desired that they should come; that we should have a mongrel race; that the Aryan character of the future of British America should be destroyed by a cross or crosses of that kind.... Let us encourage all the races which are cognate races, which cross and amalgamate naturally, and we shall see that such amalgamation will produce, as the result, a race equal if not superior to the two races which mingle. But the cross of [Aryan and non-Aryan] races, like the cross of the dog and the fox, is not successful; it cannot be, and never will be.... We are in the course of progress; this country is going on and developing, and we will have plenty of labor of our own kindred races, without introducing this element of a mongrel race to disturb the labor market, and certainly we ought not to allow them to share the Government of the country.[19]

While Macdonald employed eugenics ("race betterment") arguments and the fear of miscegenation ("race-mixing") to justify the exclusion of Asians from the rights of universal British citizenship, it is significant that some other politicians of his time were unconvinced by these arguments. For instance, L.H. Davies, a former premier of Prince Edward Island, argued for a consistent, unrestricted approach:

> If a Chinaman becomes a British subject it is not right that a brand should be placed on his forehead, so that other men may avoid him. As a member of this House, and as a Radical, I enter my protest against this reactionary proposal. It is especially unfair ... that the Chinaman, who has become a British subject, who is an honest and hardworking man, and has made up his mind to work in this country, should be excluded from taking part in the politics of the country ...

I am in favor of any one who has become a British subject and has the necessary qualifications having the right to exercise the franchise.[20]

The historic failure of non-white British subjects to gain open access to Canada by employing the rhetoric of universal-empire citizenship suggests that the drive to maintain the racial purity of Canada was more decisive than a British sense of "fair play." Thus, one of the historical discourses that designated immigrants from outside northern Europe as unsuitable settlers in Canada was their assumed inability to adapt to British civilization and democratic political traditions. In 1928, Prime Minister R.B. Bennett expressed his anxiety over the threat of non-British immigrants to British civilization:

[W]e are endeavouring to maintain our civilization at that high standard which has made the British civilization the test by which all other civilized nations in modern times are measured.... We must still maintain that measure of British civilization which will enable us to assimilate these people [immigrants] to British institutions, rather than assimilate our civilization to theirs.[21]

Two decades later, in a speech given in 1947, Prime Minister Mackenzie King affirmed before Parliament the desire by Canada's political elites to use immigration policy to maintain Canada as a white, European country:

There will, I am sure, be general agreement with the view that the people of Canada do not wish, as a result of mass immigration, to make a fundamental alteration on the character of our population. Large-scale immigration from the Orient would change the fundamental composition of the Canadian population.[22]

Explicitly restrictive immigration policy from the 1880s until the 1960s conformed to the intent of Canadian prime ministers and generations of immigration ministers and top immigration officials to develop Canada as a "white settler colony." The unease felt by at least some politicians about formulating explicitly racist policies, however, meant that in order to preserve appearances, immigration policies denied entry through bizarre orders-in-council and administrative regulations. These included the imposition of head taxes to deter Chinese immigrants, a "direct passage" regulation to prevent South Asian immigration, and reference to the challenges posed by Canada's relatively harsh climate to exclude Caribbean blacks and southern Italians.

Denial of the franchise through provincial and federal legislation reinforced the political marginality and subordination of Asians and made it harder for them to build links to party and electoral systems. The Canada Elections Act of 1920 accepted provincial racial restrictions (except for war veterans) in determining who was qualified to vote in federal elections. Since legislation had been passed in several provinces to disenfranchise the Chinese (as early as 1872 in British Columbia, and 1908 in Saskatchewan), they were barred from voting in federal elections until 1947.

Similar legal bases for discrimination existed for (East) Indian and Japanese Canadians, regardless of whether they were Canadian- or foreign-born. In British Columbia, such laws remained until the late 1940s. Exclusion from the provincial voters' list barred Asian Canadians from election to the provincial legislature, from nomination for municipal office, and from school-trustee positions and jury service.[23] In British Columbia, where the majority of Asians resided, politicians tried to outdo one another in promising to limit the economic and political involvement of Asians in Canada. Other European groups, labelled "enemy aliens" during the two world wars, also faced disenfranchisement and isolation from party, electoral, and parliamentary politics, except as objects of control.

The segregated school systems, employment, and housing and public facilities that existed for blacks in Canada (in the Maritimes and Ontario until the 1960s) undoubtedly gave rise to this group's alienation and mistrust of mainstream, white-dominated political institutions.[24] Aboriginal peoples have experienced the most profound sense of isolation from the Canadian polity, an isolation stemming from external paternalistic control (until today through the Indian Act and the Department of Indian and Northern Affairs), the reserve system, and ongoing destruction of their traditional economies and cultures.

Not surprisingly, the political marginalization of non-British, non-French groups came to be reflected in their extreme underrepresentation in mainstream political institutions. For example, in the House of Commons between 1867 and 1964, only 97 MPs were from ethnic minorities, with 40 of these being of German origin. Only two visible minorities (one Chinese and one Lebanese) made it to the House of Commons during this period.[25]

As early as the turn of the twentieth century, parties would court the "ethnic vote," and, at times, ethnic minorities were even nominated as candidates. However, those few elected MPs from non-British, non-French origins typically represented "ethnic constituencies" such as the predominantly Ukrainian ridings of Vegreville in Alberta or the heavily Jewish ridings in cities like Montreal, Toronto, and Winnipeg.[26] Even when ethnic minorities attained office in the House of Commons, they had limited impact in shaping policies in a manner favourable to minorities. Lacking a critical mass in either their parties or the House of Commons, minority politicians had little power to shape government policy in directions favourable to the interests of their ethnocultural communities.

CONTEMPORARY POLITICAL REPRESENTATION AND PARTICIPATION OF ETHNIC AND RACIAL MINORITIES

While there has been improvement since the 1960s, and particularly during the decade of the 1990s, the historical pattern of underrepresentation of visible minorities in political parties and the House of Commons has proved to be quite persistent.[27] Analyses by Jerome Black of the ethnoracial origins of the successful candidates in the last three federal elections—1993, 1997, and 2000—suggest that while progress has been made toward a more culturally diverse House of Commons, visible minorities continue to be significantly underrepresented in relation to their presence in the population. The 1993 election was particularly notable in heralding an unprecedented increase in the election of MPs of ethnic minority (non-British, non-French, non-Aboriginal) backgrounds, such that they comprised 24.1 percent of the House's membership, in comparison with only 16.1 percent in 1988.[28] While the proportion of ethnic minority MPs increased slightly in 1997 to 24.9 percent of the House, in the 2000 election it dropped to 23.6 percent.

Slow progress in representation of visible minorities, and indeed recent decline, is notable in visible-minority representation in Parliament. Thus, while visible minorities had doubled their presence in the House of Commons from 2.0 percent in 1988 to 4.4 percent in 1993, and showed a further increase to 6.3 percent in 1997, by the 2000 federal election their proportion had declined to 5.6 percent of the House of Commons. In comparison with the approximately 14 percent of the population that are visible minorities today, the visible-minority MPs thus also lost ground vis-à-vis their share of the Canadian population.[29]

Women from visible minorities are particularly unlikely to become members of Parliament. Although their numbers doubled from 1993 to 1997 from 2 to 4, a number replicated in the 2000 election, in order to reach their proportion of the population, there would need to be 21 of them. In contrast, ethnic-minority women have succeeded in increasing their presence in Parliament. Thus, while in 1988, only 1 of 48 minority ethnic MPs were female, by 1993, 11 ethnic-minority women had been elected, 17 were successful in 1997, and 19 won seats three years later.[30] As

Black has suggested, minority women may endure "double bias," but political parties, sensitive to criticism of their ethnic exclusivity, may see the "double value" of minority women.[31]

Although ethnic, racial, and gender diversity increased in the House of Commons after the 1993 and 1997 elections, why are visible minorities, and especially visible-minority women, still so underrepresented? There are two possible explanations for this. One explanation emphasizes characteristics of these groups themselves, such as immigrant status of many visible-minority communities and the presupposition that immigrants are less likely to have knowledge about or participate in the political process. As well, immigrants are also more likely to face barriers to political participation (e.g., language difficulties). Depending on the recentness of their arrival and their social class, they may be more preoccupied with economic and social survival than with political issues.

Although it may be the case that those who have recently immigrated to Canada have priorities above participating in politics (for example, finding a job),[32] and that immigrant status rather than ethnicity per se accounts for lower levels of political activity,[33] recent survey evidence suggests that there is actually little difference between immigrants and the Canadian-born when it comes to such activities as campaign involvement and voting.[34]

For this reason, the focus on immigration as an explanation for the small numbers of racial minorities in the House of Commons is insufficient. Indeed, it is important to remember that groups such as the Chinese, African Canadians, Japanese, and South Asians have had a presence in Canada since the nineteenth century and earlier. As well, among the visible-minority groups with origins in Asia, Africa, and Latin America, whose major waves of immigration date from the beginnings of the 1970s, nearly one-third (30 percent) were born in Canada.[35] Moreover, an explanation that focuses on the immigrant status of ethnic and visible minorities deflects attention from the numerous cultural, organizational, and structural barriers to participation that exist within the workings of Canada's parties and society at large.[36] Indeed, it is these features that form a more compelling argument for the underrepresentation of visible minorities in the House of Commons.

To new immigrants and to people from non-British political traditions, the culture of Canada's established political parties may be alienating and even exclusionary. Several party officials and activists have described the fear among the political establishment that ethnic and visible minorities are "taking over" the riding associations.[37] The perception both of minorities who have made it into the system (e.g., as MPs) and of those seeking entry into the political establishment is that the political gate-keepers hold negative, stereotypical views of ethnic and visible minorities.

The issues facing the major political parties in this regard may vary. It is interesting that in the 1997 federal election, Reform Party leader Preston Manning attempted to overcome the image that the party's plat-forms and members were racist by making an effort to meet with ethno-cultural communities in Toronto.[38] The Reform Party's electoral platform, entitled "Fresh Start," actually hired actors to pose as visible-minority voters. Criticized for not being a representative picture of Reform Party members, the photo was defended by the Reform campaign chairman as "a representation of those in Canada we are trying to reach."[39]

An organizational barrier to minority participation lies in the con-ventional means of recruiting party volunteers and activists, which relies heavily on personal networks within which trust and loyalty are built. It is, therefore, ironic that much of the criticism of minority ethnic activism in the 1980s and 1990s, particularly in the Liberal Party, centred on the pur-ported abuse of ethnic community networks in putting forward minority candidates.[40] This kind of criticism about minority abuse also emerged in the 1997 election. For example, in the British Columbia riding of Surrey Central, Sikh candidates ran for the Liberals, New Democrats, and Reform Party. Despite the fact that more than one-third of the population of the city of Surrey is Indo-Canadian, the Reform organizer in British Columbia argued that "They [Sikhs] don't think along the same lines [as non-Sikhs].... They're pulling out all the stops to get an MP."[41] The Reform organizer was forced by the party to resign for these comments, but it is notable that patterns of ethnic recruitment within the parties have seldom been the subject of public commentary.

Typically, networks of participants within the political parties have tended to follow traditional patterns of recruitment from white British or French (depending on the region) ethnic communities. Women from ethnic and racial minorities must also contend with the disadvantages of being excluded from the "old boys' network." Black's analysis of female immigrants and visible-minority MPs who made it into the House of Commons after the 1993 election found that such women were truly "exceptional" individuals, with more advanced degrees and skills than other male or female MPs. This suggests that female minorities need to be "more accomplished" to break through traditional networks and enter political life.[42] Structural hurdles to minority inroads within the party system include the "incumbency" factor, an unwritten rule that holds that challenges without due cause to the renomination of incumbent members of Parliament are unacceptable. This informal rule has proved to be a barrier to the placement of minority candidates within winnable or "safe" seats.[43] In the 2000 election, 247 of the 301 incumbents were re-elected. With such a low turnover from 1997 to 2000, there was little possibility of shifting the ethno-racial profile of Parliament.[44]

In addition to the cultural, organizational, and structural features of political parties that may explain the underrepresentation of visible minorities, one feature of the Canadian party system that has affected all minority groups has been the limited space for defining major political debates and issues on their own terms. The hegemonic vision of Canadian society reflected within party discourse has, at best, reflected biculturalism (and at less inclusive times, Anglo conformity).[45] This has meant that the collective identities, aspirations, and symbols of the British and (to a lesser degree) the French have been legitimized within party and state discourse, agendas, and policies. In contrast, those of the non-British, non-French groups have been suppressed. For example, while the federal Liberal party has had a long tradition of alternating French- and English-speaking leaders, this has not evolved to encompass other forms of diversity.

The downplaying of ethnocultural and racial diversity within Canadian political discourse is also reflected in the fate of multiculturalism, an official policy of the federal government since 1971. In its first two decades of existence, multiculturalism actively won the support of minority ethnic communities and the traditional federal parties (Liberals, Conservatives, and New Democrats) as a policy accommodating the symbolic aspirations of minorities. As multiculturalism was always tied to English and French bilingualism, it was mainly a symbolic policy. Nonetheless, in the 1980s there were concrete moves to provide multiculturalism with a constitutional and statutory base. The concept of multiculturalism became entrenched in section 27 of the 1982 Canadian Charter of Rights and Freedoms. The Canadian Multiculturalism Act of 1988 provided for the first time a legislative basis for the existing multiculturalism policy and programs.

However, in the 1990s and into the 2000s, the cross-party support for multiculturalism dissipated along with the shift in constellation of leading parties. For instance, both the Bloc Québécois and the Reform/Alliance Party rejected multiculturalism policy. There is a striking pattern of party affiliation among visible minorities that challenges any simple notion of visible-minority political or policy interests. Over 7 in 10 of visible-minority MPs were elected under the Liberal banner in the last three elections.[46] The Liberal Party's relative strength in electing visible-minority candidates may be partially attributed to the government's introduction of multiculturalism policy, its robust immigration record, and its relatively recent openness to minorities.

But the relationship between party policies fostering cultural and ethno-racial inclusiveness and a party's performance in electing visible minorities is not straightforward. Thus, on the one hand, the Bloc Québécois, whose sovereigntist stance has been unpopular with non-francophones, has attracted few racial minority candidates, and none that have been successful. On the other hand, the New Democrats, who have fostered the strongest affirmative-action candidate policies to convey a message of openness to minority Canadians, have indeed recruited a fair number of visible- and ethnic-minority candidates. However, given the difficulties faced by the NDP in multiparty competition, only 4.8 percent of visible-minority MPs from 1993 to 2000 have been NDP. In contrast, the Reform/Alliance Party has been able to produce the second largest percentage of visible-minority MPs from 1993 to 2000—23.8 percent—in spite of policies hostile to multiculturalism and supportive of a restrictive immigration policy, and a neoliberal stance on equality issues that downplays the historic exclusion and contemporary reality of racism in Canada. The fact that the Alliance Party has the second largest percentage of visible-minority MPs after the Liberal Party raises interesting issues around numerical versus substantive representation.[47] More broadly, since the 1990s, the declining positive (as opposed to negative) attention given in Parliament to political issues that have conventionally been identified as of concern to visible minorities and immigrant communities—such as immigration, employment equity, and multiculturalism—indicates a need to pursue closer study of the processes that hinder the substantive representation of minority issues, even when the number of minority members in the House of Commons is increasing.[48]

In sum, the underrepresentation of ethnic and visible minorities within the major parties can be explained in terms of a variety of structural, cultural, and organizational obstacles. For recent immigrants lacking official-language skills, linguistic barriers intersect with lack of familiarity with the Canadian political culture and system. Racial minorities confront discrimination practised at the highest levels of party structures. For women of colour and ethnic-minority women, the barriers are gendered as well as based on race, ethnicity, and (often) class. And for all marginalized groups, there is a legacy of exclusion that is reinforced by the hegemonic bicultural discourse of party politics, by patterns of recruitment through networks, and by party traditions such as the incumbency factor within the electoral process.

In Canada, the historical exclusion of women and many minority groups from party, electoral, and legislative politics by way of denial of the franchise, and today through less overt barriers, has meant that the political activism of minorities has often been channelled into different forums that are perceived to provide greater means for self-empowerment and the pursuit of substantive gains.

ALTERNATIVE MINORITY POLITICS

Any discussion of ethnic-minority politics in Canada must consider not only the "formal" political arena of electoral and party politics but also the "informal" political arena of communal organization and social movement activities. Concerns expressed in this arena have to do with both domestic and international developments. For instance, one common form of politics pursued in ethnic communities both historically and today is "homeland" politics, which concerns itself with providing support for political conflicts waged in the originating countries of immigrants and their descendants. Many immigrant and ethnic collectivities conceive of themselves as diasporas (i.e., as communities uprooted by physical compulsion or economic coercion) and retain the idea of return to the homeland. This is precisely the type of politics that is assumed by some critics to breed "ethnocentric hatreds," "tribalization," and a "resurgence of racism." Homeland politics, it is alleged, is an outgrowth of immigration, multiculturalism, and/or citizenship policies that encourage "divided loyalties."[49] Fuelled by the traditional stereotypes of "dangerous foreigners" held by Anglo-Celtic and French elites, the political activism of ethnic minorities in pursuit of foreign causes and "foreign ideologies" was historically met with the deportation of leaders, for example, to stem the "alien Bolshevik menace" between 1910 and the 1930s. It has also attracted excessive surveillance by security agencies such as the RCMP and the Canadian Security Intelligence Service (CSIS). This was evidenced in the responses to the Black Power movement in Canada during the 1970s and by the harassment of Arab and Muslim Canadians following September 11, 2001.

There is little question that homeland politics plays a major role in the political life of many ethnic communities, including Eastern European communities (such as Ukrainian, Polish, and Lithuanian) where there are third and fourth generations born in Canada. This form of politics in ethnic communities is either polarized along left–right divisions that correspond to different waves of migration or else factionalized according to support or opposition to homeland regimes.

In some instances, the absorption of leadership and other resources of ethnic communities in politics abroad has deflected energies away from mobilization around political issues in Canada. Thus, the waning of the spirited fight of Sikh-Canadian associations against racism in Canada in the 1970s coincided with the mobilization of some Sikh organizations around the goal of establishing a separate Sikh state in India ("Khalistan"). However, there is little evidence that an ethnic community highly politicized on homeland issues cannot simultaneously participate in Canadian politics. For example, 1950s Ukrainian Canadians, many of whom were keenly interested in the liberation of Ukraine from the Soviet Union, took great pride in the growing number of Ukrainian-Canadian elected officials, an increase that signalled their increasing acceptance in Canadian society.[50]

Moreover, it should be borne in mind that the homeland politics taken up by such communities typically address questions regarding the foreign policies of the Canadian government. The political activism of ethnic minorities in homeland causes often takes the form of lobbying Canadian politicians and senior bureaucrats in federal departments such as Foreign Affairs on issues such as whether to pursue air strikes or peacekeeping in the former Yugoslavia, aid for Palestinians in the Middle East, or the advisability of going to war with Iraq. This kind of lobbying can also mobilize support within a broader Canadian public, as witnessed in the spirited mass demonstrations during 2002 and early 2003 against a U.S.-led war against Iraq.

The extent to which the Canadian government takes up particular causes and positions put forward by ethnic groups is largely dependent on Canada's position within the international political economy (including its subordination to the U.S.) and its pre-established diplomatic relations with other countries. Thus, despite intense lobbying by Eastern European groups, the 1950s Liberal government of Louis St. Laurent refused to support the liberation of their homelands. An apparently decisive factor in this refusal was the need to avoid the appearance of interfering in the internal affairs of the Soviet Union.[51] This concern faded with the crumbling of the Soviet Union in the early 1990s, when Canada recognized the independence of the Baltic states.

While the influence of minority ethnic groups on Canadian foreign policy has generally been limited, the increasing cultural and racial diversity of Canadian society has had a decisive impact in re-shaping the politics of major Canadian social movements. In the 1920s and 1930s, the presence of "Red" Ukrainian, Finnish, Jewish, and other European workers in a variety of resource and manufacturing industries radicalized Canadian labour unions and spawned networks of grassroots foreign-language cells in the Communist and Socialist parties. Since the 1970s, visible-minority workers have formed an increasing proportion of trade-union members in unions within sectors such as the steel, auto, and garment trades. They have challenged the traditional white (and male) leadership to take up issues such as affirmative action and racism within unions, power-sharing with an ascendant minority leadership, and the construction of organizational models more appropriate to the conditions of minority workers.

Faced with discrimination in major institutions such as the labour market, policing, and education, racial- and ethnic-minority communities have engaged in prolonged and varied strategies to reform racist policies and practices. The creation of pioneering human rights legislation in Ontario is due largely to the political work of black and Jewish activists working within the labour movement and community organizations in the 1930s and 1940s.[52] Numerous police shootings of blacks in cities like Toronto and Montreal since the 1970s have kindled a sense of solidarity as well as vigorous protests against police racism within black communities. In the late 1970s, the sustained work by black and South Asian community organizations resulted in the Toronto Board of Education's adoption of an innovative anti-racist policy that sought to "deinstitutionalize" racism in Toronto's public school system.[53] Since the 1990s, mainly female foreign domestic workers from the Philippines and the Caribbean have been militant in contesting coercive Canadian immigration policies and substandard provincial employment standards.

Perhaps the social movement that has been most profoundly shaken by racism and by racial and ethnic diversity has been the women's movement. Typically in provinces with large, racially heterogeneous populations, the questions of racism and racial diversity have transformed feminist politics. Both women of colour and white women have described the experience of dealing with racism within the ranks of white-dominated women's organizations as traumatizing and silencing.[54] It has led, however, to the building of a more inclusive feminist movement that recognizes the need for numerical and substantive representation of women of colour.

For example, a Tanzanian-born woman of South Asian origins, Sunera Thobani, became the first visible-minority president of the National Action Committee on the Status of Women (NAC) in 1993. Since NAC is the main umbrella organization of the women's movement in Canada outside Quebec, Thobani's presidency (1993–1996), as well as that of her successor, Joan Grant-Cummings (1996–2001), also a visible minority, was profoundly symbolic of the growing diversity of Canadian women. Of equal significance, the leadership of women of colour in "mainstream" feminist organizations has defined fighting racism as a feminist issue rather than simply as a human rights issue supported by feminists. This has meant taking up issues and state policies previously thought outside the purview of women's issues, as exemplified by the involvement of NAC in working to expand refugee policy to provide asylum for abused women. It has also meant fundamentally rethinking some of the central categories and analyses of "old" issues such as reproductive rights, the workplace, violence against women, as well as the contradictory relations among women defined by race, ethnicity, class, and sexuality. For instance, as Sunera Thobani has observed, women of colour have highlighted the inadequacy of the pro-choice movement's focus on individual "choice," in that "women are pitted against women by technologies which enhance the fertility [and choices] of affluent, white women, and which severely curtail the reproductive capacities of poor women and of women of colour."[55]

Given these significant inclusionary developments within the women's movement, it is striking that the organizational future of NAC in Canada in the twenty-first century is uncertain. This is because of the insecure nature of state funding in an era of restructuring and neoliberal policies that have emphasized curbing social spending.[56] By 1998, then NAC president Joan Grant-Cummings announced that her organization would be forced to close its doors when the federal Liberal government cut back its financial support by about a third.[57] Federal funding for advocacy groups like NAC has not improved in the early years of the twenty-first century. This serves as a reminder of the critical importance of supportive state policies in regulating, reflecting, and challenging unequal social relations.

CONTEMPORARY STATE POLICIES OF CULTURAL DIVERSITY AND RACIAL EQUITY

While at least segments of the women's movement have come to accept that the "fundamental character" of the Canadian population is becoming more racially and culturally diverse, many state policies regulating such diversity have become the site of backlash and stagnation since the 1990s—a feature brought about by a combination of economic restructuring, neoliberal agenda shifts (see Chapter 10), and changing partisan and popular debates. Immigration and multiculturalism have been the key federal government policies at the centre of debates over support and containment of ethnic and racial diversity. Other government provisions that address issues of racial/ethnic inequality and racism are employment equity and the Charter of Rights and Freedoms. Each will be briefly discussed.

Multiculturalism and immigration policies are deeply intertwined. An officially non-discriminatory policy concerning the race/ethnicity of incoming immigrants since 1967 has allowed for greater immigration to Canada from outside of Europe, and this in turn has generated demands for more inclusive policies and symbolic representation of an increasingly diverse population. While an inter-party consensus existed for much of the 1970s and 1980s favouring multiculturalism and immigration, partisan division characterized the 1990s. Not only did the Reform Party (and its successor the Canadian Alliance) and the Bloc Québécois oppose multi-culturalism, but generally accepted features of postwar immigration policy, such as the number of immigrants allowed to enter Canada, became a question for partisan debate.[58] Added to this, since the 1990s, several national surveys indicated an increased popular purchase to the idea of abandoning government multiculturalism policies and even returning to a "white Canada" immigration policy.[59]

In this volatile political climate, the federal Liberals shifted immigration policy so that immigration is to serve first an economic function by attracting "self-sufficient" immigrants. This goal has been achieved by reducing the number of immigrants who enter through family reunification provisions and by giving preference to those who can "integrate" most quickly, for example, by having significant knowledge of an official language before immigrating.[60] These policy changes have also been motivated by federal fiscal restraint in the administration of immigration and settlement, in effect shifting the costs of immigrant integration not only onto provincial and local governments and incoming immigrants, but also onto the family and community groups most vulnerable to racism and other forms of disadvantage. This contributes to the inequality experienced by incoming immigrants, and in particular immigrant women.[61]

In addition, given the issues that are crowding the "immigration reform" agenda of the federal government in the early years of the twenty-first century, it is not likely that this trend will be reversed in the near future. Along with engaging in discussions with the United States on possibly harmonizing aspects of Canada's immigration and refugee policies to ensure the flow of goods across the U.S.–Canada border, following September 11, 2001, the federal government directed its attention to developing policies aimed at "national security." These policies included developing new anti-terrorist legislation to target both citizens and non-citizens, increasing the funds available to the Canadian Security and Intelligence Service, increasing the funds available to screen and deport refugee claimants and enforce border controls, and profiling those arriving from predominantly Muslim countries.[62] The vast majority of immigrants and refugees to Canada, including those of Muslim or Arab background, are law-abiding. Yet these policies serve to imply erroneously that all immigrants and refugees, especially those who are Muslim, are a potential threat to Canada's national security. In an immigrant-receiving society like Canada's, such practices affect the principles of both universalism of individual rights and valuing difference.

While some state policies (such as immigration) have contributed to racial/ethnic disadvantage and inequities, other state policies reflect an official recognition of the central role the state must play in eradicating racism in a pluralist society. The problems of discrimination based on race, national or ethnic origin, colour, and a number of other characteristics were explicitly recognized in section 15(1) of the 1982 Charter of Rights and Freedoms. However, the utility of the Charter as a tool for fighting racism is limited. Given that it protects individuals only from the actions of governments, it does not cover the majority of discriminatory practices (e.g., by employers in the private sector). Section 15(2) allows for but does not require affirmative-action programs for disadvantaged groups. Most cases of discrimination continue to be directed to provincial and, to a lesser degree, federal human rights commissions, where procedures for investigating complaints are notoriously slow and cumbersome, and where the penalties against discrimination are mild and ineffectual.

Constitutional expert Alan Cairns predicted in the late 1980s that as Canadians became more racially and ethnically diverse, minorities would increasingly focus on the Constitution and constitutional politics to protect and further their interests.[63] Ethnocultural minorities had fought to have section 27 in the 1982 Charter of Rights providing that "[t]his Charter shall be interpreted in a manner consistent with the preservation and enhancement of the multicultural heritage of Canadians." However, in many ways Cairns's prediction has not come to pass. Indeed, section 27 is only a very general interpretive clause (unlike the clauses in the Charter that guarantee substantive rights such as freedom of speech or minority language rights), and it is difficult to see how it could be enforced. Moreover, anti-discriminatory protections (section 15[2] of the Charter), to which racial minorities might lay claim, are subject to the provincial override clause.

One federal government policy protected by section 15(2) of the Charter is the Employment Equity Program (enacted in 1986 by the Mulroney government), whose purpose is to redress systemic discrimination in employment experienced by women, aboriginal peoples, visible minorities, and people with disabilities. Although the legislation requires employers under federal jurisdiction to prepare an annual employment equity plan with goals and timetables, it does not require them to submit this plan to the government. Since its inception, the program has drawn fire from visible-minority rights advocates. Criticisms have centred on its lack of specific goals and timetables, of systematic monitoring mechanisms, and of effective sanctions linked to the non-implementation (as opposed to mere reporting) of employment equity measures. The assumption that "public scrutiny" will provide the mechanism for enforcing the act has been called "fanciful" by human rights activists, as it places the burden of action on the victims of discrimination.[64] Indeed, it is notable that recent data suggest that while women and aboriginal peoples have achieved some improved representation in the federal public service, persons with disabilities and visible minorities (especially visible-minority women) were still underrepresented compared to their numbers in the Canadian population.[65]

The federal multiculturalism bureaucracy has made race relations programs an increasing component of its activities since 1981. The major emphasis of these programs has been to provide support for education and training within institutions in the areas of policing and justice, education, media and the arts, health and social services, and the workplace. In many instances, such support has been limited to one-time workshops and conferences and thus is unlikely to bring about any long-term anti-racist institutional reform. This has been made all the more unlikely due to cutbacks in spending on multiculturalism. Never a large program, spending on multiculturalism at its height in the early 1990s was about $27 million a year; in the early years of the twenty-first century this has fallen to about $16 million a year.

It has been suggested that the anti-racist program in multiculturalism was given its impetus by the increased racial tensions in Vancouver following the influx of wealthy Hong Kong Chinese through the "investor" stream of immigration policy.[66] In like manner, since the Liberals came to power in 1993, the rhetoric of the federal government has increasingly linked together multiculturalism, anti-racism, and good business sense in a competitive global environment. In this way, the multiculturalism program is now being justified in the language of business and trade, rather than the language of justice.[67]

From a number of angles, then, federal multiculturalism policy has been less than successful in convincing Canadians that racial and ethnic harmony as well as individual equality can be reached through government support of cultural diversity. Yet some critics of the federal multiculturalism policy have argued that far from smoothing racial tensions, multiculturalism creates and *deepens* ethnocentrism and racial hatreds. Novelist Neil Bissoondath expresses this sentiment: "In stressing the differences between groups, in failing to emphasize that this is a country with its own ideals and attitudes that demand adherence, the [multiculturalism] policy has instead aided in a hardening of hatreds."[68]

Although the arguments for rejecting multiculturalism are themselves diverse, there is little question that increasing numbers of Canadians are willing to discard government policies that promote a "cultural mosaic." Typically, recent calls to abandon multiculturalism seek to replace it with a model of liberal individualism. In other words, minorities would achieve equality by holding the same universal human rights as all other Canadians. However, given that the struggle for equality in Canada has involved, and continues to involve, both recognition of universal rights *and* also difference, it is hard to see how a framework emphasizing only universalism would be realistic or inclusionary in an increasingly ethnically and racially diverse political community.

CONCLUSION

The institution of and justifications for "racial profiling" practices targeting Arab and Muslim peoples post–September 11th counters the notion that Canada's contemporary politics of difference have provided only increased gains for ethno-racial minorities. Widespread racism, which deprives visible minorities of full recognition as Canadians, is a reminder that individuals and institutions continue to view racial distinctions as reasons to deprive people of their universal rights.

The challenge posed by ethnocultural and racial diversity—a challenge facing Canadian politicians and society as a whole—is greater than the more abstract challenge of finding a balance between the contradictory principles of *universalism*, which treats all citizens equally regardless of differences, and *difference*, which respects and promotes collective rights. Currently, there are diverse and sometimes conflicting collective interests that correspond to ethnic/racial divisions, including Quebec francophones, francophones outside Quebec, aboriginal peoples, non-Anglo and non-French minorities, and visible minorities. Each type of collective interest is fuelled by its own sense of collective origins, injustice, and destiny, and each seeks protection and enhancement through diverse political strategies and state instruments.

In addition, today there are new patterns of ethnic and racial pluralism in Canadian cities, where some recent and wealthier immigrants are setting their own terms for integration into Canada. For example, there now exist in Vancouver's residential and commercial districts Asian enclaves where store owners are known to observe with unconscious irony, "We do not see many foreigners here," referring to Canadians of European descent.[69] Many recent Hong Kong Chinese immigrants to Canada identify themselves as "global citizens," speak several languages, and feel comfortable with many different cultures. Moreover, their capacity to influence Canadian state policies may have less to do with pre-established patterns of ethnic power within Canada than with the power of international capital and the potential they represent for bringing new investment to Canada.

But global migration and Canadian immigration policies have also brought to Canada's shores Third World immigrants (foreign domestic workers, garment workers, agricultural seasonal workers, refugees) who are less privileged in class terms. The subordinate labour-market position and political marginality of these groups have much in common with oppressed Third World peoples and have spawned a more activist and global form of "ethnic politics."

The twenty-first century thus presents an opportunity for political scientists who have not traditionally engaged with the study of race and ethnicity and politics to reconsider their analyses of Canada in a way that is attuned to Canada's position within the global economy, to international migration, and to emerging forms of ethnic/racial stratification that dovetail with relations of power based on class and gender.

NOTES

1. "Racial Profiling? Yes Please," *National Post,* February 16, 2002: A19; "Profiling is No Crime," *Ottawa Citizen,* November 6, 2002: A18; and "Racial Profiling is a Proper Weapon Against Terrorism," *The Vancouver Sun,* June 7, 2002: A14.

2. Yasmeen Abu-Laban, "Liberalism, Multiculturalism and the Problem of Essentialism," *Citizenship Studies* 6, no. 4 (December 2002): 459–82.

3. Charles Taylor, *Multiculturalism and "The Politics of Recognition"* (Princeton, NJ: Princeton University Press, 1992), pp. 37–39.

4. An exception is the book by Jill Vickers, *The Politics of Race: Canada, Australia and the US* (Ottawa: Golden Dog Press, 2002).

5. See Yasmeen Abu-Laban and Daiva Stasiulis, "Ethnic Pluralism under Siege: Popular and Partisan Opposition to Multiculturalism," *Canadian Public Policy* 18 (1992): 365–86; Alan Cairns, "Political Science, Ethnicity, and the Canadian Constitution," in Douglas E. Williams, ed., *Disruptions: Constitutional Struggles from the Charter to Meech Lake* (Toronto: McClelland & Stewart, 1991), pp. 168–69; V. Seymour Wilson, "The Tapestry Vision of Canadian Multiculturalism," *Canadian Journal of Political Science* 26, no. 4 (December 1993): 645–59.

6. Canada, Statistics Canada, *Canada's Ethnocultural Portrait: The Changing Mosaic* (Ottawa: Minister of Industry, 2003), pp. 7–8. Available: <http:www.statscan.ca>. [Accessed April 6, 2003.]

7. Rick Ponting, "Racial Conflict: Turning the Heat Up," in Dan Glenday and Ann Duffy, eds., *Canadian Society: Understanding and Surviving in the 1990s* (Toronto: McClelland & Stewart, 1994), p. 89.

8. Daiva Stasiulis, "Symbolic Representation and the Numbers Game: Tory Policies on 'Race' and Visible Minorities," in F. Abele, ed., *How Ottawa Spends: The Politics of Fragmentation, 1991–1992* (Ottawa: Carleton University Press, 1991), pp. 233–36.

9. Clifford Geertz, "The Integrative Revolution: Primordial Sentiments and Civil Politics in New States," in C. Geertz, ed., *Old Societies and New States* (New York: Free Press, 1963).

10. Fredrik Barth's work on ethnic-group boundaries has been influential in the development of approaches to ethnicity that downplay ethnic culture and highlight the construction and mobilization of ethnic groups. See Fredrik Barth, *Ethnic Groups and Boundaries* (Boston: Little Brown, 1969).

11. Daiva K. Stasiulis, "The Political Structuring of Ethnic Community Action: A Reformulation," *Canadian Ethnic Studies* 12, no. 3 (1980); Audrey Kobayashi, "Representing Ethnicity: Political Statistexts," in Statistics Canada and U.S. Bureau of the Census, *Challenges of Measuring an Ethnic World: Science, Politics and Reality* (Washington, DC: U.S. Government Printing Office, 1993).

12. Kobayashi, "Representing Ethnicity," p. 520.

13. However, the program to make the federal civil service bilingual subsequent to the Royal Commission on Bilingualism and Biculturalism was, in effect, an employment equity program for francophones. Indeed, this program is the most successful Canadian affirmative-action program to date.

14. Alain Pelletier, "Politics and Ethnicity: Representation of Ethnic and Visible Minority Groups in the House of Commons," in K. Megyery, ed., *Ethnocultural Groups and Visible Minorities in Canadian Politics: The Question of Access* (Toronto: Dundurn Press, 1991), pp. 132–33.

15. Franca Iacovetta, *Such Hardworking People: Italian Immigrants in Postwar Toronto* (Montreal/Kingston: McGill-Queen's University Press, 1993), p. 22.

16. Daniel Salée, "Identities in Conflict: The Aboriginal Question and the Politics of Recognition," unpublished manuscript, School of Community and Public Affairs, Concordia University, 1994, p. 6.

17. The conceptualization of racism in terms of "differential positionality" is taken from Atvar Brah, "Difference, Diversity, Differentiation," *International Review of Sociology* 2 (April 1991): 62. For an application of the concept of "relational positionality" in the Canadian context, see Daiva K. Stasiulis, "Relational Positionalities of Nationalisms, Racisms, and Feminisms," in C. Kaplan, N. Alarcón, and M. Moallem, eds., *Between Woman and Nations: Nationalisms, Transnational Feminisms, and the State* (Durham: Duke University Press, 1999), pp. 182–218.

18. Robert A. Huttenback, *Racism and Empire: White Settlers and Colored Immigrants in the British Self-Governing Colonies, 1830–1910* (Ithaca, NY: Cornell University Press, 1976), pp. 13–25.

19. House of Commons, *Debates* (May 4, 1885), p. 1588, quoted in Daiva Stasiulis and Glen Williams, "Mapping Racial/Ethnic Hierarchy in the Canadian Social Formation, 1860–1914: An Examination of Selected Federal Policy Debates," paper presented at the Canadian Political Science Association meetings, Charlottetown, University of Prince Edward Island, June 1992.

20. Ibid., p. 1583.

21. House of Commons, *Debates* (June 7, 1928), pp. 392ff.

22. House of Commons, *Debates* (May 1, 1947), p. 2645.

23. See Peter S. Li, *The Chinese in Canada* (Toronto: Oxford University Press, 1988), pp. 2, 27–30, 86; and Ann Sunahara, *The Politics of Racism: The Uprooting of Japanese Canadians during the Second World War* (Toronto: James Lorimer, 1981), pp. 7, 17, and 151.

24. As recently as 1964, a rundown, all-black school operated in a rural area near Windsor, Ontario; white children from the area were bussed out to a newly constructed school.

The City of Windsor was reportedly the last municipality to desegregate its public facilities, in 1975. The exclusion of blacks from public facilities continues to take place to the present day. In 1991, the barring of blacks from a nightclub in Halifax resulted in street violence. See Daniel Hill, *Human Rights in Canada: A Focus on Racism* (Ottawa: Canadian Labour Congress, 1977), p. 11; Frances Henry and Carol Tator, "Racism in Canada: Social Myths and Strategies for Change," in R.M. Bienvenue and J. E. Goldstein, eds., *Ethnicity and Ethnic Relations in Canada*, 2nd ed. (Toronto: Butterworths, 1985); and Ponting, "Racial Conflict," p. 95.

25. Pelletier, "Politics and Ethnicity," p. 127.

26. Jean Burnet with Howard Palmer, *"Coming Canadians": An Introduction to a History of Canada's Peoples* (Toronto: McClelland & Stewart, 1988), p. 162.

27. Pelletier, "Politics and Ethnicity." See also Daiva K. Stasiulis and Yasmeen Abu-Laban, "The House the Parties Built: (Re)constructing Ethnic Representation in Canadian Politics," and Carole Simard et al., "Visible Minorities and the Canadian Political System," in K. Megyery, ed., *Ethnocultural Groups and Visible Minorities in Canadian Politics: The Question of Access* (Toronto: Dundurn Press, 1991).

28. Pelletier, "Politics and Ethnicity," p. 129.

29. Jerome H. Black, "Ethnoracial Minorities in the House of Commons," *Canadian Parliamentary Review* (Spring 2002): 25.

30. Jerome H. Black, "Differences That Matter: Minority Women MPs, 1993–2000," in M. Trembly and L. Trimble, eds., *Women and Electoral Politics in Canada* (Don Mills: Oxford University Press, 2003), p. 63.

31. Jerome H. Black and Aleem S. Lakhani, "Ethnoracial Diversity in the House of Commons: An Analysis of Numerical Representation in the 35th Parliament," *Canadian Ethnic Studies* (November 1997): 7; Jerome H. Black, "Differences That Matter," p. 70.

32. Yasmeen Abu-Laban, "Ethnic Politics in a Globalizing Metropolis: The Case of Vancouver, Canada," in Timothy L. Thomas, ed., *The Politics of the City: A Canadian Perspective* (Scarborough, ON: ITP Nelson, 1997), p. 83.

33. Jerome H. Black, "Ethnic Minorities and Mass Politics in Canada: Some Observations in the Toronto Setting," *International Journal of Canadian Studies* (Spring 1991): 129–51.

34. Tina W.L. Chui, James E. Curtis, and Ronald D. Lambert, "Immigrant Background and Political Participation: Examining Generational Patterns," *Canadian Journal of Sociology* 16, no. 4 (Fall 1991): 375–96.

35. Canada, Statistics Canada, "1996 Census: Ethnic Origin, Visible Minorities," *The Daily* (February 17, 1998), p. 9. <http://www.statcan.ca/Daily/English/980217/d980217.htm#ART1>.

36. The following discussion of barriers to participation of ethnic minorities in political parties is an adapted and updated version of Stasiulis and Abu-Laban, "The House the Parties Built," pp. 11–13, 41.

37. Stasiulis and Abu-Laban, "The House the Parties Built," p. 66.

38. Murray Campbell, "Manning Tackles Reform's Racist Image," *The Globe and Mail*, April 22, 1997: A6.

39. Anne McIlroy, "Staged Reform Election Photo Panned," *The Globe and Mail*, May 8, 1997: A7.

40. Stasiulis and Abu-Laban, "The House the Parties Built."

41. Ross Howard, "Reform Organizer Quits over Remarks," *The Globe and Mail*, April 23, 1997: A1, A4.

42. Jerome H. Black. "Minority Women as Parliamentary Candidates: The Case of the 1993 Canadian Election," paper delivered at the Annual General Meetings of the

Canadian Political Science Association, Newfoundland, June 1997, p. 12; and "Differences that Matter."

43. Pelletier, "Politics and Ethnicity," p. 141.

44. Black, "Ethnoracial Minorities," p. 25.

45. See Janine Brodie and Jan Jenson, *Crisis, Challenge and Change: Party and Class in Canada Revisited* (Ottawa: Carleton University Press, 1988); and Karl Peter, "The Myth of Multiculturalism," in J. Dahlie and T. Fernando, eds., *Ethnicity, Power and Politics in Canada* (Toronto: Methuen, 1981).

46. The figures for party affiliation of visible minorities are from Table 2 in Black, "Ethnoracial Minorities," p. 26.

47. Jeffrey Simpson, "Reform's Visible-Minority Members Support Its Line on Equality," *Ottawa Citizen*, October 2, 1997: A22.

48. Black and Lakhani, "Ethnoracial Diversity," p. 12.

49. See Gilles Paquet, "Multiculturalism as National Policy," *Journal of Cultural Economics* 13, no. 1 (June 1989): 17–33; and Neil Bissoondath, "A Question of Belonging: Multiculturalism and Citizenship," in W. Kaplan, ed., *Belonging: The Meaning and Future of Canadian Citizenship* (Montreal/Kingston: McGill-Queen's University Press, 1993).

50. Burnet with Palmer, *"Coming Canadians,"* pp. 174–75.

51. Ibid., pp. 171–72.

52. H. Sohn, "Human Rights Legislation in Ontario: A Study of Action," unpublished doctoral dissertation, School of Social Work, University of Toronto, 1975.

53. Daiva Stasiulis, "Minority Resistance in the Local State: Toronto in the 1970s and 1980s," *Ethnic and Racial Studies* (January 1989): 63–83.

54. Daiva Stasiulis, "'Authentic Voice': Anti-Racist Politics in Canadian Feminist Publishing and Literary Production," in S. Gunew and A. Yeatman, eds., *Feminism and the Politics of Difference* (Sydney: Allen and Unwin, 1993).

55. Sunera Thobani, "Making the Links: South Asian Women and the Struggle for Reproductive Rights," *Resources for Feminist Research* 13, no. 1 (Fall 1992): 19–20.

56. Janine Brodie, *Politics on the Margins: Restructuring and the Canadian Women's Movement* (Halifax: Fernwood Publishing, 1995).

57. "Without Funds, NAC to Fold," *The Globe and Mail*, November 26, 1998: A7.

58. Yasmeen Abu-Laban, "welcome/STAY OUT: The Contradiction of Canadian Integration and Immigration Policies at the Millennium," *Canadian Ethnic Studies*, no. 3, 1998.

59. Jack Kapica, "Canadians Want Mosaic to Melt, Survey Finds," *The Globe and Mail*, December 14, 1993: A1–2; and Geoffrey York, "Liberals to Let in 250,000 This Year," *The Globe and Mail*, February 3, 1994: A1.

60. Abu-Laban, "welcome/STAY OUT."

61. Yasmeen Abu-Laban and Christina Gabriel, *Selling Diversity: Immigration, Multiculturalism, Employment Equity and Globalization* (Peterborough: Broadview Press, 2002), pp. 61–104.

62. Ibid., p. 85.

63. Cairns, "Political Science, Ethnicity, and the Canadian Constitution," p. 173.

64. Shelagh Day, "Cries and Statistics: The Empty Heart of Federal Employment Equity," *Our Times* 9, no. 2 (April 1990): 22–25.

65. Abigail B. Bakan and Audrey Kobayashi, *Employment Equity Policy in Canada: An Interprovincial Comparison* (Ottawa: Status of Women Canada, 2000), p. 16.

66. Katharyne Mitchell, "Multiculturalism, or the United Colors of Capitalism?" *Antipode* 25, no. 4 (1993): 263–94.

67. Abu-Laban and Gabriel, *Selling Diversity,* pp. 105–28.

68. Neil Bissoondath, "A Question of Belonging," p. 376. For analyses of the diverse criticisms of multiculturalism policy, see Abu-Laban and Stasiulis, "Ethnic Pluralism under Siege," and Wilson, "The Tapestry Vision of Canadian Multiculturalism."

69. Andrew Phillips, "Lessons of Vancouver," *Maclean's* (February 7, 1994): 28.

FURTHER READINGS

Abu-Laban, Yasmeen, and Christina Gabriel. *Selling Diversity: Immigration, Multiculturalism, Employment Equity and Globalization.* Peterborough: Broadview Press, 2002.

Abu-Laban, Yasmeen, and Daiva Stasiulis. "Constructing 'Ethnic Canadians': The Implications for Public Policy and Inclusive Citizenship." *Canadian Public Policy* XXVI, no. 4 (2000): 477–87.

Abu-Laban, Yasmeen, and Tim Nieguth. "Reconsidering the Constitution, Minorities and Politics in Canada." *The Canadian Journal of Political Science* XXXIII, no. 3 (September 2000): 465–97.

Black, Jerome H. "Differences that Matter: Minority Women MPs 1993–2000." In Manon Tremblay and Linda Trimble, eds., *Women and Electoral Politics in Canada,* pp. 59–74. Don Mills: Oxford University Press, 2003.

———. "Immigrants and Ethnoracial Minorities in Canada: A Review of Their Participation in Federal Electoral Politics." *Electoral Insight* 3, no. 1 (2001): 8–13.

———. "Ethnoracial Minorities in the House of Commons." *Canadian Parliamentary Review* (Spring 2002): 24–28.

Cairns, Alan. "Political Science, Ethnicity and the Canadian Constitution." In David P. Shugarman and Reg Whitaker, eds., *Federalism and Political Community.* Peterborough, ON: Broadview Press, 1989.

Howard-Hassmann, Rhoda. "Canadian as an Ethnic Category: Implications for Multiculturalism and National Unity." *Canadian Public Policy* 25, no. 4 (1999): 523–37.

Megyery, Kathy, ed. *Ethnocultural Groups and Visible Minorities in Canadian Politics: The Question of Access.* Toronto: Dundurn Press, 1991.

Stasiulis, Daiva K. "Participation by Immigrants, Ethnocultural/Visible Minorities in the Canadian Political Process." Paper delivered to the Second National Metropolis Conference (Montreal: November 1997), <http://canada.metropolis.net/events/civic/dstasiulis_e.html>.

Stasiulis, Daiva, and Radha Jhappan. "The Fractious Politics of a Settler Society: Canada." In Daiva Stasiulis and Nira Yuval-Davis, eds., *Unsettling Settler Societies: Articulations of Gender, Race, Ethnicity and Class.* London: Sage, 1995.

Vickers, Jill. *The Politics of Race: Canada, Australia and the US.* Ottawa: Golden Dog Press, 2002.

CHAPTER 16

QUEBEC: PROVINCE, NATION, OR DISTINCT SOCIETY?

Kenneth McRoberts

For 15 years now, the term "distinct society" has assumed a central role in the continuing debate about Quebec and its place within Canada. For many English Canadians the term is anathema, as the collapse of both the Meech Lake and Charlottetown accords demonstrated. Yet, for most Quebec francophones, anything less than distinct society would not do justice to the reality of contemporary Quebec as they understand it. In fact, distinct society is only one among several different formulations of the same theme: *statut particulier, statut distinct, pas une province comme les autres,* and so on. There is, indeed, room for debate over the propriety and implications of inserting within the Constitution the statement that Quebec constitutes a distinct society. But it is difficult to dispute the underlying claim that the social and political reality of Quebec is that of a distinct society.

Clearly, Quebec is "distinct" in the sense of being "distinctive" or "different." Most obviously, it is different in terms of the first language of its residents: Quebec is the only province in which the population is primarily francophone. In 1996, 82.8 percent of its residents spoke French in the home. In New Brunswick, the province with the next-largest francophone presence, 30.5 percent spoke French at home. In Ontario, the figure was 2.9 percent, while in the other provinces it was much less. In fact, Quebec contained 90.4 percent of Canadians who use French at home.[1] The specifically cultural distinctiveness of French Quebec may be less obvious than it was in the heyday of the Roman Catholic Church, when its leaders declared French Canadians to be a preeminently Catholic people with no less than a providential mission to preserve French, Catholic civilization. Now the French language is no longer *gardienne de la foi,* thanks to the pervasive secularization that Quebec society has experienced over the last 30 years. Nonetheless, subtle sociocultural differences clearly remain.

Moreover, Quebec's *political* life is distinctive in a great many ways. In terms of political institutions, Quebec civil law is based on the Civil Code rather than on common law as in all the other provinces, and the symbols of the Crown have been markedly downplayed. Quebec provincial governments have pursued policies strikingly different from those of the other provinces. Concern with maintaining Quebec's cultural distinctiveness has led the provincial government to assume a much more important role than have the other provinces in selecting and settling immigrants and in supporting and regulating cultural activities such as book publishing and the distribution of films. Other areas of governmental activity also seem to reflect the impact of a distinctive balance of social forces. In labour relations, Quebec was the first government in North America to grant the right to strike in the public sector, and still remains the only government with an "anti-scab" law. Quebec pioneered in Canada the establishment of multi-functional public clinics, or *Centres locaux de services communautaires,* which seek to combine health and social services in a highly innovative fashion. During the 1960s, Quebec led the way among provincial governments in establishing a network of state enterprises; many observers claim that contemporary Quebec displays a distinctive form of collaboration among the state, capital, and labour, often known as "Quebec, Inc."

Beyond differences such as these, Quebec is also distinct in terms of its separateness from the other provinces. This separateness is evident, for instance, in the sources of news and entertainment to which most of its population turns—French-language media that are institutionally separate from their English-speaking Canadian counterparts. Even the public broadcasting system, ostensibly responsible to the Canadian Parliament and committed by statute to further national unity, has always been divided between the Montreal-based French-language system, Radio-Canada, and the Toronto-based English-language system, the CBC. But institutional separateness can be seen in areas other than culture. For instance, unlike their counterparts in the other provinces, most labour-union members belong to federations—the Confédération des syndicats nationaux (CSN) and the Corporation des enseignants du Québec—that are not affiliated with the Canadian Labour Congress (CLC). Historically, relations between the CLC and the Fédération des travailleurs du Québec (FTQ), which groups together the Quebec union locals that are linked to the U.S.-based international unions, have been difficult, with FTQ leaders complaining that the CLC's English-Canadian leadership cannot comprehend the distinctive concerns and needs of the FTQ's membership. Finally, in 1993 the FTQ moved to a loose, "sovereignty-association" relationship with the CLC.

As one might expect, this manifest distinctiveness of Quebec society, and the sense of uniqueness associated with it, has encouraged distinct political loyalties. Quebec's political institutions command an allegiance among Quebec francophones that has no clear parallel in the other provinces. Underlying this allegiance is the simple fact that while the federal government is responsible to a predominantly anglophone electorate, the Quebec government is responsible to a predominantly francophone electorate. Thus, it has been commonly argued (and believed) in Quebec that only the Quebec government can be entrusted with the distinctive interests of Quebec francophones.

This argument, and the attachment to Quebec that it supports, has been most dramatically reflected in the movement to secure political sovereignty for Quebec. No other part of Canada has produced a serious movement calling for parity between it and the rest of Canada (as was proposed under sovereignty-association), let alone for independence. The contention that Quebec francophones must rely first and foremost on their provincial government has been a constant theme of Quebec politics since Confederation. Indeed, it was primarily because of French-Canadian fears that Confederation took a federal form, thereby affording Quebec French Canadians an autonomous government in which they could place their full confidence. Thus, one can trace back over the decades a strong commitment among Quebec's political activists to defend Quebec's provincial autonomy and to support the Quebec government over the federal government when the two are in conflict. By and large, Quebec provincial governments have themselves taken this stance.

In fact, so profound is this sense of Quebec's distinctiveness vis-à-vis the other provinces that by the 1970s the very term "province" had fallen into disuse. Some Quebec nationalists even claimed that it harkened back to the days of the British Empire when it was used to designate divisions within such other imperial holdings as India. But whatever its connotations, "province" served to equate Quebec with Canada's other territorial units when, at least in the eyes of nationalists, Quebec manifestly was not. Thus, the Quebec provincial government became *l'état du Québec*. For the Quebec legislature, only the rather grandiloquent term *Assemblée nationale* would do.

This latter change goes to the nub of the matter: for many Quebec francophones, Quebec is not just a province with a difference; it is a nation and deserving of recognition as such. Since the early nineteenth century, nationalism has provided the set of assumptions through which francophone intellectuals have defined and interpreted their collectivity and its historical fate. To be sure, over the decades, the dominant form of this nationalism has changed radically in terms not only of the geographical boundaries of the nation, but also of the nation's fundamental characteristics and goals. In part, these changes have reflected changes in the historical condition of Quebec as a whole. But they also have reflected alterations in the balance of social forces within the Quebec nation, as members of different classes succeeded in imposing the brand of nationalism that invariably reflected the particular preoccupations and ambitions of their class. If the central theme of this nationalism has been the necessity of maintaining cultural distinctiveness against British and English-speaking Canadian threats, a recurrent theme has been the desire to break down the structures of anglophone economic and political domination. In each case, different nationalist leaderships have approached these themes in very different ways.

THE HISTORICAL ROOTS OF DISTINCTIVENESS AND NATIONALISM

To understand why Quebec's society is distinctive, and how a national consciousness has developed out of this distinctiveness, we need to trace Quebec's historical development. Unlike the rest of Canada, non-aboriginal society in Quebec first emerged within the framework of the French Empire. This formative experience established elements of distinctiveness that were to endure long after Quebec ceased to be a French colony. A common "*Canadien*" dialect was created out of the several French dialects that the colonists brought with them, predating the emergence of a national dialect in the mother country. The Roman Catholic Church was afforded a privileged position within the formal institutions of the *ancien régime*, laying the basis for the central role that it was to play throughout so much of French Canada's history. And the Civil Code was entrenched within legal structures of the *ancien régime*. The colonists soon acquired a sense of collective identity (and destiny) as they faced the common challenges of a harsh climate and periodic threats from both aboriginal peoples and the British colonies to the south. They began to call themselves "*Canadiens*" or "*habitants*" so as to distinguish themselves from the metropolitan French, as well as from English speakers. In fact, they periodically expressed resentment against the metropolitan Frenchmen who were nominated to senior positions within the colony.

The colony was never the quasi-feudal society or theocracy that was later portrayed by historians. The bishop and his colleagues regularly had to spar with secular colonial authorities over policy. Commercial values and interests were actively pursued by some secular elites, who amassed considerable personal wealth through the fur trade. And the regularity with which the *habitants* challenged the authority of parish priests or resisted paying their tithes runs counter to images of a priest-ridden society. Thus, social tensions and conflict marked French Canada from its beginning.

Although Quebec emerged as part of the French Empire, it was a relatively unimportant and neglected one. In 1759, it fell under British control and lost forever its formal ties to France. It was within the structures of the British Empire that the *Canadiens* would have to secure a future for themselves. If they were to maintain their distinctiveness, it would be on terms acceptable to the British authorities and to the English-speaking population that soon established itself within the colony. Moreover, it would be under the direction of a greatly shrunken *Canadien* leadership. With the Conquest, administrative and military structures fell into the hands of the British. And the replacement of France by England as Quebec's *metropole* ensured that the colony's trade would be controlled by the British rather than by the *Canadiens* themselves. In short, all that remained by way of a viable leadership for the *Canadiens* was the Church and, to a lesser extent, the seigneurs—the two classes that had a strong interest in the *Canadiens'* defining their distinctiveness in the most traditional of terms.

Initially, British authorities were determined to destroy all forms of cultural distinctiveness for the *Canadiens*. The Royal Proclamation of 1763 was designed to do just that. However, the proclamation was not put into effect. With time, the colonial authorities determined that the imperial interest would be better served by winning the collaboration of the *Canadien* leadership and thus, presumably, of the *Canadiens* as a whole. Under the Quebec Act of 1774, the seigneurial system was re-established, the Church was once again empowered to collect tithes, Catholics were spared the need to renounce their faith to assume office, and French civil law was re-established. At the same time, out of deference to the *Canadien* clergy and seigneurs who feared a challenge of their own positions, a representative assembly was not created.

Ostensibly, the survival of *Canadien* society was assured. Yet, it was a particular kind of *Canadien* society that was so assured. In effect, the Quebec Act served to reinforce traditional structures and values within *Canadien* society. And it formalized a cultural division of labour that was to mark Quebec for the next two centuries. *Canadiens* could count on being able to assume ecclesiastical and legal functions, at least sufficient to service the needs of their compatriots, but there was nothing to challenge the firm control over the colony's economic life that English speakers had secured in the wake of the Conquest. Much of the history of the next two centuries, including the nationalist upsurges of the 1960s and 1970s, can be seen as a struggle by various groups to break French-Canadian society out of this mould—and out of the political and economic bonds that supported it—imposed by the British colonial regime in close collaboration with French-Canadian traditional elites.

It was in the early nineteenth century that French Canada's first nationalist movement took form. It was spawned by a new class of *Canadiens*, a petite bourgeoisie of liberal professionals and small merchants that coalesced in the legislative assembly that the Constitutional Act of 1791 had created (while at the same time dividing the British colony of Quebec in two). Within the new colony of Lower Canada, French Canadians were clearly preponderant, and even with an overrepresentation of anglophones in the assembly, the *Canadiens* still had a commanding majority. In part, the nationalism of this new *Canadien* petite bourgeoisie was a response to the continuing assimilationist projects of the colony's anglophone elites. In part, it was a response to the English bourgeoisie's ambitious plans for development of the colonial economy; the *Canadiens* would not benefit directly from the projects even though they would have to assume part of the financial burden through taxation.

The French-Canadian petite bourgeoisie's nationalism also reflected its own class position. It was quite appropriate that this nationalist leadership should champion liberal political reforms and the rights of the representative assembly, given their own dominance of that assembly and relative exclusion from executive and administrative office within the colony. At the same time, the *Canadien* liberal professionals began to challenge clerical preeminence over the francophone population by sponsoring such projects as a secularized school system. Out of this protracted conflict emerged the *Patriote* movement. Championing an autonomous state for Quebec, the *Patriotes* staged an armed uprising in 1837 to secure it. With overwhelming military superiority, however, the British authorities had no difficulty putting down the rebellion. For good measure, they had the vigorous support of the French-Canadian clergy, which had long been alarmed by some of the liberal notions that the *Patriotes* had been propagating.

With the defeat of the Rebellion of 1837, the more traditional forces within French-Canadian society, led by the Church, were able to secure a new ascendancy. The Church strengthened itself by importing priests from

France (refugees from French liberalism) and by expanding the religious orders and educational institutions. In the process, a new, apolitical version of French-Canadian nationalism became hegemonic. In clerical hands, the essence of the French-Canadian nation became its Roman Catholicism. National greatness was to lie in godliness and spirituality (best achieved in a rural setting) rather than in material accomplishments. For this, French Canadians were to rely on the institutions of the Church rather than on governments and politicians, corroded as they were by liberalism and corruption. By definition, within this world-view, anglophone domination of Quebec's economic development was not a problem.

In the immediate aftermath of the rebellion of 1837, the very survival of French-Canadian society was placed in question by the British authorities. Under the Act of Union, inspired by the Durham Report, Lower Canada and Upper Canada were joined so as to encourage the assimilation of the troublesome *Canadiens*. However, French Canada survived yet another assimilationist threat as French-Canadian politicians from Canada East formed an alliance with English-Canadian reformers in Canada West and, on that basis, secured recognition of the French fact. In effect, duality became enshrined in the institutions of the United Canadas: French was made an official language along with English; hyphenated ministries were held by representatives of each of the two original colonies; and, to some extent, voting in the legislative assembly was based on a double-majority principle.

Eventually, this situation became unacceptable to many English-speaking Canadians, with the result that French Canadians in Quebec had to trade dualism for federalism. First, Canada West's population began to exceed Canada East's. In 1840, Canada East had been much more populous than Canada West; the two Canadas had been assigned an equal number of seats in the legislature so as to prevent Canada East's dominance. By the 1860s, the burgeoning population of Canada West had now become eager converts to "representation by population." Second, the English-speaking Canadian bourgeoisie found that its economic projects were being frustrated in the United Canadas assembly by French Canadians and their reformist allies. Thus, there ensued a campaign to join the several British colonies in a common union. There, French Canadians clearly would be in a minority and central political institutions would be dominated by English-speaking Canadians. To be acceptable to French Canadians, Confederation had to be based on a federalism that afforded Quebec an autonomous status for certain purposes. That French Canadians could not entrust their distinctive interests to an English-Canadian majority was a central premise of Confederation.

Nonetheless, the notion of distinctive interests contained in the division of powers of the Constitution Act of 1867 quite closely reflects the ascendancy of the Church within French-Canadian society. Along with the other provincial governments, Quebec was granted jurisdiction over matters that were central to its cultural survival (e.g., education) or that might affect the prerogatives of the Church and its institutions (e.g., health, welfare, and the solemnization of marriage). On the other hand, economic responsibilities were effectively lodged with the federal government along with exclusive access to the then primary source of government revenue—indirect taxes. In this sense, the terms of Confederation further formalized the cultural division of labour that underlay the Quebec Act of 1774. The same division of labour was reproduced within the federal government itself. In the Cabinet, anglophones effectively monopolized the major economic portfolios. In the upper levels of the bureaucracy, francophones were seriously underrepresented.

THE ECONOMIC AND SOCIAL TRANSFORMATION OF QUEBEC: SEEDS OF POLITICAL CRISIS

By the turn of the century, Quebec was undergoing social changes that eventually would result in serious challenges to the constitutional and political arrangements discussed above, and even to Confederation itself. Industrialization in Quebec can be traced back as far as the 1870s. At that time, Montreal was producing the same volume of iron and steel products as Toronto and Hamilton combined, and had a large number of manufacturing enterprises.[2] With the turn of the century, industrialization spread to other parts of Quebec. For its part, urbanization can be traced to the first part of the twentieth century. In fact, by 1921 half of Quebec's population as a whole was urban. The level of urbanization among francophones alone was not quite as high, but by 1931 it had reached 58 percent.

The full impact of these changes on Quebec's political life was delayed until the 1960s. Typically, industrialization entails an expansion of the role of the state to assist capital in its undertakings and to placate an expanded working class. And the social and economic problems of urban life usually raise demands for new government services. Moreover, one might well expect demands for state intervention to arise from the way in which English-Canadian and American capital dominated Quebec's industrial economy. Not only were francophone enterprises marginal in industry (as they had been in commerce and finance), but to a large extent the growing francophone proletariat was employed by foreigners.

Yet, especially when compared with the neighbouring province of Ontario, which was also being transformed through industrialization and urbanization, the economic and social role of the Quebec state remained limited. The provision of education and social services remained effectively under the control of the Church and its orders. Even the weakly developed public schools were subject to clerical domination through the *Conseil de l'instruction publique*, and there was no Ministry of Education in Quebec City. As for the economy, the Quebec government played a largely passive role. Industrial development was encouraged primarily by making natural resources available to American and English-Canadian firms at nominal royalty levels. As one might expect, the administrative structures of the Quebec government remained poorly developed. By and large, its personnel were political appointees and relatively few had expertise in the social sciences or public administration.

The Liberal regime of Adélard Godbout (1939–44) featured some significant reforms. The government made school attendance compulsory and granted women the right to vote, in both cases over the strong opposition of the clergy. It also established Hydro-Québec, through the nationalization of Montreal Light, Heat and Power Consolidated. But on its return to power in 1944, the Union Nationale regime of Maurice Duplessis was little inclined to follow suit by further expanding the economic and social role of the Quebec government. It did, however, intervene vigorously in one area—labour relations. Through a variety of legislative measures and deployment of the provincial police, it sought to curtail the actions of unions.

In short, the Duplessis regime faithfully reproduced the historical cultural division of labour in Quebec's economy and did little to address the mounting need of the francophone population for higher levels of education and social services than the Church-related institutions were able, or willing, to provide. Needless to say, the Duplessis administration had the close support of English-Canadian and American capitalists, who highly prized Duplessis's ability to maintain labour peace and keep taxes low. However, by the 1950s, there had emerged within French Quebec two social groups that had a clear interest in changing this state of affairs.

First, the postwar years saw the emergence within French Canada of a new middle class of salaried professionals. Within the French-language universities, formally under Church control, the numbers of lay faculty had grown rapidly both in the physical sciences and the social sciences. Especially important in the development of a critical attitude toward the passivity of the Duplessis regime was the Faculté des sciences sociales at Laval University, where lay faculty openly advocated a variety of reforms, earning Duplessis's bitter enmity in the process. Francophone intellectuals also gained a new base, and popular influence, as Radio-Canada began television broadcasting. At the same time, lay administrators and professionals acquired a new prominence in the Church-related institutions that provided health and social services. Finally, as it had for many years, l'École des hautes études commerciales continued to graduate accountants and business specialists.

Uniting these different strata of the "new middle class" was a common interest in greater state intervention, whether it be to attenuate clerical control of education and social services or to expand opportunity for francophones within the anglophone-dominated economy. This interest found expression in a variety of new middle-class movements and organizations. During the 1950s, proposals along these lines appeared in such publications as *Cité libre* and *Le Devoir*, and in the annual conferences of the *Institut Canadien des affaires publiques*. The Quebec Liberal Party, where influence of the new middle class was growing, adopted many of them. The *Rassemblement pour l'indépendance national* (RIN), the first Quebec *indépendantiste* party, was founded in 1960. Based within the francophone new middle class, the RIN called for state intervention on a variety of fronts. In 1960, francophone social workers formed a distinct professional organization in order to reduce clerical domination of their activities and carry on their lobbying for state intervention. And, in 1961, many francophone academics and teachers joined in the *Mouvement laïque de la langue française*, which forthrightly advocated a secularization of Quebec's educational system.[3]

As well, from the 1950s, Quebec's union movements displayed a new militancy. Thanks to postwar prosperity, their memberships increased rapidly. The *Confédération des travailleurs catholiques du Canada* (CTCC), founded by the Church in 1921, came under a new leadership that was much more forthright in its advocacy of workers' interests and that began to distance the CTCC from the Church. Evidence of the CTCC's new militancy was a series of bitter strikes, including the celebrated Asbestos strike of 1949, when the CTCC took on U.S. mining interests as well as Duplessis and the Quebec provincial police. This militancy was echoed by the *Fédération des unions industrielles du Québec* (FUIQ), which grouped together Quebec locals linked to the Canadian Labour Congress and the American Congress of Industrial Organizations (CIO). The CTCC and the FUIQ regularly called on the Quebec government not only to handle labour relations in a more evenhanded manner, but to meet the needs of labour directly through a variety of initiatives such as public health insurance, improved social security, increased state involvement in education, stricter regulation of working conditions, and complete public ownership of hydro production and distribution in the province.

Finally, support for much more limited state initiatives came from the precarious francophone business class, which feared it would be further marginalized by American and English-Canadian capital. In the late 1950s, the *Chambre de commerce du Québec* began to call on the Quebec government to establish an economic advisory council, with strong business representation. In particular, it was hoped that the Quebec state could help French-Canadian firms to find much-needed capital.

With the death of Duplessis in 1959, the subsequent disintegration of the Union Nationale, and the election of a Liberal government under Jean Lesage in 1960, the steadily widening demands for a major expansion of the role of the Quebec state finally found an outlet. The Liberal government was keen to project an image of progressive change, in contrast with the Duplessis regime. Moreover, unlike the Union Nationale, the Liberal Party was itself based primarily in urban Quebec. Elements of the new middle class had secured considerable influence in the Liberal Party, and the CTCC leadership had a good working relationship with Lesage and other party figures. In short, the conditions were right for what was to become a fundamental recasting of the Quebec state and Quebec politics in general. Over the next few years, Quebec underwent its "Quiet Revolution," a period of unprecedented intellectual and political ferment in which all the long-established assumptions about French–English relations and Quebec's place within Confederation were challenged.

THE QUIET REVOLUTION: STATE-BUILDING AND NATION-BUILDING

The Quiet Revolution represented first and foremost an ideological change, a transformation of mentalities. Within the new ideology, Quebec clearly was to be seen as the urban, industrial society that it had become. The state had to assume full responsibility for the social and educational functions that thus far the Church had been able to retain, just as it had to assume responsibility for planning the direction of the Quebec economy and undertaking the measures needed to modernize it and make it more competitive. In effect, the Quebec state was to assume the functions of a Keynesian state. But it was Keynesianism with a difference, since the Quebec state was also to be a "national" state. With the 1960s, French-Canadian nationalism was recast into a more explicitly Québécois nationalism. The greatness of this Quebec nation was to lie not in the past, as represented by traditional French-Canadian nationalism's glorification of the *ancien régime,* but with the future, as represented by an urban, industrial, and secular society. Responsible to a primarily francophone electorate, the Quebec state was the one institution that could enable Québécois to achieve these objectives. In particular, it was the indispensable lever for undoing the cultural division of labour within the Quebec economy, thereby making Québécois "*maîtres chez nous*"—"masters in our own house."

As with earlier formulations of nationalist ideology, the Quebec neo-nationalism of the 1960s bore the clear imprint of the class that fashioned and supported it—in this case, the new francophone middle class.[4] Because its members were fully qualified to assume managerial and technical positions, they could only be affronted by the anglophone domination of the economy. By the same token, they had every interest in the transfer of responsibilities from the Church to an expanded Quebec state with a modern bureaucracy. And they had every reason to support the Quebec government in its struggles with Ottawa, where opportunities for the francophone new middle class were few and far between. Yet resentment over anglophone domination, the desire for better educational and social services, and mistrust of the federal government were shared by a great many francophones. The various initiatives of the Lesage Liberals enjoyed unwavering support not only from the new middle class but also from organized labour (especially the CSN), and, on a more qualified basis, from francophone business and traditional liberal professional nationalists. With steady propagation by the Quebec government and intellectuals, neo-nationalism acquired a certain degree of hegemony in Quebec. Thus, young francophones entering political life in the 1960s were socialized to it en masse.

Beyond ideological change, however, the 1960s did witness real change in the role of the Quebec state and its institutions. In 1963, Quebec's private hydroelectric enterprises were all nationalized so as to give Hydro-Québec a monopoly over the production and distribution of electricity in the province. In 1968, a publicly owned steel mill, SIDBEC, was established. A *Société générale de financement* was created to inject capital into francophone-owned enterprises. On the basis of funds generated through the Quebec Pension Plan, the *Caisse de dépôt et de placement du Québec* became a major institutional investor and, when needed, a purchaser of government securities. In 1964, a Ministry of Education was created, and over subsequent years many of the *collèges classiques* were transformed into secular, government-administered *Collèges d'enseignement général et professionnel* (CEGEPs). Control over health and social services moved steadily from Church-related institutions to the Quebec bureaucracy.

Nonetheless, the overall effect of the Quiet Revolution reforms was uneven. The secularization of Quebec society progressed rapidly; as Church-held educational and social functions were transferred to the state, clerical influence in Quebec society declined at an astounding rate. However, much more limited progress was made in reversing the historical anglophone dominance over the Quebec economy, the expansion of Hydro-Québec notwithstanding. Moreover, by the mid-1960s the uneasy coalition of social forces that had supported the initiatives of the Lesage government had succumbed to its own contradictions. With the return of the Union Nationale to power in 1966, the government was formed by a party that had a different social base from its predecessors. Thus, while the momentum of change in the Quebec state was not halted, it was markedly slowed.

By the same token, mid-1960s relations between Quebec City and Ottawa became increasingly chilly. Initially, the federal government had sought to accommodate Quebec's demands to occupy its jurisdictions to the maximum, exemplified by the establishment of a Quebec Pension Plan in 1964 and other "opting-out" schemes. Under Lester Pearson's leadership, the federal government had sought to find ways to accommodate the new Quebec nationalism within the Canadian political order. Indeed, Pearson himself dubbed Quebec "a nation within a nation." In the same spirit, Pearson established a Royal Commission on Bilingualism and Biculturalism charged with making Confederation "an equal partnership" between English Canada and French Canada. However, with Pierre Trudeau's accession to power in 1968, the federal government shifted to a very different strategy. Rather than seeking to accommodate Quebec nationalism, the objective became one of confronting it and inducing Quebeckers to attach their primary allegiance to Canada as a whole. This was to be achieved in large part through the extension of French language rights, on an individual basis, throughout Canada. Rather than being afforded a distinctive status and role as the government of the province in which most of Canada's francophones are located, Quebec was to be a "province like the others."[5] A large majority of Québécois rejected what they saw as a diminished status within the Federation.

To summarize, during the 1960s, a great many Québécois had been converted to the Quiet Revolution conception of a dynamic, interventionist Quebec state. By the late 1960s, however, the Quebec state no longer seemed able to pursue the neo-nationalist agenda of economic and social change; it had reached its limits. Yet the original agenda was expanding as new concerns arose. Quebec nationalists began to fear that the continuing anglicization of immigrants threatened francophone predominance in Montreal, if not all of Quebec, especially given the radical decline in the francophone birthrate. There arose new demands for restricting access to English-language schools. At the same time, the relative failure of the Quebec state to carve out new opportunities for francophones in the upper levels of the Quebec economy fostered demands for state intervention to establish French as the language of work. These demands became all the more urgent as the 1960s expansion of the Quebec state structures wound down and fewer new positions were available to francophone university graduates. Finally, working-class organizations began to articulate their own vision of an agenda for Quebec that was not bound by the preoccupations of the new middle class. The concerns acquired urgency as labour relations in the public sector became increasingly conflict-prone.

THE PARTI QUÉBÉCOIS AND QUEBEC INDEPENDENCE

All these political frustrations provided fertile ground for the growth of the Quebec independence movement. Independence bore the promise of a Quebec state that would have the capacity and resolve to discharge a much larger agenda. Thus, it became the essential remedy for a wide variety of grievances. In addition, independence had more direct appeal. For the many francophones, especially among the youth, who had come to see themselves as preeminently Québécois, independence constituted the formal recognition of their own identity. As a result, the Quebec independence movement and its preoccupations were to colour, if not dominate, Quebec politics throughout the 1970s and early 1980s.

In 1968, the Parti Québécois (PQ), under the leadership of René Lévesque, emerged as the primary vehicle of the *indépendantiste* cause. The PQ proposed to repatriate the economic "centres of decision" through state enterprises and regulation of non-Quebec ownership in the financial sector. At the same time, this technocratic thrust was coupled with populist measures to help a variety of socially deprived groups. All this would be linked to the rest of Canada through a vaguely defined economic association, but Quebec would nonetheless achieve the full-fledged "national" status to which its centuries-old distinctiveness entitled it. Although members of the new middle class dominated the PQ leadership and the party program clearly bore their imprint, the Parti Québécois emerged as a broad-based coalition of social forces committed to Quebec sovereignty.[6]

The pressures to reinforce Quebec's distinctiveness only grew with the return of the Liberals to power in 1970, this time under Robert Bourassa. During the October Crisis of 1970, the Quebec government was effectively subordinated to Ottawa as the federal government proceeded with its hard-line response to the Front de libération du Québec (FLQ). The following year, efforts to revise the Canadian Constitution ground to a halt after the Bourassa government concluded that the Victoria Charter was insufficient to meet Quebec's needs. The government's efforts, through Bill 22, to satisfy nationalist demands for the preeminence of French within Quebec foundered over rejection of the bill by franco-phones and anglophones alike. At the same time, by retreating from state economic intervention, the government seemed to be playing down the issue of ownership within the Quebec economy. Dramatic confrontations between the Bourassa government and the union movement, especially with public-sector workers, further served to weaken the legitimacy of the existing order. As the Parti Québécois dominated opposition forces, its option of Quebec sovereignty emerged as the logical remedy to all these problems. Accordingly, the PQ was able to win power in 1976.

The election of a party formally committed to sovereignty for Quebec served to demonstrate more clearly than ever before the distinctiveness of Quebec politics. Never before had a province elected a government com-mitted to withdrawal from Canada (with the possible exception of the 1867 election of an anti-Confederation government in Nova Scotia). The PQ had not spelled out the precise nature of sovereignty; it remained committed to some form of post-independence economic association with the rest of Canada. Moreover, the party had declared that a PQ government would first need to obtain popular approval in a referendum before it could pro-ceed to secure sovereignty. Nonetheless, the mere evocation of sovereignty was sufficient to plunge the Canadian political system into a grave crisis.

As it happened, the Lévesque government moved slowly on the ques-tion of sovereignty. Three years passed before the government fully defined its proposal; another year passed before it staged its referendum. Instead, the PQ became consumed with the task of running a provincial govern-ment. In both areas, the PQ's prudence reflected the new middle-class base of its leadership. Over the previous 20 years, this class had already made very substantial gains; thus, it was disinclined to take needless risks.

The Lévesque government first moved on the language front, with Bill 101. In its final version, Bill 101 did not differ radically from Bill 22, but it did tighten non-anglophone access to English schools, and it was more stringent in requiring enterprises to conduct their operations in French. Also, by requiring French-only commercial signs, it sought to give Quebec an unmistakably French face. Coming from an *indépendantiste* government, these measures carried much more credibility than had Bill 22. In addition, the Lévesque administration reformed electoral funding practices and passed a variety of social measures, such as public automobile insurance, labour-relations reform, a limited guaranteed-income scheme, and free pre-scription medication for the elderly. In effect, the PQ went about providing good provincial government. In fact, when it came to routine federal–provincial relations, the PQ government agreed to a wide variety of joint programs with Ottawa.

This emphasis on providing good government was rationalized in terms of the PQ's *étapiste* strategy: as the population acquired confidence in the ability of the party to provide good provincial government, so it would be more prepared to support the party's option of independence. Yet this strategy carried risks common to all movements that, while committed to global change, assume office within existing structures. As party leaders and militants come to enjoy the concrete benefits associated with holding office, their own commitment to more radical change may be tempered. Party militants may become estranged from their leaders, who now have a separate base of power outside the party. Most important, efforts to provide good government may serve to make the existing system more tolerable to the discontented parts of the population, thus undercutting rather than reinforcing support for more radical change. All of these processes appear to have affected both the PQ itself and support for the independence option. Especially striking is the extent to which Bill 101 may have served to rehabilitate the existing federal order by appearing to resolve the language question to nationalists' satisfaction.

In addition, the PQ leadership applied *étapiste* logic to the goal of sovereignty itself, surrounding it with a very comprehensive economic association and committing the government to yet another referendum. In seeking to minimize the prospect of change, the government seemed to acknowledge that true independence would have catastrophic effects. On this basis, it could not address the fears of much of the population, which clearly believed that the PQ's real goal was independence. At the same time, the credibility of its option depended on whether English-speaking Canada was likely to accept it; English-Canadian politicians spared no effort to convince Québécois that this would not be the case. Whatever the explanation, the PQ government was unable to broaden support much beyond its primary electoral clientele of younger francophones, especially those based within the public sector. Thus, with only 40 percent in favour (not quite 50 percent of francophones), the referendum proposition of 1980 was soundly defeated.

QUEBEC IN THE 1980S: DISINTEGRATION AND RESURGENCE OF NATIONALIST FORCES

The failure of the 1980 referendum had a devastating effect on the nationalist movement. Even though the Parti Québécois was able to secure re-election in 1981, what had once appeared to be an inexorable movement to Quebec independence now seemed to have come to a permanent halt. The sense of defeat was only reinforced by the way in which the Canadian Constitution was amended in 1982. With the support of all provinces but Quebec, the federal government of Pierre Trudeau sent a formal request to the British Parliament to patriate the Canadian Constitution. Until that time, Canada's primary constitutional document had been the British North America (BNA) Act, a statute of the British Parliament. The Canadian government requested that the BNA Act be replaced by a Constitution Act providing a procedure for amending it in Canada. At the same time, the Constitution Act would add a new element to the Canadian Constitution: a Charter of Rights and Freedoms.

The Quebec government of René Lévesque opposed the move. Although it supported patriation as a general goal, Quebec claimed that the terms on which this was to be done ignored that province's particular concerns and diminished the powers of its government. The amending formula did not provide the Quebec government with the veto it needed to protect Quebec's interests. The Charter also reduced the Quebec government's powers by limiting its prerogatives in such matters as the regulation of access to English-language schools and the restriction of access to government services by migrants from other provinces.

The Trudeau government derided this opposition as the predictable response of a "separatist" government. Yet, the Quebec government's position was supported by a good number of Quebec federalists, including most Liberal members of the Quebec National Assembly. In fact, the Quebec government sought to have the federal move declared unconstitutional by the courts. It claimed that the initiative violated an established constitutional practice whereby Quebec, if not the other provinces, had enjoyed an effective veto over constitutional change. The Supreme Court rejected Quebec's claim, declaring that no such veto existed.

On April 17, 1982, the Constitution Act, 1982, was proclaimed by Queen Elizabeth. Canada's Constitution was patriated over the objections of Quebec, but with the approval of all nine of the other provincial governments. Quebec's distinctive demands had been simply dismissed by the federal government and a large proportion of English-speaking Canadians. The new Constitution fell squarely within the vision of Canada held by its primary author: Pierre Elliott Trudeau. It entrenched minority language rights, a primary purpose of the new Charter, and it recognized Canada's multicultural nature. But its amending formula, as well as the new Charter, placed Quebec on precisely the same level as the other provinces, and the division of powers within the federation remained effectively unchanged. Thus, not only had the dream of Quebec sovereignty been crushed, but also within Canadian federalism Quebec was denied any distinctive status relative to the other provinces. The resulting bitterness extended beyond sovereigntists to include a significant proportion of Quebec's federalist ranks.

The Parti Québécois itself became badly divided over what strategy to follow in the wake of these successive defeats of the nationalist cause. In September 1984, after the election of the Progressive Conservative government of Brian Mulroney, René Lévesque even evoked the possibility of seeking an accommodation of Quebec within the federal system. Such talk was anathema to leading PQ Cabinet members, who resigned in protest. The ensuing disarray culminated in Lévesque himself resigning from office. Under his successor, Pierre-Marc Johnson, the PQ was soundly defeated by the Liberals, led once again by Robert Bourassa. Quebec appeared to be safely back in the federalist fold.

Despite the renewed dominance of federalist forces in Quebec, there were ample signs that most Quebec francophones continued to see Quebec as their primary political community and were frustrated by the failure to find a satisfactory place for Quebec within the Canadian constitutional order.[7] But the Parti Québécois seemed unable to capitalize on this fact. Upon the accession of Jacques Parizeau to the leadership in 1987, the PQ renewed its commitment to Quebec sovereignty after the "neo-federalist" deviations of the mid-1980s. Parizeau promised to lead an all-out struggle for Quebec sovereignty. However, following the 1989 provincial election, the Parti Québécois had to content itself with nothing more than a few additional seats in the opposition benches.

As it happened, a resurgence in nationalist fortunes did come about, but it was generated by a division among the forces for Canadian federalism rather than by a new mobilization of the forces for Quebec sovereignty. Quebec federalists found themselves isolated from their ostensible allies in the rest of the country, once again over the question of Quebec's distinctiveness. The division in federalist ranks, already manifest at the time of the constitutional patriation, became far more pronounced. Ultimately, it pushed support for Quebec sovereignty to heights never seen before.

Upon their return to power, the Bourassa Liberals had turned their attention to the fact that Quebec was still not a signatory to the Canadian Constitution. In addressing this problem, the Quebec government announced five conditions that would enable Quebec to sign the document: (1) an expanded veto over constitutional change; (2) limitation of the federal government's use of the spending power in provincial jurisdictions; (3) participation in nominations to the Supreme Court; (4) recognition of Quebec's existing role in immigration; and (5) formal recognition of Quebec's status as a distinct society in a clause intended to guide the courts' interpretation of the Constitution, including the Charter of Rights and Freedoms. Collectively, these conditions represented an exceedingly modest package that fell well short of the constitutional demands that had been proposed by Quebec governments for decades.

Under the leadership of Prime Minister Brian Mulroney, the nine other premiers agreed to Quebec's demands contingent on one additional provision that was acceptable to Quebec: provincial participation in nominations to the Senate. This new document became generally known as the Meech Lake Accord.[8] At last, it seemed Quebec would formally embrace the new constitutional order created in 1982. Soon, however, the accord came under heavy attack from forces outside Quebec. There were a variety of grievances. Many claimed that negotiation of the accord had not involved sufficient consultation with the people of Canada and in particular with aboriginal First Nations. Some feared that the federal government would be weakened as a result of certain provisions of the accord, such as the restriction on the federal spending power and the tying of Supreme Court and Senate nominations to provincial lists. But it is clear from analysis of public opinion that the most important basis of English-speaking Canadian and aboriginal opposition was the clause declaring Quebec to be a distinct society.[9]

Within the vision of Canada that many Canadians had adopted under the leadership of Pierre Trudeau, there could be no justification for a provision like the distinct-society clause. Now that French had been afforded equal status to English throughout Canada, thanks to the Charter, Quebec could no longer claim to be distinct on the basis of language. With Canada composed of a multitude of cultures, as proclaimed by multiculturalism, Quebec was no longer singular for its cultural distinctiveness. In short, Quebec could only be "a province like the others."

Yet the Trudeau vision had never had many takers among Quebec francophones. For most of them, formal recognition of Quebec's distinctiveness remained the most important constitutional issue. Thus, for a great many Quebec francophones—federalists as well as sovereigntists—English-Canadian rejection of the distinct-society clause amounted to rejection of Quebec itself. In June of 1990 time finally ran out for the Meech Lake Accord. Three years had elapsed since the accord received its first ratification by a legislature, Quebec's National Assembly. It still had not been ratified by all the provincial legislatures: Newfoundland had rescinded its ratification and Manitoba had yet to ratify it. Accordingly, under the terms of the Constitution Act, 1982, the accord died.

THE 1990S: DEALING WITH THE COLLAPSE OF MEECH

The collapse of the Meech Lake Accord proved to be a watershed in Quebec's relationship with the rest of the country. During the 1990s much of Canadian political life was dominated by debate among political leaders and citizens, both federalist and sovereigntist, over what Meech's collapse really meant and what course of action should follow from it. Among Quebec francophones the sense of resentment and humiliation over English-Canadian rejection of the accord raised support for Quebec sovereignty to unprecedented levels, from 44 percent in September 1989, to 56 percent in March 1990, to 64 percent the following November, with only 30 percent opposed.[10] Arguably, with such a groundswell in favour of sovereignty, Premier Robert Bourassa could have led Quebec out of Canada if he had wished. Yet, committed to maintaining Quebec within the Canadian federation, he steadfastly resisted the sovereigntist tide. Still, to assuage the nationalist feeling sweeping Quebec, Bourassa needed to offer a genuine prospect for a renewed federal system in which Quebec's distinctiveness would at last be clearly accommodated. Moreover, for that he needed the collaboration and support of Ottawa and the other provincial governments. This was to prove to be no small undertaking, given the popular sentiments in English-speaking Canada that had caused the Meech Lake Accord's demise.

After some false starts, in August 1992 the 11 first ministers, two territorial leaders, and four national aboriginal organizations did agree on a new scheme for constitutional revision: the Charlottetown Accord. While it retained the key elements of the Meech Lake Accord, this new document reflected a two-pronged strategy to rein in the part of the Meech Lake Accord that had been objectionable and to incorporate a host of new provisions to respond to the many other demands for constitutional change that English-speaking and aboriginal Canadians had been expressing. Thus the infamous "distinct society" clause became only one of eight "fundamental characteristics" of Canada enumerated in a lengthy "Canada clause." The clause itself now sought to narrow Quebec's distinctiveness by spelling out its main elements: a francophone majority with a unique culture and civil law tradition. Moreover, constitutional revision was now also to include Senate reform, a commitment to strengthen the social and economic union, recognition of aboriginal peoples' inherent right to self-government, and reinforcement of some existing provincial jurisdictions.

Nonetheless, this attempt at constitutional reform was also to fail—in large part over the question of Quebec's distinctiveness. While recasting the distinct-society clause seemed to render it less objectionable to English-speaking Canadians, another component in the Charlottetown Accord aroused a great deal of objection. In an attempt to mollify Québécois discontent with Senate reform, as it reduced Quebec's representation to the same level as all other provinces, the accord increased Quebec's representation (along with Ontario's) in the House of Commons and guaranteed Quebec 25 percent of Commons seats in perpetuity, even if its share of the Canadian population should fall below that mark. For many Canadians this new attempt to accommodate Quebec's distinctiveness was no more acceptable than the Meech Lake Accord's distinct-society clause. At the same time, this provision seems to have won few adherents to the Charlottetown Accord in Quebec, where attention focused on the relative insignificance of Quebec's gains vis-à-vis the division of powers. All of these factors contributed to the resounding defeat of the Charlottetown Accord in a national referendum held on October 26, 1992. In Quebec, the vote split 43.3 percent for, 56.7 percent against; outside Quebec it was 45.7 percent for, 54.3 percent against.[11] The second attempt to secure Quebec's signature to the 1982 constitutional regime had ended in abject failure. Once again, it had proved impossible to find a generally acceptable constitutional formula for accommodating Quebec's distinctiveness.

These repeated failures to resolve the Quebec question within the Canadian federation provided the backdrop for the 1995 referendum, almost producing a victory for the "Yes" forces. Upon its re-election to power in September 1994, the PQ government of Jacques Parizeau was determined to move quickly on the sovereignty question, so as to avoid the erosion of support apparently incurred by the long delay of the 1980 referendum. Moreover, remembering how in 1980 fedcralist forces had undermined the sovereignty-association option by rejecting any notion of economic association, the Parizeau government resolutely sought to avoid any commitment to an association. Yet it soon became clear that the majority of Quebeckers were not prepared to support sovereignty on this basis. Under the prodding of Lucien Bouchard, head of the Bloc Québécois and leader of the Official Opposition in the House of Commons, Parizeau finally agreed, on June 12, 1995, that Quebec's accession to sovereignty must be preceded by the offer to the rest of Canada of an economic and political partnership. It was on this basis that a referendum was called for October 30, 1995.

Once sovereignty had been linked to a continuing "economic and political partnership," which sovereigntist leaders insisted the rest of Canada would be bound to accept, then most Quebeckers' fears over the economic costs of sovereignty dissipated. They were now free to vote on the basis of their dissatisfaction over Quebec's current place within Canada. During the referendum campaign, Lucien Bouchard and others made a point of stressing the repeated failures of Quebec to secure a satisfactory accommodation of its distinctiveness. It was largely on this basis that they were able to come so close to winning the referendum, with a "Yes" vote of 49.4 percent.

In the wake of the referendum, public debate outside Quebec largely focused on defining the conditions under which, after some future referendum, Quebec might accede to sovereignty. Typically, the unacknowledged objective was to demonstrate to Quebeckers that the obstacles to sovereignty, or costs it would bear, were prohibitively high. Surveys showed that Quebeckers continued to prefer an accommodation within the Canadian federation rather than full sovereignty. But past attempts to find an accommodation had failed so abysmally and the 1995 result had made a "Yes" vote a distinct possibility. Thus, the federalist response was to try to dissuade Quebeckers from voting "Yes" in a future referendum by demonstrating that sovereignty would necessarily entail heavy costs.

By the same token, now that Quebec sovereignty appeared to be a real possibility, leaders both of Quebec's aboriginal peoples and the English-speaking minority within Quebec began to prepare for a future "Yes" vote, arguing that they should not have to be part of any sovereign Quebec should they wish not to be. Contending that "if Canada is divisible then so is Quebec," leaders advocated partition so that communities should be able to determine, through local referendums, whether or not they should remain part of a sovereign Quebec. Beyond claiming that they themselves constituted nations, aboriginal leaders could invoke a constitutional fiduciary responsibility on the part of the federal government.

Indeed, some analysts began to argue that Quebec sovereignty was unattainable. The costs for Quebec of a unilateral declaration of independence would be prohibitively high. As for sovereignty on the basis of an agreement between Quebec and the rest of Canada, they pointed to a series of obstacles that they claimed virtually precluded any agreement: the complicated logistics of organizing secession negotiations, the complexity of the economic issues to be addressed, the intractable question of minority rights, the difficulty of constitutional amendment, and so on.[12] Yet other analysts made compelling arguments that these obstacles would likely be overcome given the pressures for an agreement that would come from business leaders, as well as from the U.S. government.[13]

For its part, the federal government submitted a reference to the Supreme Court to determine whether, under both Canadian and international law, Quebec had a right to declare independence unilaterally. As such, the reference responded to a widespread sense in English Canada that above all else "the rule of law" must prevail. In Quebec, the reference was seen as denial of the right of Quebeckers collectively to decide their future. Predictably, the Court responded that Quebec had no right to declare independence unilaterally. Yet it also went on to declare that along with the rule of law and constitutionalism, Canada's constitutional tradition is rooted in the principles of federalism, democracy, and the rights of minorities. Accordingly, it declared, a "clear majority" in favour of Quebec sovereignty "on a clear question" would possess considerable legitimacy.[14] The rest of Canada would be constitutionally obliged to enter into negotiations of the conditions under which Quebec might accede to sovereignty. On this basis, the decision largely defused the confrontation that had emerged between public opinion in Quebec and in the rest of Canada over Quebec's right to sovereignty.

In any event, the November 30, 1998, Quebec provincial election clearly demonstrated that Quebeckers had little disposition for another referendum on sovereignty. Despite its strong popularity as a government, the PQ secured a relatively weak popular vote of 42.9 percent, less than the Liberal vote of 43.6 percent.[15] Thanks to the functioning of the electoral system, the PQ did secure a majority of seats: 76 to the Liberals' 48. But *Péquiste* leaders had hoped to secure a popular vote that was much closer to 50 percent and that would provide the momentum for a new referendum on sovereignty. In large part, as Bouchard himself ruefully acknowledged, the failure to do so sprang from voter resistance to such a referendum.

On the other hand, the failure of the Liberals to win the victory that so many had expected, given the popularity of their new leader, Jean Charest, was in part due to Charest's failure to offer a coherent strategy for securing a new place for Quebec within the federal order. He simply declared that there would be no constitutional negotiations during the next four years. In the process, he allowed Bouchard and the PQ to assume the mantle of defenders of Quebec's interests within the Canadian federation. Beyond that, Charest opened the campaign with a social and economic program that would "turn the page" on the Quiet Revolution, and then had to backtrack in light of the negative public reaction it engendered. In effect, the Charest Liberals had abandoned the long-standing Quebec Liberal strategy, pursued under both Lesage and Bourassa, of evoking the accommodation of Quebec within a renewed federalism, along with the commitment that the Quebec state play a leading social and economic role. They paid the electoral consequences.

For good measure, the federal government proceeded in the fall of 1999 to introduce a bill, dubbed the Clarity Act, which ostensibly sought to reduce the uncertainty about precisely what would constitute a "clear majority" on a "clear question." The Act established the basis for quite stringent standards. For instance, in calling for attention to "the size of the majority of valid votes cast in favour" of the question, the act implies that a majority of 50 percent plus one would not be sufficient. Similarly, the act alludes to the proportion of eligible voters who actually have voted. Despite the publicly stated apprehension of federalist leaders in the opposition parties, *indépendantiste* leaders were unable to mobilize the kind of intense backlash among the Quebec public that they vigorously sought. The House of Commons passed the bill on March 25, 2000.

By the year 2000, it had become clear that sovereignty was no longer as compelling for many Qubeckers as it had been in the mid-1990s, let alone at the beginning of the decade when as many as 64 percent of Quebec francophones stated that they were in favour. For federal officials this proved the effectiveness of their "Plan B" strategy, with the Clarity Act as its centrepiece. For others, this decline reflected the inevitable dissipation of the visceral anger that had been generated by the collapse of the Meech Lake Accord. Beyond that, there was the indirect impact of dissatisfaction with the PQ's actions as a provincial government.

In January 2001, Lucien Bouchard resigned. The departure of Bouchard seemed to create a vacuum in Quebec politics. His successor, Bernard Landry, did not enjoy the same popularity, yet francophone voters remained dubious about the Liberals and especially their leader. Initially, it appeared that the *Action démocratique du Québec* (ADQ) might be able to fill this new space. Indeed, during the year 2002, surveys suggested that the ADQ would form the government should an election be called. Nonetheless, by the spring of 2003, the ADQ was fast losing favour, given the manifest inexperience of its leader and his mounting difficulties in putting in place a credible organization. Beyond that, as voters became more familiar with the ADQ's commitment to a radical rollback of the Quebec state, with such policies as a "flat" income tax, they began to move away from the party.

For their part, the Liberals had succeeded in defining a credible vision of Quebec's place within the Canadian federation, elaborated in *Un projet pour le Québec: affirmation, autonomie et leadership*. Morcover, during the campaign leading up to the election on April 14, 2003, Charest was able to exploit the ambiguities of the Landry government's stance on sovereignty, under which another referendum would be held only under "winning conditions." Moreover, there were serious divisions within the

PQ between "hard-line" militants, rallying around Jacques Parizeau, and the party establishment. While Charest and the Liberals continued to call for a restructuring and paring down of the Quebec state, their stance seemed quite moderate, even centrist, when compared with the explicit neoliberalism of the ADQ. By the same token, in attacking the chronic inadequacies of public health care in Quebec, Charest and the Liberals were able to break through the relatively high voter satisfaction with the Landry government. As a result, the Liberals won the election with 76 seats, leaving 45 for the Parti Québécois and only four for the ADQ. At 45.9 percent, the Liberal popular vote was not substantially larger than the 43.6 percent it had secured in 1998, but this time it was far ahead of the PQ (33.2 percent). The ADQ secured 18.2 percent.

As it went about presenting the Inaugural Speech of the new National Assembly and then tabling its first budget, the Charest government forthrightly declared that it intended to usher in a new era in Quebec politics that would represent as significant a shift in direction as did the Quiet Revolution. They intended to bring about a major "re-engineering" and downscaling of the Quebec state and, in the process, to afford a new role for private enterprise. The Inaugural Speech called for a fundamental revision of the Quebec state's structures, economic role, provision of health and education, and tax system, as well as decentralization to the regions. By the same token, the budget froze spending in all areas but health and education.

Still, it remains to be seen just how far the Charest government will go, or will be able to go, in its "reinvention" of the Quebec state. Beyond the inevitable resistance of bureaucratic structures, as well as public sector unions, there is the possibility that public opinion may also place certain limits. Quebec voters' rejection of the ADQ, with its overt neoliberalism, suggests that they were not prepared to embark on the kind of neoliberal ventures that had won the favour of voters in Ontario, with the Harris "Common Sense Revolution," or in Alberta, with the Klein Conservatives. Here too, Quebec society may continue to display a clear distinctiveness.

CONCLUSION: STILL DIVIDED OVER QUEBEC'S DISTINCTIVENESS

Thirteen years after the failure of the Meech Lake Accord, Quebeckers and Canadians outside Quebec remain as divided as ever about whether and how the Canadian political order should accommodate Quebec's distinctiveness. The anger and resentment that caused such an unprecedented surge in support for sovereignty, and almost produced a "Yes" victory in the 1995 referendum, may have dissipated. With their refusal in the 1998 election to give a clear mandate to either the PQ or the Liberals, Quebeckers demonstrated once again their overwhelming preference to remain within a *renewed* Canadian federation. For that matter, Canadians outside Quebec are as determined as ever that Quebec should remain part of Canada. They could not have been more gratified by the election of the Charest Liberals, with their unconditional commitment to federalism. Yet Canada's political leaders are no closer to finding the terms of an accommodation between Quebec and the rest of Canada. Indeed, most of them have despaired of even trying.

Over the years there has been no lack of ideas as to the form such an accommodation might take. Back in the 1960s, Lester Pearson's Liberal government had demonstrated the possibilities of an asymmetrical federalism, in which Quebec would assume responsibilities that in the rest of the country remain with Ottawa.[16] Although the Trudeau government resolutely backed away from such notions, many academics continue to develop them.[17] Similarly, a variety of scholars have shown how a confederal arrangement—in which the member states retain full sovereignty—might provide the answer.[18]

As the Meech Lake debacle so clearly demonstrated, Canadians outside Quebec have become committed to a vision of Canada that precludes even the most minimal recognition of Quebec's distinctiveness. Yet the majority of Quebec francophones remain just as determined as ever that their distinctiveness be recognized and accommodated.

There appears to be no way to escape this dilemma. Under the leadership of Pierre Trudeau, the federal government made a concerted effort to convince Quebec francophones to abandon their demands for an accommodation of Quebec and to attach their primary allegiance to Canada as a whole rather than Quebec. But these efforts were to no avail. Indeed, they only made matters worse by reinforcing English-speaking Canadians in their resistance to an accommodation. In short, there is every reason to believe that most Quebec francophones will continue to see themselves first and foremost as Quebeckers.[19] At a minimum, they will continue to see Quebec as a distinct society, and Quebec will continue to be one. Quebec will remain one of Canada's greatest challenges.

NOTES

1. Figures taken from the 1996 census as reported in Statistics Canada, *The Daily*, December 2, 1997.

2. John McCallum, *Unequal Beginnings: Agriculture and Economic Development in Quebec and Ontario until 1870* (Toronto: University of Toronto Press, 1980), p. 104.

3. These developments are traced in Michael D. Beheils, *Prelude to Quebec's Quiet Revolution* (Montreal/Kingston: McGill-Queen's University Press, 1985). See also Kenneth McRoberts, *Quebec: Social Change and Political Crisis*, 3rd ed. (Toronto: McClelland & Stewart, 1988), chap. 4.

4. The leading role of the new middle class within the Quiet Revolution coalition is discussed at length in McRoberts, *Quebec: Social Change and Political Crisis*, chap. 5. For a critique of this interpretation, see William D. Coleman, *The Independence Movement in Quebec, 1945–1980* (Toronto: University of Toronto Press, 1984).

5. These two strategies, and the shift between them, are analyzed in Kenneth McRoberts, *Misconceiving Canada: The Struggle for National Unity* (Toronto: Oxford University Press, 1997).

6. Competing approaches to classifying and explaining the ideology and class bases of the Parti Québécois are assessed in McRoberts, *Quebec: Social Change and Political Crisis*, pp. 242–59.

7. A 1988 survey found that 49 percent of Quebec francophones responded, "above all, Québécois" when asked how they identified themselves. "Le francophone est québécois, l'anglophone 'Canadian,'" *Le Devoir*, June 25, 1988: 1.

8. The Meech Lake Accord is analyzed in Peter W. Hogg, *Meech Lake Constitutional Accord Annotated* (Toronto: Carswell, 1988); Katherine W. Swinton and Carol J. Rogerson, eds., *Competing Constitutional Visions: The Meech Lake Accord* (Toronto: Carswell, 1988); and Patrick J. Monahan, *Meech Lake: The Inside Story* (Toronto: University of Toronto Press, 1991).

9. See André Blais and Jean Crête, "Pourquoi l'opinion publique au Québec a-t-elle rejeté l'Accord du lac Meech," in Raymond Hudon and Réjean Pelletier, eds., *L'engagement intellectuel: Mélanges en l'honneur de Léon Dion* (Quebec: Les Presses de l'Université Laval, 1991), p. 398.

10. "Portrait des Québécois," *L'Actualité* (January 1991): 13–16.

11. See the analyses in Kenneth McRoberts and Patrick J. Monahan, *The Charlottetown Accord, the Referendum, and the Future of Canada* (Toronto: University of Toronto Press, 1993); "The Charter, Federalism and the Constitution," *International Journal of Canadian Studies*, 7–8 (Spring–Fall, 1993); and McRoberts, *Misconceiving Canada*, chap. 8.

12. For instance, see Patrick J. Monahan, *Cooler Heads Shall Prevail: Assessing the Costs and Consequences of Quebec Separation*, C.D. Howe Institute Commentary 65, The Referendum Papers, (January 1995).

13. See Robert A. Young, *The Secession of Quebec and the Future of Canada* (Montreal/Kingston: McGill-Queen's University Press, 1995).

14. Supreme Court of Canada, *Reference re Secession of Quebec*, 1998.

15. The popular votes and seat totals include the results of the Masson by-election.

16. See McRoberts, *Misconceiving Canada*, chap. 2.

17. See, for instance, Will Kymlicka, *Finding Our Way* (Toronto: Oxford University Press, 1998); Philip Resnick, "Toward a Multinational Federalism: Asymmetrical and Confederal Alternatives," in Leslie Seidle, ed., *Seeking a New Canadian Partnership: Asymmetrical and Confederal Options* (Montreal: Institute for Research on Public Policy, 1994), pp. 71–104; Charles Taylor, *Reconciling the Solitudes: Essays on Canadian Federalism and Nationalism* (Montreal/Kingston: McGill-Queen's University Press, 1993); and Jeremy Webber, *Reimagining Canada: Language, Culture, Community and the Canadian Constitution* (Kingston/Montreal: McGill-Queen's University Press, 1994).

18. Roger Gibbins and Guy Laforest, *Beyond the Impasse: Toward Reconciliation* (Montreal: Institute for Research on Public Policy, 1998).

19. In an October 1998 Environics survey, 17 percent of Quebec francophones declared that they were "uniquely Quebecker" and another 40 percent said that they were "Quebecker first, then Canadian." The other responses were: "equally Canadian and Quebecker"—24%; "Canadian first, then Quebecker"—12%; and "uniquely Canadian"—6%. Council for Canadian Unity, *Direction* 3, no. 45 (December 17, 1998).

FURTHER READINGS

Balthazar, Louis. *Bilan du nationalisme au Québec.* Montreal: Les Éditions de l'Hexagone, 1986.

Carens, Joseph H., ed. *Is Quebec Nationalism Just? Perspectives from Anglophone Canada.* Montreal/Kingston: McGill-Queen's University Press, 1995.

Coleman, William D. *The Independence Movement in Quebec, 1945–1980.* Toronto: University of Toronto Press, 1984.

Lachapelle, Guy, Gérald Bernier, Daniel Salée, and Luc Bernier. *The Quebec Democracy: Structures, Processes and Policies.* Toronto: McGraw-Hill Ryerson, 1993.

McRoberts, Kenneth. *Quebec: Social Change and Political Crisis*, 3rd ed. Toronto: McClelland & Stewart, 1993.

———. "Canada and the Multinational State." *Canadian Journal of Political Science* XXXIV: no. 4 (December 2001): 683–713.

Maclure, Jocelyn. *Quebec Identity: The Challenge of Pluralism* (trans. from French). Montreal/Kingston: McGill-Queen's University Press, 2003.

Young, Robert A. *The Secession of Quebec and the Future of Canada.* Montreal/Kingston: McGill-Queen's University Press, 1995.

CHAPTER 17

THE MEDIA AND CANADIAN POLITICS IN AN ERA OF GLOBALIZATION

Frederick J. Fletcher and
Robert Everett

The mass media have played an important role in developing and maintaining a public space for Canadian political discourse for more than 100 years. From the time when local printer-editors published the first community newspapers, to the era of satellites and the Internet, communication systems and policies to regulate them have been central to the political process. While the public space in Canada has been fractured by linguistic and regional cleavages, the communication system has helped to maintain sufficient common elements to support a *national* political discourse, at least in times of crisis, and to permit many Canadians to identify themselves as members of an "imagined community."[1]

Most Canadians spend a high proportion of their leisure time with the media, and it is clear that the mainstream media help to set the agenda for political debate and contribute to the "psychic environment" of everyday life in Canada. The mass media, therefore, are important definers of the ideas and images that have political significance. This chapter describes the nature and operation of the Canadian media system as a public space for political and social discourse, and assesses the challenges posed by the emergence of a powerful global media system to the continued viability of Canada as a national community.

While recognizing the social and political importance of the media, it is necessary to remind ourselves that the mass media are a multibillion-dollar industry and that their business is primarily attracting audiences to sell to advertisers. While informing and entertaining us, and capturing our attention in order to increase their market share, "the media ... define what is normal and respectable in a society, what is debatable and what is beyond discussion by decent, respectable citizens."[2] Although media content is influenced by cultural, social, and economic factors, media organizations have a degree of independent influence on what we read, see, and hear. In choosing among the vast array of available drama scripts, music videos, news items, and other materials, media managers have considerable influence on the beliefs and perspectives presented to Canadians. These choices help to determine available role models, images of reality, definitions of what is political, concepts of community, and other elements of our political culture.

THE CANADIAN MASS MEDIA SYSTEM

In order to understand the importance of the mass media system in Canadian political life, it is necessary to see it both as a subject of policy and as a source of influence on policymakers and, indeed, on the values, attitudes, beliefs, and preferences of Canadians. It is in large part because of their perceived influence that the media—as sites in which meanings are constructed—have been of concern to governments. The contest to define the role of the media in our national life has created a number of tensions: (1) the debate over cross-border communication flows from the United States; (2) the conflict over control of cultural policy between Canada and the provinces (primarily Quebec); and (3) the conflict between public and private interests.

The mass media in Canada have undergone great changes in audience, philosophy, technology, and ownership since Confederation.[3] From their earliest beginnings in the eighteenth century, Canadian newspapers were highly political, with close ties to either government or opposition parties. By the 1870s, the growth of urban centres and the development of new technologies—mechanized printing, cheap newsprint, the telegraph for more rapid news gathering—contributed to the proliferation of newspapers and the emergence of a mass press with broad readership that emphasized social issues. As well, the spread of public education created an appetite for news and advertising.

Because advertising revenue freed the press from financial dependence on politicians, newspapers ceased to serve primarily as vehicles for political debate among competing elites. The competition for mass audiences, and the advertisers seeking to reach them, led to the growth of newspaper chains. By 1920, the Southam and Sifton chains were well established, and the trend toward corporate ownership of newspapers has continued up to the present. Today, a handful of large corporations control most daily newspapers and many weeklies, magazines, privately owned radio and television outlets, specialty channels, and cable systems.

The quest for mass audiences, the growth of newspaper chains with absentee ownership, and the advent of wire services selling news to a wide range of clients all contributed to the decline of the partisan press. More interested in profits than partisanship, the larger news organizations moderated their partisan loyalties to appeal to broader audiences. News services kept their reporting as neutral as possible, especially with respect to Canadian issues, so they could appeal to publishers of all parties. These factors led to the era of so-called objective journalism, which was the dominant working ideology of the news media when radio news emerged in the 1930s. Today, broadcast news is required by law to be balanced.[4]

From the beginning, Canadian broadcast news and entertainment has developed in response to and in competition with imports from the United States. CBC radio and television were created to provide a Canadian alternative to American broadcasters and, in particular, to provide a cultural space for Canadian news and entertainment. The 1968 Broadcasting Act set out some ambitious objectives for the broadcasting system: (1) that it be owned and controlled by Canadians; (2) that it "safeguard, enrich and strengthen the cultural, political, social and economic fabric of Canada"; and (3) that programming should use "predominantly Canadian creative and other resources." Both public and private broadcasters were to contribute to these goals, and the Canadian Radio-television and Telecommunications Commission (CRTC) was to implement them.

These remain the essential goals of the Canadian mass media system today but the technological, economic, and political environment has changed, requiring new thinking about how these goals can be achieved.[5] Private broadcasters increasingly recognize the necessity of differentiating themselves in a multi-channel universe and, therefore, are more open to Canadian content than they were in the past, when the low cost of American imports (with production costs already covered in their home market) made these more attractive than producing their own programming. Although serious problems of representation for Canada's many cultural communities remain, new opportunities for Canadians to tell their own stories seem to be emerging, including, for instance, a specialty cable channel featuring aboriginal programming.

THE MEDIA AND CANADA'S INTERNAL DIVISIONS

Canada's dispersed and culturally diverse population presents a formidable challenge to the development of a truly national public discourse.

The traditional goals of the federal government—to promote national identity and unity—have become too limited in an era of globalization. Hence, the 1991 Broadcasting Act directs the Canadian broadcasting system to "serve the needs and interests, and reflect the circumstances and aspirations, of Canadian men, women and children, including equal rights, the linguistic duality and multicultural and multiracial nature of Canadian society and the special place of aboriginal peoples within that society." Paradoxically, this dramatic broadening of the obligations placed on broadcasters was accompanied by substantial cuts to the CBC's budget, diminishing its capacity to fulfill this expanded mandate. In an age of deregulation, it is unlikely that the private broadcasters can be induced to meet these objectives voluntarily. The best hope may be the emergence of new services like the aboriginal specialty channel, which is available nationwide, permitting First Nations to communicate not only among themselves but also to other interested Canadians.

The Canadian media system is, in reality, two media systems—one French-language and the other English—that are only loosely related to each another. As well, there is an emerging "third media" system serving other linguistic and cultural groups. These divisions and, to a lesser extent, regional divisions within the English-language media complicate attempts to maintain a space for national public debate and also a national response to the pressures of globalization. There is relatively little crossover viewing,[6] with anglophones rarely watching programs in French. Francophone viewers of English programming most often watch American imports. However, francophone audiences spend most of their time with programming produced in Quebec, while anglophone viewers watch mostly American imports. Because of the language difference, francophone viewers are well aware that the information and values in American programs do not reflect their own culture. This is much less clear for anglophones, and it is this fact that fuels concerns about English-speaking Canadian cultural identity.

While the two language groups share many common values, the news coverage of important political issues has frequently differed significantly in the English-speaking and French-speaking media. This is particularly true of news stories with high symbolic content. For example, prior to the 1992 referendum, both English- and French-language media gave considerable attention to those municipalities outside Quebec that declared themselves to be English-only jurisdictions. In the English-language media, these gestures were often presented as responses to Quebec's French-only sign law. In the French-language media, the declarations were often presented as a rejection of the legitimacy of French in

Canada. These differing interpretations make a genuinely national dialogue more difficult, with key events in Canadian history often coming to mean quite different things in the two language communities,[7] thereby weakening any sense of national political community.

Some observers have raised concerns that the emergence of the "third media" will make the maintenance of social cohesion in Canada even more difficult by complicating efforts to integrate new immigrants into Canadian society and diminishing the meaning of Canadian citizenship. Others argue that such media can serve a dual purpose: making information about Canada more accessible to new immigrants (in their original languages) and at the same time permitting immigrant communities to tell their own stories. The key may be to encourage more interchange between the "third media" and the mainstream, broadening the sense of what it means to be Canadian.

It is clear, however, that these internal divisions do complicate Canada's response to globalization. English-speaking Canadians are more vulnerable to cultural erosion through the media than francophones, and third-language groups are increasingly using the new media to import cultural products and news from their countries of origin. Canadian policymakers seeking to preserve an effective public space in Canada in the face of globalization must work within these realities.

NEWS: "DEMOCRACY'S OXYGEN"[8]

While all media content contributes to the ideas and images available to citizens—including drama, comedy, and advertising—it is widely accepted that news in democratic societies has a central role. Because "journalism is arguably the most important form of public knowledge in contemporary society,"[9] journalists are seen to have public responsibilities. These include, in particular, informing citizens about political issues (especially those that might affect them and their communities) and exposing abuses of power, especially by governments.[10] Accordingly, reputable news organizations have specialist reporters who cover government and politics at all levels, and "the news" often deals disproportionately with political topics. While citizens do not always pay attention to political news, they still want such news to be available. Certainly, without comprehensive and comprehensible coverage of public institutions and issues, citizens could not effectively participate in democratic political life.

In recent years, however, the ways in which news organizations discharge these responsibilities have been subject to considerable criticism.

The most significant of these criticisms are (1) the lack of independence of journalists; (2) the rising political cynicism of the media; and (3) the emergence of "infotainment" at the expense of the traditions of responsible journalism. A range of factors challenges the autonomy of the news. The most important of these are the increasing sophistication of "spin doctors," who manipulate media coverage on behalf of politicians, corporations, and interest groups, and the concentration of ownership of the media into fewer and fewer hands.

The news media have become a "site of contestation," an arena in which various interests compete to influence the public agenda and the way in which issues are "framed" in news coverage. Techniques in the contest to influence the way an issue is defined include selective leaks of government information, release of research reports or audio and video materials, demonstrations and other staged "media events," celebrity endorsements, and, increasingly, advocacy advertising. One recent study notes that the some 200 journalists in the Parliamentary Press Gallery in Ottawa—with responsibility for covering all aspects of the federal government—are outnumbered not only by the politicians and their staffs but also by government communications personnel and lobbyists.[11] While the government still usually controls the media agenda, the opposition parties, through Question Period especially, can bring other issues to the fore. As well, interest groups can gain attention in a variety of ways. Indeed, the increased influence of lobbyists has shifted the power of setting the public agenda away from politicians to a considerable extent, since well-funded groups can produce a steady stream of research studies and briefs that catch media attention.

The major factors in determining the shape of news coverage and commentary include the dependence of most news media on advertising revenues, the increasing concentration of ownership in the hands of a few large corporations, and the natural tendency of owners to perceive the interests of their class as the interests of the public and to appoint publishers and editors who agree with them. As noted above, the "regime of objectivity" that constitutes the professional ideology of most journalists tends to exclude challenges to the status quo and in general to reinforce corporate dominance.[12] The appearance of objectivity, which helped the news media to project an image of credibility, has been eroding as news becomes more cynical and entertainment-oriented.

The culture of cynicism in the news media and the rise of "infotainment" have not only eroded public trust in the media but have also had a damaging effect on public debate. News managers argue that the entertainment industry has "converted citizens into audiences" and created a taste for entertaining newscasts, more drama than reality.[13] The commercial pressures on news, partly a result of increased competition, have promoted concentration of ownership, cuts in news budgets, and a "malaise" in newsrooms. Television news is under heavy pressure to be entertaining. It seems that the emphasis on scandals in the news is more about ratings and less about serving as a check on the abuse of power. Investigative journalism tends to focus its attacks on individuals, generally ignoring institutional failures. On the other hand, the real power holders—major corporations and those who run them, for example—are not subjected to the kinds of scrutiny that individual politicians face, except in rare circumstances when their actions become politicized (as in the proposed bank mergers in the past few years).

These and other factors have led to a loss of connection between newspapers and their communities. Newspapers are increasingly focused on serving the affluent readers in whom advertisers are most interested. Further, because news managers are overwhelmingly male, middle-aged, and middle-class, they have lost touch with many potential readers who fall outside these categories.[14] Radio and television newscasts may also suffer from social isolation, since they operate under the same constraints as the print media. While daily newspapers remain the major news-gathering institutions in the media system, employing many more reporters than other media, television is the most important channel for the distribution of news. In a recent survey, 57 percent of adults named television as their primary source of news, compared with only 28 percent for newspapers and 9 percent for radio.[15] Television is also the most trusted news medium.

The erosion of public broadcasting is also important to note. CBC's news services still play an important role in providing news and commentary to Canadians. However, budget cuts, commercial pressures, and, in particular, pressure from politicians are all threats to the crucial role of the CBC as a provider of public space for Canadian political discourse that ensures all legitimate viewpoints are heard and that those with power are held accountable. Many believe that the competition between public and private broadcasters in news and public affairs programming has served Canadians well. David Taras supports this perspective:

> The CBC, whatever its faults, remains a vital element in national life. It airs more news and documentaries, is more committed to "hard" news, and does more in-depth reporting than any of its rivals. To the extent that attempts have been made ... to make it more timid, the media system as a whole is damaged and weakened. Having a public broadcaster means giving its journalists the freedom to push boundaries, to take unpopular positions, and to challenge the power of the powerful if there are legitimate and compelling reasons to do so.[16]

Another important development related to news and globalization is the emergence of the Internet to serve the information needs of selected groups. However, public Internet sites come with no guarantee of accuracy and are even less accountable than the traditional media. Internet news services, often more expensive than traditional news sources, are increasingly offering specialized information to narrowly defined groups. The information is selected to provide information to various sectors of business and is also packaged for groups defined by specific tastes. These developments have prompted a number of concerns. First, there is the risk of an increasing gap between the "information rich" and the "information poor,"[17] especially as "information levelers" like public libraries are forced by budget cuts to reduce services and impose user fees. Second, there is concern that the growth of "virtual communities" will sever the connection between individuals and their geographic neighbours, undermining the foundations of community and local government. Third, the fragmentation of audiences for traditional news media may erode common public values and narrow the scope of public debate, as various "publics" limit their interaction to those who have the same interests and values. This results in a reduction of the kind of discourse that promotes compromise through awareness of the views of others.

MEDIA AND ELECTIONS

Despite their obvious flaws, election campaigns symbolize the consent of the governed by providing an opportunity for citizens to influence public decisions. In representative democracies, modern campaigns are, to a large extent, media campaigns. From the point of view of party strategists, media coverage is broadly defined to include news reports, public affairs programming, televised leaders' debates, and advertising, which are the most important sources of information for voters and, therefore, the major focus of attention for political strategists. News coverage plays a major role in shaping the images of party leaders, defining campaign issues, and influencing the tone, as well as the substance, of campaign discourse. In many respects, campaigns are contests in which media attention is the prize. The "spin doctors" of the political parties play an important role in campaigns, providing scripts for the leaders and "inside" information for journalists.

Party strategists still believe television is the best medium for reaching uncommitted voters in a campaign. With speeches written to provide a brief television "clip" (usually under 10 seconds), preferably with an appropriate visual backdrop to effectively convey the message of the day, the party leaders' tours are tailored for television. Campaign strategists generally organize campaigns around a few key themes, using leaders' speeches and advertising—mostly on television—to reinforce the message because formal election campaigns are relatively short (usually six weeks or less). The commitment to "image politics" shows up in the television ads, mainly 30-second spots, which are too brief for substantial arguments. In the 2000 federal election, the parties spent at least $20 million on the television advertising broadcast during the campaign. The major parties produced a total of 33 "spots" that were repeated many times (supplemented by radio and Internet ads).

In election campaigns, style tends to overwhelm substance because of television's dominant role. Campaigns become contests of television performance and party leaders are carefully schooled by professional trainers in television techniques. For a politician, being "telegenic" involves projecting a calm, confident demeanour and avoiding gaffes. The combination of a critical approach and the personalizing of politics, brought on in large part by television's focus on celebrities, has resulted in relentless media scrutiny of politicians. Every perceived flaw is magnified and broadcast. In contrast to U.S. politicians, however, Canadian political leaders are permitted to have a degree of privacy. This has its benefits, especially since American-style attack journalism often focuses on character flaws arguably unrelated to performance in office, but it may also have costs. Some wonder if the diffidence of Canadian journalists might be depriving voters of character-related information that would help them make "an intelligent assessment of leaders."[18]

Because of the emphasis on leaders in television coverage and party advertising, local candidates—those for whom we actually vote—do not usually play a major role in election outcomes in most federal and provincial elections. For example, at the end of the 1997 campaign, CBC news presented a "digest of the televisual moments of Election '97, distilling the entire five-week campaign down to 22 images packaged in 65 seconds."[19] More than three-quarters of the images featured a party leader, about half portrayed events on the campaign trail, and only about one-quarter even referred to an issue. Coverage of the 2000 campaign also focused heavily on leaders. The televised leaders' debates also put the leaders at the centre of the campaign, and it is plausible to argue that the influence of party leaders in Canada has strengthened to the point that our elections are somewhat more like U.S. presidential elections than is suitable for a parliamentary system.

In the end, the campaign is a product of the interaction of media logic and party strategies. As long as the parties play by media rules, focusing on the leaders and a few central issues and presenting their appeals in brief and dramatic fashion, they can set the campaign agenda.

In recent elections, however, the media have made a conscious effort to pay more attention to the concerns of voters, through polls, phone-in shows, "town hall meetings," and so on. At least one informed observer has written of considerable public dissatisfaction with election coverage in 1997 because "the terms in which the politicians spoke were not those the public would have chosen. It was as though the politicians managed to sidestep the issues and the media let them get away with it."[20] This observation applied equally to the 2000 campaign. The dilemma for journalists is to balance their responsibility to report the campaign as the parties are conducting it, against their obligation to raise other questions and provide voters with a critical perspective.

The actual effect of news and advertising on election results remains somewhat uncertain. In recent years, as campaigns have become more important with the weakening of the parties' core vote, it is logical to assume that the two major elements of national campaigns—news coverage and advertising—have an impact, especially on voters who enter the campaign period undecided (about 40 percent of voters in the 2000 federal election).[21] During the 2000 campaign, a series of news reports raised questions about the leadership capabilities of Stockwell Day, then leader of the Canadian Alliance Party, and arguably helped to prevent him from taking advantage of voters' desire for change. These reports associated him with controversial positions on creationism, abortion, and privatization of health care. Other reports raised questions about Alliance positions, such as citizen-initiated referendums. CBC satirist Rick Mercer started a campaign to have Mr. Day change his first name to Doris. The "initiative" quickly garnered more than enough signatures to trigger a referendum under Alliance-proposed rules.[22]

The televised leaders' debates, as Lawrence LeDuc has put it, "are now well known and somewhat predictable campaign events. Voters expect them, and use them to form opinions about the leaders"[23] and to gain a sense of the main issues of the campaign. The 1997 and 2000 debates, with five party leaders, featured few of the dramatic one-on-one confrontations of the past and probably had little effect on the election results. However, Joe Clark's performance in 2000—and the fact that he was declared the winner by many in the media—was arguably an important factor in the Conservative Party gaining sufficient seats to enable it to retain official party status. Even in past elections, when debates were of greater importance, they were only one among a number of key factors in voter choice. However, they do clearly influence news coverage, and the selection of the key clip or "defining moment" of a debate by the media can be important.

In this respect, "a televised debate is little more than a struggle for sound bite supremacy."[24] In the 1997 campaign, Jean Charest's patriotic pledge to keep Canada intact for his children was the sound bite that had the longest "shelf life" in the media, but it likely had limited influence on the election outcome. No lasting sound bite emerged from the 2000 leaders' debates.

In addition to the media's direct effects on voters, there are important indirect effects. Campaign contributions, public endorsements, expressions of support such as lawn signs, recruitment and enthusiasm of volunteers, and internal party morale are all affected by the tone of the coverage, the poll results reported in the media, and the quality of the national advertising campaign. Media coverage also generally influences our concepts of citizenship and democracy.

THE IMPACT OF GLOBALIZATION ON CANADIAN MEDIA AND PUBLIC POLICY

Globalization can be positive if it is designed to promote free, equal, meaningful, and constructive exchanges among societies and cultures. The often-invoked metaphor of the McLuhanesque "global village" can be appealing: new technologies hold the promise of facilitating the transfer of messages across national borders and providing Canadians with an expanded vision of the world. This is consistent with the value placed on the open expression of ideas as a cornerstone of democracy. If, however, the forces of globalization tend to bear in one direction, the consequences may be enormous for Canada. Already saturated with communications emanating from foreign sources, Canadian culture and identity may be at risk. Although the channels of communication have multiplied, it is not clear that we have access to the fullest range of voices.

We will now turn to a survey of how globalization has led to a series of related trends in the realm of Canada's cultural industries. Subject to debate is the extent to which these may erode the public space for Canadian political discourse. New policy initiatives to deal with the challenges of globalization also divide interested groups. To take one example, independent producers of television programming argued before the CRTC in 1998 in favour of subsidizing more drama and requiring higher Canadian content regulations, while those who control signal carriers insisted that quality was more important than quantity.[25]

One of the most significant overall trends in the media today involves "convergence." The term is most commonly used to describe the technical integration of telecommunications, computers, and television. This integration has led to "institutional convergence," that is, to corporate mergers, acquisitions, and joint ventures in the communications industry. Examples include the ownership of specialty channels by cable companies, or cooperative initiatives involving telephone, Internet, and cable companies. Regulators have permitted these combinations on the grounds that they will lead to efficiencies in the domestic marketplace or help establish a Canadian presence on the global stage. Deregulation of telecommunications means that various companies will either compete in sectors that were formerly governed by monopolies or seek cooperative arrangements. These developments have been accompanied by government policy that actively promotes exports, particularly of television productions. In the words of *Wired to Win*, a report issued by the Senate Committee on Transportation and Communication,

> To strengthen Canadian firms abroad, it is necessary to create a competitive domestic market-place that is tuned aggressively outwards to foreign markets.... If Canada wishes to increase its exports of services and products in the communication sector, it will have to open its domestic market to foreign services and products.[26]

Given the emphasis on economic imperatives in globalization, it is not surprising to find evidence of corresponding changes in the structure of the media system. Among these are tendencies toward privatization of state-owned institutions and relaxation or elimination of restrictions imposed by regulatory agencies. Such developments have promoted greater concentration, regional pan-media monopolies, increased cross-ownership, and partnerships between erstwhile competitors. Economic rationalization has lead to the "downsizing" of work forces in traditional media, particularly those directly engaged in news work, and the contracting out of work previously done by unionized staff.

One of the major Canadian concerns arising from these patterns is the erosion of the "public space" for political debate. Two related but distinctly different phenomena give rise to this worry. On the one hand is the tendency toward domination of the local media by transnational corporations (often U.S.-owned). On the other is a fragmentation of the media spectrum into an array of channels that makes it more difficult to cultivate a sense of national commonality.[27]

MAGAZINES

The magazine sector is perhaps the most fragile of Canada's cultural industries, despite some outward manifestations of vitality. More than 1400 magazine titles are published each year in Canada, and some three-quarters of the magazines circulating here are produced in Canada. Canadian authors, illustrators, and photographers are responsible for more than 90 percent of the content in the country's magazines.[28] Magazines cover a broad spectrum of interests and are produced by a range of groups that includes large, profitable corporations and small, essentially volunteer organizations.

Despite these benchmarks, Canadian magazines are exceptionally vulnerable in a free trade environment. Profits are generally thin in an industry reliant on postal subsidies, funding from cultural agencies, and tax incentives. The vast majority of titles circulate in small numbers to select audiences, and few off-the-shelf magazines can compete with their U.S. counterparts. Indeed, 80 percent of display space on Canadian shelves is given over to U.S. periodicals, which claim 87 percent of our retail sales.

Over the years the Canadian and U.S. governments have clashed over rules intended to support the domestic magazine industry. Challenging Canada on this issue is an important part of the overall U.S. strategy of eliminating restrictions on American cultural exports and investments around the world. The United States opposed a bundle of policy measures developed in the mid-1960s, especially those that discouraged the production of domestic versions of American magazines. Things came to a head in 1993, when *Sports Illustrated* published a so-called "split-run" version that contained a minimal amount of Canadian content but a great deal of Canadian advertising. At little cost and with no significant contribution to Canadian culture, an offshore publisher could thereby attract new revenue streams from Canadian sources. The move alarmed both representatives of the domestic industry and Canadian nationalists. Pressure exerted on government led to the creation of the Task Force on the Canadian Magazine Industry. Reporting in 1994, the task force recommended an 80 percent excise tax on split-run publishing; the government agreed, and *Sports Illustrated*'s corporate parent, Time-Warner, abandoned its project.

However, the U.S. government did not relent. The case was submitted to the newly established World Trade Organization, which accepted the American arguments. The effect of the ruling was to oblige Canada to remove the existing tariff prohibiting the importation of split-run magazines; to eliminate the excise tax on split runs distributed in Canada; to restructure the administration of the postal subsidy program to conform to the rules on subsidies by making payments directly to magazine publishers; and to harmonize the commercial postal rate for domestic and foreign publications.[29]

Virtually the only avenue left to the government was to use taxation laws to discourage Canadian advertisers from buying space in split runs.

The Foreign Publishers Advertising Services Act, or Bill C-55, was introduced on October 8, 1998. Under this legislation, companies would not be permitted to deduct the cost of advertisements placed in split-run editions. The government's move touched off a heated debate between advertisers and organizations such as the Canadian Magazine Association. The U.S. government was furious. As the bill went though parliamentary review, the United States threatened retaliation against industries unrelated to communications. Contentious negotiations between the two countries resulted in a May 1999 agreement that allows U.S. publishers to set up "Canadian" editions of their magazines and sell up to 18 percent of their ad pages to Canadian advertisers. However, Canadian advertisers cannot claim full tax deductions for advertising in U.S. magazines unless they have 80 percent Canadian content. The issue of protection for Canadian magazines remains unresolved.

TELEVISION

Numerous measures continue to underline the importance of television as Canada's primary engine of cultural transmission. Canadians spend more time watching television than they do listening to radio or reading newspapers and magazines. In 2001, Canadians over the age of two watched an average of 21.2 hours of television programming each week,[30] down slightly in the past few years.[31] Television is the primary source for news, and is the most trusted medium when it comes to delivering information, but the largest share of programming content is entertainment. Specialty and pay channels provided by cable and direct-to-home (DTH) satellite transmissions are also becoming more important.

Drama is the dominant category of programming, representing about one-quarter of all viewing time and more than 50 percent during prime time.[32] It is worrisome that Canadian drama captures a small proportion of viewers.[33] In autumn of 2001, for example, 71.4 percent of viewing time by anglophone Canadians was devoted to foreign programs, while francophone viewers watched foreign programs only 31.5 percent of the time.[34] In any given week, American programs consistently dominate the top 10 shows ranked by audience share. Only Canadian newscasts, high-profile specials, and the occasional sports program challenge this dominance.[35]

A race is on to ensure that Canadian outlets have a place on the cable and satellite spectrum. Since 1990, the CRTC has licensed many new services, including both imported and domestic channels, so that we are approaching the 500-channel universe that has long been predicted (and may be surpassed before too long). The CRTC has accepted the notion that new technologies will make it possible for viewers to choose from among hundreds of services and has worked with clients in the private sector to create, in rapid order, a menu of Canadian choices. But the results to date are questionable. If television viewing continues to be relatively stable, the biggest offshoot is likely to be the fragmentation that results as subscribers dial into dedicated programming that exclusively reflects their tastes, lifestyles, and demographic characteristics.

Other policy patterns in the television sector indicate that "industrial" objectives have greater influence on CRTC decisions than do cultural ones. The argument that profitable, market-driven services will meet the informational and cultural needs of Canadians remains unproven. Some of these patterns include the following:

- In its decisions concerning specialty television channels, the CRTC has authorized partnerships between "competing" media groups in specialty channel ventures and other media operations.
- The spate of licenses has led to a "dumbing-down" or "mainstreaming" of content on specialty channels, with little in the way of innovative new programming.
- Specialty channel licenses have been awarded to established companies with records of profitability, and it is increasingly unlikely that an independent applicant will receive favourable consideration.
- The CRTC has adopted a "2 for 1" policy in which one new U.S. channel is licensed for every two new Canadian channels, with the effect that the number of U.S. sources has expanded.
- Many programs that qualify as Canadian are actually productions or co-productions primarily designed for foreign distribution, with the result that the indigenous film and television industry is ever more reliant on subcontracts or cooperative productions with foreign producers and is dependent on international market sales.
- Privatization and budget cuts for public services have affected educational television and the networks run by the Canadian Broadcasting Corporation/Société Radio-Canada.

RADIO

Domestic commercial radio stations are owned by Canadian companies and, with few exceptions, do not compete with U.S. outlets. In 1995, stations across the border accounted for just 3.2 percent of total listenership, although 6.6 percent of adolescents were tuned into American signals. This pattern has persisted over time and shows no signs of changing. An important reason for this is the relatively limited reach of radio signals. More importantly, radio has traditionally been defined by its "localness." Listeners dial in stations according to their taste in music or talk formats, but virtually all stations carry local news, weather, sports, and traffic reports, especially during commuter hours. In the car or at the workplace, radio enjoys a nearly exclusive monopoly of media use. Stations on the FM band are increasing their share of overall audiences and the less popular AM band is turning to talk and news formats.

After years of financial challenges, the radio industry has rebounded. Profits have risen, especially for FM broadcasters, and employment is growing.[36] The CRTC has helped to boost radio by approving measures such as the 1998 decision to permit a reduction in "spoken word" programming on FM stations and to ease restrictions on ownership. The 1998 ruling permits a single owner to control more than one AM and one FM station in any single market. New technologies such as "digital radio"—clear signals delivered on demand by satellite—and various forms of Web radio, including Internet delivery of conventional stations from around the world, may further undermine conventional broadcasting in the next decade.

At present, the key question for radio turns on Canadian content. Canadian content rules were originally introduced over the objections of radio station owners. In 1998, the CRTC again raised the regulated proportion of Canadian music to 35 percent between 6:00 a.m. and 6:00 p.m. on weekdays. At the time the policy was introduced, the CRTC expressed the "hope" that "Canadian content levels will reach even higher levels in five years time" as a result of voluntary joint initiatives between commercial broadcasters and the recording industry.[37] At this writing, Canadian content is holding up fairly well and the domestic recording industry remains active.

NEWSPAPERS

The Canadian newspaper industry is for the most part owned by Canadians, a result of legislative restrictions on foreign ownership. The past decade has been marked by increased cross-media ownership (broadcast enterprises purchasing newspapers, for the most part) and shifting ownership patterns. Conrad Black, for example, purchased Canada's largest newspaper chain (Southam) and launched a new national newspaper—the National Post—to challenge The Globe and Mail. Then, within a few years, Black sold the lot to CanWest Global (controlled by the Asper family of

Winnipeg), owner of the Global Television Network and a number of other broadcast undertakings. CanWest subsequently sold some of its holdings to Osprey Media, which now owns numerous small dailies and weeklies. CanWest has a strong position in British Columbia and Saskatchewan. Other important ownership groups include Quebecor, publisher of high-circulation tabloids in French and English; TorStar, publisher of *The Toronto Star* and a number of other dailies and weeklies in Ontario; and a number of other regional chains, such as Irving (New Brunswick).

The key aspects of these developments are the high degree of ownership concentration, especially at the regional level, and increased cross-media ownership. There are real concerns about the possible constraints on political discourse when the major daily newspapers and television stations in an area are owned by the same corporation. One policy option that has been suggested is to open up the sector to foreign ownership on the grounds that this would bring more diversity. Some owners favour this option because it would create more bidders for existing properties, presumably increasing share value, or make it easier to obtain capital for expansion. It seems more likely, however, that foreign investors would simply purchase and enhance the most dominant enterprises.

As a result of this concentration and cross-media ownership, the industry has seen layoffs and consolidation. Chains are able to repackage content for local markets or distribute content very widely. Authentic competition between newspapers is rare, except in the largest cities, such as Toronto, Calgary, Ottawa, and Montreal. With the launch of the *National Post* in late 1998, however, Canadians living in urban areas have an alternative national newspaper to *The Globe and Mail.* Nevertheless, the choice remains between two dailies with an elitist style, a conservative agenda, and insensitivity to local concerns.[38]

What the policy future holds in regard to Canadian magazines, television, radio, and newspapers is open to political debate; however, different scenarios can be imagined. Pressures exerted by globalization may further undermine the willingness, and even the ability, of the state to regulate or protect cultural industries. On the other hand, it can be argued that there will be a continuing role for the state in the cultural sphere because "the political reality [of globalization] is competitive economic nationalism. The consequences include a rekindled "neo-corporatism" focused on information and cultural industries as the engines driving global capitalism in the twenty-first century."[39] Thus, the state continues to have a space in which to operate, although it currently appears all too willing to support private media interests.

THE POLITICAL SIGNIFICANCE OF MEDIA PATTERNS IN AN ERA OF GLOBALIZATION

As we move into the twenty-first century, the media picture is blurred because in a postmodern, globalizing era many traditional boundaries are eroding. The changes affecting the media can be grouped into several categories:

- *Convergent technologies:* Broadcasting, telecommunications (including telephone systems and satellites), and computers are becoming increasingly integrated into a single system.
- *Integrated production and distribution systems:* Technology has permitted and encouraged the emergence of global communications corporations that are integrated, both horizontally and vertically.
- *Erosion of geographic and cultural boundaries:* Communication systems are no longer significantly constrained by national and cultural boundaries.
- *Merging of genres:* The distinctions between such genres as news, entertainment, and even advertising are becoming increasingly less clear and less meaningful.

These developments pose both opportunities and challenges to governments and citizens. The new media create unprecedented opportunities for new forms of cultural interchange and democratic dialogue, but their equally unprecedented potential for domination by large multinational corporations—given the huge capital costs of the information highway—may limit such opportunities. As one observer has commented: "Cultural globalization is not just the spread of American cultural products ... but the implantation of an exclusively commercial model for [cultural production]."[40] This model sets up an illusion of consumer choice but, in fact, promotes a narrow version of consumerism.

David Taras has stated that "the international media cartels would prefer to be free from regulation, free from any limits on their investments, profits and products."[41] But does their freedom enhance the freedom of individuals and communities? There is little doubt that large-scale media corporations, dependent on advertising revenues, are tied closely to dominant economic interests and reflect the values of the consumer society. In helping to set the limits for public debate, the media tend to reinforce the dominant institutional and cultural patterns of authority and generally exclude serious challenges to the status quo. While most news organizations are reluctant to challenge in any direct way the dominant interests in their communities, there is nonetheless a reformist thrust in the media that angers some conservatives. So, while both business and labour can sometimes feel they are subjected to biased reporting, the absence of labour reporting in most news outlets today tends to suggest the media lean generally in the direction of business.

Among the apparent consequences of globalization and concentration of ownership has been the increasing dominance in media discourse of a neoliberal political agenda that promotes free markets and consumerism (see Chapter 10). With respect to newspapers, which tend to set the agenda for other media, "two motives—profit and influence—have tended to fuel the acquisition of Canadian newspapers during the past thirty-five years of rapid concentration."[42] There has been a sustained and concerted effort over the past two decades to legitimize neoliberal viewpoints and to ensure that they gain substantial media attention. This has led to the development of a "right-wing information infrastructure"[43] of think tanks and interest groups, employing many of the standard techniques of advocacy—research reports, conferences, news releases—to gain media attention for their point of view. Given the conservative tilt of the major newspapers, these tactics have been increasingly successful. David Radler, who was a top executive in Hollinger/Southam before its sale, made it clear that the newspapers he controlled were expected to follow a general editorial line, stating that "any Hollinger paper that wants to support a Bob Rae-type socialist government better have pretty good compelling reasons. We're not going to back a political party that seeks our destruction and the destruction of the capitalist system." This point of view has been expressed somewhat less directly by Leonard Asper of CanWest, who argued in 2002 that ownership of a media outlet reasonably includes editorial control.[44] Soon after its acquisition of the *National Post* and the Southam chain of daily newspapers, CanWest instituted regular national editorials, setting out the corporation's position on issues of the day, and prohibiting local editors from taking a different position on any issue, an unprecedented degree of centralization in Canada. This move elicited strong criticism from journalists and media analysts and the policy was eventually modified. It does, however, illustrate the potential for the control of political expression by media ownership.

While the left has countered with its own think tanks, it has notably fewer resources and its views are generally treated with less deference by the mainstream media. With the predominance of neoliberal political and economic analysis in the media, the issue becomes one of balance and diversity. As one media observer has put it: "There are lots of justifications for neoconservative economics [referred to in this chapter as neoliberalism] and theories such as global competitiveness, privatization, deregulation and paying down the deficit. But can anyone recall a single example of an argument for a thorough-going socialist alternative to capitalism presented anywhere in the Canadian mainstream media?"[45]

The obvious danger here is that the trends noted above will weaken the institutions that provide local, regional, and national communities with opportunities to learn about their shared values and history, to tell their own stories, and to debate in a public way the collective decisions that will shape the future of their communities. Citizens have some capacity to resist the messages promoted by the media giants, to seek out alternative media, to demand greater balance in news coverage and diversity in cultural programming, and to choose quality, homegrown cultural products, if they so prefer. Critics of the trends noted above worry that Canadians will be so overwhelmed by imported cultural values that they will not recognize the need for action. "[The] worry is that the growth of huge media conglomerates, the lack of support for public broadcasting, and the failures of contemporary journalism are creating a narrower and more limited media world" that threatens Canadian democracy.[46]

ACKNOWLEDGMENTS

The authors would like to express their gratitude to Daphne Gottlieb Taras, coauthor of earlier versions of this chapter, and Arlene Williams, who provided helpful research assistance, while absolving them of all responsibility.

NOTES

1. Benedict Anderson, *Imagined Communities: Reflections on the Origins and Spread of Nationalism* (London: Verso, 1991).

2. Anthony Westell, *The New Society* (Toronto: McClelland & Stewart, 1974), p. 73.

3. For a discussion of the history of the media in Canada, see Paul Rutherford, *The Making of the Canadian Media* (Toronto: McGraw-Hill Ryerson, 1978).

4. The concept of objectivity is subjected to detailed analysis in Robert A. Hackett and Yuezhi Zhao, *Sustaining Democracy? Journalism and the Politics of Objectivity* (Toronto: Garamond Press, 1998).

5. See Catherine A. Murray, ed., *Cultural Policies and Cultural Practices: Exploring Links Between Culture and Social Change*. Report of the Founding Colloquium of the Canadian Cultural Research Network, June 3–4, 1998.

6. In recent years, the CBC French and English networks have co-produced a number of television dramas and occasional major public affairs projects, such as *Canada: A People's History*.

7. For a fuller discussion of these issues, see Frederick J. Fletcher, "Media and Political Identity: Canada and Quebec in the Era of Globalization," *Canadian Journal of Communication* 23 (1998): 359–80.

8. This evocative phrase is taken from the title of James Winter, *Democracy's Oxygen: How Corporations Control the News* (Montreal: Black Rose Books, 1997).

9. Robert A. Hackett and Yuezhi Zhao, *Sustaining Democracy? Journalism and the Politics of Objectivity* (Toronto: Garamond Press, 1998), p. 1.

10. Roger Bird, *The End of News* (Toronto: Irwin Publishing, 1997), ch. 1.

11. Ibid., p. 78.

12. Hackett and Zhao, *Sustaining Democracy?* ch. 4.

13. Bird, *The End of News,* p. 133.

14. John Miller, *Yesterday's News: Why Canada's Daily Newspapers Are Failing Us* (Halifax, N.S.: Fernwood, 1998).

15. Cited in David Taras, *Power and Betrayal in the Canadian Media* (Peterborough: Broadview, 1999), p. 9. Comparable figures for the 2000 federal election: television, 52 percent; newspapers, 23 percent; radio, 11 percent. André Blais, Elisabeth Gidengil, Richard Nadeau, and Neil Nevitte, *Anatomy of a Liberal Victory: Making Sense of the Vote in the 2000 Canadian Election* (Peterborough: Broadview, 2002), p. 35.

16. Taras, *Power and Betrayal,* p. 170.

17. Bird, *The End of News,* pp. 128–29.

18. David Taras, "A Question of Character: Political Reporting in Canada and the United States," in David Thomas, ed., *Canada and the United States: Differences That Count* (Peterborough: Broadview Press, 1993), p. 340.

19. Christopher Dornan, "The Television Coverage: A History of the Election in 65 Seconds," in Alan Frizzell and Jon H. Pammett, eds., *The Canadian General Election of 1997* (Toronto: Dundurn Press, 1997), p. 157. For the 2000 election, see Jon H. Pammett and Christoper Dornan, eds., *The Canadian General Election of 2000* (Toronto: Dundurn Press, 2001), pp. 165–241. See also Blais et al., *Anatomy of a Liberal Victory,* ch. 2.

20. Dornan, "The Television Coverage," p. 154.

21. Jon H. Pammett, "The People's Verdict," in Pammett and Dornan, *The Canadian General Election of 2000,* p. 306.

22. Edward Greenspon, "Covering Campaign 2000," in Pammett and Dornan, *The Canadian General Election of 2000,* ch. 7.

23. Lawrence LeDuc, "The Leaders' Debates: (...And the Winner Is...)," in Frizzell and Pammett, *The Canadian General Election of 1997,* p. 221.

24. Dornan, "The Television Coverage," p. 156.

25. Canadian Cable Television Association, "CRTC Review of TV Policy," *Communique* 22, no. 3 (December 1998).

26. Quoted in Tony Clark and Maude Barlow, *MAI: The Multilateral Agreement on Investment and the Threat to Canadian Sovereignty* (Toronto: Stoddart, 1997), pp. 129–30.

27. Marc Starowicz, "The Gutenberg Revolution of Television: Speculation on the Impact of New Technologies," in Helen Holmes and David Taras, eds., *Seeing Ourselves: Media Power and Policy in Canada,* 2nd ed. (Toronto: Harcourt Brace, 1996), pp. 243–44.

28. Statistics Canada, *Canada's Culture, Heritage and Identity: A Statistical Perspective,* Ottawa, 1997.

29. Canada, Canadian Heritage, "New Advertising Services Measure to Promote Canadian Culture," News Release, July 29, 1998. <http://www.pch.gc.ca/newsroom/news_e.cfm?Action=Display&code=8NR064E>.

30. Statistics Canada, *The Daily,* December 2, 2002.

31. Task Force on Broadcasting Policy, *Report* (Ottawa: Ministry of Supply and Services, September 1986), p. 85.

32. Statistics Canada, *The Daily,* December 2, 2002.

33. Canada, Canadian Heritage, "Broadcasting: You Are What You Watch," 1996. Summarized at <http://www.pch.gc.ca/culture/report/HTM/3.htm>.

34. Statistics Canada, "Television Viewing Time," Catalogue 87F006XPE, December 2002.

35. See Canoe, *Canadian Regional TV Ratings*, <http://jam.canoe.ca/ TelevisionRatings/home_regionratings.html>.

36. Statistics Canada, *The Daily*, June 25, 2002.

37. Canadian Radio-Television and Telecommunications Commission, *Commercial Radio Policy 1998* <http://www.crtc.gc.ca/archive/ENG/Notices/1998/PB98-41.HTM>.

38. Miller, *Yesterday's News*, ch. 6. As well, observers wishing to keep up with these rapidly shifting ownership patterns should consult "Ownership of Canadian Daily Newspapers" on the Canadian Newspaper Association website <http://www.cna-acj.ca/ client/cna/cna.nsf/web/FactsOwnership>.

39. Marjorie Ferguson, "Media, Markets and Identities; Reflections on the Global-Local Dialectic, *Canadian Journal of Communication* 20, no. 4 (Autumn 1995): 439–60.

40. Florian Sauvageau, "Between the State and the Market: The Place of Culture," in Murray, *Cultural Policies and Cultural Practices*, p. 35.

41. Taras, "A Question of Character," pp. 91–92.

42. Miller, *Yesterday's News*, p. 72.

43. Taras, "A Question of Character," p. 210.

44. Quoted in Taras, "A Question of Character," pp. 213–14. Leonard Asper, "Inventing the Future," Speech to Canadian Club, Ottawa, December 17, 2002.

45. Miller, *Yesterday's News*, p. 52.

46. Taras, "A Question of Character," p. 27.

FURTHER READINGS

Bird, Roger. *The End of News*. Toronto: Irwin, 1997.

Dorland, Michael, ed. *The Cultural Industries in Canada: Problems, Policies, and Prospects*. Toronto: Lorimer, 1996.

Fletcher, Frederick J. *Media, Elections and Democracy*. Volume 19 of the Research Studies of the Royal Commission on Electoral Reform and Party Financing. Toronto: Dundurn, 1991.

Fletcher, Frederick J., and Rose Sottile. "Spinning Tales: Politics and the News in Ontario." In Graham White, ed., *Government and Politics of Ontario*, pp. 236–37. Toronto: University of Toronto Press, 1997.

Pammett, Jon H., and Christopher Dornan, eds., *The Canadian General Election of 2000*. Toronto: Dundurn, 2001.

Hackett, Robert A., and Yuezhi Zhao. *Sustaining Democracy? Journalism and the Politics of Objectivity*. Toronto: Garamond, 1998.

Miller, John. *Yesterday's News: Why Canada's Daily Newspapers Are Failing Us*. Halifax: Fernwood, 1998.

Nesbitt-Larking, Paul. *Politics, Society and the Media: Canadian Perspectives*. Peterborough: Broadview, 2001.

Siegel, Arthur. *Politics and the Media in Canada*, 2nd ed. Toronto: McGraw-Hill Ryerson, 1996.

Taras, David. *Power and Betrayal in the Canadian Media*, updated ed. Peterborough, ON: Broadview, 2001.

APPENDIX I

SELECTIONS FROM CONSTITUTION ACTS, 1867 AND 1982

CONSTITUTION ACT, 1867

(Originally, "The British North America Act, 1867")
(U.K. 30 & 31 Victoria, C.3)

An Act for the Union of Canada, Nova Scotia, and New Brunswick, and the Government thereof, and for Purposes connected therewith.

WHEREAS the Provinces of Canada, Nova Scotia, and New Brunswick have expressed their Desire to be federally united into One Dominion under the Crown of the United Kingdom of Great Britain and Ireland, with a Constitution similar in Principle to the United Kingdom:

AND WHEREAS such a Union would conduce to the Welfare of the Provinces and promote the Interests of the British Empire:

AND WHEREAS on the Establishment of the Union by Authority of Parliament it is expedient, not only that the Constitution of the Legislative Authority in the Dominion be provided for, but also that the Nature of the Executive Government therein be declared:

AND WHEREAS it is expedient that Provision be made for the eventual Admission into the Union of other Parts of British North America:

✶✶✶✶✶✶✶✶✶✶✶✶✶✶✶

VI. DISTRIBUTION OF LEGISLATIVE POWERS

POWERS OF PARLIAMENT

91. It shall be lawful for the Queen, by and with the Advice and Consent of the Senate and the House of Commons, to make Laws for the Peace, Order

and good Government of Canada, in relation to all Matters not coming within the Classes of Subjects by this Act assigned exclusively to the Legislatures of the Provinces; and for greater Certainty, but not so as to restrict the Generality of the foregoing Terms of the Section, it is hereby declared that (notwithstanding anything in this Act) the exclusive Legislative Authority of the Parliament of Canada extends to all Matters coming within the Classes of Subjects hereinafter enumerated; that is to say,

1. REPEALED.
1A. The Public Debt and Property.
2. The Regulation of Trade and Commerce.
2A. Unemployment insurance.
3. The raising of Money by any Mode or System of Taxation.
4. The borrowing of Money on the Public Credit.
5. Postal Service.
6. The Census and Statistics.
7. Militia, Military and Naval Service, and Defence.
8. The fixing of and providing for the Salaries and Allowances of Civil and other Officers of the Government of Canada.
9. Beacons, Buoys, Lighthouses, and Sable Island.
10. Navigation and Shipping.
11. Quarantine and the Establishment and Maintenance of Marine Hospitals.
12. Sea Coast and Inland Fisheries.
13. Ferries between a Province and any British or Foreign Country, or between Two Provinces.
14. Currency and Coinage.
15. Banking, Incorporation of Banks, and the Issue of Paper Money.
16. Savings Banks.
17. Weights and Measures.
18. Bills of Exchange and Promissory Notes.
19. Interest.
20. Legal Tender.
21. Bankruptcy and Insolvency.
22. Patents of Invention and Discovery.
23. Copyrights.
24. Indians, and Lands reserved for the Indians.
25. Naturalization and Aliens.
26. Marriage and Divorce.

27. The Criminal Law, except for the Constitution of Courts of Criminal Jurisdiction, but including the Procedure in Criminal Matters.
28. The Establishment, Maintenance, and Management of Penitentiaries.
29. Such Classes of Subjects as are expressly excepted in the Enumeration of the Classes of Subjects by this Act assigned exclusively to the Legislatures of the Provinces.

And any Matter coming within any of the Classes of Subjects enumerated in this Section shall not be deemed to come within the Class of matters of a local or private Nature comprised in the Enumeration of the Classes of Subjects by this Act assigned exclusively to the Legislatures of the Provinces.

EXCLUSIVE POWERS OF PROVINCIAL LEGISLATURES

92. In each Province the Legislature may exclusively make Laws in relation to matters coming within the Classes of Subject next hereinafter enumerated; that is to say, —

1. REPEALED.
2. Direct Taxation within the Province in order to the raising of a Revenue for Provincial Purposes.
3. The borrowing of Money on the sole Credit of the Province.
4. The Establishment and Tenure of Provincial Offices and the Appointment and Payment of Provincial Officers.
5. The Management and Sale of the Public Lands belonging to the Province and of the Timber and Wood thereon.
6. The Establishment, Maintenance, and Management of Public and Reformatory Prisons in and for the Province.
7. The Establishment, Maintenance, and Management of Hospitals, Asylums, Charities, and Eleemosynary Institutions in and for the Province, other than Marine Hospitals.
8. Municipal Institutions in the Province.
9. Shop, Saloon, Tavern, Auctioneer, and other Licences in order to the raising of a Revenue for Provincial, Local, or Municipal Purposes.
10. Local Works and Undertakings other than such as are of the following Classes:

(a) Lines of Steam or other Ships, Railways, Canals, Telegraphs, and other Works and Undertakings connecting the Province with any other or others of the Province, or extending beyond the Limits of the Province;

(b) Lines of Steam Ships between the Province and any British or Foreign Country;

(c) Such Works as, although wholly situate within the Province, are before or after their Execution declared by the Parliament of Canada to be for the general Advantage of Canada or for the Advantage of Two or more of the Provinces.

11. The Incorporation of Companies with Provincial Objects.

12. The Solemnization of Marriage in the Province.

13. Property and Civil Rights in the Province.

14. The Administration of Justice in the Province, including the Constitution, Maintenance, and Organization of Provincial Courts, both of Civil and of Criminal Jurisdiction, and including Procedure in Civil Matters in those Courts.

15. The Imposition of Punishment by Fine, Penalty, or Imprisonment for enforcing any Law of the Province made in relation to any Matter coming within any of the Classes of Subjects enumerated in this Section.

16. Generally all Matters of a merely local or private Nature in the Province.

NON-RENEWABLE NATURAL RESOURCES, FORESTRY RESOURCES, AND ELECTRICAL ENERGY

92A. (1) In each province, the legislature may exclusively make laws in relation to

(a) exploration for non-renewable natural resources in the province;

(b) development, conservation and management of non-renewable natural resources and forestry resources in the province, including laws in relation to the rate of primary production therefrom; and

(c) development, conservation and management of sites and facilities in the province for the generation and production of electrical energy.

(2) In each province, the legislature may make laws in relation to the export from the province to another part of Canada of the

primary production from non-renewable natural resources and forestry resources in the province and the production from facilities in the province for the generation of electrical energy, but such laws may not authorize or provide for discrimination in prices or in supplies exported to another part of Canada.

(3) Nothing in subsection (2) derogates from the authority of Parliament to enact laws in relation to the matters referred to in that subsection and, where such a law of Parliament and a law of a province conflict, the law of Parliament prevails to the extent of the conflict.

(4) In each province, the legislature may make laws in relation to the raising of money by any mode or system of taxation in respect of

(a) non-renewable natural resources and forestry resources in the province and the primary production therefrom, and

(b) sites and facilities in the province for the generation of electrical energy and the production therefrom,

whether or not such production is exported in whole or in part from the province, but such laws may not authorize or provide for taxation that differentiates between production exported to another part of Canada and production not exported from the province.

(5) The expression "primary production" has the meaning assigned by the Sixth Schedule.

(6) Nothing in subsections (1) to (5) derogates from any powers or rights that a legislature or government of a province had immediately before the coming into force of this section.

EDUCATION

93. In and for each Province the Legislature may exclusively make Laws in relation to Education, subject and according to the following Provisions:

(1) Nothing in any such Law shall prejudicially affect any Right or Privilege with respect to Denominational Schools which any Class of Persons have by Law in the Province at the Union.

(2) All the Powers, Privileges, and Duties at the Union by Law conferred and imposed in Upper Canada on the Separate Schools and School Trustees of the Queen's Roman Catholic Subjects shall be and the same are hereby extended to the Dissentient Schools of the Queen's Protestant and Roman Catholic Subjects in Quebec.

(3) Where in any Province a System of Separate or Dissentient Schools exists by Law at the Union or is thereafter established by the Legislature of the Province, an Appeal shall lie to the Governor General in Council from any Act or Decision of any Provincial Authority affecting any Right or Privilege of the Protestant or Roman Catholic Minority of the Queen's Subjects in relation to Education.

(4) In case any such Provincial Law as from Time to Time seems to the Governor General in Council requisite for the due Execution of the Provisions of this Section is not made, or in case any Decision of the Governor General in Council on any Appeal under this Section is not duly executed by the proper Provincial Authority in that Behalf, then and in every such Case, and as far only as the Circumstances of each Case require, the Parliament of Canada may make remedial Laws for the due Execution of the Provisions of this Section and of any Decision of the Governor General in Council under this Section.

UNIFORMITY OF LAWS IN ONTARIO, NOVA SCOTIA, AND NEW BRUNSWICK

94. Notwithstanding anything in this Act, the Parliament of Canada may make Provision for the Uniformity of all or any of the Laws relative to Property and Civil Rights in Ontario, Nova Scotia, and New Brunswick, and of the Procedure of all or any of the Courts of those Three Provinces, and from and after the passing of any Act in that Behalf the Power of the Parliament of Canada to make Laws in relation to any Matter comprised in any such Act shall, notwithstanding anything in this Act, be unrestricted; but any Act of the Parliament of Canada making Provision for such Uniformity shall not have effect in any Province unless and until it is adopted and enacted as Law by the Legislature thereof.

OLD AGE PENSIONS

94A. The Parliament of Canada may make laws in relation to old age pensions and supplementary benefits, including survivors' and disability benefits irrespective of age, but no such law shall affect the operation of any law present or future of a provincial legislature in relation to any such matter.

AGRICULTURE AND IMMIGRATION

95. In each Province the Legislature may make Laws in relation to Agriculture in the Province, and to Immigration into the Province; and it is hereby declared that the Parliament or Canada may from Time to Time make Laws in relation to Agriculture in all or any of the Provinces, and to Immigration into all or any of the Provinces; and any Law of the Legislature of a Province relative to Agriculture or to Immigration shall have effect in and for the Province as long and as far only as it is not repugnant to any Act of the Parliament of Canada.

＊＊＊＊＊＊＊＊＊＊＊＊＊＊＊＊＊＊＊＊＊＊＊＊＊＊＊＊＊＊

CONSTITUTION ACT, 1982

PART I—CANADIAN CHARTER OF RIGHTS AND FREEDOMS

Whereas Canada is founded upon principles that recognize the supremacy of God and the rule of law:

GUARANTEE OF RIGHTS AND FREEDOMS

1. The Canadian Charter of Rights and Freedoms guarantees the rights and freedoms set out in it subject only to such reasonable limits prescribed by law as can be demonstrably justified in a free and democratic society.

FUNDAMENTAL FREEDOMS

2. Everyone has the following fundamental freedoms:
   (a) freedom of conscience and religion;
   (b) freedom of thought, belief, opinion and expression, including freedom of the press and other means of communication;
   (c) freedom of peaceful assembly; and
   (d) freedom of association.

DEMOCRATIC RIGHTS

3. Every citizen of Canada has the right to vote in an election of members of the House of Commons or of a legislative assembly and to be qualified for membership therein.

4. (1) No House of Commons and no legislative assembly shall continue for longer than five years from the date fixed for the return of the writs at a general election of its members.

    (2) In time of real or apprehended war, invasion or insurrection, a House of Commons may be continued by Parliament and a legislative assembly may be continued by the legislature beyond five years if such continuation is not opposed by the votes of more than one-third of the members of the House of Commons or the legislative assembly, as the case may be.

5. There shall be a sitting of Parliament and of each legislature at least once every twelve months.

MOBILITY RIGHTS

6. (1) Every citizen of Canada has the right to enter, remain in, and leave Canada.

    (2) Every citizen of Canada and every person who has the status of a permanent resident of Canada has the right

    (a) to move to and take up residence in a province; and

    (b) to pursue the gaining of livelihood in any province.

    (3) The rights specified in subsection (2) are subject to

    (a) any laws or practices of general application in force in a province other than those that discriminate among persons primarily on the basis of present or previous residence; and

    (b) any laws providing for reasonable residency requirements as a qualification for the receipt of publicly provided social services.

    (4) Subsections (2) and (3) do not preclude any law, program or activity that has as its object the amelioration in a province of conditions of individuals in that province who are socially or economically disadvantaged if the rate of employment in that province is below the rate of employment in Canada.

LEGAL RIGHTS

7. Everyone has the right to life, liberty and security of the person and the right not to be deprived thereof except in accordance with the principles of fundamental justice.

8. Everyone has the right to be secure against unreasonable search or seizure.

9. Everyone has the right not to be arbitrarily detained or imprisoned.

10. Everyone has the right on arrest or detention
   (a) to be informed promptly of the reason therefor;
   (b) to retain and instruct counsel without delay and to be informed of that right; and
   (c) to have the validity of the detention determined by way of *habeas corpus* and to be released if the detention is not lawful.

11. Any person charged with an offence has the right
   (a) to be informed without unreasonable delay of the specific offence;
   (b) to be tried within a reasonable time;
   (c) not to be compelled to be a witness in proceedings against that person in respect of the offence;
   (d) to be presumed innocent until proven guilty according to law in a fair and public hearing by an independent and impartial tribunal;
   (e) not to be denied reasonable bail without cause;
   (f) except in the case of an offence under military law tried before a military tribunal, to the benefit of trial by jury where the maximum punishment for the offence is imprisonment for five years or a more severe punishment;
   (g) not to be found guilty on account of any act or omission unless, at the time of the act or omission, it constituted an offence under Canadian or International law or was criminal according to the general principles of law recognized by the community of nations;
   (h) if finally acquitted of the offence, not to be tried for it again and, if finally found guilty and punished for the offence, not to be tried or punished for it again; and
   (i) if found guilty of the offence and if punishment for the offence has been varied between the time of commission and the time of sentencing, to the benefit of the lesser punishment.

12. Everyone has the right not to be subjected to any cruel or unusual treatment or punishment.

13. A witness who testifies in any proceedings has the right not to have any incriminating evidence so given used to incriminate that witness in any other proceedings, except in a prosecution for perjury or for the giving of contradictory evidence.

14. A party or witness in any proceedings who does not understand or speak the language in which the proceedings are conducted or who is deaf has the right to the assistance of an interpreter.

EQUALITY RIGHTS

15. (1) Every individual is equal before and under the law and has the right to the equal protection and equal benefit of the law without discrimination based on race, national or ethnic origin, colour, religion, sex, age, or mental or physical disability.
    (2) Subsection (1) does not preclude any law, program or activity that has as its object the amelioration of conditions of disadvantaged individuals or groups including those that are disadvantaged because of race, national or ethnic origin, colour, religion, sex, age, or mental or physical disability.

OFFICIAL LANGUAGES OF CANADA

16. (1) English and French are the official languages of Canada and have equal rights and privileges as to their use in all institutions of the Parliament and government of Canada.
    (2) English and French are the official languages of New Brunswick and have equality of status and equal rights and privileges as to the use in all institutions of the legislature and government of New Brunswick.
    (3) Nothing in this Charter limits the authority of Parliament or a legislature to advance the equality of status or use of English and French.

17. (1) Everyone has the right to use English or French in any debates or other proceedings of Parliament.
    (2) Everyone has the right to use English or French in any debates and other proceedings of the legislature of New Brunswick.

18. (1) The Statutes, records and journals of Parliament shall be printed and published in English and French and both language versions are equally authoritative.

19. (1) Either English or French may be used by any person in, or in any pleading in or process issuing from any court established by Parliament.

(2) Either English or French may be used by any person in, or in any pleading in or process issuing from any court of New Brunswick.

20. (1) Any member of the public of Canada has the right to communicate with, and to receive available services from, any head or central office of an institution of the Parliament or government of Canada in English or French, and has the same right with respect to any other office of any such institution where
(a) there is significant demand for communications with and services from that office in such language; or
(b) due to the nature of the office, it is reasonable that communications with and services from that office be available in both English and French.
(2) Any member of the public in New Brunswick has the right to communicate with, and to receive available services from, any office of an institution of the legislature or government of New Brunswick in English or French.

21. Nothing in sections 16 to 20 abrogates or derogates from any right, privilege or obligation with respect to the English and French languages, or either of them, that exists or is continued by virtue of any other provision of the Constitution of Canada.

22. Nothing in sections 16 to 20 abrogates or derogates from any legal or customary right or privilege acquired or enjoyed either before or after the coming into force of this Charter with respect to any language that is not English or French.

MINORITY LANGUAGE EDUCATIONAL RIGHTS

23. (1) Citizens of Canada
(a) whose first language learned and still understood is that of the English or French linguistic minority population of the province in which they reside, or
(b) who have received their primary school instruction in Canada in English or French and reside in a province where the language in which they received that instruction is the language of the English or French linguistic minority population of the province,

have the right to have their children receive primary and secondary school instruction in that language in that province.

(2) Citizens of Canada of whom any child has received or is receiving primary or secondary school instruction in English or French in Canada, have the right to have all their children receive primary and secondary school instruction in the same language.

(3) The right of citizens of Canada under subsections (1) and (2) to have their children receive primary and secondary school instruction in the language of the English or French linguistic minority population of a province
   (a) applies wherever in the province the number of children of citizens who have such a right is sufficient to warrant the provision to them out of public funds of minority language instruction; and
   (b) includes, where the number of children so warrants, the right to have them receive that instruction in minority language educational facilities provided out of public funds.

ENFORCEMENT

24. (1) Anyone whose rights or freedoms, as guaranteed by this Charter, have been infringed or denied may apply to a court of competent jurisdiction to obtain such remedy as the court considers appropriate and just in the circumstances.
   (2) Where, in proceedings under subsection (1), a court concludes that evidence was obtained in a manner that infringed or denied any rights or freedoms guaranteed by this Charter, the evidence shall be excluded if it is established that, having regard to all the circumstances, the admission of it in the proceedings would bring the administration of justice into disrepute.

GENERAL

25. The guarantee in this Charter of certain rights and freedoms shall not be construed so as to abrogate or derogate from any aboriginal, treaty or other rights or freedoms that pertain to the aboriginal peoples of Canada including
   (a) any rights or freedoms that have been recognized by the Royal Proclamation of October 7, 1763; and

(b) any rights or freedoms that may be acquired by the aboriginal peoples of Canada by way of land claims settlement.

26. The guarantee in this Charter of certain rights and freedoms shall not be construed as denying the existence of any other rights and freedoms that exist in Canada.

27. This Charter shall be interpreted in a manner consistent with the preservation and enhancement of the multicultural heritage of Canadians.

28. Notwithstanding anything in this Charter, the rights and freedoms referred to in it are guaranteed equally to male and female persons.

29. Nothing in this Charter abrogates or derogates from any rights or privileges guaranteed by or under the Constitution of Canada in respect of denominational, separate or dissentient schools.

30. A reference in this Charter to a province or to the legislative assembly or legislature of a province shall be deemed to include a reference to the Yukon Territory and the Northwest Territories, or to the appropriate legislative authority thereof, as the case may be.

31. Nothing in this Charter extends the legislative powers of any body or authority.

APPLICATION OF CHARTER

32. (1) This Charter applies
    (a) to the Parliament and government of Canada in respect of all matters within the authority of Parliament including all matters relating to the Yukon Territory and Northwest Territories; and
    (b) to the legislatures and governments of each province in respect of all matters within the authority of the legislature of each province.
(2) Notwithstanding subsection (1), section 15 shall not have effect until three years after this section comes into force.

33. (1) Parliament or the legislature of a province may expressly declare in an Act of Parliament or of the legislature, as the case may be, that the Act or a provision thereof shall operate notwithstanding a provision included in section 2 or sections 7 to 15 of this Charter.

(2) An Act or a provision of an Act in respect of which a declaration made under this section is in effect shall have such operation as it would have but for the provision of this Charter referred to in the declaration.

(3) A declaration made under subsection (1) shall cease to have effect five years after it comes into force or on such earlier date as may be specified in the declaration.

(4) Parliament or the legislature of a province may re-enact a declaration made under subsection (1).

(5) Subsection (3) applies in respect of re-enactment made under subsection (4).

CITATION

34. This Part may be cited as the *Canadian Charter of Rights and Freedoms.*

PART II—RIGHTS OF THE ABORIGINAL PEOPLES OF CANADA

35. (1) The existing aboriginal and treaty rights of the aboriginal peoples of Canada are hereby recognized and affirmed.

(2) In this Act, "aboriginal peoples of Canada" includes the Indian, Inuit, and Metis peoples of Canada.

PART V—PROCEDURE FOR AMENDING THE CONSTITUTION OF CANADA

38. (1) An amendment to the Constitution of Canada may be made by proclamation issued by the Governor General under the Great Seal of Canada where so authorized by

(a) resolutions of the Senate and the House of Commons; and

(b) resolutions of the legislative assemblies of at least two-thirds of the provinces that have, in the aggregate, according to the then latest general census, at least fifty per cent of the population of the provinces.

(2) An amendment made under subsection (1) that derogates from the legislative powers, the proprietary rights or any other rights or privileges of the legislature or government of a province shall require a resolution supported by a majority of the members of each of the Senate, the House of Commons and the legislative assemblies required under subsection (1).

(3) An amendment referred to in subsection (2) shall not have effect in a province the legislative assembly of which has expressed its dissent thereto by resolution supported by a majority of its members prior to the issue of the proclamation to which the amendment relates unless that legislative assembly, subsequently, by resolution supported by a majority of its members, revokes its dissent and authorizes the amendment.

(4) A resolution of dissent made for the purposes of subsection (3) may be revoked at any time before or after the issue of the proclamation to which it relates.

39. (1) A proclamation shall not be issued under subsection 38(1) before the expiration of one year from the adoption of the resolution initiating the amendment procedure, unless the legislative assembly of each province has previously adopted a resolution of assent or dissent.

(2) A proclamation shall not be issued under subsection 38(1) after the expiration of three years from the adoption of the resolution initiating the amendment procedure thereunder.

40. Where an amendment is made under subsection 38(1) that transfers provincial legislative powers relating to education or other cultural matters from provincial legislatures to Parliament, Canada shall provide reasonable compensation to any province to which the amendment does not apply.

41. An amendment to the Constitution of Canada in relation to the following matters may be made by proclamation issued by the Governor General under the Great Seal of Canada only where authorized by resolutions of the Senate and House of Commons and of the legislative assemblies of each province:

    (a) the office of the Queen, the Governor General and the Lieutenant Governor of a province;

    (b) the right of a province to a number of members in the House of Commons not less than the number of Senators by which the province is entitled to be represented at the time this Part comes into force;

    (c) subject to section 43, the use of the English or the French language;

    (d) the composition of the Supreme Court of Canada; and

    (e) an amendment to this Part.

42. (1) An amendment to the Constitution of Canada in relation to the following matters may be made only in accordance with subsection 38(1):

(a) the principle of proportionate representation of the provinces in the House of Commons prescribed by the Constitution of Canada;

(b) the powers of the Senate and the method of selecting Senators;

(c) the number of members by which a province is entitled to be represented in the Senate and the residence qualifications of Senators;

(d) subject to paragraph 41(d), the Supreme Court of Canada;

(e) the extension of existing provinces into the territories; and

(f) notwithstanding any other law or practice, the establishment of new provinces;

(2) Subsections 38(2) to 38(4) do not apply in respect of amendments in relation to matters referred to in subsection (1).

43. An amendment to the Constitution of Canada in relation to any provision that applies to one or more, but not all provinces, including

(a) any alteration to boundaries between provinces, and

(b) any amendment to any provisions that relate to the use of the English or the French language within a province,

may be made by proclamation issued by the Governor General under the Great Seal of Canada only where so authorized by resolutions of the Senate and House of Commons and of the legislative assembly of each province to which the amendment applies.

44. Subject to sections 41 and 42, Parliament may exclusively make laws amending the Constitution of Canada in relation to executive government of Canada or the Senate and House of Commons.

45. Subject to section 41, the legislature of each province may exclusively make laws amending the constitution of the province.

46. (1) The procedures for amendment under sections 38, 41, 42, and 43 may be initiated either by the Senate or the House of Commons or by the legislative assembly of the province.

(2) A resolution of assent for the purposes of this Part may be revoked at any time before the issue of a proclamation authorized by it.

47.   (1) An amendment to the Constitution of Canada made by proclamation under section 38, 41, 42, or 43 may be made without a resolution of the Senate authorizing the issue of the proclamation if, within one hundred and eighty days after the adoption by the House of Commons of a resolution authorizing its issue, the Senate has not adopted such a resolution and if, at any time after the expiration of that period, the House of Commons again adopts the resolution.

(2) Any period when Parliament is prorogued or dissolved shall not be counted in computing the one hundred and eighty day period referred to in subsection (1).

48. The Queen's Privy Council for Canada shall advise the Governor General to issue a proclamation under this Part forthwith on the adoption of the resolution required for an amendment made by proclamation under this Part.

49. A constitutional conference of the Prime Minister of Canada and the first ministers shall be convened by the Prime Minister of Canada within fifteen years after this Part comes into force to review the provisions of this Part.

APPENDIX II

FEDERAL ELECTION RESULTS, 1968-2000

Election	Total Seats	Liberal	Progressive Conservative	NDP	Social Credit	Bloc Québécois	Reform/ Alliance	Others**
1968	264	155 (45)*	72 (31)	22 (17)	14 (6)			1 (2)
1972	264	109 (38)*	107 (35)	31 (18)	15 (8)			2 (1)
1974	264	141 (43)*	94 (35)	16 (15)	11 (5)			2 (1)
1979	282	114 (40)	136 (36)*	26 (18)	6 (5)			0 (2)
1980	282	147 (44)*	103 (33)	32 (20)	0 (1)			0 (2)
1984	282	40 (28)	211 (50)*	30 (19)				1 (3)
1988	295	83 (32)	169 (43)*	43 (20)				0 (3)
1993	295	177 (41)*	2 (16)	9 (7)		54 (13)	52 (19)	1 (4)
1997	301	155 (39)*	20 (19)	21 (11)		44 (11)	60 (19)	1 (2)
2000	301	172 (41)*	12 (12)	13 (9)		38 (11)	66 (26)	0 (2)

Percentage of vote in parentheses
Note: Percentages of the popular vote do not total 100 due to rounding.

* Formed government
** Covers other parties as well as independent candidates with no affiliation.

SOURCE: ELECTIONS CANADA

APPENDIX III

SELECTED INTERNET RESOURCES IN CANADIAN POLITICS

Thomson-Nelson Publications—Canadian Politics on the Web
http://www.21stcentury.nelson.com/canpol.html

Canadian Resource Page
http://www.cs.cmu.edu/Unofficial/Canadiana/README.html

National Library Guide to Political Science Resources
http://www.nlc-bnc.ca/2/25/index-e.html

Yahoo Directory of Canadian Government Sites
http://dir.yahoo.com/Regional/Countries/Canada/Government

University of British Columbia Library Canadian Politics Net Station
http://www.library.ubc.ca/poli/cpweb.html

Federal Government Institutions and Statutes
http://Canada.GC.CA/howgoc/howind_e.html

Constitution Acts, 1867 and 1982
http://laws.justice.gc.ca/en/const/index.html

House of Commons and Senate
http://www.parl.gc.ca/

Prime Minister
http://pm.gc.ca

Supreme Court
http://www.scc-csc.gc.ca

Elections Canada
http://www.elections.ca

Statistics Canada
http://www.statcan.ca

Finance Canada—Federal Budget
http://www.fin.gc.ca/access/budinfoe.html

Foreign Affairs and International Trade
http://www.dfait-maeci.gc.ca

Intergovernmental Affairs
http://www.pco-bcp.gc.ca/aia/

Canadian Publications Online
http://www-2.cs.cmu.edu/Unofficial/Canadiana/CA-zines.html

Canadian Public Opinion Polls—Centre for Research and Information on Canada
http://www.cric.ca/en_html/sondages/index.html

INDEX

politics/administration dichotomy, 57–60

polls. *See under* surveys

pork barrelling, 241

Porter, John, 90

pressure groups. *See* interest groups

prime minister, 53. *See also prime ministers*
authority of, 5, 32
Cabinet and (*see under* Cabinet)
deputy ministers and (*see* deputy ministers)
majority governments and, 45–46
order-in-council appointments by, 44
Parliament and, 10, 44–53
PCO and, 42–43
personality and, 31, 46–47
power of, 10–11, 46–47, 79
Prime Minister's Office (PMO), 43–44, 51, 64, 179
Priorities and Planning Committee (P&P), 40
private bills, 9
private members' bills, 9, 23–24
Privy Council, 32–33, 103
Clerk of the, 43, 65, 71, 74, 77, 78, 80
jurisdiction questions and, 86, 87, 88, 103
Privy Councillors, 38
Privy Council Office (PCO), 42–43
Mulroney and, 69
P&P Committee and, 40
Trudeau and, 65
Progressive Conservative Party. *See* Conservative Party
Pross, A. Paul, 221
protests, 218, 220, 227–28, 375
aboriginals and, 318–19

Ontario education, 213
police and, 319
political culture and, 318–19
race, ethnicity and, 386
provinces, large/rich and small/poor, 143–45
provincial governments
Constitution Act, 1867, and, 451–65
decentralization and (*see* decentralization)
equalization payments and, 89, 99, 143, 161
federal budget and, 233
federal fiscal policies and, 98–103
federal grants and, 100–101, 106
federalism and (*see* federalism)
federal transfer payments and, 101, 161
jurisdiction of, 75–76, 86–89, 94–98, 258
pay equity and, 358–59
populations and, 106
premiers conferences and, 107
Quebec, 400, 401, 409 (*see also* Quebec)
shared-cost programs and, 240
women and, 355
public accounts, 36
public servants. *See* bureaucracy
Public Service 2000, 70, 71
Public Service Commission, 35, 39, 59, 73, 78
Public Service Modernization Act, 78

Quebec, 399–424
Charlottetown Accord and, 418–19
Constitution Act, 1867, and, 406, 415
Constitution Act, 1982, and, 318, 415–17